DIAGNOSIS AND REMEDIATION OF THE DISABLED READER

DIAGNOSIS AND REMEDIATION OF THE DISABLED READER

Third Edition

ELDON E. EKWALL
The University of Texas at El Paso

JAMES L. SHANKER
California State University, Hayward

ALLYN AND BACON, INC.
Boston   London   Sydney   Toronto

Cover Administrator: Linda Dickinson
Cover Designer: Susan Hamant
Editorial-Production Service: Editing, Design & Production, Inc.

The photos on pages 1, 34, 86, and 339 are courtesy of Mike Penny.

Library of Congress Cataloging-in-Publication Data

Ekwall, Eldon E.
  Diagnosis and remediation of the disabled
reader.

  Includes index.
  1. Reading disability. 2. Reading—Ability
testing. 3. Reading—Remedial teaching.
I. Shanker, James L. II. Title.
LB1050.E37 1988   428.4'2   87-19591
ISBN 0-205-11174-2

Printed in the United States of America.
10 9 8 7 6 5 4   92 91 90

Eldon E. Ekwall
dedicates this book to
John H. Renner, M.D.

James L. Shanker
dedicates this book to
his most important teachers,
his parents,
Jack and Ida Shanker

Contents

Preface

This book is designed to be used by students who are taking their first course in diagnosis or remediation of reading disabilities. It was also written for practicing teachers who want to broaden their knowledge and skills in diagnostic and remedial techniques. We have assumed that anyone reading this material will have a basic knowledge of the teaching of reading as taught in a reading foundations course. However, because of the diversity of the subject matter and the manner in which foundations courses are often taught, we have, in a number of places, defined the terminology necessary to develop a general background for the discussion of major concepts.

This book begins with a chapter on the state of literacy in the United States and reasons why pupils fail in reading. We are operating under the premise that to be an effective diagnostician, as well as an effective remedial reading teacher, it is often helpful to have a broad knowledge of causal factors in reading disabilities. A number of factors have a significant correlation with reading disabilities but do not appear to exhibit a direct causal relationship. We have discussed these as well, since there is still much to learn in this ever-changing subject and to ignore any factors relating to reading would, in effect, be educating the student for obsolescence.

Chapter 2 contains a discussion of some operational procedures of which we believe all reading specialists should become aware. Portions of Chapter 2 are expanded on in later chapters; the added emphasis should serve to alert you to the importance of these topics.

Chapter 3 contains a framework for the examination of educational problems in reading diagnosis and remediation. Chapters 4 through 8 discuss diagnosis and remediation under the categories of educational, psychological, sociological, and physical factors. Because we believe that teachers must assume primary responsibility for educational factors, special emphasis is placed on topics in this area. Chapter 9 is devoted to the diagnosis and treatment of severe learning disabilities. Each of these chapters is divided into Diagnosis and Remediation sections.

The remaining chapters deal with additional diagnostic and remedial techniques and administrative procedures with which the reading specialist should become familiar. Chapter 16 covers the interpretation of tests and research results in relation to reading. If you have not had a course in educational research or educational statistics, you may wish to read Chapter 16 first. At the end of the book are appendices containing material that you should find helpful in day-to-day work with disabled readers.

In this third edition of our book we have added new information to nearly every chapter and cited new research findings in areas that are pertinent to the diagnosis or remediation of disabled readers. We have particularly expanded our coverage of new techniques for teaching students how to comprehend what they read. We have also provided a more detailed discussion of informal reading inventories and several more examples of the analyses of specific reading passages. Chapter 15 contains a comprehensive new section describes the use of the microcomputer in the diagnosis and remediation of reading difficulties.

Acknowledgments

We would like to thank a number of people who have, in some way, contributed to the completion of this book. First, we would like to thank Ethel Murphy for her research assistance, Eileen Regan for her assistance with photographs, and Ann Holly, Wedge Johnson, Karen Sheffield, Susan May, Valery Jenner, Carolyn Choate, Robert Flores, and Pam Round, who spent many hours helping document certain information. We would also like to thank Dr. Don Swink for his help in the preparation of the section on vision. Our appreciation is also extended to Roger DeSanti, University of New Orleans, Gary Anderson, Arizona State University, and Hal B. Dreyer, Mankato State University, who reviewed the manuscript and contributed many scholarly suggestions. We would also like to thank the many fine graduate students who have taken our courses in diagnosis and remedial reading, who, along with our own teachers, Dr. Ruth Strang and Dr. George Sherman, have helped us learn what we hope we have been able to communicate to the reader of this book. Our deepest appreciation is also extended to Wilson Wayne Grant, M.D., who has worked closely with one of the authors over the years and who has been unusually successful in diagnosing and treating severely disabled readers. Dr. Grant contributed a great deal to the writing of Chapter 9 on severe learning disabilities. We also extend our appreciation to Chris Baumle, Project Editor of Editing, Design & Production, Inc., and Kate Daly who spent many long hours in carefully editing the manuscript.

James Shanker would like to thank his wife Susan and his sons Kenneth and Michael for their support and assistance. And finally, Eldon Ekwall would like to extend his most sincere gratitude to his wife Carol Ann for her kindness and encouragement during the writing of his part of the third edition of this text.

To the Teacher

This is a textbook designed to be used in a first course in diagnosis and/ or remediation of reading disabilities. It is designed for either advanced under- graduates or graduate students who have had at least one course in the founda- tions of reading instruction.

You will note that Chapters 4 through 9 contain a section on diagnosis (Part A) and a section on remediation (Part B). If your institution offers sepa- rate courses in diagnosis and remediation, this format should facilitate the assignment of readings to supplement classroom activities. On the other hand, if diagnosis and remediation are combined in the same course, the student should read Parts A and B of these chapters.

We have yet to find a textbook concerning diagnosis or remediation of reading difficulties that presents various topics in the order in which we wish to present them in our classes. In this text we have presented the topics in what we believe to be a logical sequence for a student's learning needs. However, some professors may wish to cover certain topics in a different sequence. For example, you may wish to cover the administration and scoring of informal reading inventories before Chapter 11. This should present no problems.

Many students have expressed the concern that books presenting a con- stant deluge of research and long lists of references for each research study are ineffective. We have tried to make this book scholarly enough to maintain the faith and respect of both the student and the professor; also, we have tried to avoid listing many references to research that is commonly known or readily available to anyone with access to a library. Yet where issues are controversial or where the research is meager, we have tried to reference each study.

It is our hope that you will find the overall format stimulating and the material rewarding.

DIAGNOSIS AND REMEDIATION OF THE DISABLED READER

Reasons for Failure in Reading

This chapter examines the state of literacy in the United States and contains a discussion of the various factors that contribute to, or are related to, disability in reading. At this point no attempt will be made to discuss diagnostic and remedial procedures for various causal factors. The purpose of this chapter is to give an overview of these factors and the relative prevalence of each factor so that appropriate diagnostic and remedial procedures can be devised.

Experts agree that millions of adults and children in the United States cannot read. A number of major studies and considerable exposure in the national media have focused attention on the literacy problem. However, attempts to determine what percentage of individuals are illiterate are complicated by definitions of literacy and difficulty in assessing the reading performance of such a large population. In his book *Illiterate America,* Jonathan Kozol (1985) presents a disturbing, if not devastating, picture of reading problems in America:

> Twenty-five million American adults cannot read the poison warnings on a can of pesticide, a letter from their child's teacher, or the front page of a daily paper. An additional 35 million read only at a level which is less than equal to the full survival needs of our society.
>
> Together, these 60 million people represent more than one third of the entire adult population.
>
> The largest numbers of illiterate adults are white, native-born Americans. In proportion to population, however, the figures are higher for blacks and Hispanics than for whites. Sixteen percent of white adults, 44 percent of blacks, and 56 percent of Hispanic citizens are functional or marginal illiterates. Figures for the younger generation of black adults are increasing. Forty-seven percent of all black seventeen-year-olds are functionally illiterate. That figure is expected to climb to 50 percent by 1990.
>
> Fifteen percent of recent graduates of urban high schools read at less than sixth grade level. One million teenage children between twelve and seventeen cannot read above the third grade level. Eighty-five percent of juveniles who come before the courts are functionally illiterate. Half the heads of households classified below the poverty line by federal standards cannot read an eighth grade book. Over one third of mothers who receive support from welfare are functionally illiterate. Of eight million unemployed adults, four to six million lack the skills to be retrained for hi-tech jobs.
>
> The United States ranks forty-ninth among 158 member nations of the U.N. in its literacy levels.
>
> In Prince George's County, Maryland, 30,000 adults cannot read above a fourth grade level. The largest literacy program in this county reaches one hundred people yearly.
>
> In Boston, Massachusetts, 40 percent of the adult population is illiterate. The largest organization that provides funds to the literacy programs of the city reaches 700 to 1,000 people.
>
> In San Antonio, Texas, 152,000 adults have been documented as illiterate. In a single municipal district of San Antonio, over half the adult population is illiterate in English. Sixty percent of the same population sample is illiterate in Spanish. Three percent of adults in this district are at present being served.
>
> In the State of Utah, which ranks number one in the United States in the percent of total budget allocated to the education sector, 200,000

adults lack the basic skills for employment. Less than 5 percent of Utah's population is black or Hispanic.

Together, all federal, state, municipal, and private literacy programs in the nation reach a maximum of 4 percent of the illiterate population. The federal government spends $100 million yearly to address the needs of 60 million people. The President has asked that this sum be reduced to $50 million. Even at the present level, direct federal allocations represent about $1.65 per year for each illiterate.

In 1982 the Executive Director of the National Advisory Council on Adult Education estimated that the government would need to spend about $5 billion to eradicate or seriously reduce the problem. The commission he served was subsequently dismissed by presidential order.

Fourteen years ago, in his inaugural address as governor of Georgia, a future President of the United States proclaimed his dedication to the crisis of illiterate America. "Our people are our most precious possession . . . Every adult illiterate . . . is an indictment of us all . . . If Switzerland and Israel and other people can end illiteracy, then so can we. The responsibility is our own and our government's. I will not shirk this responsibility."

Today the number of identified nonreaders is three times greater than the number Jimmy Carter had in mind when he described this challenge and defined it as an obligation that he would not shirk.

On April 26, 1983, pointing to the literacy crisis and to a collapse in standards at the secondary and the college levels, the National Commission on Excellence in Education warned: "Our Nation is at risk." (pp. 4–6)*

Kozol's analysis was based primarily on data that assessed individuals' *functional illiteracy,* for example, their ability to read poison warning labels or the front page of a newspaper.

Subsequent to Kozol's book, a major study was completed by the National Assessment of Educational Progress (NAEP). It is titled *Literacy: Profiles of America's Young Adults* (1986). The findings of this study appear to be somewhat in conflict with the dire statistics presented by Kozol.

The United States Department of Education provided $2 million for the NAEP study, which was conducted to determine the reading abilities of young adults. The subjects' performance was classified according to various levels.

To complete the report, the NAEP researchers surveyed a national sample of 3,600 young adults aged twenty-one to twenty-five using techniques that were more thorough than in earlier studies. Each subject was interviewed for approximately ninety minutes, thirty minutes of which were spent to obtain important background information. The remaining time was used to de-

---

*Excerpt from *Illiterate America* by Jonathan Kozol. Copyright © 1985 by Jonathan Kozol. Reprinted by permission of Doubleday & Company, Inc.

termine the subjects' abilities to perform 105 tasks that simulated real-life situations.

The authors of the final report, Irwin S. Kirsch and Ann Jungeblut, concluded that the overwhelming majority (approximately 95 percent) of America's young adults could perform routine tasks using printed information. However, this figure refers to the percentage of young adults who meet or exceed the average reading proficiency level of *fourth-grade students.* The study found that 80 percent of the subjects could read at or above the eighth-grade level and 62 percent, at or above the eleventh-grade level.

The publication of the results of the NAEP study brought forth many responses. In *Reading Today* (1986/1987) Ronald W. Mitchell, executive director of the International Reading Association, summarized the feeling of most experts on reading instruction:

> The data give us reason to celebrate the fact that nearly all young adults are acquiring basic literacy skills. On the other hand, we are concerned by the fact that, as the report notes, a significant number of individuals are failing to develop advanced reading abilities that will enable them to achieve their full potential in a technologically advanced society. (p. 1)

However it is measured, we have reason to be concerned about individuals who because of reading difficulties are unable to benefit fully from life in our society. An alarming percentage of people who do not succeed in our society—individuals who are unemployed, on welfare, or incarcerated—cannot read. And illiterates who do manage to earn a living have to live with low self-esteem and constant fear that their inability to read will be discovered by others. There is no evidence that reading will become less important in the future. To the contrary, it is clear that greater reading ability is necessary in the midst of technological change and an increasingly complex society.

As a teacher of reading, you have an opportunity to influence dramatically the lives of your students by preventing or correcting reading difficulties. To do this is not only important but also immensely satisfying.

In 1985 another major report, *Becoming a Nation of Readers,* was published. This report, considered required for reading educators, was produced under the auspices of the National Academy of Education's Commission on Education and Public Policy, with the sponsorship of the National Institute of Education. Two quotes from this report are particularly important for you as a teacher of reading to consider:

> An indisputable conclusion of research is that the quality of teaching makes a considerable difference in children's learning. (p. 85)
> The knowledge is now available to make worthwhile improvements in reading throughout the United States. If the practices seen in the classrooms of the best teachers in the best schools could be introduced everywhere, improvements in reading would be dramatic. (p. 3)

Our goal in writing this book is to inform you about the current state of knowledge of the diagnosis and remediation of disabled readers and to describe the most appropriate practices for helping people to become successful readers.

In this chapter we shall examine in some detail the many factors that may contribute to reading problems. As you shall see, there is no *one* cause of reading failure. In almost all cases a variety of factors combine to cause an individual to fail to learn to read.

It is fascinating to see the pieces of a diagnostic puzzle begin to take shape through the process of interviewing, collecting background data, and testing. It is also extremely rewarding to see the progress of a disabled reader as the information derived from the diagnostic process is implemented in the teaching program. However, regardless of the thoroughness of the diagnostic process, you are likely to see few positive results unless it is followed by a remedial program based on the results of the original diagnosis. Likewise, a remedial program that is not based on the results of a thorough diagnosis is likely to fail. Since a child is constantly growing and changing, it is imperative that diagnosis and remediation be a continuous process.

Since reading diagnosis and remediation can seldom be separated for practical purposes, it becomes imperative that the reading specialist be well trained in both areas. As a practicing or future reading specialist, you must know what kinds of problems to look for and what to do about these problems when they are found to exist. Most of the diagnostic-remedial process for the reader deals with problems that could be classified under four major categories. These categories are illustrated in Figure 1-1.

As a reading specialist, your primary concern is the diagnosis and remediation of educational factors. However, a study of the problems related to reading disability should also make you more aware of various causal factors that

FIGURE 1–1 Factors That Influence the Reader.

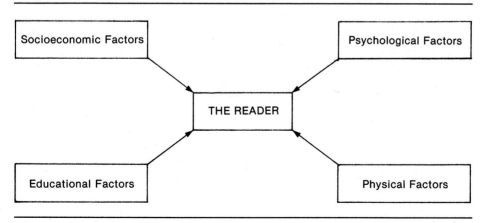

are often different from those that appear obvious when a diagnosis is made. In many cases, even though remedial procedures are instituted for a particular student, they are of less value than they might have been if some precautions had been taken to alleviate conditions or factors that caused the reading disability in the first place. Perhaps it should be emphasized at this point that there are also many factors that seem to have a close relationship to reading disability but cannot be established as having direct causal relationships. Since this textbook is not directed solely to the training of reading "technicians," it seems important to stress more than the "how to" of test administration and the "how to" of certain remedial techniques. Testing methods and materials, as well as teaching methods and materials, are constantly being updated and revised. To teach only those used at this time without examining other important aspects of reading would, in effect, be educating for obsolescence. There is still much to learn in the field of remedial reading, and although many problems are ambiguous, we cannot simply ignore them as being of little importance.

A monumental study done by Helen Robinson (1946) and described in her book entitled *Why Pupils Fail in Reading* is perhaps the best known, and it has contributed more to our knowledge about the reasons for pupil failure in reading than any other research effort. Because it was a landmark study, the results of Robinson's work will be summarized in the remainder of this chapter. Her findings will also be compared with those of more recent studies. Keep in mind, however, that it is seldom possible to determine the exact percentage of poor readers whose reading disability stems from a particular anomaly, as Robinson did in her research. This is true because we know that reading difficulties are often the result of multiple problems, or in many cases multiple problems are present that tend to mask the retarding effect of any one problem. Because of this problem many studies report only the percentage of retarded or disabled readers versus the percentage of normal readers who have exhibited certain anomalies. Other studies simply report whether there is a significant difference in the mean number of disabled readers versus the mean number of normal readers who exhibit certain anomalies. The term *disabled reader* has often been used to describe readers who are not reading well as measured by a combination of reading test scores compared to their potential as measured by intelligence tests. Or the term *disabled readers* may simply mean those students who are reading below the level of most students in their class. Chapter 13 contains a more thorough definition of the term *disabled reader* and its implications for the remedial reading program for students who have a serious discrepancy between their reading ability and their reading potential or who are not able to deal effectively with the reading materials used for instruction in their classrooms. In Robinson's study students who were below nine years of age and who had a reading grade level 0.9 years below their mental age and chronological age were accepted for study. Students who were nine years or older and had an average reading grade two years or more below their mental and chronological ages were also accepted for further study.

In conducting her study Robinson planned three steps. The first, done with the aid of various specialists, was to summarize and evaluate the literature concerning pupil failure. The second step was to identify and evaluate the causal factors in a group of severely disabled readers. The third and final step in Robinson's study was to present significant conclusions concerning causal factors and to discuss various problems needing further study.

In conducting her study Robinson enlisted the aid of various specialists. Included were a social worker, a neurologist, a psychiatrist, three ophthalmologists, an otolaryngologist, an endocrinologist, a speech specialist, and a reading specialist as well as Professor Robinson, who acted as psychologist and reading specialist. Thirty severely disabled readers with Binet IQs between 85 and 137 were examined by each of the various specialists. Following the examinations, all specialists met to present their findings. An intensive remedial program was then begun with twenty-two of the original thirty cases. During the remedial program an attempt was made to determine the "potency" of each of the possible causes listed as anomalies in the original diagnosis of each pupil.

In the initial diagnosis a number of factors were found in Robinson's disabled readers. At the conclusion of the remedial program Robinson's specialists again met to discuss the various anomalies that were considered to be probable causes of pupils' failure. Some of these factors were later determined to have had little or no impairing effect on the reading ability of the subjects. This information is summarized in Table 1–1.

As you will note, the percentages of agreement between anomalies considered important and those considered to be probable causes are not the same. This, of course, indicates the specialists did not believe that certain anomalies, even though definitely present, were necessarily contributors.

Although the number of pupils examined in Robinson's study was relatively small, the study had a number of outstanding features, some of which have been lacking in more recent studies. For example, every pupil was thoroughly examined by specialists in every area considered important to reading success or failure. Robinson was then able to carry on a remedial program and follow the progress of each student. Where necessary, students were even removed from their homes and placed in a special school to determine whether home conditions were causal factors in the pupils' failure. The social worker was able to visit homes to get a first-hand look at the students' environment. Additionally there were several specialists working in certain fields to check on any biases that any one tester might possess.

Reasons for pupils' failure are classified under the four major categories previously mentioned plus a fifth that is a combination of all four. They will be discussed in the following order:

1. Physical factors
2. Psychological factors
3. Socioeconomic factors

TABLE 1–1.   Percentage of Anomalies Considered to be Important Versus Probable Causes in Helen Robinson's Study.

	Percentage of Anomalies Considered Important	*Percentage of Anomalies Considered to be Probable Causes*
1. Visual difficulty	63.6	50.0
2. Neurological difficulty	22.7	18.1
3. Auditory difficulty	13.6	9.1
4. Speech or discrimination difficulty	27.3	18.1
5. General physical difficulty	9.1	4.5
6. Endocrine disturbance	22.7	9.1
7. Emotional maladjustment	40.9	31.8
8. Social problems	63.6	54.5
9. School methods	22.7	18.1

Reprinted by permission of the University of Chicago Press.

4. Educational factors
5. Combinations of the four major categories listed above

PHYSICAL FACTORS

The Eyes and Seeing

Robinson's initial analysis indicated that 63.6 percent of the pupils had some sort of visual difficulty. However, in the final analysis the specialists concluded that sight difficulties were the cause of reading retardation in only 50 percent of the cases.

It is almost impossible to find any substantial amount of agreement among researchers concerning exact percentages of disabled readers who exhibit seeing difficulties. It would appear, however, that Robinson's study is in general agreement with others who have studied seeing problems. For example, Howard Coleman (1968) examined eighty-seven children in grades one to six who had severe deficits in the reading and/or language arts areas. He reported that approximately 50 percent of these children had either sight or visual-perceptual dysfunctions. Coleman reported that 19.5 percent of the group with dysfunctions had refractive errors and 30 percent had visual-perceptual dysfunctions. Many researchers also agree with the position taken by Thomas Eames (1962):

One child might be greatly handicapped by a visual defect while another might perceive adequately on the basis of very poor retinal images. Statistically, it has been shown that defective visual acuity is not much more frequent among reading failures than among non-failures, although individual cases occur in which failure is definitely the result of impaired vision. Such cases are greatly benefitted by glasses if the poor vision is due to refractive error (eyes out of focus) but glasses are of no benefit when the visual deficiency is of amblyopic (insensitivity) nature. The mere existence of low acuity is to be regarded as a possible but not invariable cause of poor reading.

There is some disagreement among various researchers concerning the types of seeing problems responsible for reading disability. Certain types of eye and seeing problems do, however, tend to appear to be more closely related to reading disability than others. Chapter 8 contains a detailed discussion of these problems.

Auditory Difficulties

In discussing auditory difficulties it is necessary to make a distinction between auditory acuity and auditory discrimination. *Auditory acuity* refers to the ability to hear various frequencies at various intensities of loudness (measured in decibels). *Auditory discrimination* refers to the ability to hear major or slight differences in sounds.

It is somewhat difficult to interpret Robinson's percentages in these categories because difficulties in these areas were viewed somewhat differently than at the present time. One reason for this is that we now have better tests of auditory discrimination than were available to Robinson and her researchers. Robinson lumped speech and discrimination difficulties together. Each of these will be discussed separately.

Auditory acuity.   Robinson reports that inadequate auditory acuity was considered to be a cause of reading difficulty in 9 percent of her cases. However, Robinson also states that her study reinforces the general opinion that insufficient auditory acuity is relatively unimportant as a cause of severe reading disabilities. It would be difficult, however, to determine whether Robinson's 9 percent figure is valid for disabled readers in general, since most researchers have tended to study auditory difficulties as a whole rather than isolate auditory acuity and study it as a separate factor.

Guy Bond, Miles Tinker, Barbara Wasson, and John Wasson (1984) report that various research studies disagree on the number of children with serious hearing losses. This disagreement occurs because of the different measurement techniques used and the lack of clear standards for determining what constitutes a hearing impairment. Nonetheless, Bond, Tinker, Wasson, and Wasson estimate that approximately 5 percent of the total population of schoolchildren have serious hearing losses. They also believe that many additional children have a slight hearing loss that may develop into a serious impairment if not treated early.

Studies tend to show that there are more cases of impaired auditory acuity among groups of disabled readers than among groups of average or good readers. However, even though the differences are sometimes statistically significant, the fact that a child has impaired auditory acuity is not necessarily predictive that the child will become a disabled reader.

It appears that hearing losses in the high-frequency ranges are more likely to result in reading impairment than hearing losses in the middle or low frequency ranges. It also appears that boys tend to experience loss in the high ranges more often than girls. The fact that the percentage of women teachers in the primary grades is much higher than the percentage of men teachers also makes a loss of acuity in the high frequency range more detrimental, since women's voices tend to range closer to the high frequencies.

In summary, it appears that although inadequate auditory acuity as a whole is seldom responsible for failure in reading, it may be an important factor in some isolated cases, especially if very severe and if not detected soon enough. There is general agreement that a test for auditory acuity should be included as part of a thorough diagnosis of a disabled reader. Recommendations with respect to testing in this area follow the discussion of auditory discrimination in Chapter 8.

Auditory discrimination. Robinson combined the categories of speech, general auditory discrimination, and memory span for sounds into a category called "Speech or Discrimination Difficulty." She reported that these factors were contributing anomalies in 18 percent of her severely disabled readers. However, she believed that dyslalia (a speech impairment due to a defect in the speech organs) was responsible for 14 of the 18 percent and that only the remaining 4 percent were caused by inadequate auditory discrimination or inadequate memory span.

It should be emphasized at this point that inadequate memory span is seldom studied in conjunction with inadequate auditory discrimination; however, both are often considered to be important factors in the diagnosis of disabled readers. As mentioned previously, better instruments have also been developed for the purpose of measuring impairment in both of these areas.

It should also be emphasized that children's auditory discrimination skills improve considerably as they progress through the primary grades. Bertha Thompson (1963) conducted a longitudinal study of auditory discrimination in a group of 105 children. She concluded that "inaccurate discriminative ability is more characteristic of first grade entrants than accurate ability. The reverse is true at the end of the second grade." (p. 377) Thompson also reported that at the end of the second grade approximately 24 percent of the students had inaccurate auditory discrimination ability. Approximately half (12 percent) of this group were classified as poor readers. Thompson's view of the relationship between auditory discrimination and reading is representative of that of a number of researchers. She states, "This again points toward the importance of adequacy in auditory discrimination to success in primary reading. However, it definitely reveals that other factors are important in reading disability." (p. 377)

Reid Lyon (1977) has reviewed the research in this area and has concluded that the evidence does *not* support the view that auditory discrimination ability is necessary for later success in reading. This remains a controversy and will be discussed more fully in Chapter 8.

As stated earlier, several tests of auditory memory have been developed since Robinson completed her study; these will also be discussed in Chapter 8. Little is known concerning the relationship between auditory memory and reading. Various studies indicate that a larger percentage of disabled readers have impaired auditory memory span or ability to sequence than do good readers. The mystery that remains, however, is what to do about this problem, since the training of auditory memory per se seldom seems to have any appreciable effect on children's reading ability.

Speech.   Robinson reported that speech problems were considered to be probable causes of reading failure in 14 percent of her cases. This is in general agreement with a number of studies reported by Thomas Eames (1950) and Bond, Tinker, and Wasson (1979), although the latter authors stated that some studies showed that the number of students with speech defects was no higher among disabled readers than in a normal population.

There is some feeling that certain neurological dysfunctions contribute to inadequacy in speech as well as in reading and therefore there is a tendency to view the reading disability as stemming from the speech problem, when in reality both result from the neurological dysfunction. Some researchers also believe that emotional reactions arising from defective speech may in turn contribute to reading disability. Eames (1950) states that certain broad generalizations may be drawn concerning the relationships between reading and speech. These are as follows:

1. Neurological lesions in the language centers or their interconnections may impair both speech and reading.
2. Failure or inadequacy of auditory association and discrimination may predispose to either speech or reading trouble.
3. Speech defects occur in a certain proportion of reading failures and vice versa.
4. Emotional reactions to speech difficulties may impair reading.
5. Oral reading is more difficult for a person with a speech defect.
   (p. 53)

Laterality, Mixed Dominance, and Directional Confusion

Before beginning a discussion of the topics of laterality, mixed dominance, and directional confusion, it would be helpful first to define these terms as

they are commonly used. The definitions that follow are those of Alice Cohen
and Gerald G. Glass (1968), as derived from Albert Harris (1958).

> *Lateral Dominance* refers to the preference or superiority of one side of
> the body over the other (hand, eye, foot) in performing motor tasks.
> Right lateral dominance would indicate preference for the right hand,
> eye, and foot.
>
> *Laterality* is another term for lateral dominance.
>
> *Consistent Dominance* refers to the preferential use of one hand, eye,
> or foot.
>
> *Mixed or Incomplete (hand, eye, or foot) Dominance* exists when the
> individual does not show a consistent preference for one (eye, hand,
> or foot).
>
> *Mixed Dominance* without specific reference to hand, eye, or foot
> concludes both crossed dominance (see below) and mixed dominance.
>
> *Crossed Dominance* exists when the dominant hand and dominant eye
> are on opposite sides.
>
> *Visual Motor Consistency* occurs when the subject's dominant hand,
> eye, and foot are on the same side of the body.
>
> *Directional Confusion* refers to knowledge of left and right.
> "Knowledge of Left and Right" is demonstrated by the subject in
> response to questions such as, "show me your right hand, left eye"
> etc. (This is distinguished from actual use of the dominant hand, eye,
> or foot in performance tasks.) (p. 343)

Robinson did not attempt to determine what percentage, if any, of her disabled readers' problems resulted from mixed dominance or difficulties with
laterality. She stated that tests for mixed dominance were given but that
the specialists cooperating in her study did not know how to interpret their
findings.

The research on the relationship of laterality, mixed dominance, and directional confusion to reading is voluminous. From all of this, however, there are
still no clear-cut answers as to what we should test for and what we can do
about these problems. Some of the proponents of various approaches to the
remediation of problems in this area have been very vociferous and consequently, in our opinion, have oversold the value of remedial materials and
techniques in this area. Studies such as those of E. Shearer (1968), Steven
Forness (1968), and R. J. Capobianco (1967) are in general agreement with
the findings of Cohen and Glass (1968), who studied 120 subjects in the first
and fourth grades. Half of their sample were defined as "good" readers and
half were defined as "poor" readers. Their statistical analysis revealed the
following relationships as being significant:

1. *Knowledge of left and right and reading ability in the first grade.*
   Good readers were more likely to be "normal" and poor readers

were more likely to be "hesitant" or "confused" in their knowledge of left and right.

2. *Hand dominance and reading ability in first grade.* Good readers were more likely to have a dominant hand and poor readers were more likely to have mixed-hand dominance.

3. *Knowledge of left and right between first- and fourth-grade children.* Significantly more first-grade children than fourth-grade children were hesitant or confused in their knowledge of left and right. Significantly more fourth-grade children than first graders were normal in their knowledge of left and right.

4. *Knowledge of left and right and hand dominance.* Right-handed children were more likely to have knowledge of left and right. Left-handed and mixed children were more likely to be hesitant or confused in their knowledge of left and right.

However, no significance was found between fourth graders' reading ability and knowledge of left and right. The same was true for hand dominance. The reader may be most concerned with the factor of *crossed dominance.* This factor is what most people are referring to when the area of laterality is discussed. No significant relationship between crossed dominance and reading ability was found in the total population studied. (p. 345)[1]

Similar findings were reported by Albert Harris (1979) in a review of research on this topic.

As stated earlier, Robinson's researchers administered tests for lateral dominance but did not feel that they knew how to interpret their findings. These researchers were simply being conservative in their beliefs. Very little more is known today regarding the accurate interpretation of findings such as those reported by Cohen and Glass. Until more is known regarding effective remedial procedures for these areas that will, in turn, improve children's reading ability, a diagnosis for laterality, mixed dominance, and directional confusion seems to be of dubious value.

Neurological Problems

Laterality, mixed dominance, and directional confusion often are quite properly classified as neurological dysfunctions. They are separated here from the general heading of neurological problems for purposes of clarifying the discussion of these factors. General neurological problems also include an array of dysfunctions related to difficulties in reading. It is believed that neurological

---

[1]Reprinted by permission of the authors and the International Reading Association.

dysfunctions may stem from genetic mutations and that certain characteristics are also heritable. A further cause of neurological dysfunctions is brain injury.

Robinson and her researchers believed that neurological difficulties were an important anomaly in 22.7 percent of her retarded readers, and they were considered as a probable cause in 18.1 percent of these cases. It would be difficult to determine whether these percentages apply to disabled readers in general, since the term *neurological difficulty* is interpreted so broadly. Furthermore, some authorities also feel that neurological difficulties can be accurately diagnosed only by a neurologist; therefore, the results of a number of studies of so-called neurologically impaired disabled readers may be contaminated by other factors. A further problem exists in that many children exhibit symptoms of neurological dysfunction and yet read perfectly well. Che Kan Leong (1980) pointed out:

> The field of cerebral mechanisms underlying reading disabilities is vast, complex and touches on many disciplines: psychology, neurology, language and education. Partly because of this complexity and the interrelatedness of the workings of the brain, the findings are less than conclusive. (p. 198)

Children classified as dyslexic or alexic[2] are usually categorized as having neurological difficulties. Robinson believed, as have many others since, that children are often classified as alexic or dyslexic when in reality they do not exhibit the symptoms of the typically dyslexic or alexic child. This again complicates any attempt to determine the percentage of disabled readers who have neurological difficulties.

The fact does remain that a certain proportion of disabled readers have neurological difficulties but that neurological difficulties probably account for a small percentage of the actual causes of reading disability. However, as Barbara Bateman (1974) has stressed, the fact that a student is classified as having a minimal brain dysfunction (MBD) does not help in the diagnosis of the child's reading problem. A student who is an extremely disabled reader ultimately must be taught to read regardless of how we label his or her condition.

Other Physical Factors

Researchers who have studied other physical factors than those discussed previously have often concluded that glandular disturbances contribute to reading disabilities. Robinson and her researchers believed that endocrine disturbances

---

[2]The term *dyslexic* refers to a condition of severe reading disability. Some authors have stated that it is related to neurological dysfunctions and others simply define the term as a condition in which a student is severely disabled in reading for no apparent reason. (For a more thorough discussion of this term and of severe reading disability, see Chapter 9.)

were important in 40.9 percent of her reading disability cases. They did, however, conclude that endocrine disturbances were the actual cause in only 9.1 percent of her cases. This still, of course, represents a rather high figure and makes glandular disturbances an important factor in reading difficulties. Robinson also stressed the point that when endocrine disturbances were present, they not only retarded progress in learning but also tended to interfere with progress in other areas such as orthoptic treatment, social adjustment, and physical well-being. She stated that although this anomaly was less frequent, it did have a marked influence on certain cases.

Other researchers, such as Donald E. P. Smith (1958) and Lyman Cavanaugh (1948), have also concluded that glandular disturbances are an extremely important factor in reading disability. Cavanaugh studied 660 children and concluded that 18 percent had rather serious thyroid deficiencies that could contribute to disability in learning. Smith believed that treatment for endocrine disturbances could in some cases yield promising to dramatic results.

An article in the *Chronicle of Higher Education* (1985) reports that genetics is tied to disabilities in reading. According to Sadie Decker, a study on 100 pairs of twins found that "unquestionably, there is an important genetic factor behind the reading disabilities some individuals suffer." (p. 7) Decker evaluated the reading performance of both fraternal and identical twins and reported that where reading difficulties occurred in one fraternal twin, only 50 percent to 65 percent of the time did such a disability occur in the other fraternal twin. However, when the difficulty occurred in identical twins, 80 percent to 90 percent of the time, both twins suffered reading disorders. Decker concluded, "We still don't know how the reading disability is transmitted genetically. But the 80- to 90-percent concordance rate among identical twins indicates there is a clear genetic link." (p. 7)

Other physical factors often listed as either causal or concomitant are malnutrition, poor dentition, allergies, infected tonsils and/or adenoids, vitamin deficiencies, and susceptibility to colds. However, among these disorders Robinson found that only malnutrition could be considered a causal factor. She believed that although various physical disorders are often present in cases of reading disability, they are seldom the actual cause of reading disability.

PSYCHOLOGICAL FACTORS

A number of studies have been conducted to determine the relationship of various psychological factors to reading disability. Among the factors often studied are various emotional problems, intelligence, and self-concept. It should be stressed that all of these factors are no doubt highly interrelated, so that it becomes difficult if not impossible to completely separate them for isolated study.

Emotional Problems

In researching emotional problems the question that most often arises is whether reading disability causes or is caused by emotional problems. It appears that each tends to contribute to the other, with reading disability causing emotional problems more often than the reverse.

Robinson reported that 40.9 percent of her disabled readers had a significant degree of emotional maladjustment, but she believed that it was an anomaly that caused reading failure in only 31.8 percent of her cases. Robinson's reported percentages in this category probably vary more from those reported in other studies than do her percentages for any of the other categories. Gates (1941) reported that 75 percent of the disabled readers he studied showed personality maladjustment; Gates believed that in about 25 percent of these (or about 19 percent of the total group of disabled readers) the emotional maladjustment was a contributing cause of reading disability. Albert Harris and Edward Sipay (1980) report that of several hundred cases of reading disability seen in the Queens College Educational Clinic during a fifteen-year period, close to 100 percent showed some kind of maladjustment. Harris and Sipay report that emotional maladjustment was a causal factor in about 50 percent of the cases in this group. Harris and Sipay also report on a study by Eve Malmquist (1967). Malmquist's examination of 399 Swedish children indicated that nervous traits were probably contributing causes of reading failure in 23 percent of the disabled readers.

It is evident that there is wide disagreement not only about the percentage of disabled readers we may expect to have emotional problems, but also about the contribution of emotional maladjustment as a causal factor in reading failure. The important point, however, is that the disabled reader who comes to the educational diagnostician or to the remedial reading teacher is likely to exhibit some sort of emotional maladjustment. For this reason proper diagnosis and remediation of emotional problems must be considered a necessary part of a remedial reading program.

Intelligence

A number of research studies have been conducted to determine the relationship between achievement and intelligence. Albert Harris (1972) has pointed out:

> the relation between intelligence and reading is low to moderate at the beginning level, but increases as children get older. . . . As the nature of the reading task becomes more one of comprehension and interpretation, intelligence becomes a stronger determining factor. (p. 42)

Harris decries the use of group intelligence tests, suggesting that the nonverbal tests are unfair to disabled readers and poor measures of the abilities required for successful reading development. Harris believes that an individual verbal intelligence test, such as the Stanford-Binet or the Revised Wechsler Intelligence Scale for Children (WISC), is the best available device for estimating a child's potential to read with comprehension.

In spite of the fact that literally thousands of studies have been conducted on intelligence tests, it is not clear how useful such instruments are in diagnosing reading difficulties. For example, a study by Louise Ames and Richard Walker (1964) sought to determine whether fifth-grade reading achievement could be predicted from WISC IQ scores administered at the kindergarten level. Ames and Walker concluded that the usefulness of their reported findings did not lie in predicting fifth-grade reading scores. Rather, they offered the suggestion that individual subject characteristics other than either general intelligence or specific reading skills contributed to individual differences in reading at the above-average level as well as below average.

George and Evelyn Spache (1977) expressed a similar viewpoint:

> . . . Research studies of school beginners show that intelligence test results are not highly predictive of early reading success. If pupils are arranged in the order of their reading test scores after a period of training, the order just does not neatly parallel a ranking based on mental age or intelligence quotient. Only the extreme cases, the very superior and the mentally retarded pupils, tend to agree in their ranks in reading and intelligence. The degree of reading success for most pupils is determined not by their exact level or rank in intelligence but by other more influential factors. (pp. 156–157)

It seems evident then that we should not place a great deal of reliance on IQ scores as predictors of potential reading ability. However, as Spache and Spache point out, the IQ is a fairly good predictor of reading ability for children with extremely high IQs or for children who are mentally retarded. Most researchers agree that children with very low IQs are at a considerable disadvantage in learning to read; therefore, a low IQ is often an important hindering factor. For this reason it is often helpful to administer an individual intelligence test as part of the normal diagnostic procedure with a disabled reader. An important point to remember, however, is that many children with low IQs become good readers and many children with medium and high IQs become disabled readers. Therefore, the IQ should only be considered in conjunction with other factors.

Some estimates have been made regarding the percentage of disabled readers whose problem stemmed from having a low IQ. The authors believe, however, that any percentage figure based on IQ alone is misleading because of the interaction of low IQ with a multitude of other factors such as home environment and teaching methods.

Self-Concept

The self-concept and its close relationship with teacher expectation is a psychological factor that should not be overlooked in the diagnosis of a disabled reader. Studies such as those of William Padelford (1969) and Maxine Cohn and Donald Kornelly (1970) have shown that a significant positive relationship between reading achievement and self-concept does exist. Padelford found that this relationship exists regardless of ethnic group, socioeconomic level, or sex. Cohn and Kornelly indicate that a program of remediation for a low self-concept can produce positive achievement in reading.

Monte Smith (1979) found that the combination of word-knowledge performance, math performance, and family socioeconomic status (SES) was a significant predictor of self-concept. Interestingly, Smith also found that learning-disabled students from high-SES families possessed lower self-concepts than their counterparts from low-SES families.

Little is known regarding the percentage of disabled readers whose problems are directly related to the possession of a low self-concept. However, we do know the problem exists, and as Frances Pryor (1975) states, "Changing a poor reader's self-concept by bolstering his feelings about himself is perhaps the first step toward improving the academic problem." (p. 359) For this reason this factor should not be overlooked in the diagnosis and remediation of the reader.

SOCIOECONOMIC FACTORS

Robinson reported that maladjusted homes or poor intrafamily relationships were found to be contributing causes in 54.5 percent of her cases. As she stated, this percentage was somewhat higher than those reported in other studies. Robinson believed that we often underestimate the importance of this factor. In her study a social worker was especially diligent in obtaining information from parents concerning difficulties and problems. Robinson apparently believed that because information concerning intrafamily relationships and other related factors are somewhat difficult to obtain, the percentages of these factors that appear as causal factors in reading disability are often unrealistically low.

Socioeconomic factors are usually so closely related that it would be impossible to list any specific percentage of reading disability cases resulting from any one isolated factor. Factors often studied, however, are presence of the father in the home (or broken homes), ethnic background and its social relationships, economic level, dialect, presence of books or stimulating reading materials in the home, sibling relationships, and parent-sibling relationships.

Martin Deutsch (1967) studied family relationships, including broken homes where the father was not present. Deutsch stated that "intact homes are more crowded than broken ones, although the children from the intact homes do better in scholastic achievement. . . . Apparently, *who* lives in the home is more important than *how many*." (p. 104)

Ethnic background and its social ramifications are also important influences on reading achievement. For example, the United States Commission on Civil Rights (1971) reported as follows:

The Commission found, on the basis of information provided by school principals, that from 50 to 70 percent of Mexican American and black students in the fourth, eighth, and twelfth grades are reading below the level expected for the grade to which they are assigned. In contrast, only 25 to 34 percent of all Anglo youngsters in these grades are reading below grade level. This approaches a two to one ratio of below average reading achievement for students of minority groups. (p. 24)

Of course, economic level is in many cases related to ethnic background. Many studies have shown that the overall reading level of children from poor communities, regardless of ethnicity, is often far below that of children from more affluent communities.

Nila Banton Smith (1974) has suggested that three basic contributing factors to reading difficulties are low self-concept, impoverished environment, and poor health.

The problem of dialect and its relationship to reading difficulties has received considerable attention. Researchers and writers such as S. Alan Cohen and Thelma Cooper (1972) have stressed, however, that dialectal differences of the urban disadvantaged reader are not a hindering factor in learning to read. Studies by Richard Rystrom (1968) and W. Labov (1969) have tended to confirm Cohen and Cooper's beliefs. Rystrom (1972) stated:

There is virtually no evidence to indicate that dialect is causally related to reading failures. . . . Any regional or social dialect is, so far as has been determined, an equally effective vehicle for learning to read as any other regional or social dialect.

Studies dealing with the relationship between reading ability and such factors as the number of books found in the home or the amount of time children's parents spend reading are of little value in furnishing us with information concerning the contribution of these factors to reading achievement. The problem, of course, lies in the fact that the number of books found in a home or the amount of time that parents spend reading is so often related to a host of other factors. Among these factors are education, occupation, and economic level of the parents. Perhaps about all we can say with any certainty is that there appears to be a group of other socioeconomic factors that interact to influence reading ability.

Donald T. Searls, Nancy A. Mead, and Barbara Ward (1985) examined the relationship of students' reading skills to television watching, leisure-time reading and homework. They reported on data including those gathered by the National Assessment of Educational Progress (NAEP) during its 1979–80 evaluation assessment of reading skills of nine-, thirteen-, and seventeen-year-olds across the United States. In this survey more than 75,000 students answered questions about their backgrounds. Searls, Mead, and Ward concluded:

TV viewing does appear to be negatively associated with academic achievement—children who watch more generally tend to do less well academically—but it must be remembered that the amount of TV watched varies among population groups, with children from lower socioeconomic groups watching more. When socioeconomic status and IQ are controlled, variations in achievement by amount of television watched become smaller. (p. 160)

The NAEP findings also suggest that the effects of television watching vary according to the ages of the students, with the reading performance of younger students (9-year-olds) actually improving as the amount of television viewing increases to more than four hours daily. Older students, however, did not appear to benefit much from television watching. The optimal amounts of time for television viewing by age were three to four hours for nine-year-olds, one to two hours for thirteen-year-olds, and under one hour for seventeen-year-olds.

Not surprisingly, Searls, Mead, and Ward found that spare-time reading was associated with higher reading-achievement scores. Interestingly, the highest achievement levels occurred among students who combined one to two hours per day of spare-time reading with what appeared to be the optimal amount of television viewing for their age group.

Social relationships between siblings and/or between parents and siblings are another social factor that appears to be worthy of consideration in a thorough diagnosis. However, definite information on the percentage of reading disability cases caused by intrafamily relationships is sadly lacking due to the complexities involved in their identification.

Language Factors

Inadequate language development is undoubtedly a factor in reading failure. Unfortunately, we are unable to determine specifically the extent to which language difficulties affect reading performance. Nor are useful instruments currently available for diagnosing language problems per se. In order to be useful, such a test must not only identify specific language weaknesses but also provide information for prescriptive instruction to remediate the difficulties.

The Test of Language Development (TOLD) (Newcomer and Hammill, 1977) does enable the diagnostician to evaluate children's expressive and receptive competencies in the areas of phonology, semantics and syntax. This standardized test is sufficiently reliable and valid. It is not a lengthy test and it yields a comparative index of the child's language abilities. The TOLD is not designed to provide direct information for prescriptive instruction. As the authors point out:

The results yielded by the TOLD will focus attention upon the specific areas of language in which the child is unable to perform as well as his peers do. In effect, the results will identify his primary linguistic deficits. However, before a remedial program is planned, it will be necessary to determine through informal assessment, including criterion-referenced testing, and possibly diagnostic teaching, the specific skills within an area which are in need of remediation. (Test Manual, p. 16)

The TOLD is intended for use with most children between the ages of 4–0 and 8–11. A companion test, *The Test of Early Language Development* (TELD) (Hresko, Reid, and Hammill, 1981) was designed for use with children between the ages of 3–0 and 7–11 who possess more severe language difficulties or who are less proficient in English.

Harris and Sipay (1980) believe the most significant aspects of language are the child's (1) vocabulary, (2) understanding of sentence structure, and (3) clarity of pronunciation. Emerald Dechant (1981) adds a fourth factor, listening comprehension.

Linda S. Siegel and Ellen B. Ryan (1984) concluded that reading-disabled students have deficits in short-term memory and language-processing skills. Siegel and Ryan believe that such students will benefit from teacher modeling and direct instruction designed to develop language skills. Research by Rebecca K. Edmiaston (1984) found a moderate-to-strong statistically significant relationship between oral language and reading comprehension among third graders. Edmiaston distinguished between a correlation and cause and effect and cautioned that educators cannot assume that "increased proficiency in one area will automatically result in improvement in the other." (p. 36)

This is an emerging and exciting area of research. Recent theories, supporting research, and recommendations for instruction in language skills will be presented in Chapter 7.

EDUCATIONAL FACTORS

Robinson mentioned a number of school factors or conditions that she and others believed often influenced or were conducive to reading failure. Among these factors were teachers' personalities, methods of teaching reading, school policy on promotions, materials available, and class size. In her final analysis Robinson believed that school methods were a probable contributing causal factor in 18.1 percent of the cases she studied. She admitted, however, that there are so many factors involved in assessing educational factors that any definite conclusion is nearly impossible.

It is our opinion that Robinson's figure in this case is not representative of the total percentage of reading failures caused by educational factors. If one views educational factors contributing to reading disability as strictly those so bad that many children within any classroom fail to learn, then perhaps Robinson's figure is representative of the situation in general. However, many experts agree with John Manning,[3] who expressed the viewpoint that more than 90 percent of our reading failures could or should be blamed on poor

[3]From a speech given by John Manning at the University of Kansas, summer 1969.

teaching. Since only approximately 2 percent of our students experience learning disabilities so severe as to require the services of a specialist, it seems logical that near-perfect teaching would result in a failure rate of no more than this 2 percent.

S. Jay Samuels (1970) expresses the opinion that instruction in reading is quite likely to be less than adequate:

> It is this author's contention that the assumption of adequate instruction is probably false in numerous instances because at the present time a complete analysis of the skills which must be mastered in the process of learning to read has not been made. Without a complete analysis of each of the subskills and concepts which must be mastered in the process of learning to read, it is difficult to understand how any instruction can be considered adequate. In the absence of a complete analysis of skills necessary for reading, there is a danger that the teacher may omit teaching important skills because she does not realize they are essential; or falsely assuming that certain skills have already been mastered, she may not teach them; or she may teach nonessential skills believing they are important. (p. 267)

Gerald Duffy and Lonnie McIntyre (1981) found that even highly rated first- and second-grade teachers do not necessarily provide quality instruction. The teachers studied were rated by peers and supervisors as "good teachers," yet the researchers found that they almost never provided structured lessons or direct assistance to students during reading instruction.

Richard. L. Allington (1983 and 1984) has concluded that the amount and type of actual reading students do in school may account for some of the achievement differences between good and poor readers. Allington reports that at every grade level good readers complete more contextual reading than poor readers and that students in the higher reading groups tend to read material silently more and orally less than their less able counterparts.

The problems in assessing educational factors as a cause of reading failures are so complex that any stated percentage is at best an educated guess. The fact remains, however, that educational factors should not be overlooked in the diagnostic procedure.

Research in the area of teacher behavior and its effects on students' reading performance has begun to shed some light on this matter. Christopher Clark (1979) identified five approaches to research designed to answer the question, What makes a good teacher? Jere Brophy (1979a) reviewed much of the research in this area and summarized some of the major findings in an occasional paper written for the Institute for Research on Teaching (IRT) at Michigan State University. The IRT was established in 1976 by the National Institute of Education to serve as a center for research on teaching, a forum for communication, and a training program for researchers. Some of the findings of IRT researchers will be included in the following review of selected studies on teacher effectiveness. Particular attention will be given to findings that relate teachers' instructional behaviors to students' reading achievement.

In 1976 the California state legislature directed the superintendent of public instruction to analyze selected schools to identify the educational factors that accounted for the distinction between unusually high-performing schools and unusually low-performing schools, as determined by standard tests of school achievement. The selected schools were comparable in social and demographic factors and varied only according to pupil attainment. The result was the *California School Effectiveness Study* (1977). This study found that factors *other* than those traditionally assumed to account for pupil achievement, such as family income and parents' occupational status, were significant determinants of pupil success:

1. *Staff characteristics.* Higher-achieving schools had principals who were more effective and involved, used aides significantly more for *noninstructional* tasks, and had central office administration that was rated higher by teachers in instructional leadership and allocation of materials and resources.
2. *Measures of contact between students and staff.* Teachers at higher-achieving schools did *not* report spending more instructional time on reading and language development.
3. *Instructional and organizational characteristics.* Students in higher-achieving schools "were perceived to be happier, more engaged in their work, and less disruptive, restless, or bored." (p. 8) Teachers at higher-achieving schools placed more emphasis on students' academic performance, divided their classes into several groups (rather than providing "individualized" instruction), and participated in a reading program that was more stable or less subject to change.

Marjorie Powell (1979) reported on the six-year Beginning Teacher Evaluation Study, also conducted in California. Some of the findings:

1. The greater the proportion of time that students are engaged in their work (on task), the more they learn.
2. Some teachers were more effective than others in keeping their students on task.
3. Some teachers were more effective than others in providing their students with instructional tasks that led to a high success rate.
4. The more total time spent in reading instruction, the more students learned in that area. (This finding contradicts those of the School Effectiveness Study.)
5. Some teachers placed greater emphasis than others on "academics" and had higher expectations for students. The teachers with the high standards produced students with higher achievement.

6. In higher-achieving classrooms, teachers and students demonstrated greater respect for each other and worked in a more cooperative atmosphere.

Wilbur Brookover and Lawrence Lezotte (1979) found that emphasis on the "basics" is one of the major differences between improving and declining schools. The staffs of improving schools emphasize basic reading objectives, devote more time to achieving these objectives and believe that *all* of their students can master basic skills. Brookover and Lezotte also found that improving schools have principals who are assertive in their instructional leadership and take responsibility for evaluating student performance.

Jane Stallings and others (1978) compared classes with high gains in reading to those with low gains at the secondary school level. The authors stressed the importance of a structured program with clear expectations for pupils and minimal time wasted during instruction. It was found that in high-gain classrooms, teachers assisted students more with written assignments than with verbal directions that students were to follow on their own. Also, these teachers varied the activities, closely monitored seatwork, and provided supportive feedback to students.

In summarizing the recent research that evaluates the effect of teaching behaviors on pupil achievement, Jere Brophy (1979*b*) concluded:

1. Teachers make a difference. Some teachers produce more learning in their students than others.
2. Teacher expectations for student learning are an important factor.
3. Effective teachers possess the skills needed to organize successfully and conduct instruction. They are good classroom managers.
4. Effective teachers provide a maximum amount of instruction on critical skills, with minimal time wasted.
5. Students who receive a great deal of direct instruction in a structured curriculum have the highest achievement.

James F. Baumann (1984) also summarized the research on teacher and school effectiveness. Based on these research findings he added a list of eleven implications for reading educators:

1. If you are a principal, reading specialist, or reading coordinator, be an instructional leader. Guide your faculty in the development of your school reading program.
2. Take responsibility for teaching and learning, have confidence in your ability to instruct, assume your students are capable of learning, and expect them to learn.
3. Have objectives for every lesson you teach, know what they are, and communicate them to your students.

4. Allocate enough time for reading instruction.
5. Keep nonengaged and transition time to a minimum; that is, keep your students on task.
6. Establish high success rates; success does breed success.
7. Be an effective classroom manager—be organized and prevent misbehavior.
8. Monitor student learning, provide feedback, and reteach when necessary.
9. Administer direct instruction; that is, you teach the lessons. Do not expect textbooks, workbooks, games, or media to teach.
10. Use traditional reading groups, but individualize within and between groups.
11. Strive for a warm, nonthreatening, convivial classroom atmosphere; students will learn better when they are in a structured but secure environment. (p. 112)

We wish to point out that not all studies support the generalizations we have noted above. However, a significant amount of research is emerging to support some basic principles of teaching that are consistent with our philosophy. We hope that as you read the rest of this book, you will bear in mind that all diagnostic and remedial procedures must fit within a framework of sound principles of instruction. For example, even the best techniques for remediating a specific reading difficulty will fail if the teacher does not set high expectations for the learner, maintain the students' task attention and provide direct instruction in a well-managed environment. Some important operational procedures for the diagnostic-remedial teacher are discussed in detail in Chapter 2.

PHYSICAL, PSYCHOLOGICAL, SOCIOECONOMIC, AND EDUCATIONAL FACTOR COMBINATIONS

During the past two decades a number of combinational factors have been reported as having a moderate to high degree of relationship to reading. Robinson mentioned a number of these factors but did not study most of them in detail because of their unwieldy nature and/or because not enough was known about them at the time. Although we now know somewhat more about some of these factors, only a meager amount of information is available regarding the exact role that these factors play in reading failure. Therefore, in the discussion that follows, some of these factors will be discussed, but no attempt will be made to designate any specific percentage of disabled readers who possess these problems, nor will any attempt be made to designate the percentage of disabled readers whose problems originated from these factors.

The Relationship of Visual-Motor Perceptions to Reading Disability

A number of studies have dealt with the relationship between visual-motor perception and reading disability. Typical of the results of many of these studies is one conducted by Ernest Schellenberg (1962), who studied thirty-six matched pairs of disabled and adequate third-grade readers. Schellenberg used the Marianne Frostig Developmental Test of Visual Perception, the E. Koppitz scoring method of the Bender Visual-Motor Gestalt, and the deviation measurements of the Bender Gestalt. He also used the Silent Reading Diagnostic Tests of the Developmental Reading Tests to measure word perception. Schellenberg found that the Silent Reading Diagnostic Tests significantly differentiated the disabled and adequate readers. However, the distribution scores on the Developmental Test of Visual Perception failed to differentiate disabled from adequate readers. Also, the Bender figures drawn for the Bender Visual-Motor Gestalt Test did not differentiate disabled from adequate readers. This test did, however, show differences between matched pairs of girls when the Bender figures were measured to the nearest sixteenth of an inch. Schellenberg concluded that at the third-grade level tests such as the Silent Reading Diagnostic Test have greater usefulness than nonverbal perception tests.

Earl Heath, Patricia Cook and Nancy O'Dell (1976) conducted a study to test their belief that "smooth, coordinated ocular-motor control is closely related to efficient reading performance." (p. 435) They found that ocular control could be improved and that the Bender program was superior to two other methods studied. They reported that the students who received the Bender treatment "approached the level of significance in reading gain." (p. 443) However, an examination of the reading-gain scores reveals that the Bender group results were *not* significantly higher than the other perceptual groups. The Bender group did score significantly higher than the control group on the reading measure. However, the control group received no treatment whatever, while the Bender group received ten weeks of treatment plus additional assistance from the parents. It is reasonable to assume that any form of instruction combined with parental involvement would produce some improvement in students' reading scores. This study may justify the belief that the Bender program improves ocular-motor control, but based on the data presented by the researchers, one cannot properly conclude that this program had a significant effect on the students' reading performance.

Barbara K. Keough (1974) reviewed the research conducted to determine the effects of vision-training programs on academic readiness and remediation of learning difficulties. She concluded that the value of such programs was questionable due to inadequate methodology in the research.

Jean Harber (1979) investigated the relationship of four perceptual and perceptual-motor skills—visual perception, visual-perceptual integration, sound blending, and visual closure—to two measures of reading achievement. She found that deficits in these perceptual skills were not highly related to reading performance in learning-disabled students. She suggested that such skills may not necessarily be requisite for success in reading. It may be that a number of difficulties commonly assumed to be related to reading disability are neither related nor important to remediate. Nicholas Aliotti (1980) found that letter-reversal errors were a developmental characteristic of many children.

Although certain items of the visual-motor perception tests may relate to reading disabilities, they appear to be of dubious value in the actual diagnosis of disabled readers. It is probably more profitable simply to determine whether a child recognizes words and to examine the kinds of errors made when words are miscalled. Remediation would then be directed at obvious problems rather than at nonword perceptual training, which seems to be of little or no value in reading. Studies usually indicate that children receiving this type of training consequently perform better on perceptual tests but fail to reach a higher level of reading achievement.

The Relationship Between Teacher Expectations and Self-Concept

A number of researchers and writers have emphasized the relationship between teacher expectations and student performance growing from students' self-concepts. Among those who have studied these relationships are James M. Palardy (1968), Dale L. Carter (1970), and Robert Rosenthal and Lenore Jacobson (1966). Palardy studied the effects of teacher attitudes on the achievement of first-grade boys and girls. He found that when first-grade teachers believed that boys were far less successful in learning to read than girls, the boys did achieve significantly less than boys in classes where teachers believed that boys were as successful as girls.

Carter studied the effect of teacher expectations on the self-esteem and academic performance of seventh-grade students. He found that teacher expectations are in part determined by cumulative records and that they significantly affect students' level of confidence and scholastic potential.

In a series of extensive studies Rosenthal obtained similar results and also found that teacher expectations affect even children's measured IQs.

Results such as these leave little doubt that students' self-concepts and attitudes are often adversely affected by teacher expectations and that teacher expectation can be a major factor in reading disabilities.

Reading Disability Is Usually a Result of Multiple Factors

We have attempted to list the various factors shown by research to be responsible for reading disabilities among school-age children. It should be stressed, however, that seldom is any child's reading disability a result of any single factor. The cases studied in detail by Robinson and her group showed that nearly every student's reading disability was a result of multiple factors. In a discussion of learning disabilities, Jules Abrams (1970) states:

There is no one single etiology for all learning disabilities. Rather, learning problems can be caused by any number of a multiplicity of factors, all of which may be highly interrelated. Unfortunately, all too often the child who is experiencing learning disorders is approached with a unitary orientation so that extremely important aspects of his unique learning problem may very well be ignored. The tendency of each professional discipline to view the entire problem "through its own window of specialization" often obscures vital factors which may contribute to, or at least exacerbate, the basic difficulty. It is just as invalid to conceive of one cure, one panacea, applied randomly to all types of learning disorders. (p. 299)

Margaret Early (1969) also cautions us to be aware of multiple factors in reading diagnosis as well as in future research:

Causes of reading disability are multiple. All research points to this conclusion, either directly as in Robinson's study, or indirectly by the very inconclusiveness of studies related to single factors. Future research should be concerned with broad studies, centered in schools rather than clinics involving both retarded and able readers, to determine the interactions among causative factors. Of the physical, emotional, mental, environmental, social, and educational factors that may affect reading ability, what combinations produce results?

Three implications for the classroom teacher, in addition to those already mentioned are as follows:

1. Insight into the causes of reading failure requires study of all phases of the learner: his health, home and family, personality, experience background and learning abilities, including detailed evaluation of the complex of skills that constitute reading. Adequate study of many of these facets is beyond the teacher, or reading clinician, or psychologist. Each of these persons needs to know when to make referrals when his diagnostic tools prove inadequate.
2. Since causation is multiple, remediation must also use many approaches. A single method of attack may be detrimental as well as useless.
3. As research in causation is tentative, so is diagnosis of individual cases. As hunches are confirmed or rejected by new insights, plans for treatment must also be changed. Diagnosis of the complex process of reading is continuous. (p. 61–62)

SUMMARY

A student's ability or inability to read is affected by a number of factors, which may be classified as socioeconomic, psychological, educational, and physical. In a monumental study done a number of years ago, Helen Robinson employed the services of a number of specialists in fields that relate to reading disabilities. Robinson and her group attempted to determine the kind and number of problems that each of her cases possessed. Through subsequent study they then attempted to determine which problems were causal factors in each student's reading disability. The various causal factors listed by Robinson, as well as the percentage of students who have reading disabilities caused by these factors, are generally in agreement with more recent studies.

There are, of course, many causes of reading disabilities, and many of these cannot be completely isolated since they often appear in conjunction with other factors believed to contribute to problems in reading. The disabled reader is likely to possess combinations of physical, psychological, socioeconomic, and educational problems, all of which contribute to reading difficulties.

A number of studies have shown that certain problems such as those of a visual-perceptual nature may be related to, if not direct causal factors of, reading disability. Many studies, however, have also shown that remediation of this type of problem has little or no direct effect on a student's ability to read.

Other studies have shown that problems other than those studied by Robinson may also affect students' ability to read. For example, there appears to be a relationship among socioeconomic level, visual and auditory discrimination, and modality shifting. There is also believed to be a relationship between syntactic competence and reading disability. To date, however, little concrete research has been done that will help the remedial reading teacher diagnose and remediate these problems even when they are known to exist.

One of the most important points to be learned from Robinson's and subsequent studies is that students' reading disabilities are not usually the result of any single factor. The remedial-reading teacher should be especially careful to keep this in mind in both diagnostic and remedial work. The practitioner must also be careful not to be consumed by the search for the specific cause or causes of a student's reading disability. Attention to this area should not be so great as to detract from efforts to correct the reading problem.

REFERENCES

Abrams, J. C. (1970). Learning Disabilities—A complex phenomenon. *Reading Teacher, 23,* 299–303.

Aliotti, N. C. (1980). Tendency to mirror-image on a visual memory test. *Academic Therapy, 15,* 261–267.

Allington, R. L. (1983). The reading instruction provided readers of differing reading abilities. *Elementary School Journal, 83,* 548–559.

Allington, R. L. (1984). Content coverage and contextual reading in reading groups. *Journal of Reading Behavior, 16,* 85–97.

Ames, L. B., & Walker, R. N. (1964). Prediction of later reading ability from kindergarten rorschach and IQ scores. *Journal of Educational Psychology, 55,* 309–313.

Anderson, R. C., Hiebert, E. H., Scott, J. A., & Wilkinson, I. A. G. (1985). *Becoming a nation of readers: The report of the commission on reading.* Washington, DC: The National Institute of Education.

Bateman, B. (1974). Educational implications of minimal brain dysfunction. *Reading Teacher, 27,* 662–668.

Baumann, J. F. (1984). Implications for reading instruction from the research on teacher and school effectiveness. *Journal of Reading, 28,* 109–115.

Bond, G. L., Tinker, M. A., & Wasson, B. B. (1979). *Reading difficulties: Their diagnosis and correction* (4th ed.). Englewood Cliffs, NJ: Prentice-Hall.

Bond, G. L., Tinker, M. A., Wasson, B. B., & Wasson, John B. (1984). *Reading difficulties: Their diagnosis and correction* (5th ed.). Englewood Cliffs, NJ: Prentice-Hall.

Brookover, W. B., & Lezotte, L. W. (1979). *Changes in school characteristics coincident with changes in student achievement.* East Lansing. MI: Institute for Research on Teaching.

Brophy, J. E. (1979a). *Teacher behavior and its effects.* East Lansing, MI: Institute for Research on Teaching.

Brophy, J. E. (1979b). *Advances in teacher effectiveness research.* East Lansing, MI: Institute for Research on Teaching.

California school effectiveness study—The first year: 1974-75. (1977). Sacramento, CA: California State Department of Education.

Capobianco, R. J. (1967). Ocular-manual laterality and reading achievement in children with special learning disabilities. *American Educational Research Journal, 4,* 133–138.

Carter, D. L. (1970). *The effect of teacher expectations on the self-esteem and academic performance of seventh grade students.* Doctoral dissertation, University of Tennessee.

Cavanaugh, L. (1948). Reading behavior with regard for endocrine imbalances. *Thirteenth Yearbook of the Claremont College Reading Conference* (pp. 95–102). Claremont, CA.

Clark, C. (1979). *Five faces of research on teaching.* East Lansing, MI: The Institute for Research on Teaching.

Cohen, A., & Glass, G. G. (1968). Lateral dominance and reading ability. *Reading Teacher, 21,* 343–348.

Cohen, S. A., & Cooper, T. (1972). Seven fallacies: Reading retardation and the urban disadvantaged beginning reader. *Reading Teacher, 26,* 38–45.

Cohn, M., & Kornelly, D. (1970). For better reading—A more positive self-image. *Elementary School Journal, 70,* 199–201.

Coleman, H. M. (1968). Visual perception and reading dysfunction. *Journal of Learning Disabilities, 1,* 116–123.

Dechant, E. (1981). *Diagnosis and remediation of reading disabilities.* Englewood Cliffs, NJ: Prentice-Hall.

Deutsch, M., et al. (1967). *The disadvantaged child.* New York: Basic Books.

Duffy, G., & McIntyre, L. (1981). *A qualitative analysis of how various primary grade teachers employ the structured learning component of the direct instructional model when teaching reading.* East Lansing, MI: Institute for Research on Teaching.

Eames, T. H. (1950). The relationship of reading and speech difficulties. *Journal of Educational Psychology, 51,* 51–55.

Eames, T. H. (1962). Physical factors in reading. *Reading Teacher, 15,* 427–432.

Early, M. J. (1969). *Reading disabilities: Selections on identification and treatment.* Edited by H. Newman. Indianapolis: Odyssey Press.

Edmiaston, R. K. (1984). Oral language and reading: How are they related for third graders? *Remedial and Special Education, 5,* 33–37.

Forness, S. R. (1968). *Lateral dominance in retarded readers with signs of brain dysfunction.* Doctoral dissertation, University of California, Los Angeles.

Gates, A. J. (1941). The role of personality maladjustment and remedial reading. *Journal of Generic Psychology, 59,* 77–83.

Genetics tied to disabilities in reading. (1985). *Chronicle of Higher Education, 30,* p. 7.

Harber, J. R. (1979). Are perceptual skills necessary for success in reading? Which ones? *Reading Horizons, 20,* 7–15.

Harris, A. J. (1958). *Harris tests of lateral dominance—Manual of directions* (3d ed.). New York: Psychological Corporation.

Harris, A. J. (1972). *Readings on reading instruction.* (2d ed.). Edited by A. J. Harris & E. R. Sipay. New York: David McKay.

Harris, A. J. (1979). Lateral dominance and reading disability. *Journal of Learning Disabilities, 12,* 57–63.

Harris, A. J., & Sipay, E. R. (1980). *How to increase reading ability* (7th ed.). New York: Longman.

Heath, E. J., Cook, P., & O'Dell, N. (1976). Eye exercises and reading efficiency. *Academic Therapy, 11,* 435–445.

Hresko, W. P., Reid, D. K., & Hammill, D. D. (1981). *The test of early language development.* Austin, TX: Pro-Ed.

Keough, B. K. (1974). Optometric vision training programs for children with learning disabilities: Review of issues and research. *Journal of Learning Disabilities, 7,* 219–231.

Kirsch, I. S., & Jungeblut, A. (1986). *Literacy: Profiles of america's young adults.* Princeton, NJ: The National Assessment of Educational Progress.

Kozol, J. (1985). *Illiterate america.* Garden City, NY: Anchor Press/Doubleday.

Krippner, S. (1968). Etiological factors in reading disability of the academically talented in comparison to pupils of average and slow learning ability. *Journal of Educational Research, 61,* 275–279.

Labov, W. (1969). The logic of non-standard dialectic. Edited by J. E. Alatis. *School of Languages and Linguistics Monograph Series.*

Leong, C. K. (1980). Laterality and reading proficiency in children. *Reading Research Quarterly, 15,* 185–202.

Lyon, R. (1977). Auditory-perceptual training: The state of the art. *Journal of Learning Disabilities, 10,* 564–572.

Malmquist, E. (1967). *Reading and writing disabilities in children: Diagnosis and remedial methods.* Lund, Sweden: Gleerup.

Newcomer, P. L., & Hammill, D. (1977). *The test of language development.* Austin, TX: Pro-Ed.

Padelford, W. B. (1969). *The influence of socioeconomic level, sex, and ethnic background upon the relationship between reading achievement and self-concept.* Doctoral dissertation, University of California, Los Angeles.

Palardy, J. M. (1968). *The effect of teachers' beliefs on the achievement in reading of first-grade boys.* Doctoral dissertation, Ohio State University.

Powell, M. (1979). New evidence for old truths. *Educational Leadership, 37,* 49–51.

Pryor, F. (1975). Poor reading—Lack of self esteem? *Reading Teacher, 28,* 358–359.

Reading Today. (December, 1986/January, 1987). Newark, DE: International Reading Association.

Robinson, H. (1946). *Why pupils fail in reading.* Chicago: University of Chicago Press.

Rosenthal, R., & Jacobson, L. (1966). Teachers' expectancies: Determinants of pupils' IQ gains. *Psychological Reports, 19,* 115–118.

Rystrom, R. (1968). *Effects of standard dialect training on negro first graders being taught to read.* (Report Project No. 81–053). U.S. Dept. of HEW.

Rystrom, R. (1972, November). *Dialect differences and initial reading instruction.* Address given at National Council of Teachers of English Conference.

Samuels, S. J. (1970). Research-reading disability. *Reading Teacher, 24,* 267 + .

Schellenberg, E. D. (1962). *A study of the relationship between visual motor perception and reading disabilities of third grade pupils.* Doctoral dissertation, University of Southern California.

Searls, D. T., Mead, N. A., & Ward, B. (1985). The relationship of students' reading skills to TV watching, leisure time reading, and homework. *Journal of Reading, 29,* 158–162.

Shearer, E. (1968). Physical skills and reading backwardness. *Educational Research, 10,* 197–206.

Siegel, L. S., & Ryan, E. B. (1984). Reading disability as a language disorder. *Remedial and Special Education, 5,* 28–33.

Smith, D. E. P. (1958). A new theory of physiological basis of reading disability. *Reading for Effective Living. Conference Proceedings of the International Reading Association.* Newark, DE: International Reading Association, Yearbook No. 3, 119–121.

Smith, M. D. (1979). Prediction of self-concept among learning disabled children. *Journal of Learning Disabilities, 12,* 664–669.

Smith, N. (1974). Some basic factors in reading difficulties of the disadvantaged. *Reading Improvement, 11,* 3–9.

Spache, G. D., & Spache, E. B. (1977). *Reading in the elementary school* (4th ed). Boston: Allyn and Bacon.

Stallings, J., Cory, R., Fairweather, J., & Needles, M. (1978). *A study of basic reading skills taught in secondary schools.* Palo Alto, CA: Stanford Research Institute.

Thompson, B. B. (1963). A longitudinal study of auditory discrimination. *Journal of Educational Research, 56,* 376–378.

United States Commission on Civil Rights. (1971). *The unfinished education.* Washington, DC: U.S. Government Printing Office.

2

Some Important Operational Procedures

The experienced diagnostician and teacher have usually discovered that there are certain operational procedures that if applied, tend to make their jobs easier and the results of their labor more successful. These are sometimes discovered while working with children over a period of years, and sometimes they are learned through the professional literature and by taking courses in reading diagnosis and remediation. The first part of this chapter contains a discussion of some important operational procedures for the diagnostician. This is followed by a list of important operational procedures for the teacher. The chapter then concludes with a discussion of some common reasons for failure in the diagnostic-remedial process.

IMPORTANT OPERATIONAL PROCEDURES
FOR THE DIAGNOSTICIAN

The following operational procedures will be discussed in this section:

1. Know the amount of diagnosis necessary before remediation is begun.
2. Make sure the test information is accurately communicated.
3. Gather enough initial diagnostic information to begin a program of remediation, but make sure the program remains flexible.
4. Do not do unnecessary testing, but gather enough information to serve as a data base for measuring improvement.
5. Do not be overly concerned about the repetition involved in the teaching of a few skills already known by the child.
6. Diagnosis for a disabled reader should involve more than an appraisal of educational factors.
7. Make the diagnosis as efficient as possible.
8. Test in a situation that is analogous to actual reading.
9. Major decisions concerning the welfare of a child should be based on known facts.
10. Become aware of the strong points and limitations of group standardized, individual standardized, and informal measuring instruments.
11. Keep in mind, and properly use, materials according to whether they "teach," "test," or "reinforce."

Know the Amount of Diagnosis Necessary Before Remediation Is Begun

One of the operational procedures facing personnel in the field of reading is whether it is better to do a great deal of diagnosis before remediation is begun or to do only enough to initiate remediation and then continue the diagnosis while teaching.

Proponents of a system of doing a great deal of diagnosis before beginning remedial procedures often argue that their method of operation is better because more information is available for planning a program of remediation. They also state that time may not be wasted in doing unnecessary remediation and that a thorough initial diagnosis provides a basis for measuring progress. They also believe that children with similar difficulties can be located and grouped for more efficient instruction.

Those who oppose doing a great deal of diagnosis before beginning remediation argue that children tend to become discouraged if too much initial testing is done. Proponents of this view also believe that diagnosis continued during remediation deals with the problem as the child sees it and that when the diagnosis is continuous the remedial program is likely to be flexible.

We would suggest that the best method of operation lies somewhere between the two extremes, with the observation of certain precautions, some of which are explained in the following.

Make Sure Test Information Is Accurately Communicated

If the person doing the diagnostic work also carries out the remedial procedures, there is seldom cause for concern; however, a plan sometimes used in larger school systems is to employ a number of full-time diagnosticians. After each child is diagnosed, the diagnostician writes prescriptive procedures. Where this type of procedure is in operation, the normal problems are often compounded because of the difficulty in accurately relaying diagnostic information to the person charged with carrying out the remedial procedures.

Anyone who has read psychological testing reports or reports from educational diagnosticians would probably agree that frequently these reports leave you wondering what treatment has been prescribed. Because of this problem of communication, many people feel that the person who will eventually do the remediation should also do the testing. A typical example of what happens in the communication of test results is illustrated by the following excerpt from a test report: "Dwight exhibits problems with lateral dominance and would probably benefit from procedures to correct this problem."

A group of experienced remedial reading teachers were asked to explain what they would do with this information. Following are some of the answers:

Teacher 1: "I would have him practice pacing his reading with his hand, using a left-to-right motion."

Teacher 2: "I would start him on the Frostig program."

Teacher 3: "Research shows that there is no relationship between lateral dominance and reading, so I would ignore it."

At this point no attempt will be made to evaluate the teachers' responses, but it is evident that each teacher interpreted the information differently. Such is often the case when one person attempts to interpret what another has written.

Another problem with test reports is that they often use such statements as, "Dwight has difficulty with the initial consonant blends." This statement is too vague to be of any real significance. For example, one might then ask the following questions: Does he have difficulty with all blends? Does he not know the phonemes represented by various graphemes? Or does he lack the ability to blend various initial consonant blends with word families or phonograms? In this case the person doing the remediation would still have to do further diagnosis before meaningful teaching could begin. On the other hand, if the person who did the testing also did the remedial procedures with the same child, then there would be no communication problem.

Gather Enough Initial Diagnostic Information to Begin a Program of Remediation, but Make Sure the Program Remains Flexible

A major problem that sometimes occurs is that the program of remediation is not changed according to the changing needs of the child. For example, a child who is slightly nervous or who is reading at a frustration level is likely to make a number of substitutions for basic sight words. A child who does make substitutions for some basic sight words may in fact really know these sight words when the words are tested in isolation. The problem would then be to determine why the substitutions were made. However, if the original diagnosis indicated that the child should have instruction on the basic sight words, then that child is very likely to have to sit through a great deal of unnecessary instruction. This situation occurs more often when the original diagnosis is done by someone other than the person doing the remediation. It is also more likely to occur when one child is placed with other pupils who indicate similar weaknesses.

Do Not Do Unnecessary Testing, but Gather Enough Information to Serve as a Data Base for Measuring Improvement

In determining initial versus ending performance in a remedial program, consider such factors as (1) progression in reading-grade placement, (2) various phoneme-grapheme relationships learned, and (3) number of basic sight words learned. It is difficult to determine whether the child has actually learned from day to day if there is no accurately determined base or beginning point.

Attempting to measure progress without some base point is somewhat like being told how much your child has grown. This growth is often very difficult for the parents to notice, since they are in daily contact with the child. However, the visiting relative, who has not seen the child for a year, is very much aware of the child's growth. The parents may also get out last year's blanket sleeper as cold weather approaches and find that it is now too small for the child. The size of the child when it did fit the sleeper versus a year later when it was tried on is analogous to a beginning and ending measurement of the reading skills. That is, we become much more aware of growth from a beginning-to-ending period than we do when we are exposed to a child's daily growth in reading skills.

Since many remedial reading programs are supported by some sort of special funding, accountability becomes extremely important. Often the very existence of remedial reading programs is dependent on the demonstration of success. When such a situation occurs, no choice remains but to attempt to show improvement in students from the beginning to the end of the program.

It should be emphasized, however, that certain precautions should be observed in doing the initial testing. A very common and often deserved criticism of remedial reading programs is that a great deal of testing is done and then little time is left for remediation. One school system with which we are familiar tests candidates for the program for about one-fourth of the school year before any remedial work is done. These children often become even more discouraged about their reading than they were in a normal classroom situation, because of the testing itself. In order to find a child's IQ or frustration-reading level, the child must be taken up to a level of questioning or reading that is extremely difficult. This often results in discouragement, feelings of inadequacy, and consequently a loss of rapport between the child and the tester.

When the person who has done the initial testing later does remedial work with the child, it is often difficult to re-establish the good rapport lost during the testing periods. For this reason alone it seems that only a minimal amount of initial testing is desirable.

A highly skilled tester can usually administer a test in such a manner that almost any child will appear to enjoy it. Some children are also delighted to be excused from the classroom to participate in a testing program. This is less damaging to the self-confidence of the children than being forced to participate. The tester should, however, remember that most children soon tire of any activity in which they are not entirely successful, and in a test situation complete success for the child is nearly always lacking.

Do Not Be Overly Concerned about the Repetition Involved in the Teaching of a Few Skills Already Known by the Child

It is quite natural for a remedial reading teacher to begin work with some help in the comprehension skills, even though the teacher may know that the child's diagnosed problem is in word-attack skills. Some teachers argue that this time is wasted, since it does not focus on the exact needs of the child. If the time in which the child is to be tutored is severely limited, this argument is somewhat valid.

A number of research studies such as those of Joseph Lillich (1968) and Keith Dolan (1964) have shown, however, that the guidance and counseling aspects and establishing of rapport with a disabled reader are just as important as teaching reading skills per se. It appears that some time in working with a skill in which the child is somewhat more adept may in fact not be harmful; the benefits from the improved relationship between the disabled reader and the teacher may far outweigh the repetition of materials. Furthermore, it seems doubtful that any class can claim efficiency to such a degree that there is never repetition of known facts, even if repetition were completely undesirable.

Diagnosis for a Disabled Reader Should Involve More Than an Appraisal of Educational Factors

A teacher whose student has developed a minor problem with some phase of the reading skills, such as learning certain initial consonant sounds, may only be interested in locating and correcting that particular problem. The student may have failed to learn the skill because a day or two of school was missed; the student may not have been listening closely when the skill was initially taught; or the student may simply require more time and drill to learn them. When a student misses only an occasional concept, the teacher is not usually concerned with factors other than the educational problem itself. In the case of a somewhat severely disabled reader, however, a diagnosis should involve more than an appraisal of educational factors.

One of the major reasons that school personnel are faced with as many seriously disabled readers as they are is that teachers often fail to locate and correct incipient reading problems while they are still in an easily correctable stage. However, the reasons for failure to learn are often more complicated than for example absence from school or failure to listen closely on one occasion. When failure to learn stems from other causes, often more serious, even a teacher who is well trained in locating and correcting incipient reading problems may find certain students who do not learn. When this is the case, a much more thorough diagnosis involving more than educational factors is necessary.

When a child fails to learn in a normal educational setting, somewhat more complicated causes of the learning disability such as physical, psychological, or socioeducational factors may be responsible. Each of these factors, of course, can be broken down into a number of subfactors or subcategories that may contribute to, or in some cases result from, a reading disability. The essential point for the reading diagnostician to remember is that what often appears as a problem may be only a symptom of a more difficult and involved problem.

Make the Diagnosis as Efficient as Possible

A diagnosis should be as thorough as necessary but should not extend beyond what is required. The problem of the reading diagnostician is to determine just what is and is not necessary. Although this is often somewhat difficult, there are some definite guidelines that the diagnostician will soon learn to follow.

One of the most common problems leading to inefficient diagnosis is that the diagnostician falls into the habit of giving the same tests to each student regardless of the apparent problem or problems. In some cases certain phases of commonly used diagnostic procedures can easily be omitted and a great deal of time can be saved. For example, a child who is in the fifth or sixth grade may read orally very poorly. For a child such as this, a reasonable approach would be to diagnose a number of questionable areas such as initial, ending, and medial consonants sounds, consonant clusters, vowel, vowel-team and special letter combination sounds, vowel rules, and structural analysis skills. However, if the student can read the words on the Pronunciation of Quick Survey Words test of the Ekwall Reading Inventory (Ekwall, 1986), you can automatically eliminate testing in those areas because a child weak in them would not be able to read long nonsense words. There are also other areas where certain commonly administered tests may be omitted for certain children, such as visual screening tests for a child who has recently been examined by an optometrist or an ophthalmologist, or IQ tests for a child who definitely demonstrates ability to learn.

Just as it is easy to fall into the habit of using unnecessary tests, it is also easy to omit tests or further checks that may be indicated. The reading diagnostician should continually examine the methods of diagnosis by asking: Am I giving this test only because I am in the habit of doing so? Are there more efficient methods of locating problems than I am now using? Is the information I seek already available in the child's cumulative records? Will the cause of the child's disability also affect future attempts at remediation?

Test in a Situation That Is Analogous to Actual Reading

A serious problem with group diagnostic tests is that they often do not measure reading skills in a situation that is analogous to actual reading. This is also a criticism of some individually administered tests. Research by Eldon E. Ekwall (1973) has indicated that many types of tests do not measure what they purport to measure. It appears that only in some areas such as comprehension and vocabulary can reading diagnosticians feel fairly sure that group tests are valid. If you really want to measure certain reading skills, you must use an individually administered test.

Typical examples of misleading group tests are tests for basic sight words and for phonics skills. One of the coauthors once taught an evening reading class to a group of elementary and secondary teachers. After discussing ways of testing for knowledge of the basic sight words, one ninth-grade teacher of a group of extremely poor readers asked the writer to administer a group basic sight word test in his class. In taking this test the student is required to underline or circle one of four words that is the same as a word pronounced aloud by the person administering the test. Approximately thirty students took the test. Each student was tested on 220 words; that is, had to underline or circle 220 words from a list of 880. This meant that 220 x 30, or 6600 choices were made. When these tests were corrected, only six errors were found. Certainly this many mistakes would be expected on the basis of clerical errors alone.

Next, several consultants sat down individually with students and asked each of them to pronounce each of the 220 basic sight words on the test. This time many students missed twenty-five to fifty words each. The results in this case are quite typical of those obtained when you try to test in a situation that is not analogous to actual reading. It is much easier to pick one word pronounced by a tester from a choice of four than to see the same word and then pronounce it. The latter, however, is what you must do when you read orally. As you can see, what we wanted to know was which students did not know which words. Administration of the test to a group simply did not give us this information.

As in the case just illustrated, most group tests are multiple choice. This is simply not pertinent to what a student does when reading.

Group phonics tests present similar problems. For example, a test of initial consonant sounds may call for a student to circle one of four letters that represents the same sound as the beginning sound of a word pronounced by the teacher. Here again, it is easier to circle one of four letters (for example *d, p, b, c*) that represents the beginning sound in the word *dog* than it is to see a *d* and pronounce the "d" phoneme.

Authors of tests often claim that since the kinds of group tests mentioned above have a high correlation with individual tests, they are a valid instrument for diagnosis. You must keep in mind, however, that a high correlation between two tests only means that students who scored high on the group test also scored high on the individual test. This usually happens whenever two highly related skills are tested and the results of two groups' scores are correlated.

This type of information may be useful to the reading specialist who wishes to survey a group of students to determine which ones are most seriously deficient in the skills tested. For example, students who fail the test for initial consonant sounds mentioned above demonstrate that they are extremely weak in phonics skills. Students who pass this test may or may not have mastered their initial consonant sounds. In other words, passing this test is a necessary but not sufficient indication of mastery of this skill. This is because the test measures only *low-level* phonics knowledge. A more complete discussion of the levels of phonics knowledge will be included in Chapter 5. For now, the diagnostician should bear in mind that in order to evaluate a student's ability to apply phonics skills *in the act of reading,* the testing must be conducted individually.

This is not meant to imply that all individual tests are good. A number of individual tests contain subtests designed to measure certain skills not required in the act of reading. Chapters 4 through 6 address the testing of various educational factors in reading. Problems encountered in test construction and administration are covered in considerable depth in those chapters. The essential point for the reading diagnostician to keep in mind is that in order to obtain the information needed for prescriptive instruction, testing must be done in a situation analogous to actual reading.

Base Major Decisions
Concerning the Welfare of a Child on Known Facts

Most of us who have worked in the public schools have at some time heard about or witnessed a case of a child suddenly "taking hold" or "blooming" after having been a poor student. Even the best of teachers, psychologists, and diagnosticians are unable to predict whether this sort of thing will happen to a child. The important point is to leave the door open to the possibility of such an occurrence.

Any major decisions for prolonged remedial work that will remove a child from the normal learning environment should be based on the opinions of several people and the results of several tests. A psychologist who examines a child for several hours may develop some excellent insights; yet this same person may lack a great deal of information that has been available to the child's classroom teacher, the principal, or the parents. We once heard an elementary principal say, "When the school psychologist works with one of our children for several hours and then writes his report, it often tells us that now he knows as much about the child as we did when the psychologist started testing." This statement should not be taken to discredit the work of the school psychologist, but it does illustrate the point that no individual can hope to gain enough information about a student in an hour or two to make decisions that may affect the student's entire life.

School personnel who are involved with making decisions concerning intensive remedial work or assignment to special classes should develop procedures for placement of students. A diagnostic-referral procedure such as that outlined in Figure 2–1 will enable school personnel to place children according to the best information that can be derived from all sources.

The Non-Discrimination on the Basis of Handicap Act (Public Law 93–112, Section 504) and the Education for All Handicapped Children Act (Public Law 94–142) have had a significant impact on the services provided to disabled readers. This federal legislation includes a number of provisions that now by law affect all handicapped students between the ages of three and twenty-one.[1] The term *handicapped children* includes students who have "specific learning disabilities." Within this category are included disabled readers. These students must receive a "free, appropriate public education" designed to meet their special needs.

For each handicapped student an individualized education program (IEP) must be developed. The teacher, one or both parents, the child (where appropriate), a representative of the public school other than the child's teacher (usually the school principal), and other individuals such as the reading specialist, speech teacher, and school psychologist all participate in the development of the IEP.

According to P.L. 94–142, Section 121a.346, the IEP for each child must include:

1. a statement of the child's present levels of educational performance;
2. a statement of annual goals, including short term instructional objectives;
3. a statement of the specific special education and related services to be provided to the child, and the extent to which the child will be able to participate in regular educational programs;
4. the projected dates for initiation of services and the anticipated duration of the services; and
5. appropriate objective criteria and evaluation procedures and schedules for determining, on at least an annual basis, whether the short term instructional objectives are being achieved.

Figure 2–2 is an IEP that was completed for a ten-year-old girl.

The reading specialist should be aware of certain additional specifications of the federal legislation. Section 121a.550 describes the mandate for the least restrictive environment (mainstreaming).

Each public agency shall insure:

[1]For additional information on this legislation, we refer you to *The Rights of Parents and the Responsibilities of Schools,* compiled by James G. Meade (Cambridge, Mass.: Educators Publishing Service, 1978).

FIGURE 2–1 Student Diagnostic-Referral Procedure

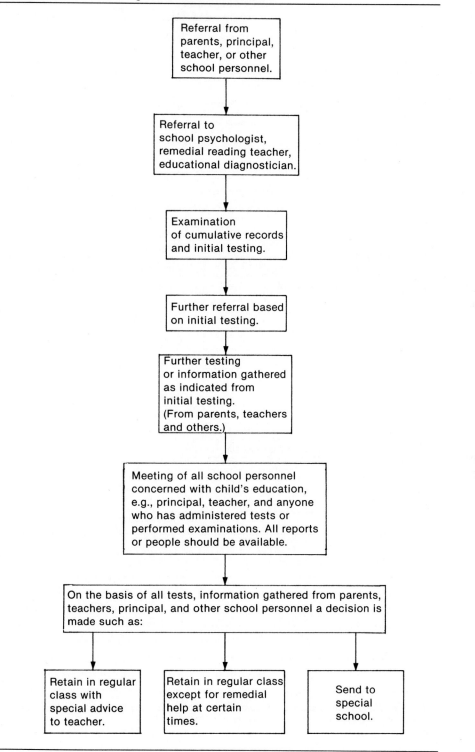

Referral from
parents, principal,
teacher, or other
school personnel.

Referral to
school psychologist,
remedial reading teacher,
educational diagnostician.

Examination
of cumulative records
and initial testing.

Further referral based
on initial testing.

Further testing
or information gathered
as indicated from
initial testing.
(From parents, teachers
and others.)

Meeting of all school personnel
concerned with child's education,
e.g., principal, teacher, and anyone
who has administered tests or
performed examinations. All reports
or people should be available.

On the basis of all tests, information gathered from parents,
teachers, principal, and other school personnel a decision is
made such as:

Retain in regular
class with
special advice
to teacher.

Retain in regular class
except for remedial
help at certain
times.

Send to
special
school.

FIGURE 2-2 Individualized Education Program Forms

INDIVIDUALIZED
EDUCATION
PROGRAM

Date: _JAN 30, 1986_   Page 1 of _4_

STUDENT
Name: _SUSAN_   M ⓕ

Annual Review Date: _2 - 87_   Tri-Annual Review Date: _2 - 89_

Number: _____   Ethnic Code * _____

Birthdate: _9-2-77_

PURPOSE OF MEETING: ☒ Initial   ☐ Annual   ☐ Tri-Annual   ☐ Exit   ☐ Other _____

Parent Name: _____   Child Resides: * _____   Primary Language: _ENGLISH_

Address: _____   Home School: _____

City: _____   Zip: _____   School of Enrollment: _____

Phone:
Home: _____   Business: _____   Current Program: _____   Grade: _____

PRESENT LEVELS OF PERFORMANCE - STRENGTHS AND WEAKNESSES -- See Page 2

ELIGIBILITY: ☐ Not Eligible   ☒ Eligible   ☐ Exit   STUDENT CLASSIFICATION NUMBER * _____

ANNUAL GOALS AND OBJECTIVES -- See Page 3

RECOMMENDED PROGRAM:	Start Date	Duration	Frequency	RELATED SERVICES
☒ Regular Education	ONGOING			☐ Transportation * _____
☒ Resource Specialist - 200	ASAP 2/86	1-2 YRS	DAILY	☐ Extended School Year
☐ Special Day Class - 300				☐ Other * _____
☐ Other * _____				STANDARD FOR PROFICIENCY TESTING
☒ Designated Instruction & Services				☐ Not Applicable
☒ Speech and Language - 725	2/86	1 YR	2 x weekly	☐ Regular Standards
☐ Adaptive P. E. -701				☐ Alternative Means and/or Modes
☐ Occupational Therapy - 731				☐ Differential Standards
☐ Other * _____				☐ To Be Determined at a Later Date
☐ Low Incidence Disability				

Extent of Regular Education: ☐ 100%   ☐ More than 50%   ☐ Less than 50%   ☐ None

This individualized education program is a statement of the services to be delivered and of the anticipated goals and objectives for the student; it is not a contract that guarantees the accomplishment of the anticipated goals and objectives. I agree with the content of this individualized education program. I have received a copy of my rights, and these rights have been reviewed with me.

_____   _____
DATE   PARENT SIGNATURE

TEAM MEMBERS
The persons whose signatures appear below have participated in the formulation of this individualized education program.

Signature	Title	Date
	Case Manager/	
	Administrator/Designee	

DISTRIBUTION: White - Special Services Office; Canary - Parent; Pink - Cum Folder; Goldenrod - Teacher
*See coding on back of page.

STUDENT
Name: SUSAN

INDIVIDUALIZED EDUCATION PROGRAM

PRESENT LEVELS OF PERFORMANCE - STRENGTHS AND WEAKNESSES

Check areas of special needs:

✔ ACADEMIC FUNCTIONING (readiness, reading, written language, math, test results)

WIDE RANGE ACHIEVEMENT TEST:	GRADE	SS	%	WOODCOCK-JOHNSON:	GR	SS	%
READING:	2.4	82	12	READING:	1.4	74	4
SPELLING:	2.7	90	25	MATH:	2.2	85	16
ARITHMETIC:	2.7	91	27	WRITTEN LANG:	1.6	78	7

TEST OF WRITTEN SPELLING: TOTAL SCORES: SA=6-9, SQ=81, GE=1.5

KAY MATH DIAG. ARITH. TEST: SCORE 2.2 (PLACED 2.5)

_____ LEARNING STYLES

APPEARS TO FAVOR THE VISUAL MODE WHEN PRESENTED WITH NEW LEARNING. NEEDS TO HAVE A STRONG MULTISENSORY APPROACH WITH MANY VISUAL REINFORCERS IN HER LESSONS.

✔ SENSORY MOTOR FUNCTIONING (visual/auditory perception, gross and fine motor)

WEPMAN (REVISED) TEST OF AUDITORY DISCRIMINATION — 4 "X" AND "Y" ERRORS

MOTOR FREE VISUAL PERCEPTION TEST: PA = >9-0 — PQ = 114 + 32/36

BEERY TEST OF VISUAL MOTOR INTEGRATION: VMIAE = 6-10 (CA = 8-3)

VISUAL AURAL DIGIT SPAN TEST: A-O=6; V-O=4; A-W=5; V-W=4   TOTAL =19

AGE	75	10	50	10	25
GRADE	90	10	75	10	25

✔ COMMUNICATION SKILLS (articulation, voice quality, fluency, expressive/receptive)

WEISS ARTICULATION TEST: SUBSTITUTES /d/ + /f/ for /th/; /b/ for /V/

T.O.L.D.-P AND WORD TESTS: STANDARD SCORES ARE WITHIN AGE EXPECTATIONS BUT SHE EXPERIENCED DIFFICULTY (DELAYS + UNCERTAINTIES WITH HER RESPONSES. RELIES HEAVILY ON CONTEXTUAL CLUES.

PEABODY PICTURE VOCABULARY: 2nd PERCENTILE, AGE EQUIVALENCY OF 6.0 INDICATES DELAYED RECEPTIVE VOCABULARY.

_____ SURVIVAL/SELF-MANAGEMENT/PRE-VOCATIONAL/CAREER DEVELOPMENT SKILLS

ADEQUATE

✔ SOCIAL SKILLS (self-concept, social interaction, behavior)

GENERALLY AGE-APPROPRIATE. UNSURE OF SELF AND LOW SELF-ESTEEM AT TIMES. OFTEN PREOCCUPIED WITH FAMILY CONCERNS; SEEMS TO INTERFERE WITH CLASSROOM WORK

_____ HEALTH/ATTENDANCE

GOOD

INDIVIDUALIZED EDUCATION PROGRAM

ANNUAL GOALS	OBJECTIVES	MEASUREMENT/ METHOD	SERVICE PROVIDER	COMPLETED DATE
IMPROVE SPEECH FUNCTIONING	1) SUSAN WILL PRODUCE /b/ AND VOICED + VOICELESS /th/ IN ALL WORD POSITIONS IN SENTENCES WITH 90% ACCURACY	1) STANDARD ARTICULATION TEST, BASELINES, CHARTING	SPEECH + LANG. SPEC.	2/87
INCREASE LANGUAGE SKILLS	1) SHOW 6 MONTHS + INCREASE IN RECEPTIVE + EXPRESSIVE VOCABULARY	1) PPVT, TOLD, WORD		2/87
	2) GIVE DEFINITION AND USE APPROPRIATELY IN SENTENCES THE FOLLOWING WHEN GIVEN ORAL STIMULI; HOMONYMS, GRADE-EQUIVALENT VOCABULARY WORDS, SYNONYMS + ANTONYMS, WITH 80% ACCURACY	2) TOLD, WORD, TEACHER DESIGNED TESTS		2/87
	3) VERBALLY EXPLAIN SIMILARITIES + DIFFERENCES AMONG OBJECTS OR IDEAS WITH 80% ACCURACY.	3) SAME AS #2		2/87

NOTE: When appropriate, the following topics will be addressed on this page: Prevocational/vocational/Career Ed/Work Experience; transition to regular class; low-incidence disabilities; linguistic goals; and alternate means of completing course requirements.

46

INDIVIDUALIZED EDUCATION PROGRAM

ANNUAL GOALS	OBJECTIVES	MEASUREMENT/ METHOD	SERVICE PROVIDER	COMPLETED DATE
IMPROVE AUDITORY AND VISUAL PERCEPTUAL SKILLS	1) SUSAN WILL DEMONSTRATE THE ABILITY TO FOLLOW 3-4 CONSECUTIVE ORAL DIRECTIONS WITH 90% ACCURACY.	TEACHER EVALUATION	RSP	2/87
	2) SUSAN WILL DEMONSTRATE AT LEAST 12 MOS. IMPROVEMENT IN VISUAL MOTOR SKILLS ON THE BEERY TEST OF VISUAL MOTOR INTEGRATION, OR OTHER STAND. VISUAL TEST.	BEERY TEST OF VISUAL MOTOR INTEG. — OR OTHER STAND. VIS. MOT. TEST	RSP	2/87
IMPROVE ACADEMIC SKILLS — READING	1) SUSAN WILL DEMONSTRATE THE ABILITY TO READ A LIST OF 25 CVC+CVCE PATTERN WORDS (BOTH LONG+SHORT VOWEL SOUNDS) WITH 80% ACCURACY.	RES. SP. EVAL. — TCHR. INPUT	RSI REG. TCHR.	2/87
	2) SUSAN WILL DECODE A LIST OF 20 WORDS WITH VOWEL COMBINATIONS (AI, AU, OW, ETC.) WITH 85% ACCURACY	TEACHER EVALUATION	RSP/ REG. TCHR.	
IMPROVE ACADEMIC SKILLS — WRITTEN LANGUAGE	1) SUSAN WILL WRITE A SHORT PARAGRAPH OF AT LEAST 3 SENTENCES WITH 80% ACCURACY.	WORK SAMPLES	RSP/ REG. TCHR.	2/87

NOTE: When appropriate, the following topics will be addressed on this page: Prevocational/vocational/Career Ed/Work Experience; transition to regular class; low-incidence disabilities; linguistic goals; and alternate means of completing course requirements.

47

1. that to the maximum extent appropriate handicapped children . . . are educated with children who are not handicapped, and
2. that special classes, separate schooling or other removal of handicapped children from the regular educational environment occurs only when the nature of severity of the handicap is such that education in regular classes with the use of supplementary aids and services cannot be achieved satisfactorily.

The student's parents must approve the IEP and consent to the placement of the student. They must also approve all changes in the program, and they have the right to pursue an impartial due-process hearing if they are dissatisfied. Assessment of the student must be conducted by a team that includes at least one teacher or other specialist with knowledge of the area of disability. Since a high percentage of specific learning disabilities are reading difficulties, the reading specialist should anticipate frequent participation in IEP assessment. The law mandates that no *single* procedure may be used to determine a student's placement or program.

Become Aware of the Strong Points and Limitations of Group Standardized, Individual Standardized, and Informal Measuring Instruments

The reading diagnostician should make every effort to become familiar with as many tests as possible. This is not to say that any one person will or should continually change the tests that are commonly used in diagnosis; however, the diagnostician should continually search for newer and better tests and methods of testing. The process of examining new tests and test procedures is certain to be excellent in-service training in itself. For example, the authors of tests are not likely to stress the weaknesses inherent in their own material; however, they are likely to explain why certain techniques or procedures they use are better than others. This explanation in itself will often enable the diagnostician to better evaluate tests and testing procedures.

The strong points of various group and individual tests and testing techniques are discussed in considerable detail in later chapters. There are, however, some inherent weaknesses and strong points in certain types of testing that are of such importance that they should receive special emphasis at this point.

Group standardized tests.   Group standardized tests are perhaps more misused than any other type on the market today. Some of this misuse can be attributed to the users of the tests, but certainly some of the blame also lies with the authors, who have a tendency to overstate the test's value for some purposes.

The most flagrant misuse of group standardized tests is in using them to make final decisions about individual students. Although the publishers of group achievement tests often claim that their tests have considerable individual diagnostic value, it is doubtful that this claim can be substantiated in most cases. For any individual, group test scores are often so unreliable that it would be difficult to place any real confidence in their results. One of the coauthors administered to a class of college students a nationally used reading achievement test designed for grades four through six. The students were not given the questions but were instructed to mark the answer sheets at random. One of the subtests on this test purports to measure children's reading vocabulary in science. The class of college students scored from a low grade level of 2.5 to a high grade level of 6.5 on this subtest. Remember, of course, that this was a situation similar to one in which none of the students could read at all! The grade placement of the students on the entire test ranged from 2.9 to 4.3, which also makes it evident that individual students' total reading scores varied too much to place any credence in them for individual grade placement. The problem here may result from a high guess factor inherent in these tests. Another problem with group standardized tests is their relative unreliability for individual students. Most experienced teachers have noticed with puzzlement that some students score *lower* on the posttest than the pretest. Surely these students did not lose learning over the course of the year. Such deviations balance out when group data are examined, but this fact is of little consolation to the parents or teacher of the individual student. While working as a specialist with groups of extremely low-achieving students, one of the coauthors discovered another weakness in using group standardized tests. The students were pre- and posttested with levels of a test that corresponded to the students' grade placement. Unfortunately, the norms of the test did not extend low enough to reflect the performance of some of the older readers (for example, sixth graders reading at or below a first-grade level). Even though these students may have grown a year or more in ability, this was not reflected in the testing, since they still had not reached the low end of the norms on this particular test. This was especially distressing because the amount of future funding for this special program was based on the students' growth as demonstrated by scores on this test. In response to this type of problem, Lawrence Smith, Jerry Johns, Leonore Ganschow, and Nancy Browning Masztal (1983) have suggested that "using test forms from a lower grade level and converting the scores may give you a more reliable estimate of achievement." (p. 550)

Yet another inherent weakness of group tests is that they cannot test many of the reading skills in a situation that is analogous to actual reading. This point was discussed in more detail earlier in this chapter. Reading skills such as vocabulary and comprehension are more amenable to testing with group tests.

One strong point of group standardized tests is that they are useful for measuring overall class achievement during a specified period of time. If one examines the subtests rather carefully, they can also be useful in determining whether overall areas such as study skills are receiving adequate attention in the curriculum. Another important point in favor of using group tests is that they are less time-consuming to administer. Group standardized tests also allow school personnel to compare the achievement of their students with that of the nation as a whole or the norm group on which the test was originally standardized. Finally, group tests can be useful for the *initial* screening of students for the remedial reading program. Many specially funded programs require that only students who score below the 50th percentile on a standardized achievement test may be served by the program. Group tests will enable you to quickly determine which students qualify. Also, many reading specialists are assigned to schools with many more problem readers than can be served directly. By using group test data, these reading specialists can select students with the greatest apparent need for individual diagnostic evaluation. If instead the reading specialist randomly selected students for diagnosis or relied only on teacher referral, then too much time would be spent diagnosing an unnecessarily large number of students.

Individual standardized tests.   Individual standardized tests are less misused than group standardized tests for several reasons. To begin with, the people who find a need to use individual standardized tests, such as the Durrell Analysis of Reading Difficulty (Durrell and Catterson, 1980), are usually more experienced in test administration and are therefore better informed about the strong points and limitations of various tests. Individual standardized tests are also more difficult to administer than group standardized tests. For this reason they are likely to be given only when needed, in contrast to group tests, which are often given simply because it is "test time."

Individual standardized tests can be given in a situation that is analogous to actual reading and thus have a tremendous advantage over group standardized tests. For example, you can ask a child to read orally while you mark the kinds of mistakes made, or the child can be asked to pronounce basic sight words. Individual standardized tests also enable you to compare a child's reading abilities with those of other children of the same age and/or grade level. A further advantage of individual standardized tests is that the tester can easily omit certain subtests not relevant to a certain student.

Perhaps the greatest disadvantage of individual standardized tests is that they are time-consuming to administer. In many cases they are somewhat difficult to administer and therefore require some special training. This can, however, be a blessing in disguise.

Informal measuring instruments.   Informal measuring instruments such as word lists, informal reading inventories, decoding-skill inventories, and cloze passages are also valuable diagnostic tools. Often these instruments are readily adaptable to the materials within the classroom. By using the standard criteria for the informal reading inventory or cloze procedure, the teacher can rather quickly and easily determine whether a certain student can read a certain book at the "instructional" or "free" reading level. The teacher can also use these procedures to determine whether a new textbook is written at a proper reading level for the students. The use of word lists from a book commonly used in the school will also enable teachers to make a rapid check on a student's ability to deal with the vocabulary load in that book. Decoding-skill inventories can be an invaluable tool for determining specific phonics or structural analysis skills a student needs to learn. Often these inventories are criterion-referenced, so that the diagnostician may compare the student's performance to the accepted criterion for mastery of the particular skills.

Informal measuring instruments have several rather serious disadvantages. They must be used by someone who can understand and use the standard criteria for their application or they are no better than simply listening to a child read and then guessing at the child's grade level. Although the procedure for using them is rather simple, they are still somewhat difficult to construct. For example, it is a tremendous task to find questions that measure more than simple recall of facts for use in an informal reading inventory. It is also difficult and time-consuming to construct and check cloze passages for measuring ability to read a certain book or tests that properly measure phonics and structured analysis skills. Other specific advantages and disadvantages of using informal measuring instruments are discussed in detail in Chapter 11.

KEEP IN MIND, AND PROPERLY USE, MATERIALS ACCORDING TO WHETHER THEY "TEACH," "TEST," OR "REINFORCE"

The diagnostician and remedial reading teacher should keep in mind that there is a distinct difference between diagnosis, teaching, and reinforcement activities. For example, one would not expect a student to "learn" anything new while completing a page in a workbook that requires the student to use concepts taught in a previous lesson. One would, however, expect to "reinforce" these previously taught concepts so that the student would become thoroughly familiar with their use and thus be less likely to forget them. On the other hand, a page in a programmed textbook would be likely to teach, as well as reinforce, various concepts. Most testing is done so that the teacher can learn more about the student, but testing, as such, has no immediate benefit to the student unless the answers are provided to the questions on which the student is being tested.

The double-column listing that follows illustrates the three categories (testing examples or diagnosis, teaching, and reinforcement or practice) and some activities that might be associated with each. As you examine the various suggestions in the following chapters for remediation of various reading skills, keep these three categories in mind. That is, do not expect a straight practice exercise to teach or do not expect a teaching exercise to test, although examination of student performance on reinforcement or practice materials will provide some diagnostic information.

In using the diagnostic, teaching, and reinforcement materials that appear in this text as well as in other textbooks and commercially or teacher-made materials you should consider your overall instructional purpose and use the appropriate materials to accomplish this purpose.

Testing and diagnostic materials	*What they are designed to accomplish*
Examples	
1. Basic sight-word lists	Provides the teacher with diagnostic information on the basic sight-word knowledge of the student. The student learns little or nothing unless the teacher pronounces each word as it is missed.
2. Cloze technique for assessing student's level of reading comprehension (see Chapter 11)	If used only for finding a percentage score of right and wrong answers to determine grade placement, little or no teaching is done. If the exercises are discussed after the student has completed them, some teaching and possibly some reinforcement takes place.
3. Informal reading inventories	Provides the teacher with an overall grade placement and considerable information on specific weaknesses. Little teaching is accomplished other than when aid is given when a word is unknown.
Teaching materials	
1. Material held in the hands of students and explained by the teacher	This is a typical teaching situation. If it is material that is being reviewed, then it may teach *and* reinforce. Unless the teacher provides for some type of feedback, little or no diagnostic information will be derived.
2. Preparation of a language experience chart or story	Provides the teacher with an opportunity to teach the student to decode new words. The student receives ample reinforcement as

Testing and diagnostic materials	*What they are designed to accomplish*
	the dictated story is reread. Provides some diagnosis of the student's language and oral reading skills.
Teaching materials	
3. Worksheets used in conjunction with a tape recorder	If the directions on the audiotape provide for instruction on how to do the worksheets, and then give the student the answers and provide an opportunity for the student to correct any that are wrong, this would teach and reinforce. If provisions are made for the teacher to see which answers were missed, some diagnosis may also take place.
Reinforcement materials	
1. Worksheets	Most worksheets only provide for reinforcement of concepts that have already been learned but which need to be mastered more thoroughly.
2. Reading games	Most games *do not* teach since they require that nothing new be learned in order to play the game, e.g., recalling and using previously learned material. If properly constructed, games will provide reinforcement. Games in which one pupil competes with another may teach, for example, if one pupil creates words from initial consonants or consonant blends and phonograms or uses words in sentences in which the other pupil learns the meaning from context.
3. Practicing words or phrases from flash cards	This can provide excellent reinforcement of sight vocabulary, if the words or phrases were previously introduced by the teacher.

IMPORTANT OPERATIONAL PROCEDURES
FOR THE TEACHER

As experience in working with disabled readers is gained, the reading teacher is likely to find that some techniques work especially well with some students and yet seem somewhat less successful with others. One of the characteristics of a successful teacher is the ability to determine whether a certain teaching procedure is producing the desired results with a particular student. When a procedure does not produce the desired results, the experienced teacher will alter the approach. Certain procedures have, however, proven to be consistently successful with almost all students regardless of such factors as their specific reading problems, age, grade, or sex. It is imperative that the remedial reading teacher become aware of these procedures and make every effort to implement them. Some of these important procedures are as follows:

1. Select a remedial reading program that is highly individualized.
2. Start at the child's level.
3. Start with the child's strongest area.
4. Provide an opportunity for success for the child.
5. Make the disabled reader aware of the progress that has been made.
6. Make the learning process meaningful to the child.
7. Use materials appropriate to the needs of the child.
8. Continue to diagnosis while you teach.
9. Be alert to pick up any clues given by the child.
10. Capitalize on the motivation the child may already possess.
11. Maintain a relaxed attitude.
12. Do not be too authoritative.
13. Have confidence in the child's ability to learn.
14. Direct the child toward self-instruction.
15. Begin each period with a summary of what you intend to do and why you intend to do it and end each period with a summary of what you did and why you did it.
16. Provide for a follow-up program.

Select a Remedial Program That Is Highly Individualized

Terms such as a *well-balanced program* and a *well-rounded program* sound good and are appropriate for a developmental-reading program, but they do not describe the type of program desirable in remedial reading. In most cases the remedial reading program must be highly individualized and directed toward correcting certain individual reading deficiencies rather than giving a child a well-rounded program. By "individualized" we do not mean that instruction must necessarily occur on a one-to-one basis. In the school setting the remedial reading teacher is generally able to group students according to their skills.

Many children in remedial reading classes are simply retarded a year or more in almost all of their reading skills; however, a large percentage of children are behind a year or more only in certain areas of reading. For students who are lacking only in certain reading skills it would prove inefficient to provide a remedial program that covered all skills. These children can be brought up to reading grade level much more rapidly by receiving an intensive instructional program only in the skills in which they are deficient. One might think of a child's progression in developmental reading as the steps or rungs on a ladder or as a continuum of skills with each step representing the accomplishment of a certain skill such as learning the initial consonant sounds, the initial consonant blends, or the short vowel sounds. Whenever a child fails to learn one of these important skills, a step is omitted from the ladder or continuum of skills. The task of the corrective or remedial reading teacher is to fill in these omitted steps or rungs in the ladder or continuum of reading skills rather than to build a whole new ladder. For this reason the remedial reading teacher must be very specific in the diagnosis and then specific in the remediation given for noted weaknesses in order to provide for efficient use of both teacher and student time.

Start at the Child's Level

The educational cliché "start where the child is" has special relevance for the remedial reading teacher who gets a child who is advanced in some areas and extremely disabled in others. As mentioned previously, a thorough diagnosis is a prerequisite for beginning the remedial program. The diagnosis must not only include the area or areas in which the child is deficient, but for the sake of efficiency should report the level of each skill in which the child is deficient. For example, it is not enough to say that John is a fourth grader who is deficient in comprehension skills; the diagnostic report should also state the level at which he does comprehend. Likewise, a student who is having difficulty with consonant blends should be reported as deficient in knowledge of the *bl, fl, pl,* etc., blends and not simply as "having trouble with consonant blends." In both cases the teacher will be able to begin at the child's level of achievement if the diagnostic report is precise. An important point of which both the remedial teacher and classroom teacher must be cognizant is that the disabled reader must not merely begin to make normal progress, but must progress faster than normal in order to catch up with children of a normal age-grade level.

Start with the Child's Strongest Area

Most readers, whether disabled or not, have at least one area in which they are strong or in which they are somewhat more competent than others. The strength may be in a certain area of reading itself, for example, knowledge of initial consonant blends, or it may be in an area such as mathematics. Because of the extreme importance of establishing proper rapport with a disabled reader, it often works well to begin remedial work by focusing on the strong area. This will allow the disabled reader to experience initial success and thus create an atmosphere in which the child can enjoy working on the reading problem. To continue work in an area in which the disabled reader is already competent would, of course, be inefficient in terms of both student and teacher time; however, the value to be gained from improving the initial attitude of the child will usually outweigh the fact that certain material in the beginning stages is repetitious.

Provide an Opportunity for Success for the Child

Most teachers realize the importance of providing lessons in which children can achieve considerable success. This concept has usually been stressed in various methods courses and in psychology courses as well. In remedial reading, however, providing an opportunity for success for the child is even more crucial and deserves special emphasis. The reason for this special emphasis is that the child who ultimately comes to the remedial-reading teacher has already suffered a series of failures that led to the disability. In spite of good teaching or at least a proper attitude on the part of the classroom reading teacher, the disabled reader is almost certain to have experienced less success than most children in the classroom.

Since the disabled reader has usually experienced considerable failures, the student's overall attitude toward learning will often need to be reoriented. This reorientation may be changed somewhat by "educational engineering," in which the teacher consistently arranges for situations in which the child is able to succeed; two examples are winning a word game and doing a series of easy exercises in which the child gets 100 percent correct. Some children, however, may need more than normal success to change their attitude. The teacher may find, for example, that the reorientation process will require not only constant success but counseling as well. A typical counseling procedure is described in Chapter 7.

Make the Disabled Reader Aware of the Progress
That Has Been Made

Disabled readers need to be aware of their progress. To say, "You're doing better" is often not sufficient to convince children that you are actually helping them. Just as students' physical growth is not clearly noticeable to them, neither is their growth in reading. If you really wanted a child to believe that physical growth was occurring, you might mark a line on the wall when the child was measured and label it: "Jane's height on February 20, 19__." A year later you could measure Jane and mark another line to show her year's growth. Most children would accept such evidence as proof that they were growing.

The remedial reading teacher should use measurements that are just as concrete as the line on the wall. One excellent method of demonstrating students' progress is to code all of the errors they make in reading materials at and slightly above their grade level. These coded errors can then be tallied, as shown in Figure 2–3.

After the students have improved in their reading, they can read the same material while the teacher again codes the various types of errors. The students can then be shown the reduction in each type of error from the first to the second reading. Tape recordings of the first and second readings are also an excellent way to demonstrate improvement to students. Tape recordings in conjunction with coded series of reading passages are still better.

FIGURE 2–3 Coded Errors of a Student's Oral Reading

TYPES OF ERRORS
(Indicate number of each type)

First Trial		Second Trial	Percent of Increase (+) or Decrease (−)
6	Omissions	2	− 66⅔
2	Insertions	0	− 100
14	Partial mispronunciations	7	− 50
0	Gross mispronunciations	0	—
2	Substitutions	0	− 100
8	Repetitions	2	− 75
3	Inversions	0	− 100
0	Aid	0	—
6	Self-corrected errors	0	− 100

CHARACTERISTICS OF THE READER
(Indicate with checkmark)

First Trial		Second Trial
✓	Poor word-analysis skills	0
✓	Head movement	0
✓	Finger pointing	0
✓	Disregard for punctuation	0
✓	Loss of place	0
✓	Overuse of phonics	0
✓	Does not read in natural voice tones	0
✓	Poor enunciation	0
✓	Word-by-word reading	0
✓	Poor phrasing	0
✓	Lack of expression	0
✓	Pauses	0

Student__*James Wilson*__ Teacher__*Anne Updike*__

Date__*9/23*__ School__*Lincoln Elementary*__

Students who make a number of errors on basic sight words or phrases can be given cards with the known words or phrases on them. As the students learn new words or phrases, they receive new cards. In this way the students can easily watch their basic sight vocabulary grow. The teacher may also elect to take cards from the students as they master words and phrases. In this way the students see their stacks of cards gradually disappear until their basic sight vocabulary "troubles" are gone.

In phonics or structural analysis the teacher can simply check or circle the elements not known and show these checklists to the students. As the students learn various elements, they erase the checkmarks or circles.

When seeing actual growth in their reading skills, students are more likely to be motivated. Also, students who are aware of their progress are more likely to take an active interest in increasing their rate of progress.

Make the Learning Process Meaningful to the Child

A college student was working with a disabled reader on a phonics problem. The disabled reader was in the fourth grade but was reading on a first-grade level. After learning several initial consonant blends and several phonograms, the child was given an opportunity to form some new words by blending the initial consonant blends with the phonograms. After forming several new words, the child exclaimed, "Hey, this helps you figure out new words!" Perhaps one may criticize the college student for not explaining why the blends and phonograms were being taught, but one must certainly be critical of the child's former teachers, who allowed the child to progress to the fourth grade without knowing why he should learn his phonics lessons. It is evident that this child simply perceived phonics as a subject or an activity completely different and unrelated to reading.

Children, until they reach the junior high level or beyond, seldom question why they are being taught various concepts and subject matter. However, this does not mean that they believe in the necessity of learning it; in fact the attitude that children often demonstrate makes it a certainty that they do not.

Most children, just like adults, when told that they must learn the basic sight words because they account for over half of the words they will ever need to read, can understand the importance of thoroughly learning them. Children also understand, if told, that they must do comprehension exercises to help them understand what they are reading so that they can get more out of their science and social studies books. Likewise, children need to be shown how learning the various word-attack skills helps them unlock new words.

Use Materials Appropriate to the Needs of the Child

The reading program in many classrooms is dictated by the kinds of materials found within each classroom. This is not desirable even in a developmental reading program, but it is completely intolerable in remedial reading. Excellent reading materials are no better than poor materials if they are not appropriate to the needs of the learner. Many remedial reading programs have failed because an untrained teacher simply gave the disabled reader "more of the same."

The remedial reading teacher must remember that referred students are for the most part disabled only in certain areas and that the weak areas must receive special attention. For example, a readily available book designed to improve a child's comprehension skills is of little value to a child with problems with word-attack skills.

Teachers and administrators should be extra cautious when buying materials to be used in remedial reading. Some materials attempt to do too many things to be really worthwhile in any one area of difficulty. For example, materials that attempt to enrich vocabulary, improve comprehension, and improve word-attack skills in each lesson are likely to be of questionable value in remedial reading, since a child is more likely to need saturation in one area rather than a well-rounded program of teaching each of these three skills. Educational research has also shown that many of the devices designed to speed up reading are of questionable value in developmental reading and may very well be detrimental to a disabled reader. In most cases there is simply no valid reason for using them. Materials appropriate for the remedial reading classroom should contain lessons designed to remedy specific reading difficulties. Chapter 16 contains considerable information on the selection and evaluation of materials for remedial and/or corrective reading.

Continue the Diagnosis While You Teach

A student who is being tested will often fail to perform as well as in the more relaxed day-to-day reading situation. If this happens, there is the danger that the student will fail certain items that are actually known. The student may be channeled into unnecessary remedial work. For example, after testing a child, you may discover that a number of phonic elements and basic sight words were missed. The student may also have missed a number of comprehension questions. You are likely to find that later in a normal classroom atmosphere the student will know some of the phonic elements and basic sight words and may improve a great deal on comprehension.

Improvement in these areas is often accounted for by the difference in stress or performance criteria between testing and actual reading. The prevalence of such cases emphasizes the need for continual diagnosis during the remediation period.

Be Alert to Pick Up Any Clues Given by the Child

Regardless of how thoroughly a disabled reader may be tested in the beginning, you will find many opportunities to expand on the initial diagnosis while you work. It is most important that you develop alertness to significant clues that children give concerning their reading disability. Some clues may lead you to change your initial diagnosis, while others allow you to expand on or confirm the original diagnosis. Following are some clues dropped by children being taught by university students:

> Casey: "Sometimes Mom makes me study in the evening for five minutes and sometimes she makes me study for three or four hours. It just depends on what kind of a mood she's in."

Casey's mother was divorced and was working full time in the daytime and dated quite often at night. Casey did his homework if his mother supervised it; however, she often simply ignored him and did not really concern herself with whether it was done. Sometimes she told him that he had to read for three hours for punishment. Most importantly, Casey did not know what to expect and had developed some poor work habits as a result of his mother's erratic behavior. Since reading was used as punishment, he had come to view reading as something to be done only when you are bad.

Counseling sessions with Casey's mother helped her to see the need to be more consistent. She also was made aware of the negative feelings that Casey was developing toward reading because it was used as punishment.

> Jeffrey: "Sometimes I can see a word and sometimes I can't."

The school nurse had tested Jeffrey's eyes earlier in the year. She reported that Jeffrey had normal vision. This clue, however, led the teacher to refer Jeffrey, through his parents, to an eye doctor who discovered that he was farsighted (had poor nearpoint vision). Glasses were prescribed and his vision and reading both improved.

> Tim: "Dad doesn't read and he gets along fine."

Tim's father was a truck driver who spent a great deal of time away from home. Tim indicated that he would like to be like his dad and he had never seen him sit down and read. During an ensuing conference with Tim's mother and father, the teacher found that both of Tim's parents read a great deal. Tim was later brought into the conference. Tim's father explained that his job depended on the ability to read. For example, he had to read road maps and road signs and a considerable amount of paperwork connected with his work, such as delivery instructions and Interstate Commerce Commission regulations. Tim's father also told Tim that when he stayed in motels at night he often read a book each night. This conference proved well worthwhile and improved Tim's attitude toward reading.

Clues such as those listed above often lead the teacher to examine certain aspects of a child's reading problem that might otherwise go unnoticed. The remedial reading teacher who is alert to such clues will often be able to add considerable worthwhile information to the original diagnosis.

Capitalize on the Motivation That the Child May Already Possess

Most children have at least one thing that seems to interest them somewhat more than others. The teacher who is able to determine that area of interest can often capitalize on it in reading. For example, Kurt came to the reading center after being referred by his classroom teacher. After his teacher at the reading center talked with him at length, she found that he had seldom, if ever, read at home, and for that matter he had seldom read anything not required. After several work sessions with Kurt, the teacher at the reading center discovered that he was interested in airplanes. His father was an Air Force pilot and had taught him to identify a great many commercial as well as Air Force planes. The teacher asked Kurt if he would be interested in reading books about airplanes. He said that he thought he might. For several succeeding sessions Kurt and his teacher searched the library for books about airplanes and flying in general. Kurt found eleven books that he expressed an interest in reading. By the end of the semester Kurt had read eight of the eleven books and had asked several times if his teacher knew where he could find some more books on the subject.

Other teachers have been successful in getting students to read about various occupations in which the students were extremely interested. Still others have motivated students to read by showing them how and why reading is a necessary part of occupations in which the student someday hoped to work. Teachers are often successful in motivating students in an area in which they previously had no interest. However, this extrinsic interest is often much more difficult to generate than intrinsic interests or motivation that the student may already possess.

Maintain a Relaxed Attitude

Children often come to remedial reading with feelings of hostility. Many of these children have failed for a number of years and can see no reason why the special class in reading should be any different. As adults, we often forget how constant failure feels. Imagine what kind of an attitude you might have toward a college statistics course if you were in it for the third time after failing it or receiving the lowest grades in the class the first two times. Certainly you would not bounce exuberantly into the class asking, "When do we get started?"

When a child brings to remedial reading a negative or hostile attitude, it becomes very easy for this same attitude to be transferred to the teacher working with the child. The teacher must, however, learn to not take such an attitude too seriously. You must maintain a relaxed attitude and teach the child that you will accept mistakes and that the child need have no fear of correction from you. Once the child sees that there is no reason for a hostile attitude, the hostility will usually disappear.

One of the coauthors worked with a young boy who almost always came to remedial reading with a negative attitude. In fact, it was very difficult for the author to maintain a pleasant attitude toward the child. During the course of the year the child's reading improved considerably, but the child's overall attitude remained pretty much the same. At the end of several years, the author happened to revisit the school and met this same boy walking back to his classroom from an outside recess period. The boy exclaimed, "Say, you're the guy who helped me learn how to read. You know, that sure helped me!" This, coming from what was probably the most hostile student the author had ever taught, is an excellent example of a child whose only defense against failure and all things connected with it was a hostile attitude.

Do Not Be Too Authoritative

As mentioned previously, the remedial reading teacher must maintain a relaxed attitude. Maintaining such an attitude should also preclude becoming too authoritarian in the classroom. This is not to say that the teacher should not be firm in demanding certain standards of work and behavior, but merely that the teacher's job should not be that of disciplinarian or authoritarian in the eyes of the child. Studies such as those of Sarah D. Muller and Charles H. Madsen, Jr. (1970), James Gardner and Grayce Ransom (1968), and Richard Cheatham (1968) indicate that the counseling aspects of teaching remedial reading are just as important as the teaching of reading per se. The teacher who is too authoritative soon becomes an ineffective counselor.

The teacher must strive to maintain a climate in which students can express their fears and resentments. Students should be spared unnecessary sermons on why they should try harder. Instead, the teacher can help students to develop motivation and self-direction by providing the success that derives from effective instruction.

Have Confidence in the Child's Ability to Learn

The remedial reading teacher must not only have confidence in the student's ability to learn but also transfer this belief to the child. A study by J. Michael Palardy (1969) demonstrated that what the teacher believes regarding students' abilities can significantly affect final student achievement. Palardy also indicated that teachers can either positively or negatively influence students' self-concepts, which in turn influence achievement.

The remedial reading teacher must be cognizant of this type of research and constantly strive to maintain a positive attitude toward each student's ability to learn. Perhaps the best way to develop this attitude is through careful record keeping as described under the earlier section entitled, "Make the Disabled Reader Aware of the Progress That Has Been Made.'' Such procedures allow both teacher and student to see the student's week-by-week progress and thus give both of them the needed confidence in the child's ability to learn.

Direct the Child Toward Self-Instruction

Although the specific instruction in a remedial reading classroom is almost always certain to be of considerable benefit, the amount that students learn on their own is often of equal or greater importance. This is true of almost any class that students attend, regardless of the subject matter involved. The learning that takes place within the classroom is, of course, of greater importance in the beginning, but it serves only as a stepping-stone to the broadening of one's knowledge. One might say that classroom learning points students in the direction of expanding and broadening their knowledge. This is especially true in remedial reading. Often the amount of time available for special tutoring is severely limited due to the lack of an adequate teaching staff. Because of these factors, the remedial reading teacher must direct the students toward self-instruction.

Self-instruction may take many different forms depending on the age-grade level of the student, the nature of the reading disability, and a host of other factors. For example, a teacher may diagnose a child as having a very limited sight vocabulary and as a result may spend many hours teaching words that should have been learned earlier. Such effort, however, can be futile if the child does not begin to read independently to gain continual exposure to the new words learned during the remedial sessions. Our work at the reading clinics at the University of Texas at El Paso and California State University, Hayward, has shown that even the brightest child needs many exposures to a word before it becomes a sight word.

Richard Allington (1980) examined the amount of actual reading assigned to students during classroom reading instruction. He found that good readers read on average more than twice as many words per session as poor readers in first- and second-grade classrooms. In addition, the poor readers had fewer opportunities to read silently, and their oral reading errors were more often treated out of context.

In a subsequent article Allington (1983) argued, ''Good and poor readers differ in their reading ability as much because of differences in instruction as variations in individual learning styles or aptitudes.'' (p. 548) Allington's review of the research persuaded him that good readers tend to receive instruction oriented toward meaningful discussion of stories, while poor readers tend to receive instruction that emphasizes words, sounds, and letters. Good readers also do considerably more silent reading, and this factor was the ''single most potent predictor of school reading achievement'' (p. 551) in several studies. Allington strongly urges teachers to provide students with more opportunities for silent reading.

Elsewhere in this book we stress the importance of substantial practice in the *act of reading*. We believe that one of the major contributors to students' reading difficulties is their limited exposure to reading in context. Though this fact may appear obvious, it bears repeating here. The implication for the remedial reading teacher is clear: The single most important form of self-instruction is to spend as much time as possible in the act of reading.

In the area of comprehension and study skills children can be taught to improve themselves by applying study techniques such as SQ3R (see Chapter 6) to reading their science and social studies lessons. They can also be taught the use of full and half signals such as "in the first place," "secondly," and "and then," which will enable their comprehension to improve while reading on their own.

Begin Each Period with a Summary of What You Intend to Do and Why You Intend to Do It, and End Each Period with a Summary of What You Did and Why You Did It

As parents, most of us have at some time or another asked our children what they learned at school today. An all-too-common answer is, "Oh nothing." As teachers, most of us also realize that the "Oh, nothing" is probably incorrect. What you must remember, however, is that "Oh, nothing" represents the child's perception of what was learned. For the purpose of stimulating or motivating a child to learn you must be cognizant of how the child feels about it. If you are successful in convincing the child that learning is in fact taking place, chances are the child will take a more active interest in what is being taught.

In order to avoid the "Oh, nothing" response, you should brief the child at the beginning of the session on what is to be learned. Then, at the end of the remedial session, you and the student should review what has been learned and why it was learned. If you follow this procedure, you will find an overall improvement in the children's attitude toward learning, and in addition, you are likely to improve your public relations program with the parents of the children you teach.

Provide for a Follow-Up Program

Remedial reading programs in which the disabled readers have been kept for a considerable length of time have tended to be more successful than those that have only brought children in for short periods. This is especially true where no follow-up program was instituted for children who were terminated from short-term remedial reading programs.

Bruce Balow (1965) reported on a study of three groups of disabled readers, some of whom were given assistance during a follow-up period:

> Continuing growth seems to depend upon continued attention to the problem. While the second and third groups received additional

remedial assistance throughout the follow-up period, few of the pupils in Sample I had any further special help. Sample I pupils did not lose the reading skill they had acquired during the time in the clinic, but neither did they continue to develop on their own. Quite in contrast is the continuing progress of the second and third groups. Given far less intensive, but nonetheless supportive, help over the follow-up period, these pupils continued to develop in reading at a pace more rapid than that preceding intensive tutoring. Rate of growth over the follow-up period was approximately 75 percent of normal growth. (p. 585)

Balow indicates that unfortunate as it may seem, short-term intensive programs have not been successful, although children are helped somewhat during the course of instruction. He believes that reading disability should probably be considered a relatively chronic illness needing long-term treatment.

Similar results were reported by Theodore A. Buerger (1968), who also did a follow-up study of remedial reading instruction. In his conclusions Buerger stated, "What is needed after a rather intensive remedial period is provision for supportive reading assistance during the follow-up period." (p. 333)

E. Shearer (1967), studying the long-term effects of remedial reading instruction, also concluded that children do make gains and that these gains can be preserved if follow-up help is given.

The activities of the follow-up in most cases will closely parallel the period of more intensive remediation. Some teachers prefer to cut the time allotted to each session, while others prefer to keep the length of sessions the same but have the child come to class less often.

REASONS FOR FAILURE IN THE DIAGNOSTIC-REMEDIAL PROCESS

Certain factors, if allowed to interfere, can seriously impede the diagnostic-remedial process. Educational diagnosticians and/or remedial teachers should constantly examine their own diagnostic-remedial procedures to insure that certain influencing factors are not adversely affecting their diagnostic or remedial procedures. Some common reasons for failure:

1. Too much time is spent on the diagnosis so that no time is left for remediation.
2. The data are inadequate.
3. A single cause of reading disability is overemphasized.
4. The diagnosis is determined by one person and the remedial work is done by another.
5. The diagnostician comes up with the same factors time after time.
6. We diagnose and work on factors that do not help children's reading.
7. Previous bias exerts an undue influence.

Too Much Time Is Spent on the Diagnosis So That No Time Is Left for Remediation

The problem of spending too much time on diagnosis is more prevalent than many people realize. In some schools the initial testing system and the initial diagnosis once the student enters the program may take up nearly one half of the first semester of school. Even if the child is not directly involved in testing every day, the admittance procedure often is so involved that the child loses out on valuable time. School personnel who deal with disabled readers should simplify procedures for initial diagnosis as much as possible in order to avoid unnecessary testing. For some children certain routine tests may be omitted. For example, hearing tests can probably be omitted for children whose problem is in an area such as reading comprehension. Likewise, individual intelligence tests may often be omitted if the child is to be admitted to the program regardless of the outcome of the test. Chances are the type of instruction given will not be influenced by the child's IQ even if it is extremely high or extremely low. In most cases a good teacher uses whatever methods or procedures that prove successful with the child.

Another problem in this area is that people involved in reading simply become curious about certain children's abilities and administer tests to satisfy their own curiosity. The teacher should be able to justify the administration of all tests given a child on the basis that the test results will ultimately help the child. Curiosity is healthful, and much good research and practical knowledge stem from it. However, unless some justifiable research is involved, children should not be subjected to unnecessary testing. The remedial reading teacher should also remember that a great deal of useful information, such as the ways children learn, their success in mastering certain concepts, and their reasons for failure, will be uncovered in working with children on a day-to-day basis.

The Data Are Inadequate

Although the diagnostic-remedial process can easily be hampered by the collection of unnecessary data, it can just as easily be hampered when the data collected are inadequate. Some children are simply referred to the remedial reading teacher, who immediately begins work on specific problems. Operating in this fashion is often wasteful of the teacher's, as well as the child's, time.

Data that could help the remedial reading teacher plan a more effective program are often readily available. For example, many children do not learn phonics through the application of rules; therefore, some children come to remedial reading with a deficiency in phonics knowledge, even after completing three years of intensive "rule type" phonics. If the remedial reading teacher is not aware of a child's inability to learn phonics through this type of approach, the child may continue to be exposed to more of the same. On the other hand, a short interview with the child's former teachers, or in some cases a check of the child's cumulative folder would inform the remedial reading teacher and avoid duplication of efforts. Another example of data that may be readily available is information on the child's physical condition that could adversely affect reading. A short interview with the child's parents can often provide information that will be helpful in planning the remedial program.

Some Single Causes of Reading Disability Are Overemphasized

Unfortunately some diagnosticians and remedial reading teachers become extremely interested in some particular aspect of reading and consequently have a tendency to overemphasize that aspect in their diagnoses and remedial work. This may happen as the result of the reading of a journal article on the subject, a report for a class, a speech at a professional meeting, and so forth. No professional person would deny the value of any of these activities; however, you should guard against becoming so involved in diagnosis in any specific area that other important deficiencies are overlooked.

Other areas that often receive undue emphasis are the learning of vowel rules, syllable principles, and accent generalizations. The remedial reading teacher should remember that the learning of any of these is merely a means to an end, that end being the ability to properly attack and pronounce an unfamiliar word. If a child can already pronounce words on or above grade level, or if the child can readily pronounce difficult nonsense words, there is little reason to learn the vowel rules, syllable principles, or accent generalizations as word-attack skills.

The diagnostician and remedial reading teacher do well to ask themselves such questions as: Do I consistently find myself teaching the same thing regardless of the original diagnosis? Do my diagnoses indicate that I consistently prescribe the same remediation? Do I use only one or two tests with which I am familiar that may tend to give me the same results each time? Do other diagnosticians concur with my findings and recommendations? Would the total number of disabled readers I have diagnosed show approximately the same percentage of reading problems in each category as reputable studies have indicated are the causes of reading disability?

The Diagnosis Is Determined by One Person and the Remedial Work Is Done by Another

When a diagnosis is done by one person and the student is turned over to another for remediation, communication problems often arise. Communication concerning reading deficiencies is sometimes difficult because of differences in reading terminology. Helen Robinson (1970) states:

> Examples of differences in terms and labels may be found by
> comparing articles dealing with reading in almost any publication. In

learning to read, a child may be expected to identify words, discriminate words, recognize words, or perceive words. (p. 78)

Unless the reading diagnostician has the ability to communicate accurately the diagnosis to the person who will be carrying out the remedial procedures, the child is quite likely to receive inadequate or unnecessary help.

Most of the problems encountered in the area of communication between the diagnostician and teacher are a result of a lack of preciseness. For example, a part of one diagnostician's report read as follows: "This child should be provided with help in word-attack skills." Such a statement is of little value to a teacher since there are so many word-attack skills. Even if the statement was narrowed to any one word-attack skill such as phonics, the diagnostician should still be exact in describing what the child needs. For example, a report that read as follows would provide much more direction for immediate remedial help:

This child should be provided with help in learning the initial consonant blends, *bl, pl, fl,* and *pr.* He should then be given help in learning to blend them with various phonograms.

Another problem encountered when the diagnosis is done by one person and then turned over to another is that children who are exposed to a strange person in a testing situation often fail to perform up to their normal standards. When this happens, the person doing the remedial work will find discrepancies with the original diagnosis, which will in turn lead to an inefficient diagnostic-remedial procedure.

The Diagnostician Comes Up with the Same Factors Time after Time

Most educational diagnosticians tend to rely on certain tests with which they have become familiar through continued use. The use of the same test or tests time after time can be beneficial in that the tester becomes more efficient in the diagnostic process. Efficiency in administration of tests is of little value, however, if the diagnostician fails to diagnose certain important causal factors and continually comes up with the same recommendations for remediation time after time.

Unfortunately, in reading psychologists' and educational diagnosticians' reports, we often find that nearly all reports even on different students diagnosed by one person contain the same recommendations. The reports on various students diagnosed by another person may contain different types of recommendations but again often contain the same recommendations for all students. All of you dealing with the diagnosis of disabled readers should continually evaluate your findings and recommendations to determine whether they are generally in line with studies showing various causal factors and the percent of time you might expect each to occur. Research by J. F. Vinsonhaler

(1979) examined three types of agreement in reading diagnosis: group agreement, intraclinician agreement, and interclinician agreement. Vinsonhaler found that reading clinicians do not agree very well with themselves or with other clinicians.

We Diagnose and Work on Factors That Do Not Help Children's Reading

In most cases there is little value in diagnosing factors for which we either do not expect to provide remediation or for which remediation has not proven effective in the past. For example, Donald Hammill, Libby Goodman, and J. Lee Wiederholt (1974) summarized the research in the areas of eye-motor coordination and visual perception. They concluded that readers with visual-perception problems, such as eye-motor coordination, discrimination of figure-ground, and position in space, were not helped by training in these areas per se. Therefore, unless these tests can be justified strictly for research purposes, there seems to be little if any value in their routine administration in the public schools. Jean Harber (1979) found that the skills of visual perception, visual-perceptual integration, sound blending, and visual closure were not highly related to reading performance in learning-disabled children. Therefore, the remedial reading teacher must question the value of instruction designed to remedy weaknesses in these areas.

A child who has difficulty in discriminating a "b" from a "d" may, for example, also score low on Frostig's (1966) *Developmental Test of Visual Perception* subtest "Position in Space." However, simply having the child read or write the letters of the alphabet will quickly enable the diagnostician to determine whether the child is making letter reversals. If letter reversals are occurring, research evidence suggests two possible approaches: either the problem should be ignored, since the child will likely outgrow it; or, if remedial procedures are employed, it is more logical to work on the *b* and *d* problem directly, rather than to do the types of exercises recommended by Frostig when children obtain a poor score on the "Position in Space" subtest. If you do the type of remediation recommended by Frostig, you can only hope that the remediation will transfer to the *b* and *d* reversal problem.

The remedial reading teacher and/or educational diagnostician should continually examine their diagnostic procedures to determine whether unnecessary testing is being done in terms of what is being provided in the remedial program. Care should also be taken to provide adequate diagnosis for any suspected areas of difficulty for which remediation has proven effective.

Previous Bias Exerts an Undue Influence

Few if any of us would deny that we are somewhat biased on matters such as politics, religion, and certain beliefs concerning education. We must, however, continually examine our own beliefs and practices to determine whether they are exerting an unhealthy influence in diagnosing and treating reading disabilities. It is all too easy to ignore research indicating that our beliefs may be wrong and look for research that tends to confirm our biases.

Reading personnel should constantly guard against developing attitudes that are likely to be detrimental to their diagnostic or remedial procedures. While serving as a reading consultant in the public schools, one of the coauthors encountered a reading teacher with very little formal training in the field. The teacher was using procedures that were far out of line with proven procedures. Still, this teacher insisted that his ideas and methods were successful. A subsequent check of the standardized test scores of this teacher's classes during the four previous years indicated that his pupils' class average had dropped about ten percentile points each year during the time he had taught them. There was no doubt that his personal bias concerning methodology was adversely affecting his pupils.

Experimentation should be encouraged, and when certain procedures prove successful, they should be adopted. On the other hand, when test results or experience proves that procedures are detrimental to the welfare of students, those procedures should be revised.

SUMMARY

Through a combination of research and experience, remedial reading teachers have found that certain procedures can make their programs more effective. It is important to know which diagnostic operational procedures have been successful and which have not. Some of these have been discussed in this chapter. It is also important to know which procedures have been successful in the remedial process. These have also been discussed in this chapter. Quite often remedial reading programs have failed to achieve the expected results. The information presented in this chapter should help remedial reading teachers avoid the same mistakes.

REFERENCES

Allington, R. L. (1980). *Poor readers don't get to read much.* East Lansing, MI: Institute for Research on Teaching.

Allington, R. L. (1983). The reading instruction provided readers of differing reading abilities. *Elementary School Journal, 83,* 548–559.

Balow, B. (1965). The long term effect of remedial reading instruction. *Reading Teacher, 18,* 581–586.

Buerger, T. A. (1968). A follow-up of remedial reading instruction. *Reading Teacher, 21,* 329–334.

Cheatham, R. B. (1968). *A study of the effects of group counseling on the self-concept and on the reading efficiency of low-achieving readers in a public intermediate school.* Doctoral dissertation, The American University.

Dolan, K. G. (1964). Effects of individual counseling on selected test scores for delayed readers. *Personnel and Guidance Journal, 42,* 914–919.

Durrell, D. D., & Catterson, J. H. (1980). *Durrell analysis of reading difficulty.* New York: Psychological Corporation.

Ekwall, E. E. (1973). *An analysis of children's test scores when tested with individually administered diagnostic tests and when tested with group administered diagnostic tests.* Final Research Report, University of Texas at El Paso, University Research Institute.

Ekwall, E. E. (1986). *Ekwall reading inventory* (2d ed.). Boston: Allyn & Bacon.

Frostig, M. (1966). *Developmental test of visual perception.* Palo Alto, CA: Consulting Psychologists Press.

Gardner, J., & Ransom, G. (1968). Academic reorientation: A counseling approach to remedial readers. *Reading Teacher, 21,* 529–536.

Hammill, D., Goodman, L. & Wiederholt, J. (1974). Visual-motor processes: Can we train them? *Reading Teacher, 27,* 469–478.

Harber, J. (1979). Are perceptual skills necessary for success in reading? Which ones? *Reading Horizons, 20,* 7–15.

Lillich, J. M. (1968, April). *Comparison of achievement in special reading classes using guidance, skill-content and combination approaches.* Paper presented at International Reading Association Conference, Boston, MA.

Muller, S. D., & Madsen, C. H., Jr., (1970). Group desensitization for anxious children with reading problems. *Psychology in the Schools, 7,* 184–189.

Palardy, J. M. (1969). For Johnny's reading sake. *Reading Teacher, 22,* 720–721.

Robinson, H. (1970). Significant unsolved problems in reading. *Reading Teacher, 14,* 77–82.

Shearer, E. (1967). The long-term effects of remedial education. *Educational Research, 9,* 219–222.

Smith, L. L., Johns, J. L., Ganschow, L., & Masztal, N. B. (1983). Using grade level vs. out-of-level reading tests with remedial students. *Reading Teacher, 36,* 550–553.

Vinsonhaler, J. F. (1979). *The consistency of reading diagnosis.* East Lansing, MI: Institute for Research on Teaching.

3

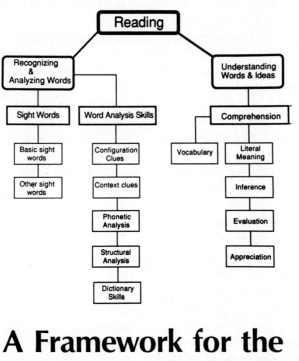

A Framework for the Diagnosis and Teaching of Educational Factors

The first purpose of this chapter is to develop a framework for the diagnosis and remediation of educational factors in reading. The second purpose is to illustrate scope and sequence of the commonly taught reading skills to enable the teacher to determine which reading skills students should have mastered at various stages in their progression through the grades. This is followed by a discussion intended to clarify the usage of materials for diagnosis, teaching, or reinforcement.

Many definitions of the act of reading have been proposed over the years. Many of these are similar to the following: reading is the act of interpreting, by the reader, what was written by the author. This definition, although somewhat useful for theoretical purposes in discussing the act of reading, is not concrete enough to be meaningful to the remedial reading or learning disabilities teacher in diagnosis and remediation. For that purpose, think of reading as a process of recognizing and analyzing words and of understanding words and ideas.

We often hear beginning teachers make such statements as, "I have a student in my class who is a good oral reader but can't seem to understand what he reads." Still others will say, "One of my students can really understand what she reads, but she just can't seem to say all of the words." When hearing this type of statement we are reminded of the story of the man who was raised in a Spanish-speaking community. He spoke both Spanish and English but learned to read and write only English. During the process of learning to read he never learned to sound out words. During his college years he began to date a young lady from Mexico City. One Christmas vacation when the young lady went home, she sent the young man a letter written in Spanish. Since the young man had only learned to speak Spanish, he could not read the letter. He solved the problem, however, by getting one of his friends to help him. His friend could not speak Spanish, but he could pronounce the words, since Spanish is a phonemic language and his friend had a good knowledge of sound-symbol relationships. The essential point here was that neither one of the young men could read the letter. One of them could pronounce the words and one of them could understand the words and ideas, but it took both of them to read the letter.

Reading, then, is a process of recognizing and analyzing words and understanding words and ideas. What the beginning teachers mentioned earlier meant was that certain students were poor in knowledge of sight words and/or word analysis skills or else in comprehension of words and ideas. A lack of knowledge in either area makes a student a disabled reader.

The scope of the reading skills discussed thus far is illustrated in Figure 3–1.

Recognizing and analyzing words is usually broken down into two subdivisions, sight words and word-attack skills. Here are two situations for a reader. Either the reader has come in contact with a word enough times to recognize it at once, or the reader must apply one or more word-attack skills to recognize and say or think that word. If the word is familiar enough to be recognized instantly, it is a sight word. The number of sight words in any reader's storehouse varies with such factors as the amount of previous reading, the grade level, and the potential for learning. For example, the word *and* becomes a sight word for most readers shortly after they begin to read because of its high utility in the English language. On the other hand, the word *sextant* does not become a sight word for most readers until much later in life.

The term *sight vocabulary* is often used by authors and reading specialists

FIGURE 3–1 Two Basic Categories of Reading Skills

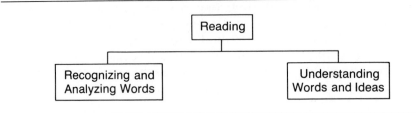

to refer to the total stock of words recognized by a student by sight. In this case they are not concerned with whether the student knows the meaning of the word but only with whether the word is recognized and pronounced instantly. Some words may be in students' "recognition" vocabularies but not in their "meaning" vocabularies, and vice versa. Still other authors reserve the word *vocabulary* strictly for "word meaning." When the term *vocabulary building* is used, most authors are referring to the building of a word-meaning vocabulary; the word may or may not also be learned as a sight word. In this book the term *sight vocabulary* means the same as "sight words," i.e., simple word recognition. The term *vocabulary* used by itself indicates "meaning vocabulary."

Under the sight-word category are two subcategories, basic sight words and other sight words. The term *basic sight word* usually refers to a certain list of *high-utility words* (words most often in print) compiled by writers and researchers in the field of reading. Examples of some of these are the Dolch List (1955), the Harris-Jacobson List (1985), and the Fry List (1980). The term *basic sight word* is also used to indicate a word of such high utility that it should not require the application of word-attack skills.

Listed under sight words is another category called other sight words. This category includes all words known instantly or known without the use of word-attack skills. The number of other sight words varies from reader to reader and within any one reader through continual contact with new words. For example, a word such as *establish* may require the application of word-attack skills quite a number of times, but it eventually becomes a sight word. It is classified here as one of the "other sight words." That is, it is known instantly but is not of such high utility as to be a "basic sight word."

The scope of reading skills explained thus far is illustrated in Figure 3–2.

As stated earlier, the other subcategory of recognizing words is word-attack skills or word-analysis skills. When a reader does not instantly recognize a word, the reader must apply one or more word-attack skills. The subcategories of word-attack skills are configuration clues, context clues, phonics, structural analysis (or morphology), and dictionary skills. Configuration clues are the hints a student receives from the overall shape or configuration of a word. The configuration of a word is influenced by such factors as length (*elephant* versus *bed*), use of capital and lower-case letters (*BED* versus *bed*), use of

FIGURE 3–2 A Partial Breakdown of the Skill of Recognizing and Analyzing Words

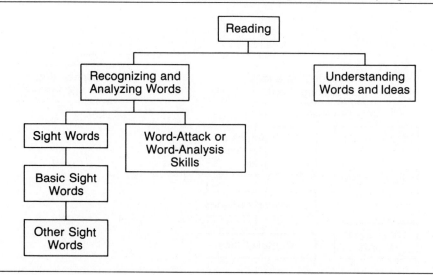

extenders and descenders (*l, b* versus *p, j*), and use of double letters (*look* versus *have*). Context clues are those that a student receives from a word by the way it is used in the sentence. (The old car rattled as the farmer drove down the country _____ [road].) Another kind of context clue that is often useful to beginning readers is the picture context clue. It tells the reader what the word might be, based on a picture illustrating the reading passage. Phonics usually refers to the sound-symbol relationships between the small, usually nonmeaning-bearing, parts of words. This includes the sounds represented by consonants, consonant blends, consonant digraphs, vowels, vowel teams, and special letter combinations. Phonics also includes phonetic generalizations, e.g., rules governing vowel sounds. Syllabication principles are also often considered a phonics skill, although they are more appropriately considered structural analysis. Structural analysis is similar to phonics; however, the term as commonly used refers to larger parts of words that bear meaning, such as root words, suffixes, prefixes, word endings, apostrophe + *s* to show possession, contractions, and compound words. Sometimes the term *structural analysis* is used to refer to the ability to *derive meaning* from word *parts.* Although this is an important skill that may serve to broaden a student's meaning vocabulary, such knowledge does not contribute directly to decoding ability. The dictionary skills apply to a number of abilities, such as alphabetizing, locating a specific word, using guide words, and interpreting spellings. With the addition of the subcategories of word-attack or 'word-analysis' skills the scope of reading skills is illustrated in Figure 3–3.

The problem of deriving subcategories to illustrate the skills required for understanding words and ideas, or what is usually referred to as comprehen-

FIGURE 3–3   A Breakdown of the Skill of Recognizing and Analyzing Words

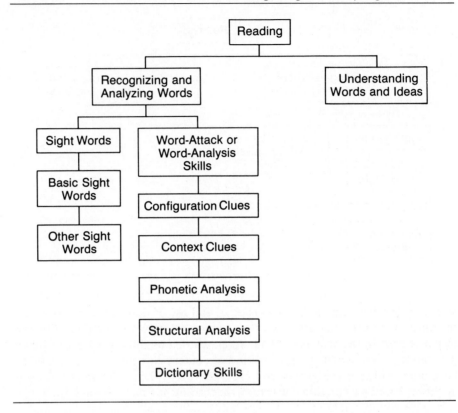

sion, is much more complicated and less clear-cut than the area of word-attack or word-analysis skills. Research to date has generally shown that investigators are not able to accurately differentiate more than two or three broad factors. According to George and Evelyn Spache (1977) the factors influencing comprehension may be arranged in three broad categories:

1. those inherent in the material being read,
2. the characteristics of the reader, and
3. the influences dependent upon the manner of reading. (p. 447)

Within these categories Spache and Spache include these prominent factors: vocabulary knowledge; the structure and style of the material being read; the ability to use reasoning processes; the beliefs, attitudes, and prejudices of the reader; the purposes of the reader; and the rate of reading.

Most commonly used measures of reading achievement attempt to measure only two broad categories of comprehension—vocabulary and reading comprehension. It appears, then, that one is justified in categorizing the subskills of comprehension as vocabulary development and other comprehension skills.

Thomas Barrett (1967) suggests that the cognitive dimension for comprehension categories might be classified as "(a) literal meaning, (b) inference, (c) evaluation, and (d) appreciation." (p. 21) Literal meaning, as defined by Barrett, is concerned with ideas and information explicitly stated in a reading selection. The first of these in terms of pupil behavior is recognition and the second, recall. Inference, as Barrett states, occurs when the student "uses the ideas and information explicitly stated in the selection, his intuition, and his personal experience as a basis for conjectures and hypotheses." (p. 22)

In explaining his concept of evaluation Barrett states:

Purposes for reading and teachers' questions, in this instance, require responses by the student which indicate that he has arrived at a judgment by comparing ideas presented in the selection with external criteria provided by the teacher, other authorities or written sources, or with internal criteria provided by the reader's experiences, knowledge, or values. In essence, evaluation deals with judgments and focuses on qualities or correctness, worthwhileness, or appropriateness, feasibility, and validity. (p. 22)

Barrett's last category of appreciation would involve all of the other mentioned levels of thought but would go beyond them. Barrett states,

Appreciation, as used here, calls for the student to be emotionally and aesthetically sensitive to the written work and to have a reaction to its psychological and artistic elements. For example, when a student verbalizes his feelings about part or all of a reading selection in terms of excitement, fear, dislike, or boredom, he is functioning at the appreciational level. (p. 23)

It should be kept in mind that Barrett's taxonomy of skills for comprehension are only suggested and cannot necessarily be defended in terms of factoral analysis studies dealing with concretely measured categories. They do, however, add meaning to our goals for viewing and teaching these skills.

Barrett's categories under other comprehension skills appear in Figure 3-4.

In addition to the subskills of comprehension mentioned by Barrett, a number of authors have listed other categories such as the ability to see main ideas, see important details, see the author's purpose, develop mental images, see a sequence of ideas, and see the author's organization.

Note the broken line from "appreciation" to "study skills." This indicates that study skills have a relationship to, or contribute to, reading comprehension. This relationship is, however, less direct than the relationship between comprehension and the other subcategories previously mentioned.

Perhaps this breakdown of the comprehension skills is not justified on the

FIGURE 3-4   Scope of the Reading Skills

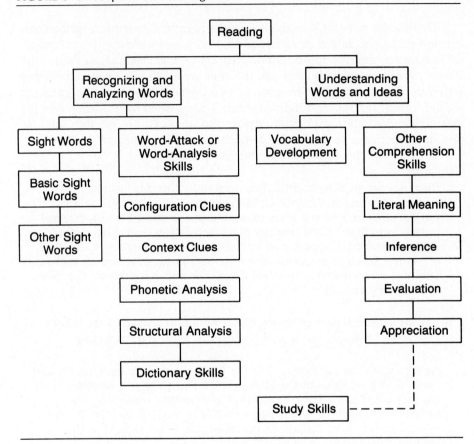

basis of research. We believe, however, that it is helpful to examine, in at least this much detail, what we have commonly believed to be some of the other subskills of comprehension.

The relationships shown in Figure 3–4 no doubt grossly oversimplify the reading act. For example, we know that the purpose and/or state of mind of a student previous to reading a passage can greatly affect comprehension. These might be considered psychological factors, and this should be shown in the comprehension part of Figure 3–4. There are so many factors of this nature that it would be virtually impossible to illustrate them in a diagram. Furthermore, at present we do not know how to measure many complex factors that are known to exist. Figure 3–4 represents relationships that are generally known to exist and the educational factors in reading that to some extent can be measured.

COMPETENCIES THAT STUDENTS SHOULD ACHIEVE
IN THEIR PROGRESSION THROUGH THE GRADES

If you were to wait until a secondary student was seriously disabled in reading, there would be no need to be concerned about which of the various skills should be tested. That is to say, you could simply assume that the student should have mastered all of the commonly tested reading skills and therefore that it would be appropriate to test any or all of the reading skills. On the other hand, with a younger and less disabled reader you must be more familiar with the scope and sequence of the reading skills in order to avoid testing beyond the point at which that student should have normally progressed. It is imperative, then, that the reading diagnostician be familiar with the scope and sequence of the reading skills. In this section reference will again be made to the skills and subskills presented in Figure 3–4. This time, however, we will be more concerned with a further breakdown of these skills and the points at which each of the various skills should have been mastered by a student with normal achievement.

It is also imperative that the classroom teacher become familiar with the scope and sequence of the reading skills in order to locate students with incipient reading problems. For example, a teacher who does not know when students should have mastered the basic sight words is not likely to notice a student with a mild disability in this area until the problem becomes obvious. At that time the problem is more difficult to correct and the student not only is more disabled, but also may have developed concurrent psychological problems resulting from this difficulty. In order to determine the point at which each of the reading skills should be mastered, seven sets of basal readers were analyzed. As one might expect, the points at which the authors of the various series of basal readers chose to introduce each of the skills varied to some extent. For the diagnostician, however, these minor disagreements as to time of introduction of the reading skills are not extremely important. What the diagnostician must be concerned with is the latest point at which all authors agree the skills should have been taught. This is the point at which the diagnostician can test for any particular skill and safely assume the student has been taught that skill.

An important point for the diagnostician to keep in mind is that some reading skills should definitely be mastered and others will be extended and refined ad infinitum. For example, the basic sight words should definitely be known by average students by the middle of their third year in school. On the other hand, a student's knowledge of other sight words will continue to expand. Likewise, there is no point at which one can assume the comprehension skills are completely mastered. The ability to make inferences from a paragraph, for example, probably continues to improve as the vocabulary and background of experiences continue to expand. Skills that are extended and refined rather than completely mastered should be learned and tested; however, keep in mind that a student who continues to learn will also continue to improve in the ability to use these skills. In the breakdown of the reading skills in Figure 3–5 you will note the use of single and cross-hatched lines under various grade levels (see key). The level at which a line appears is opposite the listing of that skill or subskill and indicates the general point at which you can assume that the skill has been taught and likewise the point at which you can logically assume the student should have mastered (in some cases) or have a knowledge of the use of that skill. In interpreting the chart you should keep in mind that the designation of grade level serves only as a general guideline. Also, in using the scope and sequence chart several precautions need to be observed. First, you should not consider any one skill that appears on the chart to be a prerequisite to a child's learning to read. For example, knowledge of vowel rules may be necessary only if a child cannot pronounce various short and long vowel sounds and if the child needs this skill to decode. The learning of vowel rules is only a means to an end. If the child can pronounce various vowel sounds and combinations of vowels and vowel controlling letters, then there is no need for the child to master that skill. Many very good adult readers can pronounce almost any word or syllable; however, it would be very difficult for many of these same adults to give the vowel sounds in isolation. Furthermore, knowledge of vowel sounds is neither necessary nor helpful for all readers. Many readers are able to decode effectively using other word-attack skills. Therefore, we are only reporting the information in Figure 3–5. We shall evaluate the relative importance of the various skills in succeeding chapters.

It should again be emphasized that Figure 3–5 does not attempt to point to a specific time when the skill should be taught. The points of time illustrated represent the stage at which all of the basal reader programs examined agree each skill should be known.

A final but very important consideration is that there are often considerably different levels of development of a certain skill. For example, a child may be able to recognize and circle one of four phonemes that is the same as the initial sound heard in a word pronounced by a tester. However, the child may not be able to pronounce the same phoneme in a strange word when it is encountered in the act of reading. This is the level of competency necessary in actual reading. This point will be emphasized again in later chapters as methods of testing for various competencies are discussed.

SUMMARY

In order to begin diagnosis work in the field of reading, the remedial reading teacher must have a thorough knowledge of the scope and sequence of the reading skills. The teacher must not only understand what educational problems need to be diagnosed but must also know when to expect each student to have mastered each of the reading skills.

In doing diagnostic work it should be kept in mind that certain skills are

FIGURE 3–5 Competencies That Students Should Achieve in Their Progression Through the Grades

SKILL	GRADE LEVEL OR YEAR IN SCHOOL						
	1	2	3	4	5	6	7+
Knowledge of Dolch Basic Sight Words (or similar)							
First Half		▨	▨	▨	▨	▨	▨
Second Half			▨	▨	▨	▨	▨
Other Sight Words							
Configuration Clues[a]	▩	▩	▩	▩	▩	▩	▩
(Word length, capital letters, double letters and letter height)	▩	▩	▩	▩	▩	▩	▩
Context Clues							
(Pictures and words)		▩	▩	▩	▩	▩	▩
Phonic Analysis							
Single initial consonants							
(all but soft *c* and *g*)		▨	▨	▨	▨	▨	▨
soft *c*			▨	▨	▨	▨	▨
soft *g*			▨	▨	▨	▨	▨
Initial consonant blends							
bl, br, fl, fr, gr, st, tr, cl, cr,		▨	▨	▨	▨	▨	▨
dr, pr, sl, sp		▨	▨	▨	▨	▨	▨
pl, gl, sk, sm		▨	▨	▨	▨	▨	▨
sn, thr, sw, wr		▨	▨	▨	▨	▨	▨
tw, sch, sc, squ, str, spl, spr, scr			▨	▨	▨	▨	▨
shr, dw			▨	▨	▨	▨	▨
Ending consonant blends							
st		▨	▨	▨	▨	▨	▨
ld, nd, ng		▨	▨	▨	▨	▨	▨
nk, nt			▨	▨	▨	▨	▨
ft, mp			▨	▨	▨	▨	▨
lt				▨	▨	▨	▨
Consonant Digraphs							
sh, th (three, this), wh (which, who),		▨	▨	▨	▨	▨	▨
ch (church)		▨	▨	▨	▨	▨	▨
ck, ng			▨	▨	▨	▨	▨
gh, ph			▨	▨	▨	▨	▨
Silent Consonants							
kn, gh(t), wr			▨	▨	▨	▨	▨
mb			▨	▨	▨	▨	▨
gn				▨	▨	▨	▨

  Skill firmly established   Skill extended and refined, but has been introduced

[a] The use of configuration clues is taught in grade one, but older students continue to use and improve in this skill as their knowledge of structural analysis increases.

(cont.)

FIGURE 3–5. (cont.)

SKILL	GRADE LEVEL OR YEAR IN SCHOOL						
	1	2	3	4	5	6	7+
Short Vowel Sounds							
a, e, i, o, u		▨	▨	▨	▨	▨	▨
Long Vowel Sounds							
a, e, i, o, u			▨	▨	▨	▨	▨
Vowel Teams and Special Letter combinations							
ay, ee			▨	▨	▨	▨	▨
oo (book), oo (moon), ea (each),				▨	▨	▨	▨
ea (bread), oe, ai, oa, ow (cow),				▨	▨	▨	▨
ow (snow), ir, ur, or, ar, aw, ou, er					▨	▨	▨
oi, oy, al, au, ew				▨	▨	▨	▨
Rules for Y sound							
at end of multi-syllable word				▨	▨	▨	▨
at end of single syllable word				▨	▨	▨	▨
Vowel Rules For Open and Closed Syllables					▨	▨	▨
Contractions							
didn't, won't, can't, isn't, don't		▨	▨	▨	▨	▨	▨
let's, it's, that's, wasn't, hadn't, I'll,			▨	▨	▨	▨	▨
I'm, he's			▨	▨	▨	▨	▨
we'll, I've, he'll, hasn't, haven't,			▨	▨	▨	▨	▨
we're, you're, what's, there's, she's,			▨	▨	▨	▨	▨
they'd, she'll, here's, ain't, couldn't,			▨	▨	▨	▨	▨
they're, you'll, she'd, weren't, I'd,			▨	▨	▨	▨	▨
you've, you'd, we'd, anybody'd, there'll,			▨	▨	▨	▨	▨
we've, who'll, he'd, who'd, doesn't,			▨	▨	▨	▨	▨
where's, they've, they'll			▨	▨	▨	▨	▨
aren't, wouldn't			▨	▨	▨	▨	▨
Possessives							
Accent Rules[b]							
1. In two syllable words the first is usually accented.					▨	▨	▨
2. In inflected or derived forms the primary accent usually falls on or within the root word.					▨	▨	▨
3. If two vowels are together in the last syllable of a word it may be a clue to an accented final syllable.						▨	▨
4. If there are two unlike consonants within a word, the syllable before the double consonants is usually accented.						▨	▨

[b] At present no definitive research is available as to which accent generalizations are of high enough utility to make them worthwhile to teach. The four listed here are believed to be quite consistent and also of high utility.

(cont.)

FIGURE 3–5. (cont.)

SKILL	1	2	3	4	5	6	7+
Prefixes (recognition only)[c]							
a		▨	▨	▨	▨	▨	▨
un, re			▨	▨	▨	▨	▨
dis			▨	▨	▨	▨	▨
in, per, pre, al, be, de, con				▨	▨	▨	▨
im, under, mid				▨	▨	▨	▨
for, ex, over, ad, sub, photo, en,				▨	▨	▨	▨
com, pro, non, fore, anti, out					▨	▨	▨
auto, mis, trans					▨	▨	▨
inter, self, tele, counter, ab						▨	▨
Prefixes (meaning only)							
re (back or again), un (not)			▨	▨	▨	▨	▨
pre (before, prior to)				▨	▨	▨	▨
ex (out, forth, from)				▨	▨	▨	▨
de (from, away, from off)				▨	▨	▨	▨
dis (apart, away from), in (into), in (not)					▨	▨	▨
en (in, to make, put into), sub (under)					▨	▨	▨
com (with, together)					▨	▨	▨
Suffixes (recognition only)							
ly		▨	▨	▨	▨	▨	▨
est, er			▨	▨	▨	▨	▨
y, less			▨	▨	▨	▨	▨
fully, self, en, full, ness, ily, ty				▨	▨	▨	▨
an, ier, some, ish				▨	▨	▨	▨
ern, ite, ion, able, ment, ology, ous,					▨	▨	▨
or, ward, al, th, ious, ese, hood, ship,					▨	▨	▨
ist, ure, ive, ible, age					▨	▨	▨
ity, ation, ant, ian, ent					▨	▨	▨
ance, ence, ic, ical, ling, eer, ery,						▨	▨
ey, most, wise						▨	▨
ary							▨
Syllable Principles							
1. When two like consonants stand between two vowels the word is usually divided between the consonants.				▨	▨	▨	▨

GRADE LEVEL OR YEAR IN SCHOOL

[c] The prefixes *un* and *re* should be known by the middle of the third year in school. From that point on, the student should continue to extend and refine his or her knowledge of prefixes. This extension and refinement would continue throughout his or her elementary and high school years. The same is true of the suffixes such as *est* and *er* which should be known by the end of the second year of school but would be extended and refined throughout the student's elementary and high school years. (The authors suggest that "known" in this case only means that the student recognizes the prefix and/or suffix, but that he or she not be required to know its meaning.)

(cont.)

FIGURE 3–5. (cont.)

GRADE LEVEL OR YEAR IN SCHOOL

2. When two unlike consonants stand between two vowels the word is usually divided between the consonants.
3. When a word ends in a consonant and *le,* the consonant usually begins the last syllable.
4. Divide between compound words.
5. Prefixes and suffixes are usually separate syllables.
6. Do not divide letters in consonant blends and consonant digraphs.

Dictionary Skills
  Alphabet in order
  Alphabetizing letters
  Alphabetizing words to first letter
  Alphabetizing words to second letter
  Estimating location of a word
  Alphabetizing words to third letter
  Using guide words
  Interpreting symbols
  Interpreting accent and stress
  Selecting word meaning from context
  Interpreting pronunciation key
  Using cross reference
  First and second spellings
  Word origin
  Parts of speech

Study Skills
  Table of Contents
  Index
  Glossary
  Encyclopedia (Find topic)
  Encyclopedia (Use index volume)
  Encyclopedia (Use cross-reference)
  Almanac
  Telephone Directory
  Interpret tables
  Library card index
  Read maps
  Read graphs, charts, and diagrams
  Skimming

Skill	1	2	3	4	5	6	7+
2. Two unlike consonants between two vowels				■	■	■	■
3. Word ends in consonant and *le*				■	■	■	■
4. Divide between compound words				■	■	■	■
5. Prefixes and suffixes separate syllables				■	■	■	■
6. Do not divide consonant blends and digraphs				■	■	■	
Alphabet in order		■	■	■	■	■	■
Alphabetizing letters			■	■	■	■	■
Alphabetizing words to first letter			■	■	■	■	■
Alphabetizing words to second letter				■	■	■	■
Estimating location of a word				■	■	■	■
Alphabetizing words to third letter					■	■	■
Using guide words					■	■	■
Interpreting symbols					■	■	■
Interpreting accent and stress					■	■	■
Selecting word meaning from context					■	■	■
Interpreting pronunciation key					■	■	■
Using cross reference					■	■	■
First and second spellings						■	■
Word origin						■	■
Parts of speech						■	■
Table of Contents		■	■	■	■	■	■
Index				■	■	■	■
Glossary				■	■	■	■
Encyclopedia (Find topic)				■	■	■	■
Encyclopedia (Use index volume)					■	■	■
Encyclopedia (Use cross-reference)					■	■	■
Almanac					■	■	■
Telephone Directory					■	■	■
Interpret tables						▨	▨
Library card index						■	■
Read maps					▨	▨	▨
Read graphs, charts, and diagrams							▨
Skimming			▨	▨	▨	▨	▨

definitely necessary for a student to learn to read. On the other hand, skills are helpful to some readers but not known by other excellent readers. In other words, some reading skills are only a means to an end, and if the student has already reached the end there is no use in diagnosing the skills that lead to it.

We have also discussed the classification of diagnostic, teaching, and reinforcement activities.

REFERENCES

Barrett, T. C. (1967). The evaluation of children's reading achievement. *Perspectives in reading no. 8,* Newark, DE: International Reading Association.

Dolch, E. W. (1955). *Methods in reading.* Champaign, IL: Garrard Publishing Co.

Fry, E. (1980). The new instant word list. *Reading Teacher, 34,* 284–89.

Harris, A. J., & Jacobson, M. D. (1985). *How to increase reading ability* (8th ed., pp. 376–78). New York: Longman.

Spache, G. D., & Spache, E. B. (1977). *Reading in the elementary school* (4th ed.). Boston: Allyn and Bacon.

4

Diagnosis and Remediation of Educational Factors: *Letter Knowledge and Sight Words*

One purpose of this chapter is to examine the need for and methods of testing for letter knowledge and knowledge of sight words and basic sight words. A second purpose is to examine some of the pros and cons of each method. A third purpose is to discuss some ways of teaching letter knowledge, sight words, and basic sight words.

Part A: DIAGNOSIS

ALPHABET KNOWLEDGE

A number of research studies have shown that letter knowledge is not necessarily a prerequisite for learning to read. On the other hand, numerous studies have also shown that children who begin their schooling with a knowledge of the ABC's are likely to become better readers than children who lack this knowledge. For some time this was taken to mean that letter knowledge was helpful or necessary in learning to read. Diane Chisholm and June Knafle (1978) found that first-grade pupils who knew letter names were able to learn words in significantly fewer trials than their counterparts who did not. Olga Speer and George Lamb (1976) found that speed of letter-name recognition was the critical factor. Many authorities believe that knowledge of the ABC's for entering school-age children is simply indicative of a host of factors that are often conducive to learning to read. Among these factors are a natural potential for learning to read, educational level of parents, and good reading environment in the home. However, after a thorough review of the research on the value of learning letter names, Patrick Groff (1984) stated:

> At present, the following conclusion seems tenable: Letter name teaching is appropriate if done concurrently with instruction in phonics. Those who contend that the time of letter name teaching is unimportant probably are wrong.
> Since letter name knowledge and phonics knowledge are highly correlated, it makes sense to view them as functionally related areas of information. Thus simultaneous teaching appears to be the best way to exploit their potential for helping children to learn to read. (p. 387)

It should be stressed that children who reach the middle or upper elementary grades without a thorough knowledge of the alphabet are quite likely to be disabled readers. Although children *can* learn to read without being able to identify the name of each letter, it becomes difficult in most classrooms simply because of communication problems. Furthermore, children who cannot distinguish a *b* from a *d* or a *q* from a *p* are likely to encounter a great deal of difficulty in learning to read. For these reasons a check on children's knowledge of the alphabet should be included as a regular part of the diagnostic procedure.

Beginning teachers and inexperienced diagnosticians are likely to take it for granted that children in the middle and upper grade levels possess a thorough knowledge of the alphabet. Testing at this level soon reveals, however, that a rather large percentage of disabled readers still have difficulty in this area. Since the diagnosis for alphabet knowledge is so quick and simple, it should be included as one of the beginning procedures.

One procedure that is relatively easy is to put the letters of the alphabet on two cards approximately 5 × 8. Put the lower-case alphabet on one card and the upper-case alphabet on the other. On one side of the card you may wish to type the letters with a primary typewriter or print them by hand. On side two of the card you reproduce what is on side one plus any directions you may wish to look at while the child looks at side one. It is also better to put the letters in random order, since some children have learned the alphabet song or the alphabet in order, which makes it appear they know letters that they do not know.

Another procedure is to ask the child to write the alphabet. After the child finishes you may wish to ask the child to write any omitted letters or any that appeared to give difficulty.

Flash cards with one letter on each card also work well for testing alphabet knowledge. Some disabled readers perfer to work with flash cards, since they tend to have an aversion to a typical reading-type situation in which the letters are printed on a line. In either case it will be necessary to note letters with which the student has difficulty. The best way to do this is always to present the letters in the same (not alphabetical) order and tape record the testing. The tape can be played back later to compare the student's responses to a prepared record sheet that lists the letters in the same order as they were presented to the student.

Some children have a great deal of difficulty with many or nearly all letters. When this is the case, you should proceed to the next easiest task in alphabet knowledge. This involves having the child identify letters as you call them. The 5 × 8 card will work well for this, or you may wish to arrange flash cards so the child can see at least five to ten of them at a time. A few extremely disabled readers will not even be able to accomplish this task. When this is the case, you may wish to determine whether the child is able to match letters, which is easier still.

The *Durrell Analysis of Reading Difficulty* (Durrell and Catterson, 1980) contains a series of eight readiness-level tests, called the Prereading Phonics Abilities Inventories. These tests include Syntax Matching (measuring students' awareness of separate words in spoken sentences), Identifying Letter Names in Spoken Words, Identifying Phonemes in Spoken Words, Naming Letters—Lower Case and Upper Case, Writing Letters—from Dictation and from Copy, and Identifying Letters Named. If this test is available, you may wish to use it instead of constructing your own materials.

SIGHT-WORD KNOWLEDGE

Sometimes *sight vocabulary* refers to overall sight-word knowledge. Although this is proper, this discussion will be concerned only with instant recognition of words and not with meaning vocabulary. The difference between sight words and basic sight words was discussed in Chapter 3. However, it should again be stressed that the terms are not being used interchangeably. *Sight words* refer to all words any one reader can recognize instantly, while *basic sight words* refer to a designated list of words, usually of high utility, that appear on someone's list. Any word if read enough times can become a sight word, and thus each of us possesses a different sight vocabulary depending on such factors as occupation, reading interests, and ability to remember. However, anyone reading above middle third-grade level has the same basic sight-word vocabulary.

Because of the difference in meaning of the terms *sight-word vocabulary* and *basic sight-word vocabulary,* techniques for diagnosis of each will be discussed separately. In testing for sight-word knowledge we usually use a sampling of words referred to as a *graded sight-word list,* while in testing for basic sight-word knowledge we usually test the entire population of words on a designated list. The following discussion explains the need for, and methods of testing for, knowledge of basic sight words.

A number of researchers and writers have studied the utility of various words (Curtis, 1938; Hockett, 1938; Stone, 1939, 1941). Although these studies are seldom in exact agreement because of the differences in the materials they choose to study, they are in general agreement concerning the percentage of total running words[1] that are accounted for by certain numbers of words. Table 4–1 shows a general summary of the results of these studies. In interpreting these figures you should keep in mind that the percent of total running words for each specific number of words is likely to be slightly higher for beginning reading materials and slightly lower for adult reading materials.

Words such as *I, the,* and *and* appear so often in reading matter that it is imperative that children know these as sight words. As Table 4–1 also shows, even in learning approximately 200 words a child is likely to have mastered considerably more than one half of the words he or she is likely to encounter in reading. As you will also note, the percentage of utility begins to drop off rather rapidly after the 500 words most used in reading. For this reason most basic sight-word lists contain two hundred to five hundred words.

The importance of learning to read and spell high-utility words was emphasized by Richard Madden (1959) in a study of low- and high-utility words. Madden pointed out that there is very little value in attempting to teach students to spell words of lower utility until they have completely mastered the words of high utility. To illustrate this futility Madden states that a child in grade five with only 5 percent misspellings in a random sample of the first 500 words in frequency will make more errors in writing than if the child misspells all 600 words in the commonly designated list for grade five. The same concept is true for reading.

---

[1]*Total running words* are all the words that appear in a particular selection.

TABLE 4-1 The Percentage of Total, Running Words in Reading Materials Accounted for by Various Numbers of Words.

Number of Words	Percentage of Total Running Words
3	8 —12
10	20 —25
100	60 —65
200	66 —70
500	75 —80
1000	83 —85
1500	87 —88
2000	89 —90
3000	91 —92
5000	92.5—93.5

William Durr (1973) studied the high-frequency words in popular juvenile trade books. He found that in the eighty books studied, ten words were of such high frequency that a young reader could expect to meet one in nearly every four words read. Durr further stated that the 188 high-frequency words he listed, although making up only 6 percent of all the different words found, made up nearly 70 percent of the running words in print in the eighty library books he studied.

Such studies illustrate the importance of learning certain core or basic sight words so that no word-analysis skills are required when a student encounters them in print. Furthermore, many of these high-utility words are not phonetically regular and do not lend themselves to phonic word attack. Glen Gagon (1966) quotes Arthur Heilman as saying that approximately 35 percent of the usual primary reading vocabulary is phonetically regular. We have analyzed other basic sight-word lists and find them to be 30 percent to 77 percent phonetically regular depending on the number of phonic rules applied.

Testing for knowledge of basic sight words may at first appear so elementary that almost anyone would be likely to find this an easy task. During the past several years, however, we have researched several different methods and found the results differ considerably depending on the method employed. There has also been considerable controversy over whether basic sight words should be tested in or out of context.

Many people assume that children know more basic sight words, or *service words,* when they are used in context than when they are not. However, there is little evidence that this is true. H. Alan Robinson (1963), in a study of techniques of word identification, found that only about one-seventh of 1 percent of the words he studied were identified by students through context clues alone. Even when context, configuration, and phonic and structural elements in initial and final positions were all used together, students only scored 3.93 correct out of twenty-two possible responses.

We have also heard reading specialists say it is not fair to the child to test a word out of context. First of all, we might say, "What is fair?" Even if context were a valuable aid some of the time, you would not want a child not to know the same word at another time when it was not used in as helpful a context. What seems unfair to the child then, is to test the child on a word in meaningful context and later find that the child does not really know the word when it is not in a meaningful context. If identifying words in isolation is more difficult, then you should test them that way, since you are more likely to discover words that may later prove difficult for the child. Again, remember that basic sight words appear so often that children cannot afford to miss or be unsure of any of them. In reality, testing a word in context may be depriving them of the opportunity to learn it. This should not be construed to mean, however, that we are necessarily suggesting that basic sight words be "taught" in isolation. The issue of teaching basic sight vocabulary in isolation versus in context will be discussed in the remediation section of this chapter.

One of the points stressed in Chapter 2 was that you should always try to test in a situation that is analogous to actually reading. This principle is extremely important in the case of basic sight words. A common mistake by beginning reading teachers is thinking that they can use a group test to assess children's knowledge of basic sight words. A group test often used for this purpose is the Dolch Basic Sight Word Test (Dolch, 1942). In using it the teacher gives each student a sheet of paper that has numbers down the left-hand column of the page. Opposite each number are four words. The teacher calls out one of the four words, and each child is expected to mark the word called by the teacher. One of the problems with this type of test is that even if a child did not know any of the words, he or she would be likely to get one-fourth of them right by guessing. A second problem is that it is not analogous to reading; i.e., underlining a word when you hear it is much easier than seeing a word and saying it. Our experience has shown that many children who get almost every word right on this type of test miss twenty-five to fifty words on a test in which they are to look at words and say them. Because of these problems we conclude that any attempt to assess children's basic-sight-word knowledge with a group test is of little value.

The problem is how to best test the child in a one-to-one situation. This is not difficult, but even here there are some important considerations. One can simply give a child a list of words and ask the child to read them while you mark the right and wrong responses on a similar list. We have found, however, in trying this method with children in our university reading centers, that disabled readers often get tense when confronted with a long list of words and make more errors than if the words are presented one at a time on flash cards. A further problem with the former method is that it is difficult to control the length of exposure to each word. This often becomes a word-analysis test when the child has time to apply word-attack skills. This can be prevented to some extent by using a card and sliding it over each word after the child has been exposed to the word for about one second. This, however, is difficult to judge and some children resent having you cover the word if it is difficult for them.

We have also found that many students learn the sight words only in isolation and are unable to correctly pronounce these same words when reading a passage orally. This is the major reason for testing, and later teaching, the sight-word phrases, which build a bridge between isolated pronunciation and contextual reading.

We have found the computer to be an excellent tool for testing a student's knowledge of basic sight words. The computer is programmed to present the student with a flash presentation of a basic sight word every second and a half or second and three-fourths. A student can recognize the words considerably faster than this, but the teacher needs at least one and one-half seconds to mark the answer sheet. In this system the student is seated. The teacher explains that the computer will flash words to the student rather rapidly. The student should be told to pronounce the words as they are flashed and to ignore any words that are not known. All of the 299 words on the *Ekwall Basic Sight Word List* can be tested, in this manner, in about seven and one-half minutes.

A computer has an advantage over a tachistoscope in that it is nearly noise-free. For students who do not know the basic sight words well the rate of presentation will be too rapid. However, it should be kept in mind that basic sight words should be known instantly and that the ultimate goal for any student is to know them well enough to recognize them at a rapid rate. Students who cannot pronounce the words as rapidly as they are presented may be slightly resentful at the rapid rate. However, when words are presented by the computer, students will generally not feel hostility toward the teacher. On the other hand, if teachers use flash cards and present them so fast, the student is somewhat likely to direct hostility toward the teacher. The test should be stopped when the student has missed four or five consecutive words. In using such a test, words should be presented in lower case. Most modern computers permit programming in both upper and lower case; however, some use only upper case. If this is the case, it would probably be better to use the method described below.

We have found the following method to be practical for teachers and diagnosticians to use in evaluating students' knowledge of basic sight words.

The examiner will need the following materials:

1. A tape recorder.
2. Prepared scoring lists (or protocols) for the assessment of basic sight

words and phrases. Copies of the scoring lists for *both* words and phrases are necessary for each student tested.

3. Prepared flash cards, arranged in the same order as the word lists.

The examiner turns on the tape recorder and places the microphone on the table, then lifts off twenty to thirty words from the ordered stack. These are flashed individually to the student at a rate of *one second or less* per flash card. Since the examiner's purpose is to test *instant* sight-word recognition, it is critical for the words to be flashed quickly enough to prevent the student from sounding them out.

The examiner's attention should be focused on flashing the cards, not on the student's responses. Do *not* separate the cards into "right" and "wrong" piles, since this may serve to distract the examiner, upset the student, and confuse the order of the flash cards. Continue flashing the cards until the student does not respond to four or five consecutive words, or otherwise indicates an inability to successfully complete the test. If the student appears to be pronouncing most of the words correctly, continue the procedure until all cards are flashed.

To complete the scoring procedure, the examiner rewinds the audio tape, selects the appropriate prepared list, and indicates by marking + or − whether the student correctly or incorrectly pronounced each word. (The scoring procedure is usually completed after the student has left the testing site.) In scoring, *only the first response counts*. Having mastered a word, the student recognizes it instantly. If the student hesitates, the flashed word is not known by *sight*.

The same procedure is repeated for the testing and scoring of sight-word phrases. The examiner may allow up to two seconds per phrase when flashing the cards. Each sight-word test takes approximately six minutes to administer and score.

By examining the prepared lists the examiner can determine specifically which basic sight words and phrases have not been mastered by the student. These can then be taught without having to misuse instructional time teaching words or phrases that are already known.

A reasonable criterion for mastery is 90 percent or better. Even students who know all of the basic sight words quite well will often miscall a few words because of the speed of the test. The examiner may wish to recheck missed words or phrases a second time to determine whether they were errors of the speed of the test or of the student's lack of knowledge.

The examiner must use judgment in evaluating a students' performance on the sight-word tests. Young children may have greater difficulty with a speed of one word per second, although ultimately it is essential that the words be recognized at this rate. Similarly, students with speech difficulties may need an adjustment in the rate of flashing.

The examiner must be sure that the student is not excessively nervous and that the setting is conducive to the student's best performance. It is suggested that this assessment procedure be presented as a kind of game or fun activity. Paraprofessionals may be trained to conduct this testing. The sight-word tests may be repeated periodically while instruction is taking place, in order to check students' progress.

There has been a debate among reading experts about which sight-word list to use. A number of investigators have suggested that the Dolch list is outdated and therefore no longer appropriate. Robert Hillerich (1974) has questioned not the datedness, but rather the appropriateness, of the Dolch list. On the other hand John Mangieri and Michael Kahn (1977), A. J. Lowe and John Foilman (1974), and Jerry Johns (1974) all agree that the Dolch list remains as relevant for today's students as for those of the 1930s.

Other newer lists have appeared from time to time. Edward Fry (1980) has offered an updated version of his "Instant Word List." The newer version of the Fry list contains 300 items. A well researched list that we also recommend is the Harris-Jacobson list (1985).

We believe that it really does not matter which of the many basic word lists are used for testing and teaching basic sight vocabulary. Almost all contain the same high-frequency words. For example, excluding nouns which Dolch listed separately, there is an 88 percent overlap between the words on the Durr list (1973) and the older Dolch list. Basic sight words do not go in and out of fashion. What does matter is that the teacher provide effective instruction to enable students to master the basic sight words taught.

The modified Dolch list that follows includes the 220 Dolch words reordered according to frequency of occurrence as found in the Durr list. The 220 individual words are then divided into eleven sublists of twenty words each for ease of scoring and instruction.

The list is presented based on the assumption that not all students will master all the words. It is therefore reasonable to begin by teaching the words that appear most often.

The phrase list is compiled so that each word from the isolated words list is presented in a phrase. Only seventeen new words are added to complete phrases. These are nouns that are all drawn from the preprimer level of a popular basal series.

The lists are presented as facsimiles of the scoring sheets you may use in following the procedure outlined above.

QUICK CHECK FOR BASIC SIGHT WORD KNOWLEDGE

The *Quick Check for Basic Sight Word Knowledge*[2] may be used as a quick way to test students' knowledge of basic sight words. The test consists of thirty-six words taken from Eldon E. Ekwall's basic-sight-word list. It may be

---

[2]Reprinted by permission of Charles E. Merrill Publishers, adapted from: Ekwall, Eldon E. *Locating and correcting reading difficulties* (4th ed.). Columbus, Ohio: Charles E. Merrill, 1985, 200–03.

Individual Diagnosis of Dolch Words
(Listed in Descending Order of Frequencies)   *Pre* [/220] *Post* [/220]

LIST I

	Pre	Post
1. the		
2. to		
3. and		
4. he		
5. a		
6. I		
7. you		
8. it		
9. of		
10. in		
11. was		
12. said		
13. his		
14. that		
15. she		
16. for		
17. on		
18. they		
19. but		
20. had		
*	/20	/20

LIST II

	Pre	Post
1. at		
2. him		
3. with		
4. up		
5. all		
6. look		
7. is		
8. her		
9. there		
10. some		
11. out		
12. as		
13. be		
14. have		
15. go		
16. we		
17. am		
18. then		
19. little		
20. down		
*	/20	/20

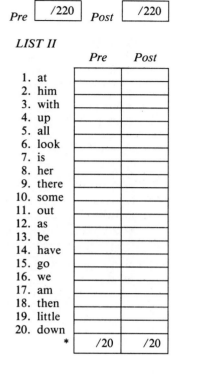

LIST III

	Pre	Post
1. do		
2. can		
3. could		
4. when		
5. did		
6. what		
7. so		
8. see		
9. not		
10. were		
11. get		
12. them		
13. like		
14. one		
15. this		
16. my		
17. would		
18. me		
19. will		
20. yes		
*	/20	/20

LIST IV

	Pre	Post
1. big		
2. went		
3. are		
4. come		
5. if		
6. now		
7. long		
8. no		
9. came		
10. ask		
11. very		
12. an		
13. over		
14. your		
15. its		
16. ride		
17. into		
18. just		
19. blue		
20. red		
*	/20	/20

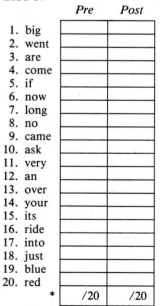

*Number of words read correctly.

LIST V

	Pre	Post
1. from		
2. good		
3. any		
4. about		
5. around		
6. want		
7. don't		
8. how		
9. know		
10. right		
11. put		
12. too		
13. got		
14. take		
15. where		
16. every		
17. pretty		
18. jump		
19. green		
20. four		
*	/20	/20

LIST VI

	Pre	Post
1. away		
2. old		
3. by		
4. their		
5. here		
6. saw		
7. call		
8. after		
9. well		
10. think		
11. ran		
12. let		
13. help		
14. make		
15. going		
16. sleep		
17. brown		
18. yellow		
19. five		
20. six		
*	/20	/20

LIST VII

	Pre	Post
1. walk		
2. two		
3. or		
4. before		
5. eat		
6. again		
7. play		
8. who		
9. been		
10. may		
11. stop		
12. off		
13. never		
14. seven		
15. eight		
16. cold		
17. today		
18. fly		
19. myself		
20. round		
*	/20	/20

LIST VIII

	Pre	Post
1. tell		
2. much		
3. keep		
4. give		
5. work		
6. first		
7. try		
8. new		
9. must		
10. start		
11. black		
12. white		
13. ten		
14. does		
15. bring		
16. goes		
17. write		
18. always		
19. drink		
20. once		
*	/20	/20

*Number of words read correctly.

LIST IX

	Pre	Post
1. soon		
2. made		
3. run		
4. gave		
5. open		
6. has		
7. find		
8. only		
9. us		
10. three		
11. our		
12. better		
13. hold		
14. buy		
15. funny		
16. warm		
17. ate		
18. full		
19. those		
20. done		
*	/20	/20

LIST X

	Pre	Post
1. use		
2. fast		
3. say		
4. light		
5. pick		
6. hurt		
7. pull		
8. cut		
9. kind		
10. both		
11. sit		
12. which		
13. fall		
14. carry		
15. small		
16. under		
17. read		
18. why		
19. own		
20. found		
*	/20	/20

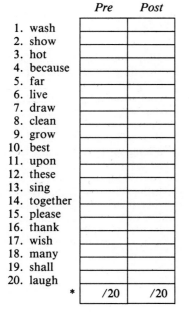

LIST XI

	Pre	Post
1. wash		
2. show		
3. hot		
4. because		
5. far		
6. live		
7. draw		
8. clean		
9. grow		
10. best		
11. upon		
12. these		
13. sing		
14. together		
15. please		
16. thank		
17. wish		
18. many		
19. shall		
20. laugh		
*	/20	/20

SCORE

LIST	Pre	Post
I		
II		
III		
IV		
V		
VI		
VII		
VIII		
IX		
X		
XI		
TOTAL		

*Number of words read correctly.

Individual Diagnosis of Sight Word Phrases

Pre ⬚ /143 Post ⬚ /143

LIST I	Pre	Post
1. he had to		
2. she said that		
3. to the		
4. you and I		
5. but they said		
6. on a		
7. for his		
8. of that		
9. that was in		
10. it was		
*	/10	/10

LIST II	Pre	Post
1. look at him		
2. as little		
3. at all		
4. I have a		
5. have some		
6. there is		
7. down there		
8. then we have		
9. to go		
10. to be there		
11. look up		
12. look at her		
13. we go out		
14. I am		
*	/14	/14

LIST III	Pre	Post
1. look at me		
2. can you		
3. a little one		
4. you will see		
5. what is that		
6. my *cat*		
7. I will get		
8. when did he		
9. like this		
10. get them		
11. so you will see		
12. I could		
13. we were		
14. would not		
15. yes, I do		
*	/15	/15

LIST IV	Pre	Post
1. a big ride		
2. went into		
3. if I ask		
4. come over with		
5. they went		
6. I am very		
7. there are blue		
8. a long *book*		
9. an *apple*		
10. your red *book*		
11. its *name*		
12. they came		
13. just now		
*	/13	/13

*Number of phrases read correctly.

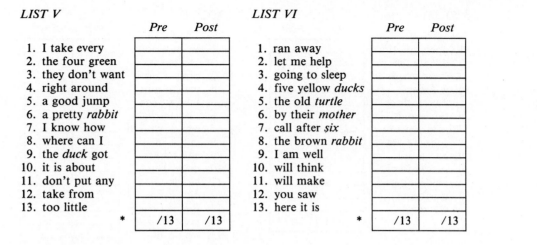

LIST V

	Pre	Post
1. I take every		
2. the four green		
3. they don't want		
4. right around		
5. a good jump		
6. a pretty *rabbit*		
7. I know how		
8. where can I		
9. the *duck* got		
10. it is about		
11. don't put any		
12. take from		
13. too little		
*	/13	/13

LIST VI

	Pre	Post
1. ran away		
2. let me help		
3. going to sleep		
4. five yellow *ducks*		
5. the old *turtle*		
6. by their *mother*		
7. call after *six*		
8. the brown *rabbit*		
9. I am well		
10. will think		
11. will make		
12. you saw		
13. here it is		
*	/13	/13

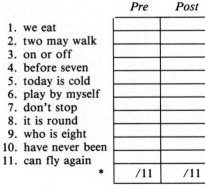

LIST VII

	Pre	Post
1. we eat		
2. two may walk		
3. on or off		
4. before seven		
5. today is cold		
6. play by myself		
7. don't stop		
8. it is round		
9. who is eight		
10. have never been		
11. can fly again		
*	/11	/11

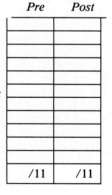

LIST VIII

	Pre	Post
1. black and white		
2. start a new		
3. must try once		
4. don't keep much		
5. it does go		
6. always drink *milk*		
7. will bring ten		
8. *Lad* goes		
9. write and tell		
10. work is first		
11. can give it		
*	/11	/11

*Number of phrases read correctly.

LIST IX

	Pre	Post
1. open and find		
2. *Jill* ate the		
3. those are done		
4. is funny		
5. buy us three		
6. this is only		
7. gave a warm		
8. soon we ate		
9. had a full		
10. run and hold		
11. made a big		
12. it is better		
13. our *duck*		
*	/13	/13

LIST X

	Pre	Post
1. sit with both		
2. you use it		
3. carry a small		
4. the cut hurt		
5. the fast *car*		
6. then the light		
7. which will fall		
8. pull it in		
9. had found		
10. under here		
11. be kind		
12. pick it up		
13. *Bill* can read		
14. my own *bed*		
15. why is it		
16. I can say		
*	/16	/16

LIST XI

	Pre	Post
1. wash in hot		
2. because it is		
3. grow best		
4. once upon		
5. sing and laugh		
6. please thank		
7. we draw these		
8. shall we show		
9. the wish is		
10. we clean		
11. they live		
12. too far		
13. all together		
14. many *turtles*		
*	/14	/14

SCORE

LIST	Pre	Post
I		
II		
III		
IV		
V		
VI		
VII		
VIII		
IX		
X		
XI		
TOTAL		

*Number of phrases read correctly.

FIGURE 4-1   Quick Check for Basic Sight Word Knowledge

ANSWER SHEET

Name: _____   Date: _____

School: _____   Tester: _____

Directions: After the student reads the words from flash cards, mark those read correctly with a plus (+) and those read incorrectly with a minus (−) or write in the word substituted. If the student says he or she does not know an answer then mark it with a (?) and consider it an error.
(IF A STUDENT MISSES ANY WORDS ON THIS TEST, THEN HE OR SHE SHOULD BE GIVEN THE FULL LIST OF BASIC SIGHT WORDS.)

1. I _____
2. the _____
3. you _____
4. down _____
5. here _____
6. he _____
7. fly _____
8. help _____
9. this _____
10. happy _____
11. tree _____
12. his _____
13. hot _____
14. end _____
15. ride _____
16. saw _____
17. light _____
18. sat _____
19. pretty _____
20. again _____
21. thank _____
22. only _____
23. well _____
24. first _____
25. thing _____
26. any _____
27. also _____
28. while _____
29. should _____
30. upon _____
31. sure _____
32. always _____
33. than _____
34. present _____
35. such _____
36. hurt _____

given to students who you suspect are deficient in their knowledge of basic sight words. It was developed by giving Ekwall's basic sight word list to 500 students in grades two through six. One hundred students were tested at each of these five grade levels. A computer analysis then listed in ascending order of difficulty the words most often missed. From this list approximately every eighth word was taken, so that the words at the beginning are the easiest and the words at the end are the most difficult. We suggest that you administer this test in the same manner as that described previously. A student who misses even one word on this test should be given the entire basic sight word list.

Sight Words in General

Graded word lists are usually used to assess children's knowledge of sight words in general or reading level in relation to word knowledge. In doing this it is also possible in many cases to make a close estimation of a child's overall reading level. These tests are also useful for placing students for further testing in informal reading inventories. A number of graded word lists are available; however, one that we have found to be useful is the San Diego Quick Assessment List. A description of the list, directions for its use, and the list itself follow:[3]

PP	*Primer*	*1*	*2*	*3*
see	you	road	our	city
play	come	live	please	middle
me	not	thank	myself	moment
at	with	when	town	frightened
run	jump	bigger	early	exclaimed
go	help	how	send	several
and	is	always	wide	lonely
look	work	night	believe	drew
can	are	spring	quietly	since
here	this	today	carefully	straight

4	*5*	*6*	*7*
decided	scanty	bridge	amber
served	business	commercial	dominion
amazed	develop	abolish	sundry
silent	considered	trucker	capillary
wrecked	discussed	apparatus	impetuous
improved	behaved	elementary	blight

[3]La Pray, Margaret, and Ross, Ramon. "The Graded Word List: Quick Gauge of Reading Ability." *Journal of Reading,* Vol. 12 (January 1969): 305–307. (Reprinted with permission of the authors and the International Reading Association.)

certainly	splendid	comment	wrest
entered	acquainted	necessity	enumerate
realized	escaped	gallery	daunted
interrupted	grim	relativity	condescend

8	*9*	*10*	*11*
capacious	conscientious	zany	galore
limitation	isolation	jerkin	rotunda
pretext	molecule	nausea	capitalism
intrigue	ritual	gratuitous	prevaricate
delusion	momentous	linear	risible
immaculate	vulnerable	inept	exonerate
ascent	kinship	legality	superannuate
acrid	conservatism	aspen	luxuriate
binocular	jaunty	amnesty	piebald
embankment	inventive	barometer	crunch

Administration
1. Type out each list of ten words on index cards.
2. Begin with a card that is at least two years below the student's grade-level assignment.
3. Ask the student to read the words aloud to you. If he misreads any on the list, drop to easier lists until he makes no errors. This indicates the base level.
4. Write down all incorrect responses, or use diacritical marks on your copy of the test. For example, *lonely* might be read and recorded as *lovely. Apparatus* might be recorded as *a per' a tus.*
5. Encourage the student to read words he does not know so that you can identify the techniques he uses for word identification.
6. Have the student read from increasingly difficult lists until he misses at least three words.

Analysis
1. The list in which a student misses no more than one of the ten words is the level at which he can read independently. Two errors indicate his instructional level. Three or more errors identify the level at which reading material will be too difficult for him.
2. An analysis of a student's errors is useful. Among those which occur with greatest frequency are the following:

Error	*Example*
reversal	*ton* for *not*
consonant	*now* for *how*
consonant clusters	*state* for *straight*
short vowel	*cane* for *can*
long vowel	*wid* for *wide*
prefix	*inproved* for *improved*
suffix	*improve* for *improved*
miscellaneous	(accent, omission of)

3. As with other reading tasks, teacher observation of student behavior is essential. Such things as posture, facial expression, and voice quality may signal restlessness, lack of assurance, or frustration while reading.

Other sources of graded word lists are the *Botel Reading Inventory* (1978), the *Diagnostic Reading Scales* (1981), the *Wide Range Achievement Test* (Jastak and Jastak, 1978), *Bader Reading and Language Inventory* (1983), *Informal Reading Inventory* (1985), *Diagnostic Reading Inventory* (1979), *Basic Reading Inventory* (1985), *The Contemporary Classroom Reading Inventory* (1980), *Classroom Reading Inventory* (1981), and the *Analytical Reading Inventory* (1981).

Graded word lists may also be constructed from basal readers or from social studies and science books. These can be helpful in assessing children's sight-word knowledge in materials they are likely to have to read. When constructing your own graded word lists, you should expect children to know approximately 95 percent of the words at their instructional level.

In using graded sight-word lists you should keep their limitations in mind. For example, remember that you are sampling only a few words at each level as an overall estimate of a child's ability to pronounce words at that level. A child who is very good at word-attack skills may tend to correctly pronounce quite a few words that are not in his or her sight vocabulary. You should be able to determine to some extent whether this is happening based on the time and ease with which the child responds to each word. You should also keep in mind that many children are disabled in reading because of their inability to comprehend what they read. For this type of child the graded word list is quite likely to be inaccurate in terms of placement level.

Part B: REMEDIATION

This part of the chapter will present techniques for teaching sight words in general and basic sight words. There is no separate section devoted exclusively to teaching letter knowledge. Many of the techniques and principles that apply to the teaching of sight words are also useful in teaching the alphabet. It should also be emphasized that the techniques for teaching sight words as a remedial procedure differ very little from those used in teaching sight words in a developmental program. Quite often, in fact, the same techniques and materials are used. For that reason many of the suggested procedures and materials will be the same as those used in many developmental programs. There are, however, a few specialized procedures for children who meet severe difficulties in learning. These procedures will also be discussed in this part of Chapter 4.

In teaching any sight word, one of the most basic things to remember is that for any normal child without problems in reading, a word is not likely to become a sight word until the child has encountered it many times. Studies have tended to disagree on how many times it takes a child to learn a word well enough so that it is instantly known. However, we do know that before most words are instantly recognized, a student must encounter them a number of times (probably a minimum of around twenty for most words). The number of exposures depends on such factors as the potential of the child for word-learning tasks, the meaning or relevance of the word for a child, the configuration of the word, and the context in which it is used. The important point is that in teaching any word you must arrange for the child to come into contact with it many times before expecting him or her to recognize it instantly.

One of the most important questions that must be addressed in teaching basic sight vocabulary is, Will students learn these words most easily if they are taught in isolation or in context? Kathryn Hampton (1979) compared the effectiveness of two methods of teaching basic sight vocabulary to fourth- and fifth-grade remedial readers. In the first method the words were taught in isolation. In the second method the words were presented in isolation, in phrases, and in sentences. The results favored the isolated approach; that is, students learned to *pronounce* more words when the words were taught in isolation.

Linnea Ehri and Lee Wilce (1980) found that multiple aspects of the basic sight words are learned by beginning readers. First graders were able to pronounce the words faster and more accurately when they were practiced in isolation. However, the students learned more about the syntactic/semantic identities of the words when they were practiced in sentence context. The researchers concluded that perhaps the best approach is to provide both types of word-reading practice.

More recent researchers have criticized earlier studies for not testing both methods of teaching (isolation and context) in similar settings. In doing this Barbara Nemko (1984) found that subjects who were trained in using words in context performed no better than subjects trained in isolation. She reported that the only difference in methods was associated with the subjects who were both trained and tested in isolation. Nemco reported that these subjects performed better than all of the other training/testing groups. On the other hand,

Judy Rash, Terry D. Johnson, and Norman Gleadow (1984) obtained results that appeared to conflict with those of Nemco. In a study in which they too attempted to eliminate the training/test bias they reported that kindergarten children learned new words in significantly fewer trials when the target words were presented in context. These researchers reported that the word-in-context method was also superior to teaching words in isolation when both short- and long-term retention was tested. Based on the results of these studies perhaps Ehri and Wilce's advice mentioned above would seem most prudent: to provide both types of word-reading practice.

A similar controversy centers on the role of pictures in learning new words. The focal-attention theory proposed by S. Jay Samuels suggests that words should be learned in isolation and that picture and context clues actually deter the acquisition of sight vocabulary because they enable the child to identify the word without focusing on its graphic features. A number of studies support this hypothesis, including those reported by Harry Singer, S. Jay Samuels, and Jean Spiroff (1973–1974) and Samuels (1977). However, Marshall Arlin, Mary Scott, and Janet Webster (1978–1979) dissent. They concluded from their research that pictures presented with words facilitate rather than hinder learning. Singer (1980) suggested that methodological and analytical flaws in the research conducted by Arlin and colleagues made their results questionable. Arlene Strikwerda (1976) found that pictures neither aided nor interfered with the learning of sight words by first-grade children if the time of exposure to pictures was limited. Maria A. Ceprano (1981) reviewed selected research on methods of teaching sight words. After reviewing the information on the use of pictures in the teaching of sight words she stated,

> The studies reviewed thus far leave us unsure as to whether pictures do or do not help or hinder beginners in learning sight words. We are perhaps surprised because we expect more consistent results from studies that display so many similarities in research design. Moreover, the subjects were comparable in age and level of readiness. Nevertheless, these studies yielded disturbingly inconsistent results. (p. 317)

Such controversy among researchers provides little help to the practitioner who must decide daily which approach to use. Our recommendation is to use a *combination* approach.

One of the first problems often encountered is how to group remedial students for instruction on basic sight words. One very effective solution is to buy a number of different colored 3 in. × 5 in. (or smaller) cards. Designate a color for each of the levels on the basic-sight-word lists shown earlier in this chapter, for example, green for list one, pink for list two, etc. After the tests are completed, the teacher should have little difficulty organizing groups according to the students' performance. The teacher may wish to write each word or phrase missed on a separate card color-coded according to level. Children file these cards in junior-sized shoe boxes by color. It is usually most efficient to teach students in groups by level. Thus, the teacher may ask that all students with pink cards bring their cards with them when they come to the group for instruction.

TEACHING SIGHT WORDS IN GENERAL

There are many ways to teach a student or a group of students; a method similar to the following often proves successful:

1. Write a sentence on the chalkboard with the new word used in context. Underline the word.
2. Let students read the sentence and attempt to say the new word using context clues along with other word-attack skills. If you are introducing a new story, it is especially important that you not tell them each new word in advance, as this deprives them of the opportunity to apply word-attack skills themselves.
3. Discuss the meaning of the word or how it is used in talking and writing. Try to tie it to something in their experience. If possible, illustrate the word with a picture or concrete object.
4. Write the word as students watch. Ask them to look for certain configuration clues such as double letters, extenders, and descenders. Also ask them to look for any well-known phonograms or word families, e.g., *ill, ant, ake,* but do not call attention to little words in longer words.
5. Ask students to write the word themselves and to be sure and say the word while they write it. Research by the Socony-Vacuum Oil Co. showed that people tend to remember about 90 percent of what they say as they do a thing, 70 percent of what they say as they talk, 50 percent of what they see and hear, and only 10 to 20 percent of what they read or hear.
6. Have students make up and write sentences in which the word is used in context. Have them read these sentences to each other and discuss them.

TEACHING BASIC SIGHT VOCABULARY

In order to learn basic sight vocabulary, remedial readers frequently require a systematic and intensive approach. The following techniques have proven effective not only in our university clinics but also in remedial and developmental classrooms. Formal, systematic instruction does not usually begin until students have completed a primer-level reader. If by the end of third grade students have not mastered the lists of basic sight words and phrases, then specific, direct instruction is imperative.

When teaching children individually or in small groups, introduce the words a few at a time. The number of words to be learned per week will vary from student to student. Success, however, is critical. *It is better to learn fewer words well.* The students should see mastery as a challenging goal. Often the students themselves can best determine the number of new words to be learned at a time. If in doubt, begin with five words.

When presenting sight words, always be sure that the student is *looking at the word,* not at you. If possible, the teacher should try to spend a few minutes with the student individually when presenting the words for the first time. The following sample represents a thorough approach. Usually not all of the steps noted are necessary.

Teacher: (Hold up flash card.) "Look at this word. The word is *the.*"
(Use it in a sentence.) "I am *the* teacher. Say the word."
Student: "The."
T: "Good. Now say it five times."
S: "The, the, the, the, the."
T: "Outstanding. Now say it really loud."
S: "The."
T: "No, that's not loud enough. Let me hear you say it really loud."
S: "The."
T: "Here, I'll show you. THE!"
S: (chuckle) "THE!"
T: "Fantastic. Now let me hear you whisper it."
S: (whispering) "The."
T: "Excellent. Now close your eyes. Can you see the word on your eyelids?"
S: "Yup."
T: "Spell it."
S: "T-h-e."
T: "Good. Now describe the word. What does it look like?"
S: "Well, it's kinda small."
T: "How are you going to remember it?"
S: "Uh, it has two letters that stick up."
T: "Terrific! Now, what's going to happen to you if you forget this word?"
S: "I don't know. What?"
T: "I'm going to kill you!" (chuckle)
S: "Oh."

Humor aside, the previous dialogue included some of the critical factors in the learning of sight words: the student's attention is focused on the word, the student visualizes the word, and strong reinforcement is provided.

Each new word should be presented using the "overlearning" procedure: 1, 2; 1, 2, 3; 1, 2, 3, 4; 1, 2, 3, 4, 5. For example, *the, to; the, to, and; the, to, and, he;* etc. If, after all the new words have been presented, the student still has difficulty pronouncing them quickly, the following steps may be taken:

1. Have the student trace the word, write it on paper, or use chalk or magic slates.
2. Have the student repeat the word each time it is written.
3. Have the student write the word without looking at the flash card; then compare the two.

Other tactile-kinesthetic approaches may be used. These are described more fully in a later section in this chapter.

As many of the procedures as necessary should be repeated for each new word. For many students it is sufficient to show them the word, use it in a sentence, and provide brief reinforcement. For a very few students even heroic procedures yield only intermittent success.

Immediate follow-up (lots of practice) is essential for the student to remember the new words. Some suggestions:

1. Create "study buddies." Match learners in the classroom with fellow students who have mastered the words. Take time to teach the "tutors" how to reinforce new words. Provide a big reward to both tutor and learner once the learner has attained the goal.
2. Provide reinforcement games for students to use on their own or with their study buddies. Games may be open-ended game boards or developed by levels according to the sublists. Specific suggestions for written exercises and games are provided later in this chapter.
3. Provide charts, graphs, and other devices for students to display their progress. These serve as excellent motivators, especially since students are competing with themselves rather than each other.
4. Use your imagination. Have students dramatize phrases, build a sight-word "cave," practice words while lining up, read sight-word "plays," etc.

It is important for the teacher to provide regular posttests on sublists to establish mastery. Remember to mix the flash cards to be sure that students have not merely memorized the words by order. The following technique may be used for posttesting: If the student says the word or phrase correctly on the test, put a star or sticker on the back. The word or phrase is not mastered until five stars are accumulated. If at any time the word is missed on a test, all of the previous stars are removed and the process must begin again. This is painful but important. If teachers did this, students would not forget words once learned. *"Mastery" means the student will know the word instantly forever!*

When twenty-five words are mastered, the student qualifies for "time trials." Using a stopwatch the teacher tests the students and graphs and displays the results. By flashing the cards more slowly in the beginning trials, the teacher can insure that improvement will be demonstrated on the graphs.

To be certain that mastery of individual words translates to recognition of words in the reading act, *it is important to repeat the entire procedure for the sight word phrases on completion of each sublist of words.* Thus, teach word list I, followed by phrase list I, word list II, phrase list II, and so on. Once the phrases for each sublist have been mastered, students should practice reading these phrases embedded in complete sentences or brief stories, which may be teacher-constructed. In addition, students will need generous exposure to low-level trade books.

THE USE OF THE LANGUAGE-EXPERIENCE APPROACH

Some severely disabled readers will know hardly any words at all. In this case it is difficult to follow the procedures explained above. When this occurs, the methods used in the language-experience approach are often quite successful. Furthermore, the language-experience approach, in its latter stages, can also be used with great success with average or better readers. As Nancy Smith (1985) has pointed out, the computer when used as a word processor can be exciting for students and enhance the value of the language-experience approach. A discussion of the use of the computer in the language-experience approach appears in Chapter 16. In using the language-experience approach with a group of disabled readers a method similar to the following may be used:

1. Discuss some event of great interest. Afterward ask students if they would like to write a story about it.
2. As students dictate the story, write it on chart paper using the following methods:
   a. Use manuscript or cursive writing, whichever is common to the age-grade level of the group.
   b. Use a heavy writing instrument such as a felt-tip pen.
   c. Use the language of the students and do not attempt to alter it.
   d. Make sure students see the words as they are being written.
   e. Try to adhere to the one important event and follow a sequence of events.
   f. Use one-line sentences for severely disabled readers and gradually increase sentence length as improvement is noted.
   g. In beginning each new sentence, emphasize the fact that you start on the left and proceed to the right.
   h. Emphasize the return sweep from the end of one sentence to the beginning of the next.

3. After the story has been completed, reread it as a choral exercise. Either you or a child may point to each word as it is read. It is important that the word being read is the same one being pointed to.
4. Have individual children take turns rereading the story sentence by sentence.
5. Duplicate the story on a large piece of tagboard and have students cut it into sentence strips. These can then be put in a pocket chart to form the original story. Go back to the original chart when necessary. Also let students rearrange the sentences to form a different order of events.
6. After students have read the story over many times, you may wish to cut the tagboard sentences up into words and let students form the original sentences and new sentences.
7. As more stories are dictated and read and as students build a larger sight vocabulary, you may wish to duplicate stories on ditto paper and give each student a copy to be cut up into sentences and/or words for building varying story order and new sentences.
8. As students' reading ability grows, you should begin to let each student write and illustrate his or her own stories. These can be bound into booklets with attractive covers on them indicating the author of each book. Students should then begin to read each other's books.
9. A great deal of emphasis should always be placed on rereading materials that were written earlier, as children require a great many exposures to each word before it becomes a sight word. After sight vocabularies begin to grow considerably, students can begin to read library or trade books.

When using the language-experience approach with an individual student, you may wish to use a process somewhat similar to the following:

1. As with a group, find some event of interest to the student and ask the student to record the event on paper.
2. As the student dictates, you write on a piece of paper with the student seated so that the words can be observed as they are written. The same methods listed in steps 2(a) through (h) above for a group should be observed, except the writing may be done on 8½″ × 11″ paper with a pencil or felt-tip pen.
3. After the story has been completed, you may wish to type it on a pica or primary-size typewriter as appropriate to the grade level of the student. (For third grade and above use regular pica type.)
4. Have the student reread the story, with either you or the student (if able to do it properly) pointing to each word as it is read. Depending on the ability of the student at this stage, the story may be reread sentence by sentence in varying order.
5. Let the student illustrate the story or apply stickers, pictures, or other

decoration. Finally, the story should be placed in a booklet to be kept and reviewed each time you meet.

6. You may wish to duplicate the typewritten copies of these stories so that students can cut them up and rearrange first the sentences and later the words within each sentence.

7. Bind groups of stories into booklets with illustrated covers and encourage students to exchange and read each other's booklets.

8. Gradually encourage the student to branch out into the reading of trade books.[4]

The language-experience approach is especially appropriate for disabled readers because it is immediately meaningful to them—they are writing about events in their own lives and using their own speaking vocabularies. Another advantage is that it develops a feeling of security and success and keeps pace with their development. It also gives meaning to their reading because students learn to associate printed stories with their own experiences.

Although the language-experience approach offers a number of advantages for beginning or disabled readers, there are also some disadvantages of which the teacher should be aware. For example, there is no step-by-step teacher's manual, and an inexperienced or untrained teacher is likely not to present a complete program. That is, the teacher may not use certain high-utility words enough times. Or, the teacher may fail to diagnose specific problems with various word-analysis skills. There may also be difficulty in transferring the students from reading material written by students to that written by adult authors. Most of the problems encountered in using the language-experience approach can, however, be overcome if the teacher is well trained and aware of the problems that are likely to come up when using this approach.

THE USE OF THE TACHISTOSCOPE

As stated earlier, words should be taught in both isolation and context; however, a tachistoscopic presentation of words is also helpful for some students. Such an approach may be especially useful with words that are easily confused. For example, for the student who confuses words such as *that* and *them* or *what* and *when,* a few sessions with a tachistoscopic presentation of these

[4]For a more detailed explanation of this approach see the following sources: Hall, Mary Anne, *Teaching Reading as a Language Experience,* 3rd ed., Columbus, Ohio: Charles E. Merrill, 1981. Lee, Dorris M., and Allen, R. V. *Learning to Read through Experience,* 2d ed., Englewood Cliffs, New Jersey: Prentice-Hall, Inc., 1966. Stauffer, Russell G. *The Language Experience Approach to the Teaching of Reading,* 2d ed., New York: Harper & Row, 1980. Veatch, Jeannette; Sawicki, F.; Elliott, G.; Flake, E.; and Blakey, J. *Key Words to Reading,* 2d ed., Columbus, Ohio: Charles E. Merrill, 1979.

words mixed in with other more familiar combinations can be extremely helpful.

The use of the tachistoscope and controlled reading devices tended to fall into disrepute during the 1960s because a number of studies showed that tachistoscopic presentations of gradually widening spans of numbers and phrases did not contribute appreciably to reading speed. Furthermore, studies indicated that hand pacing in a book was equal to or in some cases more effective than controlled reading devices. This kind of research information should not be interpreted as meaning that the tachistoscope has no value in a reading program. The same is true for controlled reading devices. Although often expensive, they can serve as excellent motivating devices and are useful in helping children overcome problems with habitual repetitions.

A tachistoscopic presentation of phrases can also be of considerable value in helping children learn sight words. When using either words or phrases, a good technique is to let several children work together and yell out the words and phrases as they appear on the screen or the window of a hand-held tachistoscope. Although this is noisy, most children love it. As with any other reading activity, most of the words (95 percent or more) should be previously known by the students.

We have contrasted various factors (Table 4–2) that we believe have tended to separate studies reporting successful results with the use of the tachistoscope from those reporting less success.

It should be stressed that the factors noted only represent a general trend toward the more successful versus the less successful use of the tachistoscope. It

TABLE 4–2 Factors Affecting Use of the Tachistoscope.

Successful	*Less Successful*
Elementary school students (grades 1–6)	*Older students of high school or college level*
1. Tachistoscope was used for giving multiple exposures of words or phrases or to get children to attend to the configuration of words.	1. Tachistoscope was used to attempt to widen vision span and thus increase reading speed.
2. Students had follow-up activity writing words or words and phrases after each lesson.	2. There was no written follow-up.
3. Children yelled out or read words and phrases aloud.	3. Reading was usually done silently.
4. Tachistoscope was used by someone who believed in its effectiveness. (This factor tends to make any device or material appear superior.)	4. Tachistoscope was used as just another device.

should, however, be useful in establishing guidelines for the use of the tachistoscope in your own remedial program.

ADDITIONAL RESEARCH FINDINGS

Several studies have provided information on how students learn words and/or letters that is important in using the tachistoscope and other learning devices. For example, Joanna Williams, Ellen Blumberg, and David Williams (1970) studied the cues used in visual word recognition. They concluded, as have several other researchers, that the overall shape or configuration of a word may not be as important for beginning readers as is knowledge of first and last letters. They found that beginning readers used initial letters as an important clue in word recognition and that ending letters also provided an important clue. They did, however, state that older or adult readers tended to use a different method of word recognition strategy that depends more on overall configuration. These authors' research indicates that for younger readers, it may be highly important to discuss beginning and ending letter differences in unknown words and in words with similar configurations that are often confused. Patrick Groff (1974) believes, "The statements made by most modern writers about how children recognize sight words generally are wrong. The shape of a word is the least-used cue to its recognition by beginning readers." (p. 577)

Ralph Norman Haber and Lyn R. Haber (1981) studied the importance of configuration clues and concluded that configuration clues are an important source of information. It appears to us, however, that the research mentioned by these authors had some serious flaws. For example, Haber and Haber based their study only on adults' ability to derive an unknown word from the shape of that word. Kindergarten and first-grade children do not have the benefit of the background with words of the adults in the Haber and Haber study. Perhaps the most important thing these studies reveal is that our knowledge of the importance of word configuration is still sadly lacking.

Richard Allington (1973) studied the use of color cues to focus attention during discrimination, visual memory, and paired-associate tasks. He found that such tasks all improved on letter-like figures when maximum color was added and then taken away. His study also indicated that the vanishing color was superior to no color at all or to a maximum color added and remaining. Mark Goodman and Bert Cundick (1976) obtained similar results. These studies may indicate that it would be helpful to some students to learn letters and/or words if they were first presented with a strong color cue in order to focus their attention. It may also be helpful to add color cues to words that have similar configurations such as *though* and *through, county* and *country,* and *when* and *what* in order to help students distinguish between these words when they are confused.

A study done by Joanna Williams (1969) also indicates that some methods of teaching letters or letter discrimination are more effective than others. She concluded that too much time is often spent in copying and tracing. She suggested that more time be devoted to discrimination training that involves comparison of letters with their transformations. It should be stressed, however, that Williams's recommendations were based on children in kindergarten or first grade and may not necessarily apply to older students.

Charles Hargis and Edward Gickling (1978) found that the imagery level of basic sight words appears to be an important factor in the rate of learning and retention of the words. Low-imagery words are more difficult to recall than are high-imagery words and therefore require more repetition.

A study by Ernest Adams (1970) indicated that when words were introduced via a tape recording (referred to as *response familiarization*) before they were introduced visually, they were learned more easily. Adams also found that words of high meaningfulness were easier to learn than words of low meaningfulness. This evidently means that words should always be in a student's listening-speaking vocabulary before they are introduced in their printed form. Most reading specialists are aware of this but perhaps often fail to take it into consideration when teaching. However, in Adams's study even basic sight words, which were probably already in students' speaking-listening vocabulary, were learned more easily when students heard words before seeing them.

WRITTEN EXERCISES AND GAMES

In using any type of written exercise with disabled readers, keep in mind that certain students are likely to fail a great deal if they are simply left on their own. It is helpful to have a teacher's aide or a student tutor work closely with the student to help with difficult words and to provide immediate feedback and correction. It is also helpful to tape record written exercises so that the student can listen to the material if unable to read all of the words. The tape recorder can also provide immediate feedback by giving the answers after each question. Most important of all, the teacher must remember that written exercises and games serve only to reinforce or supplement previous instruction. Such activities must never be used as a substitute for directed teaching. Similarly, activities such as those described below do not take the place of substantial practice in the act of reading, which is essential for sight-word mastery.

Examples of Written Exercises and Games

Many different types of written exercises are helpful in teaching sight words. Some examples of these are as follows:

1. Have students fill in the blanks in sentences from a choice of sight words that are often confused, as in the following example:
   a. Jim _____ he could run faster than Ann. (though, thought, through)
2. Have students write sentences using as many sight words from a list of about ten as they can in the same sentence. Have students underline all sight words used. (See example below)

   (Sample list)

go	him
not	am
she	will
with	when
from	after

   a. When I go after him, she will not be with me.

3. Make students aware of context and teach them to read up to the word and slightly beyond and then attempt to get the word from a combination of context and beginning and/or ending phonemes. This is a good way to give practice on words that present a great deal of difficulty.
   a. Fred liked his new t_____r very much. (teacher)
   b. Amy found a b_____r way to do the job. (better)
4. Have students draw pictures of scenes that represent certain words such as *wash, throw,* and *run.* Be sure to label each scene.
5. Give students lists of words and several different-colored crayons or pencils. Give them directions as follows:
   a. "Use your yellow pencil to circle all of the things that are alive."
   b. "Use your red pencil to circle all of the words that show action."
   c. "Use your blue pencil to circle all of the words that could be used to describe something."

   (Sample list)

cow	throw
the	did
when	go
dog	run
pretty	man
ugly	brown

   This is a good scanning exercise to be done in *x* number of seconds (depending, of course, on the age of the students and the length of the list).
6. Give students envelopes containing about ten words on cards. Place a

pocket chart in the front of the room and then give directions such as the following:

a. "Place any cards in the pocket chart that tell (a) what we eat, (b) where we go in the morning, (c) what you like to do, etc."

(Sample list)

home	food
table	work
chair	apple
room	have
school	pie

These are but a few examples of the many types of exercises for the remediation of difficulties with sight words. Games are also beneficial in teaching sight words. They have the added benefit of presenting the reading task in a new dimension in which the child has not known failure.

Mark Kolb (1977) found that a game approach was as effective as worksheets in the reinforcement of basic sight words taught to first and second graders. Not surprisingly, the students showed a significant preference for the games compared to the traditional reinforcement approach. Dolores Pawley Dickerson (1982) also studied the use of games to reinforce sight vocabulary:

> These results lend support to educators who believe that games are worthwhile learning tools. Statistically it was shown that games that involved the most movement were more effective than the more passive ones, although both types were more effective than worksheet activities. (p. 49)

Head-chair game.   Line up chairs and designate the chair on one end as the "head chair." Students occupy the chairs. The teacher flashes words to the student in the head chair. The student in the head chair continues to occupy that chair until missing a word. After missing, the student goes to the end of the line and everyone moves up one chair. The idea is to see who can stay in the head chair.

Sight-word bee.   Use the same rules as you would for a spelling bee, but instead of spelling words have students say words as they are flashed.

Sight-word hunt.   Two or more students are blindfolded; other students hide sight-word cards around the room. When the signal is given, the blindfolded students remove the blindfolds and begin to hunt the sight-word cards. After the hunt students must say all of the words on the cards they have found in order to keep them. The one who has the most cards after saying the words is the winner.

What word?   Fill the pocket chart with sight words. Let children take turns trying to answer questions such as: "What word tells a number?" "What word is a color?" "What word begins with the *p* sound?" etc. Either the teacher or students can make up the questions.

These are only a sample of the many effective games for teaching sight words. Many commonly played games can be adapted; for example, Bingo, rummy, checkers, etc. Appendix C also contains a listing of commercial programs, games, and other materials useful in teaching sight words and basic sight words.

THE USE OF THE TAPE RECORDER

One of the best aids a teacher can have for teaching sight words is the tape recorder. Although Chapter 16 deals with using the tape recorder in reading, we would also like to illustrate several of its many uses in teaching sight words in this chapter. One of the values of the tape recorder is that it never gets bored or tired with simple tasks. It is also a great motivator for children and can provide homework to extend the lessons carried on in the regular classroom. Following are some specific ways in which the tape recorder can be used in teaching sight words:

1. Write words a student has missed in sentences and give the student the list of sentences. The taped script to accompany the student's list would be as follows:
   "Read sentence number one. (*Pause.*) Now let's check to see if you got it right. It says, 'John and Bill were going to go fishing.' Read it once more to be sure you have it right. (*Pause.*) Now read sentence number two. . . . ."
2. Give the student a list of numbered sight words. The tape-recorded script to accompany the student's list is as follows:
   "I will say number one and then wait two seconds and then say the word by number one. You are to try to say the word before I say it. Be sure to listen each time to see if you got it right. Number one (*two-second pause*) 'at,' number two (*two-second pause*) 'go,' number three. . . ."
3. Make up a group of eight sight words—one on each card. Number the cards on the back from one through eight. The tape-recorded script to accompany the cards is as follows:
   "Lay the cards out in front of you in two rows. Place four cards in each row. Turn the tape recorder off until you have done this. (*Four-second pause.*) As the words are called, pick up the word and place it on a pile in front of you. Place the second card over the first card, the third card over the second, and so on. Here are the words: 'go' (five), 'do' (five), 'of' (four), 'from' (four), 'went' (three), 'want' (three),

'had' (three), 'have' (three). Now turn the pile of cards over and check to see if they are numbered from one to eight with one on top and eight on the bottom. If they are not in that order, change them so that they are in that order. Turn the tape recorder off until you have done this. (*Four-second pause.*) If they were all in the right order you knew all of the words and you may rewind the tape and put the tape and the cards away. If they were not in the right order, turn the cards over and pick each one up and say it after me. Ready 'go,' 'do,' 'of,' 'from,' 'went,' 'want,' 'had,' 'have.' Now rewind the tape and begin again."

This exercise is completely self-correcting with the number system. Students who miss words are given a chance to learn the word by hearing and saying it, and they are automatically channeled back into the same exercise again and again until they learn all of the words. The numbers after the words the first time through represent the number of seconds you should pause before giving the next word. Keep in mind that the student needs a slightly longer pause on the first words than on the last because the student has more words from which to choose. The words must be called in the same order as they are numbered on the back. Also note the four-second pause after the instructions to turn the tape recorder off. In recording the directions you should not stop the recorder but simply pause for four seconds. This is just about the right amount of time for the student to respond to the directions when the student hears it and *does* have to shut it off.

Again, these are but a few of the many ways in which the tape recorder can be used in teaching basic sight words. Trial and experience will bring to mind many more ideas.

Another type of instrument useful in teaching letters, sight words, and phrases in the electronic card reader such as Language Master® shown in Figure 4–2. The Language Master is used for recording and playback of a strip of audio tape attached to the bottom of a card. These cards are available in various sizes in either blank or prepared form. The device contains a built-in microphone and a Student-Instructor switch. When the switch is set on Student mode, the student can pronounce a word written on a card while pressing the record button. This will record the student's voice on the tape. The student can then insert the card again and listen to the word as he or she pronounced it. When using a prepared card, the student can set the selector switch to Instructor mode and again insert the card. This time a voice will pronounce the word written on the card. The student then has an opportunity to compare, and correct if necessary, the response in accordance with the one pronounced by the instructor.

Since blank cards are available, this and similar instruments allow the teacher to record on cards those words, letters, phonemes, phrases, etc., missed by a particular student. This allows the student to work alone and correct errors, making the program highly individualized. Prepared cards also come in a wide selection.

FIGURE 4–2   The Language Master® Card Reader/Recorder

Reproduced by permission of the Bell & Howell Audio Visual Products Division, 7100 McCormick Road, Chicago, IL 60645. (The "Language Master" is a registered trademark of the Bell & Howell Co.)

CHILDREN WITH ESPECIALLY DIFFICULT LEARNING PROBLEMS

Children who do not learn by normal sight or auditory approaches are sometimes quite successful when taught by use of a kinesthetic approach, described in detail by Grace Fernald (1943); however, since then a number of variations of her original method have been used. In teaching words using the kinesthetic approach the procedure is usually somewhat like this.[5]

1. Show the child a word and pronounce it. The word may be written on the chalkboard, on a large sheet of paper, or on a flash card approxi-

[5]For a thorough explanation of the Fernald Technique similar to this, see Chapter 9.

mately 3″ high by 9″ wide. The letters should be about two inches high. A very broad felt-tip marking pen works well for writing on tagboard flashcards. It may be written either in manuscript or cursive writing, whichever is more familiar or being used in school.

2. Ask the child to trace the word while saying it. The child should say each part of the word while tracing that part; however, the word should not be sounded out letter by letter. It is also important that the child's finger or fingers contact the surface of the paper or tagboard at all times while the child is tracing the word. Some teachers have children use only their index finger. We would suggest, however, that you have the child use the middle and index fingers at the same time as though they, both together, were one large pencil or piece of chalk. The child should continue this tracing until you are relatively sure the child knows the word.

3. Then ask the child to write the word while looking at the original copy, in letters about two inches high. Direct the child to say each word part as it is being written.

4. In the final step of this procedure, tell the child to write the word again, but this time from memory. Also tell the child to say the word again as it is written.

In using the kinesthetic approach some teachers prefer to have the child write the words in sand or in salt sprinkled in a container such as a shoebox lid. Another approach that works well is to lay paper over a piece of window screen and then write the words with a crayon. This has the advantage of leaving a series of raised areas on the paper that the child can actually feel when tracing.

For children who have a great deal of difficulty with some words or letters you may wish to cut letters or words out of sandpaper so that they are easily felt. The same effect can also be achieved by using felt material or by forming letters or words with white glue and then sprinkling them with salt or sand. When dry, these have a texture that can easily be felt.

The kinesthetic approach has an advantage over other forms of instruction in that it combines the sense of touch (tactile) and kinesthesia (muscle and/or body movement perception) with the normal auditory and visual modes of learning. The disadvantage is that it is time consuming. Studies have not shown the kinesthetic approach to be superior to other modes of learning for groups of children as a whole. Its superiority is evident only for children who are not successful with a traditional approach.

Frequently, children who have difficulty learning the letters of the alphabet or sight words are identified as suffering from perceptual disorders or learning disabilities. Teachers should be cautious in forming such conclusions. Sandra Moyer and Phyllis Newcomer (1977), in reviewing research studies related to reversals, found that reversals are often a result of the child's unfamiliarity with directionality as it relates to letter discrimination, not of a perceptual disorder. Richard Allington, Kathleen Gormley, and Sharon Truex (1976) sought to determine whether poor readers exhibited perceptual confusions in words of high frequency, low discriminability, and low meaningfulness (basic sight words). They concluded that a visual perceptual deficit is unlikely to be a major factor in reading disability. Thomas Kampwirth and Marion Bates (1980) reviewed twenty-two studies that compared auditory and visual preferences with visual and auditory methods of teaching words in children under ten years of age. After examining the research on the "modalities preference" approach, the writers concluded that there is little research supporting the efficacy of matching children's auditory and visual preferred modalities to teaching approaches. They stated:

> Indeed, with this sort of evidence available, one is hard pressed to justify the continued reliance on this supposed "truth" in the learning disabilities field, that teaching according to preferred modalities, however measured, will lead to greater success than doing the opposite. . . . Obviously, it is imperative that we look much more closely at this idea than we have done in the past. (p. 604)

These issues will be examined in depth in Chapters 9 and 10.

SUMMARY

Although it is possible to learn to read without complete letter knowledge, most teachers would agree that letter knowledge is an important part of learning to read. However, reading teachers often feel that any student above the first-grade level will automatically know the alphabet. Such is often not the case even for older students, and a part of the diagnostic procedure should include testing for letter knowledge.

An extremely important part of the diagnostic procedure is the testing of sight-word knowledge, including basic sight words. Students can never expect to become fluent readers until they have mastered the basic sight words or the high-utility words that appear so often in print. Basic sight words and phrases should be tested using flash cards so that you can be assured that students have instant recognition of these words. Sight-word knowledge in general is usually determined by using a graded list of words that samples representative sight words at each grade level.

We have reviewed pertinent research on letter and word learning and presented some general and specific techniques for teaching letter knowledge and sight words. Among these are methods for teaching sight words in general, a systematic procedure for teaching basic sight vocabulary, the language-experience approach, the use of the tachistoscope, the Fernald Technique, and methods of using the tape recorder as a teaching device.

REFERENCES

Adams, E. L. (1970). *Influence of meaningfulness and familiarization training on basic sight vocabulary learning with first-graders.* Doctoral dissertation, Michigan State University, East Lansing.

Allington, R. L. (1974–75). An evaluation of the use of color cues to focus attention in discrimination and paired-associate learning. *Reading Research Quarterly, 10,* 244–247.

Allington, R. L., Gormley, K., & Truex, S. (1976). Poor and normal readers' achievement on visual tasks involving high frequency, low discriminability words. *Journal of Learning Disabilities, 9,* 292–296.

Arlin, M., Scott, M., & Webster, J. (1978–79). The effects of pictures on rate of learning sight words: A critique of the focal attention hypothesis. *Reading Research Quarterly, 14,* 645–660.

Bader, L. A. (1983). *Bader reading and language inventory.* New York: Macmillan.

Burns, P. C., & Roe, B. D. (1985). *Informal reading assessment* (2d ed.). Chicago: Rand McNally.

Botel, M. (1978). *Botel reading inventory.* Chicago: Follett.

Chisholm, D., & Knafle, J. (1978). Letter-name knowledge as a prerequisite to learning to read. *Reading Improvement, 15,* 2–7.

Curtis, H. M. (1938). Wide reading for beginners. *Journal of Educational Research, 38,* 255–262.

Dickerson, D. W. (1982). A study of use of games to reinforce sight vocabulary. *Reading Teacher, 36,* 46–49.

Dolch, E. W. (1942). *Basic sight word test.* Champaign, IL: Garrard Press.

Durr, W. K. (1973). Computer study of high frequency words in popular trade juveniles. *Reading Teacher, 27,* 37–42.

Durrell, D. D., & Catterson, J. H. (1980). *Durrell analysis of reading difficulty.* New York: Psychological Corporation.

Ehri, L. C., & Wilce, L. S. (1980). Do beginners learn to read function words better in sentences or in lists? *Reading Research Quarterly, 15,* 451–476.

Fernald, G. (1943). *Remedial techniques in basic school subjects.* New York: McGraw-Hill.

Fry, E. (1980). The new instant word list. *Reading Teacher, 34,* 284–289.

Gagon, G. (1966). Modern research and word perception. *Education, 86,* 464–472.

Goodman, M. D., & Cundick, B. P. (1976). Learning rates with black and colored letters. *Journal of Learning Disabilities, 9,* 600–602.

Groff, P. J. (1984). Resolving the letter name controversy. *Reading Teacher, 4,* 384–388.

Hampton, K. (1979). *An investigation of the effectiveness of two methods teaching basic sight vocabulary.* Master's thesis, California State University, Hayward.

Hargis, C. H., & Gickling, E. E. (1978). The function of imagery in word recognition development. *Reading Teacher, 31,* 870–873.

Harris, A. J., & Sipay, E. R. (1985). *How to increase reading ability* (8th ed.). New York: Longman. 376–378.

Hillerich, R. L. (1974). Word lists: Getting it all together. *Reading Teacher, 27,* 353–360.

Hockett, J. A. (1938). Comparative analysis of the vocabularies of twenty-nine second-grade readers. *Journal of Educational Research, 31,* 665–671.

Jastak, J. F., & Jastak, S. R. (1978). *Wide range achievement test.* Wilmington, DE: Guidance Associates.

Jacobs, D. (1979). *Diagnostic reading inventory.* Dubuque, IA: Kendall/Hunt.

Johns, J. L. (1985). *Basic reading inventory* (2nd ed.). Dubuque, IA: Kendall/Hunt.

Johns, J. L. (1974). *Some comparisons between the Dolch basic sight vocabulary and the word list for the 1970's.* U.S. Educational Resources Information Center. (ERIC Document ED 098 541)

Kampwirth, T. J., & Bates, M. (1980). Modality preference and teaching method: A review of the research. *Academic Therapy, 15,* 597–605.

Kolb, M. C. (1977). *A game activity approach versus a traditional approach in the reinforcement of sight words taught to first and second graders.* Master's thesis, California State University, Hayward.

Lowe, A. J., & Foilman, J. (1974). Comparison of the Dolch list with other lists. *Reading Teacher, 28,* 40–44.

Madden, R. (1959). *Language arts notes-number 11.* New York: World Book Co.

Mangieri, J. N., & Kahn, M. S. (1977). Is the Dolch list of 220 basic sight words irrelevant? *Reading Teacher, 30,* 649–651.

Moyer, S. B., & Newcomer, P. L. (1977). Reversals in reading: Diagnosis and remediation. *Exceptional Children, 43,* 424–429.

Nemco, B. (1984). Context versus isolation: Another look at beginning readers. *Reading Research Quarterly, 19,* 461–467.

Rash, J., Johnson, T. D., & Gleadow, N. (1984). Acquisition and retention of written words by kindergarten children under varying learning conditions. *Reading Research Quarterly, 19,* 452–460.

Rinsky, L. A., & de Fossard, E. (1980). *The contemporary classroom inventory.* Dubuque, IA: Gorsuch Scarisbrick.

Robinson, H. A. (1963). A study of the techniques of word identification. *Reading Teacher, 16,* 238–242.

Samuels, S. J. (1977). Can pictures distract students from the printed word: A rebuttal. *Journal of Reading Behavior, 9,* 361–364.

Silvaroli, N. J. (1982). *Classroom reading inventory* (4th ed.). Dubuque, IA: William C. Brown.

Sipay, E. R. (1974). *Sipay word analysis tests.* Cambridge, MA: Educators Publishing Service.

Singer, H. (1980). Sight word learning with and without pictures: A critique of Arlin, Scott and Webster's research. *Reading Research Quarterly, 15,* 290–298.

Singer, H., Samuels, S. J., & Spiroff, J. (1973–74). The effect of pictures and contextual conditions on learning responses to printed words. *Reading Research Quarterly, 9,* 555–567.

Slosson, R. L. (1963). *Slosson oral reading test.* East Aurora, NY: Slosson Educational Publications.

Smith, N. J. (1985). The word processing approach to language experience. *Reading Teacher, 38,* 556–559.

Spache, G. (1981). *Diagnostic reading scales* (3rd ed.). Monterey, CA: California Test Bureau.

Speer, O. B., & Lamb, G. S. (1976). First grade reading ability and fluency in naming verbal symbols. *Reading Teacher, 29,* 572–576.

Stone, C. R. (1939). Most important 150 words for beginning reading. *Educational Method, 18,* 192–195.

Stone, C. R. (1941). Vocabularies of twenty preprimers. *Elementary School Journal, 41,* 423–429.

Strikwerda, A. W. (1976). *The effect of pictorial stimuli on the instruction of sight words to first graders.* Master's thesis, California State University, Hayward.

Wangberg, E. G., Thompson, B., & Levitov, J. E. (1984). First steps toward an adult basic word list. *Journal of Reading, 28,* 244–247.

Williams, J. P. (1969). Training kindergarten children to discriminate letterlike forms. *American Educational Research Journal, 6,* 501–514.

Williams, J. P., Blumberg, E. L., & Williams, D. V. (1970). Cues used in visual word recognition. *Journal of Educational Psychology, 61,* 310–315.

Woods, M. L., & Moe, A. J. (1981). *Analytical reading inventory.* Columbus, OH: Charles E. Merrill.

5

Diagnosis and Remediation of Educational Factors:
Word-Analysis Skills

The first part of this chapter contains a discussion and examples of the problems involved in various types of testing for word-analysis skills. This is followed by a description of some of the more commonly used commercial tests and surveys along with a discussion of their strengths and weaknesses. A method of constructing your own phonics survey is then described along with the rationale for use of the El Paso Phonics Survey, which appears in Appendix A. The remainder of the chapter deals with specific methods of diagnosing and remediating reading difficulties in other word-analysis skills.

Part A: DIAGNOSIS

PHONICS AND STRUCTURAL ANALYSIS

Testing for Knowledge and Sound-Symbol Correspondence

Before making a decision about which test to use in phonics and structural analysis, you must decide how you are going to use the information obtained. For example, if you plan to group a number of children who are simply labeled "weak" in overall phonics knowledge, chances are a *group* diagnostic test will suffice for your needs. On the other hand, if you intend to teach to students' specific weaknesses, for example, lack of knowledge of the initial consonant sounds *p, f,* and *g,* and consonant blends *fl, gr,* and *pl,* you will need to administer an *individual* diagnostic test.

It is often believed that an accurate assessment of students' knowledge of sound-symbol correspondence can be done using a group assessment device. Research in the El Paso Reading Center has shown that this is not so (Ekwall, 1973). Once again, you should test in a situation that is analogous to actual reading. The test should require that the student perform the task being tested in the same manner as when he or she actually reads. Group diagnostic tests usually do not permit this. For example, the directions are often somewhat similar to the following:

"Write the beginning sound you hear in the following words: Number one, *need,* number two, *teach,* etc."

The student in this case is to write an *n* in blank number one and a *t* in blank number two. A second set of directions for group testing for knowledge of the *n* and *t* sounds might be as follows:

"On your papers are four letters. Circle the beginning sound you hear in the following words. The first word is *need.* The second word is *teach,* etc."

In this case the students' answer sheets would be similar to the following:

1. p f n d
2. g t h r

At first glance both tests may appear to be valid; however, on examining them more closely you will realize that hearing the words *need* and *teach* and writing *n* and *t* in a blank or hearing *need* and *teach* and circling their beginning sounds from a choice of four letters is simply not the same skill as is required for seeing the *n* and *t* graphemes and responding with the *n* and *t* phonemes. Extensive research in the El Paso Reading Center has shown that the item-by-item agreement on items missed on various group and individual-type tests is extremely low and that group diagnostic tests do not diagnose accurately enough for prescriptive teaching. Since remedial reading is usually a process of filling in the gaps in a student's reading skills, prescriptive teaching is a necessity. And in most cases remedial reading teachers will need to give individual diagnostic tests in order to accurately diagnose and remediate specific problems in phonics and structural analysis. In all fairness to the authors and publishers of group diagnostic tests it should also be stated that much of the teaching of phonics and structural analysis is done by simply grouping children with the lowest overall scores and teaching them practically everything covered on the test. When a teacher is dealing with a large number of children in a group, this approach, although somewhat inefficient in terms of the students' time, is quite efficient in terms of the teacher's time. If this type of teaching is to be done, a group diagnostic test will serve the purpose; that is, it will generally separate students who are extremely poor in word-attack skills from those who are at a medium or higher level. In some cases this information is valuable in making *initial* determinations about students' word-attack skills. The examiner may use a group-test format to identify the students who are most deficient in word-attack skills so that those students may be given individual tests to identify specific weaknesses for prescriptive instruction.

Although it would seem that testing phonics knowledge is an easy task, this is not necessarily the case. Listed below are some commonly used methods of assessing children's phonics knowledge and what we believe to be the shortcomings of each method.

Method 1: Children are shown letters, e.g., *a, b, c,* and told to give the sounds of these letters. First of all, although perhaps a minor point, the letters do not "have" sounds, they represent sounds, and we should ask the child to tell us the sounds that these letters stand for. One of the major problems with this method is in determining whether a response is correct. In playing tape recordings of children taking this type of test in our classes, we find that the scorers do not agree on which answers are right and which are wrong. This type of test then lacks interscorer reliability. The main problem is that scorers do not "hear" the same thing. For example, they cannot agree on whether they hear *er* or *ruh* for the *r* sound. Another problem with this method is that some children who know their sounds in the context of a word do not know the sounds in isolation. Testing sounds in isolation yields irrelevant information in such cases.

Method 2: Children are given a piece of paper on which four letters, blends, etc., appear by each number. They are told to circle or underline the letter, blend, etc., that begins or ends or has the same middle sound as a word pronounced by the tester. The problem with this type of test, as stated earlier, is that hearing a word and circling a sound heard in it is not the same as actual reading. Furthermore, if there are four possible choices on each question, the student has a one in four chance of guessing the correct answer. There is a fairly high correlation between being able to do this and actually attacking a new word, and thus children who are good at this task will probably be good at attacking words and vice versa; however, our research shows that this type of test is simply not accurate enough for prescriptive teaching purposes.

Method 3: Children are given a sheet of paper with a blank by each number. They are then instructed to write down the beginning sound, beginning blend, vowel sounds, etc., heard in a word pronounced by the tester. This method has the same weaknesses as those described in method 2. That is, it is not analogous to actual word attack in reading. This method does, however, have the advantage of eliminating the guessing factor.

Method 4: Children are shown nonsense words that contain the initial consonants, blends, vowels, etc., to be tested. For example, in a test for knowledge of the "p" sound a child may be given the nonsense word *pide*. For some children this presents major problems. In order to pronounce the nonsense word *pide* they have to know the following:

a. The long and/or short vowel sound for *i*;

b. The *d* sound;

c. The vowel rule stating that when there is a vowel-consonant-final *e* the first vowel is usually long and the *e* is silent.

In addition, the student must possess the ability to *blend* the various phonemes together. As you can see, all of the points listed in (a), (b), and (c) above are equal to or more difficult than simple knowledge of the *p* sound. Therefore, if the child does not respond, you do not know if it was because the child did not know the *p* sound, or one, two, or all three areas listed above, or how to blend the letters. It should also be kept in mind that vowel sounds and vowel rules are usually taught somewhat later than initial consonant sounds. Therefore, many children having difficulty with initial consonant sounds are likely to have even more problems with vowel sounds and/or vowel rules. A final problem with this method is that many students simply resist reading nonsense words. These students, even when told that the words are not real words, have difficulty pronouncing nonsense syllables. It may be that for these pupils pronunciation of nonsense words represents a task that is more difficult than reading real words.

Method 5: Children are given a list of real words, each beginning with a specific initial consonant, blend, etc., to be tested. The problem is that if the words are already in the child's sight vocabulary, it is not a test of word-attack skills at all, and if the words are not in the child's sight vocabulary, many of the same problems encountered in using method 4 are also encountered here.

In order to understand why the foregoing methods are inadequate for diagnosing phonics weaknesses, it may be helpful to think of the testing and teaching of phonics skills as occurring at three stages: low-level skills, high-level skills, and blending skills.

A student who masters low-level skills is able to recognize the correct letter(s) when the sound is provided. In this situation the student is going from sound to symbol, which is the easiest phonics task. Methods 2 and 3 above will adequately test for this ability. However, in order for a student to utilize phonics as an aid to decoding, he or she must go from symbol to sound, a more difficult skill. When reading, the student first sees the letter(s) or symbol(s) and then must think of the associated sound. This can be thought of as high-level phonics. Methods 1, 4, and 5 above purport to test this level; however, there are a number of testing problems that were noted in our discussion of these methods.

Successful application of phonics skills requires not only high-level skills but also blending ability; that is, the student must blend the sounds or phonemes together to pronounce the whole word. Methods 4 and 5 above attempt to do this but do not sufficiently control the exposure of new skills or prevent recognition of the whole word by sight. Later in this chapter we will present an alternative method for testing that will enable you to diagnose accurately specific phonics weaknesses.

Some Commercially Published Tests and Surveys: Their Strengths and Weaknesses

In this section a number of tests are described in detail, along with their strengths and weaknesses. The purpose of the somewhat lengthy descriptions is to make the user aware of the common shortcomings of some of our most popular reading diagnostic tests. The information gained in this section should also help you in critically analyzing other reading tests.

We have chosen seven of the more commonly used tests for this analysis. In Part I of Appendix B you will find some of the above listed tests as well as other tests commonly used in the diagnosis of reading and reading-related difficulties. For each test you will find three columns. The first column lists the items tested by each subtest. The second column gives the purpose of the subtest. The third column describes how each subtest is administered. After reading our analysis of various methods of testing you should be able to study each of the subtests and decide whether each is valid.

In Part II of Appendix B you will also find some of the above listed tests and a number of other reading and reading-related tests as well as the following information:

1. Name and date of test
2. Subskills measured
3. Time for administration
4. Number of forms
5. Grade level for which test is appropriate
6. Whether the test is administered individually or in a group setting
7. Publisher of test

The *Botel Reading Inventory* (Botel, 1978) contains a Decoding Test, a Spelling Placement Test, a Word Recognition Test, and a Word Opposites Test. The latter two tests have two forms each and are designed for use as reading placement tests. The Decoding Test includes twelve subtests:

1.   "Letter Naming"
2.   "Beginning Consonant Sound/Letter Awareness"
3.   "Rhyme Sound/Letter Pattern Awareness"
4–12. "Decoding Syllable/Spelling Patterns"

The first three decoding tests are group tests; the remaining ones are individually administered.

On the "Letter Naming" subtest the students circle the letters named by the examiner. On the "Beginning Consonant Sound/Letter Awareness" subtest the students circle or underline words that begin with the same sound as pairs read by the examiner. This format is similar to that noted in method 2 above and has the same advantages and disadvantages. The test does provide a measure of low-level phonics ability, but it evaluates only ten beginning single-consonant sounds. High-level skills and blending are not measured.

The "Rhyme Sound/Letter Pattern Awareness" subtest uses the same group format and measures students' ability to recognize ten rhyming patterns or ending phonograms, such as *-ed, -ake,* and *-ot.*

The individually administered "Decoding Syllable/Spelling Patterns" subtests consist of nine lists of ten words each, grouped according to spelling patterns. The student is to read the words on the lists aloud until two or more errors (80 percent correct) are made on one of the lists. These tests are essentially a series of sight-word tests of increasing difficulty much like method 5 above. If a student misses a word, there is no way of determining whether the error was caused by the student's failure to decode the beginning sound, vowel sound, or ending sound or by an inability to blend the various sounds together.

The last three lists contain multisyllable words, and in these cases we would have to add structural-analysis weaknesses to the list of possible reasons why a student might fail to pronounce a word correctly.

The last list is perhaps the most useful of the entire test. It contains a number of difficult nonsense words such as *pegflitting* and *quidderish*. Although the author of the test does not point it out, it is quite logical to assume that a student who can pronounce these words has an adequate knowledge of single consonant sounds, consonant blends and digraphs, vowel rules, structural analysis, and to some extent accent generalizations. This test is therefore useful as a quick screening device; if a student can pronounce the words on this list, the above-mentioned skills need not be tested, thus saving a considerable amount of time.

In short, the *Botel Reading Inventory,* although somewhat time-consuming to administer, does not provide the examiner with the kind of information required to plan prescriptive instruction.

The *Diagnostic Reading Scales* (DRS) (Spache, 1981) contains twelve word-analysis and phonics tests to supplement a series of graded reading passages. The word-analysis and phonics tests are vastly improved over the eight subtests that appeared in the earlier (1972) edition. Apparently, Spache has responded resourcefully to criticism of the earlier subtests.

The twelve subtests of the DRS are as follows:

Test 1: "Initial Consonants." In this subtest, the student is to read aloud nine one-syllable real words and thirteen one-syllable nonsense words that begin with a consonant. Words such as *bam, cam,* and *dam* are used. Although the use of nonsense words may present a problem for some students, as we pointed out in our discussion of method 4, accurate testing for higher-level phonics skills requires some use of nonsense words. In this subtest Spache provides a good mixture of real and nonsense words. In this way, the examiner can determine whether only nonsense words were missed and can be sure that the student is not recognizing all the words by sight.

Test 2: "Final Consonants." Using a similar format, this test evaluates a student's ability to pronounce (go from symbol to sound) fifteen different final consonants in one-syllable words.

Test 3: "Consonant Digraphs." Similar to tests 1 and 2, this measures a student's ability to pronounce various consonant digraphs in both initial and final positions. This test is somewhat more difficult because a variety of beginning and ending parts are used to complete the syllables in which the consonant digraphs appear. However, Spache wisely cautions the examiner to "disregard mispronunciations of vowels and consonants appearing with the digraphs.''

Test 4: ''Consonant Blends.'' Similar to test three.

Test 5: ''Initial Consonant Substitution.'' This test measures ability to substitute beginning consonant sounds and to do simple blending. The sample items present a one-syllable word, then the ending phonogram of the word, then a new word with the substituted consonant, as follows:

dark   ark   bark

The student is given three trials with this format, then is asked to perform the substitution task on items that are presented as follows:

c   bake

The student must pronounce *bake* and *cake,* though the examiner may provide additional aid if necessary. A similar subtest in the earlier edition was criticized for being too difficult for primary children. This new test represents a considerable improvement. However, it is most effective (i.e., least confusing) to present all items in the same way as the sample items are presented. Or the test items might be presented as follows:

bake   cake

There is reason to believe, based on our experience testing students on initial-consonant substitution tasks, that the *c   bake* format represents a formidable visual task for the student—one that may interfere with measuring the decoding skill, which is the purpose of the test.

Test 6: ''Initial Consonant Sounds Recognized Auditorily.'' The student names the letter that begins the word pronounced by the examiner. This is similar to method 3 described previously and measures only low-level phonics ability (sound to symbol). Our criticism of this test is not so much with the format but rather with its placement. It seems logical to place this test before test 1, since it evaluates a lower-level, or prerequisite, skill. Otherwise, this test will be necessary only for students who failed test 1. Since any student who fails test 1 will be likely to fail tests 2 through 5, it makes most sense to place test 6 before test 1.

Test 7: ''Auditory Discrimination.'' This test uses the common format of having the student identify identical and contrasting pairs of words that are pronounced by the examiner; for example, *end-end* and *bin-pin*. The placement of this test is even more puzzling than that of the previous one. Auditory discrimination is a pre-phonics skill that requires no visual skill whatever. Surely this test should be the first in the battery, or instructions should be given to skip this test for students who attain mastery on any of the other tests.

Test 8: "Short and Long Vowel Sounds." This test consists of sixteen one-syllable word pairs with one word in each pair having a short vowel sound and the other a long vowel sound; for example, *red-ride*. Some of the words are real words and some are nonsense words. Vowel-sound abilities are perhaps the most difficult of all phonics skills to test accurately. This test has the virtue of requiring the student to read words rather than recite rules. Some of the problems mentioned under method 4 appear because the student must read words that contain a number of different consonants, consonant blends, and consonant digraphs. However, it is probably reasonable to assume that students will master these skills prior to learning short and long vowel patterns.

Test 9: "Vowels with *r*." The student pronounces ten words that contain the *r*-controlled vowel pattern.

Test 10: "Vowel Diphthongs and Digraphs." The student pronounces thirty real and nonsense words that contain common vowel digraphs and diphthongs.

Test 11: "Common Syllables or Phonograms." The student pronounces thirty-four common syllables or phonograms that occur frequently in primary reading materials, such as *tion, atch,* and *ile*. For some reason, in this test the syllables appear in isolation, instead of in real or nonsense words as in previous tests. Also, this test seems to be misplaced, since the skill tested is probably easier than those evaluated on tests 9 and 10.

Test 12: "Blending." This test consists of ten nonsense words divided into phonograms, such as *gr-ell-on*. The student is asked to pronounce each word element and then blend them into one word. The student is evaluated on the ability to blend the elements rather than on the ability to pronounce the phonograms. This does test the ability to blend. It seems reasonable, however, to present words with fewer and easier phonograms. Even though the pronunciation of the phonograms is not to be taken into account in the scoring, it is likely that students will be frustrated by this aspect of the task and fail to demonstrate blending skill that may exist.

As noted earlier, the new DRS subtests are significantly improved over those in the earlier edition. Most diagnosticians will find these tests useful in the evaluation of various phonics skills. Since the author continues to present the tests in a puzzling order, we recommend that the examiner alter the order of administration.

Sally Lipa (1985) summarized her review of the *Diagnostic Reading Scales:*

The releveling of passages reduces the credibility of the instrument even with the author's detailed rationale. The battery is an alternative to an informal reading inventory but does not yield different or additional information about a student's reading behavior. Further, using the same set of passages for oral and silent reading as well as for obtaining a potential level can lead to problems in both administration and interpretation. There appears to be little real advantage in using the DRS in preference to other publisher IRIs now available. (p. 667)

The *Durrell Analysis of Reading Difficulty* (3rd edition) (Durrell and Catterson, 1980) does not contain enough depth in phonics testing to plan prescriptive instruction. The "Identifying Sounds in Words" subtest provides for evaluation, similar to method 2, of low-level phonics skills. It tests for only seven beginning consonants, eight beginning blends and digraphs, five ending consonants, and nine items where the student must identify both beginning and ending sounds. The "Sounds in Isolation" subtest tests sixteen beginning consonants, sixteen consonant blends and digraphs, and twenty phonograms. This testing is done in isolation and therefore suffers from the problems mentioned in method 1. Perhaps the real value of the *Durrell Analysis of Reading Difficulty* is in the training it can provide the diagnostician on what to observe in students' reading abilities. Once this has been learned, however, many diagnosticians and teachers find that the administration of the various subtests is too time-consuming for the diagnostic information that it provides.

The *Gates-McKillop-Horowitz Reading Diagnostic Tests* (2nd edition) (Gates, McKillop, and Horowitz, 1981) contains a series of nine tests designed to evaluate a student's word-attack skills. The order of these subtests is as follows: "Syllabication," "Recognizing and Blending Common Word Parts," "Reading Words," "Giving Letter Sounds," "Naming Capital Letters," "Naming Lower Case Letters," "Vowels," "Auditory Blending," and "Auditory Discrimination."

In "Syllabication" the student is shown a series of seventeen nonsense words, such as *rivlob* and *acdengist,* and told to pronounce them. This test purports to measure the student's "ability to combine syllables into words." However, the nonsense words are quite difficult, and in order to pronounce them the student must also have mastered phoneme-grapheme correspondence and structural analysis. Therefore, it is more appropriate to use this test as a quick screening device to determine which students possess adequate phonics and structural-analysis skills to eliminate further testing in these areas. This is the recommendation we made for the last test in the Botel battery.

"Recognizing and Blending Common Word Parts" tests the student's ability to pronounce nonsense words such as *spack* and *twable.* If the student cannot pronounce the word, he or she is shown each part separately, for example, *sp* and *ack.* After pronouncing each part, the student attempts to blend the parts into a whole word. This subtest will provide a gross measure of the student's knowledge of blends, digraphs, diphthongs, and phonograms or word families as well as of the student's ability to blend these word parts. However, the presentation of various beginning sounds with a variety of ending sounds makes the task somewhat difficult. The blending skill itself could be better measured if only one or two ending phonograms were used. As the test is constructed, a student may miss an item, and the examiner will find it difficult to determine whether the error results from an inability to blend or from a failure to recognize the beginning or ending sounds. The authors do provide a scoring system for the various subtasks, and this should aid the careful examiner.

"Reading Words" requires the student to read fifteen one-syllable nonsense words, such as *rus* and *soat*. The authors wisely caution that "some children have difficulty handling a [nonsense word] task, and poor performance may not indicate poor phonetic skills." With this caution in mind, this subtest provides a gross measure of a student's ability to apply phonic analysis to isolated words.

"Giving Letter Sounds," as the name implies, is a test for the letter sounds of the consonants and vowels. Each sound is tested in isolation. All consonants are presented along with ten vowels and vowel combinations, and the results should be thorough enough for prescriptive teaching. However, since the sounds are tested in isolation, this subtest suffers from the problems described in method 1. The inclusion of the vowels is somewhat unusual, and the child is expected to provide more than one sound where appropriate. It is not reasonable to ask a child to give long and short sounds for vowels in isolation, let alone provide alternate sounds for the *ea* digraph. What we should be concerned with is not the ability to produce from memory the vowel sounds in isolation, but rather the ability to apply the correct sound in the context of reading words.

"Naming Capital Letters" and "Naming Lower Case Letters" require the child to say the name of each of the letters.

The "Vowels" subtest follows the format described in method 2. This test evaluates the student's ability to recognize (sound to symbol) the long and short vowel sounds. As pointed out earlier, this low-level skill is not the same as that required of the student when reading.

In "Auditory Blending" the examiner reads word parts to the child, such as *b-ox* and the child is to pronounce the whole word, *box*. Auditory blending is considered a prerequisite to blending while reading.

The subtest "Auditory Discrimination" is administered by having the student sit with his or her back to the examiner while the examiner reads a number of pairs of words. The student is to say whether the words are the same or different. This should serve as a sufficient screening device for auditory discrimination.

The various subtests of the *Gates-McKillop-Horowitz Reading Diagnostic Tests* evaluate a range of prereading and word-attack skills. The examiner compares the student's test performance on various subtests. Some of the tests could be constructed differently, and the examiner may have difficulty planning prescriptive instruction based on the results of the subtests. Nonetheless, this individually administered inventory does provide useful information to the reading diagnostician.

The *Sipay Word Analysis Tests* (SWAT) (Sipay, 1974) are seventeen subtests, administered individually, to test students' knowledge of word-analysis skills: "Survey Test," "Letter Names (Lower-Case and Upper-Case)," "Symbol-Sound Association: Single Letters (Sounds and Words)," "Substitution: Single Letters (Initial Consonants, Final Consonants, and Medial Vowels)," "Consonant-Vowel-Consonant Trigrams," "Initial Consonant Blends and Digraphs (Blends, Digraphs and Triple Clusters)," "Final Consonant Blends and Digraphs (Blends and Digraphs)," "Vowel Combinations (Most Common and Consistent Vowel Digraphs, Most Common and Consistent Diphthongs, More Common Vowel Combinations That Usually Represent One of Two Sounds, Less Common Vowel Combinations That May Represent One of Two Sounds)," "Open Syllable Generalization," "Final Silent *e* Generalization," "Vowel Versatility," "Vowels + *r* (Single Vowel + *r,* Two Vowels + *r,* Single Vowel + *r* + Silent *e*)," "Silent Consonants," "Vowel Sounds of *y,*" "Visual Analysis (Monosyllabic Words, Root Words and Affixes, Syllabication)," "Visual Blending (Component Elements into Syllables, Syllables into Words)," and "Contractions."

Each of the SWAT subtests has four components: a mini-manual, a set of test cards (approximately 57 mm × 90 mm), an answer sheet, and an individual report form. The mini-manuals provide general information on the subtest, what skills are measured, how to administer and score it, how to analyze and interpret the results, and suggestions for follow-up testing. The test cards are used to present the stimuli to the student. The answer sheets are used for recording the student's responses and to allow the examiner to make a more detailed analysis of the learner's performance. The individual report forms are used by the examiner to summarize and report findings.

Because of the length of this test we will not analyze each subtest in this section. However, the author of this test recognized that word-attack skills generally cannot be tested in a group and took considerable care to construct a test that will allow the student to perform on each subtest as if actually reading. He also did considerable research to find which graphemes were of high enough utility to make them worthwhile to test. This test should yield results accurate enough for exact prescriptive teaching.

One feature of the test that some teachers may find undesirable is that they are required to handle a great many cards while administering the subtests. However, this is also an advantage, since it takes the test materials out of the traditional setting and puts them into a context that a student is more likely to perceive as a game.

The *Stanford Diagnostic Reading Test* (Karlsen, Madden, and Gardner, 1976) is a group of diagnostic tests in four levels, with two parallel forms (A and B) at each level. The Red Level is intended for use at the end of grade one, in grade two, and with low-achieving students in grade three and above.

It evaluates auditory discrimination, the basic phonics skills, auditory vocabulary, word recognition, and comprehension of short sentences and paragraphs. The Green Level is intended for use in grades three and four and with low-achieving students in grade five and above. It evaluates auditory discrimination, phonetic and structural analysis, auditory vocabulary, and literal and inferential comprehension. The Brown Level is intended for use in grades five through eight and with low-achieving high school students. It evaluates phonetic and structural analysis, auditory vocabulary, literal and inferential comprehension, and reading rate. The Blue Level was published in 1974. It is also called the SDRT Level III. It is intended for use with high school and community-college students. It evaluates phonetic and structural analysis, reading vocabulary, literal and inferential comprehension, reading rate, and scanning and skimming.

This battery offers both content-referenced and norm-referenced scores and is well constructed and standardized. Administration of it should enable a teacher to determine appropriate placements for students; that is, which ones are good, fair, or poor readers. However, by its nature (it is group-administered) it allows you to evaluate only low-level skills. Thus, the test provides only a gross measure of a few word-attack skills, not sufficient information for prescriptive teaching.

The *Woodcock Reading Mastery Tests* (Woodcock, 1973) are five tests designed for individual administration. They are for kindergarten to grade twelve. One tests word-attack skills. Two alternate forms of the battery are available. The author of this test states:

> This battery of tests is particularly useful for clinical or research purposes and in any situation for which precise measures of reading achievement are desired. Raw scores can be converted to traditional normative scores including grade scores, age scores, percentile ranks and standard scores. Primary interpretative emphasis, however, is directed toward using the specially designed Mastery Scale, which predicts the individual's relative success with reading tasks at different levels of difficulty. Separate norms are available for boys and girls in addition to total group norms. An innovative feature is the provision of SES (socioeconomic status) adjusted norms based on communities having SES characteristics similar to the local community. (Page 1, *Teacher's Manual.*)

> The Word Attack Skill Test contains 50 items which measure the subject's ability to identify nonsense words through application of phonic and structural analysis skills. Items are arranged in order of difficulty. At the lower end of the test the nonsense words are simple consonant-vowel or consonant-vowel-consonant combinations such as "dee" and "lat." Multisyllable words such as "ipdan" and "depnonlel" are presented at the upper end of the test. Represented within the set of nonsense words are most consonant and vowel sounds, common prefixes and suffixes, and frequently appearing irregular

spellings of vowels and consonants (*ph* for *f* and *igh* for long *i*). (Page 3, *Teacher's Manual.*)

This test has the advantage of being rather easy to administer and is contained in a functional easel-type notebook. The student who is able to read all of the nonsense words no doubt has adequate word-attack skills. However, as described earlier in method 4, the use of nonsense words presents a number of problems. If the student does not respond, the tester does not know whether the student does not know the initial consonant, the medial vowel, the ending consonant, etc., or whether the student does not know how to blend. For this reason the only "precise measurement" is whether the student does or does not possess adequate word-attack skills. This test would not be adequate for prescriptive teaching of specific phonemes.

Constructing Your Own Test or Using the El Paso Phonics Survey

Before choosing or constructing a test for phoneme-grapheme relationships, you should examine the research on which graphemes are of high enough utility or represent a specific sound or phoneme to a degree that makes them worthwhile to test and teach. For example, Lou Burmeister (1968), in examining the 17,310 words from a study by P. R. Hanna and others (1966), found that the vowel pair *ie* appeared 156 times. In those 156 words the *ie* grapheme represented six different phonemes as heard in the following words (p. 448):

Word	Frequency	Percent
thief	56	35.9
Lassie	30	19.2
die	26	16.7
patient	23	14.7
cashier	17	10.9
friend	4	2.6

Heard in the word *thief,* the "ie" sound accounted for 35.9 percent of the total words; in *Lassie,* for 19.2 percent, etc. It would not be practical to try to teach students all six of the "ie" variations. For this reason decisions need to be made concerning which graphemes are of high enough utility to make them worthwhile teaching, based on such factors as the percent of time that vowel combinations represent certain phonemes, frequency of appearance in children's literature, etc. Oswald and Ekwall (1971) developed a list of phonic elements to be tested and taught to children in grades one through three and to older disabled readers. These are the graphemes tested in the El Paso Phonics Survey shown in Appendix A. In that survey you will note that some graphemes represent two phonemes. Where it is recommended that both be taught, it is because they are approximately equal in utility.

There is a way of testing for the various phonic elements that is nearly analogous to actual reading and that does not possess the innate disadvantages of the methods used in many commercial tests. An example of this type of test along with complete directions for its administration is shown in Appendix A. The procedure for constructing such a test and the rationale for its use:

1. Choose about three small stimulus words that are usually known by children in their early reading. The words should contain only one syllable and should begin with a vowel. Eldon Ekwall (1986) suggests these:

   > in
   > up
   > am

   Print these words on three flash cards or all on one larger card or at the top of the stimulus sheet.

2. Place each initial consonant, consonant blend, or consonant digraph before one of these small words to form a nonsense word. The element to be tested and the stimulus word should precede the nonsense word on the same line:

   a. m   in   min

   b. t   up   tup

   c. p   am   pam

   d. s   up   sup

   e. pl   up   plup

   f. ch   am   cham

   g. qu   am   quam

   The use of at least three stimulus words will enable you to form nonsense words with any combination of initial consonants, blends, and digraphs.

3. In constructing the test be sure to place eight to twelve of the easier consonants first, e.g., the following: *p, n, s, t, r, m, b,* and *d*. These are later used in nonsense words to test for vowel knowledge.

4. Combine each vowel, vowel team (vowel digraphs and diphthongs), and special letter combinations (*r-, l-,* and *w*-controlled vowels, etc.) with one or two of the easier consonants listed above to form a nonsense word as shown below:

   a. a   bam

   b. i   mip

c. o   tope

d. a   mape

e. oi   poi

Be careful to construct long-vowel and short-vowel nonsense words that do not violate common vowel rules. For example, put short vowels between two consonants to conform to the cvc pattern in which we expect the vowel to be short. Put the long vowels in a pattern of cv final *e* or *cv*[1] in which we would expect the vowel to be long.

The procedure for administering the test:

1. Make sure that all children to be tested know the three stimulus words so they can say them without any hesitation. Before administering the test always show the student these words and ask the student to pronounce them. If the student misses one or more of them, teach them and have the student come back later, having learned them thoroughly. Do not attempt to teach the stimulus words and immediately test the student, as the overall concept load will be too heavy; the learning of the new stimulus words in conjunction with the testing of various initial consonants and consonant clusters is more than the student can deal with at one time.

2. Have the student respond to each line by saying the name of the letter or letters (not the sound), the small stimulus word, and then the nonsense word. It is important that the student say all three exactly as outlined here.

3. In the vowel section the student should respond by saying the name of the vowel and then the nonsense word. Before administering the vowel section you should make sure the student knows the initial consonant letter sounds chosen to combine with the vowels, vowel teams, and special letter combinations. In the *El Paso Phonics Survey* these are the first eight letters (initial consonants) tested. It is not likely that the student will know the vowel sounds without knowing these initial consonant sounds, so you may feel relatively sure that missed vowel combinations result from a lack of knowledge of vowel sounds rather than of consonants.

Administering a test of this nature is not at all difficult, and the results are gratifying. You will also find this type of test to be highly reliable. Some of the advantages of this type of test:

[1]Although there are some exceptions to the rule that vowels are usually long in the cv pattern in "words" (it is not a good rule when dealing with syllables), many more words do have the long vowel sound in this pattern, e.g., *go, me, he,* and *she.* A few exceptions are *do, to,* and *the* when *the* is pronounced with a schwa sound at the end.

1. You test in a situation that is analogous to actual reading. That is, the student has to react as in reading, to decode words rather than encode them, as one does in spelling. Also, sounds are not tested in isolation when this method is used.

2. Although nonsense words are used, you can presume that the student will know all of the word but the element being tested. This way if the student fails to respond properly, you can be reasonably sure it is because the student does not know the element being tested and not some other part of the word. In a few instances students fail to respond because they do not know how to blend. If you find that a student does not respond, then you can easily check to see if blending is a problem by having the student give the sounds in isolation. If the student can give them in isolation, you can assume that blending is a problem. If the student cannot do that, you can assume that he or she does not know the letter sounds.

3. The student is not being tested on words that may already be in his or her sight vocabulary; therefore, if the student responds correctly, you are assured that he or she does know the element being tested.

4. When the student responds, it is not at all difficult to determine whether the response is correct or incorrect. When this test is administered via an audio tape with a number of different teachers scoring the answers, you will get near-perfect agreement on most answers, which indicates that this kind of test is highly reliable. On the other hand, when the same number of teachers are asked to score a student's responses on a test in which the student gives answers in isolation, it is very difficult to reach a consensus on many items and there is a great deal of disagreement on certain items, such as the sounds represented by *r, w, l,* etc.

Albert Harris and Edward Sipay (1985) have made the point that testing sound-symbol correspondence in nonsense words takes a higher degree of knowledge than testing in the context of a word:

> In assessing decoding ability, two points should be considered. First, it is easier to decode words that are in your listening vocabulary. Second, words in context are easier to recognize and decode than words in isolation because additional cues are available. These two points lead to the conclusion that a test employing nonwords in isolation requires a higher degree of decoding ability than is necessary for decoding real words in context. On such tests, therefore, one should be willing to accept a mastery level below that which might be desirable if real words were used. (p. 221)

The *El Paso Phonics Survey* does use nonsense words in testing students' knowledge of sound-symbol or phoneme-grapheme correspondence. However, since the teacher, before giving the test, will have made sure the student knows the word endings, such as those suggested in the *El Paso Phonics Survey* (*in, up,* and *an*), this type of test does not pose the difficulties normally associated with using nonsense words in testing phonics knowledge. Because of this factor, which is not taken into consideration in testing with the use of nonsense words in general, we do not suggest that the teacher accept a lowered mastery level. In fact, we believe that a student's mastery level on this test should be at or near 100 percent.

In the *El Paso Phonics Survey* the student is first asked to give the name of the letter, not the sound it stands for, then pronounce the short stimulus word, then give the nonsense word formed by the two. Some teachers assume that having students pronounce the name of the letter rather than the letter sound will pose undue difficulty. In fact, once the student understands what is expected, he or she will pronounce the letter name and blend the parts of the nonsense word as easily as if the letter sound were first pronounced. Having the student pronounce the letter name avoids problems of interscorer reliability that often arise with letter sounds. We recommend the format of the *El Paso Phonics Survey,* not because it is without problems, but rather because we believe its approach is the best of the available options.

We also caution the diagnostician to use judgment when planning instruction based on the results of any phonics test. The student's performance on a variety of reading tasks should be considered. The examiner should not assume that just because a student fails to pass certain items on a phonics test, instruction on these items is necessarily indicated. Many students have difficulty pronouncing vowel patterns correctly. Yet an analysis of the oral reading performance of these students may show that they can successfully decode real words in which these vowel patterns occur. Similarly, these students may demonstrate sufficient comprehension of silently read material that contains words with these vowel patterns. In this case further instruction on these vowel patterns is not justified. What we are concerned with is the student's ability to use certain phonic skills *when necessary* to decode unknown words. If the student is able to decode successfully using context clues and beginning letter-sound associations with an ample sight vocabulary, instructional efforts are well directed to other areas of need. Since it is possible to decode words in context even when all of the vowels have been removed, diagnosticians must be especially careful when prescribing instruction on the letter-sound correspondences of vowels and vowel combinations.

A complete diagnosis for a disabled reader's knowledge of phonics skills usually includes testing for weaknesses in consonants, consonant blends and digraphs, and various vowel sounds. Frequently such testing also includes an evaluation of the student's ability to pronounce representative phonograms or word families. Thorough testing in this area can easily consume one half hour. And after all of this time the diagnostician may find that the disabled reader is really not weak in phonics ability at all.

For students who have adequate phonics word-attack skills the examiner can save a great deal of time by simply administering a group of long nonsense words such as those in the Quick Survey Word List found in the *Ekwall Reading Inventory* (Ekwall, 1986). These are words such as *pramminciling* and *twayfrall*. Similar word lists are found in the *Botel Reading Inventory* and the *Gates-McKillop-Horowitz Reading Diagnostics Tests*. If the student is able to pronounce these words, there is really no need to test in the areas of phonics mentioned above or for that matter in structural analysis. You should keep in mind that the learning of vowel rules, syllable principles, and so on is simply a means to an end. The student who is able to decode new words does not need to be able to tell you the vowel rules or syllable principles. Indeed, in this case there is no need for the student to pronounce vowel or consonant sounds in isolation. Many students in reading-methods courses can pronounce almost any word, but they have long since forgotten, or never knew, how they learned to do so. For this reason, we recommend that students above the third-grade level, where most of these skills should have been mastered, be given a list of nonsense words at the beginning of the diagnostic procedure to determine whether they know the various phonics word-attack skills. If after attempting one or two of these words it becomes obvious that the student cannot pronounce them, the examiner should put the list aside and conduct further diagnosis to determine the specific phonics skills in which the student is weak.

Vowel Rules or Principles and Accent Generalizations

Research during the past two decades has shown that some vowel rules formerly taught are of very little value. As a result most textbooks are beginning to reflect this change. Although some research has been done on word accent, there is still very little definitive information to guide us in selecting worthwhile generalizations for teaching.

In testing for knowledge in these areas you should again remember to devise or use a test that is analogous to what the student does when actually reading. For example, in testing for knowledge of various vowel rules you should ask the student to respond to a nonsense word such as *rup* rather than have the student recite the rule. (A single vowel in a closed syllable usually has the short sound.) Many students are able to recite rules they are unable to apply, and conversely, many students seem to have a sixth sense for the application of rules they cannot recite. What the teacher should remember in testing is that rules and generalizations are a means to an end. If a student can already apply the rule or generalization, he or she has achieved that end and there is little or no value in discussing or teaching the means to the end.

It should also be remembered that in most cases a student is not ready to apply vowel rules without mastery of all of the vowel sounds. Therefore the teaching of vowel rules other than the cvc and vc final "e" rules is premature until the student has mastered the vowel sounds.

Vowel Rules.   In this discussion the most useful rules will be listed, and then a method or methods of testing for knowledge of the rule will be presented.

1. In *words* containing a single vowel letter at the end of the word, the vowel letter usually has the long vowel sound. (Note that this rule refers to words and not just syllables. There is a similar rule for single vowel letters at the end of syllables—see number 2 below.)

   Testing: Write several nonsense words with the pattern shown below and say to the student, "If these were real words, how would you say them?"

   > sho
   > bri
   > na

   Note that it is assumed the student will know the *sh, br,* and *n* sounds as well as short and long vowel sounds. If not, you should test for vowel rule knowledge anyway. It should also be noted that three words are used in each set when testing for knowledge of most rules. The student should get the correct pronunciation of each of the vowels correct to avoid the possibility of guessing. When choosing nonsense words, use words that are not very similar to words the student is likely to have in his or her sight vocabulary.

2. In syllables containing a single vowel letter at the end of the syllable, the vowel letter may have either the long or short vowel sound. Try the long sound first. (Note that this has the same effect as number 1 above. Research indicates that a single-syllable word with a vowel at the end, as in number 1 above, is much likelier to be long than short. On the other hand, a vowel at the end of a syllable *in a multisyllable word* is only likelier to be long than short; therefore, we express the rule as *try the long sound first.*

   Testing: Use the same test as in number 1 above. However, when teaching this rule be sure to stress that the student should be flexible, i.e., try the short vowel sound if the long one does not form a word in the student's speaking-listening vocabulary.

3. A single vowel in a syllable usually has the short vowel sound if it is not the last letter or is not followed by *r, w,* or *l.* When explaining this to students it is often helpful to indicate that a single vowel in a closed syllable is usually short. Students should be taught that a closed syllable is one in which there is a consonant on the right-hand side. They will also need to know, as indicated above, the *r, w,* and *l* control rules.

   Testing: Write several nonsense words with the pattern shown below and say to the student, "If these were real words, how would you say them?"

   > pid
   > pud
   > lat

4. Vowels followed by *r* usually have a sound that is neither long nor short.

Testing: The directions for this are the same as in number 3. Use nonsense words such as the following:

bur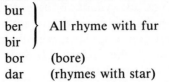
ber   All rhyme with fur
bir
bor   (bore)
dar   (rhymes with star)

5. A *y* at the beginning of a word has the "y" consonant sound; *y* at the end of a single-syllable word, when preceded by a consonant, usually has the long *i* sound; and *y* at the end of a multisyllable word, when preceded by a consonant, usually has the long *e* sound. (Some people hear it as short *i*.)

Testing: The directions for this are the same as in number 3. Use nonsense words:

cly
fory
mippy
yint
yand

6. In words ending with vowel-consonant-silent *e* the *e* is silent and the first vowel may be either long or short. Try the long sound first.

Testing: The directions for this are the same as in number 3. Use nonsense words:

tete
pape
mide

In teaching this rule, stress that the student should be flexible; i.e., try the short vowel sound if the long one does not form a word in his or her speaking-listening vocabulary. It has been demonstrated that students who are taught to be flexible in attacking words when applying rules such as this become more adept at using word-attack skills than those who are not taught this flexibility.

7. When *ai, ay, ea, ee,* and *oa* are found together, the first vowel is usually long and the second is usually silent.

Testing: This is normally tested under the vowels, vowel teams, and special letter combinations section of the test described earlier in the chapter and shown in Appendix A. The directions are the same as in number 3. Use nonsense words:

dea
dee
boap

8. The vowel pair *ow* may have either the sound heard in *cow* or the sound heard in *crow*.

Testing: This is also normally tested under the vowels, vowel teams, and special letter combinations section of the test described earlier in the chapter; otherwise, show the student a nonsense word such as *fow* and say, "If this were a real word, how would you say it?" If the student says it so it rhymes with *cow* then say, "Yes, and how else could we say it?" The student should then pronounce it so it then rhymes with *crow* if the student knows both common pronunciations. If not, you need to teach whichever one the student did not give you.

9. When *au, aw, ou, oi,* and *oy* are found together, they usually blend to form a diphthong.

    Testing: This is also normally tested under the vowels, vowel teams, and special letter combinations section of the test described in Appendix A. If not, handle the testing the same as described in number 3.

10. The *oo* sound is either long as in *moon* or short as in *book*.

    Testing: This is the same situation and can be handled the same as *ow* described in number 8 above.

11. If *a* is the only vowel in a syllable and is followed by *l* or *w*, then the *a* is usually neither long nor short.

    Testing: This is the same situation and can be handled the same as the *r* control rule listed in number 4 above.

Accent Generalizations. These are of less importance for a disabled reader than the vowel rules. This is true partially because a student who properly attacks a new word in his or her speaking-listening vocabulary but not sight vocabulary is likely to get the right accent without any knowledge of accent generalizations. Although Carol Winkley (1966), gives some guidance as to which accent generalizations to teach, information is still lacking concerning the utility of various accent generalizations. For these reasons the testing of a disabled reader's knowledge of accent generalizations is probably not worthwhile.

Contractions

An area of structural analysis that often causes problems for children is contractions. The method of testing them is very similar to that of basic sight words, i.e., give the student a list of them and ask the student to read the contractions and then tell what two words each contraction stands for. In scoring keep in mind that a student must know each contraction, since contractions appear so often in print. Although it is less important, the student should also know what two words each contraction stands for. Table 5–1 is a list of contractions taken from five commonly used sets of basal readers that may be used for testing purposes. Although many of them do not appear on basic sight word lists, at least one of the two words from which these contractions

TABLE 5.1 When Contractions are Known.

Word	Grade Level	Word	Grade Level
let's	2.9	wouldn't	3.5
didn't	2.9	she'll	3.5
it's	2.9	here's	3.5
won't	2.9	ain't	3.9
that's	2.9	couldn't	3.9
can't	2.9	they're	3.9
wasn't	2.9	they'd	3.9
isn't	2.9	you'll	4.5
hadn't	2.9	she'd	4.5
don't	3.5	weren't	4.5
I'll	3.5	I'd	4.5
we'll	3.5	you've	4.5
I've	3.5	you'd	4.5
he'll	3.5	we'd	4.5
hasn't	3.5	anybody'd	4.5
haven't	3.5	there'll	4.5
aren't	3.5	we've	4.5
I'm	3.5	who'll	4.5
he's	3.5	he'd	4.5
we're	3.5	who'd	4.5
you're	3.5	doesn't	4.5
what's	3.5	where's	4.5
there's	3.5	they've	4.5
she's	3.5	they'll	4.5

were derived does appear on these lists. Because writing styles vary a great deal, it would be difficult to find an "average" utility value for these words. However, it is known that contractions do cause some students considerable difficulty, and remedial exercises with contractions improve their reading. Note that following each contraction is a grade-level designation. This represents the point at which you can expect most students to know that contraction. Remember, however, that the grade-level designations are only guidelines.

Inflectional Endings

Inflectional endings include -*s* and -*es, 's, -d* and -*ed, -ing, -er,* and -*est*. These suffixes indicate a change in number or tense, possessive, comparison, present participle, or third-person singular verbs. Sometimes -*y* and -*ly* are also considered to be inflectional endings. These word parts are introduced at the beginning of the reading program, and students must learn to recognize them in order to decode successfully. You may test for inflectional endings by placing the following word list in front of the student:

bake	*pale*	*slow*
baker	paler	slower
baked	paling	slowest
bakes	palest	slows

Say to the student: "Read these words. I will read the first one in each column." Then observe to see if the student can pronounce each word with the added ending. It is acceptable to use real words, since you are not concerned with the student's ability to pronounce the base word but rather to recognize and correctly pronounce the added inflectional ending.

Affixes

The term *structural analysis* refers to two quite different processes. Sometimes the term refers to a student's ability to derive *meaning* from word parts. Although this skill may serve to broaden a student's meaning vocabulary, such knowledge does not contribute directly to decoding ability. We are concerned here with structural analysis as a tool to aid the student in analyzing (decoding) multisyllable words. This distinction is particularly important in diagnosing prefix and suffix knowledge.

Studies such as that by Russell Stauffer (1969, pp. 348–351) suggest that the diagnostician not be concerned with the *meaning* of any suffixes and of only fifteen prefixes, based on the consistency of these meanings each time they are used. The fifteen prefixes suggested include *in-* and *de-*. The prefix *in-* means "input," "into" or "not." The prefix *de-* means "from," "away from" or "off." It is doubtful that knowledge of the meanings of even these "consistent" prefixes will aid the student in understanding words such as *intense, decode, defeat,* or many others.

However, a high percentage of the words that students encounter as their reading level increases contain prefixes, suffixes, or both. Usually these affixes are easily recognizable and have consistently regular pronunciations. The student who can learn to *recognize* and *pronounce* these word parts will be greatly assisted in decoding the big words that are frequently troublesome.

Experts disagree about which prefixes and suffixes should be tested and how they should be tested and taught. The following tests present ten of the most common prefixes and nine of the most common suffixes. These affixes are presented in an attempt to provide a consensus and an appropriate scope for testing and teaching these critical skills. Our experience has shown that students who master these affixes have little difficulty in transferring this skill to other structural parts. Specific teaching procedures will be presented in the remediation section of this chapter.

There are three simple tests that you can give to evaluate a student's ability to recognize and pronounce prefixes and suffixes. The first two use the same format and rationale as the test for inflectional endings presented in the previous section.

Prefix Test.   Place the following word list in front of the student:

play	*mote*	*form*
replay	remote	conform
display	promote	inform
misplay	demote	deform

take	*tend*	*pack*
retake	intend	unpack
intake	contend	prepack
mistake	extend	repack
	distend	
	pretend	

Say to the student: "Read these words. I will read the first one in each column." Then observe to see if the student can pronounce each base with the added prefix. Some of the prefixes are tested more than once. Thus you can judge if the student consistently misses this word part. If the student misses any of the items, you must determine whether the failure resulted from the student's inability to pronounce the prefix, blend the prefix with the base, or both. This will determine the remedial approach you will employ. The same procedure is used for the suffix test that follows.

Suffix Test.   Place the following word list in front of the student:

joy	*invent*	*base*	*elect*
joyous	inventive	basement	election
joyful	inventable	baseness	elective
joyless		baseless	

The third test requires the student to pronounce two-syllable words containing one common affix. On this test the examiner does not pronounce the base word, so the task is significantly more difficult for the student than the two previous tests.

Affix Test.   Place the following word list in front of the student:

uncall	treeness
proclaim	sunning
indeem	bookful
demark	raytion
prestrain	darkous

Say to the student: "Read as many of these words as you can. Some are not real words." The student must use all three steps of decoding through structural analysis: (1) separating the word parts; (2) pronouncing the word parts; and (3) blending the separate parts to pronounce the whole word. Failure to pronounce the base word correctly suggests that the student lacks sufficient word recognition or phonics ability to decode through structural analysis.

Syllabication Principles

The testing and teaching of syllabication is the most controversial area of structural analysis. Many authorities believe that syllabication should not be taught at all. We agree with Patrick Groff (1981) who after reviewing the literature concluded:

> The number of studies that support the teaching of syllables for word recognition stands in contrast to those that advise against this kind of teaching. It is difficult, in fact, to find empirical data to support the contentions that the successful decoding of words is not related to syllabication skills, that the syllable is too complex a phenomenon to be used by children for word recognition, or that it is impossible for a child to work out the pronunciation of a word through an analysis of the sound of its syllables. (p. 662)

Part of the problem results from adherence by many experts and practitioners to syllabication instruction based on dictionary word divisions. Diagnosticians should not be concerned with the student's ability to identify the *specific* points in words where syllable division takes place according to the dictionary. This skill, often called *end-of-line division,* is frequently tested. Unfortunately, it is not useful for decoding purposes. Indeed, the only time that this skill is required is when one is engaged in formal writing and there is no dictionary at hand. To complicate the matter, dictionaries do not always agree on where words should be divided. Groff states:

> The syllabication taught children for learning to read should not be traditional dictionary syllabication. Despite the fact that dictionary syllabication has often been recommended to teachers, its rules are not based on linguistic research but rather on the arbitrary decisions of typesetters from the early days. Dictionary syllabication rules have little to do with the actual sound patterns of syllables, are often impossible to apply because they are inconsistent, and are not truly usable by children for word recognition. . . . (p. 663)

Much controversy surrounding the teaching of syllabication arises from teachers' lack of knowledge of how students use this skill. Syllabication is taught so that when words are divided between certain letters, the student will know what sound to give the vowel(s) in each syllable. Suppose a student did not know how to pronounce the word "consonant." Assuming the student knew the consonant sounds, the student would be presented with the following possibilities for pronouncing the vowel sounds:

First Vowel	Second Vowel	Last Vowel
Long *o*	Long *o*	Long *a*
Long *o*	Long *o*	Short *a*
Long *o*	Short *o*	Short *a*
Long *o*	Short *o*	Short *a*
Short *o*	Long *o*	Short *a*
Short *o*	Short *o*	Short *a*
Short *o*	Long *o*	Short *a*
Long *o*	Long *o*	Short *a*
Short *o*	Short *o*	Long *a*

It should be noted that with a three-syllable word there are nine possible combinations of vowel pronunciations (3 × 3), with four syllables, sixteen (4 × 4), with a five-syllable word, twenty-five (5 × 5), and so on. Obviously, it is not practical for a student to struggle through each combination until the correct pronunciation is found. Most of us have learned what sound to give various vowels from simply looking at the word; however, remember that this only comes with years of practice.

If in the example above the student knew how to divide the word "consonant" into syllables and knew the vowel rules, he or she would cut the possible pronunciations from nine to one. Even if there were an exception to the rules, the possible pronunciations would be cut from nine to possibly two. From this example it becomes clear that if a student knows the vowel rules and syllable principles innately, even if not able to recite them, they can be very helpful. On the other hand, Diana E. Wolff, Peter Desbert, and George Marsh (1985) have pointed out that learning-disabled readers have more difficulty in learning and applying rule-based phonics.

Before beginning the teaching of syllabication rules, you will first want to know if the student understands the concept of syllabication. First determine if the student can hear the separate syllables of words. Then test for the following decoding steps: (1) separate the word parts (this is a visual task); (2) pronounce the word parts (usually a base word with an inflectional ending and/or one or two affixes); and (3) blend the separate parts to pronounce the whole word.

This process is analogous to that of phonic analysis on words of one syllable. With phonic analysis the student separates, pronounces, and blends individual sounds or phonemes. With structural analysis, of which syllabication is a key component, the student separates, pronounces, and blends larger units or syllables.

In order to test a student's ability to hear the separate parts (syllables) of words, you need only give the following direction: "Listen carefully. I am going to say some words. Tell me how many syllables or parts you hear in each word." Then pronounce a series of words containing one to four sylla- bles, such as *cowboy, intention, steam, disagreement,* and *randomly.* The words should be pronounced slowly and clearly, without, however, exaggerat- ing the syllable divisions in the words. After only a few words it will be easy to determine whether the student possesses sufficient auditory understanding of syllabication. This skill is not what is required of a student when decoding, it is a necessary prerequisite. The student who fails this test will require instruc- tion at this level before proceeding to the next step.

One way to evaluate the student's ability to use syllabication as a decoding tool is to observe the student's performance when reading orally material that contains a number of multisyllabic words. If the student does not attack these words at all or merely gives the appropriate beginning sound and then guesses wildly, he or she will likely need instruction in syllabication.

To test for knowledge of specific syllable principles, give the student some nonsense words or long words that are not likely to be in the student's sight vocabulary and ask the student to draw lines separating the syllables. Below is a list of some of the most commonly taught and generally accepted syllable principles, as well as words you can use to test students' knowledge of these principles.

1. When two consonants stand between two vowels, the word is usually divided between the consonants, e.g., *dag-ger* and *cir-cus.*
   botnap
   daggal
   In some of the newer materials words are divided after the double consonant, e.g., *dagg-er.* It should be remembered that in reading we are usually teaching syllabication as a means of word attack.
   Therefore, you should also accept a division after double consonants as correct even though the dictionary would not show it that way.

2. When one consonant stands between two vowels, try dividing first so that the consonant goes with the second vowel, *e.g., pa-per* and *mo- tor.* Students should be taught that flexibility is required in using this rule; if this does not give a word in the student's speaking-listening vocabulary, then the student should divide it so that the consonant goes with the first vowel, as in *riv-er* and *lev-er.*
   lador
   mafel

3. When a word ends in a consonant and *le,* the consonant usually begins the last syllable, e.g., *ta-ble* and *hum-ble.*
   nable
   frable
   (The *le* sound is usually heard as *ul.*)

4. Compound words are usually divided between word parts and
   between syllables in these parts, e.g., *hen-house* and *po-lice-man.*
   cowperson
   dogthrower
5. Prefixes and suffixes usually form separate syllables.
   rebaseness
   distendable

As indicated above, principles 1 and 2 have many exceptions. When evaluating students' performance on these items you should be most concerned with whether the student divided the word at an *appropriate place* rather than precisely according to the rule. For example, in the real word *basket,* a student could appropriately divide the word as *ba-sket, bas-ket,* or *bask-et* and still end up with pronounceable units. However, the following divisions would be clearly unacceptable: *b-asket* or *baske-t.*

Another way to test a student's ability to syllabicate is to present a list of real words sufficiently difficult that the student is unlikely to recognize them as sight words. Such a list of words follows:

automotive	premeditate
displacement	imperfection
conformation	unreasonable
remarkable	misplaying
impeachable	complicated

By observing the student's attempts to decode these words, the examiner should be able to determine whether the student has difficulty (1) dividing the words into appropriate (pronounceable) units; (2) pronouncing the parts; (3) blending the parts into whole words; or (4) some combination of all three difficulties.

Two additional facts bear mentioning. First, the goal here, much as with instruction in phonics for smaller words, is to give the student sufficient word-attack skills to be able to use them, together with context, to decode unfamiliar words *in the act of reading.* If the student possesses some ability to use context, it is seldom necessary to arrive at a "perfect" pronunciation through phonics or structural analysis. Second, all of the word-attack skills will be insufficient if the student has a severely limited vocabulary. New words must be at least minimally recognizable in order for the student to arrive at the correct pronunciation.

These facts were well illustrated by a student named Tony. When his teacher presented multisyllabic words to Tony in list form, he had great difficulty pronouncing them in spite of excellent direct instruction. However, when the teacher presented the same words in sentences, Tony was able to decode them with but a moment's hesitation. For example, when presented the word *engagement* in isolation, Tony read *en-gag-uh-ment*. Yet when reading the sentence, *The boy gave his girl an engagement ring,* Tony pronounced the word correctly. In this case, Tony had sufficient vocabulary knowledge for context to assist him in combination with this structural-analysis skills. Incidentally, after substantial practice in the act of reading, big words like *engagement* became easily recognizable sight words for Tony.

The example of Tony serves not only as a conclusion to this section but also as an introduction to the next section.

CONTEXT CLUES

Research such as that done by Alan Robinson (1963) on context clues indicates that a student is able to attack an unfamiliar word with the use of context clues alone only a small percentage of the time. However, when a student uses context clues, it is usually in conjunction with phonics or structural analysis. A student may read up to an unfamiliar word, sound the first letter, and then, using the clues gained from both, say the word. (He saw the man who was coming h _____ [home].) Or the student may read up to a word and pronounce the first syllable. (When the dis _____ was determined, they stopped the measurement [distance].) The use of context clues is one of the most important word-attack skills a student can possess. Paul Burns and Leo Schell (1975) suggest that "the use of context may well be the major skill which distinguishes connected meaningful reading from reading of word lists." (p. 90)

They quote Nita Wyatt's observation that "the good reader uses context to predict what an unknown word may be *before* the analysis process or *as* the process begins." (p. 90)

Beginning teachers often make the mistake of thinking that children will automatically learn to use context clues without any instruction. Many children do seem to use both picture clues as well as written context clues almost innately; however, some children, especially those who become disabled readers, need specific instruction in this important skill.

For teaching purposes context clues are often categorized according to type such as "summary clues," "experience clues," and "synonym or definition clues," as explained by Ruth Strang, McCullough, and Traxler (1967). However, for testing purposes this is not necessary.

In constructing exercises for testing you should obtain several short paragraphs written at varying grade levels, e.g., first, third, and fifth grade. Be sure not to employ materials commonly used, such as well-known graded reading inventories, as many children will have already been given these reading passages or are quite likely to encounter them later. Type or print the passage on one side of a 5 in. × 8 in. card and leave out several words. Passages written for first or second graders should be typed with primary type or printed in letters of an equivalent size or larger. Omitted words should be those for which few or no substitutions could be made in the context in which they are used. They should also be easily derived from the context if the student is able to use context clues. Where words are omitted, you should substitute an *X* or dash for each letter in the word. This also gives the student a clue as to word length, which again is analogous to the clues that he or she would have in actually reading. On the back of the card you may wish to include the directions along with the reading passage and answers to be supplied in each of the blanks.

The front of the card might appear as in Figure 5–1, the back of the card as in Figure 5–2.

The testing of context clues in this manner should not be confused with the cloze technique, a method of testing students' comprehension explained in Chapter 6. In using the standard cloze procedure every fifth word is omitted and a standard-sized line is left on which the student is to write the word that he or she thinks was omitted. In this procedure there is no standard number of words to be omitted or percentage of right and wrong answers. Your judgment of the student's ability to supply oral answers in the reading passages used for context clues will be based on your opinion of how well the student does in relation to other average readers of the same grade level.

If students are unable to use context clues when they read, they should be tested on their ability to use them orally. For example, you may wish to read a sentence, leaving out a word, and then ask the student what word might be used where the blank appeared in oral context. Students who do considerably better on oral than on written context clues may be lacking so severely in word-recognition skills that they are unable to concentrate their efforts on the use

FIGURE 5–1

Fred had a pet cat.

Its name xxx Jiffy.

Jiffy liked xx run xxx play.

Jiffy xxx not like Fred's dog.

And, Fred's dog xxx not xxxx Jiffy.

FIGURE 5–2

> Read this story. Some of the words have been left out.
> When a word was left out some x's were put in its place.
> As you read the story try to say the words that you think
> belong in the story where the x's are.
>
> > Fred had a pet dog.
> >
> > Its name was Jiffy.
> >
> > Jiffy liked to run and play.
> >
> > Jiffy did not like Fred's dog.
> >
> > And, Fred's dog did not like Jiffy.

of context clues. Students who do no better in oral exercises using context clues than in written exercises are usually unaware of the value and use of context clues and need to be taught. The teacher should also be aware that sufficient oral vocabulary and the ability to use speech effectively are essential prerequisites for teaching context clues. A child who says "me go" or "her does that" is not ready to profit from instruction in context clues.

An alternative or additional procedure for assessing a student's ability to use context clues is to ask the student to read orally from material where he or she will make five to ten errors per page. While the student reads, note whether miscalled words are logical replacements; that is, does the student rely on context clues when other word-attack skills are inadequate? As the difficulty of the material increases, the student's ability to derive meaning from context naturally decreases. Because this is a potentially frustrating task, you should be sure to keep this part of the evaluation brief.

Bear in mind that students' difficulties with context clues may be reflected in two opposite behaviors. Many students fail to use context clues adequately and appear to read word by word. A common example of this type of problem is the student who reads the sentence *The boy went into the house* as *The . . . boy . . . went . . . into . . . the . . . house.* This student apparently overrelies on graphic information at the expense of meaning clues. At the other extreme are students who overrely on context. These students appear to be reading fluently, but what they read may not be what was written. Such a student might read the sentence given above as, *The boy went into the garage.* Both forms of context-clue difficulties are detrimental to reading ability.

Paul Burns and Leo Schell (1975) listed several common traits associated with *not* using context clues:

1. Stops when meeting an unknown word
2. Overrelies on other skills, such as configuration and beginning/ending sounds
3. Practices less effective analysis techniques, such as relying on signals from the teacher or on picture clues

EFFICIENCY SKILLS

Some students have mastered the decoding skills of phonic, structural, and contextual analysis and possess an adequate sight vocabulary yet still have difficulty reading fluently. Most often these students lack the ability to read with appropriate speed, accuracy, or both. They may try to read too quickly and thus inaccurately, or their reading rate may be unusually slow. They may lack the ability to read with proper phrasing or expression. Some of these students consistently ignore punctuation; some persist in finger pointing or subvocalizing when reading silently. We consider students who have these difficulties and others like them to have problems with efficiency skills. Somehow, in the process of learning to read, these students failed to put together the various pieces of the puzzle of reading. Often they have merely picked up faulty habits along the way. Unfortunately, teachers do not always realize that these students have efficiency problems that can be remedied with a host of appropriate and effective procedures. Sometimes teachers continue to drill these students on phonics or basic sight words, which may only make the problem worse.

In the remediation section of this chapter we offer specific methods for assisting students who have difficulty reading efficiently. Usually no specific diagnosis is necessary to spot these problems. Teachers who have carefully observed their students when reading and who have conducted a thorough enough diagnosis to eliminate other decoding-skill problems may reasonably assume that these students will benefit from techniques designed to overcome reading-efficiency difficulties. A specific procedure for assessing students' reading-efficiency skills follows.

The examiner should have the student read passages orally at two different levels—one at a comfort or independent reading level and a second at the instructional level. As the student reads, the examiner should complete transcriptions on copies of the passages as described in Chapter 11 and evaluate the student's performance in the following areas:

1. *Speed*—Did the student read too fast, causing unnecessary word-recognition errors, or was the reading speed too slow for acceptable comprehension and adequate rate of learning?
2. *Phrasing*—Was the phrasing appropriate, or did the student read word by word or with other inappropriate phrasing?

3. *Punctuation*—Were punctuation cues followed, or did the student ignore or misinterpret punctuation marks?
4. *Accuracy*—Did the student correctly pronounce the words in the selection, or were words miscalled due to excessive speed or poor phrasing? If omissions, repetitions, insertions, or substitutions occurred, were these the result of poor decoding skills, efficiency problems, or both? (See Chapter 11 for a discussion of techniques for remediating problems of omissions, repetitions, or substitutions.)

The following efficiency-skill weaknesses may be observed by the examiner while the student is reading silently: lip movements, finger pointing, and head movements. An examination of the student's performance on the basic sight-word tests described in Chapter 4 will also provide a clue to efficiency skills. A student whose performance is significantly better on the test of basic sight words in isolation than in phrases is likely to have a problem with efficiency skills.

CONFIGURATION CLUES

Some authorities believe it is helpful for beginning and disabled readers to receive instruction in the use of configuration clues. We suggest that in your day-to-day teaching procedures you note whether the student is confusing words of similar configuration and whether the student seems to be aware of differences in words with extenders and descenders, capital and lower-case letters, and with double letters.

Where it is apparent the student is not fully aware of these differences, remediation as described in Part B of this chapter under the heading "Configuration Clues" is appropriate.

DICTIONARY SKILLS

Although few would argue the importance of a thorough knowledge of the use of the dictionary for students from the middle elementary grades through their adult lives, the lack of dictionary skills is not a serious problem for disabled readers. Most of the basic word-analysis skills should be achieved by the time students begin to work with the dictionary. Furthermore, only a small percentage of one's total meaning vocabulary is achieved through the use of the dictionary. Therefore, for seriously disabled readers it is not recommended that a test for knowledge of dictionary skills even be included in the initial diagnosis. For older, less disabled readers, however, you may wish to take inventory of their ability to use the dictionary.

Part B: REMEDIATION

The whole-word or sight approach to the learning of words is rapid at first, but as students begin to encounter many new words, they usually find that they must use some method of word analysis. Linnea C. Ehri and Lee S. Wilce (1985) found that as kindergarten children progressed from the beginning stages of reading to more mature stages they gradually shifted from visual cue processing to phonetic cue processing. As students became more dependent on phonetic cue processing, most began using a combination of methods such as phonics, structural analysis (morphology), configuration, and context clues. Many readers become disabled because they have failed to develop one or more of these word-attack skills. Before beginning work on word-attack skills you should first determine whether the student is lacking in only one kind or whether he or she needs to start from scratch and learn all of them.

There are several ways of teaching word-attack skills. Some commercial programs present a great many rules for long and short vowel sounds, vowel combinations, syllabication, etc. Students are expected to memorize these rules as well as their application. Other programs present lists of graphemes for which the students are to learn phoneme equivalents either in isolation or when blended with a familiar phonogram. In this type of program few rules are taught. Instead an attempt is made to get the student to the automatic-response level. Before beginning a specific program of remediation you should attempt to discover what type of word-attack program each student has had. If a student has been through a rule-oriented phonics program and failed to learn, it may be more productive to instruct the student in techniques that do not require learning and application of many rules. On the other hand, a student who has been taught under a program in which few if any rules are taught can often benefit by learning rules and principles.

Most students are unable to describe the type of program they have been through and are unaware of the publisher of the materials from which they have been taught. However, these students can be asked about certain characters that appear in basal readers. From students' familiarity with certain characters or stories you can often determine the student's basal reader series. For this reason we suggest that a part of your diagnostic kit be a list of characters from the basal readers and supplementary readers or phonics programs most commonly used in your state and by your transfer students during the past three to five years. This can easily be compiled by looking through the materials. You will, of course, need to be somewhat familiar with the word-attack program presented in each series.

In teaching remedial word-attack skills you should consider that students may be deficient because they were not able to learn by the method used by their regular classroom teacher. An eclectic approach to word-analysis skills may have been used, and a student predisposed to learning through any one approach may not have gotten enough instruction in that one approach. On the other hand, the student's classroom teacher may have used a rule-oriented program, as mentioned previously, at which some students succeed, yet at which some are doomed to almost certain failure.

In beginning a program of word-attack skills with a new student, you should first discover whether the student is immediately successful with whatever approach you choose in the beginning. If the student is still not successful, be prepared to switch to another approach. You should also examine your own methods of teaching from time to time to insure that you are not wedded to any one approach. The use of any one approach that seems best to you may often be beneficial in teaching developmental reading. However, being a one-approach teacher in remedial reading is highly undesirable.

PHONICS AND STRUCTURAL ANALYSIS

Many of the activities that follow will seem to the student to be tests if wrong responses are not immediately corrected. Remedial reading if done properly is a highly individualized procedure. When the student responds incorrectly on either written or oral exercises, he or she should be corrected immediately so as not to reinforce a wrong response. These correctional procedures can be carried out while the student works by the teacher, by a teacher's aide or by an older student who is familiar with the material.

It is essential for the remedial teacher to recognize that substantial direct instruction is usually required for disabled readers to master the various word-attack skills. The teacher must demonstrate the skill to be learned, present the subtasks in a systematic way, and assist the student in practicing the new skill *before* resorting to seatwork or other reinforcement material that will help the student to practice the skill. We also strongly recommend that teachers provide sentences or stories for students to read as they are learning each new skill so that they can immediately apply their new knowledge in the act of reading. We want students to rely on context clues as they are learning phonics and structural analysis skills. We also want to be sure that students understand that the purpose of our instruction is to aid them in decoding so that they can obtain *meaning* from printed words.

Phonic Elements

The term *phonic elements* is often used to define various letter combinations and the sounds they represent. We have chosen to use this term rather than *phoneme* for sounds and *grapheme* for its written equivalent because some letter combinations (phonic elements) consist of more than one phoneme and consequently more than one grapheme.

There are many methods of teaching the phonic elements. One typical procedure:

1. Developing awareness of hearing the sound:
    1.1. Say, "Listen to these words. Each of them begins with the *bl* sound. Circle the *bl* on each word on your paper as you hear the sound. *Blow—blue—blunder,* etc."
2. Developing awareness of seeing the sound:
    2.1. Tell the student to circle all of the words in a passage that begin with *bl*.
3. Providing practice in saying words with the *bl* sound:
    3.1. Pronounce each word and have students pronounce it after you.

    blow
    blue
    blunder
    bleed
    blast

4. Providing practice in blending the *bl* sound with common word families or phonograms:
    4.1. Teach or use several phonograms with which students are already familiar such as *ock* and *ush*. Put the *bl* in one column, the phonogram in a second column, and the two combined in a third column as follows:

bl	ock	block
bl	ack	black
bl	ur	blur
bl	under	blunder

    Instruct the student to say *bl* (the two letters and not the sound) and then the phonogram (this time sound represented by the letters in the phonogram) and then the word formed by the two.
    4.2. Another similar exercise that works well and gives practice in blending is to place the letters and words as follows:

bl	<u>f</u>lock	(block)
bl	<u>la</u>ck	(black)
bl	<u>fu</u>r	(blur)
bl	<u>thu</u>nder	(blunder)

    Instruct the student to say *bl*, then the middle word, and then take off the underlined letters from the middle column word and replace it or them with *bl* and say the new word that is formed. If students cannot do this mentally, have them write the complete word shown in column 3 above.
5. Asking the student to make a list of some words that begin with *bl*. If this is too difficult, provide a list of some phonograms from which some *bl* words can be formed. Ask the student to say each word as he or she writes it.
6. Providing practice in reading *bl* words. Either present a paragraph or story that has a number of *bl* words in it or write a paragraph using the *bl* blend in a number of words.

This procedure takes the student through the critical steps in learning a new phonic element. Steps 1, 2, and 3 help the student to recognize the association between the letter(s) and sound you are teaching. This provides the foundation for the low-level phonics knowledge (sound to symbol) described in the diagnosis section of this chapter. Steps 4 and 5 teach the student high-level phonics (symbol to sound) and blending ability, which are required to apply phonics as a decoding tool. Step 6 not only reinforces the previous learning but also gives the student an opportunity to apply the skill in the act of reading.

One important factor to remember in teaching any phonic element is that you should not expect to teach it and then assume the student has full recall and use of it from then on. To begin with, you are likely to have received the student because he or she did not learn at a normal rate or through whatever methods the classroom teacher used initially. Furthermore, it takes many exposures to a word before it becomes a known sight word. It is unlikely that a student can learn a certain phonic element without some initial teaching and then repeated exposures to that element in various types of written and oral exercises.

When teaching a group of students to listen for sounds in words, you can increase participation by giving everyone three cards on which are printed the numbers 1, 2, and 3 or the words *beginning, middle,* and *end.* As you say words, have each student respond by holding up the appropriate card; for example, "I am going to say some words that have the *n* sound in them. If you hear it at the beginning of the word, hold up your number 1 card. If you hear it in the middle of the word, hold up your number 2 card. And if you hear it at the end of the word, hold up your number 3 card. Some words may have more than one *n* sound in them. If you hear the *n* sound at the beginning and middle, hold up your number 1 and 2," etc. This type of exercise will show you which students are learning to recognize the *n* sound and which are not. When only calling on one student there is often a tendency to overlook other students who do not respond.

The activity just described is an example of an *every pupil response technique* (EPRT). Such techniques are very effective. They not only increase the number of student responses but also tend to improve the on-task time of all students, who know that they must be prepared to respond at all times. This way less time is wasted and the learning rate for all pupils increases. In addition, EPRT enables the teacher to conduct diagnosis while teaching. Other examples:

1. *Yes-no cards*—to provide group response to "yes-no" or "right-wrong" questions. For example, the teacher might say, "I am going to read some words that start with the *b* sound and some that start with other sounds. If the word I read starts with the *b* sound, hold up your 'yes' card. If it starts with another sound, hold up your 'no' card. Does everybody understand? Good. Ready? *ball, tree, house, bat, Bill, dig,*" etc.

2. *Thumbs up, thumbs down*—the same as yes-no cards; thumbs up indicates "yes," thumbs down indicates "no."

3. *Open eyes, close eyes*—the same as above; this method has the added advantage of eliminating the possibility that students will mimic the responses of others.

4. *1, 2, 3* . . . —to provide a group repetition response. The teacher might say, "Printed on this chart are a number of words that begin and end with sounds you know, so I know you will be able to read them. Say each word on the signal as I point to it. Ready? . . . " The teacher points to each word, saying: "1, 2, 3 . . . " The students read the word quickly. After the list is read in order, the teacher may point to words quickly in random order. Students enjoy the speed and challenge of this technique and it provides excellent practice.

Note that the first three techniques listed above are appropriate for practicing low-level (recognition) phonics tasks, while the last method may be used to have students practice high-level (production) skills, blending skills, or both.

Some other types of exercises for practicing phonics skills follow. Most of these should be used only after direct instruction has taken place.

1. Omit letters from a word used in context and give several choices to be filled in. This usually encourages the student to try several sounds in order to arrive at the correct answer.

   1.1. Sue and Fred like to go _____ ishing.
        (*g, f, b, h*)
   1.2. Sam forgot his _____ ooks at school.
        (*d, p, b, q*)
   1.3. Paul did a goo _____ job of washing the car.
        (*d, p, b, g*)

2. Give each student an envelope with several cards in it. On the front and back of each card print one letter. For example, each student might have five cards: *c, f, g, h,* and *d.* As you say words, have students hold up the card that has a letter representing the sound they hear at the beginning, middle, and end of various words. Do this again having students hold up various vowel letters and vowel pairs that they hear in words.

3. Have students write and read their own and other students' alliterative stories. For example, a junior high student's paragraph illustrating the use of *f:*

Once in a fir forest there were four fast fireflies. The four fireflies like to fly forward and backward. Once on the fourth of February the four fireflies flew fast forward and then fast backward into a flaming fire. Now there are not four fireflies in the fir forest.

4. Have students scan the newspaper and circle or underline learned phonic elements. Discuss the words found.

5. Start a "thing box" in which you put many miscellaneous articles such as a ball, book, bike (toy), toothbrush, tank, dress (doll), and drum. Have boxes labeled *b, d, t,* etc. As students pick up each article, they say the name of the article, listen for the initial sound, and then sort the items into their respective boxes. This type of exercise can be made self-corrective by using a label maker to put the correct beginning letter on the bottom of each item.

6. The same type of exercise can be done using a file folder in which an envelope is glued or taped to one inside fold. This envelope can contain many pictures representing various initial consonants, blends, digraphs, vowels, etc. On the other side of the inside fold make pockets by cutting out pieces of tagboard and taping them on the sides and bottom. Students take pictures out of the envelope and sort them into the proper pockets. This exercise can also be made self-correcting by writing the correct letter (grapheme) on the back of the pictures. A file folder done in this manner to teach vowel sounds is illustrated in Figure 5–3.

7. Tell the students to put an *X* in front of each word in the list on the right that has the same beginning sound as the thing shown in the picture on the left.

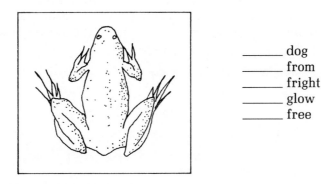

       _____ dog
       _____ from
       _____ fright
       _____ glow
       _____ free

8. Tell the class to say the words below and listen for the long or short vowel sound in each word. They should write *long* in the blank after the word if they hear the long vowel sound and *short* if they hear the short vowel sound.

     bid _____   he _____

     make _____   lake _____

     up _____   three _____

FIGURE 5–3 File Folder for Vowel Sounds

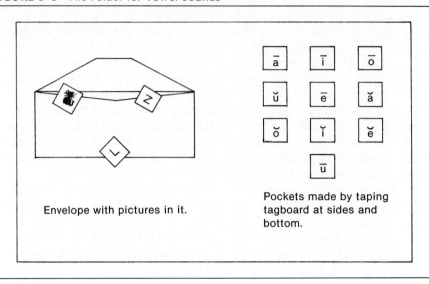

Envelope with pictures in it.

Pockets made by taping
tagboard at sides and
bottom.

Another similar exercise calls for the student to say each word and
mark the long and short vowels over each vowel letter using the
breve (˘) and macrom (—).

9. Instruct the class to say each of the words on the list to themselves
   and listen for the vowel sound. Then have them write the words
   from the top list under the word with the same vowel sound.

Spain	came	mood
freight	Mike	piece
ate	each	trial
me	ran	Sue
blue	meat	sleigh

too	*line*	*tree*	*lake*	*cat*
___	___	___	___	___
___	___	___	___	___
___	___	___	___	___

10. Instruct the students, "Find the vowel sound that is heard in each
    blank by looking at the key word preceding each sentence. Then
    find the correct word from the list that has that vowel sound in it."
    (Help the student with the stimulus words to the left of the
    numbers if he or she does not know them before beginning the
    exercise.)

let—hop—lid—lake—lad—like

(Ed)   1. Father _____ me go with him.

(cat)   2. The small _____ went with his mother.

(cake)   3. We went to the _____ to go fishing.

(it)   4. Father put the _____ on the pot.

(kite)   5. I _____ to go fishing.

(top)   6. Can you _____ over the fence?

There are many ways the tape recorder can be used in teaching phonic elements. Several of these are illustrated below.

11. Tape record a number of words for the student in order to determine whether he or she hears the long or short vowel sound: "First, number your paper from one to twenty. Turn the tape recorder off until you have done this (*pause*). Now you will hear some words called. As you hear each word, write *long* or *short* after the number of that word. Here are the words: number one— *dog,* number two—*lake,* number three—*rod,*" etc. You may wish to have the student mark each blank with a breve (⌣) or macron (—) if the student has already learned diacritical marking. A more advanced exercise using the same type of script is to have the student write the word *long* or *short* and the vowel sound he or she hears in each word. This can also be done with initial consonants, consonant digraphs, etc.

One major advantage of the tape recorder is that it can act as a self-correcting device, as below:

12. Each student is given a sheet of paper prepared as follows:

    1. d f g t   f r b n
    2. t c v w   p l s n
    3. etc.

    The tape recorder script: "On your paper are numbers, and after each number are four letters, a space, and then four more letters. Now you will hear some words called. You are to circle the letter you hear at the beginning of each word from the first group of four letters and the letter you hear at the end of the word from the second set of letters. Here are the words. Be sure to listen carefully. Number one—*din,* number two—*camps.* . . . Now we will check your work. The first word was *din.* You should have circled the *d* from the first group of letters and the *n* from the second group of letters. Circle these two letters now if you did not get them right the first time. The second word was *camps*. You should have circled the *c* from the first group of letters and the *s* from the second group of letters. Circle the two letters now if you did not get them right the first time. The third word was . . . '' etc.

When using the tape recorder keep in mind that almost any material that you can check as a class exercise can be checked by the tape recorder. Although it takes a little more time to record these exercises in the beginning, it will certainly save much time in the long run.

Blending

Many students learn the consonant and vowel sounds in isolation or are able to give the sounds in isolation but are unable to blend them to form words. The inexperienced teacher who tests sounds in isolation may be led to believe some students have no problem with sounds, when in reality their inability to blend known sounds may be as disabling as not knowing the sounds at all. The importance of the blending skill in the word-attack process cannot be overstressed. A study by Jill Whaley and Michael Kibby (1980) found that word synthesis (blending) was related to beginning reading achievement regardless of the reading strategy employed by the students. Research by Wanda Homen (1977) determined that blending skill was equally predictive of first graders' reading success as knowledge of letter names.

If the testing procedure described in Part A of this chapter is followed, students' ability to blend will be tested along with their knowledge of grapheme-phoneme relationships. In another article, Jill Whaley (1975) presents some excellent procedures for the direct teaching of blending skills:

1. Teach the child to use his or her voice to ''slide'' through the sounds of unfamiliar words. The teacher tells the student to say the sound when the teacher points to a letter and continue saying the sound until the teacher's finger points to the next letter. After some practice at this, the finger pointing is eliminated and the child is told to read through a word as if the teacher were still pointing to it.
2. Use analogies between blending and other activities, such as skating. Place large letters on the floor and have the child ''skate'' from one to another while saying the letter sounds out loud or have the student stretch a rubber band between words.
3. Provide kinesthetic reinforcement by tapping the child near the shoulder for the beginning sound and lower down the arm for subsequent sounds while the teacher pronounces the word. Then the teacher says the whole word while sliding a hand the length of the student's arm. The student may practice the exercise on his or her own arm.
4. Use letter tiles or other movable letters, which may be gradually moved

apart while a word is sounded slowly, then brought back together as the whole word is pronounced. Again, after the teacher demonstrates, the child may move the letters.

5. Tell the child to form his or her mouth in preparation for saying the beginning sound of a syllable, but then to say the following vowel instead. This forces the child to think ahead and be prepared for the second sound rather than concentrating solely on the first sound, eliminating an undesirable stuttering, letter-by-letter attack.

The following exercises may be assigned for additional assistance to students who have blending difficulties:

1. After students have learned to hear beginning, middle, and ending sounds, they can begin blending using the technique called *double substitution*. In using this technique you should start by using an oral presentation, for example:

   1.1. "What word begins like *down* and ends like *hog?*" (*dog*)
   1.2. "What word begins like *dig* and ends like *log?*" (*dog*)
   1.3. "What word has two letters that begin like *white* and end like *hen?*" (*when*)

   After considerable practice using an oral presentation you may wish to give students word lists and directions as follows:

   "Using the beginning sound from the word in the first column and the ending sound from the word in the second column, write a new word in the blank in the third column. Say the word as you write it."

   Initial consonants

1. can	2. bar	3. _____ (car)
1. name	2. go	3. _____ (no)
1. to	2. lake	3. _____ (take)
etc.		

   Initial consonant blends

1. from	2. crank	3. _____ (Frank)
1. stair	2. land	3. _____ (stand)
1. plum	2. clay	3. _____ (play)
etc.		

   Initial consonant digraphs

1. champ	2. blew	3. _____ (chew)
1. wheel	2. gale	3. _____ (whale)
1. thin	2. sing	3. _____ (thing)
etc.		

2. Put several initial consonants, blends, or digraphs on the chalkboard in a column. To the right of these put several familiar phonograms (see example below).

    ch op

    sl ap

Tell students that you will quickly point to a beginning consonant or blend on the left and then to one of the phonograms on the right. They are to say the word formed by the combination of the two. This exercise works well with three to four students. You should use your hand and sweep across from the initial sound to the phonogram very rapidly. Do not hesitate to use combinations that form nonsense words.

3. "Read the questions below. Letters are missing from the beginning of each word. Write the missing letters in the blank using one of the sets from the row at the top to answer the question."

    br   cr   dr   fr   gr   pr   tr   bl   cl   fl   pl   thr

    1. What do you do when you are thirsty?   _____ink

    2. What do you do when you get bigger?   _____ow

    3. What does a baseball pitcher do?   _____ow

    4. What does a rooster do?   _____ow

    5. What does the wind do?   _____ow

    6. What do you do at recess time?   _____ay

Rules for Hard and Soft *C* and *G*

Most reading specialists agree that students are more likely to learn and remember rules, generalizations, and principles governing sounds when they have been learned inductively or by the discovery technique. The rule governing the hard and soft sounds of *c* and *g*: "When *c* and *g* are followed by *e, i,* or *y,* they usually retain their soft sounds; if they are followed by any other letter, they usually retain their hard sounds." In teaching this to a student or to a group of students the procedure is as follows. (Only *c* is illustrated; however, *g* is done in the same manner.)

1. Discuss the fact that the letter *c* stands for more than one sound.
2. Discuss the fact that rules can help us to remember which sound to use in various situations.
3. Suggest that a list be made to examine a number of *c* words to see if students can make up their own rule.
4. Have students think of a number of *c* words while you list them on the chalkboard. Examples might be as follows:

can	came	cry
cent	cycle	cog
cigar	century	color
cancer	cut	certain
come	curve	cavity
cell	city	circus

5. Have students reread all the words to determine how many different sounds the *c* represents. (In this exercise the answer should be two—the *k* sound as in *cut* and the *s* sound as in *cell*.)

6. Group all words under the following two headings:

k-sound	*s-sound*
can	cent
cancer	cigar
come	cell
came	cycle
cut	century
curve	city
cry	certain
cog	circus
color	cancer
cavity	
circus	

7. At this point after some discussion students will usually come up with the correct generalization. Do not rush them. Also, if necessary, find more words to make sure that all parts of the rule are covered.

8. Provide practice in applying the rule by giving students a list of *c* words and letting them mark a *k* or *s* over or after each *c*:

s			
cent	*or*	cent	s
k			
came		came	k

9. Provide practice in applying the rule in the act of reading by having students read short sentences or stories containing words with the *c* sounds.

The rules governing the various *y* sounds may be taught the same way. This technique works well with most other generalizations of fairly high utility.

R Control Rule

The *r* control rule can easily be taught using a technique similar to that described above concerning the rules for hard and soft *c* and *g*. A typical procedure would be as follows:

1. Discuss the fact that when *r* follows a vowel it usually controls or
   modifies the sound of the vowel.
2. Again, discuss the fact that rules can usually be made to help
   remember various *r*-controlled vowel sounds.
3. List a number of words in which *r* follows a vowel:

fir	brother	cur	bird
fur	corn	torn	Ford
far	scorn	morning	herd
jar	happier	mar	

4. Categorize the different sounds:

ar *as in car*	or *as in corn*	er *as in herd*
far	scorn	fir
jar	torn	fur
mar	morning	brother
	Ford	happier
		cur
		bird

5. Let students make up a generalization: e.g., "*ir, ur,* and *er* usually
   have the sound heard in *herd. Ar* usually has the sound heard in
   car. Or usually has the sound heard in *corn.*"
6. Give students a chance to practice using their newly gained
   knowledge by giving exercises such as the following:
   6.1. Write the correct vowel plus *r* in the blanks below.
        I ate breakfast this m___ ___ning.
        Many animals are covered with f___ ___.
        Father came home in a new c___ ___.
        etc.
7. Give students an opportunity to practice in the act of reading by
   having them read short sentences or stories containing words with
   r-controlled vowels.

As stated earlier, learning various vowel rules can be of considerable benefit
to a disabled reader. However, the commonly taught accent generalizations
are of less utility. First of all, there is insufficient research regarding what
accent generalizations are of high enough utility to make them worthwhile

teaching. Secondly, we need to consider *why* we teach accent generalizations. When students encounter words in their speaking-listening vocabularies, but not in their sight vocabularies, they will have to apply one or more word-attack skills to determine that word. For example, a student may not know the word *cabin* in the sentence, *The Smiths went to their cabin by the lake.* After applying the necessary word-attack skills, the student is left with accenting the word as *cab-in'* or *cab'-in.* With the help of context clues, the student quite likely to accent it properly if *cabin* is in the student's speaking-listening vocabulary, since there are only two choices to begin with. It is only when words are not in a student's speaking-listening vocabulary that accents really become useful. Since most disabled readers' reading levels are likely to be one or more years behind their speaking-listening vocabularies, they have less need for learning accent generalizations than a normal reader does. It is only when their reading level approaches normal that this need becomes more apparent.

One of the problems that teachers and students encounter when learning the vowel rules is the many exceptions. Teachers can alleviate this problem somewhat in the beginning by using words that do follow the rules. However, students will discover that there are many exceptions, and they should be taught to be flexible in their word attack. For example, "When a vowel comes at the end of a syllable, it is usually long" should be taught as "When a vowel comes at the end of a syllable, try the long sound first." Even when exceptions appear, students usually accept this fact quite well if you explain to them that rules and generalizations cannot fully describe our complex language. Were it possible to design a language to fit a set of existing rules, it would be different.

The initial procedure for the introduction of vowel rules is somewhat the same as for teaching the hard and soft *c* and *g* sounds, i.e., by use of the discovery technique. In introducing the vowel rules, however, you may wish to introduce a word list, prepared prior to the lesson, from which your students can derive various rules and generalizations. This word list should contain no exceptions to the rule or principle being taught. In the initial introduction use words that are already familiar to most students.

After the various vowel rules have been introduced, provide students with the opportunity to practice applying the material they have learned. Just as you would not expect most students to learn a new word well enough for it to become a sight word after one or two exposures, you should not expect students to learn the application of a particular vowel rule from only applying it one or two times.

Word Families, or Phonograms

The teaching of word families, or phonograms, to disabled readers is often very beneficial. The practice of looking for little words in big words has usually been discouraged because the pronunciation of the little word often changes when it becomes part of a longer word. Phonograms, however, tend to have fairly consistent pronunciations from one word to another. Phonograms are also extremely useful in teaching blending of initial consonants, blends, and digraphs.

One technique you may want to use in teaching word families is to call students' attention to the fact that certain clusters of letters tend to have similar sounds from one word to another. Students can compile lists of the common phonograms, and these can be used in exercises:

1. Have the students see how many words they can make by combining the list of initial consonants or consonant clusters on the left and the word families on the right.

   br   ell

   b   ank

   sh   all

   cr   anch

   c   eak

2. Have students make, or you can make, a flash card for each phonogram with which they have difficulty. Pair students for study using exercises as described above. Also have students test each other on their own and other students' phonogram lists or groups of flash cards.

The teacher may also prepare simple sentences or short stories that frequently repeat a few phonograms. A number of supplementary readers are available from publishers that do the same thing. Teachers should also consider using the so-called linguistic readers that present word families a few at a time and with much repetition.

Contractions

Contractions often present difficulties for normal as well as disabled readers. Although a lack of knowledge of contractions alone will not cause a student to become a disabled reader, it can be an important factor in the overall error pattern. One of the major reasons that students encounter difficulties with contractions is that their oral language is often less formal than what is found on the printed page. Therefore, students find a discrepancy between what it seems natural to say and what they read. Many contracted forms that are apparent in students' oral language are seldom seen in print and therefore are not thoroughly learned.

The teaching of contractions then becomes a matter, for most teachers, of providing for multiple exposures to each contraction and insuring that each trial is practiced correctly. The procedures outlined in Chapter 4 for teaching basic sight words will work equally well for contractions. Since contractions are common in oral language, the tape recorder can also be used as a device for reinforcement of contractions. Some examples follow:

1. Give each student a numbered sheet of paper in which two to four contractions appear to the right of each number.
   1.1. they've   they're   they'd
   1.2. wouldn't   would've
   Tape record sentences and have students circle the contraction they hear in the sentences. In numbers 1 and 2 above the sentences would be as follows:
   1.3. The boys said they'd rather not go.
   1.4. We would've gone if they had asked us.
2. Do the type of exercise shown above, only give students sentences in which the contracted word is blank. Students are to pick the correct contraction from a choice of several to make the sentence read correctly.
3. Give students numbered lists of contractions and have them write the two contracted words beside the contraction. Use a tape recorder to correct each answer immediately. The papers appear as follows:
   3.1. I've _____
   3.2. Haven't _____
   The tape recorder script: "Write the two words that stand for the contraction in the blank in number one. (*Beep.*) The contraction is *I've* and the two words it stands for are *I have*. Now do number two. (*Beep.*) The contraction is *haven't* and the two words are *have not*. Now do number three," etc. (The beep is a signal to turn off the tape recorder.)

Possessives

Possessives usually present few problems for students; however, a few disabled readers tend to confuse them with contractions, and when pronouncing words with possessive endings, they attempt to contract the word in some manner. Disabled readers can usually correct this problem rather easily if they are simply told that whenever the apostrophe is followed by or comes after *s*, it means that the word is pronounced as though the apostrophe were not there. A few practice sentences or phrases including contractions or possessives will be helpful in reinforcing students' learning:

1. Jim's hat was lost.
2. I'd like to go.
3. Sam lost Frank's watch.
4. The boys found Frank's watch.
5. The boys said they'd like to go.

Inflectional Endings

To recognize and pronounce inflectional endings the student must learn to apply structural analysis: identify word parts, visually separate word parts, pronounce word parts, and blend the parts together to form the whole word. The following procedure will teach students to do this with the inflectional endings -*s, -ed,* and -*ing.* The same procedures may be used with other inflectional endings:[2]

Step I: Identify Word Parts

1. Review the following base words to be sure students can pronounce them: *clean, born, cover, dress*
2. Write the following word lists on the chalkboard:

look	asks
looks	works
looked	called
looking	asking
	calls
	worked
	calling
	asked
	working

3. Direct the students' attention to the first list. Say, "How are these words alike?"
4. Circle the base word *look:*

look	s
look	ed
look	ing

Say, "How are these words different?"

5. Write these headings across the chalkboard:

   s   *ed*   *ing*

6. Direct the students' attention to the second list. Say, "These words have some of the same endings you saw on the word *look*. Which column would you place the word *asks* under?"
7. Repeat number 6 with the other words in the second list.

Step II: Separate Word Parts

(*Note:* This step is optional. If students appear to have little difficulty separating the words parts, move to step III.)

---

[2]We are indebted to Cheryl Milner, principal, Hayward, California Unified School District, and William Radulovich, reading specialist, San Ramon Valley, California Unified School District, for their assistance in developing and field testing specific procedures for teaching structural analysis skills.

1. Review the base words *turn* and *help*.
2. Give each student a page or large card that has the following words printed on it in boxes approximately 3 in. × 4 in.: *turned, helping, helps, turns, turning, helped.* Also give each student an envelope and a pair of scissors.
3. Say, "The words on this paper each have one of the three word endings we have been studying."
4. Write the endings on the chalkboard: *s, ed, ing.*
5. Write the word *turned* on the chalkboard. Say, "Find the word *turned* on your paper. Cut it out." Check to be certain that students cut out the correct word. Say, "Which ending does this word have?" Then say, "Cut off the *ed.*" Then say, "What is left?" Then say, "Excellent. Put the word *turn* and the ending *ed* in your envelope."
6. Repeat number 5 for the other words.

Step III: Blend Word Parts
(This step also will not be necessary for all students.)

1. Direct the students to place their word parts face up in front of them. Make certain all cards are face up and right side up.
2. Say, "Find the word *turn*. Find the ending *ed*. Put the parts together. What is the word?" Then say, "If you take away the *ed*, what is left?" Then say, "If you take away *turn,* what is left?" Then say, "What is the whole word?"
3. Repeat number 2 for the other words.
4. Ask each student to read the words on his or her table aloud.

In order to reinforce this skill, the students will need ample practice in reading whole words that contain these inflectional endings and in reading sentences or stories that contain these words. A list of words and sample sentences and a story for practicing the *-s, -ed,* and *-ing* endings:

walks	watering
watered	plays
playing	started
starts	opening
opened	waits
waiting	walking
walked	waters

She turns and helps the girls.
She turned and helped the girl.
She is turning and helping the girl.
Mother knows when the family eats, plays, and sleeps.
The family likes being mothered.
The family will be eating, playing, and sleeping here.

He opens the doors for his friends.
He opened the door and called his friend.
He is opening the door and calling his friend.
Bob stops and looks up and down the street.
Bob looked before he crossed the street.
Bob is looking before crossing the street.
Sis likes trees, walks, and dogs.
Sis watered and walked the dog.
Sis will be watering and walking my dog.
Sam waits and thinks about how many days it takes.
Sam played while he waited.
Sam is waiting and thinking about the day.

A Long Camping Trip

It all started when I came home from camp. I was walking home from the bus stop. As I turned down my street, I saw some friends a block away. I called hello, but they acted as if they did not hear me.

I was feeling a little sad as I opened the doors to our house. I needed a snack, so I went to find mom and get some nuts and apples. When I saw her I laughed and said, "Here I am!" Mom seemed not to hear or see me. I started yelling. I jumped up and down. It was no use. She just went on cooking. "She does not look the same as before," I thought.

I walked out the back door. First my friends, and now my mother! What had I done? Was no one glad to see me? The trees were blowing, and the birds were singing, but I felt like crying as I climbed a tall tree near the gate.

I started thinking. My dog Rags would be happy to see me! I jumped from the tree and ran to find Rags. He would be in my room sleeping. I ran up the steps. When I walked into my room I was shocked to find it filled with trunks, junk, and all kinds of odds and ends.

Just then my little sister Kate ran up the stairs. To my surprise she walked right by me too. She looked to be about five years too old to be little Kate! As I walked down stairs I saw the date in the hall: July 16, 1992. But this is only 1987!

The steps outlined above may seem unnecessarily long and tedious for teaching three relatively simple endings. In fact, it will not be possible to go through all of the steps with most students in one session. However, we are persuaded that if the structural analysis skills are initially taught thoroughly and carefully, reteaching will not be required, and subsequent skills can be taught more rapidly.

Affixes

As explained in the section on testing students' knowledge in this area, instruction should focus on pronunciation of affixes and not on meaning. The procedures for teaching prefixes and suffixes are identical to those for inflectional endings. The remedial reading teacher will find that for students who have mastered basic sight vocabulary and phonics skills, effective teaching of structural analysis will result in dramatic improvement in decoding ability.

Listed below are words and sentences that may be used to teach the prefixes *re-* and *un-* following the steps previously outlined. The teacher may use similar lists and sentences, as well as stories, to teach and reinforce the other prefixes and suffixes tested in Part A of this chapter.

For teaching:

unclean	reclaim
reclean	uncover
unborn	recover
reborn	undress
uncap	redress
recap	untouch
unclaim	retouch

For practice:

redone	unfair
undone	renew
recall	unjust
unbroken	repay
refresh	unplug
redo	unseen
relay	untrue

The weather announcer will repeat the report on our pleasant weather at six o'clock.

My dog will refuse to unclench his teeth and release the stick after I throw it.

Unlace and remove your shoes, unzip your coat, and relax until dinner is ready.

Unless we repair the old chair, it will be unsafe, and we will be unable to sit in it.

Please remind me to unload the washer after we return from the store.

Bob was feeling a little uncertain and very uneasy about trying out for the class play.

As a wind came up, they had to unwind the ropes and release the sails in order to return the boat to the dock.

It would be unwise to unfasten the ribbon and unwrap the present before the party.

You must review the story and rewrite this paper before I retest you.

As he began to unsaddle his horse and unpack the saddlebags, the sheriff said, "I regret having to lock you up, Sam, but I can't let you get revenge for your brother's death."

Listed below are some commonly used exercises that are also intended to assist students with prefixes and suffixes:

1. Have students underline all the affixes they can find in a newspaper article. Compile a list of the ones found. Discuss each affix and then compile a master list of all the different affixes found for a period of time.
2. Do the same thing as described in number 1 above, but furnish the students with lists of affixed words.
3. Give students one or more root words such as *do* and have a contest to see who can make the most variations of the word. For example:
   a. undo
   b. doing
   c. doer
   d. redo
4. Have each student make flash cards for any affixes with which he or she has trouble. On one side of the flash card write the affix and several words illustrating its use. On the other side of the card write a sentence using the affix on a word in a sentence.

Syllabication

Students who have learned to identify, separate, pronounce, and blend affixes in whole words will already have mastered the ability to decode most two- and three-syllable words, such as *payment* and *promotion*. The only words that will remain difficult for them are words that are not in their listening vocabularies (i.e., words that are not recognized by students when the teacher pronounces them) and unusually long or difficult words. There is nothing the teacher can do to assist students to decode words in the former category. Instruction must focus on methods of increasing the students' meaning vocabularies before students will be able to read words that they do not presently recognize. However, these six syllabication generalizations will help them to decode difficult words that they recognize when they hear them. Examples of long words for which the generalizations may apply are *decompression, craftsmanship, unreasonable,* and *composition.*

The six generalizations:

1. Look for prefixes and suffixes.
2. Look for a known base or root word.
3. Read to the end of the sentence. Think of a word with the parts you know that makes sense.
4. If necessary, try different divisions of the base word to form syllables.
5. Try different sounds, syllables, and accents until you form a word that makes sense.
6. If you still can't figure the word out, use a dictionary.

These guidelines are not perfect; however, experience leads us to conclude that they are the most helpful available generalizations. The first three are usually sufficient to unlock the unknown word. If the root word is difficult, as in *investigate,* the fourth and fifth steps probably represent the best guidelines. Here's why: Using the word *investigate,* we will assume that (1) the student will recognize it if he or she gets close enough with decoding skills; (2) the student has used step 1 and can pronounce *in* and *ate* or *gate;* steps 2 and 3 were not helpful and the student is stuck on the *vesti* or *vestig* part of the word. One traditional syllabication rule tells the student to divide between two consonants; however, another rule says not to divide between consonant blends. A third rule tells students to treat consonant blends as though they were a single letter and divide before the blend when the blend stands between two vowels. The student who is able to remember these rules and identify the consonant blend (both of which are doubtful under the circumstances) is likely to end up thoroughly confused and no closer to decoding *investigate.* In any case it does not matter, for the student may be able to decode the word if he or she divides it before the *s,* between the *s* and the *t,* or after the *t.* Incidentally, trying to decode the word by analyzing the vowel sounds will probably prove as frustrating for the student as trying to apply syllabication rules that do not work.

Thus, we provide steps 4 and 5, which tell the student to try different divisions of sounds, syllables, and accents in hopes of arriving at the proper pronunciation. These steps are similar to the one rule offered by Shirley Rosati (1973), who wryly suggested, "Either divide before or between consonants or don't."

When all else fails, there is step 6. If the teacher observes students following this step too often, either the students are not satisfactorily applying the previous steps or the material is too difficult for them.

The best way to teach the syllabication steps we have listed is first to model the use of the steps yourself while students observe. Select a few difficult words, put them in sentences, and demonstrate for students how to go through the steps one at a time to decode the unknown word in a sentence. Do this with enough words to go through the various steps and use a different number of steps each time to arrive at the pronunciation. Always go through the steps in order. You want to convince students that the first three steps are in order the most helpful. Reassure students that this system works and that with practice they will learn to read great big words with little difficulty. Of course, you must be sure that students have mastered the prerequisite skills of phonic analysis, basic sight word mastery, and mastery of prefixes, suffixes, and inflectional endings. The students must also have some ability to use context clues.

After you have demonstrated the syllabication strategy, provide students with sentences that they may use to apply the steps themselves; guide their work if necessary. It is a good idea to list the steps on a chart and have the students memorize the steps so that they will *use* them. If they are able to decode the words quickly, so much the better. If they are not, then you want them to use a systematic approach. For students who have severe difficulties with multisyllabic words, the strategy usually consists of one glance and panic. You will be showing them a concrete, systematic, and helpful approach to decoding these most challenging words.

Following your demonstration of the steps and the students' attempt to use the strategy with multisyllabic words in sentences, all that remains is for the students to apply the skills continually in the act of reading. You must persuade students at this level that they will need to read *a lot* for their new word-attack skills to become automatic.

You may use this list of sentences to teach and practice the syllabication steps. These are difficult sentences, since most contain more than one multisyllabic word. We recommend that if these prove too difficult for your students initially, then you prepare more sentences like the first and third.

The amplifier made the music louder.
The archaeologist studied the bones of the dinosaur and the other artifacts found near the caves.
Sara is a kind, compassionate person.
The twelve contributors contributed five hundred dollars to the charity.
That delicatessen has delicious potato salad.
After the explosion there was an evacuation of the building.
The horizontal lines on the television screen make it impossible to see the picture.
The intricate puzzle is very frustrating.
The hurricane did substantial damage to our neighborhood.
The barometric pressure is falling rapidly.

CONTEXT CLUES

Context clues are a very important word-attack skill as well as an important means of vocabulary development. Although today's basal-reader teacher's manuals usually thoroughly teach the use of this skill, many readers in the past were seldom given any instruction in the use of context clues. Even today many disabled readers have failed to learn to use context as a word-attack skill. Evidently teachers sometimes believe that the use of context is so obvious that students are likely to learn this skill with little or no instruction. This is simply not true. Many readers need a considerable amount of instruction and a great deal of practice in using this skill. Susanna Pflaum and Ernest Pascarella (1980) reported on a study that found that learning-disabled students whose initial instructional level was at or above grade two benefited significantly from instruction in the use of context clues. Eunice Askov and Karlyn Kamm (1976) found that students in grades three, four, and five who were taught a classification of context clues, such as cause-effect and direct description, demonstrated improved reading performance.

A study of considerable significance for remedial reading teachers was done by Margaret McKeown (1985). McKeown found that "low-ability" students (those who scored low on an achievement test) were less able to use context clues than abler readers:

> . . . Thus, even under what would appear to be optimal conditions, that is, the correct identification of constraints and availability of meaning choices, successful testing of a choice within constraints does not automatically occur, at least for children of lower ability. (p. 493)

McKeown found teacher modeling appropriate as a technique for helping low-ability students to improve their contextual skills:

> . . . A teacher could communicate important concepts of acquiring word meaning from context by demonstrating the use of context to derive contextual constraints, test candidates, compile information about the word's meaning, and eventually interpret subsequent contexts. (p. 494)

One of the first and most important techniques for teaching context clues is simply to talk with students about their use. Many disabled readers do not have any idea that a word can often be attacked by the use of the context. Some students apparently figure it out for themselves, but the disabled reader is often less adept at reaching these conclusions without some help.

The following general techniques will assist students in using context clues to decode unknown words:

1. Have students preread material silently before reading orally. Discuss troublesome vocabulary.
2. Set purposes for reading. Stress accuracy in reading, not speed.
3. Use short, easy selections. Have students stop frequently to explain what they have read in their own words.
4. Use high-interest material, including student-authored language-experience stories.
5. Encourage students to read *past* unknown words to the end of the sentence and then to come back. Research indicates that words that come after are often more helpful than those that come before unknown words.
6. Have students scan for important words. Have them guess the content and then read to see if the guess was accurate.
7. Encourage practice in the act of reading. There is no better technique for students to learn to read for meaning. Provide time, appropriate

materials, the proper setting, and encouragement for sustained silent reading.

Other ideas and exercises are listed below:

1. The tape recorder can be used to advantage in first making students aware of context clues in oral exercises. Note: Wait five seconds after reading each sentence. The script:
"I am going to read a short story. Once in a while I will leave out a word. Where a word is left out you will hear a beep sound. When you hear the beep, try to fill in the word that belongs there before I give the answer. Here is the story.
    "Once Jack and Jim were going to _____ fishing. (*go*)
First they dug _____ worms. (*some*) Then they took. . . . ''
2. Give students sentences with words left blank. For every blank give the student several choices of words that might belong in the blanks:
    2.1. Mary was _____ to visit her Uncle George.
        (*they - going - did - being*)
    2.2. Frank's dog did _____ like cats.
        (*that - give - not - be*)
3. Give students sentences such as those listed in number 2 but give only the first letter of the missing word:
    3.1. Mary was g_____ to visit her Uncle George.
    3.2. Frank's dog did n_____ like cats.
4. Give students sentences such as those listed in number 2 but do not give any clues as to what word or words might be used in the blanks. After students have completed the blanks, have each student read his or her sentence and hold a discussion about the appropriateness of the words chosen.
5. Use cloze passages where approximately every eighth to tenth word is omitted. Ask students to fill in the blanks. After students have completed the exercise, hold a discussion about what words were used in each blank. Research in the use of this technique has generally shown that this type of exercise has little value without the discussion that follows, so do not omit that part. An example of a cloze passage follows:
    5.1. George was going to visit _____ Grandpa and Grandma.
        He _____ going to go on an airplane. His father
        _____ with him to buy his ticket. The clerk _____
        the desk asked George _____ he wanted to. . . . , etc.

Context clues aid the student not only in word attack but also in comprehension. For this reason, additional suggestions for using the cloze procedure as a teaching technique (number 5 above) will be included in the next chapter.

A WORD-ATTACK STRATEGY

Thus far in this chapter we have described techniques and procedures for diagnosing and remediating the following word-analysis skills: phonics, structural analysis, and context clues. In the previous chapter, we discussed testing and teaching letter knowledge and sight words. If you have been successful in your instruction to this point, you have provided students with the necessary tools to decode. It is possible, however, for students to overrely on one or more of these skills or to apply the wrong skill in certain situations. Also, your students will need to learn to use their skills in situations where you will not be present to assist them. Therefore, you can help your students by teaching them a word-attack strategy. This strategy will assist students in incorporating the various decoding skills when they meet unfamiliar words in the act of reading.

The strategy consists of four simple steps, similar to those for syllabication; however, these are appropriate for readers in the earlier decoding stages. You may wish to present the following on a chart:

When you come to a word you don't know:
1. Say the beginning sound.
2. Read the rest of the sentence. THINK.
3. Say the parts that you know. GUESS.
4. Ask someone or skip it and go on.

These steps may appear obvious to the teacher; however, the remedial student frequently lacks a systematic approach to decoding and will likely benefit from applying the four steps. The first step—applying initial letter-sound associations—is the one most students will do automatically. We know from research and experience that beginning sounds are often the most helpful. The second step requires the student to use context clues *before* applying additional phonics or structural analysis. Most often the combination of initial letter sounds and context will result in correct identification of the unknown word. It seems reasonable to ask the student to use context clues before resorting to less helpful word-analysis techniques. Also, step 2 requires the student to read to the end of the sentence to take advantage of the context clues that may come after the unknown word.

If the student still has not decoded the word, step 3 is to apply other word-analysis clues, such as ending sounds, vowel sounds, and structural analysis. Depending on the level of instruction, the teacher may wish to be more specific at this step. The student is encouraged to guess, if necessary, so as not to spend too much time trying to decode a single unknown word. The last step encourages the student to ask for help or continue reading if all else fails. It is quite possible that context clues picked up in reading further will permit the student to identify the unknown word.

If students must resort to step 4 often, the student should be given easier material to read. Similarly, if the student encounters more than one unknown word in a single sentence, the strategy is likely to break down, indicating that the material is too difficult.

To teach the strategy to students, the teacher should follow the same steps outlined for teaching the syllabication generalizations presented in the previous section:

1. Present the steps, using a written chart that students can remember and refer to.
2. Model use of the steps yourself with sample sentences.
3. Reassure students that the strategy works.
4. Provide students with sentences that they may use to apply the steps as you provide guidance.
5. Insure that students use the steps as they practice in the act of reading.

At the end of this paragraph is a list of sentences that you may use to teach, and give students practice in, the four-step strategy. The numbers after each sentence indicate which steps are *likely* to assist students. It is not possible to determine exactly which steps will help students. Some students will recognize unknown words at sight. Others will use only one or two steps. Some may not succeed at all. The teacher will need to provide other examples for students based on their specific knowledge of the students' needs.

1. The *light* is red. (1, 2)
2. I will *take* you there. (1, 2)
3. I cannot *remember* your name. (1, 2, 3)
4. I like *chocolate* cake. (1, 2, 3)
5. The *cat* is my pet. (1, 2)
6. The *hamster* is my pet. (1, 2, 3)
7. The *armadillo* is my pet. (1, 2, 3, 4?)

EFFICIENCY SKILLS

In Part A of this chapter we pointed out that some students master decoding skills but fail to read efficiently. They may possess faulty reading habits, such as inappropriate reading rate, inaccurate reading, improper phrasing or expression, inability to recognize punctuation, lip movements, finger pointing, and head movements. This section contains a number of general suggestions as well as specific procedures for remediating these difficulties.

General Suggestions
1. Make sure the decoding skills of basic sight vocabulary, phonics, structural analysis and contextual analysis have been mastered. If not, provide remedial instruction in these areas.

2. Take time to discuss with students the specific nature of their efficiency skill problems and suggest general approaches to solving them. It is often helpful to tape record the student while he or she is reading orally, then play back the recording so the student can become aware of the specific problem.
3. Do not expect students to read material above their meaning-vocabulary level. Generally use *easy* materials, which encourage students to read in great quantity.
4. Encourage wide reading from a *variety* of materials. In addition to the necessary practice this provides, students can be directed to read different types of materials at different speeds and for different purposes, such as pleasure, information, instruction, and so forth.

For problems with reading rate, accuracy, phrasing, or expression we recommend that teachers use a variety of oral reading methods, not because oral reading is the goal, but because it often helps students to identify and correct specific reading difficulties. Oral reading is most effective if it is done in a one-to-one fashion or with very small groups so that students participate as much as possible. In using these methods, it is important for the teacher to stress to students that oral reading is only one way of reading and that this practice will ultimately lead the student to greater ability in silent reading. Also, oral reading practice is not substituted for silent reading. Rather, it is presented to give students additional experience with the printed word.

Betty Anderson (1981), Claire Ashby-Davis (1981), and Albert Harris (1981) among others have described three different oral reading techniques and reviewed the evidence that supports their use. These techniques are (1) the neurological impress method, (2) echo reading or imitative reading, and (3) repeated readings.

The neurological impress method (NIM) was developed by R.G. Heckelman, who first described its value in 1966. The method, which has some variations, generally consists of having the student and teacher (or other adult) read the same material out loud at the same time. Initially the instructor reads slightly louder and faster than the student. The instructor points to the words as they are read and directs his or her voice into the student's ear. Sentences or passages may be reread to achieve fluency. A variation we have found to be particularly effective is for the instructor to use easy material and read slightly behind the student. In this case the teacher's voice is like an instant echo of the student's, serving to reinforce the student's word recognition. (This is not to be confused with echo reading, which will be described presently.) When using this variation of NIM, the instructor can usually anticipate which words a student will miss in a particular selection and pronounce these ahead of the student to minimize the student's failure and discouragement.

When using NIM, specific correction is seldom if ever offered, nor is questioning or testing of the content. As the student's ability improves, he or she may take over the finger movements and more challenging materials may be read. Advocates of NIM recommend that it be used for up to fifteen minutes daily for a total time of eight to twelve hours. Usually students show progress after only a few sessions; the method should be discontinued after four hours if the student fails to respond positively.

In echo reading the instructor reads first and the student repeats what the instructor read. Material can be read in either phrases or sentences, and finger pointing is used in this method also. A common variation uses recorded texts; students first listen straight through while following the written text and then read along with the recording. An advantage of this method is that an instructor need not be present. On the other hand, this variation lacks the immediacy and psychological force of the teacher's presence. At present there are a number of high-interest, low-vocabulary read-along materials available in varying formats with accompanying records, tapes, or slides. Students seem to enjoy these, and if used properly, they can be beneficial. The teacher must be sure that students *can* read the materials and that they stay on task and *do* read when they are supposed to.

Repeated readings is a method suggested by S. J. Samuels (1979), Lopardo and Sadow (1982), and Cunningham (1979). Students are given selections that consist of 50 to 200 words. The student is instructed to practice the selections and then is timed, after which reading rate and number of errors are recorded on a chart. While the teacher is checking other students, the student rereads the material along with a recording of the text. The rereading may be done over and over. When the student feels ready, another test is given. When the student achieves a rate of eighty-five words per minute, another selection is provided. Comprehension checks may also take place. Graphing the student's results serves as a positive motivator for continued progress.

We believe that the repeated-readings method is excellent, but we would add one caution. Our experience has led us to conclude that a primary cause of efficiency or fluency difficulties is that remedial students often try to read too fast. For most students (excepting overanalytical readers) it is helpful first to encourage them to read accurately and then work to improve their speed. This is analogous to learning to play the guitar. Initially the budding musician should concentrate on picking the notes cleanly. Speed will come later.

To this end we have developed a technique we call precision reading, which has been used successfully at the California State University, Hayward Reading Clinic. This adaptation of other fluency techniques emphasizes first accuracy, then speed. While the student reads, the evaluator (the teacher, another adult, or another student) records the student's accuracy sentence by sentence. A form is prepared to record the student's reading efficiency. The form has spaces to indicate the beginning and ending page numbers of the material read, the total number of *sentences* read, the number of sentences read perfectly, and the number of sentences read with one or more errors. At the beginning the student is given relatively easy material and reads a set number of sentences, such as twenty-five. The evaluator records the student's accuracy on each sentence, so that on completion a fraction of correct sentences out of the total is derived; for example, 20/25. This indicates that the student read twenty sentences perfectly and made one or more errors on five of the sentences. The fraction is then changed to a percentage—in this case, 80 percent accuracy—and the percentage figure is graphed daily. The students enjoy seeing their performance graphed, and this serves as a powerful motivator for continued progress. It is important to select material where the accuracy rate is unlikely to drop below 75 percent. Also, the teacher may select different material for the student to read each day. However, it is helpful if the passage is chosen at least one day in advance so that the student can begin practicing the material in advance as part of his or her homework. As the student improves and begins to read consistently at or near 100 percent accuracy, the teacher may provide more difficult material or add the factor of speed. To do the latter, you may have the student read as many sentences as possible within a prescribed time, as long as the accuracy rate does not drop below, say, 90 percent. Then the number of sentences read perfectly is graphed daily.

Other authors and researchers have reported positive results with repeated readings. Miriam Martinez and Nancy Roser (1985) found that students' responses to children's stories improved with repeated readings. They stated that reading a variety of books should remain a priority with children; however, they also found that repetition of literature created more divergent responses and helped provide an opportunity the better to appreciate books as "old friends." On the other hand, Carol A. Rashotte and Joseph K. Torgesen (1985) found that if speed was the only aspect of a student's reading you wish to improve, repeated reading was no better than reading new material each time.

Oral reading for meaning has been suggested by Barbara M. Taylor and Linda Nosbush (1985) as a technique for improving students' word identification skills. They suggest a four-step procedure. First the teacher works with a student for ten to fifteen minutes. During this time the student is asked to read 100 to 300 words and the teacher records any miscues. The student should be interrupted as little as possible. In the second step the student is given praise for positive aspects of his or her oral reading. Taylor and Nosbush note that the student should especially be praised for any self-corrected errors. The third step is a discussion of various miscues made by the student. This could include a discussion of how substitutions can change the meaning of a sentence and how to monitor these substitutions using context as well as by giving more attention to word endings, etc. The fourth step is on-the-spot instruction for specific word-attack deficiencies. For example, a student who read "know" for "now" might be given instruction on the two most common sounds represented by *ow*.

Additional suggestions for oral reading activities:

1. The teacher and student take turns reading the material out loud by alternating paragraphs, sentences, or lines.
2. The student prereads silently first, notes difficult vocabulary, and re-

views the vocabulary with the teacher; then the student and teacher read together.

3. The teacher provides choral reading activities for small groups of students.

4. The teacher provides plays for students to read. A number of kits are available with simple two-, three-, or four-person plays; or teachers and students write their own plays.

5. Many students enjoy relaxed paired reading. A student and a friend select two copies of a good book and then take turns reading it out loud together.

6. Younger students read selections using puppets.

7. Older students enjoy participating in reader's theater activities.

8. The teacher may provide a reinforcer, such as clicking a counter or putting a chip in a bank, each time the student reads a sentence perfectly.

9. The teacher may use favorite games such as tic-tac-toe, hangman, and dots to score reading accuracy. For example, a student reads while the other draws part of the hangman if the student who is reading makes an error. (Numbers 8 and 9 are variations of the precision-reading method described above.)

10. The use of controlled readers or reading pacers is *not* recommended unless great care is taken to guard against the frustration likely to occur if the student is unable to keep up with the machine.

The audio tape recorder may also serve as an excellent device for students to practice oral reading. The teacher might set up a "recording studio" in the classroom. In addition to the tape recorder the teacher will need a microphone and cassette tapes for the students. If possible, provide a cassette for each student. The cassettes may be hung on a pegboard for easy access. The tape recorder may be used for commercially prepared read-along materials. The following activities may also be provided:

1. The student reads orally into the tape recorder, plays back the tape, and
   a. listens to the recording noting errors; or
   b. reads along silently; or
   c. reads along orally.

2. The teacher or another person reads a selection into the tape recorder and the student plays it back as above. The teacher may make purposeful errors or exhibit poor efficiency skills, such as inadequate phrasing, excessive speed, ignoring punctuation, etc. The student evaluates the teacher's performance and tries to apply this to his or her own reading.

3. Two or more students read into a tape recorder together, using some of the above techniques.

4. The student uses the Language Master® or equivalent machine to practice phrase or sentence reading. (For a description of the Language Master®, see Chapter 4, "The Use of the Tape Recorder.")

The following procedures may be used with students who are having difficulty with phrasing.

1. Have students practice reading phrase flash cards. Dolch phrases are commercially available, or you may make your own (see Chapter 4). Chart the students' progress.
2. Use tachistoscopic devices with phrases.
3. Type up material with words separated in phrase units. Have the student practice reading this out loud.
4. Use vertical marks to indicate the phrases in written material. Phrases may be divided at any appropriate place.
5. Use other oral reading techniques noted above.

Students who habitually ignore punctuation are bound to have difficulties in reading efficiently. The teacher should not assume that students have been taught the function of common punctuation marks. You may use the tape recorder to help the student become aware of the problem and then teach the uses of the period, comma, question mark, quotation marks, apostrophe, and colon. Some specific suggestions:

1. Prepare a paragraph with no punctuation marks. Have the student try to read it. Then you and the student together punctuate and read the selection.
2. Use short written paragraphs to demonstrate how punctuation affects the pitch and stress of your voice. Have the student repeat and then reread the paragraphs.
3. Use guides—three counts for periods, two for commas.
4. Use an overhead projector with paragraphs without punctuation. Together fill in appropriate marks and read.
5. Dictate simple paragraphs. The student provides the punctuation, in part by the inflections of your voice.
6. Use the language-experience approach and leave out all punctuation marks from the student's dictated story. Then have the student fill them in.
7. Provide cards with words or phrases and cards with punctuation marks. Have the student arrange them properly.

There are a number of silent-reading difficulties that reflect poor efficiency skills. These include lip movements, finger pointing, head movements, and skipping unfamiliar words. Procedures for remediating these difficulties follow:

1. Lip movements
   a. Have the student place a finger against his or her lips when reading silently.
   b. Have the student place a small piece of paper between his or her lips when reading silently.
   c. Temporarily reduce the amount of oral reading.
   d. Discuss with the student the importance of forming mental pictures when reading. Explain that it is not necessary to say each word.
2. Finger pointing
   a. Have the student's eyes checked if you suspect a vision problem.
   b. Have the student use a marker *temporarily.*
   c. Provide practice in phrase reading.
   d. Provide practice in reading from charts and the chalkboard, where finger pointing is impossible.
   e. Have the student use both hands to hold the book.
   f. Use material with large, clear print.
3. Head movements
   a. Have the student place elbows on the table and index fingers against his or her temples.
   b. Demonstrate how to use the eyes to scan a page while the head remains stationary.
4. Skipping unfamiliar words
   a. Have the student read orally first, then silently.
   b. Increase vocabulary instruction before silent reading.
   c. Use easier material.
   d. Deemphasize speed. Stress the importance of reading each word accurately.
   e. Make sure the student has mastered the basic decoding skills.
   f. Teach word-attack strategy.
   g. Teach the student how to use the glossary and dictionary in emergencies.

CONFIGURATION CLUES

Although the use of configuration clues is an important skill in word analysis, there is little concrete information on effective ways of teaching students to become more aware of it. Most research shows that traditional methods are of little value. For example, many textbooks on reading have suggested that lines be drawn around words printed in lower case to show contrasting shapes as in the words what and when. However, research by Gabrielle Marchbanks and Harry Levin (1965), as well as others, has shown that in practice this technique has very little value. The problem probably lies in the fact that so many words have exactly the same shape when outlined. If this technique has any value at all, it is probably for the student who constantly confuses two somewhat similar words. This technique might then be used to emphasize slight differences in the configuration of those two words only.

We also know that words printed in lower case tend to be easier to read than words printed in upper case, when the lower half of the word is masked. Thus, it seems that using the lower-case alphabet in beginning reading would be more effective. However, the research does not support even this argument. It does not seem to make any difference in students' overall reading achievement whether they are instructed in lower case, upper case, or as is normally done, by combining the two.

Occasionally a student has considerable difficulty with words such as *though, through,* and *thought.* Where this is the case, point out differences such as the "t" sound and the *t* letter at the end of *thought* and the *r* in *through.* You also improve students' ability to note configuration in teaching word families—phonograms—such as *all* and *ate.* Generally speaking, however, unless a student is confusing two similar words such as *county* and *country,* you should probably spend your time on more effective methods of word attack than configuration clues.

DICTIONARY SKILLS

As stated in Part A of this chapter, students do not become seriously disabled readers from a lack of knowledge of dictionary skills. This is not to belittle the importance of thoroughly learning the use of the dictionary. However, from the standpoint of economy of time the remedial reading teacher will probably spend most of his or her time in remediating problems that have a more immediate effect on most students' reading.

There are numerous filmstrips, workbooks, etc., that effectively cover the teaching of dictionary skills. Because of these factors, we have not included discussion of the teaching of the dictionary skills. A list of sources for teaching the dictionary skills is shown in Appendix C.

SUMMARY

For the teacher who has no experience in the testing of word-attack skills the problem of assessing students' knowledge in this area may seem quite simple. The experienced diagnostician, who is familiar with an array of tests in this area, will know that there are many different ways of testing word-attack skills. Research has shown that although the correlations between any two of these tests may be rather high, you are not likely to obtain item-by-item agreement on particular skills or phonemes when using one test as contrasted with another. If the remedial reading teacher is to do exact diagnostic teaching on the basis of test results, it will be necessary to examine the type of test to be used to make sure it tests students' word-attack skills in a situation comparable to the act of reading.

A number of tests that contain subtests for word-attack skills have been discussed in this chapter. The beginning teacher and even the experienced diagnostician would do well to familiarize themselves with a number of these tests. In many cases it is better to use a combination of subtests from several different test batteries. In many cases you can construct testing materials as good as, and in many cases more appropriate than, some commercial materials.

Part B of this chapter contains a thorough description of procedures for teaching and reinforcing each of the word-attack skills.

REFERENCES

Anderson, B. (1981). The missing ingredient: Fluent oral reading. *Elementary School Journal, 81,* 173–177.

Ashby-Davis, C. (1981). A review of three techniques for use with remedial readers. *Reading Teacher, 34,* 534–538.

Askov, E. N., & Kamm, K. (1976). Context clues: Should we teach children to use a classification system in reading? *Journal of Educational Research, 69,* 341–344.

Botel, M. (1978). *Botel reading inventory.* Chicago: Follett.

Burmeister, L. (1968). Vowel pairs. *Reading Teacher, 21,* 445–542.

Burns, P. C., & Schell, L. M. (1975). Instructional strategies for teaching usage of context clues. *Reading World, 15,* 89–96.

Cunningham, J. W. (1979). An automatic pilot for decoding. *Reading Teacher, 32,* 420–424.

Durrell, D. D., & Catterson, J. H. (1980). *Durrell analysis of reading difficulty* (3rd ed.). New York: Psychological Corporation.

Ehri, L. C., & Wilce, L. S. (1983). Development of word identification speed in skilled and less skilled beginning readers. *Journal of Educational Psychology, 75,* 3–18.

Ehri, L. C., & Wilce, L. S. (1985). Movement into reading: Is the first stage of printed word learning visual or phonetic? *Reading Research Quarterly, 20,* 163–169.

Ekwall, E. E. (1973). *An analysis of children's test scores when tested with individually administered diagnostic tests and when tested with group administration tests,* Final research report, University of Texas at El Paso.

Ekwall, E. E. (1986). *Ekwall reading inventory* (2nd ed.). Newton, MA: Allyn and Bacon.

Ekwall, E. E., & Oswald, L. D. (1971). *Rx reading program.* Glenview, IL: Psychotechnics.

Ekwall, E. E. (1986). *Teacher's handbook on diagnosis and remediation in reading* (2nd ed.). Newton, MA: Allyn & Bacon.

Gates, A. I., McKillop, A. S., & Horowitz, E. C. (1981). *Gates-McKillop-Horowitz reading diagnostic tests* (2nd ed.). New York: Teachers College Press.

Groff, P. (1981). Teaching reading by syllables. *Reading Teacher, 34,* 659–664.

Hanna, P. R., Hanna, J. S., Holdges, R. G., & Rudorf, E. H., Jr. (1966). *Phoneme-grapheme correspondence as cues to spelling improvement.* Washington, DC: Office of Education, United States Department of Health, Education, and Welfare.

Harris, A. J. (1981). What is new in remedial reading? *Reading Teacher, 34,* 405–410.

Harris, A. J., & Sipay, E. R. (1985). *How to increase reading ability* (8th ed.). New York: Longman.

Heckelman, R. G. (1966). Using the neurological impress remedial technique. *Academic Therapy Quarterly, 1,* 235–239.

Hislop, M. J., & King, E. M. (1973). Application of phonic generalizations by beginning readers. *Journal of Educational Research, 56,* 405–412.

Homen, W. J. (1977). *Predicting first grade reading success with a test in letter-sounds and synthesis.* Master's thesis, California State University, Hayward.

Karlsen, B., Madden, R., & Gardner, E. F. (1976). *Stanford diagnostic reading test.* New York: Harcourt Brace Jovanovich.

Kochnower, J., Richardson, E., & DiBenedetto, B. (1983). A comparison of the phonic decoding ability of normal and learning disabled children. *Journal of Learning Disabled, 16,* 348–351.

Lopardo, G., & Sadow, M. W. (1982). Criteria and procedures for the method of repeated readings. *Journal of Reading, 26,* 156–160.

Lips, S. (1985). Test review: Diagnostic reading scales. *Reading Teacher, 38,* 664–667.

Marchbanks, G., & Levin, H. (1965). Cues by which children recognize words. *Journal of Educational Psychology, 56,* 57–61.

Martinez, M., & Roser, N. (1985). Read it again: The value of repeated readings during storytime. *Reading Teacher, 38,* 782–786.

McKeown, M. G. (1985). The acquisition of word meaning from context by children of high and low ability. *Reading Research Quarterly, 20,* 482–496.

Pflaum, S. W., & Pascarella, E. T. (1980). Interactive effects of prior reading achievement and training in context on the reading of learning-disabled children. *Reading Research Quarterly, 16,* 138–158.

Rashotte, C. A., & Torgesen, J. K. (1985). Repeated reading and reading fluency in learning disabled children. *Reading Research Quarterly, 20,* 180–188.

Robinson, H. A. (1963). A study of the techniques of word identification. *Reading Teacher, 16,* 238–242.

Rosati, S. (1973). Emancipate syllabication. *Reading Teacher, 26,* 397–398.

Samuels, S. J. (1979). The method of repeated readings. *Reading Teacher, 32,* 403–406.

Sipay, E. R. (1974). *Sipay word analysis tests.* Cambridge, MA: Educators Publishing Service.

Spache, G. D. (1981). *Diagnostic reading scales.* Monterey, CA: Hill.

Stauffer, R. G. (1969). *Teaching reading as a thinking process.* New York: Harper & Row.

Strang, R., McCullough, C. M., & Traxler, A. E. (1967). *The improvement of reading* (4th ed.). New York: McGraw-Hill.

Taylor, B. M., & Nosbush, L. (1985). Oral reading for meaning: A technique for improving word identification skills. *Reading Teacher, 37,* 234–237.

Whaley, J. W. (1975). Closing the blending gap. *Reading World, 15,* 97–100.

Whaley, J. W., & Kibby, M. W. (1980). Word synthesis and beginning reading achievement. *Journal of Educational Research, 73,* 132–138.

Winkley, C. (1966). Which accent generalizations are worth teaching. *Reading Teacher, 20,* 219–224.

Woodcock, R. W. (1973). *Woodcock reading mastery tests.* Circle Pines, MN: American Guidance Service.

Diagnosis and Remediation of Educational Factors: *Comprehension, Vocabulary Development, and Study Skills*

One purpose of this chapter is to discuss methods as well as limitations of diagnosing students' reading comprehension and vocabulary development. The first section contains a general description of commonly used methods of diagnosing general comprehension and vocabulary development. Following this general section are specific suggestions for diagnosing difficulties with comprehension. Another purpose of this chapter is to identify methods of diagnosing study skills that are likely to contribute to students' failure in school. The last purpose of Chapter 6 is to discuss some practical methods for dealing with students who are disabled in these areas.

Part A: DIAGNOSIS

OUR CHANGING VIEW OF READING COMPREHENSION

During the past decade there has been a renaissance in the study of comprehension. As a result of this renewed interest there have also emerged a number of concrete procedures that if used by the classroom teacher can greatly improve on previous methods of teaching reading comprehension. According to P. David Pearson (1985), who has written extensively on the subject of reading comprehension:

> There can be no doubt that children's reading comprehension performance concerns educators at all three levels today. More than ever before, we are devoting more intellectual and emotional energy to helping students better understand the texts we require them to read in our schools. (p. 724)

Pearson believes that one of the reasons we have made considerable strides in teaching reading comprehension is the efforts of researchers and writers in the field of cognitive psychology. We agree with Pearson; researchers have learned more about the teaching of reading comprehension in the past four or five years than in the past four or five *hundred* years.

Of the new information in *how* to teach reading comprehension, the methods classified under the name of metacognitive techniques have the most to offer. Other procedures, rarely mentioned or unheard of a decade or more ago, include semantic mapping or semantic webbing and various procedures referred to as schema theory. Following the section on methods of diagnosis for general comprehension level we will discuss each technique and illustrate how they can be implemented.

THE NATURE OF COMPREHENSION

Over the years reading-methods textbooks and basal reader teacher's manuals have often listed a host of different comprehension skills that students should supposedly master during their progression through the grades. Some skills commonly listed: noting and grasping details, main ideas, and the author's purpose; underlining or noting key words; making generalizations; and predicting outcomes. As mentioned in Chapter 3, however, research in reading comprehension does not support the theory that these skills actually exist as separate entities. A statistical technique that is often used to locate or measure separate variables is factor analysis. If separate comprehension abilities actually exist, then through factor analysis one should be able to identify each of these separate factors. Once these factors are located and identified, one can devise tests over each factor or skill and administer them to groups of students. If the factors are measurable entities, one would expect to obtain rather low correlations among them. That is, one would expect students to exhibit strengths in some factors and weaknesses in others. For example, musical ability and mathematical ability are not highly related. If tests were given to ten students measuring their abilities in each area, quite likely there would be little relationship between the two. In other words, some students who were extremely talented in music might do quite poorly in math and vice versa. This would produce a low correlation. One would obtain a high correlation if all óf the students who were talented in music were also talented in mathematics and if all of the students who did poorly in music also did poorly in mathematics.

According to George Spache (1981*a*):

> . . . No factor analysis of reading tests has yet shown that different types of thinking are really assessed by [the] various types of questions. The components of the reading act appear to be vocabulary difficulty, relationships among ideas, and inductive and deductive reasoning, not the types of ideas identified by labeling questions such as main ideas, details, conclusions, inferences, and the like. (p. 209)

Michael Strange (1980) describes the present debate among experts as a disagreement about whether reading comprehension is a bottom-up or top-down process. Proponents of the bottom-up or text-driven position argue that "the page brings more information to the reader than the reader brings to the page." (p. 392) Those who believe in the top-down or concept-driven model take the other point of view: "When someone is reading s/he has a good deal of prior knowledge about the world and this prior knowledge is used to make good guesses about the nature (relationships, episodes, characters, etc.) of the text." (p. 392) Strange suggests that a third conceptualization, an interactive model, properly describes the process as both concept- and text-driven, wherein the reader and the text work together to elicit meaning.

An additional concept known as *schema theory* is also being explored. Studies have shown that individuals' presuppositions, or "schemata," about a passage can have a strong influence on comprehension. Indeed, some readers may not accept text information that conflicts with their presuppositions. Schema theory is related to the top-down or concept-driven model, although the assumption is made that schemata are adaptable or changeable. Tom Nicholson and Robert Imlach (1981) studied the inferences children make when answering questions about narrative stories and found that text data competed with background knowledge for priority in question answering. The results tended to provide more support for a text-driven or bottom-up view, however. A crosscultural study conducted by Margaret Steffensen, Chitra Joag-Dev, and Richard Anderson (1979) was interpreted as showing opposite results, favoring the influence of prior knowledge of the content on comprehension. In this study, subjects from the United States and India read letters and answered questions about an American and an Indian wedding. The subjects read the native passage more rapidly and with better comprehension. The researchers concluded that the reader's schemata greatly influenced their understanding of the written material.

Teachers can expect to see more conflicting results from research as concepts and research methods continue to develop in this complex field. While a clear direction for the diagnostician has not yet emerged, the continued interest in comprehension research should eventually help all teachers to understand this most essential component of the reading act.

From a testing standpoint, based on what we know about comprehension at this time, it does not seem justified to attempt to diagnose a student's comprehension abilities beyond separating them into one category of word or vocabulary knowledge and another category of other comprehension in general.

METHODS OF DIAGNOSIS FOR GENERAL COMPREHENSION LEVEL

Traditional methods of diagnosing students' level of comprehension can be divided into five main categories: group standardized tests, individual standardized tests, informal reading inventories, informal recall procedures, and the cloze procedure. The cloze procedure is somewhat newer than the other four. A sixth method, deep structure, or the analysis of sentence meaning from its structure, has been used somewhat in the development of standardized tests.

Group Standardized Achievement and Diagnostic Tests

The use of standardized tests is by far the most common method for diagnosis in group situations. Although they have some major disadvantages, standardized tests do have several advantages that make them popular. One is that they are quite efficient in terms of teacher time. Also, you can compare the performance of a group of students with that of other students. As we have said in earlier chapters, one criterion for any reading test is that it should measure reading skills in a situation that is analogous to actually reading. Although it is nearly impossible to do this with group tests of word-attack or word-recognition skills, it does appear feasible to test reading comprehension with groups of students, since this can be done in a situation nearly analogous to actually reading. Another often-claimed advantage of group standardized tests is that they are written by "experts." On the other hand, a number of critics have pointed out that certain standardized tests, although well known and much used, contain many questions that tend to make them of dubious value.

Most group standardized tests do not attempt to classify various subskills of general reading comprehension beyond one category, vocabulary knowledge, and another usually referred to as comprehension. This is somewhat confusing, since vocabulary knowledge itself is such an important factor in general reading comprehension. It is important to emphasize that when test writers purport to measure vocabulary *and* comprehension, what they really mean is vocabulary knowledge and *other* comprehension skills. Both of their categories collectively measure general comprehension, or what has been referred to in the scope of the reading skills in Chapter 3 as recognizing and understanding ideas.

As mentioned above, most group standardized tests do not attempt to categorize the subskills of vocabulary and comprehension. The *Stanford Diagnostic Reading Test* (Karlsen, Madden, and Gardner, 1976) does, however, break reading comprehension down into two categories called "literal" and "inferential." The authors have provided norms for each of these two subcategories. However, because of the fill-in format of items it is difficult to believe that they can accurately measure these categories. A separate subtest for vocabulary is also provided. Within the category of comprehension most test authors have tried to devise questions that measure the student's ability to make inferences, remember important details, understand the author's purpose, see a sequence of events, etc. A careful reading of the questions on some of even the best-known group standardized tests often disenchants the well-trained reading specialist. For example, in reading the passages and then reading the questions pertaining to these passages it soon becomes obvious that some generalizations the student is expected to make cannot possibly be made from the information presented in the material itself. Success with a particular question of this nature may depend entirely on the student's background of experiences. For more information on this and other problems with group standardized tests, consult the article by Howard F. Livingston (1972) entitled, "What the Reading Test Doesn't Test—Reading." In that article Livingston discusses in much more detail some of the problems with group standardized tests.

Nearly all group standardized tests lump the various types of questions mentioned above into a broad category, comprehension, from which you get only a grade-level score.

One of the disadvantages of group standardized tests is that they do not allow the teacher to check on total recall in most cases, since the student is usually able to look back over the material and find answers to the questions at the end of the reading passage. However, the most serious problem encountered with group standardized tests, as far as disabled readers are concerned, is that students can often simply guess at all answers and yet make a somewhat respectable score. To illustrate this problem, we have often given to students who are beginning their first course in reading the machine-scorable answer sheet for the intermediate battery (grades four to six) of a nationally known reading test. We instructed them to mark their answers at random. In this case they do not even see the test questions. This is similar to a situation in which every student is a complete nonreader. When all answers are marked, the class members grade their own papers and their grade-level scores are computed. Invariably the class average is 3.2 to 3.5, with individual subtest scores ranging as high as 6.5. You see the futility of attempting to derive any meaningful grade-level scores for extremely disabled readers. Perhaps a good rule in interpreting individuals' test scores on group standardized tests is to ignore any score at or below what could be achieved by chance.

In summary look at some ways group standardized tests may be useful and some ways they should not be used. Some ways they may be used:

1. To measure the achievement of a group from the beginning to the end of a remedial period. However, even then you must keep in mind that for students who cannot read at all, or for those who are severely disabled, you are not likely to obtain an accurate beginning measurement, and thus the full extent of student gains will not be shown.
2. To measure overall class or group weaknesses in certain areas, e.g., general vocabulary, study skills, or social science vocabulary. This should in turn point to specific areas for upgrading the instructional program. This may, however, have little relevance for the remedial program.
3. To look at the specific types of questions that any one student or small group of students are missing.
4. To initiate a beginning point in the diagnosis of individuals.

Some ways group standardized tests should not be used:

1. For grade placement of disabled readers or in making any major decision concerning the welfare of a single student based on a grade-placement score.
2. For judgment of the amount of gain in overall reading ability, for a single student, from the beginning to the end of an instructional period.

In summary, you should use a great deal of caution in interpreting the results of group standardized tests before making judgments concerning individual students unless you are simply examining the types of questions on which a student was and was not successful or unless the tests serve as a beginning point for a more thorough diagnosis.

Appendix B lists some commonly used group standardized reading tests, the grade levels for which they are appropriate, and the skills that each test purports to measure.

Individual Standardized Reading Tests

Individual standardized reading tests have been popular with reading specialists for many years. They have the disadvantage of being more time consuming to administer, but while administering the test the teacher has the distinct advantage of being able to observe various characteristics displayed by the reader. Individual standardized tests are also available for measuring oral as well as silent reading. This is also an advantage over group standardized tests, which, of course, are limited to the measurement of students' *silent* reading ability.

The *Durrell Analysis of Reading Difficulty* (Durrell and Catterson, 1980), which is well known among reading specialists, contains subtests for both oral and silent reading. In the oral reading subtest the student reads a series of graded passages. After each passage the student answers literal comprehension questions about what was read. Norms for oral reading are based primarily on reading speed and only secondarily on comprehension ability. These norms are intended to provide an estimate of the child's instructional reading level. In the silent-reading passages the student is merely told to read the passage and try to remember what was read. The score sheet or record booklet contains an exact reproduction of each passage, phrase by phrase or idea by idea. After reading the passage the student tells all he or she can remember about the story. The examiner records the unaided memories on the score sheet. The student is later asked specific questions about memories that were not voluntarily recalled. These memories are also recorded but are not included in determining the norm scored. Norms are based on time of reading and the amount of recall and are intended to provide an estimate of the student's independent reading level. Suggestions are also given for evaluating students' imagery in silent reading; however, the term is not carefully defined, and the examiner is given neither criteria for measurement nor directions for diagnostic application.

Leo Schell and Robert Jennings (1981) have criticized a number of aspects of the Durrell inventory. They believe that comprehension would be better measured using traditional examiner-asked questions. Durrell and Catterson, the authors of the Durrell inventory, stress the importance of observing and recording students' strengths and weaknesses.

The *Diagnostic Reading Scales* (revised 1981 edition) by George D. Spache (1981*b*) is another well-known individual standardized reading test. The DRS contains a special bound test book or student reading book, an examiner's manual and a consumable examiner's record book. Three sets of word-recognition lists are used for placing students for further testing of oral and silent reading to determine three reading levels for each student: an instructional level, an independent level, and a potential level. Spache defines the instructional level as a measure of oral reading and comprehension that indicates appropriate basal-reader placement. The independent level is defined as a measure of silent reading ability and is said to designate the highest level for supplemental instruction or recreational reading. The potential level is a measure of auditory comprehension that suggests the upper limit of a student's present capability. Spache's use of the terms *instructional level* and *independent level* is quite different from that of most experts in the field and in contrast with the standards of traditional informal reading inventories (IRIs) (see the next section). Normally we expect that students' independent levels will be lower than their instructional levels. With Spache's test the opposite is usually the case. Although Spache offers justification for his approach, most test reviewers and practitioners have found that the DRS inflates students' scores relative to other measures and typical basal-reader placements.

The DRS contains two sets of reading passages (a total of 22 selections) ranging from grade level 1.4 to 7.5. This is in contrast to some of the commercially published IRIs, which contain four sets of comparable passages at each grade level for ease and flexibility of administration. The Durrell battery contains one set each for oral and silent reading. Since Spache's passages are used for oral, silent, and potential-level reading assessment, the examiner may find that the DRS, like the Durrell battery, contains an insufficient number of passages for pre- and posttest evaluation. Although Spache (1981*a*) claims, "I have added a third series of parallel, equated reading selections in the latest revision to meet this situation" (p. 211), no third set of passages can be found in the new edition of the DRS.

In spite of this and other criticisms, the DRS has been widely used and can be an effective instrument for observing and evaluating individual students' comprehension strengths and weaknesses, if not their reading grade placement.

Another standardized test is the *Gilmore Oral Reading Test* (Gilmore and Gilmore, 1968). It contains a subtest for oral reading comprehension, and the norms provide for interpretation in terms of grade-level score, a stanine score, and a general rating for the actual grade level of the student being tested. The general rating is "poor," "below average," "average," or "superior." The student is told to read carefully because he or she will be asked some questions about each story after it is read. For each paragraph there are five questions designed to test the student's ability to comprehend beyond the recall level. The authors present some guidance in interpreting the answers.

This type of test can be very useful, especially for the beginning reading diagnostician, since it provides norms and gives other criteria by which to judge a student's reading. The norm group was also fairly large for a test of this nature. Gilmore and Gilmore report that the performance ratings for their scores were based on a distribution of scores of 4455 pupils from six school systems in various locations throughout the United States.

Certain individual diagnostic tests, although standardized for certain subtests, do not contain norms or standardized information for grading either silent or oral reading comprehension. Although Durrell and Catterson present comprehension norms for their silent reading subtest in the *Durrell Analysis of Reading Difficulty,* no comprehension norms are presented for the oral reading subtest. For that subtest, norms are based essentially on time. The *Gray Oral Reading Tests* (Gray, 1967) also provide questions to be asked of students after reading each passage. Again, however, the norms are based on time and number of errors; comprehension was not considered in the norming.

Informal Reading Inventories

Informal reading inventories (IRIs) as a measure of students' comprehension abilities have become quite popular during the past twenty years and especially the past decade. Part of the reason for this is that there are now many more well-qualified reading specialists than formerly. Another is increased mistrust of group standardized test results, which at one time were more or less the standard by which reading was judged.

Informal reading inventories are usually constructed from materials that students will be expected to use in the course of their normal instruction, or they are written at specific grade levels using one of the better-known readability formulas as the criterion for difficulty. Usually two or more reading passages are written or found for each grade level. The student alternates from silent to oral reading at each grade level and is asked four to ten comprehension questions on each reading passage.

When constructing IRIs teachers usually attempt to devise questions that cover main ideas, important details, vocabulary, and inferences. There is a more or less standard set of criteria for judging performance on the comprehension section of IRIs; however, there is still some disagreement among authorities on the exact percentage necessary for placement at the free or independent, instructional, and frustration reading levels.

Constructing the IRI from the actual materials a student will use lets the student deal with vocabulary, concepts, and syntax that truly serve his or her instructional needs. On the other hand, it is difficult to write good comprehension questions. Shauker (1984) of this text is the author of a commercial IRI. It took several years to develop the passages and corresponding questions, and many questions that appeared to be valid were seldom answered correctly, while others were nearly always answered correctly. We conclude that writing valid questions for an IRI is surprisingly difficult, and for this reason the use of teacher-made IRIs is questionable.

A further difficulty is the accurate interpretation of the adequacy of inferential-type questions. A teacher may feel that he or she is accurately interpreting a student's answers; however, when the rating is compared with that of several other grades, a rather large discrepancy is often revealed.

Peter H. Johnston and Richard L. Allington (1983) have also questioned the validity of teacher-made IRIs. They suggest, as does M. M. Clay (1979), that perhaps it would be best for teachers to "take running records of children's reading behaviors while they read whatever they are currently placed on." (p. 500).

Leo Schell and Gerald Hanna (1981) have pointed out that at present commercially published IRIs do not accurately assess the various *subskills* of comprehension because the IRIs:

(1) fail to demonstrate objective classifications of questions, (2) neglect to provide and to demonstrate comparable scores across subskill

categories, (3) fail to provide evidence of uniform passage dependence and passage independence of questions across categories of comprehension, and (4) fail to provide reliable subskill scales and evidence thereof. (p. 267)

Schell and Hanna noted, however, that these deficiencies can be corrected with more careful construction of commercial IRIs.

In spite of their limitations informal reading inventories have become and will probably continue to be one of the most useful instruments that the reading diagnostician may possess. Chapter 11 is devoted to the construction and use of IRIs and the cloze procedure. For this reason we will not discuss either of these methods of measuring reading comprehension in great detail in this chapter.

Informal Recall Procedures

Although not often publicized by this term, *informal recall procedures* have largely been used as a measure of students' comprehension for as long as reading has been taught. This procedure may take the form of a teacher asking a student a number of questions from a teacher's manual or "off the top of the teacher's head" after the student has read a passage. Sometimes the teacher may simply ask the student to tell about what was read. One of the major disadvantages of this system is that there are no criteria by which to judge the answer. Teachers often compare one student's answers against those of other students in the class, but even this is often misleading if the teacher has a low-ability group, a high-ability group, or students from a community with an extremely low or high socioeconomic level. Although this procedure has some advantages for the classroom teacher, it usually has limited usefulness for the reading diagnostician.

The Cloze Procedure

The cloze procedure is a technique whereby every *n*th word is omitted from a reading passage, and a blank is left in place of each omitted word. The student is given the passage and told to fill in the blanks with proper words to fit the context of the sentences. Many authorities believe this technique to be one of the better measures of reading comprehension. They contend that filling in the blanks requires deeper comprehension of a reading passage than can generally be measured with oral or written questions or with multiple-choice questions. In fact, anyone who doubts the fact that thorough comprehension of a reading passage is required to obtain a high score on a mutilated passage has but to try one.

A great deal of research has been done in an attempt to develop a standardized procedure for building and scoring cloze passages. Much of this research is concerned with developing specific percentages of correct responses equivalent to a student's independent, instructional, and frustration reading levels. By comparing students' scores on cloze passages with those of the same passages in multiple-choice form (and in some cases administered as IRIs), researchers such as John Bormuth (1967) and Earl Rankin and Joseph Culhane (1969) have developed what is now generally recognized as a standardized procedure for the percentage of words to be omitted as well as the percentage of correct responses corresponding to the three reading levels mentioned above. Most of the percentages have been developed on the basis of leaving out every fifth word and replacing each word with uniform blanks. Based on the omission of one word in five, the percentage of correct responses equivalent to the commonly recognized reading levels are as follows:

> 57 percent plus = free or independent reading level
> 44 through 56 percent = instructional reading level
> 43 percent minus = frustration reading level

Cloze passages have the advantage of group tests in that they can be administered to more than one student at a time. When used with a plastic overlay to check the answers, they are also quite easy to score and interpret. See Chapter 11 for details of the construction, use, and scoring of cloze passages.

Sentence Structure or Deep Structure

Very little formal research has been done on the use of the recovery of sentence structure as a measure of students' comprehension. Herbert Simons (1971) believes that through linguistic theory and psycholinguistic research better comprehension tests may emerge. As Simons points out, transformational grammar is the theory of the inherent structure of natural language. It includes a study of the way words are put together to form sentences; meanings vary according to the way in which words are strung together. Simons stresses the point that comprehension cannot take place without the recovery of the original underlying relationships in a reading passage.

Simons suggests several methods of using knowledge of sentence structure as a measure of comprehension. One of these methods is to determine which two of three sentences is a paraphrase of another, as in the following example:

a. He painted the red house.
b. He painted the house red.
c. He painted the house that was red.

Another method of recovering sentence structure suggested by Simons is filling in blanks to make sentences having the same meaning, as follows:

1. For the girl to leave is what the boy would like.
   What the _____ would like is for the _____ to leave.

2. He painted the house that was red.
   He painted the ＿＿＿＿＿ ＿＿＿＿＿ .
3. The girl asked the boy when to leave.
   The girl asked the boy when ＿＿＿＿ should leave.   (p. 359)

A third method suggested by Simons is to have students paraphrase what was read. In order to do this you need very objective scoring criteria. Simons's suggestions seem to hold a great deal of promise for research in the construction of comprehension tests and could be adapted to some extent by reading specialists in their day-to-day diagnostic procedures.

DIAGNOSIS FOR VOCABULARY KNOWLEDGE

Some of the most commonly used methods of testing for vocabulary knowledge include group standardized tests, the vocabulary sections of individual standardized reading tests and individual intelligence tests, informal questioning, and informal reading inventories.

Group Standardized Tests

Group standardized tests have traditionally been popular as a measure of both group and individual vocabulary development. They are easy to administer and are generally efficient in terms of teacher time. Most of the other advantages as well as disadvantages of group standardized tests for general comprehension also apply for vocabulary development. However, most critics of group standardized tests have tended to be less critical of the vocabulary sections of these tests than of general comprehension. Perhaps this is because questions designed to measure vocabulary knowledge are inherently easier to construct.

Most group standardized tests report vocabulary development in terms of grade-level placement. See Appendix B for a listing of a number of commonly used group standardized tests containing vocabulary subtests, publishers, and grade levels for which they are appropriate.

Some ways you can use group standardized tests in vocabulary measurement:

1. To measure the overall vocabulary development of a group.
2. To compare a group's vocabulary development with its general comprehension development.
3. To find particular areas of weakness or strength, such as mathematics or social studies vocabulary.
4. To establish a beginning point in examining the vocabulary of an individual, providing he or she scores above the level that could be achieved by chance.

5. To measure overall class achievement from beginning to end of an instructional period, providing that most beginning group scores are above the level that could be achieved by chance.

Avoid using group standardized vocabulary tests for the following:

1. To determine grade placement of disabled readers or to make any major decision concerning the welfare of a student.
2. To judge the amount of gain in vocabulary development, for a single student, from the beginning to the end of an instructional period, especially where the initial score is low enough so that it could have been achieved by chance.

In using group standardized tests, keep in mind that you are measuring not only students' knowledge of words but also their ability to read the words being tested and in most tests a number of other words and synonyms. The fact that a student does not score high on a group standardized test does not necessarily mean that he or she has a low listening or speaking vocabulary. If a student has poor word-analysis skills and cannot read the stimulus words on a group standardized test, then regardless of the level of the student's vocabulary, the score on a standardized test will not reflect the true level of the student's performance.

The Vocabulary Sections of Individual Standardized Reading Tests

Certain individual standardized tests, such as the *Durrell Analysis of Reading Difficulty,* contain subtests for diagnosing individual students' oral word knowledge. In the Durrell battery, this subtest is called the "Listening Vocabulary" test. It measures not reading word knowledge, but rather knowledge of word meanings when students hear the words read to them. The authors of the Durrell battery suggest that oral vocabulary may be thought of as a good indicator of reading capacity. In taking the subtest, the student looks at three pictures, such as a clock, an elephant and a rainbow. The examiner explains to the student that the first picture is for words about time, the second for words that mean "big," and the third for words about color. The examiner then reads a series of words, such as *red, large,* and *century,* while the student points to the appropriate picture. The Durrell battery also tests the student's ability to *read* these same words in another subtest, so that the examiner may have a clue as to whether word recognition weaknesses are a function of vocabulary deficiencies. The tests are constructed to minimize learning transfer between the two subtests.

The Vocabulary Sections of Individual Intelligence Tests

The vocabulary sections of certain individual intelligence tests, such as the *Wechsler Intelligence Scale for Children*—Revised (WISC-R) (Wechsler,

1974), the *Wechsler Adult Intelligence Scale*—Revised (WAIS-R) (Wechsler, 1981), and the *Stanford-Binet Intelligence Scale* (Terman and Merrill, 1972) can also be useful in assessing children's oral vocabularies. The WISC-R and WAIS-R both contain a vocabulary subtest from which a raw score is obtained. This score is converted to a scaled score from which interpretations can be made in terms of IQ, percentile rating, grade equivalent, etc. (See Figure 16-1, Chapter 16.) The Stanford-Binet also contains a subtest for oral vocabulary from which it is possible to derive a mental age and thus a grade equivalent. The real value of tests of oral vocabulary, or any of the three intelligence tests mentioned in this section, is to determine whether there is a discrepancy between a student's oral and reading vocabularies. When test results reveal a normal or near-normal reading vocabulary, very little is gained by administering these tests. On the other hand, for the student who achieves a low reading-vocabulary score, the information obtained from an oral vocabulary test can be useful in determining whether the difficulty lies in a low oral or overall vocabulary. The use of informal questioning can be valuable in determining whether a student is having difficulty with the vocabulary of a reading passage. You need only say, "What did the word _____ mean in this passage?" There is no need to prepare questions prior to the student's reading the passage, as is necessary for assessing general comprehension. In informal questioning you also have the opportunity to delve further into questionable answers, which enables you to place further confidence in the validity of your assessment. The major problem with informal questioning, as with any method of informal assessment, is that there are no standards with which you can compare the answers you obtain, other than the answers given by other students. Where a teacher is working with very bright or very dull students, this sometimes presents a problem.

Informal Reading Inventories

IRIs can also be used in assessing vocabulary knowledge and have the same advantages and disadvantages as informal questioning techniques. However, because IRIs are prepared in advance, they are more likely to contain a vocabulary representative of a particular book or grade level.

A SUGGESTED SEQUENCE FOR DIAGNOSIS OF READING COMPREHENSION AND VOCABULARY DEVELOPMENT

Most diagnosticians include an assessment of vocabulary as a part of a diagnosis for general reading comprehension. Our heading, "reading comprehension *and* vocabulary development," reflects this.

As a starting point for the diagnostician there are generally two situations—one in which a fairly recent (six months or less) group achievement or diagnostic test score is available and one in which no group scores are available. When group achievement or diagnostic test scores are available, they can serve as a guideline for further diagnosis. Where these scores are available, there will be several possibilities:

1. Average-to-high vocabulary and average-to-high comprehension
2. Average-to-high vocabulary and low comprehension
3. Low vocabulary and low comprehension
4. Low vocabulary and average-to-high comprehension

Situation 1. A student has an average-to-high score (at grade level or above) in both vocabulary and comprehension. Overall comprehension (vocabulary and comprehension) is probably not a contributing factor to reading difficulty. On some tests it is possible to score within six months to one year of grade level by guessing; however, when guessing the chances of achieving a score at grade level or above on the entire battery are remote. In addition you may wish to verify the group score using an informal reading inventory. This will also provide for a check on the student's comprehension while reading orally and will enable you to verify the group achievement test scores on vocabulary and comprehension. Although the IRI is not a necessity, major decisions concerning the welfare of a student should not be made on the basis of one test score. Furthermore, the time spent in giving the IRI is not wasted, since it can give valuable information on problems in word-attack skills.

Situation 2. A student achieves an average-to-high vocabulary score and a low comprehension score. This is fairly common when students have problems with units larger than single words. You must determine the level at which comprehension breaks down. Since most group tests use reading passages of several paragraphs, you can feel fairly sure the difficulty is with units of two to three paragraphs or quite likely a paragraph or less. Since the group test score indicates a difficulty with silent reading, you should also check to see if the student has the same problem when reading orally. An informal reading inventory will allow you to check on all of these things. In giving the IRI note the level at which comprehension breaks down and then give the student individual sentences to read and ask the student to paraphrase them for you. This can be done on both the oral and silent passages; i.e., have the student read sentences from oral passages aloud and then paraphrase them and then have the student read sentences from silent passages silently and paraphrase them also. If the student seems to comprehend sentences but has difficulty with entire paragraphs, he or she is likely to need remediation in the understanding of larger units. While administering the IRI you can also ask informal questions on the vocabulary of the reading passages and verify the results of the vocabulary score obtained on the group test.

A student who does not understand sentence units will need further diagnosis. During oral reading, note whether the student phrases properly. Also note whether the student is aware of punctuation marks.

Another factor that affects group scores is the student's reading speed, since these tests are timed. It may be necessary to check certain students' reading rates to see if they fall considerably below the norm for their grade levels. This can be done with the "Oral Reading" subtest of the *Durrell Analysis of Reading Difficulty,* or it can be done by giving a student a timed reading test. Albert Harris and Edward Sipay (1985) present an excellent set of norms in their book entitled *How to Increase Reading Ability.* (p. 554)

For students with average-to-high vocabulary scores and low comprehension scores it is often helpful to administer a listening comprehension test. This will tell you to some extent whether the student's problem is the mechanics of reading or remembering facts and restructuring a sequence of events. The student who cannot do appreciably better in comprehending a passage read orally to him or her will need remediation in restructuring events, remembering details by forming visual images, etc. On the other hand, the student who does well in listening comprehension but poorly on reading comprehension will likely need help with the mechanics of reading. Some students do not comprehend well because they lack an adequate sight vocabulary. Consequently, while reading, so much effort is spent on word attack that overall comprehension suffers. Use a test such as the "Listening Comprehension" subtest of the *Durrell Analysis of Reading Difficulty* or use IRI passages and apply the criteria as described in Chapter 10.

Situation 3. A student receives a low vocabulary and a low comprehension score. In this case, first determine whether the student's problem is actually one of comprehension or whether the comprehension score is symptomatic of a problem in word-attack skills. As a first step, administer a word pronunciation test such as the *San Diego Quick Assessment* list described in Chapter 4, or the word pronunciation section of the *Wide Range Achievement Test.* If a serious problem is indicated, very little can be done with overall comprehension until remediation is provided for the difficulty with word attack.

If the problem is not in word attack, determine whether the student has an adequate oral vocabulary. Check the results of the WISC-R for ages 5–15 and WAIS-R for ages 16+ or Stanford-Binet if available. If they are not available, administer an oral vocabulary test.

If the student's problem is not word attack or oral vocabulary, proceed much the same as in situation 2; i.e., administer an IRI, check for problems at the paragraph, sentence, and phrase level, and check for the student's knowledge of the vocabulary in each passage. Also check the possibility that lack of speed was a factor. If you do not have an IRI available or do not feel proficient in their use, you may wish to administer the "Oral and Silent Reading" subtests of the *Durrell Analysis of Reading Difficulty.* If you choose to use the "Silent Reading" subtest of the Durrell, however, we recommend that it be supplemented with a few vocabulary and interpretation questions that measure beyond the simple recall level.

As in situation 2, it may prove helpful to administer a listening comprehension test. When a student has a low vocabulary and a low comprehension score, you may also wish to check the results of individual IQ tests, or administer one yourself if you are qualified, to determine if the student is having problems because of mental deficiency. As in any mental testing program, however, you should not let a slightly low IQ score influence your expectations, since many students with low IQs read perfectly well. It serves little purpose to administer an IQ test if the remedial procedures will remain the same regardless of the outcome.

Situation 4. A student scores low on the vocabulary section and average to high on comprehension. This is somewhat less common than the first three situations. Your first step might be to determine whether the student has a low oral vocabulary by checking the subtest scores of the WISC-R or WAIS-R or Stanford-Binet or by administering an oral vocabulary subtest. If the student's oral vocabulary is low, chances are his or her reading vocabulary will not improve unless remediation is provided in that area first.

If the student's oral vocabulary is above the reading vocabulary, you may wish to verify the results of the group vocabulary test using an IRI with informal questions concerning the vocabulary. If the reading vocabulary (in terms of meaning) is low, you will need to provide remediation in word meaning and provide for wide reading experiences.

In cases where there are no recent group achievement tests or group diagnostic tests, the procedure follows a somewhat standard pattern. A good beginning point is to administer a word pronunciation test such as the *San Diego Quick Assessment* or the "Word Pronunciation" subtest of the *Wide Range Achievement Test*. A student who is considerably below grade level on this type of test is not likely to improve in comprehension until he or she receives remediation for word-analysis difficulties.

If the student is somewhere near grade level on the word pronunciation test, the diagnosis should continue. At this point you may wish to use an IRI or an oral reading test such as the *Gilmore Oral Reading Test*. If you choose one of these oral reading tests, you should also give a silent reading test. The *Durrell Analysis of Reading Difficulty* contains a normed subtest for silent reading comprehension, but you should supplement it with vocabulary and inference-type questions, since the norms provide only for literal recall.

In administering either an IRI or a combination of the other silent and oral tests, be careful to note whether the student is having a great deal of trouble with vocabulary. If it is evident that the student is encountering vocabulary problems, administer an oral vocabulary subtest or check the student's scores on the vocabulary subtest of the WISC-R, WAIS-R, or Stanford-Binet if they are available. The student who scores low on oral vocabulary will need remediation in that area before you can expect reading vocabulary to improve to any great degree. However, the two probably should be remediated simultaneously. If the student's oral vocabulary is extremely low, you may wish to check on previous IQ tests, or administer an individual IQ test, to determine whether the student has an extremely low IQ. However, the vocabulary subtest itself is a good measure of reading potential, and in many cases little is gained by administering an entire IQ test. The student whose oral vocabulary is considerably higher than his or her reading vocabulary needs work in improving understanding of written words. Such work should include broad reading experiences.

If the student's vocabulary proves adequate, the diagnosis should focus on other comprehension problems. Check to see if the student has difficulty only with passages longer than a paragraph or even at the paragraph level. If the student has difficulty with paragraphs, see whether he or she can read and understand single sentences. This should be done in both oral and silent reading by having the student paraphrase each sentence after it is read.

If the student cannot comprehend sentences adequately, check the phrasing as the student reads orally for correct intonation, pitch, and stress. Also determine whether a lack of knowledge of punctuation is interfering with proper phrasing. Look for pauses before words that should be sight words. Students who have to expend a great deal of effort in analyzing words in a passage are not likely to comprehend well. If frequent pauses are noted, the student needs to build up a larger sight vocabulary before comprehension will improve to any great extent.

For the student with an adequate reading vocabulary but inadequate comprehension, a listening comprehension test can be of considerable help in the diagnosis. Students who cannot comprehend well on either type of test will need help in skills such as structuring events and developing visual images. Students who do well on listening comprehension tests but poorly on reading comprehension usually have difficulty in sight-word knowledge, word attack, punctuation, or some combination of the three.

DIAGNOSIS OF STUDENTS' KNOWLEDGE OF STUDY SKILLS

A number of study skills are of considerable importance to the student in developing a background for working in an academic setting. Any student who did not develop most of these skills would be somewhat handicapped in the elementary grades and even more handicapped in high school. However, failure to develop adequate study skills is not likely to cause a student to become a disabled reader even though it may cause the same student to fail in an academic setting. The end result is, of course, the same. For this reason the diagnosis of an older student who is doing poorly in school work should include an analysis of the student's study skills.

Diagnosis of study skills is relatively easy, since most of the skills involved can easily be tested using a group informal inventory. Some commonly listed study skills and methods of assessing students' ability to use them:

Skill	*Method of Assessment*
1. Using table of contents	Using students' textbooks, ask questions such as, ''What chapter contains a discussion of wild animals?'' ''On what page does Chapter 10 begin?''
2. Using index	Using students' textbooks, ask questions such as, ''On what page can you find information on the topic of polar bears?''
3. Using glossary	Using students' textbooks, ask questions such as, ''What does your book say the word *armature* means?''
4. Using encyclopedia	Ask questions such as, ''On what page of what volume can you find information on the life of Abraham Lincoln?'' ''What other topics would you look under to find more information on Lincoln?''
5. Using almanac	Ask questions such as, ''What city has the largest population in the world?''
6. Using telephone directory	Ask questions such as, ''What is the telephone number for Amos Abrams?'' ''List the telephone numbers for three companies that sell firewood.''
7. Using library card index	Use questions such as, ''How many cards have a listing for the book *World War Two Airplanes?*'' ''What does the author card include?'' ''What does the subject card include?'' ''What does the title card include?'' ''What is the call number of the book *Hitler?*''
8. Learning to skim	Using a newspaper, give timed exercises for finding such things as an article on atomic energy or auto accidents; or using students' textbooks, give timed exercises in finding a certain date, sentence, etc., in a specific chapter.
9–12. Learning to read maps, graphs, tables, and diagrams	Use students' textbooks to derive questions. This will be more meaningful than questions commonly asked on standardized achievement tests.
13. Learning to take notes	Play a short tape recording of a lecture or radio program on a subject in which the students are interested and ask them to take notes.

| 14. Using time to good advantage | Use a time analysis sheet (see "Methods of Remediating Deficiencies in Study Skills," later in chapter). |

Part B: REMEDIATION

COMPREHENSION TODAY

As we mentioned earlier in this chapter, a sort of renaissance has occurred in the teaching of reading comprehension. Terms often heard today are metacognition, schema theory, and semantic webbing or semantic mapping. Each has something to offer; we believe the various metacognitive techniques have the most to offer.

Before we describe these techniques, perhaps it should be said that in the past very little teaching of reading comprehension has taken place in the average classroom. This was documented by Dolores Durkin (1978–1979). Durkin reported on an observational study to determine whether elementary school teachers provide instruction in reading comprehension, and if so, how much time is allotted to this task. Durkin selected middle- and upper-grade classrooms on the assumption that more instruction in comprehension was likely to be found at this level. Durkin and two assistants conducted observations during reading and social studies periods for a total of 300 class hours. Durkin writes:

> Major findings included the fact that almost no comprehension instruction was found. The attention that did go to comprehension focused on assessment, which was carried on through teacher questions. Instruction other than that for comprehension was also rare. It could not be concluded, therefore, that teachers neglect comprehension because they are busy teaching phonics, structural analysis, or word meanings. What they do attend to are written assignments. As a result, time spent on giving, completing, and checking assignments consumed a large part of the observed periods. Sizeable amounts of time also went to activities categorized as "Transition" and "Non-instruction." (p. 481)

Carol Hodges (1980) responded to Durkin by suggesting that a broader definition of comprehension instruction would yield different results. Instead of the less than 1 percent of the observation time that Durkin found accounted for instruction, Hodges's analysis with the broader definition found that 23 percent of the time was spent in comprehension instruction.

Regardless of which definition of instruction is applied, the findings of

Durkin's research are distressing. It does not matter which of the various methodologies are used if substantial direct instruction is not provided to students.

If you assume that comprehension skills can be taught with teacher-directed instruction, then the next logical question is, What kinds of programs and/or techniques are needed to develop students' comprehension skills? Leo Schell (1972) indicates that regardless of the type of program involved, you cannot expect it to succeed unless it is carried out on a long-term basis. Schell suggests that ten minutes once a week for ten weeks will not accomplish it. He suggests that a reasonable minimal amount of time to see comprehension growth is three lessons per week for ten weeks. He further suggests that the student will continue to need periodic reinforcement after termination of the formal lessons.

METHODS OF REMEDIATING
GENERAL COMPREHENSION DIFFICULTIES

Using Metacognitive Techniques

Metacognitive techniques, if used consistently and correctly, can quickly improve difficulties with comprehension for most disabled readers. Since metacognitive techniques involve immediate help with a student's overall comprehension problems, they can perhaps be of more benefit to a student in remedial reading than any other reading comprehension techniques.

The prefix "meta-" means "knowledge of." Therefore metacognition means knowledge of cognition or knowledge of thought processes. Stated more simply, it is the ability to monitor one's thought processes while reading.

Metacognition is not necessarily the ability to understand what is being read, but rather knowledge of whether the student is understanding what is read. In teaching students to monitor their thought processes while reading, focus on their ability to understand *how to use* metacognitive processes and not just teach them *about* metacognitive processes.

Apparently students who comprehend well consistently use metacognitive strategies. Margaret Mier (1984) indicates that good or experienced readers constantly monitor, revise, observe, and test their understanding of material being read. Sharon Pugh Smith (1985) states:

> Experienced readers, it was found, proceed on a trial-and-error basis but within a systematically organized repertoire of strategies. . . . experienced readers, when left to their own devices, do not confine themselves to a given text but readily resort to outside information when the text is judged inaccessible. At the same time, they also used such strategies as reorganization, paraphrasing, and diagramming to build meaning from the language of the text. (p. 292)

Mier and Sharon Pugh Smith (1985) have pointed out that young, inexperienced, and low-ability students consistently fail to test or revise their understanding of what is read. It has also been found that poor readers tend to lack a clear picture of the purpose of reading. They tend to view it as a decoding process even when lacking adequate decoding skills; they also have a tendency to view reading as a passive act of translating symbol into sound (Erickson, Stahl, and Rinehart, 1985).

Mier indicates that the monitoring strategies of poor readers of high school age tend to be the same as those of low-ability and younger students. She states that comprehension monitoring does develop automatically with age or maturity but depends on knowledge and expertise. Mier summarizes her information on metacognition:

> What does seem clear from the research is that comprehension monitoring, a developmental skill generally only emerging fully with adolescence, can be strengthened through careful classroom training. Training in monitoring strategies is effective, however, only if it is used discriminatingly, by teachers who are aware of their students' varying abilities and maturity and are able to adapt classroom procedures to these differences. (p. 773)

The lack of poor readers' and younger students' knowledge of their own reading strategies was emphasized by Pat Cunningham (1984):

> While the research is still at a beginning stage, it is shocking to discover that so much of what we thought children "naturally" did as they read, it appears they don't do until much later than we assumed and that poor readers may never learn to do. (p. 84)

Generating Questions While Reading

Oran Stewart and Ebo Tei (1983) have given a number of suggestions for teaching students to monitor their thought processes. One is to ask students to generate their own questions while they read. They described a study by Palincsar (1981) in which students were shown how to model the questioning behavior of the teacher. Once students had learned how to ask appropriate questions, their comprehension improved very rapidly—from an average of 15 percent to about 80 percent correct.

Rereading, Awareness of New Words, and Predicting What Lies Ahead

In the same article Stewart and Tei reported on a study in which tenth-grade good and poor readers were compared in their ability to comprehend. Good readers tended to identify unknown words, to reread when the meaning was unclear, and to predict what might lie ahead more than did poor readers. Thus it appears that poor readers should be instructed to monitor their thought processes while reading and encouraged to reread when they do not understand what they have just read. Diane L. August, John H. Flavell, and

Renee Clift (1984) as well as Ruth Garner, Victoria Chou Hare, Patricia Alexander, Jacqueline Haynes, and Peter Winograd (1984) have reported on the success of text "lookback" procedures. Students should also be taught to be aware of unknown words and to anticipate what will happen or will be described next.

Making Students Aware of the Purpose of Reading, the Vocabulary of Reading, and Some Possible Stumbling Blocks in Reading

Stewart and Tei also emphasized the importance of knowing about reading. They suggest that you: Teach the vocabulary of reading, i.e., the meaning of such concepts as *word, sentence, paragraph, beginning sound,* etc. Instruct children that meaning is the ultimate goal of reading and show them how stories progress from page to page through a book. Teach children awareness of stumbling blocks and strategies to use in overcoming them. Help children to know when the text does and does not make sense. For this last Stewart and Tei suggest inserting material that does not make sense and then have children search for it in the text.

Learning to Get Mental Images and Changing Reading Rate

Stewart and Tei (1983) and Frances L. Clark et. al. (1984) also suggest having students stop periodically to get a mental image from the text and to predict what may lie ahead based upon previous text content. Ask students to read a sentence or two of a descriptive passage and then ask if they were able to get a mental image of the scene or event described. Have students draw what they saw in their mind's eye and then compare these drawings and discuss important features that were or were not included.

Stewart and Tei also suggest emphasizing the necessity of changing reading rate when the text becomes more or less difficult.

Developing Awareness of Paragraph Meaning

Richard J. Smith and Velma L. Dauer (1984) have described another metacognitive technique, which has been used by this writer in a number of situations with students from third grade to adult level. It has always created a great deal of interest and works extremely well in making students aware of the strategies for getting meaning from a paragraph.

First, find a page of descriptive or narrative material that is slightly difficult for the group. Then instruct the class to read one paragraph from the selection.

Tell the group that while they read the material they are to think about what they have to do in order to understand the material, e.g., reread, use context to determine the meaning of a word, etc. Have them read the assigned paragraph and then stop.

When everyone is through, use the overhead projector or a piece of chart paper to record the various strategies students used to understand the paragraph. Call on one student to describe what happened as he or she read the paragraph. In one seventh-grade group the first response was that the student got a mental image of the item described in the paragraph. The teacher said, "Good. Let's use the letters 'AVI' to indicate that you were able to get a visual image." Other students gave the following responses; note the designated abbreviations.

AVI—Able to get a visual image
NAVI—Not able to get a visual image
RR—Had to reread the material to understand it
W—Why am I reading this?
CQ—Can I think of a question over this material?
LS—Listening for sounds (The student was reading about a battle in which there were running horses and the student was listening in her mind for the sounds.)
UC—Used the context to get the meaning of a word
UEC—Used expanded context (The student said that the meaning of the word was not apparent from the context of the sentence in the assigned paragraph, but he saw the word in a paragraph preceding the one he was told to read. Therefore, he went back to that paragraph and was able to derive the meaning of the word.)
U—Understood just fine
DNU—Did not understand what was read
D—Disagreed with the author of the passage
DN—Distracted by noise in the room

Place this list on the overhead projector or on a piece of chart paper (24″ × 36″) so that it is always in full view of all the students in the class. Then give each student a strip of paper about the width of one of the margins and the length of the page they are to read. Tell students to place the strip of paper over the margin of the page and read each paragraph. Have them mark each paragraph according to the code that was just developed.

After everyone has finished reading the page, discuss what was done by various students and ask if any further abbreviations are needed. If they are, add them to the list.

This exercise can be used with students' basal readers and social studies and science books. Students who used not to know what to do when they did not understand soon begin to use the techniques of good reading comprehension. Smith and Dauer emphasize that this strategy makes students aware of what they are and are not getting from each selection, aids motivation, deters mind-wandering, and aids postreading discussions.

Insertion of Questions

Joseph Sanacore (1984) suggests interspersing questions about the passage being read so that some require lookbacks and retrieval while others do not, as the questions should not disrupt the flow of meaning to a significant degree. He advises instructing students on *how* to generate the following questions while they read: "1. Who is the leading character? 2. What is the leading character trying to accomplish in the story? 3. What stands in the way of the leading character reaching the desired goal?" (p. 710)

Recognizing Unknown Words

Most readers become somewhat expert at ignoring words they do not know. This can be illustrated by asking a group of students if they have ever looked up a word in the dictionary and then found that they kept coming across that same word in the ensuing weeks. Most will have had this experience. This tells us that the student had probably seen the word a number of times before, but simply ignored it. In order to break this habit you should call students' attention to it. You may also wish to have contests in which students are rewarded for finding new words that others missed or ignored.

Determining When Something Does or Does Not Make Sense

Ask students to read a paragraph at a time and then stop and ask if the material made sense to everyone. If some students say it did not make sense, attempt to determine why not. Doing this will call students' attention to the fact that all reading should be meaningful. You may also wish to insert in the passages a few sentences that do not make sense or have no relation to the rest of the material. Ask them to draw a line through sentences that do not make sense in relation to the rest of the passage. From time to time you may also wish to ask students to draw a line through sentences that add no meaning to the material being read and so can be eliminated.

Stress the Need to Vary Reading Rates

Discuss the fact that some materials should be read very carefully, almost word for word, while others can be read much faster or even skimmed. Discuss what materials are appropriate for skimming or scanning and which require more careful reading.

Predicting What May Lie Ahead

Attempt to get students in the habit of continually predicting what may lie ahead as they read. Many basal reader teacher's manuals suggest this practice in teaching reading comprehension; however, many students do not seem to make the transfer to materials other than the stories in their basal readers. Show students how doing this with nearly everything they read will make them much more aware of what they are reading and how if done consistently, it will improve their overall comprehension.

Learning to Paraphrase

Jack E. Haynes and H. Thompson Fillmer (1984), Sherrie L. Shugarman and Joe B. Hurst (1986), and James R. Kalmbach (1986) suggest teaching students to paraphrase as a method of improving reading comprehension. In doing this, begin at the sentence level and ask students to paraphrase each sentence. After students become adept at this, ask them to do the same at the paragraph level. Have them take turns paraphrasing what they have read. Ask other students whether they agree that the paraphrase was an accurate account of the reading passage. Discuss points of difference and why there may have been several different interpretations of the material.

Learning to Ask Who, What, When, Where, and Why

Although for a number of years this exercise has been suggested as an aid to comprehension, few students have been taught to use it consistently. Give them practice with short passages such as often appear in the left-hand column of newspaper pages. As they become adept at these, they should progress to longer passages.

Ruth Cohen (1983) found that students at third-grade level could be taught to ask meaningful questions. She stressed the fact that students are often not taught techniques such as SQ3R until they are in the upper grades or at the high school level:

> In summary, these findings suggest that training in self-generated questions can start as early as the primary grades and that this type of training may improve students' comprehension of stories. (p. 775)

Help Students Distinguish What Is Already Known and What Is Not Known

Mary F. Heller (1986) has suggested a method of helping students become aware of what they know and do not know as they read. Before students read their content area lessons, they should set up three columns on a sheet of paper:

Column A	*Column B*	*Column C*
What I already knew	What I now know	What I don't know

Before beginning to read, each student places the three headings at the top of a piece of paper. In a discussion and with the help of the teacher, the class lists first what is already known about the subject. After reading the assignment, they write what they have learned. Following this they discuss what they still do not know and what additional information they need in order to understand the information in the reading assignment.

This is a very brief version of the procedure Heller described. We encourage you to read Heller's entire article.

Learning to Use Monitoring Cards

Patricia J. Babbs (1984) suggests that students use nine monitoring cards as they read:

(1) Click—"I understand." (2) Clunk—"I don't understand." (3) Read on. (4) Reread the sentence. (5) Go back and reread the paragraph. (6) Look in the glossary. (7) Ask someone. (8) What did it say? (to check comprehension at the paragraph level). (9) What do I remember? (to check comprehension at the page level.) (pp. 201–202)

Babbs suggests that the 1 and 2 cards be 4.5 in. × 2.5 in.; 3 through 7, 4.5 in. × 1.5 in.; and 8 and 9, 8.5 in. × 2.5 in. While students read they should respond to each sentence with the 1 or 2 card. If the student raises the 1 (Click) card, he or she goes on to the next sentence. If the 2 (Clunk) card is raised, the student looks at cards 3 through 7 and then attempts to resolve the problem by using one of these strategy cards. Babbs suggests that in order to save time the strategies should be used in this order:

If (a) does not resolve the problem, (b) is tried, and so on. If the problem is with a word:

(a) Reread the sentence.
(b) Read on. (Read the next sentence.)
(c) Look in the glossary. (Only if she thinks the word will be defined there.)
(d) Ask someone.

If the problem is with the sentence as a whole:

(a) Read the sentence.
(b) Go back and reread the paragraph.
(c) Read on.
(d) Ask someone. (p. 202)

After the student has read each paragraph, he or she looks away from the page, raises the "What did it say?" card, and attempts to answer that question. If unable to answer the question, he or she rereads the paragraph without using the 1 or 2 cards.

After reading each page, the student looks away from the page and raises the card (9) that says, "What do I remember?" If the student cannot remember, he or she rereads the page using the "What did it say?" card (8).

Using Story Frames

Gerald Fowler (1982) presented a unique idea for getting students to monitor their thought process while reading. This was what he terms story frames. Ekwall/Shauker has introduced them to many teachers who have found them of great benefit to students.

It has long been known that if questions are asked of students before they begin reading a story, they will read to find the answers to those questions; however, overall comprehension is likely to suffer, as they concentrate too narrowly on the prereading questions. On the other hand, if we tell students we would like them to read a story and we will ask them some questions when they have finished reading, they are likely to remember somewhat more than if we did not tell them that they would be tested. Since it is nearly impossible to ask prereading questions on everything we wish students to remember, we are left in a quandary as to what kind of questioning we should do. The use of story frames seems to answer this problem. The story frame is an outline of what students will be expected to remember from the story. As they read the story, they are forced to monitor their thought processes in order to complete the story frame. As students become more adept at completing a particular story frame, another is added. When all story frames are implemented with each story, students are required to remember nearly every important part of the story, which greatly enhances overall comprehension.

Students should be introduced to one story frame at a time. Start with this one:

FIGURE 6–1   Story Summary With One Character Included

Our story is about_____

_____ is an

important character in our story. _____

tried to _____

The story ends when _____

_____

_____

Reprinted by permission of the author and the International Reading Association.

Fowler originally recommended five types of story frame. First give students a copy of the first story frame [Figure 6–1] and explain that the blanks are to be filled in after students have read the story. The teacher should then discuss the story frame with students, illustrating what will be required in most stories. Students read the story and fill in the missing information. Following this, discuss the story and have several students read what they have inserted in the story frame. Students should reread any part of which they are uncertain before they complete the story frame.

After most students become adept at doing the simplest story frame, stop using it and introduce the second kind. Instruct students to use the second type just as they did the first. When they have mastered the second kind of story frame, they should begin using the first and second kinds together. After students become proficient at both the first and second kinds, withdraw them and introduce a third. After they can do the third kind, the first, second, and third are done together, and so on. Fowler's other four story frames:

FIGURE 6–2   Important Idea or Plot

In this story the problem starts when _____. After that, _____. Next, _____. Then, _____. The problem is finally solved when _____. The story ends _____

_____.

_____

Reprinted by permission of the author and the International Reading Association.

FIGURE 6–3   Setting

This story takes place _____. I know this because the author uses the words "_____." Other clues that show when the story takes place are _____.

Reprinted by permission of the author and the International Reading Association.

FIGURE 6–4   Character Analysis

_____ is an important character in our story. _____ is important because _____. Once, he/she _____. Another time, _____. I think that _____is

                                        (character's name)

_____ because _____.

(character trait)

Reprinted by permission of the author and the International Reading Association.

FIGURE 6–5   Character Comparison

_____ and _____ are two characters in our story. _____ is _____

        (character's name)   (trait)

while _____is _____.

        (other character)   (trait)

For instance, _____ tries to _____ and _____ tries to _____.

_____ learns a lesson when _____.

Reprinted by permission of the author and the International Reading Association.

Fowler (1986) has also presented two other types of story frames to be used with biographies and mystery stories:

FIGURE 6-6 Biography Story Frame

_____

Biography Story Frame

_____

_____ is famous because _____

_____. Before this could happen

_____°_____ had to _____

_____, and _____

_____. If _____ had _____

_____, today _____

_____

° add pronoun

Reprinted by permission of the author and the Maryland State Reading Association.

To complete the biography frame in Figure 6-6, students identify accomplishments, locate events that relate to these accomplishments, and possibly infer consequences had the person of interest not been successful.

The mystery story frame (Figure 6-7) was created by using the same procedure. It requires students to identify a detective and the evidence and to uncover a solution to the mystery. (p. 68)

STRUCTURED COMPREHENSION

When it was introduced, this was not known as a metacognitive technique; nevertheless, the structured comprehension technique, introduced by Marvin Cohn (1969), works extremely well.

For this technique Cohn suggests choosing factual material just difficult enough to be beyond the comprehension of the students who will be reading it. Students read the first sentence and answer the question, ''Do I know what

FIGURE 6–7 Mystery Story Frame

Mystery Story Frame

_____

This Mystery is about _____

_____. To solve this mystery _____

_____ decide(s) to _____

_____

_____, and _____

_____ conclude(s) that _____

The story ends _____

_____.

° add pronoun

_____

this sentence means?'' This forces each reader to be an active participant rather than a passive reader. If the reader does not understand all or part of the sentence, he or she is to ask the teacher or a peer as many questions as are necessary to comprehend fully. After all student questions have been answered, the teacher asks one or more questions about the sentence, and the students write the answers. This again forces all students to participate actively. Next, the question is discussed and answers are checked. Cohn points out that when answers have been written, the student cannot rationalize that a mental answer was right. In the beginning you should stress literal meaning more than relationships. Ask for the antecedent of every pronoun, the meaning of figurative expressions, and any new or uncommon vocabulary words. After the teacher has set a pattern for questioning, the students should use the same type of question in their search for meaning. The book should remain open during the entire process. After ten questions have been answered, each student scores his or her own paper and compares it with those done previously.

ReQuest Procedure

Another highly successful technique, at first not called metacognitive, is the ReQuest Procedure. Originated by Anthony Manzo (1969), it is similar to structured comprehension, just described.

In the request procedure the teacher begins by telling the student to ask the kind of questions pertaining to each sentence that the student thinks the teacher might ask. Each question is to be answered as fully and as honestly as possible; it is unfair for the teacher to pretend not to know the answer in order to draw out the student. It is also unfair for the student to say, "I don't know," since the student should at least explain why he or she cannot answer the question.

The game begins by having the teacher and student read the first sentences silently. The teacher then closes his or her book and the student asks questions concerning the content of the sentence. Then the student closes his or her book and the teacher asks questions. The teacher should provide a model for good questions, using thought-provoking questions that call for reasoning rather than strictly factual recall. After several sentences have been read, the teacher should ask questions that call for integration and evaluation of sentences read previously. Questioning is to continue until the student can answer the questions, "What do you think will happen in the rest of the selection?" "Why?" Manzo (1969) recommends:

1. Questions for which there is an *immediate reference,* e.g., "What was the second word in the sentence?" or "What did John call his dog?"
2. Questions which relate to *common knowledge* and for which answers can be reasonably expected, e.g., "What kind of animal has been associated with the name Lassie?"
3. Questions for which the teacher does not expect a "correct" response, but for which he can provide *related information,* e.g., "Do you happen to know how many varieties of dogs there are? . . . well I just happen to. . . . "
4. Questions for which neither the teacher nor the selection is likely to supply a "right" answer but which are nonetheless worth pondering or discussing; "I wonder why some animals make better pets than do others?"
5. Questions of a *personalized type* which only the student can answer, e.g., "Would you like to have a pet?", "Why?", "How did the different members of your family react to your first pet?"
6. Questions which are answerable, but are not answered by the selection being analyzed; *further reference* is needed, e.g., "I wonder what is the average height and weight of a collie?"
7. Questions requiring *translation.* Translation questions frequently call upon students to change words, ideas, and pictures into a different symbolic form, e.g., translation from one level of abstraction to

another, from one symbolic form to another, from one verbal form to another. "In a few words, how would you summarize what happened to Lassie?" "What is happening in this picture?" "What do you suppose the ex-convict meant by 'up at the big house'?" (p. 126)[1]

SQ3R

In our opinion one of the most effective aids to comprehension ever devised is the SQ3R procedure. It was not known as a metacognitive procedure when it was originally described by Francis Robinson (1941). Since that time a number of variations have been devised. However, none of these has proven more successful than Robinson's original technique.

SQ3R stands for "survey, question, read, recite and review." This method is best adapted to material in which subject headings are used, as in social studies and science books. The technique in brief form:

Survey: The student reads the introductory sentences at the beginning of the chapter and then all boldface headings, captions, and questions at the end of the chapter. Students who use this technique should at first be timed to make sure they *only* survey. They have a tendency to read the material as they have been doing if they are not put under some time pressure. Two to three minutes is usually sufficient; however, time will depend on the age and proficiency of the readers and the length of the chapter.

Question: Each heading is turned into a question. For example, in a science book, "Iron is an important metal." This changes to, "Why is iron an important metal?" When students first use this technique, you should help them devise questions. One way is to develop a list of common beginnings for questions such as, "When did," "Why are," "Why did," and "Why is."

Read: Students read down to the next boldface heading to find the answer to the question.

Recite: After reading, the student looks up from the book and attempts to answer the question. When students are first learning this technique, this can be done orally as a class procedure. After they have had a chance to practice, they should recite silently to themselves. If a student cannot answer a question, he or she should read the material under that boldface heading again.

Review: After the entire chapter has been read, students go back and read only the questions derived from the boldface headings and

[1]Reprinted by permission of the author and the International Reading Association.

see if they can answer them. If any questions cannot be answered, they would read the material under that question again.

The Use of Schema Theory

Schema (pl. *schemata*) theory is designed to help reading teachers understand how knowledge already in a student's mind is integrated with the information read from a printed page. Most of us in the field of reading refer to this as background of experience. We know that the more a reader knows about a subject, the more he or she is likely to comprehend when reading about it. Also, if a group of readers is lacking in experience background on a specific subject, we can improve reading comprehension by discussing the subject about which they are to read. Schema theory provides a more logical approach to integrating students' prior knowledge with what they read.

P. David Pearson (1982) says:

A basic premise of schema theory is that human memory is organized semantically (as opposed, say, to phonologically or alphabetically). In other words, memory is organized like a thesaurus rather than a dictionary. Presumably, one can possess schemata for all manner of things, ranging from simple objects (chair, boat), to abstract entities (love, hope, fear), to actions (buy, dive, run), to complex events (attending a conference or a football game), to very complex entities (story, novel, world affairs). (p. 26).

Any two individuals are likely to possess differing schemata for a specific object, entity, etc. For example, a very young child's schema of *dog* would be very simple compared to that of an adult. The child is likely to think of a dog as possessing all of the characteristics of the one with which he is most familiar. An adult's schema of *dog* encompasses many facets such as various breeds, colors, temperament, uses, etc. No two students are likely to construct the same schema of any subject or object.

You may logically ask, "What can I learn or what can I do differently as a result of knowing about schema theory?" Reading teachers must determine the best approach to bring about the most economical (in terms of time) integration of students' past schemata with those gained by reading. This is no small task, and we have still learned very little about the best processes for accomplishing it.

In answer to the question of the value of schema theory, Pearson suggests that five kinds of problems can be explained in terms of schema theory:

Schema Availability

Prior knowledge has been shown to be of more importance than measured reading ability. Thus, if students do not possess a certain amount of knowledge about a subject, they are not likely to comprehend material about it. Pearson suggests that a teacher can more quickly learn about students' knowledge of a subject by using free association and that semantic mapping, explained in the next section, may be appropriate for the purpose. In a group situation, it is helpful to add to the knowledge of many students.

Schema Selection

Pearson says, "Some students have the prior knowledge but neglect to call it into focus at the appropriate time." (p. 31) Helping students learn to do this may be difficult; however, most teachers help students do this by use of the guided reading activities at the beginning of a basal reader lesson. Metacognitive techniques can also help the student to take an active role in selecting his or her schemata in order to interact with the material being read.

Schema Maintenance

This is the ability of the student to maintain either the schema selected prior to reading the story or the interaction between the reader and the material being read. Pearson says that none of the instructional advice for schema maintenance has been tested and that this "might be accomplished either through systematic questioning techniques or the use of visual representations of the way texts are organized." (p. 31) We believe metacognitive approaches can also be helpful in schema maintenance.

Overreliance on Bottom-up Processing

Pearson found that students who overrely on bottom-up processing are likely to make errors because of attention to graphic features rather than to semantic concerns and they tend to give verbatim answers from the text rather than rely on what they actually know about the subject. According to Pearson, in order to help this we need to teach the student (1) that reading should make as much sense as listening and (2) that in order to comprehend it is often necessary to go beyond the text.

For the first part of the problem Pearson suggests an exercise such as placing in the text material that does not make sense in relation to the rest of the text. The student is to determine which material could be deleted.

For the second, Pearson suggests asking the student questions concerning information in the text. These questions are followed by various answers. Some answers should be directly from the text and others not direct from the text but correct based on the information in the text and on inferences the student should be able to make. The remaining answers are those that cannot be derived from either the text or from drawing inferences. The purpose of this exercise is to help the student understand that there are times when nontextual answers are as appropriate as textual answers.

Overreliance on Top-down Processing

Pearson says that the student who overrelies on top-down processing, or "schema-based processing," is likely to make semantically appropriate oral reading errors. That their answers to questions, while being generally correct, are not likely to be exactly right. He points out that this can often be a disadvantage when careful reading is called for, as in experiments, poetry, and evaluative reading. Pearson suggests that students be given fill-in-the-blank exercises in which all answers denote a response that is semantically correct, "(e.g., *walked, skipped, trudged),* but only one carries the appropriate connotation (e.g., *Susan felt so happy that she _____ through the park)."* (p. 32)

In his article on schema theory Pearson writes:

> In conclusion, schema theory can be a useful tool in approaching students' reading problems. By providing a framework for how students understand or fail to understand a text, a teacher can develop strategies like those explained above to remedy the reading problem. (p. 32)

Using Story Maps and Semantic Mapping

Ray D. Reutzel (1985) describes story maps as visual representations somewhat similar to a semantic map, which helps the student to integrate and organize the concepts and events within a story. Reutzel believes story maps can help teachers do a better job of organizing reading instruction and help students better understand the organization of a story, especially during the introductory phase. He also believes they can help students summarize or better reflect upon what they have read: "Story maps organize a story visually so specific relationships of selected story elements are highlighted." (p. 400)

Richard C. Sinatra, Josephine Stahl-Gemake, and David N. Berg (1984) describe a semantic map as " . . . a graphic arrangement showing the major ideas and relationships in text or among word meanings." (p. 22) These authors find semantic mapping especially appealing because it integrates schema theory with reading comprehension in a practical and holistic way. Reutzel, as well as Sinatra, Stahl-Gemake, and Berg, reports superior results in students' comprehension with story maps or semantic webbing than with a more traditional approach.

We believe, however, that one of the major points the remedial reading teacher should keep in mind is this: while semantic maps or semantic webbing can be very helpful in teaching from a basal reader or a social studies or science book, there is less carryover for future assignments than is obtained from metacognitive techniques.

Sinatra, Stahl-Gemake, and Berg have illustrated a classification map for "Our New Age-Old Foods:"

FIGURE 6-8　Classification Map for "Our New Age-Old Foods"

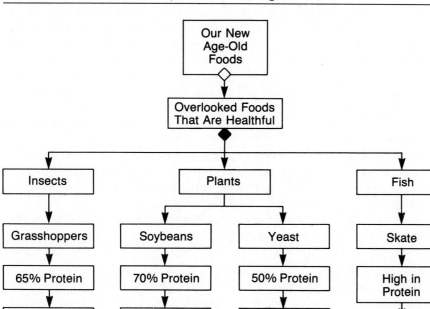

Reutzel says that the use of story maps can help the teacher as well as the student plan and execute more meaningful and purposeful or focused reading lessons. Story maps can organize efforts to reach specific comprehension objectives and help students build an organized structure for retrieving important information from a story within a text. They help in visually summarizing the text and in developing a structure for guiding prereading experiences. Story maps also, according to Reutzel, provide a model for integrating text information from within the content areas and a framework for facilitating recollection of background experiences. Finally, they encourage students to think about monitoring their reading.

Questioning

It is sometimes difficult to separate diagnosis from remediation in reading, since in some cases they appear to be one and the same. For example, the technique of questioning appears to be one of the best methods we have found for teaching comprehension. Although effective, this technique could be improved if teachers asked more questions beyond the simple recall level. Frank Guszak (1967) found that over half the questions asked by teachers he observed dealt with recall of facts. Other researchers have found that 10 percent or less of teachers' questions required students to use interpretative skills. Helen J. Caskey (1970) suggests that teachers attempt to cure themselves and their students of the "right-answer syndrome," i.e., the idea that there is a correct answer that must exactly correspond with the material in the text. She suggests that teachers often condition pupils to respond with the "right answer" to the point that they are afraid to attempt to answer questions that call for them to speculate.

Be aware that disabled readers can answer inference questions as well as normal readers. Jane Hansen and Ruth Hubbard (1984) found that if disabled readers were given material at their own instructional level, they were able to answer questions as well as normal-achieving readers.

Robert Willford (1968) reported that researchers with whom he worked had a great deal of success asking negative questions:

> Watch a five- or six-year-old. You put a picture up and you say, "Okay, what can you do with a horse?" Out of a group of 10, five of them have had an experience. The others don't know what you can do with a horse. We turn it completely around and say, "What can't you do with a horse?" You ought to see the differences in responses we get. Every child can tell you what you *can't* do with a horse. "What can't you do?" "Well you can't take a horse to bed with you." Someone else might say, "You can too if you live in a barn." This kid never thought about this. So now we find, what can you do with a horse? You can take a horse to bed with you if you live in a barn. You can flip the thing over by using a negative question as a stimulus to get a variety of answers. Kids love to do this. You may get more conversation out of a single picture than any single thing you can do. (p. 103)

Linda Gambrell (1980) presents evidence that one of the critical aspects of questioning is to allow "think-time." She suggests that teachers allow a minimum of five seconds after posing a question to permit students to think about a response. Think-time should also be provided after a student responds, to stimulate higher-level thinking. Gambrell believes that students verbalize in spurts and need extra time to process information to higher levels. She is persuaded that providing think-time is difficult but that teachers can be trained to do this and will find the results most gratifying.

James D. Riley (1979) believes that teachers' responses may be as important as the questions themselves. He suggests that teachers carefully observe student responses, try to guess what underlies these responses, make students aware that their statements and thoughts are valued, and then assist students to generalize or expand on their responses.

Signal Words

Teaching students to become aware of signal words can do a great deal to help them understand and follow a sequence of ideas or events. Some authors classify full signals and half signals. Words such as *first, second, third, one, two,* and *three* are full signals; words such as *then, after, that,* and *furthermore* are half signals. Note the use of full signals in the paragraph below:

> *First,* I would like to recommend Mr. Edwards for this position. *Second,* I would like to elaborate on some of his accomplishments during his tenure in his former position. *Third,* I would like to discuss some of his fine qualities as a husband and a father.

Note the use of half signals in the following paragraph:

> When hybrid corn first came on the market most farmers ignored it. *Then* they began to note the increased yields obtained by the farmers who used it. *After* that it was not long until nearly every farmer planted it. *Now* it would be almost impossible to find a farmer who plants anything but hybrid seed corn.

Kathleen C. Stevens (1982) has listed a number of signal words that help students understand difficult sentences:

Connectives that add ideas

also	both. . . . and	moreover
and	furthermore	then
besides	likewise	

Connectives that contrast ideas

but	nevertheless	yet
however	still	

Connectives that express choice

either . . . or	nor	or
neither . . . nor	otherwise	

Connectives that express result

accordingly	hence
consequently	therefore

Words that express time

whichever	after	until
while	since	when

Words that express cause or reason

since   as

whereas   because

Words that express purpose or result

in order that   that   so that

Words that express condition

unless   provided

if   although (pp. 187–88)

Often there is a mixture of half and full signals in books such as those of the social studies field. Sometimes authors make points or lead the reader through a series of events or ideas without any formal signals. They are, however, used consistently enough for it to be necessary to make students aware of the value of recognizing them. In teaching students to become aware of signal words you can use the students' own textbooks as a source of material. In the initial stages you will need to read paragraph by paragraph and count signals as you go.

Cloze Procedure

Cloze procedure as a teaching technique is becoming more useful as teachers uncover more and better ways to use it. Some past attempts to teach with it have ended in failure. Subsequent research has shown that it cannot successfully be used as a teaching device in the same manner in which it is used as a testing device. For example, as a standard test procedure most teachers omit every fifth word. Therefore there is no omission of specific types of words in the beginning stages. Passages in which every fifth word is deleted are extremely difficult for some students and, furthermore, the omission of certain words makes it almost impossible for the student to reconstruct the original passage. Also, as mentioned earlier, in the testing procedure synonyms are not counted as correct answers.

Several authors have suggested modifications of the cloze technique. Among the most important is discussing why certain answers either are or are not correct. J. Wesley Schneyer (1965) made this important point a number of years ago, when he stated that merely giving a student blanks to fill in without a discussion of why certain words are or are not correct is like a method of teaching comprehension in which a pupil reads a passage and then answers questions calling for knowledge of word meaning, main ideas, and conclusions. Schneyer emphasizes that a student checking which answers *are* correct and incorrect may never learn *why* they are correct or incorrect: "The reasons for the appropriate responses must be verbalized." (p. 178)

Lea McGee (1981) conducted a study suggesting that cloze passages should initially be constructed so that blanks are easily supplied with correct words. Others have recommended that aural practice with the cloze procedure be provided prior to written work. Materials from which cloze passages are developed should be of high interest and not require excessive knowledge apart from the students' experiences.

Leo Schell (1972) and Robert Bortnick and Genevieve Lopardo (1973) have offered additional specific suggestions for using the cloze procedure as a teaching technique. Some of these suggestions are as follows:

1. In the beginning stages use a multiple-choice format rather than simply leaving blanks and forcing the reader to come up with answers on his or her own. As the student gains confidence and the ability to make correct choices, gradually switch to the standard format of simply deleting words altogether.
2. In the beginning delete only selected words such as nouns and verbs and do not be concerned about deleting every fifth or even every tenth word.
3. After students have been allowed time to read a paragraph silently, read it aloud, sentence by sentence. Students can then offer suggestions on what might fit in the blanks. Semantically and syntactically correct answers should be accepted, but students should be asked to justify their answers. Compare the original passage with students' answers.
4. As students improve their ability to read mutilated passages, you should increase the difficulty of the material. This can be done by using material of a higher reading level, by omitting a larger percentage of the words, or both.

Illustrating Paragraph Structure

Drawing various-sized rectangles to illustrate paragraphs and show the relationship between main ideas and important details is a technique that incorporates writing with reading. This is somewhat similar to having students underline key sentences and/or words but gives students a better overall understanding of the relationships among sentences. In using this technique, main idea sentences are represented by rectangles slightly larger than sentences that represent important details. Note the following paragraph and the corresponding illustration (Figure 6–9).

Meadowlarks are wonderful birds. They sing pretty songs. They are very beautiful. And they destroy insects that would harm our gardens.

The large rectangle at the top of Figure 6–9 represents the main idea sentence, "Meadowlarks are wonderful birds." Each of the three supporting detail sentences are illustrated below it.

In using this system to teach paragraph structure, start out by explaining

FIGURE 6–9   Meadowlarks are Wonderful Birds. They Sing Pretty Songs. They are Very Beautiful. And, They Destroy Insects That Would Harm our Gardens.

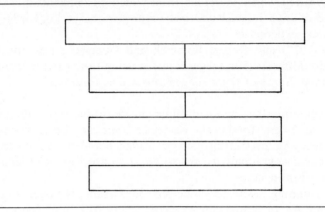

that various-sized rectangles represent main ideas and important details, and then have students write their own paragraphs to fit various structural patterns. Students seem to find it easier in the beginning to write paragraphs of their own to fit a specific pattern than to analyze the structure of someone else's paragraph. This has the added advantage of helping students to improve their ability to write well-structured paragraphs, and for some, to understand what defines a paragraph. To use this as a method of instruction we suggest the following procedure:

1. Introduce the idea as explained above.
2. Draw a simple structural form and have students work in small groups to write a paragraph to fit the form.
3. Change the structure by putting the main idea at the end and then have students rewrite their paragraphs to fit the new form.
4. Illustrate different forms, e.g., a main-idea sentence at the beginning, then several important-detail sentences, and finally a summary sentence. (See Figure 6–10.)
5. Provide students with well-written paragraphs that clearly show main-idea and important-detail sentences; have students illustrate them. Gradually increase the difficulty of the patterns.
6. When students are both writing their own and illustrating others' paragraphs, discuss their responses and allow them to justify what they write or draw. Be sure to accept reasonable alternatives. The important point is not that all students agree on how a paragraph form should be drawn, but that students be able to justify their own illustrations.
7. Have students illustrate each new form and place it on a chart showing various forms. Use colors to differentiate the main-idea rectangles from the important-detail rectangles on the permanent models.

FIGURE 6–10

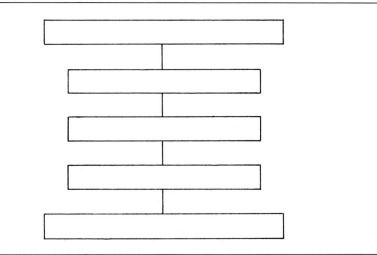

8. Students also enjoy naming different forms; one group of students named the one shown in Figure 6–1 the "natural" and the one with a larger rectangle at both the beginning and the end (Figure 6–2) the "double natural."

In using this method of instruction you should remember that not all paragraphs have a main-idea sentence. It is very frustrating for students if they do not realize this in the early stages of looking for a structural pattern in paragraphs written by others. There are also paragraphs that have the main idea somewhere near the middle, and still others that have two main ideas with supporting detail sentences for only one of the two.

Alternative Procedures for Teaching Main Idea

It is frequently helpful to provide students with a specific strategy for finding the main idea of a paragraph or selection. If students have mastered the prerequisite skills of decoding the words, understanding the vocabulary, and remembering and understanding the details of the paragraph, the following steps will assist them in finding the main idea:[2]

1. Read the paragraph.
2. Study each sentence and restate it in your own words.
3. Ask yourself what one thing most of the sentences were about.
4. Find or state the main idea.
5. Check your answer.

[2]This strategy and these teaching steps were developed by Cheryl Milner, principal, Hayward, California Unified School District.

The last step is very important, though somewhat tedious initially. To "check your answer," students will need to review *each* sentence and ask themselves: "Does this sentence tell about or support the main idea?"

In order to teach this strategy:

1. Introduce the steps.
2. Demonstrate or model the use of the steps with a sample paragraph that all students can follow; one way is to write it on a large chart.
3. Provide a substantial amount of guided practice. This can be accomplished by giving the students a series of short paragraphs and going through each step together.
4. Provide independent practice only after the students have demonstrated ability to complete the steps under teacher guidance.
5. Provide review as needed.

Each of the teaching steps listed above is important if students are to master this skill. Present the strategy on a chart for students to view. Tell the students that you are about to show them how the steps work. It is critical to *show* the students by thinking out loud as the steps are demonstrated. Next, work *with* the students to practice the steps on sample paragraphs. This is a good time for students to discuss their interpretations of sentences and main ideas. The independent practice and later review will enable students to cement the new skill if the previous instruction was effective. A similar strategy and teaching steps may be utilized to teach other specific comprehension skills, such as sequence, cause and effect, and predicting outcomes.

David Moore and John Readence (1980) suggest that teachers can use "parallel lessons" to teach main idea. These lessons progressively develop students' comprehension abilities by moving from the concrete to the abstract and from the simple to the complex.

Moore and Readence begin by providing pictures for students to view. Students locate the main idea of the picture and its supporting details after the teacher has modeled the task and provided multiple-choice samples. The next step is listening, in which the teacher reads a passage aloud or has the students listen to a recorded tape. Again the teacher first demonstrates and then tells the students to find the main idea. The next step is group oral reading, such as choral reading, reader's theater, or play reading. As before, the teacher models and provides a multiple-choice task, and then students determine the main idea. Finally the steps are applied to silent reading.

Phrase Training

A growing body of research indicates that certain types of phrase training can be helpful in a program designed to improve disabled readers' comprehension. In some studies the breaking of material into natural linguistic units is called "chunking." A chunked sentence using slash marks:

Emil was/a small man/but he was/also very strong.

The same chunked sentence using dashes:

Emil was—a small man—but he was—also very strong.

William G. Brozo, Ronald V. Schmelzer, and Hillar A. Spires (1983) studied the use of phrase training and found: "Several studies have shown that poor readers' comprehension is improved when words are preorganized into meaningful groupings for them. . . . Few, however, have shown that word grouping aids comprehension for competent readers." (p. 442)

Kathleen C. Stevens (1981) also studied the use of a chunking procedure. Her study was done with an all-male group of tenth-grade students in a parochial high school. In Stevens's study teachers discussed the use of chunking with students, and the whole procedure, according to Stevens, took approximately ten to fifteen minutes. She found that students who used the chunked passages read significantly better than students who read regular passages. Stevens's recommendations:

> As a first step in teaching "chunking," teachers might present
> "chunked" reading material to students for discussion. Then, students
> might point out the phrase units in prose for themselves. The need to
> "chunk" for every reading task should make the discussion of phrasing
> and of thought units an ongoing activity. This can be emphasized to
> students by reading meaningfully and nonmeaningfully "chunked"
> material. (pp. 128–29)

In an older study Rollin Steiner, Morton Wiener, and Ward Cromer (1971) compared a group of fifth-grade poor readers with a group of good readers. Steiner stated that as contrasted with good readers, the poor readers failed to use syntactic and contextual cues in materials. He believed that poor readers tend to treat words as unrelated items in a series. Other researchers, such as John Downing (1969), have reported that children in the early stages of reading development encounter the same problems; i.e., they do not understand words and phrases in relationship to meaning.

Past studies using the tachistoscope for training in reading skills have tended to indicate that some training at least is of very little value. It appears, however, that certain types of tachistoscope training can be especially helpful to the comprehension process. For example, Bruce Amble (1966) used a series of phrase-training films to provide tachistoscopic practice in phrase reading with a group of fifth- and sixth-grade students. Students using the phrase-training filmstrips made significant gains in comprehension over a control group that did not use the phrase-training films. Amble suggested several reasons why his students may have made more progress than students in other programs who have been instructed using a tachistoscopic technique:

1. Students in Amble's group were at the elementary school level rather than at the high school or adult level as was often the case where tachistoscopic training was not successful.
2. Students were trained using meaningful phrases rather than abstract symbols or numbers or even letters.
3. Practice trials were increased to over 5000 rather than the average of around 1000 in former studies.

The case for phrase training is also supported by Leo Schell (1972), who quotes Carl Lefevre as saying that students must learn to master clause markers such as *if, that,* and *now.* Lefevre said, "Reading clause markers quickly and accurately . . . is a first requirement of effective comprehension of meaning." (p. 423)

In phrase training students should also be taught the meaning of punctuation marks and how these influence the intonation, stress, and pitch of the reader. This can be illustrated by tape recording the oral reading of a student who phrases properly and comparing it with that of a student who does not read punctuation marks properly and thus fails to phrase correctly. Play the tape recording and then discuss why it is easier to derive meaning from material when the phrasing is accurate. Also construct exercises in which commas are omitted and show how the meaning of a phrase can often be influenced by the placement or omission of a comma.

Figures of Speech

Some students, especially those who are bilingual or who have meager language backgrounds, have difficulty with figures of speech. For these students it is often necessary to spend considerable time in discussing what is meant by commonly used figures of speech such as "She was very upset," "She's sitting on top of the world," "He's sitting on a gold mine." The problem in the case of many students is that they do not use these figures of speech in their conversations with their families at home and have not had a chance to hear them often enough elsewhere to know what they mean. There are no fast or sure cures for this problem, but you should note whether disabled readers come from bilingual or non-English-speaking homes. For these students you will need to provide more opportunities for conversation time with their peers who do come from English-speaking homes. In most cases the free interchange of conversation with other students in various school settings will do more to improve their language backgrounds than the remedial teacher has time for or is trained to do. If you use a highlighting pen or some other method of marking figures of speech in materials commonly used for remediation, you will quickly and easily be able to locate them and prepare students for their meanings before they read them.

Mental Imagery

Peter Wolff and Joel Levin (1972) have demonstrated the importance of visual imagery in reading. In several studies they have shown that students who were told to develop a mental image of a scene or of word pairs were able to remember details of the scene or the word pairs better than students who did not use this technique. They also found that good readers seem to possess a greater innate ability to form mental images. Wolff and Levin also point out that in line with the theories of Piaget, children in the first grade or younger age-grade level equivalent cannot generate mental images as well as older children without the aid of a picture or a concrete object. Research done prior to that of Levin and Wolff also demonstrated that children from low socioeconomic levels were not able to develop visual images as well as children from middle or upper socioeconomic levels.

Sandra Steingart and Marvin Glock (1979) found that students instructed in the use of mental imagery recalled significantly more correct text relations, had better recall, and had a higher level of inference ability than students instructed with a repetition technique. Ellen D. Gagné and David Memory (1978) found that general comprehension was better among students who were told to form a mental image than among students who read the same passages after being told to read carefully.

There is also some evidence to indicate that students adept at developing mental images also read more for pleasure, especially fiction. In order to enjoy certain fictional sequences one must develop some mental image of the scene. Also, a mental image of a sequence of events aids recall. There is evidence that some students tend to be image thinkers. It is not known whether this trait is inherited or developed; however, most authorities believe it is amenable to training.

One of the easiest methods of developing mental imagery is through listening to short descriptions. For disabled readers listening exercises are especially helpful, since students can concentrate on developing a mental image rather than expending all of their energies on word-attack skills. Read or play tape-recorded short descriptive passages and then ask students to illustrate what they heard. In the beginning you may wish to have students close their eyes as they listen. After the illustrations have been completed, ask students to compare them. At this time note important features that should have been included and also any details that are not based on the material. As students improve in illustrating scenes from descriptions they hear, have them read and illustrate short descriptive passages. Then discuss these, using the original reading passage as a check on the accuracy of the illustrations.

Following Directions

The ability to follow directions is an important comprehension skill. It is also one that is amenable to teaching, as shown by Clarence Calder, Jr. and

Suleiman Zalatimo (1970), who designed a program in which twenty-six fourth-grade pupils participated for thirty-six weeks. The twenty-six pupils received the same language arts program as a group of twenty-four pupils in a control group, but were requested to work in instructional booklets designed to teach the skill of following directions as related to science, mathematics, art, social studies, and arts and crafts. Students in the experimental group did significantly better on a written test of following directions at the end of the experimental program.

Exercises for teaching the ability to follow directions are simple to devise, and most students find them amusing and challenging to do. Some examples of exercises and materials that are helpful in developing this skill:

1. Have students write directions for getting from one place in the schoolroom to another. Then have a student (or students) read these written directions to see if they end up in the right place. For those who do not, analyze what went wrong.
2. Have students read directions for drawing a certain design, and attempt to draw it as they read or afterward. Show the correctly drawn design on the back of the direction sheet and analyze any obvious errors.
3. Have students work in pairs and assemble model cars and airplanes using the directions enclosed in the kits.
4. Have students practice following directions for paper folding. (There are several books on *origami* that both illustrate and give written directions.)

Sequence of Events

Learning to place a sequence of events in the correct order is a skill that is important in reading social studies and science materials. Exercises for improving students' skills in this area can easily be devised by cutting short stories into paragraphs or by cutting paragraphs up into individual sentences. Exercises can also be made self-correcting by numbering the sentences or paragraphs on the back so that when the student has arranged all parts, he or she has only to turn them over to check the arrangement. Workbook exercises designed to give students practice in this skill have traditionally presented a story and then a series of events that the student is to place in a logical order by placing numbers by each event. The problem with this is that after completing most of the work the student may find he or she has left out one or more events at or near the beginning. This necessitates erasing all the numbers. This can be avoided by cutting up the workbook pages into individual exercises and placing each set of events in an envelope. The events can then be arranged in sequential order and, if in doing the exercise the student discovers an event was omitted at the beginning, he or she only has to slide it into its proper place. When using this system each exercise can be used many times.

When devising exercises for giving students practice in ordering events properly, you may want to begin by using only three or four short sentences for a paragraph as follows:

> They saw many animals.
> Soon Josie was tired and wanted to go home.
> Josie and her father went to the zoo.
> One of the animals was an elephant.

In the beginning stages of instruction discuss why a certain paragraph, such as the one illustrated above, could only be sequenced in one way. Also discuss any other logical sequences if they exist. After students become adept at arranging sentences in paragraphs, they can begin work on longer exercises such as paragraphs into stories. In devising exercises of this nature be sure to use stories or paragraphs that show a definite sequence of events that can be determined through careful reasoning. Comic strips work well as beginning exercises, since most of them contain clues to their logical sequence.

Use of Pictures or Objects

The use of pictures and/or cartoons is often a good beginning point in helping students develop the higher-level comprehension skills such as making interpretations and evaluations. Since the stimulus in a picture is continuously present, it is somewhat easier for beginning students to make evaluations of them than of written materials. The suggestions that follow are similar to part of the parallel-lessons procedure that Moore and Readence developed and which is described earlier in this chapter.

As students look at a cartoon you can ask such questions as, "Why do you think the artist showed the president looking so mean?" "Does he usually look this way?" "Would you have shown him this way if you had been drawing the cartoon?" "What effect is this likely to have on the people who read it?" After students have begun to indicate that they understand interpretative and evaluative questions, you can switch to short reading passages and use questions that call for the same types of skills used in interpreting and evaluating the pictures.

Pictures also work well as a beginning point in teaching students to make inferences; e.g., in a picture of a high snow-capped mountain you might ask, "What do you think the weather is like at the top?" "Why?" "Do you think anyone lives at the top of this mountain?" "Why?" From working with pictures you can proceed to simple paragraphs:

> Norma put on her bathing suit.
> She sat down beside the pool.
> The water was very still.
> She soon moved under the umbrella.

Ask questions such as, "What kind of a day do you think it was?" "Why?" "Were there other people in the pool?" "How do you know?" One important point is that the use of pictures to accompany written prose does not in most cases improve comprehension. In a review of the research, S. Jay Samuels (1970) found that the use of pictures tended to interfere with the acquisition of a sight vocabulary when children were learning to read and that pictures did not facilitate comprehension. He did, however, find that pictures depicting multiethnic groups resulted in a positive change of students' attitude toward the ethnic groups that were depicted.

Stephen Elliot and James Carroll (1980) reported that manipulation of objects may assist students in comprehending what they read. Elliot and Carroll recommend the use of a storyboard to accompany children's reading. After the student completes a sentence, he or she manipulates objects on the board to provide a concrete demonstration of what was read. It is suggested that this active involvement on the part of the reader will not only increase the student's comprehension but also serve as a visual check of the reader's understanding.

Other Methods for Remediating Comprehension Difficulties

Linda Henderson and James Shanker (1978) reported on the use of interpretive dramatics activities in place of basal-reader workbooks to develop the comprehension skills of recognition and recall of details, sequencing of events, and generalizing the main idea. They found that comprehension among second-grade students was significantly higher in all three areas, as measured by written tests, when using interpretive dramatics. In addition, the pupils strongly preferred this approach. The method, which took no longer than workbook activities, consisted of (1) a predrama discussion to determine the number of characters and identify roles, (2) acting out of the story with no or minimal props, (3) discussion to determine whether the critical elements of the story were portrayed. Since all children were required to participate in acting out each story, most stories were dramatized more than once. Additional findings included an increased interest in the stories by the students who would later act them out and spontaneous dramatization of stories by children after pleasure reading at the classroom library center. The increased comprehension of the students after interpretative dramatics may be explained by a number of factors. These include (1) the fact that students might have read more carefully knowing that they would later have to act out the story, (2) increased motivation, and (3) the reinforcing effect of the dramatizations.

Samuel Perez (1981) recommends a method that he calls the "retelling technique," in which students are asked to elaborate on what was read by retelling a story in their own words. The teacher's role is to prompt responses, practice active listening, and wait patiently without interrupting the student's retelling.

James Christie (1980) is one of a number of writers who recommend the use of sentence-combining activities to promote reading comprehension. Originally, sentence-combining exercises were used to improve students' writing skills. However, Warren Combs (1977) suggests that this approach will improve students' reading comprehension by helping them understand complex syntactic structures. Sentence combining involves changing simple sentences into complex sentences by using signal words, such as *that, what,* and *because:*

1. Bob did not know SOMETHING.
   His cat escaped. (that)
   He forgot to close the door. (because)
2. Bob did not know that his cat escaped because he forgot to close the door.

Combs's article provides specific suggestions for teachers who wish to develop their own sentence-combining exercises. Or use commercially prepared activities. (See Horst and Rosenberger, 1981; Strong, 1973.)

One of the most effective means of increasing students' comprehension is by getting them to do a great deal of free or recreational reading. Wide reading usually results in an increase in students' vocabularies as well as in their general knowledge of their environment. Although some students need instruction in aspects of comprehension such as following directions or seeing a sequence of events, there is no substitute for time spent in simply practicing the art of reading. Perhaps an analogy to sports is appropriate. Athletes never make all-American by sitting on the bench listening to the coach tell them how they should play. Likewise, students never become expert readers by listening to the teacher tell them how they should read. Once the basics are mastered, the secret is to read, read, read.

There are many commercial materials designed to aid students in developing comprehension skills. Most of these are books or kits that provide reading materials at various levels of difficulty with accompanying questions. There is still a dearth of material actually designed to show the student how to comprehend. You will find a list of programs for teaching comprehension, the level for which they are appropriate, and the publishers of the materials in Appendix C.

METHODS OF REMEDIATING VOCABULARY DEFICIENCIES

There are many ways of remediating vocabulary deficiencies, but there is no substitute for wide reading. Many students in the beginning stages of remedial reading are unable to read widely, and others, if they could, would not. However, as you begin a program of remediation in vocabulary skills you should always encourage students to read as much as possible on their own. Since the meanings of many words can be learned through context and through repeated exposure, it is not necessary to teach every new word. Only a very small percentage of the total meaning vocabulary of adults is achieved through specific vocabulary instruction or through the use of the dictionary. One of the most serious problems that we are likely to encounter is that fact that students in remedial reading often get very little practice in the act of reading. Richard Allington (1977) and his assistants visited a number of remedial reading classrooms to determine the amount of reading students were required to do. He found that in the course of any one period no student read over 110 words in context and none read less than 24. Allington stated, "If, in a typical week of reading instruction, students only encounter 150–500 words in context, one has to ask: How are they ever gonna get good?" (p. 58)

Another important point to remember in starting a program of vocabulary development is to try to break the habit of skipping unknown words. Not only disabled readers but most people have this habit to some extent. Most people remember a number of times when they have learned a new word from a discussion of its meaning or by looking it up in the dictionary. They then found that during the next few weeks they came across the word a number of times in their reading. Common sense tells that they did not just "happen" to read the new word during the weeks following learning it, but that it had probably appeared many times before and gone unnoticed. The problem is that many people train themselves *not* to notice words because it is much more convenient. You can help break this habit in disabled readers by simply talking about it and by calling their attention to new words by using games and contests. Give several disabled readers the same reading passage and see who can find the most words for which other students do not know the meaning. Or have students read short passages and look up any words they do not know. Then let other students give the ones who read the passage an oral quiz on the meanings of various words found in the passage. Another method of calling attention to new words is to have students carry a pack of 3 in. × 5 in. cards with them. Each time they find a new vocabulary word, they are to write the word on one of the cards. They should also write the original sentence in which it was found and then look it up in the dictionary and write its definition and a new sentence using it in the same context as the original sentence. At the end of the week have each student discuss new words he or she has learned with several other students.

The important point is that the number of new words learned is not so important as the fact that you are helping students break the habit of skipping unknown words. And the development of an awareness to word meaning is an important first step in vocabulary building.

A large part of everyone's vocabulary is developed through both oral and written context. Although the exact meaning of a word often cannot be derived from the context, the sheer volume of words that one hears and reads in context insures that many words will be repeated in context enough times so that word meanings gradually become known. Many students realize that word meanings can to some extent be derived by noting their use in context.

However, some students need specific instruction and reinforcement in the use of context clues as an aid to word meaning.

In the beginning stages of instruction in the use of context clues, use sentences that contain obvious clues to word meaning, e.g., "It has been dry for some time, but now it is very *humid.*" Ask questions such as, "What do you think *humid* means?" "How did you figure it out?" and "Are we often able to do this with other words?" After students have become somewhat adept at deriving the meaning of obvious context clues, you should use their own textbooks for instruction. The use of students' textbooks will give them a feeling of the immediacy of application of the skill. Find a certain paragraph that contains one or more new words, and have students read silently and find these words. Then discuss the possible meanings of these words based on the way they were used and the position they occupy in the sentence. The teaching of the use of context clues should be a long-term effort, i.e., should continue on a somewhat regular basis for a long time, even after the formal teaching has been completed.

The use of the dictionary should be taught to any student who is at a third- to fourth-grade level or above and is not adept at it. You should keep in mind, however, that only a rather small percentage of total vocabulary is developed through it. Furthermore, the dictionary is usually effective only if used in conjunction with other techniques. For example, once when one of us worked as a reading consultant we checked several classes who had just had an hour of work on word meaning with the dictionary. Immediately following the one-hour period students were checked to see what percentage of the word meanings they had retained. These students were able to accurately recall the meanings of only about 20 percent of the words.

After conducting research designed to investigate the relative effectiveness of four techniques for teaching word meanings, Joan Gipe (1978–1979) concluded:

> Findings were interpreted as supportive of vocabulary instruction, which includes using new words in sentences that provide examples of appropriate usage of the new word within the context of familiar events. Associating new words with familiar synonyms was also supported. Use of category labels and dictionary practice was not strongly supported. (p. 624)

Mary Ann Jiganti and Mary Ann Tindall (1986) cite research indicating that a new word is more easily learned if it is incorporated into existing cognitive schemes and that methods that excite student interest are more effective. Jiganti and Tindall did a study in which they used a set of categorization exercises to help students tie words into existing schema of knowledge. They also experimented with the use of drama techniques to excite student interest. These techniques were compared with a traditional method in which students were asked to find the meanings of words in the dictionary and then write a sentence to demonstrate knowledge of the word.

Jiganti and Tindall found categorization and drama exercises to be superior to the traditional approach on multiple choice tests and on sentence tests of word usage. The results held true for immediate recall as well as long-term retention. In discussing the results of their study the authors stated:

> While supporting the effectiveness of category and dramatic activities, our data did not show any clear advantage of one classroom technique over the other. The similar results obtained from both methods suggest that their common ingredients (e.g., group interaction and enthusiasm, use of new words in correct context, and exploration of word relationships) may provide the most effective recipe for vocabulary learning. (p. 447)

A number of other researchers and writers (Pearson, 1985; Schwartz and Raphael, 1985) have also reached the same conclusion, that words are more easily learned if they are incorporated into students' existing cognitive schemes. The semantic mapping procedure illustrated by Sinatra, Stahl-Gemake and Berg and by Dale Johnson (1983), and discussed in this chapter, can easily be used for this purpose.

Ula Price Casale (1985) has found the use of motor imaging to some extent successful. Casale noted that when students attempted to recall word meanings, they tended to make slight hand gestures similar to the ones Casale used in teaching the same words. Casale's other observations confirmed the original theory that most people use subtle hand or body gestures when they search for a word in memory. From these observations Casale developed the following six-step procedure for teaching a word through motor imaging:

Step 1: The teacher writes a word on the chalkboard or overhead projector, pronounces it, and finally tells the class what it means.

Step 2: The teacher instructs the class to imagine how they might pantomime the word to show its meaning.

Step 3: The teacher instructs the class to pantomime the word. Upon being given a specific cue, all begin.

Step 4: The teacher watches the class to determine the most common pantomime, then explains it to the class. The students pantomime the word while saying it.

Step 5: The teacher repeats each new word and directs the class to pantomime it and say a brief meaning or synonym.

Step 6: The students read the selection that contains the new words.

Casale states that even quite abstract words can be defined for students in language that translates easily into motor imaging. For example, the word *appropriate* can be defined as "right or fit for a certain purpose." (p. 620) An example of the language meaning and motor meaning for this and several other words:

New Word	*Language Meaning*	*Motor Meaning*
appropriate	right or fit for a certain purpose	both palms together, matching perfectly
woe	great sadness or trouble	one or both hands over the eyes, head slanted forward
abode	place where you live	hands meeting above the head in a triangular "roof" shape

(p. 620)

Dale Johnson has written widely on the subject of vocabulary development. Among his excellent writings is "Three Sound Strategies for Vocabulary Development." The strategies:[3]

All words, like all real-world objects and events, can be placed in categories. In fact, the ability of the human mind to categorize, to examine the similarities and differences between two or more concepts, to draw relationships, is what enables humans to learn. Nothing can be learned in isolation. Try to think of anything you have ever learned and how you learned it and you will quickly recollect that you learned it in relation to something you already knew. You categorized it. You might have learned the meaning of *lavender* in relation to your knowledge of blue or red or purple or pink. *Spindle* might have been learned in relation to bend, fold, and mutilate and your experience with computer-card mentality. A child may not know the meaning of *mammoth* but can be helped to relate it to big, large, huge, and gigantic. The meaning of *Albasa* will remain a mystery unless you are able to relate it to things already known—that is to categorize it.

The three instructional strategies for vocabulary development described in the pages that follow are built upon this understanding. Semantic associations, semantic mapping, and semantic feature analysis are activities that stress relationships and which involve classification.

[3]Reprinted by permission of the author and Ginn & Company from "Three Sound Strategies for Vocabulary Development." *Ginn Occasional Papers,* 1983.

SEMANTIC ASSOCIATIONS

The object of semantic associations is to expand vocabulary by involving children with words that share some common feature. Begin this as a group or independent activity, but in either case it must culminate in group discussion to be worthwhile. The following are the steps in the procedure; creative teachers will think of ways to vary them.

1. Choose any word or words of interest to you or to the class. They may be words from the day's basal reader story, or from a social studies lesson, or from another source of common interest or need.
2. Write the word(s) on the chalkboard. For example, you might write the words *chew* and *meat* before the students read a story about the digestive system.
3. Ask half the class to write as many things as they can think of that can be done to meat. Have the other half write as many chewable things as they can think of. Allow time for the class to think and write independently or in groups.
4. On the chalkboard compile lists of all the words the students thought of. For example:

Meat

cook	marinate	buy	braise
eat	broil	pound	heat
chew	bake	cut	baste
taste	fry	hunt	put on black eye
savor	wrap	package	slice
season	sell	tenderize	smell

5. As an additional activity, you may have children use six of the words in sentences.

Chew

gum	cud	bread	taffy
candy	the fat	knuckles	apples
fingernails	food	paper	pens
pencils	caramels	someone out	toothpick
hair	meat	paper clips	grass

6. Lead a discussion on the meanings and uses of any of the words that are new to any class members. Many may know what it means to *season,*

or *salt* and *pepper* meat, but have never heard the word *marinate*. Others understand *cook, fry,* and *bake* but are unfamiliar with *broil* and *braise*. Thus new words can be learned by classifying them with words already known: things that affect flavor, types of cooking, preparation for cooking. In addition to learning new words, new meaning or associations for known words will develop. Most students probably associate *pound* with nails rather than meat. They can expand their conceptualization of *pound* by realizing it is something that is done to different objects for different purposes. With the word *chew* students begin to see classes of edibles and inedibles, denotative and connotative uses of *chew*. They can explore purposes. When do people chew fingernails as opposed to blades of grass? Discussion is crucial to extension of vocabulary because it helps expand categories.

With semantic association new knowledge can be gained and old knowledge can be re-examined, mulled, recategorized.

SEMANTIC MAPPING

This is not a new strategy. It has been around for a long time and has been called by several different names: cognitive networks, semantic webbing, semantic network, and plot map. For the purpose of vocabulary expansion, semantic mapping extends knowledge by displaying in categories words related to another word. This differs from semantic association essentially by showing the categories. The following steps constitute the procedure. Again, the procedures can be varied to suit different purposes. SEEING "OLD" WORDS IN A NEW LIGHT AND SEEING THE RELATIONSHIPS AMONG WORDS ARE THE DESIRABLE AND INEVITABLE OUTCOMES OF SEMANTIC MAPPING.

1. Select a word central to the story to be read, or from any other source of classroom interest or need.
2. Write the word on the chalkboard.
3. Ask the class to think of as many words as they can that are in some way related to the word you have written, and jot them on paper in categories.
4. Have individuals share the words they have written and as they do, write them on the board and attempt to put them into categories. For example, if the word you wrote on the board was *school,* the compiled semantic map might look like Figure 6–11:

FIGURE 6–11 Semantic Map of School

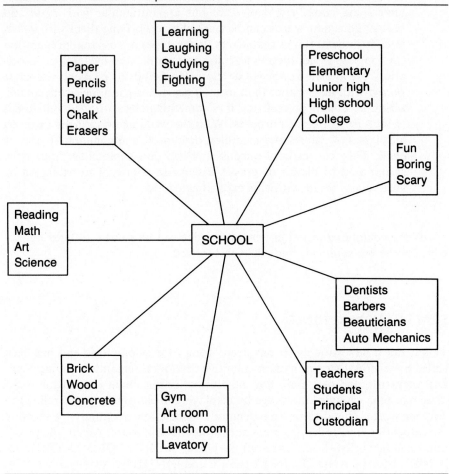

5. Next, number the categories and have the students name them:
   1. School subjects
   2. Things we use in school
   3. Places in school
   4. Kinds of schools
   5. Things school can be, etc.
6. As with semantic association, discussion is crucial to the success of semantic mapping. The meanings and uses of new words, new meanings for known words, seeing "old" words in a new light, and seeing the relationships among words are the desirable (and inevitable) outcomes of semantic mapping. Be ready for some disagreement; you may have put a word in one category when it could as sensibly be put in

another. Some words will end up in several categories. New words will typically be added as the discussion ensues.

7. As the discussion concludes, it is often necessary to focus attention on one or two categories mapped from the central concept. For example, you may need to say something like this:

"We've prepared quite a map about school and have listed words in nine categories! That's great! The selection we're going to read is about the different kind of schools to be found in our society. It describes public, private, and parochial schools as well as trade schools and specialty schools. Which two category lists on our semantic map contain words descriptive of different kinds of schools? Let's talk about these words."

This type of focusing discussion, which directs students' attention to specific words on the map, is appropriate when you are using semantic mapping as a selection-specific prereading activity. Often semantic mapping is done for general vocabulary development instead of prereading (e.g., using a current event, holiday, film, etc., as the central concept) and then focusing is not a necessary part of the discussion.

SEMANTIC FEATURE ANALYSIS

Semantic feature analysis, like the other strategies, can be done with students of any age. It capitalizes on a reader's prior knowledge (and the ways it is organized) and has considerable potential for greatly expanding vocabulary in a logical and sensible way. Like semantic association and semantic mapping, semantic feature analysis stresses the relationships among concepts within categories.

The procedure is very simple. Begin with a list of known words that share some features. If the words are known to the students, you might begin with types of tools: hammer, saw, scissors, hoe, pliers. These words are listed in a column on the chalkboard or on paper. Next have the students suggest features that at least one of the words usually possesses. These features are listed in a row across the top of the board or paper. Then have the children fill in the matrix by putting a plus or a minus beside each word under each feature as is shown in Figure 6–12. WITH EVEN THE MOST SYNONYMOUS PAIRS OR CLUSTERS OF WORDS, THE PATTERN WILL EVENTUALLY BECOME DIFFERENT ONCE ENOUGH SEMANTIC FEATURES HAVE BEEN LISTED.

This semantic feature grid shows that a hammer is used to pound, is used with wood, and has a handle. It does not usually cut or grip cloth or dirt. A hoe is a tool with a handle and is usually used to cut in dirt.

We favor the use of pluses ($+$) and minuses ($-$) to indicate whether or not a word usually has a given feature even though many features of words

FIGURE 6–12

TOPIC: TOOLS

Features

Words	Pounds	Cuts	Grips	Wood	Cloth	Dirt	Handle
hammer	+	–	–	+	–	–	+
saw	–	+	–	+	–	–	+
scissors	–	+	–	–	+	–	+
pliers	–	–	+	+	–	–	+
hoe	–	+	–	–	–	+	+

Feature

Word									

exist in varying degrees. As children learn to read better and become more skilled with feature analysis, it is appropriate to substitute a scale of numbers (1 to 3 or 0 to 10, for example) for pluses and minuses. This will allow for greater precision, for few things in life are all black or all white.

After the grid has been completed, you can introduce two more activities. Ask the children to suggest more words that share some of the features (screwdriver, rake, beater, or thimble, file, blade), and then have them suggest more features shared by some of these words (metal, kitchen, garden, two hands). Unless you have enormous chalkboards or lots of paper in your room, you will probably run out of space or time before you run out of features or words. Have the children complete the remainder of the matrix by adding pluses and minuses. Finally, help them discover that no two words have the identical pattern of pluses and minuses; thus no two words are identical in meaning. With even the most synonymous pairs of clusters of words the pattern will eventually become different once enough semantic features have been listed. In addition to discovering the uniqueness of words, children learn new words within a category and new semantic features they perhaps had not thought about. Group discussion of the words and their features is essential.

It is very important for children to grasp the fact that the term synonym refers to "something like," not "the same as." Until they clearly realize this truth, a good deal of semantic precision is lost to children, both as they read and as they write. Semantic feature analysis is a worthwhile activity for two reasons. First of all, it helps to demonstrate clearly the uniqueness of each individual word, and secondly, it is useful for direct instruction to add "something-like" synonyms to the individual's vocabulary.

Children asked to list the semantic features of the word carrot might very quickly mention "something to eat," "something to cook," "something to chew," but eventually might add "something to plant," "something to sell," "something to cut," "something to buy," and so on. In other words, they begin to discover what they already knew but hadn't thought of, and they begin to view words in more complex and precise ways.

Semantic feature charts can be constructed for any categories of words. Begin with categories that are concrete and within the experience of your pupils and then progress to more abstract or less familiar categories. A few beginning categories:

games	vegetables	pets
occupations	food	clothing
tools	buildings	animals
plants	vehicles	furniture

Later categories:

moods	sizes	entertainment
feelings	shapes	musical instruments
commands	modes of communication	machines

The categories of words in our language would make a lengthy list, as would the words and features within many categories.

In summary, semantic feature analysis involves the following steps:

1. Select a category (tools).
2. List in a column some words within the category (hammer, saw).
3. List in a row some features shared by some of the words (pounds, cuts).
4. Put a plus or a minus beside each word beneath each feature.
5. Add words.
6. Add features.
7. Complete the expanded matrix with pluses and minuses.
8. Discover and discuss the uniqueness of each word. This is crucial.
9. Repeat the process with another category.

As children gain experience with semantic feature analysis, they will begin to see that some words share the same features but vary in the amounts or degrees of that feature. (Both illnesses and diseases are serious, but diseases are more serious.) At that time you may want to switch from a plus and minus system to a numerical system (0 = none; 1 = few or some; 2 = most or much; 3 = all) so that greater precision can be attained. [In Figure 6–12 hammer received a minus under grips, which would equal a 0. But since not all hammers are used on wood, the plus under wood might become a 2.]

Semantic feature analysis works for learners of all ages, preschool (as an oral activity) through college. It is a powerful procedure with content-area materials as well as with intensive vocabulary instruction.

Reading comprehension involves processing textual material and integrating it with the experiences, prior knowledge and attitudes already in a reader's mind. Comprehending is, in metaphor, "building bridges between the new and the known" (Johnson). Semantic association, semantic mapping, and semantic feature analysis are three sound and exciting instructional strategies based on that metaphor and designed to get at the relationships among concepts through classification.

SUMMARY

There has been a renaissance in the study of reading comprehension. Apparently, more reading educators are interested in this subject than in any other subject in the field of reading. This interest has brought about a number of new techniques for the teaching of both reading comprehension and reading vocabulary. However, we still know very little about the nature of reading comprehension and whether the so-called subskills usually identified on our most popular testing instruments actually exist as separate entities. Our most-used methods of testing reading comprehension include the use of group standardized reading achievement tests, individualized standardized reading tests, informal reading inventories (IRIs), informal recall procedures, and the cloze procedure. The most popular methods of diagnosing knowledge of reading vocabulary include group standardized reading achievement tests, the subtests of individualized intelligence tests, IRIs, and informal questioning.

Although little is yet known about the so-called subskills of reading comprehension, we believe that the techniques classified as metacognition and used for teaching reading comprehension are especially helpful to disabled readers. We also believe that the techniques called "semantic webbing" and "semantic mapping" can be helpful in teaching reading comprehension and especially in teaching reading vocabulary to disabled readers.

One of the most important points, of which all beginning and practicing teachers should be aware, is that students need lots of practice in the act of reading. Unfortunately, research indicated that students in reading disability classes often get less practice in the act of reading than those in a normally achieving classroom.

REFERENCES

Allington, R. L. (1977). If they don't read much, how are they ever gonna get good? *Journal of Reading, 21,* 57–61.

Amble, B. R. (1966). Phrase reading training and reading achievement of school children. *Reading Teacher, 20,* 210–215.

Asher, S. R., Hymel, S., & Wigfield, A. (1978). Influence of topic behavior. *Journal of Reading Behavior, 10,* 35–47.

August, D. L., Flavell, J. H., & Clift, R. (1984). Comparison of comprehension monitoring of skilled and less skilled readers. *Reading Research Quarterly, 20,* 39–53.

Babbs, P. J. (1984). Monitoring cards help improve comprehension. *Reading Teacher, 38,* 200–204.

Bormuth, J. R. (1967). Comparable cloze and multiple-choice comprehension test scores. *Journal of Reading, 10,* 291–299.

Bortnick, R., & Lopardo, G. S. (1973). An instructional application of the cloze procedure. *Journal of Reading, 16,* 296–300.

Brozo, W. G., Schmelzer, R. V., & Spires, H. A. (1983). The beneficial effect of chunking on good readers' comprehension of expository prose. *Journal of Reading, 26,* 442–445.

Calder, C. R., Jr., & Zalatimo, S. D. (1970). Improving children's ability to follow directions. *Reading Teacher, 24,* 227–231 +.

Casale, U. P. (1985). Motor imaging: A reading-vocabulary strategy. *Journal of Reading, 28,* 619–621.

Christie, J. F. (1980). Syntax: A key to reading comprehension. *Reading Improvement, 17,* 313–317.

Clark, F. L., Deshler, D. D., Schumaker, J. B., Alley, G. R., & Warner, M. M. (1984). Visual imagery and self-questioning strategies to improve comprehension of written material. *Journal of Learning Disabilities, 17,* 145–149.

Clay, M. M. (1979). *The early detection of reading difficulties* (2nd ed.). Exeter, NH: Heinemann.

Cohen, R. (1983). Self-generated questions as an aid to reading comprehension. *Reading Teacher, 36,* 770–775.

Cohn, M. L. (1969). Structured comprehension. *Reading Teacher, 22,* 440–444 +.

Combs, W. (1977). Sentence-combining practice aids reading comprehension. *Journal of Reading, 21,* 18–24.

Cunningham, P. (1984). Curriculum trends in reading. *Educational Leadership, 41,* 83–84.

Downing, J. (1969). How children think about reading. *Reading Teacher, 23,* 217–230.

Durkin, D. (1978-1979). What classroom observations reveal about reading comprehension instruction. *Reading Research Quarterly, 14,* 481–533.

Durrell, D. D., & Catterson, J. H. (1980). *Durrell analysis of reading difficulty.* New York: Psychological Corporation.

Elliot, S. N., & Carroll, J. L. (1980). Strategies to help children remember what they read. *Reading Improvement, 17,* 272–277.

Erickson, L. G., Stahl, S. A., & Rinehart, S. D. (1985). Metacognitive abilities of above and below average readers: Effects of conceptual tempo, passage level, and error type on error detection. *Journal of Reading Behavior, 3,* 235–251.

Fowler, G. (1982). Developing comprehension skills in primary students through the use of story frames. *Reading Teacher, 36,* 176–179.

Fowler, G., & Coley, J. D. (1986). Using story frames with various literary genres. In L. B. Gambrell, J. D. Coley, & E. M. McLaughlin (Eds.), *1986 Yearbook of The State of Maryland International Reading Association:* (pp. 66–72).

Gagné, E. D., & Memory, D. (1978). Instructional events and comprehension: Generalization across passages. *Journal of Reading Behavior, 10,* 321–335.

Gambrell, L. B. (1980). Think-time implications for reading instruction. *Reading Teacher, 32,* 534–537.

Garner, R., Hare, V. C., Alexander, P., Haynes, J., & Winograd, P. (1984). Introducing use of a text lookback strategy among unsuccessful readers. *American Educational Research Journal, 21,* 789–798.

Gilmore, J. V., & Gilmore, E. C. (1968). *Gilmore oral reading test.* New York: Harcourt, Brace & World.

Gipe, J. (1978–1979). Investigating techniques for teaching word meanings. *Reading Research Quarterly, 14,* 624–644.

Gray, W. S. (1967). *Gray oral reading tests* (rev. ed.). Edited by H. M. Robinson. Indianapolis: Bobbs-Merrill.

Guszak, F. (1967). Teacher questioning and reading. *Reading Teacher, 21,* 227–234.

Hansen, J., & Hubbard, R. (1984). Poor readers can draw inferences. *Reading Teacher, 37,* 586–589.

Harris, A. J., & Sipay, E. R. (1985). *How to increase reading ability* (8th ed.). New York: Longman.

Haynes, J. E., & Fillmer, H. T. (1984). Paraphrasing and reading comprehension. *Reading World, 24,* 76–79.

Heller, M. F. (1986). How do you know? Metacognitive modeling in the content areas. *Journal of Reading, 29,* 415–422.

Henderson, L. C., & Shanker, J. L. (1978). The use of interpretive dramatics versus basal reader workbooks for developing comprehension skills. *Reading World, 17,* 239–243.

Hodges, C. A. (1980). Toward a broader definition of comprehension instruction. *Reading Research Quarterly, 15,* 299–306.

Horst, W. H., & Rosenberger, D. A. (1981). *Sentence combining.* Evanston, IL: Littell & Company.

Hansen, J., & Hubbard, R. (1984). Poor readers can draw inferences. *Reading Teacher, 37,* 586–589.

Jiganti, M. A., & Tindall, M. A. (1986). An interactive approach to teaching vocabulary. *Reading Teacher, 39,* 444–448.

Johnson, D. D. (1983). Three sound strategies for vocabulary development. *Occasional paper no. 3.* Columbus, OH: Ginn and Company.

Johnston, P. H., & Allington, R. L. (1983). Commentary: How sharp is a unicorn's horn? *Reading Research Quarterly, 18,* 498–500.

Kalmbach, J. R. (1986). Getting at the point of retellings. *Journal of Reading, 29,* 326–333.

Karlsen, G., Madden, R., & Gardner, E. F. (1976). *Stanford diagnostic reading tests.* New York: Harcourt, Brace & Jovanovich.

Livingston, H. F. (1972). What the reading test doesn't test—reading, *Journal of Reading, 15,* 402–410.

McGee, L. M. (1981). Effects of the Cloze procedure on good and poor readers' comprehension. *Journal of Reading Behavior, 13,* 145–156.

Manzo, A. V. (1969). The request procedure. *Journal of Reading, 13,* 123–126+.

Mier, M. (1984). Comprehension monitoring in the elementary classroom. *Reading Teacher, 37,* 770–774.

Moore, D. W., & Readence, J. B. (1980). Processing main ideas through parallel lesson transfer. *Journal of Reading, 23,* 589–593.

Neville, D. D., & Hoffman, R. R. (1981). The effect of personalized stories on the cloze comprehension of seventh grade retarded readers. *Journal of Reading, 24,* 475–478.

Nicholson, T., & Imlach, R. (1981). Where do their answers come from? A study of the inferences which children make when answering questions about narrative stories. *Journal of Reading Behavior, 13,* 111–129.

Pallincsar, A. (1981). *Corrective feedback and strategy training to improve comprehension of poor readers.* Unpublished manuscript, University of Illinois, Urbana, IL.

Pearson, P. D. (1985). Changing the face of reading comprehension instruction. *Reading Teacher, 38,* 724–738.

Pearson, P. D. (1982). A primer for schema theory. *The Volta Review, 84,* 25–33.

Perez, S. A. (1981). Effective approaches for improving the reading comprehension of problem readers. *Reading Horizons, 22,* 57–65.

Rankin, E. F., & Culhane, J. W. (1969). Comparable cloze and multiple choice comprehension test scores. *Journal of Reading, 13,* 193–198.

Reutzel, R. D. (1985). Story maps improve comprehension. *Reading Teacher, 38,* 400–404.

Riley, J. D. (1979). Teachers' responses are as important as the questions they ask. *Reading Teacher, 32,* 534–537.

Robinson, F. P. (1941). *Effective study.* New York: Harper & Row.

Samuels, S. J. (1979). Effects of pictures on learning to read, comprehension and attitudes. *Review of Educational Research, 40,* 397–407.

Sanacore, J. (1984). Metacognition and the improvement of reading: Some important links. *Journal of Reading, 27,* 706–712.

Schell, L. M., & Hanna, G. S. (1981). Can informal reading inventories reveal strengths and weaknesses in comprehension subskills? *Reading Teacher, 35,* 263–268.

Schell, L. M., & Jennings, R. E. (1981). Test review: Durrell analysis of reading difficulty (3rd ed.). *Reading Teacher, 35,* 204–210.

Schneyer, J. W. (1965). Use of the cloze procedure for improving reading comprehension. *Reading Teacher, 19,* 174–179.

Schwartz, R. M., & Raphale, T. E. (1985). Concept definition: A key to improving students' vocabulary. *Reading Teacher, 39,* 198–205.

Shores, J. H. (1968). Dimensions of reading speed and comprehension. *Elementary English, 45,* 23–28.

Shugarman, S. L., & Hurst, J. B. (1986). Purposeful paraphrasing: Promoting a nontrivial pursuit for meaning. *Journal of Reading, 29,* 396–399.

Simons, H. (1971). Reading comprehension: The need for a new perspective. *Reading Research Quarterly, 6,* 338–362.

Sinatra, R. C., Stahl-Gemake, J., & Berg, D. N. (1984). Improving reading comprehension of disabled readers through semantic mapping. *Reading Teacher, 38,* 22–29.

Smith, R. J., & Dauer, V. L. (1984). A comprehension-monitoring strategy for reading content area materials. *Journal of Reading, 28,* 144–147.

Smith, S. P. (1985). Comprehension and comprehension monitoring by experienced readers. *Journal of Reading, 28,* 292–300.

Spache, G. D. (1981a). *Diagnosing and correcting reading disabilities* (2d ed.). Boston: Allyn and Bacon.

Spache, G. D. (1981b). *Diagnostic reading scales* (rev. ed.). Monterey, CA: CTB/McGraw-Hill.

Steffensen, M. S., Joag-Dev, C., & Anderson, R. C. (1979). A cross-cultural perspective on reading comprehension. *Reading Research Quarterly, 15,* 10–29.

Steiner, R., Wiener, M., & Cromer, W. (1971). Comprehension training and identification for poor and good readers. *Journal of Educational Psychology, 62,* 506–513.

Steingart, S. K., & Glock, M. D. (1979). Imagery and the recall of connected discourse. *Reading Research Quarterly, 15,* 66–83.

Stevens, K. C. (1981). Chunking material as an aid to reading comprehension. *Journal of Reading, 25,* 126–129.

Stevens, K. C. (1982). Helping students understand complicated sentences. *Reading Horizons, 22,* 184–190.

Stevens, K. C. (1980). The effect of topic interest on the reading comprehension of higher ability students. *Journal of Education Research, 73,* 365–368.

Stewart, O., & Ebo, T. (1983). Some implications of metacognition for reading instruction. *Journal of Reading, 27,* 36–43.

Strange, M. (1980). Instructional implications of a conceptual theory of reading comprehension. *Reading Teacher, 33,* 391–397.

Strong, W. (1973). *Sentence combining.* New York: Random House.

Terman, L., & Merril, M. A. (1972). *Stanford-Binet intelligence scale* (rev. ed.). Boston: Houghton Mifflin.

Wechsler, D. (1955). *Wechsler adult intelligence scale.* New York: Psychological Corporation.

Wechsler, D. (1974). *Wechsler intelligence scale for children* (rev. ed.). New York: Psychological Corporation.

Willford, Robert. Comprehension: What reading's all about. *Grade Teacher, 85,* 99–103.

Wolff, P., & Levin, J. R. (1972). Role of overt activity in children's imagery production. *Report from the project on variables and processes in cognitive learning in program 1, conditions and processes of learning, Wisconsin Research and Development Center for Cognitive Learning.* Madison: University of Wisconsin Press.

7

Diagnosis and Remediation of Psychological and Sociological Problems

The first purpose of this chapter is to present information on the importance and nature of diagnosis for psychological and sociological problems that the disabled reader may possess; a second purpose is to discuss some specific diagnostic procedures; and the last is to present some techniques for dealing with problems in this area.

Part A: DIAGNOSIS

AN OVERVIEW OF PSYCHOLOGICAL AND SOCIOLOGICAL PROBLEMS

The psychological and sociological problems with which teachers and diagnosticians are concerned in reading are so often entwined that it is difficult to deal with one and not the other. For this reason, in this chapter no attempt will be made to deal with the diagnosis and remediation of psychological and sociological difficulties as separate entities. However, it will be obvious at times that certain discussions deal with one much more than the other.

One of the major problems you face in diagnosing psychological problems is whether certain apparent emotional problems are the causes or effects of reading disabilities. As mentioned in Chapter 1, Arthur Gates (1941) believed that 75 percent of the students who came to remedial reading were likely to have a concomitant personality maladjustment. He also estimated that one fourth of these, or about 18.75 percent of the total group, would have a reading disability as a result of the personality maladjustment. On the other hand, Helen Robinson (1946) believed that emotional maladjustment was present in 40.9 percent of her disabled readers and that it was a contributing factor in 31.8 percent of the cases. Robinson also believed that social problems were present in 63.6 percent of her cases and that these social problems were a disabling factor in 54.5 percent of her cases. Exact agreement in this area is, of course, quite unlikely because of the nature of the measuring instruments. Stanley Krippner (1968) also studied various etiological factors in reading disability and stated, "Almost all children with reading disabilities have some degree of emotional disturbance, generally as a result of their academic frustration." (p. 277) Krippner concluded, "Rarely is one etiological factor responsible for a reading problem. . . . Isolating the major factor was extremely subjective in many instances and the multifactor causation of reading disabilities became apparent to the clinicians involved in this study." (p. 277)

From the standpoint of remediation of psychosocial (combinations of emotional and social) problems, it usually does not matter whether the problem is a cause or result of a reading disability. You will simply need to recognize that it exists and that you must deal with it.

John B. Fotheringham and Dorothy Creal (1980) concluded, after a review of the literature and as a result of their own studies, that "the major influence on the differences in academic achievement among children is the family." (p. 316) Although educators cannot realistically hope to solve all of the problems that affect children when they are not in school, you should do everything within your power to improve the psychosocial aspects of students' learning. Studies such as those of D. Lawrence (1971) have shown that the counseling aspects of remedial reading are just as important as remediation of specific reading skills. Lawrence divided a group of disabled readers into four sub-groups. One group received remedial reading only, a second group received remedial reading plus counseling, a third group received counseling only, and a fourth group received no treatment. At the end of a six-month period the group that had received only counseling had made significantly greater gains than any of the other groups except the one that had received both counseling and remedial reading. Lawrence also stated that the type of counseling received by the students in his program could have been done by any intelligent, sympathetic lay person with only brief instruction in his techniques.

H. Wade Lewis (1984) also studied the effects of group counseling. He compared the effectiveness of a structured versus a nonstructured group counseling program on the reading achievement of twenty-four elementary school children. In the Wade study students who received structured group counseling produced significantly greater gains in reading comprehension than a similar group of students in a nonstructured program. The structured-counseling group began with a warm-up exercise, then viewed videotape vignettes of adult and peer models discussing their thoughts and feelings regarding reading, their self-concept, and their anxiety in simulated natural situations. After viewing each vignette the group leader led a discussion of the material. The group leader also attempted to reinforce positive statements in relation to students' self-concepts, anxieties, and attempts at reading improvement. After these sessions the group had a relaxation session in which the leader gave positive suggestions regarding students' self-concept, anxieties, and reading progress.

The techniques presented in the following pages can be effective even if you lack sophisticated psychological training. However, you must remember that your primary role is to assist remedial students with their educational problems. As we hope will be clear, the techniques presented are merely a part of sound instructional procedures. Put another way, effective reading instruction improves not only the student's reading ability but also the student's feelings of self-worth.

IDENTIFYING PSYCHOSOCIAL PROBLEMS

A number of techniques for identifying students with psychosocial problems have been suggested. However, most of these methods are somewhat unreliable. Furthermore, as Lawrence indicated in his study, some of the students in his groups did not display any of the so-called typical signs of emotional disturbance and yet seemed to benefit from the counseling. In spite of their shortcomings, you may wish to use observation, interviews, introspective and retrospective reports, projective techniques, personality inventories, and referrals to the school psychologist or counselor.

Teacher Observation

Observation of a student during day-to-day activities is a simple technique, and it can often be valuable. The advantage of teacher observation is that it is not a one-shot affair, as are some of the commonly used tests and inventories. You have the opportunity to watch students in many situations that cause stress. For example, you may observe the student's attitude relative to coming to the remedial class and toward the peer group, work habits, and the ability to concentrate for a sustained period. Since the school psychologist is likely to work with the student for only a short time, these traits are difficult for the psychologist to observe. The use of guided observation also has an advantage over the use of surveys or inventories for the same reason; i.e., you are not merely taking a sample of a student's feelings at one time.

The use of teacher observation also has some distinct disadvantages. One of these is the bias of the teacher; i.e., we are prone to see what we expect to see and ignore characteristics not in keeping with our expectations. Another major problem with teacher observation is that apparently some students who are emotionally disturbed display no outward signs of this disturbance. Some psychologists also claim that to be effective an observer must be highly trained.

The characteristics most commonly listed as indicative of some degree of emotional disturbance are that the student:

1. Fails to sustain interest and effort.
2. Does not work well with other students.
3. Is hostile toward adults.
4. Has withdrawal tendencies.
5. Is overly dependent.
6. Has low self-esteem.
7. Cannot sit quietly.
8. Has a fear of failure in group situations.
9. Is nervous.
10. Refuses to read orally.
11. Has a strong desire for attention from teacher.
12. Prefers to play alone.
13. Has difficulty in separation of important from unimportant aspects of assignments.
14. Prefers routine over new activities and assignments.
15. Brags and continually seeks approval for accomplishments.
16. Lacks initiative.
17. Has a tendency to be impulsive in oral reading, skipping unknown words and miscalling words without analyzing them.
18. Exhibits nail biting.

In using an observation checklist such as this it should be stressed that any conclusions or referrals for psychological help should be based on a cluster of these tendencies rather than on one or two. Yet most students, even though they do possess some degree of emotional disturbance, are not likely to display all or even most of these symptoms.

Interviews

Interviews are advantageous because the skilled interviewer can often gain a great deal of information in a relatively short time. Another important advantage of the interview is that it allows you immediately to delve further into any area that appears to have diagnostic significance. Certain answers a student may give either on written reports or in conversation often prove to be more than superficial when pursued by a skilled interviewer. For example, the interviewer can quickly gain a great deal of insight into a student's self-confidence by pursuing remarks such as, "I don't think I can do that."

The use of open-ended questions in the interview can also give a great deal of insight as to how the student perceives his or her own reading ability. One important step in the remedial process is to get the student to perceive and verbalize the reading problem. Through open-ended questions such as, "What do you think about your reading?" you can quickly determine the accuracy of the student's perception of the reading problem. Chapter 12 is devoted exclusively to the development of the techniques of interviewing.

Introspective and Retrospective Reports

Ruth Strang (1969) lists several kinds of introspective and/or retrospective reporting methods that we have found to be especially effective with older students. One of these is the reading autobiography. This may be either oral or written; as its name implies, it is a biography of the student's life experiences in reading. As Strang indicated, the amount of information you are able to obtain depends to some extent on the number and types of questions asked. For example, when asking the student to write the reading autobiography you may want to provide a list of questions such as, "Did you learn to read before starting school?" "Do you read materials other than those assigned at school?" "How many books have you read in your lifetime?" "Do other members of your family read a great deal?" "How do you feel about your reading?" "When did you first realize you had a reading problem?" "What were some things you especially liked about reading?" The kinds of questions illustrated here are designed to encourage discussion of the student's feelings toward reading and reading-related subjects. You may also wish to include questions that assess other factors such as the kinds of material the student likes to read and use of the school and public library.

Some students respond quite freely to a completely unstructured reading autobiography. In using the unstructured autobiography you merely ask the student to write everything important about his or her life as a reader, with no time limit or guiding questions.

Another technique suggested by Strang is the use of retrospective questioning following reading or reading-related tasks. Immediately following a student's reading of a story, ask questions such as, "Did you like that story?" "How did you feel when you were reading it?" If you wish to get information concerning *how* the student reads, ask such things as, "What did you do when you came to a word you did not know?" "When you paused at the word *government* and then understood it, what did you do?" "How did you remember all of the details?"

Another introspective-retrospective technique is the use of short student essays on reading tasks. Subjects may vary according to the area in which you need more information. For example, if you feel the student does not work well with others, ask for a short essay entitled, "Working with Groups at School"; or from the student who continually disturbs others, ask for a short essay entitled, "My Behavior at School." When using this technique, be sure that the student does not perceive the writing of the essay as punishment. This can be done by explaining to the student that you will be able to provide more assistance with reading if you know more about how the student writes. Writing short essays also serves as a good catharsis for students who have strong feelings that they are hesitant to express orally.

Projective Techniques

Projective techniques have been used by psychologists and psychiatrists for years; however, most techniques require rather extensive training and should not be attempted by someone who is not well versed in their use. These include such instruments as the *House-Tree-Person Projective Technique* (Buck and Jolles, 1955), the *Draw-a-Person Quality Scale* (Wagner and Schubert, 1955), the *Thematic Apperception Test* (Murray, 1951), and the *Rorschach* (Rorschach, 1960). There are other projective techniques that can be used by someone with less training. One of these is incomplete sentences. Although interpretation of this type of instrument is somewhat difficult, it often uncovers obvious areas for further exploration. See Figure 7–1 for an example of this type of instrument and the results that were obtained from a sixth-grade student.

It does not take an expert to spot some potentially important information derived from this student. She is evidently upset about her parents' divorce (10, 26) and appears to be somewhat insecure (3, 8). It is highly apparent that she has a negative attitude toward reading and her reading class (9, 13, 15, 18, 20, 23, 24, 25). There is also a suggestion of a physical problem with her eyes (1, 5, 11).

Another projective technique that often provides useful information for the remedial reading teacher is the use of wishes. In using this technique the student is simply asked, "If you had three wishes, what would you wish for?" The three sets of examples shown below reveal the type of responses you might expect from this technique.

Student A:
1. I would wish my family would be happy.
2. I would wish I would get good grades at school.
3. I would wish we were still living in Louisiana.

FIGURE 7-1 Sentence Completion Exercise

Sentence Completion   Reading Center
Date: February 19, 19___ Grade: 6th   Name: Nancy _____   Age: 11 years
Directions: On each line below add words to make a good sentence. Each time tell what you think. There are no wrong answers, and no right answers. Write the first thing you think of. Work quickly.

1. When I read _my eyes get dizzy_
2. I don't like to read when _I'm having fun._
3. I wish I could _Live forever_
4. I seem to understand what I read best when _I wan't to read_
5. When I read, my eyes _hurt._
6. I like to read when _I feel like Reading_
7. School is ~~Okay~~ _Alright_
8. The most important thing to me _is Life_
9. I don't understand what I read when _I feel Sick_
10. My father _Is divorced from my Mom_
11. When I read words seem _mixed together_
12. My family _is Great!_
13. When I have to read _I ~~felt mad~~ feel mad_
14. I can't seem to _Get together with some people_
15. New words _seem Very different like a new word_
16. The easiest thing I read _is Baby Books_
17. My mother _Loves dogs_
18. When I read, my body _feels like a ~~Big~~ block of ice_
19. Teachers seem to _get meaner & Nicer_
20. Reading classes always seem _terrible_
21. Other classes are always _great_
22. The hardest thing I read _is colledge work_
23. When I read, my mind _almost falls apart_
24. I would read more if _I liked reading_
25. Compared to reading, TV is _much Better_
26. I wish my parents _would go back together_
27. I am afraid _of gangsters_

Written by Eldon E. Ekwall and Everett E. Davis.

270

Student B:
1. I would like to have a new ten-speed bicycle.
2. I would like to have lots of money.
3. My third wish would be that I could have all the wishes I wanted.

Student C:
1. I would wish my Mom didn't have to work so hard.
2. I would wish I could read better.
3. I would wish I was the smartest person in the whole world.

These are verbatim responses of three disabled readers who visited the El Paso Reading Center. Although responses such as these must be interpreted with some caution, they do help provide more information about these students. For example, because of the responses given by Student A, further questioning was done and revealed that his father and mother were in the process of getting a divorce, and he was very anxious about the outcome in terms of where he would live, etc. He was also being berated by both parents for making poor grades in reading, social studies, and science. Also, he had a desire to go back to the past, when his family lived in Louisiana and at which time life, for him, was understandably happier.

The responses of Student B are less revealing than for either of the other two. His wishes did, however, reveal that the school situation, including his low grades and his inability to read, was not uppermost in his mind. Students often have a desire to please adults by telling them what they perceive the adult wants to hear. This student, however, was not overly concerned with pleasing anyone other than himself. He also had a very high IQ, as shown from his school records. Later work with him revealed that he did not perceive himself as having a reading disability.

Student C was the only child in the family and was often left in the care of a maid because his mother and father both worked. He realized he was a very poor reader and had a strong desire to improve. His classroom teacher revealed that his peer group had sometimes poked fun at him for not being able to read well in class.

Although the three-wish technique often fails to reveal anything of significant value, it is not time consuming and is usually enjoyed by the student making the wishes. The responses you receive are not likely to be especially revealing by themselves; however, they often lead to further, more meaningful diagnosis.

Another technique similar to the three wishes is to ask the student, "What would you do if you had a million dollars?" This tends to elicit similar responses to those from the three-wish technique. You may want to try this in addition to the three wishes.

Other projective techniques are the use of student drawings and illustrated picture stories. We suggest, however, that unless you have had extensive training in the interpretation of student drawings, you would be better off not to attempt to use this technique. First of all, the natural artistic ability of students varies a great deal. Secondly, minor recent events in the student's life may greatly influence the drawings. And thirdly, the interpretation of students' drawings often tells more about the interpreter than the student!

Personality Inventories

Through numerous research studies a number of personality variables have been shown to have a relationship to reading. Some of these variables and the researchers who found them are as follows:

David Bell (1969)—Poor Readers' Characteristics:
1. Negative attitude or lack of acquiescence to authority (important among Caucasians)
2. Passivity
3. Aggression
4. Excitability
5. Impulsivity

R. J. Brunkan and F. Shen (1966)—Low Rate Ineffective Readers' Characteristics:
1. Preferred to follow rather than lead
2. Tendency to be passive
3. Need for constant reassurance

Glen Chronister (1964)—Significant Correlations Between Reading and Personality for the Following Variables:
1. Self-reliance (in other words, good readers were more self-reliant and poor readers less self-reliant)
2. Personal worth
3. Personal freedom
4. Feeling of belonging
5. Freedom from withdrawal tendencies
6. Freedom from nervous symptoms
7. Social standards
8. Social skills
9. Freedom from antisocial tendencies
10. Family relations
11. School relations
12. Community relations
13. Cooperation
14. Friendliness
15. Integrity
16. Leadership responsibility

Chronister also studied these relationships for boys and girls separately. All correlations between reading and these variables were statistically significant for the boys (p < .01), but only freedom from nervous symptoms was significant (p < .01) for the girls.

George Spache (1957)—Disabled Readers:

1. Showed more hostility and overt aggressiveness than normal readers.
2. Showed less ability to accept blame than normal readers.
3. Were poor in knowing how to handle conflict with adults.
4. Exhibited a passive but defensive attitude or negativism toward authority figures.

Albert J. Harris and Edward R. Sipay (1985):

1. Student becomes convinced he/she is dumb or stupid
2. Tense and emotionally upset
3. Inattentive
4. Very sensitive to the opinions of others
5. Attempt to make themselves inconspicuous
6. Daydreaming to excess
7. Nervous habits of twitching, nail-biting, stuttering, and general fidgetiness
8. Boasting, bluffing, and exaggeration (p. 317)

As you will note from these studies, several characteristics appear with some regularity. On the other hand, there seem to be some characteristics peculiar to each study, depending to some extent on the measuring instrument. Most researchers are of the opinion that disabled readers as a whole possess personality characteristics somewhat different from those of normal readers. These same people, however, are quick to point out that within any group of disabled readers you are likely to find a great deal of variation in personality patterns.

The logical question for the educational diagnostician or remedial reading teacher to ask at this point might be, "Should I use personality inventories in the normal course of my diagnostic work with disabled readers?" We suggest that as a rule your time could be better spent in other endeavors. Most group personality tests do not discriminate between various levels of personality adjustment sufficiently to allow one accurately to adjust the course of remediation to suit a particular individual. They do, however, in many cases allow you to distinguish a student with serious personality problems from one who was relatively free of such problems. You should keep in mind, however, that the simple fact that a student is a disabled reader is quite likely to mean that personality problems will exist to some degree. And unless giving a personality test, or any other test, will alter the course of the remediation, there is nothing to be gained by giving the test.

Self-Concept

The self-concept is a personality factor and could have quite logically been discussed under the previous section. However, because of the extreme importance of the self-concept for students in remedial reading, it will be discussed here in a separate section. The importance of the self-concept has been illustrated in numerous research studies, such as those of Mary Lamy (1962), and William Wattenberg and Clifford Clare (1964). Lamy found that the self-concepts of kindergarten children correlated as highly with their success in beginning reading as did their IQ scores. Wattenberg and Clare found that measures of self-concept and of ego strength taken at the kindergarten level were predictive of reading achievement two and a half years later. Michael Thomson and Gill Hartley (1980) examined the other side of this "chicken and egg" issue. They concluded that a primary reading difficulty often affects a child's social and emotional development. Thomson and Hartley urge teachers to recognize these problems early on and suggest that efforts be focused on areas such as teacher-pupil relations and support from the home.

George F. Kwash and Janet L. Clewes (1986) suggest the use of the *Children's Personality Questionnaire* (CPQ) by Porter and Cattell (1979) as a useful instrument in determing students' self-concepts, as a student with a low self-concept is likely to show low scores on factors "'C' (low ego strength) and 'H' (low venturesomeness) and elevation on 'O' (worrisomeness) and 'Q4' (tension)." (p. 216) They report that students with high self-esteem have a tendency to be emotionally mature and stable and they are more likely to maintain a realistic approach to life. They are also likely to be sociably uninhibited and spontaneous, be placid, be secure, and have a good frustration tolerance.

Clearly there is a strong relationship between self-concept and reading achievement. Therefore, we believe that every effort should be made to improve the self-concepts of students with low self-esteem.

A well-trained counselor or the school psychologist should in most cases be able to diagnose a student's self-concept with some degree of accuracy. If you refer a student, you should make it a point to ask for a report on this aspect of the student's personality. However, there will be many students whom you will not be able to refer for a psychological evaluation. For these students you will need to make some sort of evaluation on your own. This can be done through observation and informal questioning and inventories. Although the psychologist has the advantage of formal training and more sophisticated instruments, the remedial reading teacher has the distinct advantage of being able to observe students over a longer period.

Students with low self-concepts are likely to give up easily and are often inattentive. They may also be antagonistic and insecure and show signs of loneliness and indecision. Although they may at times present a braggadocio attitude, in the long run it will usually be apparent that this is a defensive mechanism.

One of the best ways of determining the self-concept of a student is simply to talk with the student. During the conversation ask questions such as, "Tell me about how you learn." and "Why do you think you have had problems in learning how to read?" Sometimes students are hesitant to say things that they will quite readily put in writing. You can take advantage of this by having students write short essays with titles such as, "What I Think about Myself" or "My Ability to Learn." The use of incomplete sentences as explained under the section on projective techniques can also be helpful in assessing self-concept. In using this technique include incomplete sentences such as, "My ability to learn . . . " and "Compared to other students. . . . "

Referrals

In making referrals to the school counselor or school psychologist you should consider several factors:

1. Is the student making satisfactory progress in the tutoring situation?
2. Does the student exhibit a cluster of abnormal behavioral symptoms?
3. What is the student's attitude toward me and toward remedial reading?

The student who is progressing well and who is not antagonistic toward remedial reading is not likely to need psychological help even though the student may possess a poor self-concept or appear to be slightly negative about certain aspects of school life. If you are somewhat familiar with general counseling techniques and attempt to provide materials and activities that foster improvement in students' self-concepts, you are quite likely to find a corresponding improvement in their attitudes. However, if the student does not respond to your teaching after several weeks, you should consider referring the student for further evaluation and counseling. Lastly, if after several weeks the student's overall attitude toward you or the remedial reading program has not improved, a referral is in order.

IQ and Reading

It has been a fairly regular practice over the years to include an IQ test as part of the diagnostic procedure with disabled readers. To some extent this may be justified, but in many cases it was probably wasted time and effort. As mentioned in Chapter 2, you should attempt to make the diagnosis as efficiently as possible by eliminating any testing that will not ultimately affect the course of the remedial procedures. If this criterion were applied to the practice of IQ testing, there would be considerably fewer IQ tests given.

As a beginning point you should examine the reasons IQ tests are given. Probably the most often-stated reason is to determine whether there is a match between the student's reading potential and reading achievement. Another is that it allows one to see how the student functions while taking the test and to examine the scores on various subtests. The thought behind this line of reasoning is that the student can be helped by receiving remediation in areas where there are weaknesses and that this in turn should help the student's reading.

In examining the validity of these reasons we will first look at the relationship of reading and IQ, which, as stated in Chapter 1, is statistically significant. It appears, however, that the reason for this is that the very high IQ students usually read well and the very low IQ students do poorly in reading. It is doubtful that if one eliminated the high- and low-IQ students from the studies (perhaps above 115 and below 85), the remaining group's IQ scores would correlate significantly with their reading achievement scores. Yet it is likely that approximately 70 percent of the students you will deal with lie within the 85–115 IQ range. Furthermore, the innate abilities that are required for learning to read are evidently not completely the same as those that are measured by IQ tests. This was illustrated in a study by Berj Harootunian (1966), who studied the relationship between reading achievement and various intelligence variables: "The results suggest two conclusions: first, that several of the tests measure variables that are relevant in reading; second, that these variables are not being elicited by intelligence tests." (p. 391) Harootunian also stressed the fact that intelligence is composed of many factors and that you should not use a "single haphazardly composed score."

If the innate abilities required for learning to read were measured by intelligence tests, it would certainly seem logical to use intelligence tests as a predictor of future reading ability. However, since studies such as those of Harootunian and others indicate that many of the abilities required for learning to read are not being measured by intelligence tests, the argument for administering intelligence tests to measure students' reading potential loses a great deal of its validity.

How then do we measure a student's reading potential? Perhaps a more logical approach is to teach the student a sample of whatever must be learned about reading and see if the student is able to retain it. If the student can do this, do you really care whether the IQ is 80 or 150? You might also consider whether the actual course of instruction would be changed had the student's IQ been 150 versus 80. The answer to this in most cases is *no*.

The second reason for giving IQ tests is to observe the way the student works and to observe and analyze performance on various subtests. There is certainly something to be gained by the reading diagnostician in analyzing the way the student works and in analyzing performance on various subtests. For example, it is helpful to know how well a student did on the subtest of vocabulary on the *Wechsler Adult Intelligence Scale—Revised (WAIS-R),* the *Wechsler Intelligence Scale for Children—Revised (WISC-R)* or the *Stanford-Binet Intelligence Scale (S-B)*. This information can be especially beneficial in the diagnosis of comprehension difficulties as explained in Chapter 6. Scores achieved in the "Information" and "Comprehension" subtests of *WISC-R* and *WAIS-R* provide information on the student's awareness of his or her environment and ability to reason. You also gain information on how a student performs by watching him or her duplicate designs on the "Block Designs" subtest and assemble the puzzles of the "Object Assembly" subtests.

Hubert Vance, Fred Wallbrown, and John Blaha (1978) identified five meaningful *WISC-R* profiles, each of which was used to define a syndrome or cluster of behaviors related to disabled readers. However, the investigators pointed out that a substantial number of disabled readers have profiles that do not correspond to the five found in the study.

The question you must ultimately ask, then, is, "Do you get enough worthwhile information to warrant giving the test?" This, of course, must be answered by each diagnostician while working with students in various testing situations. After administering over 500 *WISC-R, WAIS-R,* and *S-B* tests to children and adults, we find that seldom if ever is enough information obtained about the way the student worked or about the subtest scores to justify taking the time to give the test. If the information could not be obtained in any other way, perhaps this would not be so, but there are short vocabulary tests that will give you an estimate of the student's word knowledge. And may it not be better to observe the way the student works and reacts in a reading task than in an intelligence-testing situation?

Psychological reports pertaining to students' performance often contain statements such as, "Juan seems to have difficulty integrating pieces into wholes," or "Frank has difficulty with eye-motor coordination." These statements may be quite true, but what do they tell us about how to teach Juan or Frank to read? Problems integrating pieces into wholes may show up in learning to sound words after learning phonemes, and problems with eye-motor coordination may show up in writing words. The problem you face is that programs designed to teach part-to-whole integration and eye-motor coordination have not as a rule been successful in carrying over into reading instruction. What has generally been successful is a more direct attack on the problem, i.e., actual teaching of phonic blending or actual teaching of handwriting. Furthermore, problems with phonic blending can easily be located by giving a phonics test, and problems in handwriting can easily be spotted by having the student write.

As the preceding information indicates, teachers and diagnosticians probably administer intelligence tests in many cases where it is not necessary. In spite of this there are times when information from intelligence tests can be beneficial. For example, if the student does not improve after receiving instruction for a period of time, an intelligence test might help you determine whether the student is an unusually slow learner as indicated by an extremely low IQ. Also, if intelligence test scores are already available when you receive a student in remedial reading, the subtest scores can provide information on vocabulary, ability to reason, etc., which may eliminate the need for certain reading tests. (See Chapter 17 for methods of interpreting scores made on the *WISC-R* and *WAIS-R.*)

You may also find yourself in a school system where intelligence test scores are used as a partial basis for accepting or rejecting students in a remedial reading program. Although we believe there are better ways of doing this (see Chapter 14), the practice still occurs; therefore, most remedial reading teachers should be familiar with the most commonly used intelligence tests.

One important point is that group intelligence tests that require reading (often referred to as verbal intelligence tests) are usually not suitable for use with disabled readers. Researchers such as Donald Neville (1961) have generally concluded that for children in the intermediate grades, a reading level of 4.0 is required for obtaining reasonably valid IQs on group tests that require any reading at all. Since many disabled readers do not read at, or even near, the 4.0 grade level, these tests do not accurately measure these students' intelligence. There are other group intelligence tests that do not require reading, but these tests have an extremely low correlation with reading ability, or in other words, do not measure reading potential to a degree that makes their administration worthwhile.

If intelligence tests are to be used as a measure of reading potential, you must use individual tests in order to achieve any degree of accuracy. The most commonly used tests of this kind are the *Wechsler Intelligence Scale for Children—Revised (WISC-R),* the *Wechsler Adult Intelligence Scale (WAIS),* and the *Stanford-Binet Intelligence Scale (S-B).* The *Slosson Intelligence Test (SIT)* (Slosson, 1963), and the *Peabody Picture Vocabulary Test (PPVT)* (Dunn and Dunn, 1981), which take considerably less time to administer, have also been used for this purpose. You are likely to find that many of the students referred for remediation have already been given an individual intelligence test; and there may be times when you request that one of these tests be given to a student with whom you have been working. In order to help you interpret the results of these tests a short description of each one follows.

WISC-R and WAIS

The *WISC-R* is designed for students ages five to fifteen and must be given by a skilled examiner who has had special training in the administration and interpretation of this test. It contains a verbal scale with six subtests and a performance scale that also consists of six subtests. In most cases only ten or eleven of the twelve subtests are used. Scores are given for the verbal scale, the performance scale, and a combined measure referred to as the full scale. The verbal scale consists of the following subtests:

"Information."   This consists of thirty questions designed to measure subjects' general range of knowledge and information. It may be influenced to a small degree by culture and background; however, care was taken to include only questions that could normally be answered by anyone alert to their environment. One of the easier questions deals with the number of legs on a well-known animal and one of the more difficult questions deals with the use of a specific weather instrument.

"Comprehension."   This consists of seventeen questions. Wechsler believes it is a test of common sense that evaluates the subject's ability to use past information and to evaluate past experience. One of the easier questions deals with the student's knowledge of what to do when he or she has a certain type of injury, and one of the more difficult questions deals with the ethics of keeping a promise.

"Arithmetic."   This subtest of eighteen questions evaluates the subject's ability to solve arithmetical problems. All questions are to be answered orally, and the subject is not allowed to use paper and pencil.

"Similarities."   This subtest of seventeen questions measures the subject's ability to use logical reasoning processes to see similarities. One of the easier questions deals with the similarities between a wheel and a ball, and one of the more difficult questions deals with the similarities between two numbers.

"Vocabulary."   This subtest containing thirty-two words measures the student's knowledge of the meaning of words. This type of subtest, although influenced to some extent by formal education, has traditionally been one of the best predictors of academic potential.

"Digit Span."   This is a measure of the subject's ability to recall a series of digits forward and backward. Wechsler does not maintain it is an especially good measure of intelligence at the higher levels, but he believes that the results of this subtest often have diagnostic value.

All of these subtests are administered verbally. The subject has no visual stimulus and is in no case allowed to use paper and pencil.

The performance scale consists of the following subtests:

"Picture Completion."   This consists of a series of twenty-six pictures, each of which has something missing. The subject is required to indicate, either by pointing or with a verbal answer, which part is missing. Wechsler states this test measures the subject's perceptual and conceptual abilities and the ability of the individual to differentiate essential from nonessential details.

"Picture Arrangement."   The consists of twelve different series of pictures. Each series is placed in front of the subject in mixed order. The subject must place them in order so as to make a sensible story. Wechsler believes this subtest measures the subject's ability to comprehend and assess a total situation.

"Block Design."   The subject is given blocks with varying designs on them. The subject must arrange the blocks so as to match a pictured design

shown by the examiner. Wechsler believes that this is a good test of overall intelligence, and he also believes that the way the subject goes about the task has considerable diagnostic significance.

"Object Assembly."   This subtest consists of four form boards that the subject is required to complete. Each is a timed exercise. Wechsler believes it measures the subject's ability to see whole-part relationships and tells something about the subject's thinking and working habits.

"Coding (digit symbol)."   The subject is required to make associations between various symbols. This subtest gives some information about the subject's speed and accuracy of learning.

"Mazes."   This is seldom used unless one of the other subtests is spoiled in the administration of the test. It consists of a series of eight pictured mazes that the subject is to find his or her way through.

The *WAIS-R* is very similar to the *WISC-R,* but it is designed for subjects of age sixteen and older, and it does not include "Mazes." Both tests take approximately forty-five minutes to two hours, depending on the subject.

In scoring each subtest the examiner first determines the raw score, which is transferred to a scaled score through the use of tables found in the manual. The scaled scores are easy to interpret, since each has a mean of ten and a standard deviation of three. It is also easy to find a percentile rating for each subtest using Figure 17–1. The scaled scores of each subtest are added and tables are consulted to determine the subject's verbal scale, performance scale, and full scale intelligence quotients.

A number of studies have shown that disabled readers tend to have higher performance scale than verbal scale IQs. However, the verbal scale tends to have a higher correlation with the ability to read.

Irla Lee Zimmerman, Theron M. Covin, and J. M. Woo-Sam (1986) have made the point that many individuals received lower scores on the revised WISC (WISC-R) than on the WAIS. They believed that this was because of the higher age norm in the WAIS before it was revised. In a longitudinal study of students who took the WISC-R and later the newer WAIS-R, Zimmerman, Covin, and Woo-Sam found that this situation had improved. However, they still cautioned that one could expect to find higher scores for any students on the WAIS-R than on the WISC-R, especially for students who had been classified as mentally retarded. Thus, they believed many children could be expected to lose the mentally retarded classification when later tested with the WAIS-R.

Stanford-Binet

The *Stanford-Binet Intelligence Scale* is designed to test children of two years through adults. Although it is an excellent all-around intelligence test, it has less diagnostic significance than the *WISC* and *WAIS,* since most of the subtests are not scored separately. It is, however, possible to obtain a subtest score for the "Vocabulary" section, which in most cases is of greatest concern to the reading specialist. The scoring manual gives age-level standards for passing the "Vocabulary" section. This serves as a guide in judging the age level of a subject's vocabulary. You will find this information in the manual at the beginning of the section on the scoring of the "Vocabulary" subtest.

SIT

The *Slosson Intelligence Test* takes only twenty to forty-five minutes to administer. Although a shorter time is listed in the manual, our experience has shown that the times that we have listed are more realistic. In devising this test the author adapted and used a number of items from the *S-B*. In most cases these were the items that are easy to administer. Since many of the items are the same, the *SIT* naturally has a rather high validity when the *S-B* and/or *WISC* is used as the criterion for validity measurement. In spite of its brevity the research on its use in reading diagnosis has been quite favorable. Furthermore, it is easy to administer and does not require extensive training. Although Slosson suggests that classroom teachers can easily learn to give it by reading the manual, we feel it is wise, if possible, to practice giving it under the supervision of someone who is trained in the administration of the *WISC, WAIS* and/or *S-B*.

Jerome M. Sattler and Theron M. Covin (1986) did a comparison of the *Slosson Intelligence Test* and *WISC-R* scores of students with learning problems and students who were gifted. They concluded that with the newer SIT norms (1982, 2nd ed.) one could expect to find the SIT scores to be approximately seven points higher and that their study supported the concurrent validity of the revised SIT norms using the WISC-R as the criterion. However, they did not consider the scores on the two tests to be interchangeable.

It should be remembered that the SIT will provide only an overall intelligence quotient and that no subtest scores are reported in the scoring. However, by examining the pattern of correct and incorrect responses, the diagnostician can estimate the student's strengths and weaknesses in such areas as general knowledge, vocabulary, computation ability, and auditory memory.

PPVT

The *Peabody Picture Vocabulary Test—Revised,* as its name implies, consists of a series of plates (pictures) that the subject is to identify as they are shown. Administration time may run from fifteen to twenty minutes. It can be somewhat useful to the reading specialist to determine the range of the subject's vocabulary and experiences as reflected by the subject's knowledge of pictures. Studies concerning its reliability and validity vary a great deal depending on the type of students studied. Our own research in its administration and our examination of students' records in a large district where both the A and B forms are routinely given indicate that it is a highly unreliable measure of intelligence for individual students. The apparent reason for rather large discrepancies between its scores and those of the *WISC* and *S-B* is that the *PPVT* measures a much narrower spectrum of intelligence than either the *WISC* or *S-B*. The reading specialist should keep this in mind while working with it and in most cases merely interpret the score as a measure of vocabulary and experience and not as an overall measure of intelligence.

Cultural Influences

Although it is often difficult to diagnose cultural factors per se, there are some cultural and/or socioeconomic factors that research has shown to have a relation to, or to contribute to, reading difficulties. As a reading specialist you should be aware that these relationships exist.

The studies of M. Deutsh as reported by Edith Grotberg (1970) illustrate some of the problems common to students from impoverished backgrounds. Deutsh found that impoverished children have inferior visual and auditory discrimination and inferior time and number concepts. No specific physical defects of the eyes, ears, or brain could be found in these children that would contribute to these problems. Grotberg suggested that impoverishment might create conditions of sensory deprivation, language restrictions, and low motivation for achievement and that all of these conditions acting together may produce a child with the same characteristics as those referred to as learning disabilities.

Cultural and socioeconomic level also tend to influence overall attitudes toward school. James Stedman and Richard McKenzie (1971) found that middle-class Mexican-American attitudes were similar to those of Anglo middle-class Americans, but Mexican-Americans of lower-class backgrounds tended not to place emphasis on formal education.

A multitude of cultural and/or socioeconomic factors apparently work together to produce disabled versus normal readers. This is well illustrated in a study by Catherine Thurston et al. (1969), who studied the differences between able and disabled black readers. The following differences were found:

1. The able readers came from families with more than one car.
2. More able than disabled readers liked to read poetry.
3. More able than disabled readers received money for working.
4. More able than disabled readers felt close to their friends.
5. More able than disabled readers had fathers who worked.
6. More able than disabled readers had mothers who worked away from home.
7. More able than disabled readers got a daily newspaper other than the local paper.
8. More able than disabled readers had an encyclopedia set in their home.

9. More able than disabled readers had taken a trip on a bus other than a school bus.
10. More able than disabled readers had been to a county fair.
11. More able than disabled readers had ridden in an elevator.
12. More able than disabled readers had been hiking through the woods and hills.
13. More able than disabled readers played a musical instrument.
14. More able than disabled readers had been to more than one town to do their shopping.

Thurston and her group also studied a group of white able and disabled readers. In that group they found the following differences:

1. More disabled than able readers had only one car in the family.
2. More disabled readers had their own room. (This was a rather surprising finding.)
3. More able than disabled readers had parents who attended PTA meetings.
4. More able than disabled readers had been to a music recital.
5. More able than disabled readers got a daily newspaper other than the local paper.
6. More able than disabled readers had taken a trip on a train.
7. More able than disabled readers had been in a building higher than eight stories.
8. More able than disabled readers had parents who visited their classrooms.
9. More able than disabled readers received the local newspaper.

It is evident from the foregoing information that various cultural and socioeconomic factors tend to influence students' reading ability as well as their academic functioning in general. However, it is also evident that seldom, if ever, could any one variable be identified as the primary cause of reading disability in a specific student. The reading specialist should be aware of the many variables that evidently contribute to reading difficulties. At times reading procedures will need to be modified to fit the special needs of students from impoverished backgrounds.

Language Factors

Many experts now consider reading to be a language-related or language-centered process. Kenneth Goodman (1967) presented a model of reading based on psycholinguistic theory. Indeed, Goodman suggested that reading is a "psycholinguistic guessing game," wherein the reader relies on three types of information when confronting the reading task. The first two are semantic (meaning) and syntactic (sentence sense) clues, which the reader uses to anticipate the content of the material. The third type is graphic (sound-symbol, or instant word recognition) clues, which the reader uses when necessary. The reader continually checks reading accuracy based on the sense of the passage. If necessary, the reader will reread the material in search of clear meaning. (You may have just demonstrated this theory if you reread the last few sentences.) According to Goodman the reader comprehends by using only as many of the semantic, syntactic, and graphic cues as required. As the reader's skill improves, less reliance is placed on graphic cues. Since semantic and syntactic cues are dependent on the reader's linguistic competence, the development of language skills is crucial to successful reading.

John Downing (1971–1972) used the term *cognitive clarity* to refer to the young reader's search for understanding of the written code based on what is already known about the oral language system. Barbara Fox (1976), in a review of research, found that many beginning readers do not understand the terms *word, sound,* and *letter* and thus are unable to separate spoken and written language into units. Albert Harris (1979) added to the list of misunderstood terms *page, sentence, line, first, last, middle, before, after, above, below.* Harris also indicated that beginning readers may fail to understand that printed words are arranged sequentially from left to right and lines from top to bottom on a page of print.

The further to complicate matters, Susan Glazer and Lesley Morrow (1978) found that written materials prepared for six-, seven-, and eight-year-olds were more complex syntactically than the oral language of the children for whom the materials were intended.

As noted in Chapter 1, useful tests for diagnosing language disabilities are not available. However, Martha Evans, Nancy Taylor, and Irene Blum (1979) described the development of an instrument that identifies and measures certain aspects of written language awareness related to beginning reading achievement. They found that the best predictors of future reading ability were tasks that stressed the *relationship* between oral and written language codes, rather than those that evaluated characteristics specific to the writing system.

For the present the diagnostician can best evaluate children's language abilities through careful observation and awareness of how individual students compare with their peers with respect to (1) vocabulary range, (2) knowledge of sentence structure, (3) clarity of pronunciation, and (4) listening comprehension.

SOME IMPORTANT CAUTIONS FOR THE REMEDIAL READING TEACHER IN THE DIAGNOSIS AND REMEDIATION OF PSYCHOSOCIAL PROBLEMS

Studies showing that children from a low socioeconomic level tend to read more poorly than children from homes of a higher socioeconomic level should be interpreted with a great amount of care; so should such factors as those listed under "Cultural Influences." For example, the fact that more able readers had parents who had visited their classroom may mean that the parents took an active interest in their children and thus created an overall environment that was conducive to reading. On the other hand, the fact that more able than disabled readers had visited a building of eight stories or higher probably has very little practical value for the remedial reading teacher. Many disabled readers are simply lacking in the experience background necessary to learn to comprehend as well as can children from homes with richer backgrounds of experience. A student's reading ability will not be improved by a visit to a building of eight stories or higher. However, providing a rich background through audiovisual materials, field trips, discussion, etc., may in time develop the students sufficiently to affect reading comprehension.

Part B: REMEDIATION

TECHNIQUES FOR REMEDIATION OF PSYCHOSOCIAL PROBLEMS

General Techniques

Most of the techniques generally suggested for working with disabled readers with psychosocial problems are simply good overall teaching procedures that would prove effective with any student. However, because of the low teacher-pupil ratio in many classrooms and because of the tendency of some teachers to become overly occupied with the subject matter, some of these techniques are often overlooked.

Set appropriately high expectations for students. Regrettably, teachers sometimes contribute to students' poor self-concepts by expecting too little of them. Many remedial students have been for years the designated plant waterers in their classrooms. Instead of receiving challenging and rewarding instruction they are given custodial tasks. Every remedial teacher should seek to provide the maximum amount of *purposeful* and *meaningful* instruction that requires students to work to the limits of their ability. All students, especially remedial readers, deserve the opportunity to experience the special satisfaction that comes from a job well done. A number of research studies reviewed elsewhere in this chapter and in Chapter 1 have shown that the teacher's expectations are a critical determinant of students' achievement.

Certainly it takes time and experience for the remedial teacher to know just how much to expect or demand of a student at a particular time. However, we urge you not to fall into the trap of expecting too little of students simply because they have experienced failure in the past. The situation is not unlike that faced by the teacher of children who are physically handicapped. It is difficult not to feel sorry for the children. Yet their improvement depends to some extent on their teacher's ability to overcome feelings of pity and to set high expectations within the limits of the students' capability.

We have observed remedial students in classrooms, special programs, and clinical settings and have noticed that they often balk at high expectations, exhibiting any number of behaviors designed to reduce the teacher's demands. At the Elementary Reading Clinic at California State University, Hayward, the following countermeasures have proven effective:

1. Inform the student that you are sure he or she is not "dumb," that you are positive that the student will learn, that some effort will be required, and that most of the activities will be enjoyable.
2. Show the student the daily lesson plan and ask the student to assist you by checking off each activity as it is completed. Point out that a number of particularly enjoyable activities will occur along the way, but that other, more rigorous activities must also be pursued.
3. Keep the student actively involved, maintain a brisk pace, and do everything possible to keep the student on task at all times.
4. Praise the student's efforts when warranted after each activity and at the end of the session.
5. Communicate with the student's parents, preferably in writing, indicating what the student accomplished, your pride in the student's efforts, and the specifics about the homework assignment.

These procedures can be used effectively with groups of students in either classrooms or school remedial programs.

While setting high expectations is essential, you must be careful not to make unreasonable demands of students. Psychologists have known for years that some students become the class clown because it provides a justification for other students laughing at them. Students soon realize that in certain classes they are likely to be called on to perform tasks such as working a difficult math problem or reading a difficult passage and that they are likely to be laughed at when and if they fail to do a good job. Students who feel assured that they will have no unreasonable demands made of them are much less likely to need to anticipate others' laughter by trying to provoke it. You can help assure students that unreasonable demands will not be made of them by letting them know that you are aware of their abilities and weaknesses and that in no case will you embarrass them or ask them to perform tasks for which they are not ready.

A number of the principles alluded to in this section will be repeated for emphasis in the discussion of the other general techniques that follow.

It is important that the student participate in planning the remedial program. One of the important steps in a good counseling procedure is to encourage students to verbalize their educational problems and to discuss the kinds of activities that would probably prove helpful in remediating these problems. Students who have had a hand in planning their remedial program are more likely to see a need for each day's activities and become more enthusiastic about them. For example, students often fail to see that an activity as crucial as practice in the act of reading is relevant to their problem. Help students understand how important this practice is by pointing out that all complex skills, such as playing a musical instrument, swimming, or even riding a bicycle, require substantial practice for improvement. Present the student with a wide selection of books and other materials written at the student's independent level. Let the student choose some and plan together specific times for practice during and after remedial sessions.

In cooperative planning do not leave the student with the impression that you are not sure what should be done. Be positive, confident, and persuasive in discussing the student's diagnosed needs, but work cooperatively to help the student understand why certain activities are necessary.

Cooperative planning sessions with students can also do much to improve their self-concept. Many students come to view themselves negatively because they believe they are a part of an overall curriculum in which they have consistently failed. This leads them to believe they are not as intelligent as other members of their class. However, when a student sees that the teacher is willing to take time to discuss what needs to be done and then begins to experience consistent success, the student's overall self-concept is likely to improve.

Students need to be constantly aware of their improvement.   In a general classroom environment it is difficult for remedial students to know whether they are learning or improving various skills. In fact, disabled readers are quite likely to believe that they are getting worse, since their faster-achieving classmates constantly seem to be doing everything faster and better than they are. It is also difficult for disabled readers to achieve success because they have no measure with which to compare their progress. For example, most disabled readers are not aware of the scores they achieve on standardized tests, and even if they were, their progress as indicated by these scores would not be meaningful to them.

In remedial reading you can make students aware of their progress in many ways. For example, a basic sight word test administered to a student at the beginning of a remedial program can be used as the basis for cooperative program planning. File this test in the student's record folder. After a number of words have been learned, give the student the original test and show his or her progress. The same sort of thing can be done with phonic elements. Student progress can also be shown by tape recording a somewhat difficult reading passage at the beginning of a remedial period and then tape recording it a second time after the student's reading has improved. Students are often startled at hearing their improvement. Another method of showing improvement is to point out things the student has learned on a daily basis, e.g., making such comments as, "Look, Sam, you knew the 'fl' sound today. Do you remember you didn't know it yesterday?" Or, "Did you notice you have learned the two hard words that you didn't know last week?'' It is important not only to talk about these indicators of improvement but also to get students to say that they too notice. Another effective technique is to use charts or graphs of the student's progress and to display them prominently in the instructional area. We have found this technique to be as effective with older students as with elementary-age pupils.

The student needs to learn by methods that are enjoyable.   Many students in remedial reading come to view school, and especially reading, as drudgery. Most adults as well as children do not seek activities that they do not perceive as somewhat pleasurable, let alone those that they perceive as drudgery. One of the best methods of determining the type of activities students enjoy is to ask them. It is also a good idea occasionally to provide several alternatives, if possible, and let the students decide which alternative to choose. Many reading activities, for example, can be taught by games. Although at times games may be a less efficient method of learning than teacher-directed activities, students' change of attitudes may more than make them worthwhile.

Avoid unfavorable comparisons with other students.   These comparisons should be avoided whether it be on the basis of academic achievement, behavior, or other social or ethnic factors. Most experienced teachers have found that comparisons really never serve to improve the student being compared but more than likely make the student antagonistic. If comparisons are made, they should be done on the basis of present behavior versus previous work or behavior. This gives the student no reason to become antagonistic.

Provide the student with as much success as possible.   Although this may sound like a cliché, it is an important technique in working with disabled readers. A number of studies have shown that a large percentage of disabled readers possess a low self-concept. The reason in many cases is repeated failure in reading and other reading-related activities. This means that many students must constantly experience success until they come to see themselves as successful. Other studies have shown that as children grow older their self-concepts become more stable and resistant to change. This means that older students must receive large dosages of success over a long period if their self-concepts are to change.

You can provide success for your students in a number of ways. One of these is to apply the IRI criteria to books students choose to read so as to insure that they are at their free or independent reading level (see Chapter 11 for a thorough explanation of this procedure). You should also make sure that most seatwork lessons are comparatively short and well understood before students attempt to do them. One of the most successful methods of providing success is to let students read to children in the lower grades or if their home situation permits, to a younger brother or sister. Students who are skilled in a particular area of reading can also achieve a measure of success by helping other students who are disabled in that area. This also frees the teacher to do more individualized instruction.

David M. Brown, Doan W. Gugua, and David A. Otts (1986) reported on a program wherein tutors provided small stickers to students. Each student was allowed to accumulate up to three stickers during a thirty-minute tutoring session. The stickers had rewarding comments printed on them: "Super," "Keep it up," "Nice work," etc. Stickers were given to students for paying attention, working hard, etc. They were also given a larger ribbon sticker when they had accumulated thirty of the smaller stickers. Although no statistical analysis was done, tutors reported "a large-scale improvement in the attitudes and reading performance of the tutees." (p. 603)

Provide a friendly atmosphere in which students feel free to express their opinions.   Many students perceive their teachers as authority figures with whom they are not free to discuss their likes and dislikes and opinions in general. You can easily let students know they are free to discuss their opinions without the necessity of receiving your stamp of approval or without being criticized for opinions that happen to be contrary to yours. As a remedial reading teacher you should also attempt to ignore antagonistic attitudes or at least not take them too seriously. Some disabled readers will be extremely antagonistic about reading, and this antagonism will often appear to be directed toward you. However, most teachers find that as disabled readers begin to improve and perceive the teacher as being directly responsible for much of this improvement, their attitudes also improve.

Be consistent in your behavior toward students.   Many students come from homes where they receive verbal or physical punishment one day for behavior that would be accepted or tolerated on another day. You should as nearly as possible set up standards for behavior and expectations for completion of assignments in the beginning and then be consistent in these behaviors and expectations. Few things bother students (regardless of age) more than not knowing what to expect. When students do not know what to expect, they are more likely to experiment to determine what behavior on their part is likely to bring about a change of behavior on the part of their teacher. All students, and especially disabled readers, need the security of consistent behavior patterns from their teacher.

Attempt to improve students' relationships with their peers.   Studies such as that of Deon Stevens (1971) have shown that disabled readers are not as well accepted socially as their normal-achieving peers. To some extent this can be altered by arranging for disabled readers to demonstrate their strengths in other areas. If remedial activities are conducted outside of the student's classroom, the remedial reading teacher may need to work in conjunction with the homeroom teacher to arrange for this type of success experience. These experiences might include such things as demonstrating hobbies or reading aloud after practicing.

Counseling Disabled Readers

Most disabled readers can be expected to possess some degree of emotional maladjustment, even though it is not always apparent. For this reason counseling should be an integral part of the remedial reading program. Contrary to the beliefs of some people, effective counseling can be done by the remedial reading teacher with brief training in a few specific techniques. This point has been emphasized by Lawrence and others who have carried on extremely effective counseling programs for disabled readers. The technique described by Lawrence had nine steps:

1. The counselor introduced himself or herself as a person who was interested in students and concerned about their happiness in school.
2. The counselor attempted to establish an atmosphere in which he or she was uncritical, friendly, and accepting of the student's personality.
3. The counselor attempted to provide a sounding board for the student's feelings. No attempt was made to interpret these feelings.
4. The interviews were student-centered.
5. In most cases direct questioning was avoided. Any questions were asked in a general way.
6. In the beginning stages discussion was possible only through the use of drawings and pictures done by the student. In the later stages other pictures such as those of the *Children's Apperception Test* were used as a stimulus.
7. The student was asked for three main wishes, and these wishes were discussed fully.
8. During the interviews the counselor attempted to find opportunities to praise the student's personality (not skills). In doing this the counselor attempted to build the student's self-image.
9. Various areas of the student's life were covered. These included the following: "relationship with parents; relationship with siblings; relationship with peers; relationship with other relatives; hobbies and interests; aspirations immediate and long-term; worries, fears, anxieties; attitude toward school; and attitude toward self." (p. 120)

A counseling technique that has been used effectively for some time in the Reading Center at the University of Texas at El Paso is one described by James Gardner and Grayce Ransom (1968). It is a rather comprehensive eight-step procedure that can easily be adapted to the needs of specific individuals. Teachers can learn it with only a minimum amount of study.

1. *Provide the subject with an adequate rationale for his or her learning problem.* The counselor is attempting to find something that does not reflect on the intelligence of the student to blame the problem on. In this step the counselor (C) attempts to determine why the subject (S) believes he or she has failed to some degree in reading. As Gardner and Ransom point out, many students manifest a strong underlying fear that they are mentally retarded or have serious brain dysfunction although the subject may mask this belief to some extent. C then attempts to help S realize that S does not fit the pattern of a mentally retarded or brain-injured student. In doing this C can point out that S is not in any of the special classes for this type of student. S is also made aware of his or her intelligent behaviors, such as knowing the rules of complicated games—Monopoly, baseball, and football— and/or competencies that C and S may find. S's background is then discussed in terms of possible reasons for failure. These might include such things as prolonged absence from school in the beginning years, or lack of continuity of instruction because of family moves or because of perceptual immaturity. C should fully explain to S how these factors can impede learning progress so that S can accept one or more of these reasons as an explanation or rationale for the learning problem.

2. *Provide social reinforcement for S's positive statements about school.* Whenever S makes a positive statement about school, a teacher, or school-related activity, C smiles and shows heightened or overall interest. The theory behind these actions on the part of C is that changing the verbal responses of S may lead to a corresponding change in behavior.

3. *Help the subject learn basic discriminations about his or her own behavior.* In doing this C attempts to discover circumstances that lead to S's failure to complete assignments or S's failure to act in a manner in keeping with a healthy academic orientation. This is done by asking S to discuss the circumstances that lead to failure. After C discovers these circumstances, S is helped to become aware of his or her undesirable behavior. This can be done by role playing in which S assumes the role of a student in the classroom and C plays the teacher. Gardner and Ransom emphasize that C must attempt to get an exact conception of precisely what S does.

4. *Teach the subject the aversive consequences involved in the continued use of avoidance patterns.* In this step C attempts to show S the immediate consequences rather than delayed consequences of avoidance patterns. As Gardner and Ransom aptly point out, we often tell students that they are likely to be unable to obtain a certain job or they will be unable to accomplish some other long-term goal. In most cases these long-term goals are unrealistic as far as children are concerned. In this step, however, the authors suggest showing short-term consequences such as those of the S who daydreams:

You look out the window because you feel you are not a good reader. But now you are in a practice situation, with reading material that you know you can handle. But you have the *habit* of looking out the window. You must break that habit. It will cause nothing but trouble, for you look out the window and you miss the word. When you miss the word, you fall behind and lose your place. When this happens, you start foundering around, getting scared, thinking you are stupid, and getting mad at yourself and the teacher and the book. These are the things that happen when you start to look out the window. (p. 533)

5. *Help the subject to develop alternative modes of responding.* In this process C may help S to develop alternative modes by assuming the role of S and demonstrating S's avoidance behaviors. S may then be asked to suggest alternative modes of responding or C and S may both discuss alternative modes. Gardner and Ransom also emphasize the importance of maintaining communication with other teachers of S so that they can be alerted to the types of behavior being developed. The responses can be reinforced as other teachers note them.

6. *Help the subject label his or her feelings.* As Gardner and Ransom point out, most students are not able to discriminate among their moods or feelings. In this step C should attempt to explain concepts such as avoidance and anger. In doing this the authors suggest stopping the student as he or she is reading something that appears to be difficult and asking how S is feeling *right now.* Although, as the authors state, many S's will report feeling "funny," later discussion will often prove that S is angry or disgusted at not being an able reader. Do not force S to admit to feelings S does not possess; however, you may find that suggesting possibilities such as "afraid," "angry," "wanting to stop," "angry at the teacher," "angry with myself," or "tired" often helps S to discover how he or she really feels.

7. *Maintain a positive attitude toward the personality and academic potentiality of the subject.* This is a quality that often requires some reorientation on the part of the teacher doing the counseling. However, knowing that most studies show that all but about 2 percent of the school population *can* learn to read should help C maintain a positive attitude. C must show his or her belief in the worth of S by everything C says and does.

8. *Maintain communication with the subject's teachers.* Be sure that S's other teachers know what goals you are attempting to achieve and what responses are currently being developed so that they can reinforce these responses when they occur.

This procedure can easily be adapted to the particular needs of each student. Some students may display considerably less avoidance behavior than others. When this is the case, less time should be spent in steps 3, 4, and 5. You should be careful, however, not to overlook less apparent, yet important, avoidance behaviors.

Another important step in the counseling process with disabled readers is to make sure they understand and verbalize their diagnosed reading problems. Perhaps there is an appropriate analogy between remedial reading and Alcoholics Anonymous. Spokespersons for AA say that there is little hope in rehabilitating people who do not first *admit* that they are alcoholics. Likewise, in remedial reading, it is important that students recognize and verbalize their problems. An initial interview with the student can readily reveal whether the student is aware of the problem. Ask such questions as, "What do you think about your reading?" or "Now that you have told me you do not read very well, can you tell me why you say that?"

Students often respond to questions such as these with statements such as, "Well, I don't seem to understand what I read," or "I can't seem to figure out new words."

Some students with apparent problems will insist that they really have no difficulty in reading. For this type of student it is often helpful to tape record their oral reading and let them listen to it as it is replayed. While listening they can be asked to circle any words missed, repeated, or substituted. When doing this you should avoid argument with the students, and you should not appear to be trying to prove that the student has a reading problem.

After students recognize their problem, they should be encouraged to talk about it. You can show them the kinds of things you plan to do to remediate the difficulty.

It is important to note that the procedures outlined here for counseling disabled readers are by no means meant to supplant the normal cognitive or academic aspects of the program. Rather, they should serve as a most important supplement to these activities.

The Use of Suggestopedia or Hypnosis

Albert Harris (1981) reported on the use of *suggestopedia* as a method of improving the performance of disabled readers. It emphasizes the use of positive suggestion, relaxation, and visualization. Its proponents believe that most students have much greater potential for learning than is realized. Harris states, "Suggestopedia is a new development in the application of psychological techniques to education, and one worth watching." (p. 408)

O. A. "Buff" Oldridge (1982); H. Thompson Fillmer, Sherrie L. Nist, and Elois M. Scott (1983); and H. Thompson Fillmer and Forrest W. Parkey (1985) have reported on the use of positive suggestion or hypnosis in their work with disabled readers. Oldridge reported on a program in which students participated for six weeks. Students in his program were put in a medium trance twice a week during this time. The following points were emphasized to students: 1. They were intelligent enough to read well. 2. They had no impairment of the eyes or ears. 3. Students seemed to be having difficulty because the students themselves thought they could not learn to read. 4. Students probably thought they could not learn to read because they had gotten off to a poor start. 5. Everything was now right; all students had to do was relax and concentrate while reading. Oldridge reported a number of positive comments from the tutors, such as:

> Jimmy seems to have relaxed considerably during the last two weeks. Reading doesn't seem to be such a chore—yesterday he read 14 pages to me and said it felt like two. Also, he has willingly taken books home. (p. 283)

Oldridge made the following recommendations for teachers using nonhypnotic suggestion:

1. Base suggestions on fact, i.e., on tests and other information known by the student.
2. The suggestions are most effective when made by an authority figure.
3. Suggestions should be made in a direct, no-nonsense manner.
4. In making suggestions emphasize the positive but do not try to eliminate the negative.
5. All suggestions should be in direct support of the later behavior of the teacher and none should contradict later behavior of the teacher.
6. The student's self-concept should be the focus of a large percentage of the suggestions.
7. Suggestions are most effective when the students are relaxed.

Oldridge's method is to ask students to lay their heads on their desks and close their eyes and relax. Tell them to forget what they have been doing and to listen very carefully while you explain the next classroom activity. Emphasize that the activity will be easier than the time before and that it will become easier each time the students perform the task.

Fillmer and Parkay (1985) say there are many definitions of hypnosis but that virtually all of these definitions include two elements: *relaxation* and *imagery*. In using hypnosis with students Fillmer and Parkay suggest a three-step process:

1. Relaxing the subjects
2. Improving imagery
3. Restoring pupils to a state of alertness

These authors suggest that four elements are essential in the relaxation response. (a) a quiet environment; (b) a mental device such as a word or phrase, which should be repeated in a specific fashion over and over again; (c) the adoption of a passive attitude; and (d) a comfortable position. (p. 62)

In improving imagery students receive positive suggestions concerning their reading and test-taking behavior: "See yourself reading a book or magazine in a familiar location. It might be in a room at home . . . Imagine that the letters, words, and sentences are flying off the pages of the book right into your head. . . . (p. 63)

In restoring students to a state of alertness you can first suggest that as you count from one to five, the students will become more alert, until by the count of five they will be fully awake.

In concluding their article Fillmer and Parkay state:

> . . . There is evidence to suggest that the combination of relaxation and imagery (hypnosis) can markedly improve pupils' reading proficiency. Classroom research is needed so that the use of hypnosis in reading instruction may be further refined. (p. 63)

COUNSELING PARENTS OF DISABLED READERS

Because of the close relationships between inability to read and emotional problems connected with the home environment, parent counseling can be an important part of the remedial reading program. Although concrete research is lacking on the effectiveness of large-scale or intensive programs, there is some evidence that parent counseling can improve student achievement as well as parental attitudes. For example, Janice Studholms (1964) studied the results of group guidance with mothers of disabled readers. She found that the group guidance sessions improved not only the attitudes of the mothers, but also the attitudes of the students towards their lessons. The students who developed the greatest positive change in attitudes also made greater achievement. Studholms noted, however, that the attitudes of the students tended to regress after the termination of the counseling sessions.

The type of counseling program instituted tends to vary a great deal depending on the orientation of the counselor. It is not advisable for a remedial reading teacher who is not highly trained in counseling to attempt to provide parents with anything more than a general orientation to the remedial reading program. This orientation might include the following types of activities:

1. A discussion of the basis for students' acceptance to the program with an emphasis on the fact that students in remedial reading are not mentally retarded but disabled readers who usually have considerably more potential than is being demonstrated.
2. Discussion of the fact that pressuring disabled readers to achieve usually results in more harm than good.
3. Coordinating activities of home and school.

At the Elementary Reading Clinic at California State University, Hayward, parents participate in a number of activities designed to ease their feelings of guilt, improve their effectiveness in helping their children with reading problems, and enhance communication with the clinic staff and other educational agencies:

1. An initial meeting to discuss the clinic experience, to provide an overview of the program, to meet the staff, to become aware of the facilities and resources, to discuss remedial reading problems generally, and to discuss expectations for parents, children, clinicians, and the clinic director.
2. A home visit by the clinician to learn about the child from the parents in the home environment, to discuss the specifics of the initial diagnosis and remediation plans, to clarify how the parents may assist with home assignments, and to answer questions.
3. An evening program for parents at the clinic site to describe coming events in clinic; to allow for questions, answers, and discussion; to share materials and techniques that parents may use to assist their children at home; and to provide for a private conference between parents and clinicians for discussing the pupil's progress and scheduling the clinic visit.
4. A clinic visit in which the parents spend a morning with their child in the program. At their discretion, the clinicians may have the parents assist with some of the activities to determine which if any of the instructional procedures can be utilized effectively by the parents at home. The parents also have an opportunity from this direct participation to become more aware of the clinic program and the needs and progress of their children.
5. The Clinic Fair, a culminating day of reading games, activities, and an awards presentation (for all participating children) to which all family members are invited.
6. An optional final conference to discuss the final report (a copy of which is sent to the child's school), to review specific recommendations, and to advise the parents about future educational options. When this conference is not held, the reports are mailed to the parents.
7. A written evaluation form sent to all parents seeking feedback on various aspects of the clinic program. Interestingly, many parents report that their participation in the above activities, in addition to the time they spent with their children in transporting them daily, had a strong positive impact on their relationship with their children.

Many of these activities have been adapted by reading specialists for use in their school programs. Although the activities require much time to plan and conduct, the reading specialists insist that they are a valuable part of the remedial services.

If the parent counseling is to be done by an expert counselor experienced in group techniques, the sessions should include activities such as those mentioned above but might also include information such as that used in a counseling program described by Patricia Bricklin (1970):

1. Information to "help parents understand their child's behavior as it refers to typical child development and to sort out those behaviors growing out of his learning disability. And . . . learn to recognize and accept their own feelings as well as those of the child." (p. 338)
2. " . . . Help parents set more effective limits, accept and acknowledge feelings and develop appropriate independence in the child." (p. 338)
3. Help parents learn to cope with their own feelings about their child's problems.

Improving the Disabled Reader's Self-Concept

During the past two decades many studies have been done on the relationship between students' self-concepts and reading ability. Following are a few important generalizations that could be derived from these studies:

1. There is a fairly high correlation between the self-concept of beginning readers and their achievement in reading in the elementary grades.
2. The self-concept is learned and is amenable to change.
3. The self-concept of a first grader seems to be easier to change than the self-concept of upper elementary school or junior or senior high school students.
4. There is a fairly high degree of relationship between teachers' and parents' expectations and students' self-concepts.

These generalizations have some important implications for remedial reading teachers. One is that the remedial reading program should have built-in provisions for the improvement of students' self-concepts as well as for the improvement of students' cognitive skills. This means that the remedial reading teacher should be constantly alert to capitalize on any opportunity to build the student's self-image. Some ways of doing this:

1. Accept the student as a worthy individual who is capable of learning.
2. Constantly look for things in which the student is successful and point these out. For example, Lee Mountain (1986) has suggested the use of successful experiences in creative dramatics as a way to improve students' self-concepts.
3. If possible, arrange for older disabled readers to help beginning readers by reading to them or by helping them with other tasks.
4. Keep careful records of progress and share these with students.
5. Make sure disabled readers do not attempt to read at their frustration level. Before checking books out to them to take home to read for pleasure, apply the IRI criteria as explained in Chapter 11. Or if you

know the independent reading level of the student, make sure that any books the student chooses to read for pleasure are not written above that level, as measured by one of the better-known readability formulas.

6. Make certain that assignments are understood and can be done without a great deal of difficulty.
7. Encourage students to bring their hobbies to class, and show materials relating to these hobbies to other members of the class.
8. Encourage students to think about and constantly imagine themselves being excellent readers.

Another implication from the generalizations mentioned earlier is that students with mild reading disabilities should be located and corrective work should begin as soon as possible. Because of the inability of many classroom teachers to spot incipient reading problems, some students' reading problems do not receive attention until they become severe enough to make them clearly noticeable. If a student does not receive remediation until the reading disability becomes clearly apparent, the remedial reading teacher is likely to have to deal with a student with a negative self-concept that will be much less amenable to change than it would have been during the student's earlier years in school.

Improving Language Skills

Socioeconomic factors frequently cause or contribute to students' language difficulties. Therefore, a discussion of appropriate procedures is included here, even though language development might properly be considered within the realm of cognitive skills.

Guy Bond, Miles Tinker, and Barbara Wasson (1979) discuss the reading problems of children who are learning to speak English as a second language. Their recommendations have equal relevance for native English speakers who have difficulty in understanding or speaking English:

> The procedures ordinarily used in teaching beginning reading in our schools assume that each child already has learned to understand and speak the language. Language-handicapped children first need a program to improve their English. A preparatory instructional period ordinarily should have three simultaneous activities: first, building up a basic vocabulary for understanding and speaking; second, improvement of facility in oral communication; and third, providing a background of meaningful experiences. Words and concepts associated with experiences must be in English. Thus the child learns to speak and understand a vocabulary before he encounters it in reading. (p. 105)

Psycholinguists such as Kenneth Goodman (1967) and Frank Smith (1971, 1977) believe that once oral language facility has developed, reading should occur as a natural outgrowth of the child's language. These writers believe that teachers should deemphasize instruction in specific decoding skills and should instead present reading as a contextual activity. For applications of language-centered reading models, also refer to David Pearson (1978) and Carol Chomsky (1972, 1979).

MaryAnne Hall (1979) recommends five language-centered approaches for pre- and beginning readers. A discussion of each of these follows below. Other resources for specific language development activities include books by Doris Lee and Joseph Rubin (1979) and Walter Petty and others (1976).

1. *Provide exposure to written language in prereading.* Reading readiness activities should focus on experiences with the printed word rather than pictures and other nonprint materials. Children can best learn the specific prereading skills, such as visual discrimination, left to right progression, the important terms (word, sound, letter, etc.), and letter knowledge through lessons that rely on actual word forms. A critical concept for children to learn at the beginning stage is that writing represents talk written down; that is, the written language is a code for meaning.

2. *Use the language-experience approach for beginning reading.* A variety of language-experience techniques for the purpose of building students' general sight vocabulary were discussed in Chapter 4. We strongly endorse this approach as a vehicle for helping children to bridge the gap between oral and written language forms. Research and experience have shown that this is a particularly motivating and satisfying approach for both children and teachers.

3. *Make reading comprehension-centered.* Every effort should be made to teach reading as a meaning-getting activity. In our opinion this does not mean that there is no place for instruction in phonics or basic sight vocabulary in the reading program. Rather, you must relate this instruction to the goal of reading comprehension. The best way to do this is to teach specific decoding skills in the more meaningful context of phrases, sentences, and stories. Also, you should make frequent checks to be sure that pupils understand what they are decoding and take time to *discuss* with children the meaning of what the children have read.

4. *Correlate reading and writing.* This is easy to do if the language-experience approach is used. Evidence suggests that writing activities not only improve children's reading comprehension but also serve to reinforce the learning of decoding skills.

5. *Immerse children in an environment of language and literature.* One of the most fundamental, important, and enjoyable teaching activities is to read to children of all ages. Children who have been read to extensively prior to school are generally at an advantage. Teachers must provide for children who have not had this experience. Immersion in language is also reflected in the classroom environment. Objects should

be labeled. Books and other printed materials, such as children's language-experience stories, should be attractively displayed and available. Time must be provided for children to express themselves verbally and to look at, read, discuss, and enjoy their written materials.

Improving Teacher Expectations

A number of studies done during the 1960s have shown that teacher expectation can have a strong influence on the achievement of students. There also seems to be a never-ending circular pattern between teacher expectation and students' self-concepts. For example, a teacher who has low expectations for a student is likely to relay those feelings to the student in one way or another without openly admitting it. The student sensing this feeling will tend to develop a poor self-concept and will consequently be likely to achieve less, which, in turn, will verify the teacher's expectations for the student and make the teacher even more likely to have lower expectations for the student.

Through a series of studies Robert Rosenthal (1968) and other researchers have found that teachers are able to communicate their expectations to students, whether these expectations are high or low, without even being aware of doing so. For example, Rosenthal found that when the interactions between experimenters and subjects were recorded on film and then reviewed, only 12 percent of the examiners ever smiled at their male subjects, while 70 percent smiled at their female subjects. In another study examiners were to examine subjects who were behind a screen out of their sight. The examiners were told that one group of subjects was brighter than another group. It was found that the examiners tended to obtain greater success from the so-called bright group even without being able to see them. Evidently verbal clues are relayed to the subject even when the examiner is not aware of doing so.

Perhaps the most heartening thing about some of these experiments, however, is that some researchers have shown that many teachers are not influenced by information on students' achievement and IQs. The type of phenomenon mentioned earlier often need not happen if teachers are aware that their low expectations can influence students' self-concepts and achievement. For example, a study conducted by David Elijah (1980) found that first-grade teachers' expectations were not altered by falsified scores on reading readiness tests. The results also indicated that the teachers' rankings of students' readiness were as reliable as rankings obtained using a popular reading readiness test. In a somewhat related study, Hilary Schofield (1980) found a correlation between the attitude and achievement of teachers and pupils. Findings indicated that high achievement and high attitude in teachers were positively associated with high achievement and high attitudes in students.

This type of information has a great deal of relevance for the remedial reading teacher. Some specific suggestions for dealing with the influence of teacher expectation are as follows:

1. Read the research of Robert Rosenthal and Lenore Jacobson (1968) and others and become aware of the ways in which teacher expectations are relayed to students. Simply knowing of this phenomenon is much more likely to prevent you from forming and thus relaying low expectations to your students.
2. Realize that every student is a worthy human being and that every student is capable of learning.
3. Look for the strengths that students possess and focus on these rather than on reasons for their inability to learn.
4. Do not be unduly influenced by IQ scores. Remember that many students with high IQ scores have reading problems and that many students with comparatively low IQ scores become excellent readers.

SUMMARY

Psychological and sociological problems are often less visible in disabled readers. For this reason they are often likely to receive less attention in the overall remediation planned for disabled readers. Studies have shown, however, that remedial programs that incorporated counseling, along with teaching of the cognitive skills of reading, have been considerably more successful than those that omit these aspects of the overall remedial reading program.

Methods of diagnosing psychosocial problems are not as exacting as the methods used for diagnosing the cognitive skills of reading. However, certain observation procedures and informal assessment techniques can be useful in gaining insight into students' problems in these areas.

Counseling procedures that can quite easily be learned by the remedial reading teacher have been developed. There are also some important procedures developed from psychological theories that can rather easily be learned and applied by remedial reading teachers.

Language factors and their relation to reading disability were discussed, and some techniques for improving students' language abilities were presented.

REFERENCES

Armstrong, R. J., & Mooney, R. F. (1971). The Slosson intelligence test: Implications for reading specialists. *Reading Teacher, 24,* 336–340.

Bell, D. B. (1969). *The motivational and personality factors in reading retardation among two racial groups of adolescent males.* Unpublished doctoral dissertation, Texas Tech University, Lubbock.

Bond, G. L., Tinker, M. A., & Wasson, B. B. (1979). *Reading difficulties: Their diagnosis and correction* (4th ed.). Englewood Cliffs, NJ: Prentice-Hall.

Brown, D. M., Fugua, J. W., & Otts, D. A. (1986). Helping reluctant readers "stick" to it. *Academic Therapy, 21,* 599–605.

Brunken, R. J., & Shen, F. (1966). Personality characteristics of ineffective, effective, and efficient readers. *Personnel and Guidance Journal, 44,* 837–843.

Buck, J. N., & Jolles, I. (1955). *House-tree-person projective technique.* Los Angeles: Western Psychological Service.

Chomsky, C. (1972). Stages in language development and reading exposure. *Harvard Educational Review, 42,* 1–33.

Chomsky, C. (1979). Language and reading. In R. E. Shafer (Ed.), *Applied linguistics and reading* (pp. 112–128). Newark, DE: International Reading Association.

Chronister, G. M. (1964). Personality and reading achievement. *Elementary School Journal, 64,* 253–260.

Downing, J. (1971–1972). Children's developing concept of spoken and written language. *Journal of Reading Behavior, 4,* 1–19.

Dunn, L. M., & Dunn, L. M. (1981). *Peabody picture vocabulary test revised.* Circle Rines, MN: American Guidance Service.

Elijah, D. (1980). Teacher expectations: Determinants of pupils' reading achievement. *Reading Improvement, 17,* 117–121.

Evans, M. T., Taylor, N., & Plum, I. (1979). Children's written language awareness and its relation to reading acquisition. *Journal of Reading Behavior, 11,* 7–19.

Fillmer, H. T., Nist, S. L., & Scott, E. M. (1983). The use of hypnosis in improving reading performance. *Community College Review, 11,* 23–27.

Fillmer, H. T., & Parkay, F. W. (1985). How can hypnosis improve reading proficiency? *The Clearing House, 59,* 61–63.

Fotheringham, J. B., & Creal, D. (1980). Family socioeconomic and educational-emotional characteristics as predictors of school achievement. *Journal of Educational Research, 73,* 311–317.

Fox, B. C. (1976). How children analyze language: Implications for beginning reading instruction. *Reading Improvement, 13,* 229–234.

Gardner, J., & Ransom, G. (1968). Academic reorientation: A counseling approach to remedial readers. *Reading Teacher, 21,* 529–536.

Gates, A. (1941). The role of personality maladjustment and remedial reading. *Journal of Generic Psychology, 59,* 77–83.

Glazer, S. M., & Morrow, L. M. (1978). The syntactic complexity of primary grade children's oral language and primary grade reading materials: A comparative analysis. *Journal of Reading Behavior, 10,* 200–203.

Goodman, K. S. (1967). Reading: A psycholinguistic guessing game. *Journal of the Reading Specialist, 6,* 126–135.

Grotberg, E. H. (1970). Neurological aspects of learning disabilities: A case for the disadvantaged. *Journal of Learning Disabilities, 3,* 321–327.

Hall, M. A. (1979). Language-centered reading: Premises and recommendations. *Language Arts, 56,* 664–670.

Harootunian, B. (1966). Intellectual abilities and reading achievement. *Elementary School Journal, 66,* 386–392.

Harris, A. J. (1979). Discussion: Linguistic awareness and cognitive clarity in learning to read. In M. L. Kamil, & A. J. Moe (Eds.), *Reading research: Studies and applications* (pp. 295–296). Twenty-eighth Yearbook of the National Reading Conference.

Harris, A. J. (1981). What is new in remedial reading? *Reading Teacher, 34,* 405–410.

Harris, A. J., & Sipay, E. R. (1985). *How to increase reading ability* (8th ed.). New York: Longman.

Kawash, G. F., & Clewes, J. L. (1986). Inferring a child's level of self-esteem from a knowledge of other personality factors. *Psychology in the Schools, 23,* 214–217.

Krippner, S. (1968). Etiological factors in reading disability of the academically talented in comparison to pupils of average and slow learning ability. *Journal of Educational Research, 61,* 275–279.

Lamy, M. (1962). *Relationship of self-perception of early primary children to achievement in reading.* Unpublished doctoral dissertation, University of Florida, Gainsville.

Lawrence, D. (1971). The effects of counseling on retarded readers. *Educational Research, 13,* 119–124.

Lee, D., & Rubin, J. B. (1979). *Children and language.* Belmont, CA: Wadsworth Publishing.

Lewis, H. W. (1984). A structured group counseling program for reading disabled elementary students. *The School Counselor, 31,* 454–459.

Mountain, L. (1986). Releasing the remedial reader's creative power. *Journal of Learning Disabilities, 19,* 5–7.

Murray, H. A. (1951). *Thematic apperception test.* Los Angeles: Western Psychological Services.

Neville, D. (1961). A comparison of the WISC patterns of male retarded and nonretarded readers. *Journal of Educational Research, 54,* 195–197.

Oldridge, O. A. (1982). Positive suggestion: It helps LD students learn. *Academic Therapy, 17,* 279–287.

Pearson, P. D. (1978). Some practical applications of a psycholinguistic model of reading. In S. J. Samuels (Ed.), *What research has to say about reading instruction* (pp. 84–97). Newark, DE: International Reading Association.

Petty, W. T., et al. (1976). *Experiences in language: tools and techniques for language arts methods.* Boston: Allyn and Bacon.

Porter, R. B., & Cattell, R. B. (1979). *Handbook for the children's personality questionnaire (CPQ).* Champaign, IL: Institute for Personality and Ability Testing.

Robinson, H. (1946). *Why pupils fail in reading.* Chicago: University of Chicago Press.

Rorschach, H. (1960). *Rorschach psychodiagnostic plates.* Los Angeles: Western Psychological Services.

Rosenthal, R. (1968). Self-fulfilling prophecies in behavioral research and everyday life. *Reading conference yearbook 32* (pp. 15–33). Claremont, CA: Claremont Reading Conference.

Rosenthal, R., & Jacobson, L. (1968). *Pygmalion in the classroom.* New York: Holt, Rinehart, & Winston.

Sattler, J. M., & Covin, T. M. (1986). Comparison of the Slosson intelligence test, revised norms and WISC-R for children with learning problems and gifted children. *Psychology in the Schools, 23,* 259–264.

Schofield, H. L. (1980). Reading attitude and achievement: Teacher-pupil relationships. *Journal of Educational Research, 74,* 111–119.

Slosson, R. L. (1982). *Slosson intelligence test* (2nd ed.). East Aurora, NY: Slosson Educational Publications.

Smith, F. (1971). *Understanding reading: A psycholinguistic analysis of reading and learning to read.* New York: Holt, Rinehart & Winston.

Smith, F. (1977). Making sense of reading—and of reading instruction. *Harvard Educational Review, 47,* 386–395.

Spache, G. D. (1957). Personality problems of retarded readers. *Journal of Education, 50,* 461–469.

Stedman, J. M., & McKenzie, R. E. (1971). Family factors related to competence in young disadvantaged Mexican-American children. *Child Development, 42,* 1602–1607.

Stevens, D. O. (1971). Reading difficulty and classroom acceptance. *Reading Teacher, 25,* 52–55.

Strang, R. (1969). *Diagnostic teaching of reading* (2nd ed.). New York: McGraw-Hill,

Studholms, J. M. (1964). Group guidance with mothers of retarded readers. *Reading Teacher, 17,* 528–530.

Thomson, M. E., & Hartley, G. M. (1980). Self-concept in dyslexic children. *Academic Therapy, 16,* 19–36.

Hodges, K. M., Pool, L. B., Calloway, B., & Thurston, C. E. (1969). Cultural background study in relation to reading ability. In J. A. Figurel (Ed.), *Reading and realism* (pp. 554–559). Newark, DE: International Reading Association.

Vance, H., Wallbrown, F. H., & Blaha, J. (1978). Determining WISC-R profiles for reading disabled children. *Journal of Learning Disabilities, 11,* 657–661.

Wagner, M. E., & Schubert, H. J. P. (1955). *Draw-a-person quality scale.* Los Angeles: Western Psychological Services.

Wattenberg, W. W. (1964). Relation of self-concepts to beginning achievement in reading. *Child Development, 35,* 461–467.

Zimmerman, I. L., Theron, M. C., & Woo-Sam, J. M. (1986). A longitudinal comparison of the WISC-R and WAIS-R. *Psychology in the Schools, 23,* 148–151.

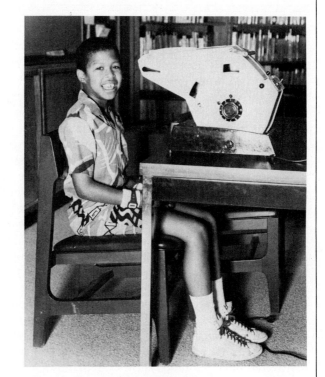

Diagnosis and Remediation of Physical Disabilities

The first part of this chapter contains a review of those physical disabilities that research and experience have indicated tend to affect reading ability. Following this discussion we present methods for diagnosing disabilities serious enough to require referral or remediation. The last part of this chapter contains specific suggestions for the remediation of disabilities that fall within the realm of the school.

Part A: DIAGNOSIS

As indicated in Chapter 1, most of the physical disabilities with which you are concerned in reading can be classified under the headings of problems of the eye, problems of the ear, problems with speech, neurologically impaired functions, and problems of general health. Because of the difficulties you will encounter in dealing with neurological disabilities, this subject is discussed in detail in Chapter 9. As so often happens in the remediation of reading disabilities, you will find that many of these areas overlap so that it becomes difficult, if not impossible, to determine which factors are actively contributing to a student's reading disability and which are merely concomitant.

In the diagnosis of educational problems you also face a number of problems that may not be of great concern to the medical doctor. For example, the physician may find a student's ear to be healthy and the student's auditory acuity normal. From an educational standpoint, however, you cannot assume that this same student has no problems in listening. Even with normal acuity, the student's auditory discrimination may not be adequate to learn without difficulties with certain phonemes. In addition to possible problems with auditory acuity and discrimination the student may experience difficulty with auditory memory. Such problems will be discussed later; however, it should be remembered that only rarely are difficulties with anything but auditory acuity discovered in a routine physical examination.

The diagnosis of reading difficulties as related to physical disabilities requires much more than a report from the family physician. This chapter deals not only with those problems of the eye, ear, speech, and general health that are likely to become apparent in a physical examination, but also with some less visible problems that are likely to surface only through diagnostic teaching and careful observation. In addition to testing and diagnostic teaching you should also keep in mind that a parent interview can yield valuable information concerning possible physical disabilities that contribute to the student's reading problem.

DIAGNOSIS OF PROBLEMS OF THE EYE

To understand a discussion of seeing as it relates to reading and learning it is important to understand the terms. It has become popular for many authors to create their own terms and definitions. This causes much confusion. Terms here will be as common and as obvious as this complex subject will allow.

Seeing

This is a general and all-inclusive term.

Sight Versus Vision

It is imperative that teachers and all others concerned with diagnosis of problems of the eye realize that in reading, we are concerned with more than sight. Although the exact terms may vary slightly, the term *sight* often refers to the ability to see, or the eye's responses to light, whereas *vision* refers to the student's ability to interpret information that comes through the eyes. Obviously then, a student without proper sight, unless corrected, can never have adequate vision. On the other hand, a student who has adequate sight may lack the vision or perceptual ability to interpret various symbols.

Sight concerns the ability of the eye to resolve detail. This is a mechanical or physical process. The measurement of this ability to resolve detail is called *acuity*. Sight, then, is the production of acuity. Sight can be likened to a snapshot camera and drugstore prints. Sight includes the snapping of the shutter; that is, the making of the optical image or picture in the back of the eye. This back part, called the *retina*, is like the film in the camera. Sight includes sending the image to the brain; that is, taking the film to be developed. Good sight means good acuity. The Snellen measure is 20/20 for good acuity. The larger the denominator, the less the acuity. That is, the person with 20/80 acuity would need to be four times as close to an object as a person with 20/20 acuity to see it as well. Acuity has no relationship to how the student understands or perceives the detail or how efficiently the student can read. Poor readers, in fact, often have good sight.

Vision is the processing of sight to give location, memory, and intersensory relationships. Vision is a mental process. It cannot be compared to the camera. Vision might be thought of as the work of a skilled darkroom artist, which consists of not just developing film but retouching the negative, deciding the portion of the negative to use, and getting the right shade of color to the picture.

Proper processing of sight should tell the student where the object is in space as well as its orientation. This processing should also give the student memory of similar past experiences to compare, and it should evaluate this with the other senses such as hearing and touch.

Perception is the end result of sight and vision, the output. Reading ability seems to be dependent not only on visual perception, but also on auditory and tactual perception. If the student cannot differentiate *b* from *d*, the processing of sight for location is not good (visual-spacial perception). If the student draws a triangle after being shown a square, the student's processing to give memory is not adequate (visual memory). If the student cannot visualize the sequence of the letters *c-h-a-l-k* when the word *chalk* is spoken, or cannot relate visual stimulus to touch stimulus, then there is a deficiency in intersensory processing.

Vision is also often used as an all-inclusive term to designate several aspects of the use of the eye. Stanley Krippner (1971) cites the writing of N. Flax as having developed a definition that should help clarify the word for all professions. Flax refers to disorders of the peripheral nervous system (PNS) and the central nervous system (CNS). Krippner states:

> To Flax, PNS disorders refer to deficiencies of the end-organ system of vision (i.e., the eye); they include visual acuity, refractive error, fusion, convergence, and accommodation, all of which involve the eye mechanism and which are responsible for producing clear, single, binocular vision. CNS disorders involve deficiencies in organizing and interpreting images received by the eyes and sent to the brain. In CNS disorders, a clear, single visual image may be present but the child cannot decode the printed word because of problems in organization and interpretation of what is seen. (p. 74)

In reading, the CNS problems described here are usually referred to as visual perceptual problems.

Irwin Suchoff (1981) reports that the relationship between vision and reading is unclear; some studies reveal that particular visual defects occur more often among disabled readers than among the general population, while other studies refute that claim. Similarly, research findings disagree about whether remediation of visual difficulties actually improves reading ability. Michael Rouse and Julie Ryan (1984) claim that visual acuity has little correlation with reading ability except in extreme cases. They point out, however, that visual deficiencies may affect reading in two ways:

> First, the child may experience asthenopia (visual fatigue) or a number of other symptoms that cause reading to be laborious and inefficient. Second, the child may avoid dealing with the problem, resulting in behaviors such as inattentiveness, daydreaming, and a general avoidance of nearpoint activities. (p. 307)

The incidence of eye disorders often varies considerably depending on whether the research is discussing what Flax referred to as possessing problems of the PNS category, or both. These differences are often evidenced in the writings of ophthalmologists versus optometrists on the subject of vision.

The ophthalmologist (also called an oculist), a physician (M.D.) who specializes in the care of the eye, is licensed to prescribe glasses and other medication and to perform surgery to correct visual problems. The optometrist receives a Doctor of Optometry degree (O.D.) in a college of optometry and is a specialist in sight and vision. As Krippner points out, many optometrists also take more advanced study in developmental vision and become proficient in visual training concerned with the CNS aspects of vision. Because of the nature of their training there is a tendency for ophthalmologists to concern themselves more with the PNS aspects of the eyes and for optometrists to be more concerned with both the PNS and CNS aspects. This, of course, is a rather broad generalization, but to a large extent it accounts for the large differences often reported on visual problems as causative factors in reading disability.

Regardless of the type of doctor doing the testing it is generally agreed that certain disorders of the eye do contribute to, or may be causal factors in, cases of reading disability. The following are eye and sight skills and anomalies that are involved with seeing and reading.

Accommodation. This is commonly called focusing. Like a camera, the eye must adjust the optics to make a clear picture. The eye must accommodate the printed words in a book at twelve inches or the words on the chalkboard at fifteen feet. As the student's book gets closer, the amount of accommodation must be increased. There is a neurological connection between this center and the center that causes the eyes to turn in. When the student increases accommodation, this other center causes the eyes to turn in. A student can have inaccurate accommodation or spasm (hypertonicity) of the muscles (ciliary muscles) controlling accommodation.

Convergence. This is the turning in of the eyes. As a single point moves closer to the two eyes, they must converge to insure that the image in each eye is centered. It is accomplished first by the neurological connection with accommodation. The more stimulus to accommodate, the more stimulus is put into *accommodative convergence,* or automatic convergence as a result of increased accommodation. Accommodative convergence does not perfectly align the eyes on a point at the distance for which they are accommodated. Therefore, manual convergence (turning the eyes in or out to complete the alignment after automatic or accommodative convergence has occurred) must now be used to obtain perfect centering of the image in each eye. This centering is called *fusion,* and the manual convergence is *fusional convergence.* A student can have insufficient accommodative convergence, thus requiring more manual convergence. The student can also have excessive accommodative convergence, which means the student must manually diverge the eyes to get fusion. The student can also have limited ability to converge the eyes manually for a very near point. This would mean that converging to the normal reading distance requires a high percentage of the student's total ability to converge.

Fusion. This refers to the aligning of each eye so that the image in each is centered. They center in identical places on the retinas (back of the eye) where each eye has maximum acuity. The point in the back of the eye with maximum acuity is called the *macula.* If the images are not properly centered, the student will see double.

Hyperopia. This is commonly called *farsightedness.* It is congenital and anatomical. Among the various refractive errors listed as causing reading disabilities this is perhaps listed most often. Hyperopia causes excessive accommodation and convergence. Therefore, when it is present, two of the ocular motor skills function improperly. This results in blurring, eye fatigue, head-ache, and loss of interest in close work.

Myopia.   The common name for this is *nearsightedness.* It is a refractive error, and the symptoms are the reverse of hyperopia. There is a great deal of evidence that most myopia is developmental. Myopia does not interfere with reading; in fact, this is a common condition with good readers. Since the myo-pic eye is focused for a near point, this eye will require less accommodation. Uncorrected myopia will, however, give the student problems with board work or other tasks requiring seeing at a distance.

Astigmatism.   This condition, like hyperopia and myopia, is an optical or refractive one. Astigmatism can exist with hyperopia and with myopia. In fact, it is not usually found by itself, and when it is, the eye is partly myopic and partly hyperopic. To understand astigmatism, consider the power of the optics of a narrow vertical section through the eye, and the power of a narrow horizontal section. If the power in the vertical is different from the power in the horizontal, the optical system has astigmatism.

Astigmatism causes blurred print and eye fatigue. Since there are different focuses in the eye, the eye will do more changing focus trying to make the image clear. This can also cause headaches and interfere with reading effi-ciency.

Both hyperopia and astigmatism can cause suppression and strabismus. High amounts of hyperopia frequently cause crossed eyes due to the excessive accommodative convergence. If these children are properly fitted with lenses at an early age, the excessive convergence is usually relieved and the eyes will straighten. Delwyn Schubert (1982) reports that astigmatism occurs equally among good and poor readers, except in severe cases, where it is correlated with reading difficulty.

Aniseikonia.   This is a condition in which there is a different size and/or shape of the image of each eye. When there is no difference in refractive error of the two eyes, a difference in image size is due to a different physical size of the eyeball. A student with this condition has difficulty fusing. Therefore, it contributes to reading disability.

Anisomatropia.   This is a condition in which there is a different refrac-tive power in each eye. This is almost always accompanied by aniseikonia.

Heterophoria.   This refers to the basic position of the eyes at rest as they relate to each other. The eyes assume this position of rest when one or both are closed. This removes any need to converge to align one eye with the other. There is no stimulus to fusion. The eyes are disassociated. When there is no stimulus to fusion and the eyes are outward from each other, the condition is *exophoria.* When there is no stimulus to fusion and the eyes deviate inward, it is known as *esophoria.* When disassociated (no stimulus to fusion) and one is turned above the other, it is termed *hyperphoria* (up) or *hypophoria* (down). Heterophoria means that any one of these conditions exists. The student can overcome heterophoria and obtain fusion without treatment. However, when the condition is severe, it is known as heterotropia and cannot be overcome without treatment.

Suppression.   This is a neurological block of the picture stimulus from the macula so that the picture in that eye is not seen. This is done at the brain. Any time the student has difficulty with fusion, one eye may become suppressed. This relieves the need to fuse and there is no longer a fusion problem. Suppression works to block out the picture only in the central area. This is the point at which the student is looking—the fixation target. The suppressor does not suppress the sight to the sides. If a student develops suppression at an early age, *amblyopia* almost always results.

Amblyopia.   This is commonly called *lazy eye.* It is lowered acuity in the suppressed eye. This is true even when the other eye (the good eye) cannot see. When suppression is not developed until school age, there is usually less loss of acuity.

Heterotropia.   When heterophoria (tendency of one eye to deviate in one or another direction) is great and cannot be overcome, the eyes will not fuse. One might say a heterotropia is a heterophoria that cannot be overcome. Deviation outward is *exotropia;* inward, *esotropia;* and vertical, *hypo-* or *hypertropia.* If the student is able to hold the eyes in alignment part of the time, it is termed *intermittent tropia.* When one eye deviates at one time and the other eye at other times, it is an *alternating tropia.* The student with a tropic condition either sees double or suppresses the deviating eye when the eyes are not fused (one deviated).

Hysteria.   This is a condition in which emotional upsets frequently cause lowered acuity, reduced sight to the sides, and difficulty in accommodation. There are usually no other signs of the hysteria.

Fixation (ocular fixation).   This is the ability to hold fusion precisely on a given target.

Pursuit.   This is the ability to maintain fixation on a moving target.

Saccadic skills.   This is the ability to fixate on a sequence of different targets. This may be back and forth on targets, to the left and to the right, several in a row left to right, or from far to near and back.

Ocular motor skills.   This refers to the movement skills of the eyes. This would include heterophorias, convergence, accommodation, pursuit, fixation, and saccadics.

Instruments for Checking Vision

The Snellen Chart.   For years the most popular instrument for testing sight has been the Snellen Chart, which originated in 1862. The fact that it is used so widely is unfortunate, since there is an overwhelming amount of evidence to indicate that it is inadequate for testing vision in schools. One of the earlier studies criticizing it was by George Spache (1939), who listed a number of reasons why it was inadequate for use in schools. Among them:

1. It does not measure the efficiency of the eyes at reading distance.
2. "Only 20–40 percent of all the children are identified who really need the help of an eye specialist." (p. 623)
3. It does not measure the coordination of the eyes (phoria tests).
4. It does not detect astigmatism.
5. If it is used with a group of children, some of the group who take the test last are likely to have memorized the letters. Spache also stated that some of the lines were especially difficult or easy to read because of the groupings of certain configurations of letters.

Somewhat later the Snellen type of test was criticized in a study by Malmquist (1965), who stated that the instruments did not take into account vision defects at normal reading distance. Malmquist also mentioned that a number of other defects of vision were found to remain undetected when instruments of the Snellen type were used. On the other hand, the Keystone Telebinocular (another type of eye-testing instrument) succeeded in identifying all the cases of visual difficulties, given the criteria of the visual examinations made by a group of medical eye specialists. A strong indictment of the use of the Snellen Chart also came from Gordon Bixel (1966), who believed that although it was a valid test in itself, its use was often detrimental because the results could ruin a child's future. Bixel points out that when children pass the Snellen test, they are expected to perform tasks that many simply cannot see to do. They are then considered to be lazy or stupid. Bixel says:

No one would consider putting a thermometer in a child's mouth and, when the temperature registered normal, proclaim good health. But that is just what is being done visually. Letters are placed on the wall and if the child can read standard size letters, he is told he needs no glasses, his eyes are all right. (p. 181)

Other vision testers that have proven satisfactory for disabled readers are the Bausch & Lomb Vision Tester (and School Vision Tester), the Keystone

Visual Survey Telebinocular, the Massachusetts Vision Test, the Sight Screener, and the Titmus School Vision Tester. A description and illustration of the first two:

The Bausch & Lomb vision tester and the Bausch & Lomb school vision tester. These are essentially the same instrument; however, a different set of slides is used for school vision testing. The School Vision Tester (see Figure 8–1) includes the following tests: Acuity Far (right eye), Acuity Far (left eye), Far Sightedness (right eye), Far Sightedness (left eye), Phoria Far, and Phoria Near. All tests can be completed in approximately two minutes. The Bausch & Lomb Vision Tester is used more frequently in industry. In addition to the tests listed for the School Vision Tester it also includes tests for depth perception and color blindness.

The Keystone Visual Survey Telebinocular Instrument. This instrument is used for the following tests: Simultaneous Perception, Vertical Imbalance, Lateral Posture at Far Point, Fusion at Far Point, Usable Vision of Both Eyes at Far Point, Usable Vision of Right Eye at Far Point, Usable Vision of Left Eye at Far Point, Stereopsis, Color Blindness, Lateral Posture at Near Point, Fusion at Near Point, Visual Acuity of Both Eyes at Near Point, Visual Acuity

FIGURE 8–1 The Bausch & Lomb School Vision Tester

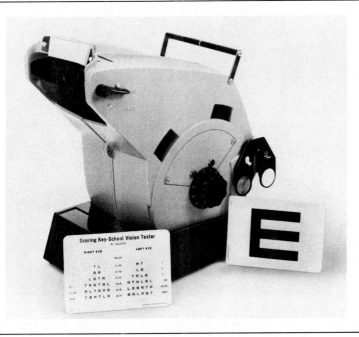

Reproduced by permission of Bausch & Lomb, Rochester, New York 14802.

of Right Eye at Near Point, and Visual Acuity of Left Eye at Near Point. (See Figure 8–2.)

Vision Screening

Although research definitely indicates a need for near-point vision testing, it does present some problems for younger children. Arthur Keeney (1969), an ophthalmologist, stated that visual screening is more reliable at far point than at near point or reading range and that near-point range is influenced by age, refractive error, light, accommodative effort, pupillary diameter, and convergence stability. He stated that the coefficient of reliability in near-point acuity is .75 to .78 and for far-point acuity is .95 to .97. He also emphasized that the plus-lens screening procedure often used for farsightedness is somewhat unreliable, and that no screening instrument takes the place of professional eye

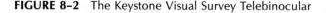

FIGURE 8–2   The Keystone Visual Survey Telebinocular

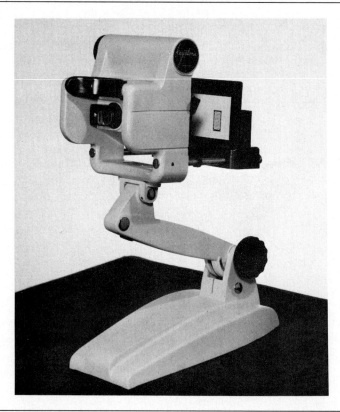

Reproduced by permission of Keystone View Company, 2212 E. 12th St., Davenport, Iowa 52803.

care but should be thought of as an assisting device used to identify individuals needing care on the basis of a few salient points.

Gail Weber (1980), in a study of fifty elementary-age pupils, found that children with deficient visual skills may experience greater problems academically. Weber found that two simple vision tests used in her study could be more useful than customary screening in identifying vision problems. The first test was the Pursuit, Centering, and Alignment Test, which identifies a child who cannot track a moving target. The Convergence Test identifies children who have difficulty converging the eyes to look at a near object. This test purports to measure fusion, fixation, and binocular vision ability.

All students in remedial reading should be given a visual screening test as part of their initial testing upon entering the program. But, as William Smith (1969), an optometrist, points out:

> Even the most sophisticated and carefully performed tests are neither final nor absolutely conclusive. In doubtful cases, it is my practice to repeat tests on different instruments and at different times. It is not unusual to obtain variable findings when performed in such a manner. However, when results are repeatedly and relatively compatible, it is safe to draw conclusions as to probable complicity. (p. 148)

In discussing a group of students with whom he had worked, Smith said, "Again using experience as the basis for evidence, I can add that many of the children in the group reported and in others (before and since), whose reading became markedly improved with orthoptic treatment, were, according to earlier reports, supposed to have had normally functioning, blameless visual systems." (p. 148)

During a four-year period in which accurate records were kept on the visual problems of students in the Reading Center at the University of Texas at El Paso, it was found that approximately 50 percent of the students, all of whom were disabled readers, had visual problems that had been undetected through normal school screening procedures. It is also interesting to note that the results in testing substantiate the statement made by Smith that tests made at different times produce differing results. Referrals to eye doctors are made only after at least two visual screening tests in which *both* indicate that a referral is called for.

The problem encountered in obtaining differing results in visual screening lies not so much with the screening device but with students themselves. For example, a student's eye muscles may be able to compensate for a slight muscle imbalance on one day, whereas on another day the problem may be somewhat more severe. Because of this it is imperative that the remedial reading teacher, as well as students' other teachers, know something about the observable symptoms of visual difficulties. A checklist to guide your observations is shown in Figure 8–3. In using such a device remember that referrals should

FIGURE 8-3   Educator's Checklist

Observable Clues to Classroom Vision Problems

Student's
name_____ Date_____

1.   Appearance of Eyes:
    One eye turns in or out at any time   _____
    Reddened eyes or lids   _____
    Eyes tear excessively   _____
    Encrusted eyelids   _____
    Frequent styes on lids   _____
2.   Complaints When Using Eyes at Desk:
    Headaches in forehead or temples   _____
    Burning or itching after reading or desk work   _____
    Nausea or dizziness   _____
    Print blurs after reading a short time   _____
3.   Behavioral Signs of Visual Problems:
    A.   *Eye Movement Abilities (Ocular Motility)*
        Head turns as reads across page   _____
        Loses place often during reading   _____
        Needs finger or marker to keep place   _____
        Displays short attention span in reading or copying   _____
        Too frequently omits words   _____
        Repeatedly omits "small" words   _____
        Writes up or down hill on paper   _____
        Rereads or skips lines unknowingly   _____
        Orients drawings poorly on page   _____
    B.   *Eye Teaming Abilities (Binocularity)*
        Complains of seeing double (diplopia)   _____
        Repeats letters within words   _____
        Omits letters, numbers or phrases   _____
        Misaligns digits in number columns   _____
        Squints, closes or covers one eye   _____
        Tilts head extremely while working at desk   _____
        Consistently shows gross postural deviations at all desk
            activities   _____
    C.   *Eye-Hand Coordination Abilities*
        Must feel things to assist in any interpretation required _____
        Eyes not used to "steer" hand movements (extreme lack of
            orientation, placement of words or drawings on page)   _____
        Writes crookedly, poorly spaced: cannot stay on ruled lines _____
        Misaligns both horizontal and vertical series of numbers   _____
        Uses his hand or fingers to keep his place on the page   _____
        Uses other hand as "spacer" to control spacing and align-
            ment on page   _____
        Repeatedly confuses left-right directions   _____
    D.   *Visual Form Perception (Visual Comparison, Visual Imagery,
        Visualization)*
        Mistakes words with same or similar beginnings   _____
        Fails to recognize same word in next sentence   _____

Reverses letters and/or words in writing and copying   _____

Confuses likenesses and minor differences   _____

Confuses same word in same sentence   _____

Repeatedly confuses similar beginnings and endings of
words   _____

Fails to visualize what is read either silently or orally   _____

Whispers to self for reinforcement while reading silently   _____

Returns to "drawing with fingers" to decide likes and differences   _____

   E.   *Refractive Status (Nearsightedness, Farsightedness Focus
Problems, etc.)*

Comprehension reduces as reading continues; loses interest
too quickly   _____

Mispronounces similar words as continues reading   _____

Blinks excessively at desk tasks and/or reading; not elsewhere   _____

Holds book too closely; face too close to desk surface   _____

Avoids all possible near-centered tasks   _____

Complains of discomfort in tasks that demand visual interpretation   _____

Closes or covers one eye when reading or doing desk work   _____

Makes errors in copying from chalkboard to paper on desk   _____

Makes errors in copying from reference book to notebook   _____

Squints to see chalkboard, or requests to move nearer   _____

Rubs eyes during or after short periods of visual activity   _____

Fatigues easily; blinks to make chalkboard clear up after
desk task   _____

Observer's Suggestions:

Signed_____

    (Encircle): Teacher; Nurse; Remedial Teacher; Psychologist; Vision Consultant;
Other.

Address_____

_____

not usually be made on the basis of one symptom, but rather on observation of a cluster of these symptoms.

Visual Discrimination

Research by Raj Gupta, Stephen Ceci, and Alan Slater (1978) and by Rosemarie Park (1978–1979) has shown that students' abilities to discriminate letters and words are the most reliable of the many visual perception tasks for predicting later reading achievement. Hal Seaton (1977) and other researchers have found that there is little or no benefit from visual discrimination training with pictures or geometric shapes. William Rupley, Michael Ashe, and Pearl Buckland (1979) found that even utilizing forms that looked like letters but were not did not yield positive results.

Thus it appears to be most helpful for visual discrimination activities to focus on the recognition of letters and words. Diagnosis is generally accomplished by having students select from a row of letters or words those items that exactly match the stimulus letter or word. It is not necessary for the student to name the letter(s) or pronounce the word(s) in such a test, but rather to identify the appropriate item(s) through visual discrimination. Research by Edward Paradis (1974), among others, has shown that most students have mastered this ability by the time they enter school.

Eye Movements and Reading Speed

Contrary to the belief of many people unfamiliar with the work of the eye in reading, the eye does not sweep smoothly across the page. As we read, the eye stops and starts, making a series of short, quick movements. These are often referred to as *saccadic movements*. We do not see clearly as the eye moves; therefore, in order to see a word or group of words, our eyes must stop and fixate, move to the next word or small group of words, fixate again, etc.

The time it takes to fixate varies, according to our studies, between 1/4 and 1/6 second, with the average time for a good reader running between 1/5 and 1/6 second. Most researchers also agree that it takes 1/25 to 1/30 second for the eye to move from one fixation to the next and 1/25 to 1/30 second for the eye to sweep from the end of one line of print to the beginning of the next. According to Albert Harris and Edward Sipay (1985), the average number of words it is possible to see clearly during each fixation runs from .45 for an average first grader to 1.11 for an average college student. Naturally one can see something to the right and left of each word or group of words as one fixates. However, most researchers agree that even for the very best reader, it is impossible to see an average of more than three words clearly enough to read them. In reading, then, one shows a pattern similar to Figure 8–4.

If you were to check the reading (or word seeing) speed of someone, assuming this person had the widest span of recognition (three words), the fastest fixation time (1/6 second), the fastest sweep time from one fixation to another

FIGURE 8-4 Eye Movements and Reading Speed

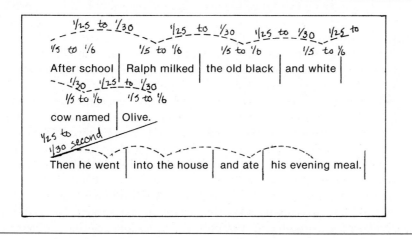

(1/30 second), and the fastest return sweep from one line to the next (1/30 second), the greatest number of words read (or seen) per minute would be computed as follows:

6 fixations/second multiplied by 3 words/fixation
$6 \times 3 = 18$ words/second
18 words/second multiplied by 60 seconds
$18 \times 60 = 1080$ words/minute

For every six fixations you would have five movements from one fixation to the next ($1/30 \times 5 = 5/30$ seconds). If you assume that for every six fixations you also have one return sweep, that adds another 1/30 second. Therefore, for every six fixations you have $5/30 + 1/30$ or $6/30 = 1/5$ second lost in sweep time. Roughly, then, you subtract 1/5 of the 1080 words/minute for sweep time. Therefore, the total number of words this reader could read (or see):

$1/5 \times 1080 = 217$
$1080 - 217 = 864$

Even under ideal conditions this reader could not *see* more than 864 words/minute.

Some writers have claimed that the reader gets enough clues through peripheral vision, even though not all words are seen clearly, to read as many as 3500 words/minute. It is our opinion that the evidence does not support this belief, but there is a possibility that a few people do have this capability. Note in our calculations that we have differentiated between *reading* and *seeing* words. This is because there is a semantic difference between the two. If we consider *reading* to mean getting a general idea of what is contained in a passage, then it is often possible to read only the first few words or first sentence of each paragraph and still *read* the material. On the other hand, it is probably not possible for even the best readers to *see* more than 800 to 900 words/ minute.

The diagnosis of eye movements became somewhat commonplace during the 1960s. Although instruments for measuring eye movements had been available since the late 1800s, the influx of federal money through ESEA Title I Programs enabled many schools to buy devices for recording eye movements. One such device is the Reading Eye Camera,[1] which makes a recording of students' eye movements as they read. The older models recorded eye movements on film that had to be developed after the student had completed reading. A newer model records the student's eye movements directly on paper similar to a graph. These recordings can be analyzed to discover the number of fixations and regressions that a student makes while reading.

Studies such as those of Miles Tinker (1958) have shown that undesirable eye movements are usually only symptomatic of various reading problems such as lack of word recognition; when the word-recognition problem is remediated, the student's eye-movement pattern becomes normal. More recent research has sometimes relied on modern technology. This includes studies by R. D. Elterman and others (1980), who used an infrared recording technique, and Ruby Den Buurman, Theo Roersema, and Jack Gerrissen (1981), who used a display system controlled by the reader's eye movements. Lester Lefton, Richard Nagle, and Gwendolyn Johnson (1979) compared the eye movements of good- and poor-reading third graders, fifth graders, and adults. The authors concluded that the eye movements of poor readers were quantitatively and qualitatively different from those of normal readers. The poor readers' eye movements were chaotic, frequent, of longer duration, and generally unsystematic. In another study, Lefton, Benjamin Lahey, and David Stagg (1978) reached similar conclusions and found that disabled readers' problems resulted not from inability to discriminate letters, but rather from an unsystematic search strategy.

However, Keith Rayner (1983) argues that eye movements are not the cause of severe reading disabilities but rather "reflect underlying cognitive or neurological problems." (p. 171) David Moore (1983) warns educators not to confuse cause and effect. The fact that poor readers tend to have faulty eye movements does not mean that the eye movement irregularities *cause* reading problems. In the absence of clear research, it is just as logical to assume that the reading problems cause the irregularities.

Further research in this area may lead to specific procedures to be used in remediating reading difficulties. However, at present it appears to be a misuse of time and money for the classroom teacher, reading specialist, or reading clinician to diagnose eye movements as a part of normal remedial procedures.

---

[1]Manufactured and distributed by Educational Development Laboratories, Huntington, New York.

DIAGNOSIS OF PROBLEMS OF THE EAR

Classification of Auditory Problems

Auditory problems that are of concern to reading specialists can be classified under three categories, discrimination, acuity, and memory. Studies such as that of Pauline Flynn and Margaret Byrne (1970) have sometimes shown that disabled readers as a group have inferior auditory abilities as compared with average or advanced readers. Other studies report results conflicting with those of the Flynn and Byrne study. The correlation between auditory disabilities and reading disabilities is low or insignificant. In other words, there are likely to be a few severe cases of auditory disabilities within a group of disabled readers; however, the most disabled readers are not necessarily the students with serious auditory disabilities. Guy Bond, Miles Tinker, Barbara Wasson, and John Wasson (1984) suggest that both research and clinical experience provide evidence that some children overcome auditory difficulties, while others do not. Various factors affect the outcome, according to Bond, Tinker, and Wasson, including the severity and type of auditory disability, the amount of time that passes before remediation is begun, the quality of the treatment, the desire of the student to read, and the coordination of the efforts of the parents, specialists, and others.

Auditory discrimination and auditory perception.   Auditory discrimination is generally considered to be the ability to discriminate between various combinations of sounds. In reading, of course, you are usually concerned with the ability to discriminate between or among similar-sounding phonemes. You are also concerned with a student's ability to *mask,* which is the ability to hear a certain sound when interfering sounds or noises are present.

It is reasonable to assume that auditory discrimination is important to learning to read, since the student must hear the difference between similar sounds in order to reproduce these sounds. It is also important that a student have the ability to mask other extraneous noises so that what the teacher or another student is saying can be heard.

However, controversy exists regarding the role of auditory discrimination in learning to read. Many practitioners assume that skill in this area is essential for later reading success, even though much of the research does not show a significant relationship between performance on tests of auditory discrimination and reading tests.

Some earlier research, such as that reported by Jerome Rosner (1973) and Gerald Strag and Bert Richmond (1973) did show a positive relationship between auditory discrimination and reading.

Patrick Groff (1975) reviewed the results of relevant empirical research on this issue and concluded, "There is enough negative evidence as to the causal effect of auditory discrimination on reading success to warrant further examination on this supposed relationship." (p. 746) Groff suggested, "A cautious, skeptical outlook to the importance of auditory discrimination on reading ability is needed.'' (p. 746)

In a response to Groff, Shirley Finnegan (1979) suggested that problems of definition and testing clouded the data Groff analyzed. Finnegan asserted that adequately defining the term *auditory discrimination* and conducting a proper study show a relationship between auditory skills and word calling.

Nonetheless, research has borne out Groff's skepticism. Susan Neuman (1981) conducted a study in which first-grade children were taught various auditory perceptual skills, including attention, discrimination, blending and closure, and memory and comprehension. She found that although the training did produce superior growth in auditory skills, these gains did not transfer to reading achievement among the experimental group. Indeed, the control group, which had been involved in individual activities such as reading and math games and special art projects, showed a slightly greater increase in tested reading ability.

Barbara Matthews and Charlena Seymour (1981) found that tests of auditory discrimination were not likely to differentiate between learning-disabled children and nonlearning-disabled children, unless both groups also had difficulties in speech articulation.

Karl Koenke (1978) compared three of the most frequently used tests of auditory discrimination—Wepman's *Auditory Discrimination Test,* the Goldman-Fristoe-Woodcock *Test of Auditory Discrimination,* and the Kimmell-Wahl *Screening Test of Auditory Perception.* Fifty-two third-grade students were evaluated on all three tests, using different random sequences to control for testing effects. Koenke found that when the cutoff scores recommended by the various authors were used as the criterion, the numbers of students passing or failing the three tests were significantly different from each other. Of the fifty-two students, only two passed all three tests and only twelve failed all three tests. Thirty-eight of the students (73 percent) passed one or two of the tests and failed the others. Understandably, Koenke woefully concluded, ''Auditory discrimination is that which auditory discrimination tests measure.'' Mary Ann Geissal and June Knafle (1977) pointed out that auditory discrimination tests and exercises are complicated by such factors as dialect differences, vocabulary range, previous experience, differing views on the nature of the task, examiner bias, and the lack of visual cues.

After reviewing the literature concerned with the relationship of auditory-perceptual skills to reading ability, Reid Lyon (1977) concluded that there was insufficient evidence to support the view that intact auditory-perceptual skills are necessary for the adequate development of reading ability:

> Although many of the investigations cited indicate that poor readers do manifest difficulties in auditory perception, an equal number of studies found good readers who demonstrated deficits in auditory skills and poor readers who demonstrated adequate auditory-perceptual abilities. (p. 570)

Lyon also points out that correlational studies must be interpreted with caution. In a correlation between two factors either may be the cause, or both may be caused by a third, unknown factor. This fact notwithstanding, Lyon states, "Evidence indicates that the relationships obtained between auditory-perceptual ability and reading skills reach a higher correlational value when the samples selected for study consist of younger children rather than older children." (p. 569)

Clearly, the practitioner faces a dilemma. In light of the evidence presented above, perhaps it would be best to ignore problems of auditory perception when completing the diagnosis and carrying out remediation procedures. On the other hand, some studies have shown positive correlations between auditory-perceptual abilities in the prereading period and future success in reading. In addition, many teachers and reading specialists report that auditory discrimination training is successful with kindergarten and first-grade children who lack that ability.

Unfortunately, the research evidence does not tell us whether auditory discrimination should or should not be taught. We believe the practitioner should take a cautious approach. The procedures for diagnosing and remediating auditory discrimination problems are relatively simple and need not be too time-consuming. We recommend that teachers and reading specialists test and teach auditory discrimination skills to young children (ages five to seven) when such an approach appears to be warranted. Not all children in a particular class will require this instruction, and for those who do, the amount of time should not be so great as to detract from other, more important reading-skill areas.

Students with auditory discrimination problems may exhibit certain difficulties. Following is a list of some of these. It should, however, be stressed that any student may exhibit one or more of these symptoms from time to time and not have problems with auditory discrimination. This list should serve only to alert you that the problem might exist:

1. Phonics knowledge inadequate
2. Frequent requests for a repeat of oral material presented by the teacher
3. Difficulty in understanding what was said by the teacher or another student
4. Pronunciation of certain words unclear
5. Tendency to hold mouth open while listening
6. Tilting of head while listening

The best-known and most-used test for auditory discrimination is *The Auditory Discrimination Test* (Wepman, 1978). This is an individual test in which the examiner pronounces a number of pairs of words that are either alike or alike except for one phoneme, e.g., *lack-lack,* and *tub-tug.* The student is to respond by telling whether the two words are the same or different.

When taking *The Auditory Discrimination Test* it is important that the student understand that "same" and "different" refer to the *sounds* of the words and not to the *meaning* of the words. If a student does poorly, it is a good idea to wait several days and give the same test or an alternate form to insure that the results of the first administration were valid. If a great many students fail, consider having a sample of that group tested by another person to insure that your pronunciation is not at fault.

It is important to note that *The Auditory Discrimination Test* is only a test for minimal pairs and does not test other auditory discrimination skills such as the ability to mask sounds. If you suspect a student is having difficulty with masking, the best way to confirm your suspicions is to ask the student to respond in writing to various questions in a normal classroom setting. For example, pronounce words and ask the student to write the initial consonant sounds, ending sounds, or medial vowel sounds. When doing this, however, it is important that the student know the sound-symbol relationships involved.

Auditory acuity.   This is the ability to hear sounds of varying pitch (frequencies or vibrations) heard at different degrees of loudness (measured in decibels). Normal speech frequency runs from 125 up to as high as 8000 cycles per second, with more in the 130-to-4000 range. It has been noted that students with hearing loss in the higher frequency ranges (500+) often have difficulties in school because they are taught by female teachers, whose voices tend to be higher than those of male teachers. It is also important to note that certain consonant sounds such as *s, z,* and *t* are of higher frequencies than the vowel sounds. Students also experience hearing loss in terms of loudness. A loss of up to five decibels would probably cause the student very little difficulty. A loss of six to ten decibels may cause slight difficulty, and a loss above ten to fifteen decibels normally causes difficulty, especially if the student is not seated near the front of the room and does not wear any corrective hearing device. Students with a hearing loss in any two frequencies in one ear or at a six or above decibel level are considered to have a problem serious enough to be referred for clinical evaluation.

Auditory acuity is measured by using an audiometer such as the MA–19 manufactured by Maico Hearing Instruments, shown in Figure 8–5. This portable instrument can be used for conducting tests for either individuals or groups.

Manufacturers of audiometers:

Maico Hearing Instruments
7375 Bush Lake Road
Minneapolis, Minnesota 55435

Auditory Instrument Division
Zenith Radio Corporation
6501 W. Grand Ave.
Chicago, Illinois 60635

Precision Acoustics Corporation
55 W. 42 Street
New York, New York 10036

Royal Industries
Audiotone Division
P.O. Box 2905
Phoenix, Arizona 85036

Beltone Electronics Corporation
Hearing Test Instruments Division
4201 W. Victoria Street
Chicago, Illinois 60646

FIGURE 8–5 The Maico Model MA-19

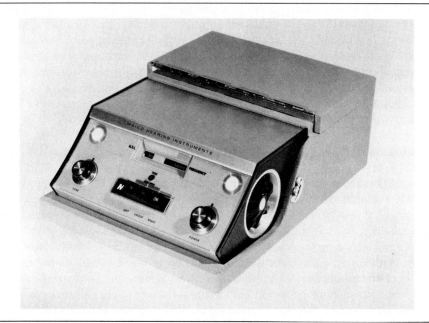

Reproduced by permission of Maico Hearing Instruments, 7573 Bush Lake Road, Minneapolis, Minnesota 55435.

Many remedial reading teachers do not have an audiometer available for their use; however, in many cases audiometric testing is available through the school nurse. In some remedial reading programs audiometric testing is done as a matter of course. Where a school nurse is available and willing to do this testing, we recommend that it be done. On the other hand, routine audiometric testing is not necessary unless it is indicated because of a student's failure on an auditory discrimination test or because you note these symptoms of hearing loss:

1. Cupping hand behind the ear.
2. Complaints of buzzing or ringing in the ear.
3. Gives the appearance of being lazy or of not paying attention.
4. Drainage or discharge of ears.
5. Tilts head at angle or turns head while listening.
6. Opens mouth while listening.
7. Frequent head colds.
8. Does not respond well to oral directions.
9. Reads in unnatural voice tones.
10. Does not enunciate clearly.
11. Stiff or strained posture while listening.

Certain other informal tests—such as the watch tick, coin click, and whisper tests—have also been used by classroom teachers and reading specialists for many years. You should keep in mind, however, that hearing a watch tick or two coins click is not the same as hearing the human voice in the classroom. These tests are therefore unlikely to be reliable measures of a student's hearing ability. The whisper test, in which the tester whispers a word or phrase at various distances, is somewhat more practical than either the watch tick or coin click but is still a poor substitute for *The Auditory Discrimination Test,* testing with an audiometer, and careful observation in the classroom.

Auditory memory. This refers to the ability to listen to, remember, and repeat a series of words or digits, a sentence, nonsense symbols, etc. This ability is important in learning to read. For example, in sounding a three-letter word the student must hold the first two sounds in memory to put them with the third letter in order to analyze the word. As word analysis becomes more difficult, e.g., in applying various syllabication principles, vowel rules, and individual grapheme sounds, the student needs a great deal of both visual and auditory memory. Comprehension of oral and to some extent silent reading also depends on the student's auditory memory. Interestingly, a study by Cermak and others (1980) found that learning-disabled children were not at a significant disadvantage on a short-term retention assessment task. Three groups of learning-disabled children and one control group of normal readers were required to remember verbal information over intervals up to eighteen seconds while being distracted. All of the learning-disabled groups performed at least as well as the normal controls.

Although auditory memory is important for reading and the measurement of the skill is not difficult, there is some doubt about the importance of measuring it. The problem lies in the fact that few research studies have shown that training in the improvement of auditory memory skills results in an increase in reading ability, although auditory memory per se can be improved. Part of the problem in the past, however, may have been in training students in digits and nonsense rather than in materials directly related to reading. Research at the Reading Center at the University of Texas at El Paso has shown that students who cannot remember and repeat at least a five-word sentence benefit from auditory memory training that deals directly with listening to and repeating sentences. You should also remember that many exercises in phonics and structural analysis actually train students in auditory memory skills.

If you wanted a standardized test for auditory memory of digits, you could administer either the "Digit Span" subtest of the *WISC-R* or the *WAIS*. You should note, however, that remembering a series of digits is not necessarily parallel to the auditory memory abilities required for reading. Memory for sentences can be assessed to some extent by using the "memory for sentence" items on either the *Stanford-Binet Intelligence Scale* or the *Slosson Intelligence Test*. It is also easy to develop your own test of sentence memory by writing several four-word sentences, several five-word sentences, etc., until you reach a point where few or no students can repeat them. This can be standardized by giving it to normal students at each grade level to determine the average sentence length remembered at each grade level.

From a practical standpoint, however, most remedial reading teachers can best diagnose auditory memory by careful diagnostic teaching, i.e., noting whether students can remember such things as a five- to eight-word sentence, a series of directions, or four to five letters in a word.

DIAGNOSIS OF SPEECH PROBLEMS

There is some disagreement concerning the relationships between various speech disorders and reading disability. Some studies have found the incidence of speech disorders among disabled readers to be no higher than among normal readers, while others have reported that 20 percent to 35 percent of groups of disabled readers have speech disorders. One of the major reasons for these discrepancies is probably that in some studies reading ability was assessed with an oral test and in others with silent tests. There is also considerable evidence that many speech disorders cannot easily be recognized by a lay person. Also, when certain speech disorders are in evidence, it is sometimes difficult to determine whether they are a hindering factor in reading.

There is often a relationship between problems of auditory acuity and/or auditory discrimination and speech disorders. If a student shows evidence of either of these auditory difficulties, you should note whether the student also shows evidence of a speech problem.

Most speech disorders, especially those of an organic nature, should be diagnosed and treated by a speech specialist. The remedial reading teacher, however, should be aware of the symptoms of speech disorders, and whenever a cluster of these symptoms appears, or when one or more appear to a serious degree, the student should be referred to a speech specialist. Some of these symptoms:

1. Inability to produce clear phonic elements as shown on the test in Appendix A.
2. Inability to reproduce certain phonic elements after hearing them (closely related to auditory acuity and/or auditory discrimination).
3. Peculiar movements of the head and/or mouth on phonic elements, or words mispronounced. Also watch for difficulty in forming lips to make certain sounds.
4. Too much or too little volume (closely related to auditory acuity).
5. Long pauses before certain phonemes or phonograms.
6. Refusal (or resistance) to talk.
7. Use of improper tonal quality (closely related to auditory difficulties).

8. Skipping or slurring certain words, phonemes, or phonograms.
9. Stuttering.

DIAGNOSIS OF GENERAL HEALTH PROBLEMS

In most cases the educator is neither trained nor equipped to diagnose problems of general health. For this reason the remedial reading teacher will need to rely on information gained from the student's past health history and from careful observation. The parent interview can be an important source of information concerning general health. In interviewing the parents of disabled readers check into health background concerning any chronic illnesses or allergies, any medication taken for allergies or other illnesses, childhood injuries or diseases that kept the student out of school for extended periods, eating habits, general stamina as evidenced by outside activity, and sleep habits. Information from parents can be especially helpful, since they know the student and have in most cases had an opportunity to observe the student longer than anyone else. We have found information gained from parents to be especially helpful where there are other children in the family with whom they can compare your student. Information coming from parents of an only child is often less objective, since they have no norm with which to compare that child.

Some health problems will not be apparent even with careful observation; however, others do manifest observable symptoms. Some symptoms that may have relevance to a reading disability:

1. Lack of energy, listlessness, or general fatigue (including falling asleep).
2. Poor eating habits.
3. Susceptibility to colds.
4. Labored breathing.
5. Complaints of dizziness and/or headaches.
6. Inability to concentrate for sustained periods of time.
7. Irritability, especially after physical exercise or near end of the day.
8. Evidence of much better work at the beginning of the day.
9. Complaints of stomach ache or nausea.
10. Considerable overweight or underweight.
11. Unsteadiness in writing or small motor activities.
12. Chronic absenteeism.

When a cluster of these symptoms appears, or when any one symptom appears to a strong degree, the student should be referred to the school nurse; or the student's parents should be contacted concerning referral to a medical doctor.

Part B: REMEDIATION

REMEDIATION OF PROBLEMS OF THE EYE

In many situations the responsibilities of the teacher in eye treatment cease once a referral to an optometrist or ophthalmologist has been made. The only problem with which the teacher is then concerned is the remediation of educational disabilities that may have been caused by eye problems. There are also many instances in which the teacher should work with the eye doctor to carry out a total program adapted to the special needs of visually handicapped students. For this reason a clear channel of communication between the teacher and the student's doctor needs to exist. Generally teachers are not concerned with eye disorders involving the peripheral nervous system, i.e., visual acuity, refractive error, fusion, convergence, and accommodation, after an eye doctor has examined the student and prescribed accordingly.

There is considerable disagreement between optometrists and ophthalmologists as well as some disagreement within each group concerning the value of orthoptic training and school-related visual perceptual training. A typical statement of the beliefs of many ophthalmologists comes from Harold Martin (1971) in describing the beliefs of Dr. George Campian, a clinical professor of ophthalmology:

> He feels that if an orthoptic program aimed at muscle balance and convergence is associated with any improvement in reading, the reading improvement must result from the patient's increased concentration rather than from the exercises themselves. He also points out that refractive errors are of negligible importance in reading disorders. (p. 470)

The opposite viewpoint, perhaps more typical of many optometrists, is expressed by William Swanson (1972) in describing the results of his study of the effectiveness of optometric vision therapy:

> Study of 100 consecutive cases of learning disorders revealed that optometric vision therapy was successful in 93 percent of the cases. The accuracy of this figure was verified by a registered psychologist. The criterion for success was a definite indication of improvement in the person's learning ability, as verified by subsequent tests, by report of the parent, the patient, or the teacher. Fifty-seven parents reported improvement in their child. The teachers reported improvement in 48 percent, and retesting showed improvement in 82 percent. (p. 42)

These conflicting viewpoints make it difficult for the reading specialist to judge the value of orthoptic training. Existing research offers little help. Harris and Sipay (1985) refer to Barbara Keogh's (1974) review of the research on optometric vision training programs:

> Keough . . . concluded that inadequacies of research methodology precluded any conclusive finding regarding the value of orthoptic training for developing school readiness and for the remediation of learning disabilities. Little has appeared in the last decade to alter this conclusion. (p. 293)

In work with disabled readers in our reading clinics, we have found that many children who do not improve with previous orthoptic training make excellent progress with instruction that does *not* focus on vision. Of course, this does not prove that such training will not benefit some students. Because of the disagreement among various eye doctors and the equivocal research findings, it seems best to recommend that a clear channel of communication be established between remedial teachers and optometrists or ophthalmologists and that suggestions for teacher work with specific students come directly from the examining doctor.

Schubert (1982) offers seven specific suggestions for teachers to promote the visual health of all children in the classroom:

1. Point out to children that proper reading distance (usually 12 to 16 inches) is equal to the length of the arm from knuckles to elbow.
2. Encourage children to use a bookholder or to tilt their books when reading. A book lying flat on a desk or lap when it is being read places more stress on the eyes while reading the lower part of a page as compared to reading the top of the page. In addition, it is fatiguing to bend over a book for long periods of time.
3. Help children's writing posture by having writing surfaces at elbow height. Put a rubber band around the pencil about an inch from its tip or use a triangular pencil gripper. These will encourage proper pencil grip and will provide more seeing room when writing. Proper pencil grip and proper posture make it easier for children to maintain a distance of 12 to 16 inches from the writing surface.
4. Protect children against glare. Glare can be avoided by having children read with their backs toward the source of light. This can be accomplished by positioning pupils' chairs so that light passes over the shoulder opposite their writing hand. Not only is glare avoided when this is done but the possibility of casting shadows on writing or reading materials is minimized.
5. Tell children to refrain from reading for extended periods when they are ill. During a weakened condition, the muscles involved in

accommodating and converging the eyes are also weak. Undue strain at such a time can be harmful.

6. Encourage children to rest their eyes periodically when reading. A good way to do this is to look up at a distant object for a few seconds before turning a page.

7. Give special attention to myopic children who wear glasses. Ask whether they have been instructed by their eye doctor to wear their glasses when reading at nearpoint. If the child does not know, have the parents check with the eye specialist. (pp. 120–121)[2]

REMEDIATION OF PROBLEMS OF THE EAR

As stated in the section on diagnosis, problems of the ear can be divided into three categories in dealing with reading disabilities. These categories are discrimination, acuity, and memory. Although all three areas are of importance to teachers who deal with auditory deficiencies, remediation is usually not within the realm of the remedial reading teacher.

Auditory Discrimination

Although practice in auditory discrimination in general may be somewhat beneficial, it is usually necessary to provide remediation only in those combinations with which the student has particular difficulty. These can easily be determined by giving *The Auditory Discrimination Test*. For example, a student who cannot hear the difference between *vow* and *thou* will need practice in discriminating between the "v" and "th" phonemes. There are also certain combinations that cause difficulty for specific ethnic groups. For example, native Spanish speakers often have difficulty with the short "i" and short "e" sounds and with the *ch* and *sh* digraphs. You should be especially aware of these difficulties. However, many children, as in the case of blacks from certain areas, can hear these differences in others' speech, and seem to be aware of them in reading, yet do not pronounce them correctly in their own speech. In some black dialects, for example, the *s* is often omitted in speaking, yet many of the students who speak them seem to have no difficulty in answering questions concerning singular and plural. Where these problems appear only in students' speech and do not appear to be detrimental to their reading, it is probably best to ignore them.

Remedial exercises for auditory discrimination may be done orally, but putting them on audio tape will save much time in the long run. These can be

---

[2]As listed in D. G. Shubert, What Every Reading Teacher Should Know About Vision, *Claremont Reading Conference Yearbook, 46* (1982), 115–121.

categorized and retrieved when needed. (Teacher-made tapes should not be used unless the reproduction quality is very good.) Practice exercises for various pairs may be done as follows:

A. (Beginning level) Hearing likenesses and differences—*v* and *th*. (Try to avoid using the same combinations as those on the test so that it will not be repetitious for later use.)
Tape Script: "Listen to each pair of words I pronounce and decide whether they are the same or different. If they are the same, circle the word *same* on your answer sheet. If they are different, circle the word *different* on your answer sheet. Number one is *van* and *than*. Number two is *then* and *then*."
The answer sheet:
1. Same-Different
2. Same-Different
The answer part of the script:
"The first two words were different. They were *van* and *than*. Circle *different* if you did not do so before. The next words were the same. They were *then* and *then*. Circle *same* if you did not do so before."

B. (Second level) Hearing beginning sounds—*v* and *th*. (This requires a knowledge of phonics.)
Tape Script: "Look at row one on your answer sheet. Circle the letter or combination that begins the same as *very*. Now look at row two. Circle the letter or combination that begins the same as *though*."
The answer sheet:
1. th   v   b   c
2. v   b   th   f
In making exercises of this nature it is important to give the answers on the same script. This will teach and reinforce the concept and will also conserve the teacher's time. The correction part of the script for the examples would be as follows:
"Now we will check the answers. Number one was *very;* the answer should have been *v,* the second letter in the row. Circle it now if you did not get it right. Number two was *th;* these letters are third in the row. Circle them now if you did not get them right," etc.

C. (Third level) Writing beginning sounds—*v* and *th*. (This also requires a knowledge of phonics.)
Tape Script: "Listen to the words I pronounce. They all begin with either *v* or *th*. After you hear each word I pronounce, write the beginning sound you hear in the blank by the number. Number one is *van*. Number two is *than*."
The answer sheet:
1. _____
2. _____

The answer part of the script: "The first word was *van*. It begins with *v*. You should have written a *v* by number one. The second word was *than*. It begins with *th*. You should have written *th* by number two."

This type of exercise takes the beginning reader from simple discrimination of similar sounds to the more difficult process of writing sounds when they are heard. When developing exercises of this nature you should also keep in mind that some students have difficulty with medial and ending sounds. Exercises for the remediation of these types of auditory discrimination problems can easily be devised with slight changes in the tape scripts.

Commercial materials are also available for the remediation of problems of auditory discrimination. These materials are listed in Appendix C. You should remember, however, that it is usually very difficult to select lessons to remediate a specific problem without requiring the student to go through a considerable amount of other material that in many cases would be of little value. Reid Lyon (1977) adds the following observation:

> Although programs, methods, and techniques designed to enhance auditory-perceptual skills continue to be manufactured and sold commercially, their value in facilitating reading achievement remains doubtful. . . . A major problem impeding endorsement of auditory-perceptual training programs is that the developers of these methods and materials do not usually provide research evidence that their products are actually effective in improving the auditory skills they purport to train. Moreover, even if such training were found to increase selected auditory abilities, the effect of this improvement on subsequent reading achievement is rarely documented. (p. 570)

Auditory Acuity

Auditory acuity difficulties should normally be treated by a medical doctor. However, in some cases the doctor is likely to feel that from a medical standpoint the student's hearing is not impaired enough to treat. The physician may recommend that allowance be made in school for the student's problem. When such is the case, you should if possible consult directly with the physician concerning measures for dealing with the problem. In most cases recommendations are like these:

1. Place the student near the front of the room for any instruction in which the teacher or other students speak from the front of the room.
2. Face the student when talking to him or her, and speak slowly and clearly.
3. If outside noises interfere through windows, seat the student as far away from these as possible.

4. Teach the student to use a visual mode for learning spelling and word attack whenever possible.
5. To make sure the student is correctly receiving directions, have the student write them from time to time. Also check immediately, once the student has begun to work, to make sure the directions were heard properly.
6. Use programmed materials if they are available for teaching certain concepts.
7. Try to use written directions along with oral directions.
8. Have the student use headphones when listening to recorded material.

Auditory Memory

This is an important skill for reading; however, some studies have shown that although certain memory factors can be improved, a corresponding increase in reading ability does not necessarily follow. Perhaps one of the major problems in the past has been in training areas not necessarily related to reading. For example, a student who cannot remember a series of digits forward or backward is also somewhat likely to experience reading problems in remembering a sequence of events. However, remediation that focuses on practice in remembering a series of digits is not likely to result in a corresponding increase in remembering details or a series of events in reading.

Although research on the effectiveness of specific kinds of auditory memory training directly related to reading is lacking, a more logical approach would seem to be through exercises such as giving practice in having the student listen to and repeat sentences. Start with sentences containing as many words as the student can remember and work up to sentences equivalent to those remembered by other students of the same age group. Another approach is to attempt to associate auditory sequences with visualization of the process. For example, have the student attempt to see in the mind's eye what is read or heard. This, in our experience, aids in recall.

REMEDIATION OF SPEECH PROBLEMS

Students who have any speech defects should be referred to a speech therapist for an evaluation. After this make it a point to consult personally with the speech therapist concerning any special treatment that should be afforded the student. In some cases the recommendations of the speech therapist may require that certain precautions be taken in teaching the student, e.g., teaching the student in a one-to-one situation without the necessity of performing before a group. In other cases the therapist may feel that exposure to group situations may be appropriate and even desirable. Because speech problems are so diverse and the problem of any one student may be entirely unique, general recommendations for the treatment of speech problems would be inappropriate.

However, the speech therapist should be informed about the nature of the remedial reading program, including such factors as the amount of time the student spends in remedial reading, the amount of individual versus group work, possible reasons for the disability, and the degree of the disability. Armed with this information, the speech therapist and remedial reading teacher can combine efforts to plan a dual program of remediation.

REMEDIATION OF GENERAL HEALTH PROBLEMS

Once a student has been referred to a medical doctor for problems of general health, there is usually little or nothing that can be done by the remedial reading teacher. However, the teacher should stay alert to the symptoms mentioned in the section "Diagnosis of General Health Problems" and consult with the parents concerning any recommendations by the physician for maximizing learning conditions. For example, some students may require more breaks for rest and relaxation, provision for mid-morning and/or mid-afternoon snacks, etc. The problem, however, as with dealing with other specialists, is to insure that channels of communication are always open.

SUMMARY

The physical problems with which the remedial reading teacher is usually concerned might be classified as problems of the eye, of the ear, and with speech, neurologically impaired functions, and problems of general health. Because of the complexity of neurological problems they have not been discussed in this chapter, but they are thoroughly covered in Chapter 9. Problems of the eye are prevalent in a number of cases of students with reading disability. The teacher should become familiar with instruments for vision screening and learn to recognize symptoms of visual difficulties. The teacher should also learn to test for auditory discrimination and to give auditory acuity tests; or refer to the school nurse or a hearing specialist any students who have inadequate auditory discrimination. Auditory memory is also an important skill for reading. However, research clearly indicating that training in auditory memory will improve students' ability to read is lacking.

There is some disagreement as to whether speech difficulties actually contribute to reading disability. In reality, a common factor such as inadequate hearing is probably responsible for both.

The teacher should be familiar with symptoms of problems with general health. When a cluster of these symptoms appears in a student, or when any one symptom appears to a strong degree, then that student should be referred to the school nurse, or the parents should be contacted so that the student can receive attention from a medical doctor.

The remedial reading teacher is usually not concerned with the treatment of physical disabilities but should learn to recognize various symptoms when they occur so that a proper referral can be made. However, some types of exercises can be done to improve auditory discrimination.

REFERENCES

Bixel, G. (1966). Vision—Key to learning or not learning. *Education, 87,* 180–184.

Bond, G. L., Tinker, M. A., & Wasson, B. B. (1979). *Reading difficulties—Their diagnosis and correction* (4th ed.). Englewood Cliffs, NJ: Prentice-Hall.

Bond, G. L., Tinker, M. A., Wasson, B. B., & Wasson, J. B. (1984). *Reading difficulties: Their diagnosis and correction* (5th ed.). Englewood Cliffs, NJ: Prentice-Hall.

Cermak, L. S., Goldberg, J., Cermak, S., & Drake, C. (1980). The short-term memory ability of children with learning disabilities. *Journal of Learning Disabilities, 13,* 25–29.

Den Buurman, R., Roersema, T., & Gerrissen, J. F. (1981). Eye movements and the perceptual span in reading. *Reading Research Quarterly, 16,* 227–235.

Elterman, R. D., Abel, L. A., Daroff, R. B., Del'Osso, L. F., & Bornstein, J. L. (1980). Eye movement patterns in dyslexic children. *Journal of Learning Disabilities, 13,* 16–21.

Finnegan, S. D. (1979). Auditory skills and word calling ability. *Academic Therapy, 14,* 299–309.

Flynn, P. T., & Byrne, M. (1970). Relationship between reading and selected auditory abilities of third-grade children. *Journal of Speech and Hearing Research, 13,* 731–740.

Geissal, M. A., & Knafle, J. (1977). A linguistic view of auditory discrimination tests and exercises. *Reading Teacher, 31,* 134–140.

Groff, P. (1975). Reading ability and auditory discrimination: Are they related? *Reading Teacher, 28,* 742–747.

Gupta, R., Ceci, S., & Slater, A. (1978). Visual discrimination in good and poor readers. *Journal of Special Education, 72,* 409–416.

Harris, A. J., & Sipay, E. R. (1980). *How to increase reading ability* (7th ed.). New York: Longman.

Harris, A. J., & Sipay, E. R. (1985). *How to increase reading ability* (8th ed.). New York: Longman.

Keeney, A. H. (1969). Paper presented at the Annual Conference of the National Society for the Prevention of Blindness, Milwaukee, WI.

Keough, B. K. (1974). Optometric vision training programs for children with learning disabilities: Review of issues and research. *Journal of Learning Disabilities, 7,* 219–231.

Koenke, K. (1978). A comparison of three auditory discrimination-perception tests. *Academic Therapy, 13,* 463–468.

Krippner, S. (1971). On research in visual training and reading disability. *Journal of Learning Disabilities, 4,* 66–76.

Lefton, L. A., Lahey, B. B., & Stagg, D. I. (1978). Eye movements in reading disabled and normal children: A study of systems and strategies. *Journal of Learning Disabilities, 11,* 549–558.

Lefton, L. A., Nagle, R. J., & Johnson, G. (1979). Eye movement dynamics of good and poor readers: Then and now. *Journal of Reading Behavior, 11,* 319–328.

Lyon, R. (1977). Auditory-perceptual training: The state of the art. *Journal of Learning Disabilities, 10,* 564–572.

Malmquist, E. (1965). A study of vision defects in relation to reading disabilities and a test of the validity of certain vision screening programmes in elementary school. *Slow Learning Child, 12,* 38–48.

Martin, H. (1971). Vision and its role in reading disability and dyslexia. *Journal of School Health, 41,* 468–472.

Matthews, B. A. J., & Seymour, C. M. (1981). The performance of learning disabled children on tests of auditory discrimination. *Journal of Learning Disabilities, 14,* 9–12.

Moore, D. W. (1983). What research did *not* say to the reading teacher: A case study. *Reading Teacher, 37,* 14–19.

Neuman, S. B. (1981). Effect of teaching auditory perceptual skills on reading achievement in first grade. *Reading Teacher, 34,* 422–426.

Paradis, E. (1974). The appropriateness of visual readiness materials. *Journal of Educational Research, 67,* 276–278.

Park, R. (1978–1979). Performance on geometric figure copying tests as predictors of types of errors in decoding. *Reading Research Quarterly, 14,* 100–118.

Rayner, K. (1983). Eye movements, perceptual span, and reading disability. *Annals of Dyslexia, 33,* 163–173.

Rosner, J. (1973). Language arts and arithmetic achievement and specifically related perceptual skills. *American Educational Research Journal, 10,* 59–68.

Rouse, M. W., & Ryan, J. B. (1984). Teacher's guide to vision problems. *Reading Teacher, 38,* 306–317.

Rupley, W., Ashe, M., & Buckland, P. (1979). The relations between the discrimination and letter-like forms and word recognition. *Reading World, 19,* 113–123.

Seaton, H. (1977). The effects of a visual perception training program and reading achievement. *Journal of Reading Behavior, 9,* 188–192.

Schubert, D. G. (1982). What every reading teacher should know about vision. *Claremont reading conference yearbook, 46,* 115–121.

Smith, W. (1969). The visual system in reading and learning disabilities. *Journal of School Health, 39,* 144–150.

Spache, G. (1939). Testing vision. *Education, 59,* 623–626.

Strag, G. A., & Richmond, B. O. (1973). Auditory discrimination techniques for young children. *Elementary School Journal, 73,* 447–454.

Suchoff, I. B. (1981). Research in the relationship between reading and vision—What does it mean? *Journal of Learning Disabilities, 14,* 573–576.

Swanson, W. (1972). Optometric vision therapy—How successful is it in the treatment of learning disorders? *Journal of Learning Disabilities, 5,* 37–42.

Tinker, M. (1958). Recent studies of eye movements in reading. *Psychological Bulletin, 54,* 215–231.

Weber, G. Y., (1980). Visual disabilities—Their identification and relationship with academic achievement. *Journal of Learning Disabilities, 13,* 301–305.

Wepman, J. M. (1978). *Auditory discrimination test.* Palm Springs, CA: Language Research Associates.

Diagnosis and Remediation
of Severe Reading Disabilities[1]

The first part of this chapter is a discussion of the dilemma of the reading specialist in dealing with severe reading disabilities. As you will note, even the terminology presents a problem. Information is presented on the history of diagnosis and modern-day diagnostic aspects including typical symptoms and precautions to be observed. The last part of the chapter deals with prior theories of remediation and their success, followed by present-day theory and its implementation.

[1]Chapter 9 was written by Wilson Wayne Grant, M.D., Fellow, American Academy of Pediatrics; Assistant Clinical Professor, Texas Tech School of Medicine.

THE DILEMMA OF THE HARD-TO-TEACH CHILD

Most problem readers encountered during a teaching career have clearcut, easily diagnosed reasons for their failure to learn. Such students do respond to remediation efforts, which can vary from mild to prolonged.

But what about the student who underachieves in reading, writing, math, and other cognitive tasks, for whom ordinary remedial methods are of limited success? Both the classroom teacher and the remedial reading specialist experience the frustration and challenge of such a student. "This student seems capable but just doesn't catch on to what we're doing" is a common observation. And not infrequently such students have normal to high intelligence, appear to be free of emotional problems, have adequate vision and hearing, and present no obvious health problems—thereby adding to the dilemma.

Many labels and descriptive terms have been applied to these children over the years. Around the turn of the century they were labeled *problem* children and were described as lazy or unmotivated. Later educators, physicians, and psychologists began to sense that these were in fact *children with a problem,* for some reason unable to process information as other children were able to.

Today the accepted term for these children is *learning disabled.* In this chapter we will be addressing two general classes of disorders, or learning disabilities, that commonly interfere with the learning process. The first is the broad spectrum of disorders commonly called specific learning disabilities, and the second is attentional deficit disorders, also known as hyperactivity.

Part A: DIAGNOSIS

SPECIFIC LEARNING DISABILITIES

One of the first reports of a child with a learning disability to appear in the literature was authored by a British general practitioner, W. Pringle Morgan (1896). In his case report Morgan wrote:

> Percy F.—a well-grown lad, aged 14 . . . is the eldest son of intelligent parents, the second child in a family of seven. He has always been a bright and intelligent boy, quick at games and in no way inferior to others of his age. His greatest difficulty . . . his inability to learn to read . . . is remarkable, and is pronounced, and I have no doubt it is due to some congenital defect. He has been at school or under tutors since he was seven years old, and the greatest efforts have been made to teach him to read, but in spite of this laborious and persistent training, he can only with difficulty spell words of one syllable. . . . The

schoolmaster who has taught him for some years says that he would be the smartest lad in the school if the instruction were entirely oral. . . .

Many teachers will recognize this boy; he has been in their class at one time or another.

During the first quarter of the twentieth century, interest in reading and learning problems grew. Other case reports appeared in the literature, especially those made by ophthalmologists, who were often the first physicians consulted about failure to read.

J. A. Fisher (1910), an ophthalmologist and early observer of reading problems, felt that such disabilities were due to structural damage of the brain. For others, functional neuromaturational delays rather than anatomical abnormalities were more likely causes. Out of this debate Samuel Orton expanded the neurological model and developed one of the first comprehensive theories of learning disabilities in children. Based on his work in the 1930s, Orton (1937) coined the term *strephosymbolia,* meaning "twisted symbols," and postulated that mixed or incomplete dominance was the underlying reason for the learning (reading) difficulties. He based these views on his observations of frequent left-handedness and ambidexterity and the tendency toward reversals in writing and reading among the reading-disabled children. Orton believed that this abnormality of brain development was genetically determined, given its increased incidence in certain families. With his assistant, Ann Gillingham, he developed a variety of teaching strategies and remediation techniques. Many of Orton's theories have not stood the test of time, but as pointed out by developmental pediatrician Melvin Levine (1980), Orton's pioneering work encouraged further research.

In the 1940s and 1950s research from educational, psychological, and medical disciplines attempted to establish causative factors and remedial techniques. *Dyslexia* was one of the earliest labels used to define a child such as was described by Dr. Morgan in 1896.

From the beginning researchers had difficulty defining dyslexia, which literally means "inability to recognize words." The term has come to mean such different things to different people that it has limited value today. During the 1950s and 1960s a number of terms were coined that derived from the belief that learning disabilities were due to anatomic damage to the brain. These were replaced by the term *minimal brain dysfunction* because no *apparent* brain injury could be found in most learning-disabled children.

By the late 1960s it was the consensus that these previous labels were too emotionally charged as well as inadequate; professionals moved increasingly toward more functional classifications, finally arriving at the term *specific learning disabilities.* Perhaps due in part to its incorporation into federal legislation, this new classification has persisted in the language of most disciplines.

In April of 1967 the Council for Exceptional Children during a meeting in St. Louis prepared a definition of *learning disabilities.* N. Dale Bryant (1972) states their conclusions:

A child with learning disabilities is one with adequate mental abilities, sensory processes, and emotional stability, who has a limited number of specific deficits in perceptive, integrative, or expressive processes which severely impair learning efficiency. This includes children who have a central nervous system dysfunction, which is expressed primarily in impaired learning efficiency.

Bryant also noted another definition emphasizing the basic nature of the language process, adopted by the National Advisory Committee on Handicapped Children in January of 1968:

Children with special learning disabilities exhibit a disorder in one or more of the basic psychological processes involved in understanding or in using spoken or written languages. These may be manifested in disorders of listening, thinking, talking, reading, writing, spelling, or arithmetic. They include conditions which have been referred to as perceptual handicaps, brain injury, minimal brain dysfunction, dyslexia, developmental aphasia, and so on. They do not include learning problems which are due primarily to visual, hearing, or motor handicaps, to mental retardation, emotional disturbance, or environmental disadvantages.

This definition was incorporated into the landmark federal legislation of 1975 concerning education of the handicapped (P.L. 94, 1975, p. 142).

The term *dyslexia* is still used by some professionals. Developmental dyslexia is today defined as "a constitutional and often genetically determined deficit in written language skills such as reading, writing, and spelling." It may ᴗ or may not be associated with difficulty in symbol recognition, disordered development of time concepts, or disordered concepts of space. Al Benton (1975) has specified that dyslexia implies a constitutional, neurological basis for reading and learning failure. More often than not, however, you'll find *dyslexia* being used interchangeably with *reading and learning disability.*

Characteristics of Learning Disabilities

Let us briefly review the steps in the learning process, outlined in Figure 9–1 and discussed below.

Learning begins with a stimulus; that is, a particular piece of information to be processed such as the alphabet or a series of words. The learner must *attend to* the stimulus for a sufficient length of time for it to be fixed in the mind. The learner having attended to the information, the sense organs register the information, transmitting it via nerves to the brain for processing. For normal processing to occur the brain must *perceive accurate information.* That means, for example, words or proper shape and orientation are received, not upside-down or misshapen versions.

With the stimulus accurately received in the brain, a complex *processing*

FIGURE 9–1 The Process of Learning

Stimulus ——→ Reception ——→ Information ——→ Short-term ——→ Long-term ——→ Retrieval ——→ Expression
(Information)   processing   memory   memory

                    eyes   perception   vocal cords
                    ears   association   muscles
                    touch   integration
                                    closure

of information occurs. This information is stored in the *short-term memory* for a limited period. Depending on the degree of relevance of the stimulus to the learner and its association with existing stored knowledge, it may be transferred to *long-term memory.* Only as information is firmly fixed in the long-term memory is it really learned. The learner should then be able to *retrieve* the information when needed and *express* it in a meaningful way.

Blocks to learning can occur at any point in the learning cycle. Initially the child must attend to the stimulus long enough to latch on to, or learn it. Failure to concentrate results in inefficient, inconsistent learning. This brings us to disorders of attention and their effect on learning, which will be discussed later in this chapter. Sensory disorders that interfere with information reception were discussed in Chapter 8.

Careful observation during the teaching-learning process is most helpful in identifying students with severe reading disability. But you must know what to look for to make meaningful observations. A number of symptoms are typical of the learning-disabled child. Note, however, that these symptoms can be present in any student. Also, most severely disabled readers exhibit a number of symptoms, since one problem interacts with another to produce varying degrees of disability and thus varying symptoms.

What follows is a list of symptoms associated with cases of severe reading disability and common to learning disability cases in general.

1. *Reversals of letters or words.* In the case of letters, the student may reverse *b*'s and *d*'s, *p*'s and *q*'s, or less commonly *n*'s and *u*'s, thus making *bad* read *dab* or *baby* read *dady*; in the case of words, parts of words may be reversed as in *ant* to *nat,* or entire words may be reversed as in *saw* to *was* or *on* to *no.*
2. *Short or erratic memory for words.* Words that a normal reader would learn in teaching-learning situations may require many more exposures for the disabled reader. Also, a word could be remembered and spoken correctly one time and not recognized the next time. This failure to recognize may occur within minutes.
3. *Oral rereading not improved following silent reading or a first oral reading.*

4. *Inability to hold information in memory until needed.* Memory problems are exhibited in the use of context clues; that is, the student cannot remember what has just been read and so cannot derive a new word from context. Problems are also exhibited in use of phonics or structural analysis for word attack. In sounding a word with three phonemes the student may forget the first one or two by the time the third appears.

5. *Difficulty with concentration.* Some students cannot attend to a paragraph or story as it is being read or cannot listen for periods of beyond a half minute. This problem becomes apparent when dealing with abstract relationships such as sound-symbol correspondence. Students with difficulty in concentrating may not have obvious hyperactivity or other behavior problems.

6. *Inability to see whole relationships or form a gestalt.* This difficulty is illustrated by the phonetic speller who is unable to form a mental image of a word. Also, words are often spelled exactly as they sound, e.g., *liks* for likes or *hav* for *have.*

7. *Emotional instability.* Most students become irritated in the absence of success. Students with severe reading disability, however, have a tendency to become extremely irritable on meeting a task at which they are not immediately successful. Their moods may also change rapidly.

8. *Impulsiveness.* This problem is illustrated by the student who guesses at words rather than working them out using word-attack skills. Impulsiveness is best demonstrated when pictures are represented on a page. The student may say "bunny" for "rabbit" when the word *rabbit* is accompanied by an illustration of a rabbit.

9. *Poor eye-motor coordination.* This problem can be measured using tests. It can also be noted by observing the student write or engage in motor activities such as cutting with scissors or coloring. Tests have the advantage of providing scoring criteria or norms from which to judge the student's performance. However, the eye of an experienced teacher may be just as capable in identifying eye-motor coordination problems.

10. *Difficulty with sequencing.* This problem arises in poor spelling but may be more common in reading, when the student has difficulty remembering the specific order of words in a sentence, events in a paragraph, days in a week, or months in a year.

11. *Inability to work rapidly.* This problem arises in reading assignments but is equally common in written work. The student is always behind the pace set by others and gets irritable if rushed. There is also a tendency to perseverate, or dwell on a particular point for an extra long time.

12. *Omissions of words and phrases.* It should be emphasized that many students omit an occasional word, but some severely disabled readers

consistently omit words, especially unknown words. There is also a tendency to skip whole phrases or lines and to lose place.

13. *Directional confusion.*   This may show up in lack of ability to distinguish *b* and *d*, and so forth. Confusion can extend to inability to distinguish left and right, front and back, before and after. Bernard L. Heydorn (1984) studied the reading achievement of first-grade students who made reversals and those who did not. Heydorn found that poor readers made significantly more errors than normal readers. He hypothesized that a higher-order process might control both reading and reversals. Keith Stanovich (1985), after reviewing the literature, stated: "Systematic studies of the distribution of error types across reading ability have indicated that poor readers make more errors of all types, but that their number of reversal errors as a *proportion* of the total number of errors is no higher than that displayed by good readers." (p. 70)

14. *Poor auditory discrimination.*   This condition may be present even when the student's auditory acuity is excellent. Again, many students have difficulty with auditory discrimination, but the severely disabled reader has trouble learning minute differences in words such as *pen* and *pin* or even *him* and *hen*. Disabled readers are also erratic in their ability to discriminate sounds.

15. *Hyperactivity.*   The hyperactive student frequently has a short attention span and is wiggling and squirming, tapping fingers, etc. These signs are more apparent when the student is under stress, as when completing an assignment. (See the next section for additional description of hyperactivity.)

16. *Poor syntax, stuttering, and halting speech.*   The student who exhibits speech problems seems to need to think ahead when talking; that is, words do not flow smoothly, or when they do the order of the words is illogical.

17. *Achievement in arithmetic considerably higher than in reading and spelling.*   Perhaps there is a physiological explanation for this. Some people who have suffered strokes have been left unable to read but still able to solve difficult math problems.

CAUSES OF LEARNING DISABILITIES

With specific learning disabilities dysfunction of the central nervous system interferes with the learning process, specifically the *perception, organization, storage, retrieval,* and *expression of information.* This process is quite complex and not fully understood. At one time most reading and learning difficulties were attributed to disorders of visual perception. This assumption derived from the difficulty observed in the disabled learner with reversals of letters and words as well as difficulty with space orientation and figure-ground pattern. Such aberrations being fairly obvious and readily observed, it is understandable that they received considerable attention. Many and varied remedial techniques grew out of this theoretical position. Prominent among these were the teaching methods of Marianne Frostig (1973).

Recent evidence suggests that perceptual dysfunction may not be as significant as once thought. According to F. R. Vellutino (1977), remedial programs based on perceptual techniques alone have had limited effectiveness in teaching children to read. The problem shared by most disabled readers is not perception of letters and words but association of symbols with their spoken counterparts. Vellutino (1977) illustrated this distinction in two separate experiments involving carefully selected samples of school children in grades two through eight (ages seven to fifteen). His findings suggest that with poor readers verbal rather than visual information is lacking, which limits the utility of visual discrimination exercises.

Ronald MacKeith (1977), in a review of reading disability research, concluded that remedial measures for reading readiness derived from theories of visual deficits have no usefulness. In his view most learning disabilities are related to dysfunction of information processing, such as the association, integration, memory, and expression of information.

Definitive testing of these intricate steps in the learning process is unfortunately limited. As this text points out, more is to be gained from evaluating the child from a functional standpoint; in other words, posing questions such as, How does this child read? In what skills is the child deficient? How are learning tasks approached? (Diagnosis of information-processing skills is discussed in detail in Chapter 10.)

In reaction to theoretical positions emphasizing neurological factors in the cause of learning disabilities, other professionals turned to environmental and emotional factors. Bruce Balow (1971) expressed this view:

> Obviously some few cases arise from an unusual neurological switchboard, scrambled circuitry, crossed wires or blown fuses, but the large mass of learning disabled are far more likely to derive from an innate or acquired vulnerability coupled with an environment in home and school that is inhospitable or downright hostile to learning in the basic skills. (p. 513)

Most experts today subscribe to the concept that multiple factors—genetic, neurological, and environmental—interplay to produce a learning-disabled child (Levine, 1980). Most experts would agree with Kinsbourne (1979): "We know in principle that a lag in cognitive development can derive either from an individual variation in genetic programming or from early damage to an area of the brain destined to control the behavior in question." The child's ability to cope with this developmental lag certainly is influenced by the emotional and educational environment. Nevertheless, those of us who spend time working with these children recognize the child who comes from one of the best families, has the best educational opportunities, and yet still is unable to learn.

It is clear from this discussion that we have much to learn about the causes of learning disabilities. But caution is in order about too much emphasis on causation. The important task is to teach the child how to read, count, and spell, and that can be done without a detailed knowledge of causative factors.

TESTS USED IN THE EVALUATION OF SPECIFIC LEARNING DISABILITIES

Teachers and diagnosticians will be confronted with a variety of tests and test scores in the evaluation of children with learning disabilities. Each test has a purpose and a degree of usefulness to the teacher in planning a remedial program. In evaluating tests, it is helpful to consider what information a test is designed to give and what use that information has. For example, some tests give information of practical value in determining the cause and expected natural course of the child's disability but of limited value in planning a remedial program. Neurological tests (of handedness, dominance, soft signs, etc.) fall into this category. On the other hand, a neurological test may document that a student has a physical, developmental reason for clumsiness, indicating that messy writing or disorganized approach to tasks is not due to laziness or poor habits. Other neurological tests are designed to provide specific data about information processing and may be of more practical help in planning a remedial program.

The following list of tests is not exhaustive. It gives only a sample of the more widely accepted tests available.

1. *The WISC-R and WAIS-R.*   These tests have been used extensively in reading diagnosis and are discussed in other chapters in this text. It is possible for a psychologist trained in learning and reading diagnosis to gain some evaluation of a student's information-processing capabilities from performance on the WAIS-R or WISC-R. Too often, however, these are not as helpful as they should be considering the time required to administer them.
2. *Tests for handedness, dominance, and knowledge of left and right.* These tests have been used and researched extensively in the diagnosis of severe as well as mild reading disabilities. One such battery is the *Harris Tests of Lateral Dominance* (Harris, 1958). It tests such factors as knowledge of left and right, hand preferences, eye dominance, and foot dominance. Other researchers and diagnosticians have used similar but unpublished testing instruments. It should be noted that at certain age-grade levels significantly more children who are severely disabled may, as Harris points out (1958, p. 20), show more confusion in identifying left and right and mixed hand dominance, or at other age-

grade levels show strong left preferences. However, this does not mean that a student who exhibits these symptoms is disabled in reading, nor does this knowledge provide us with any information of significant value in planning a program of remediation for a severely disabled reader. In most cases, based on what is now known about severe reading disability, there is little to be gained from tests for handedness, dominance, or knowledge of left and right.

3. *Other tests used in diagnosis of disabled readers.* The *Bender Visual-Motor Gestalt Test (BVMG)* (Bender, 1958) and the *Developmental Test of Visual Perception (DTVP)* (Frostig, 1964) have been used in diagnosis of severely disabled readers. However, as in the case above, the fact that a student does poorly on the *BVMG* is not conclusive evidence of a disability; or, if a disability is present, the information derived from the test scores is of little use in prescribing meaningful remedial activities. The *DTVP* attempts to identify students who have problems with perception in space and with eye-motor coordination. Many studies indicate, however, that the type of activities prescribed for the remediation of weaknesses found on this test are of little or no value in the remediation of concomitant difficulties in reading. (For a review of such studies, see Hammill, Goodman, and Wiederholt, 1974.)

The *Illinois Test of Psycholinguistic Abilities (ITPA)* (Kirk, McCarthy, and Kirk, 1968) attempts to measure what you do need to know about the seriously disabled reader. That is, it tends to indicate weaknesses in such areas as auditory decoding, visual decoding, and auditory association. However, the reliability and validity of the subtests have not been clearly established. Furthermore, it is somewhat difficult and time-consuming to administer. And since no clear-cut information exists concerning the relationship of subtest weaknesses to reading disabilities, the information derived from it is in most cases not worth the time and effort required for its administration.

The causes of cases of severe learning disabilities cannot be easily discovered by any of our most commonly used diagnostic tests. In an article on the study of psychoeducational assessment of learning disabilities, David Sabatino, William Wickham, and Calvin Burnett (1968) indicated that global measures such as IQ are of little value in assessing severe reading and learning disability. What they believe is needed is "specific information processing behaviors"; that is, information on how the student learns so that you may capitalize on strong modes of learning and strengthen weaker modes. Gathering information on specific processing behaviors may enable you to modify the classroom environment to achieve the best results with this type of student (Sabatino, Wickham, and Burnett, 1968).

Marjorie Youmans Lipson and Karen K. Wixson (1986) have more recently made the same point:

Our general thesis in this paper is that research on reading disability must move away from the search for causative factors within the reader and toward the specification of the conditions under which different readers can and will learn. (p. 111)

The information-processing behaviors can to some extent be assessed by a psychologist or diagnostician using information derived from the tests discussed here as well as other commonly used tests. However, the classroom teacher or the remedial reading teacher can in most cases gain a working knowledge of a student's information-processing behaviors by careful observation and diagnostic teaching. (The diagnosis of information-processing behaviors and teaching techniques are covered in detail in Chapter 10.)

HYPERACTIVITY AND ATTENTIONAL DEFICIT DISORDER

Few subjects in child development have received as much attention in recent years as hyperactivity. Nevertheless, confusion and misunderstanding surround this subject. Yet there is little need for confusion. In the past decade more precise information has clarified many of the issues.

Prominent among the reasons for confusion about this topic is the term *hyperactivity* itself. To begin with, not all that is active is hyperactive. A variety of factors can cause a normal child to appear more active than the child's peers. Preschoolers and toddlers by nature are active. Nervous, anxious children may appear more active than other children. And some children by nature are more active, alert, and inquisitive but still learn in a normal way. They exhibit problem behaviors when bored or understimulated.

Characteristics of Hyperactivity

The truly hyperactive (or hyperkinetic) child with an attentional deficit disorder has a set of characteristics that in combination impair learning and social adjustment to a significant degree. According to Marcel Kinsbourne and Paula Caplan (1979), such attentional deficits, alone or in combination with learning disabilities, are common precursors to underachievement in the classroom.

While the appearance of increased body activity is often the most noticeable symptom in a child with hyperactivity, this is not necessarily the most significant symptom. These children present a cluster of disruptive characteristics that when seen together are easily recognized:

1. *Disordered activity.* One of the most prominent characteristics of hyperactive children is a quality of physical activity that is disruptive. They do appear more active than most normal children of their age and maturity. In the extreme they are restless, incessantly moving from one activity to another. At play they tend to be loud and boisterous,

constantly changing activity and disrupting the play of other children. In the classroom they are restless, frequently getting out of their seats. They run when they should walk and invariably talk when they should listen. They crave attention and priase, but seem always to act in ways that get them into trouble.

Thus, these children do appear *hyper*active—that is, to have increased activity—but in reality they may not be. Researchers have placed a modified pedometer, a watchlike instrument that measures body movement, on normal children and children with hyperkinetic syndrome. Surprisingly, in such experiments children with the hyperkinetic syndrome do not always have a greatly increased rate of activity. But the *nature* of the activity in the hyperkinetic child differs vastly. Behaviors tend to be random, disorganized, and nongoal-directed. It is the *quality,* not necessarily the *quantity,* of activity that is abnormal. The random and disorganized nature of their movements does, however, give the appearance of increased activity.

2. *Disordered attention.*   Parents and teachers of hyperactive children frequently complain that the child won't pay attention to anything. The teacher says, "He has a short attention span" or "She can't concentrate on her work." However it is expressed, hyperkinetic children are unable to control and modulate their attention. They are unable to focus on one task or activity for any length of time. When one observes them, their minds appear to be bouncing from one interest to another with rapidity and lack of order.

Concentration is the ability to focus one's mind on a limited number of activities and stimuli for a given period while simultaneously screening out all other unrelated stimuli. The hyperactive child cannot do this and is therefore not consistently productive; the hyperactive child is *stimulus bound*. This means that all stimuli are attended to, and sometimes simultaneously. Only a very strong stimulus can override all others and capture the hyperactive child's undivided attention. More often than not the child does not pay effective attention to instructions or material being presented. When an assignment is begun, the child is often distracted before completing the task. Decisions are made before all the data are in, and all too often the child stops listening before hearing all the questions. Choices are thus made impulsively.

3. *Disordered impulse control.*   The ability of hyperactive children to control their impulses is impaired, so they literally act before they think. To a greater or lesser degree they are unable to stop, look, and listen. Strong impulse control is a sign of maturity that gradually develops through childhood. The hyperkinetic child fails to do this as well as other children. In class the child repeatedly speaks without being called on. Another perplexing symptom related to impulsiveness is disordered emotional control: "One moment she is happy and the next she's crying." Just as hyperkinetic children have trouble controlling

and organizing their activity, attention, and impulses, so they cannot organize and control their emotions well either. At one moment they may change from a happy and peaceful mood to crying and frustration.

As mentioned earlier, the term *hyperactive child* is confusing. One reason is that the physical hyperactivity, while at times disruptive, has the least effect on the child's ability to learn. The destructive factor is the disorganized, unstructured attention. In fact the physical hyperactivity is largely a by-product of the attentional deficit. It is the body following the distractible, disorganized mind.

Recognizing this, the latest edition of *Diagnostic and Statistical Manual of Mental Disorders* (DSM III) of the American Psychiatric Association has introduced a new term, *attentional deficit disorder*. This is a much better diagnostic term because it focuses the emphasis on the most relevant problem. For the remainder of this chapter this term will be used in place of, or interchangeably with, *hyperactivity*.

Causes of Hyperactivity, or Attentional Deficit Disorder

As with specific learning disability, many causative factors have been proposed for hyperactivity, or attentional deficit. The linkage of hyperactive, impulsive, and attentional deficit behaviors with organic brain lesions has a long history with reports occurring as early as 1900. The consequences of a major encephalitis epidemic in 1918 further linked behavior changes with organic brain damage. Survivors of encephalitis were found to have significant behavior changes, including persistent hyperactivity, distractibility, irritability, and impulsivity. In 1937 Charles Bradley published a study on the use of stimulant drugs in the treatment of children in a residential center. Previously hyperactive, distractible children showed improvement in schoolwork and social adjustment.

Some interesting circumstantial evidence suggests that genetics may play a role in producing attentional deficit disorders. For a long time it has been known that both hyperactivity and learning disorders are more common in males, suggesting genetic factors. Those working with children are struck by the frequency of a father or mother remarking, "I was just like him when I was a child. I almost didn't finish school." And it is not uncommon to have two or more siblings in the family with similar problems. Of course, there are many other such children whose families have no history of learning problems. It seems then that genetics may play a role in some cases, but the extent or nature of the role is still undefined.

Some professionals, albeit a small group, claim that hyperkinesis and learning disabilities are not due to physical factors at all but to emotional stresses and poor environment. An unsuitable emotional environment can produce unhealthy mental and emotional development, and this in turn can affect the child's school performance. However, the emotionally disturbed child and the hyperactive child differ on several counts, and it is very important that a proper distinction be made between the two during the diagnostic and treatment process.

Children from an economically and socially deprived environment may underachieve in school and may not behave in the way middle-class teachers expect. But this does not make them hyperactive or learning disabled. It is important when forming judgments about a particular child to consider all possible factors before applying labels, particularly where disorders are concerned.

As with specific learning disabilities, attentional deficit disorders are most likely caused by several factors working conjointly. The right constitutional background (neurological and genetic) acted on by certain environmental factors facilitates the expression of the attentional deficit.

Evaluation of the Child with Hyperactivity, or Attentional Deficit

Although either may occur alone in a given student, hyperactivity will occur with some frequency in conjunction with specific learning disability and delayed motor development. Figure 9–2 illustrates the various combinations.

FIGURE 9–2   The Spectrum of Learning Disability

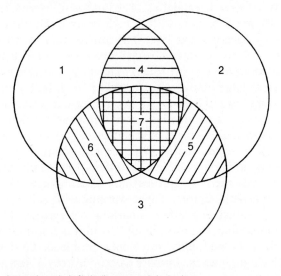

1. Attentional deficit (hyperactivity) alone
2. Specific learning disability alone
3. Motor coordination deficit alone
4. Attentional deficit + specific learning disability
5. Specific learning disability + motor coordination deficit
6. Attentional deficit + motor coordination deficit
7. Attentional deficit + specific learning disability + coordination deficit

Part B: REMEDIATION

SPECIFIC LEARNING DISABILITIES

Most of the early theories of severe reading disabilities and their concomitant remedial techniques have met with little success. Since new programs and materials constantly appear, it is important for the remedial reading teacher to know what programs have been unsuccessful in the past to avoid unfruitful duplication of efforts.

Probably the best-known of the early theories was proposed by the neuropathologist Samuel Orton (1928), who believed that the two halves of the brain were alike in size and design and reversed in pattern. That is, the left hemisphere would bear the same relation to the right hemisphere that the left hand bears to the right hand. Orton concluded that records, or *engrams* as they were called, of one hemisphere would be mirror copies of the other. If a student failed to establish the normal physiological habit of using exclusively engrams of one hemisphere, a confusion in orientation would result, causing a student to be unable to recognize differences between pairs of words that could be spelled backwards. Orton and his associates reported considerable success in the use of certain physical exercises, along with intensive remediation in reading, in overcoming the reading difficulties of a number of children. It is somewhat difficult now to assess the significance of the physical therapy in relation to the direct remediation in reading. Orton was not given to making idle claims, and his work has been of considerable value in furthering an understanding of possible causes of severe reading disabilities. In interpreting his work one must keep in mind that even if his explanation was correct, or partially correct, one should not automatically assume that a physical training program could correct damage already done.

Carl Delacato, working on Orton's theory that severe reading disability was often caused by failure to develop proper neurological organization, developed a program designed to overcome these difficulties. Delacato (1959) suggested physical exercises and remedial procedures dealing with sleep patterns, tonality, handedness, visual control, and so forth. Most medical and educational professionals find little evidence in the literature for the general application of Delacato's or other motor training programs in the treatment of learning problems. The use of various types of perceptual training programs at one time appeared to hold great promise. Present evidence, however, indicates that this area too shows limited success. Many disabled students do have various kinds and degrees of perceptual handicaps. In simple terms, however, the remediation of perceptual handicaps does not improve the ability to read or even the potential for reading. In a very thorough review of the literature on perceptual training programs, Hammill, Goodman, and Wiederholt (1974) concluded that "the results of attempts to implement the Frostig-Horne materials and Kephart-Getman techniques in the schools have for the most part been unrewarding.'' (p. 476)

After reviewing a number of more recent studies, Stanovich (1985) stated, ''It is generally accepted that visual perception training programs have been ineffective in promoting reading acquisition.'' (p. 71)

Bruce Balow (1971) had a similar assessment in an earlier review:

> . . . While motor and perceptual skill weaknesses are frequently found in learning disabled pupils, there is great likelihood that these are most often simply concomitants without causal relevance; thus the argument cannot depend upon assumed etiologies for learning disabilities. (p. 523)

Despite his conclusions, Balow cites six reasons to consider the addition of visual-motor activities to the curriculum for all primary-age students, including students who suffer serious deficiencies in school skills. In summary, Balow's reasons address the importance of visual-motor skills in mastering schoolwork in general and the fact that such skills are ''ordinarily left to develop incidentally.'' Similar reasoning is proposed by other authors who believe that such training will allow students to concentrate better after flexing their muscles and that the development of motor skills may simply contribute to the good mental health of students.

It is our view that these same benefits can be derived from activities more directly related to reading. Furthermore, personal observation suggests that teachers come to view such activities as ends in themselves. Perhaps most important, however, time spent in perceptual training usurps time for activities dealing more directly with reading disabilities.

Some Important Considerations in the Remediation of Severe Reading Disability

A few considerations are of special significance when dealing with severely disabled readers. One is an overall plan in dealing with these problems. Three steps of such a plan:

1. Early identification of children of normal intelligence who exhibit difficulty with reading and reading-related activities.
2. Formulation of an educational plan based on the student's specific strengths and weaknesses.
3. Continual assessment of the original plan as measured by diagnostic teaching.

Another important consideration in remediation is that severely disabled readers are more likely to benefit from a long-term intensive program than from the less intensive programs often found in the public schools. Jules

Abrams and Herman Belmont (1969) found that full-time specialized reading instruction was superior to that usually carried on in most remedial programs. John Heckerl and Russell Sansbury (1968) also studied severely disabled readers and concluded that remedial therapy should be a daily occurrence. In their view an hour is the minimum time for each session, with the exception of sessions for younger children, who cannot tolerate lengthy periods. They cautioned that long-term programs should be anticipated with little accomplished during the first six months or even the first year. They emphasized that provisions should be made for the severely disabled reader to receive intensive remediation for as long as profitable or until a functional reading level is achieved.

It is especially important to ensure that the program remains flexible. Once a program has been devised, tried, and evaluated, it should be reevaluated in terms of its success. If little or no success results, another plan should be tried and evaluated. This is an ongoing process in any remedial reading program, but it is of special significance to the severely disabled reader.

Techniques for Remediation of Specific Learning Disability

It should be emphasized that the techniques and materials recommended in this text for the mildly disabled reader are often successful for the learning-disabled child. It may be necessary at times, however, to modify techniques for more severely disabled children. For example, the methods for teaching basic sight words suggested in Chapter 4 can be used but will need to be repeated more often and used over a longer time. Likewise, the methods suggested here are appropriate for the mildly disabled reader but are more time-consuming and require individualized teaching.

The Fernald Approach. This is often referred to as the kinesthetic method. It was first described by Grace M. Fernald and Helen B. Keller in 1921. The following description of their approach, with minor changes, was taken from Fernald's book published in 1943.[2]

In the early stages of the Fernald approach no commercially prepared materials are used. The teacher solicits words to be learned from the student. These words are taught until they are mastered. When a storehouse of words is acquired, the student is asked to compose a story. The story is written by the teacher, and any new words that appear are taught. The story is then typed by the teacher so that the student can read it the following day. You will note that this approach is essentially the language-experience method used so often in regular classrooms today.

Four stages are identified in teaching words, depending on the student's ability to learn:

[2]The Fernald approach is reproduced here with minor changes by permission of McGraw-Hill Book Company.

Stage 1. tracing.   The word is first written for the student on the chalk-board or on a strip of paper or tagboard measuring approximately 3 in. × 9 in. or 4 in. × 10 in. The word may be written in manuscript or cursive style depending on the type of writing used for the student's normal classroom activities. The student is asked to trace the word with the index finger or a combination of index and middle fingers and says each *word part* as it is being traced (not sounding the word letter by letter). This procedure is used until the word can be traced from memory. The student then writes the word from memory, again saying each word part as it is written. The word is later typed and read in typed form. New words are filed in a box in alphabetical order.

In this stage certain points of technique are stressed:

1. The finger or fingers must contact the paper. Writing in the air is less successful.
2. The student should never copy a word but always write it from memory.
3. The whole word should be learned at once or as a unit.
4. Each word part should be said aloud as it is traced or written.
5. Whatever the student writes is typed by the teacher and read by the student before too long an interval has passed. This provides transfer from the written to the printed form.
6. The student should not be allowed to write a word incorrectly. If the student cannot remember a word, the session stops and initial tracing practice is resumed.

Stage 2. writing without tracing.   At some point words will not need to be traced. The student looks at the word in script, says it several times, and then writes it from memory. At this stage library cards are substituted for the larger cards. The words can be typed on one side of the card and written in manuscript or cursive on the other side. These cards are filed alphabetically, as in stage 1.

Stage 3. recognition in print.   At this stage it is unnecessary to write each word in print. The student looks at the word and is told what it is. The word is pronounced once or twice and written from memory. Reading in books is usually started during this stage.

Stage 4. word analysis.   The student is encouraged to look at new words and to try to identify familiar word parts (families or phonograms) and apply them to new words. Phonic sounding is discouraged, but the student is encouraged to develop the habit of looking for familiar parts of words.

In most cases the total nonreader starts in stage 1 and students with partial disabilities, in stage 2. No special techniques are used to overcome word reversals, since the method teaches words in a left-to-right sequence.

Research on the effectiveness of the Fernald approach shows little difference in its effectiveness compared to other approaches. This is probably due to the fact that students with very severe reading disabilities who are predisposed to learning by this method are simply not grouped together in the studies. It should be stressed, however, that this method is not for large groups of students; it is intended for the student who fails to learn by more commonly used methods.

Saroj Sutaria (1984) has reported on an adaptation of the Fernald approach by Thomas Stich and his colleagues at the Northern Tier Learning and Diagnostic Center of Mansfield (Pennsylvania) State College. The Stich method combines writing of stories with illustrations. In using it material is typed and reviewed each day. Those who use the Fernald technique may wish to investigate the Stich method, although no research on its effectiveness is presented by the author.

Nonvisual auditory-kinesthetic-tactile (AKT) method. Harold Blau and Harriet Blau (1968) report that many children seem to learn well using the kinesthetic method just described. For other children there occurs a short circuit between the eye and the brain; that is, something happens to the message the student sees before it reaches the brain, causing words to come out scrambled. To remedy this the authors describe a method similar to the visual-auditory kinesthetic-tactile method but bypassing the visual channel.

The nonvisual AKT approach has been used at the Reading Center of the University of Texas at El Paso for a number of years with students who seem unable to process information when it comes through the visual channel. A description of this approach:

> Non-Visual AKT differs from VAKT in several ways, and variations of Non-VAKT are possible too. Primarily, however, the child is blindfolded or closes his eyes, and the word to be learned is traced on his back. As the teacher traces the word, she spells it aloud, letter by letter. Often, the second or third time around, the student can identify the letters being traced and he too spells out the word. Usually (until the student becomes too advanced for this) three-dimensional letters, arranged to spell out the word, are placed before the student and, still blindfolded, he traces these with his fingertips as he feels the letters being traced on his back. The letters are then scrambled, and still blindfolded, the student arranges the letters in the proper sequence. The blindfold is then removed, the student sees what he has done (often his first experience with coherent sequencing) and writes the word on paper, or at the board, and then on a file card for future review. (Blau and Blau, 1968, pp. 127–128)

Diagnosticians cannot be sure that the student's problem is a malfunction of the visual channel. It may simply be that blindfolding facilitates concentration in the auditory and kinesthetic aspects of the learning process.

General Teaching Procedures

Certain teaching procedures seem to be successful with many severely disabled readers, although in most cases these procedures are tedious and time consuming. For example, severely disabled readers require repetition and drill to a point often referred to as overlearning. This means that something has been learned so well that it evokes an automatic response. This response level is often successful with the severely disabled reader. Whether you are teaching word-attack skills or sight words, the automatic response level must be reached. For example, the sight word *no* should be presented enough times that the student automatically says "no" without any hesitation whatsoever when he or she sees the written word; this is the case regardless of the approach used.

With most severely disabled readers it is also helpful, if not absolutely necessary, to focus on one concept at a time. For example, do not try to teach the *d* sound with the *og* phonogram unless the phonogram has been previously learned. The need for a narrow focus makes the analytic system of teaching phonics often inappropriate with the severely disabled reader. The *d* sound may need to be learned in isolation until it evokes an automatic response.

A modified analytic approach may be used. For example, after teaching the *d* and *l* sounds to the automatic level, you could then teach the *og* phonogram by using the words *dog* and *log*. Note, however, that no new concepts should be introduced until the prior concepts are automatic.

Many severely disabled readers can learn through the kinesthetic and tactile senses regardless of the degree of impairment of their auditory and visual channels. A number of learning activities using this approach are available. The type will depend on the age-grade level of the student and the concept to be taught. Some examples of this approach:

1. Use of modeling clay to form letters and short words.
2. Use of three-dimensional letters available commercially. (Some have magnetic backing to stick to a metal easel.)
3. Use of salt or fine sand in a shallow box such as a shoe-box lid in which the student can trace letters and words.
4. Use of paper placed over screen wire (such as that used on screen doors) on which the student writes with a crayon. This leaves a raised surface on the paper, and the letters and words can be felt.

The use of immediate reinforcement in the accomplishment of goals is advised for all students, and it is especially helpful when working with the severely disabled reader. Reinforcement of short-term goals such as learning the *p* sound or the word *go* is more productive than attempting to reinforce longer-term goals such as "learning to read well enough so that you can read this book." The importance of reinforcement was illustrated by Barbara Batemen (1974). A young cerebral-palsied girl learned to type at a rate of two to three letters a minute with the aid of a stylus held in both hands. Her performance was praised and visitors were often "treated" to her typing demonstration. When the girl was given the opportunity to earn playing time with a prized magnetic board contingent on an increase in her typing rate, however, she soon increased to twenty-five to thirty words per minute.

Careful diagnostic teaching is probably the most important procedure to be followed in working with the severely disabled reader. Although this is not easy for the inexperienced teacher, it can be learned. When working with a student on learning a new word, be sure to note carefully any areas in which the student appears to have difficulty. In teaching the word *man* consider carefully such questions as these:

1. Were the *m* and *n* reversed?
2. Does the student seem to learn the word best as a gestalt (learning the whole word picture), or by concentrating on the phoneme-grapheme relationships?
3. Was there anything I did that made this word easier or more difficult to learn than others?
4. Does writing the word enable the student to learn it faster than previous words taught?
5. Does the student learn this and other words faster when they are used in a sentence?
6. Is the student, when working with the sounds, able to discriminate between the *m* and *n*?
7. What does the student think helps him or her learn best?
8. Does the student learn faster when the word is spoken aloud or when spelled aloud?
9. Did the student know all the phoneme-grapheme relationships before we started, or do I need to go back and teach those if this is the preferred method? Did the student even know the letter names?
10. After mastering the names and the letter sounds, did the student have trouble blending? Is blending a problem on other words as well?

See Appendix C for a brief description of some commercial materials designed specifically for the severely disabled reader.

Specific Teaching Procedures and Classroom Modifications

To list a specific set of procedures appropriate for all severely disabled readers would be futile, since the symptoms of each student differ. There are, however, some specific teaching procedures and classroom modifications that you may wish to consider depending on the particular diagnosed needs of any one student. Some of these specific procedures and modifications follow:

1. Review materials previously learned as often as possible until responses are automatic.
2. Illustrate new concepts with verbal explanations.
3. Limit directions for oral and written assignments. For example, divide a three-part assignment into three parts and give directions for each part separately. (As with all suggestions in this section, procedures used depend on the capabilities of the student.)
4. Provide a working environment that is as free of distractions as possible. Use study carrels or reading and study areas isolated from other students.
5. Introduce new or distracting words with color cues such as a green letter at the beginning of a word and a red letter at the end of a word.
6. Give the student sufficient time to respond to oral questions. One study showed that teachers allow on average about two to three seconds for a student to answer. Allow at least five to ten seconds if needed; in some cases half a minute may be more appropriate.
7. Encourage the student to verbalize the response when writing something new.
8. Encourage the student to use a finger, pencil, ruler, or piece of paper with a window cut in it when reading, if needed.
9. Many experts have suggested permitting students to give oral answers to tests in their regular classroom if unable to produce adequate written responses. However, this reinforces an undesirable habit. It is usually better to modify the time allowed for completion or to provide questions that require short answers.

Some Cautions in the Treatment of Severe Reading Disability

Regardless of the label attached to the condition, students still need to be taught. While labels have some validity with regard to causation, they are often of little help in designing a remedial program. Beyond using the term *learning disabled,* labeling is not only unnecessary; it is often damaging.

Several years ago a professor's son was brought to the El Paso Reading Center for help with his reading. The professor and his wife said their child had experienced a great deal of difficulty in learning to read because he was "dyslexic." When the boy (age fourteen) was interviewed, he said, "You know, I can't read because I have dyslexia." The clinic director and the teacher assured the boy that at his age most people automatically get over dyslexia (probably true to some extent). Within six months the boy's grades in high school went from Ds and Fs to As and Bs, and he no longer had any trouble with reading.

A fairly typical program of remediation was undertaken with this student, focusing on his specific weaknesses in reading and especially in study skills. An important part of the remediation, however, involved enhancing this student's self-concept and getting him to realize that he was not saddled with some awesome disease from which he would never recover. The point of all this is, of course, that the use of the label *dyslexia* was in his case highly damaging.

If you are new to the field of reading, you may feel that there is very little here in terms of concrete procedures for identifying and working with severely disabled readers. This is quite true. The results of some of the most commonly used tests provide some help, but for all practical purposes the diagnosis and treatment of students with severe reading disability can best be handled by the teacher through careful, guided observation and diagnostic teaching.

ATTENTIONAL DEFICIT DISORDER, OR HYPERACTIVITY

Remediation of attentional deficit involves a three-pronged approach:

1. Provide a proper environmental cocoon for the child to optimize strengths and overcome weaknesses.
2. Alleviate inciting factors.
3. Use medical therapy in a careful, considered way.

Providing an Environmental Cocoon

The goal of remediation is breaking through the distractibility and impulsiveness to facilitate learning. Since the root of the problem is the child's unstructured and disorganized approach to most tasks, the first step is to provide a structured, well-organized, nondistracting environment. This involves the child's whole life—at home and at school. In this effort the teacher plays an important role. A regular schedule with minimum interruption is important, as is a consistent approach to learning tasks.

The demands of the classroom excite the major features of the attentional deficit disorder. In the classroom the child faces failure, punishment, demands for attention, and motor inhibition unparalleled in other spheres of the child's life. The child who is mildly disturbing at home can become a severe problem at school.

Techniques for Dealing with Attentional Deficit Disorder in the Classroom

1. Seat the child near the teacher's desk in a reassuring, nonthreatening way.
2. Address the child by name before eliciting a response or calling attention to the child. It is helpful to stand near or touch the child when giving instructions to the class or eliciting a response.
3. Remember that physical features of the work environment influence the child's activity and distractibility levels. Consider these guidelines:

a. Reduce stimuli in the child's visual field (place construction paper over windows, eliminate posters, pictures, etc.).

b. Use lighting of medium intensity; no flickering or bright lights.

c. Plan the schedule so that the child is not expected to concentrate when there is distracting noise in the hallway. Music set at a low volume can be helpful in masking continuous distractions.

d. Create a private study office by screening off a work area for children with significant attentional deficits.

4. Give shorter assignments with immediate feedback on results. Stress quality, not quantity. An attentional deficit child often has difficulty finishing work. Also give shorter tests. (McNutt, 1984)

5. Use techniques that assist the short-term memory. Use a preprogrammed assignment card that is reviewed daily and kept at the student's desk.

a. List each activity separately. If necessary, list specific steps.

b. Require that the child have activities checked off as progress is made.

c. Set approximate time limits for an activity. It may be helpful to provide a timer; however, some children become more disorganized under time pressure.

d. For maximum retention in short-term memory, use the following steps:

Step 1. "Please pay attention. Tell me when you are ready." "Very good; now listen carefully to [these words]," etc.

Step 2. Break the material to be retained into small units.

Step 3. Use a multisensory approach to allow rehearsal of the material, i.e., speaking orally, writing down key words, drawing pictures, etc.

Step 4. Have the child repeat orally the material to be committed to long-term memory.

Step 5. Provide frequent rehearsals.

Step 6. "Chunk" material; that is, combine it into meaningful units.

Step 7. Strongly reinforce any increment in amount of material remembered (with verbal praise and/or privileges).

6. Use techniques for dealing with impulsivity and what appears to be an increased activity level; confinement for long periods will be felt as pressure. The child should be given legitimate opportunities for physical movement.

a. Lesson plans should include sorting, cutting, printing, and manipulating counters and gadgets.

b. Allow the child to work standing or moving at times.

c. Provide outlets for physical movements (running errands, sharpening pencils, etc.).

d. Provide an adequate physical education program that allows for gross body movement without involving competitive team sports; this is essential.

Frequently you will find a student who shows symptoms of both attentional deficit and specific learning disability. With this student deal early with the learning impairment using whatever techniques are necessary to remediate the reading and learning problems. If the child senses pressure or failure in the learning area, attentional deficit and related behavior problems are likely to worsen; this exacerbates learning difficulties and increases pressure and stress. Providing educational opportunities that complement the child's strengths and weaknesses in an important aspect of creating an environmental cocoon.

Alleviating Inciting Factors

The physician in evaluating a hyperactive child looks for factors that cause or aggravate the attentional deficit and related behavior problems. The child's emotional environment is of great importance here. Undue stress or pressure at home or at school worsens the attentional deficit. Efforts to reduce stress through counseling and instruction can be helpful. Benjamin Feingold (1974) has popularized the use of special diets in the treatment of hyperactive and learning-disabled children. While this thesis has yet to be adequately tested, preliminary evidence suggests that behavior is aggravated by certain specific foods or additives for a minority of hyperactive children.

While the rare child may be helped by a restricted diet, no evidence supports the use of a special diet with most attentional deficit and learning-disabled children. The institution of such a diet is no simple matter—it takes much effort and can stigmatize the child, reinforcing a sense of inferiority. Diet therapy should be used only for carefully documented reasons and under the supervision of a knowledgeable physician.

Seeking Medical Treatment

As Paul Wender points out, a large body of evidence for the effectiveness of medical treatment of attentional deficit and related behavioral problems of hyperactivity and impulsiveness has been accumulated since Bradley's work in 1937. A variety of drugs were used, but the most effective have been the stimulants Ritalin and Dexedrine. Holly O'Donnell (1982) also suggests that the drug Cylert is one of the more common, along with Ritalin and Dexedrine.

C. Wishher, G. Atkins, and P. Manfield (1985) reported on the effect of Piracetam on "dyslexics'" reading ability. In their study forty-six children were administered either Piracetam or a placebo in a double-blind experiment that lasted for eight weeks. They found no significant group effects; however, they reported improvements in reading speed and accuracy in the individuals treated with Piracetam.

Rachel Gittelman, Donald F. Klein, and Ingrid Feingold (1983) reported on the effects of Methylphenidate in combination with reading remediation: "The fact that the reading improvement was not observed in more instances suggests that the effect of methylphenidate on reading is not a strong one." (p. 207)

Just how the stimulants work is unclear, although it is believed they affect the balance of neurotransmitters in the brain. (These are chemicals, present in minute quantities, that participate in the transmission of impulses from one brain cell to another.)

Whatever the mechanism, proper medical therapy improves the attention span, decreases abnormal activity, increases frustration tolerance, and decreases impulsivity and emotional outbursts. Performance on psychological tests and in the classroom may be improved, but this is not due to any increase in actual intelligence. Rather, the medication allows the child to use native intelligence without interference, primarily by improving the attention span and mental organization.

The use of medication does not reverse specific learning disabilities. This is important: The simple fact that a child is underachieving in school is no reason to consider medical therapy. In fact, medical therapy should be undertaken only after a thorough evaluation and for specific indications. When given for the proper reasons and carefully supervised by a knowledgeable physician, medical therapy with stimulants is quite safe and has minimal side effects.

The Importance of Communication Between Professionals

One of the most serious problems in effective use of combined educational and medical approaches has been the lack of communication between personnel in the two fields. Teachers, of course, cannot accurately diagnose which students may benefit from medical treatment. On the other hand, a student who climbs the walls in a normal classroom setting may be perfectly calm when visiting the doctor's office and thus appear normal. As a result, the doctor may believe that the teacher is overly concerned about a few minor incidents in the student's behavior. The teacher has no chance to describe the way the student reacts in the classroom and is told by the student's parents that the medical doctor believed nothing was wrong.

Teachers should remember that only a medical doctor can prescribe medication. But the medical doctor must remember that the student's classroom teacher or remedial reading teacher, having a chance to compare the student's behavior with that of many other students, is in a far better position to judge a student's behavior in relation to that of other students. A short standard teacher evaluation questionnaire summarizing the child's behavior in the classroom can be most effective in improving communication between physician and teacher.

A FINAL NOTE ON TEACHING TECHNIQUES FOR THE DISABLED CHILD

Dealing with the disabled child can be likened to finding a cure for cancer. Some medical researchers contend that there are so many different types of cancer that it is unrealistic to hope for a single cure. You, no doubt, face the same problem dealing with severely disabled readers. Most reading specialists now agree that the use of one term to describe problems of so varying a nature is unrealistic and makes the problem appear less complicated than it actually is.

It would be less than honest to leave the impression that magical techniques and procedures will work wonders for the learning-disabled child. More is known about it today than twenty years ago, but progress has been slow, and few, if any, miracle techniques have appeared. Luckily, most of the serious cases of reading disability, given intensive remediation over a long time, do show improvement.

It is important to remember that the learning-disabled child is a person whose problems often result in complete disequilibrium with the environment. Such a child is a unique combination of strengths and weaknesses and remains through it all an individual.

At present very little is known about students who exhibit learning disabilities, including severe reading disability. Perhaps Harold Martin (1971) was correct in his assessment:

> At present, it seems most prudent to try to understand how the child can best learn rather than only focusing on the reasons he doesn't learn when taught by traditional methods. If educators and other professionals can recognize the factors and the environment in which the child will best learn—including motivation, perceptual strengths, style of learning—individualization of that child's teaching to capitalize on those strengths presently holds our most promising assistance to the handicapped child. (p. 471)

In summary, Balow's statement (1971) concerning learning disabilities seems especially relevant. He said, "Until experimentally proven otherwise, it may be that the simplest explanation of success obtained with any treatment for learning disabilities is the power and skill of the teacher who believes in it." (p. 519)

SUMMARY

Students with severe learning disabilities have presented a dilemma to teachers and other professionals in the past, and in many cases this dilemma is still present today. Our diagnostic tools are limited, and pinpointing the nature and cause of a student's difficulties is not easy. There are, however, certain characteristics that cluster and point to the appropriate diagnosis and treatment. Some students have disorders of information processing; others have disturbances in their style or approach to the learning situation; and some students have deficiencies in both areas.

Earlier programs for the remediation of severe reading disability have generally failed to prove their worth when thoroughly researched. However, some procedures are highly effective in specific cases. But what appears to work well with one student often fails to bring results with another.

There is a need for close cooperation among all professionals working with learning-disabled children, particularly teachers and physicians. Medical therapy is indicated for only a limited number of students—those with attentional deficit disorder, otherwise known as hyperactivity.

REFERENCES

Abrams, J. C., & Belmont, H. S. (1969). Different approaches to the remediation of severe reading disability in children. *Journal of Learning Disabilities, 2,* 136–140.

Adams, R. B. (1969). Dyslexia: A discussion of its definition. *Journal of Learning Disabilities, 2,* 616–626.

American Psychiatric Association. (1981). *Diagnostic and statistical manual of mental disorders* (3rd ed.). Washington, DC: Author.

Balow, B. (1971). Perceptual-motor activities in the treatment of severe reading disability. *Reading Teacher, 24,* 512–525.

Bateman, B. D. (1974). Educational implications of minimal brain dysfunction. *Reading Teacher, 27,* 662–668.

Bender, L. (1958). *Bender visual-motor gestalt test.* NY: Psychological Corporation.

Benton, A. (1975). Developmental dyslexia: Neurological aspects. In W. J. Friedlander (Ed.), *Advances in Neurology.* NY: Raven Press.

Blau, H., & Blau, H. (1968). A theory of learning to read. *Reading Teacher, 22,* 126–129+.

Bradley, C. (1937). The behavior of children receiving Benzedrine. *American Journal of Psychiatry, 94,* 577–584.

Bryant, H. D. (1972). Learning disabilities. *Instructor, 81,* 49–56.

Delacato, C. H. (1959). *The treatment and prevention of reading problems.* Springfield, IL: Charles C. Thomas.

Feingold, B. (1974). *Why your child is hyperactive.* NY: Random House.

Fernald, G. M. (1943). *Remedial techniques in basic school subjects.* NY: McGraw-Hill.

Fisher, J. A. (1910). Congenital word blindness, trans. *Ophthalmological Society United Kingdom, 30,* 216.

Frostig, M. (1973). *Learning problems in the classroom.* NY: Grune & Stratton.

Gittleman, R., Klein, D. F., & Feingold, I. (1983). Children with reading disorders—II. Effects of Methylphenidate in combination with reading remediation. *Journal of Child Psychology, 24,* 193–212.

Hammill, D., Goodman, L., & Wiederholdt, J. L. (1974). Visual-motor processes: Can we train them? *Reading Teacher, 27,* 469–478.

Harris, A. J. (1958). *Harris tests of lateral dominance-manual of directions.* NY: Psychological Corporation.

Heckerl, J., & Sansbury, R. (1969). A study of severe reading retardation. *Reading Teacher, 21,* 724–729.

Heydorn, B. L. (1984). A comparative study of reading achievement in terms of symbol reversals in first grade children. *Reading Improvement, 21,* 210–211.

Kinsbourne, M., & Caplan, P. (1979). *Children's learning and attention problems.* Boston: Little, Brown.

Kirk, S. A., McCarthy, J. J., & Kirk, W. D. (1968). *The Illinois test of psycholinguistic abilities* (rev. ed.). Urbana, IL: University of Illinois Press.

Levine, M. (1980). *A pediatric approach to learning disorders.* NY: Wiley.

Lipson, M. Y., Wixon, K. K. (1986). Reading disability research: An interactionist perspective. *Review of Educational Research, 56,* 111–136.

MacKeith, R. (1977). Do disorders of perception occur? *Developmental Medicine and Child Neurology, 19,* 821.

Martin, H. P. (1971). Vision and its role in reading disability and dyslexia. *Journal of School Health, 41,* 468–472.

McNutte, G. (1984). Alternative testing for slow readers. *Reading Teacher, 37,* 669–670.

O'Donnel, H. (1982). The hyperactive child and drug treatment. *Reading Teacher, 36,* 106–109.

Orton, S. (1928). An impediment to learning to read—A neurological explanation of the reading disability. *School and Society, 28,* 286–290.

Orton, S. (1937). *Reading, writing and speech problems in children.* NY: Norton.

Sabatino, D. A., Wickham, W., Jr., & Burnett, C. (1968). The psychoeducational assessment of learning disabilities. *Catholic Education Review, 66,* 327–341.

Stanovich, K. E. (1985). Explaining the variance in reading ability in terms of psychological processes: What have we learned? *Annals of Dyslexia, 35,* 67–96.

Sutaria, S. (1984). A stitch in time: Adapting Fernald's method. *Academic Therapy, 19,* 309–315.

Vellutino, F. R. (1977). Has the perceptual deficit hypothesis led us astray? *Journal of Learning Disabilities, 10,* 375–385.

Wender, P. (1971). *Minimal brain dysfunction in children.* NY: Wiley.

Wilsher, C., Atkins, G., & Manfield, P. (1985). Effect of Piracetam on dyslexics' reading ability. *Journal of Learning Disabilities, 18,* 19–25.

10

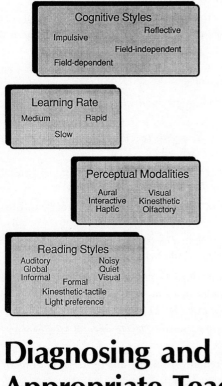

Cognitive Styles
Reflective
Impulsive
Field-independent
Field-dependent

Learning Rate
Medium   Rapid
Slow

Perceptual Modalities
Aural   Visual
Interactive Kinesthetic
Haptic   Olfactory

Reading Styles
Auditory   Noisy
Global   Quiet
Informal   Visual
        Formal
Kinesthetic-tactile
Light preference

Diagnosing and Using Appropriate Teaching Techniques for the Disabled Reader

The first part of this chapter contains a discussion of the need for diagnosis beyond students' knowledge of skills. This is followed by a discussion of how humans learn and the theory of diagnosis for learning modalities. The last part of this chapter contains information on diagnosing and teaching to specific learning modalities and cognitive styles. We also present information on diagnosing and using the concept of learning rate, and finally on the diagnosis and use of learning styles.

DIAGNOSIS BEYOND KNOWLEDGE OF SKILLS

Often in teaching disabled readers little more is needed than a simple diagnosis of skill deficiencies. With prescriptive teaching based on them, skill deficiencies, success is often obtained in a matter of months. However, with the seriously disabled reader, it is not uncommon to work for one or two years with a student and still see very little progress. As Waynne B. James and Michael W. Galbraith (1985) have pointed out, "Experts generally concede that every person has a unique approach to learning. . . . "(p. 20) For this reason it seems all the more important that we thoroughly examine whether teaching to certain modality strengths and weaknesses and to differing learning styles will produce superior results to those obtained by slower and longer teaching of students with severe learning disabilities.

We are implying that the view of the severely disabled reader is often much too simplistic. As a result of this view teachers may use too simplistic a method of testing, which results in inefficient teaching. A number of years ago Edward Wolpert (1971) stressed the point that various ambiguities arise when the modality concept is applied to the process of learning rather than to the act of reading. He stated, as we have, that the tests often do not test in a situation analogous to the act of reading. For example, a student may be given certain subtests of the *WISC-R* that have little relationship to reading, and on the basis of these subtests be classified as poor in visual perceptual skills. Although the student may grade poorly on the subtests, this does not necessarily mean that he or she will not be a good visual learner in reading-type tasks. Wolpert also pointed out that even to divide tasks as indicated on most tests into auditory and visual is probably a false dichotomy, since most tasks call for the use of both modalities.

Perhaps a more realistic view of the learning task for a severely disabled reader was described by Jean Piaget as related by John Blackie (1968). Piaget portrayed learning as composed of two processes, assimilation and accommodation. Blackie said, "Assimilation is what is done to what has to be learned so that it can be learned, and accommodation is what the learner has to do within himself in order to learn." (p. 40) In diagnosis beyond the level of skills it is assimilation and accommodation that matter.

When you face the question of how to teach the severely disabled reader, it is easy to believe there must be a miracle cure or magical approach if only you can identify it. Our experience as teachers and as supervisors of clinics that serve students with severe reading problems has led us to the following conclusions:

1. Most disabled readers learn successfully if sound diagnostic-remedial procedures (particularly those described in Chapters 4, 5, and 6) are employed over time and if the readers have sufficient opportunities to apply the skills in the act of reading.
2. For those who still do not succeed, the best hope lies in providing tradi-

tional instructional procedures, but doing it better. *Better* may mean more instruction with smaller increments of learning over a longer period. It should be noted that traditional procedures encompass the wide range of approaches heretofore described.

3. For the *very few* students who fail to read successfully after the best reading instruction you can reasonably provide, it may make sense to try other approaches, even if there is a lack of sound research evidence to support them.

4. Some approaches that do not appear justified at this time may prove to be valuable as understanding of the reading process and how individuals learn expands. Also, new approaches to teaching the severely disabled reader will continue to emerge.

It is in this context that we present this chapter. We shall be discussing theories that have yet to be proven and critically examining some of the existing evidence about them. A reading specialist may reject a particular approach after becoming aware of the lack of evidence supporting it; we hope no one would continue to embrace an approach *in spite* of evidence to the contrary. Instead, we welcome future research that may modify what we know.

HOW HUMANS LEARN

The Socony Vacuum Oil Company (Ekwall and Oswald) did an interesting study on how humans learn in terms of retention. It has some important implications for diagnosis and remediation:

Students' Power of Retention
1. 10 percent of what they read
2. 20 percent of what they hear
3. 30 percent of what they see
4. 50 percent of what they see and hear
5. 70 percent of what they say as they talk
6. 90 percent of what they say as they do a thing

The information in this study is of a general nature, and the relative efficiency of one method of presentation over another often depends on several factors discussed in the section "Research on Methods of Presentation of Modalities." However, it is evident that some of the teaching procedures most often used are of little value in getting students to retain what you teach them. Consider the value of telling students something (20 percent retention) versus getting them to say a thing as they do it (90 percent retention). Even if you were able to cover twice as much information in a lecture, it would be less efficient in the end than if only half as much information were covered but in one of the more efficient ways. Based on this, in teaching you might use more of the following types of procedures:

1. Whenever teaching a new concept, at least illustrate it using the chalk-board or overhead projector so students can hear and see the information at the same time. This brings retention up to 50 percent versus 20 percent from an oral presentation alone.
2. Whenever possible have students voice a new principle, rule, word, etc., shortly after it has been taught (70 percent).
3. Whenever something new is taught, get students to do something with it: write or illustrate the rule, use a new word in a written sentence while they say the word and sentence, or get them to act out suitable words as they say them. This can easily be done with words such as *wash, throw, run.*

It is evident why the kinesthetic-tactile or Fernald approach is often of considerable value. The procedure automatically incorporates the most effective techniques discussed in this study.

THE THEORY OF MODALITY DIAGNOSIS AND ITS IMPLICATIONS

There is controversy among reading and learning-disabilities specialists about the value of modality-based diagnoses and instruction. The notion that individual students possess varying strengths and weaknesses in their sensory modality capabilities is logical. Furthermore, it seems reasonable to believe that one can identify students' modality preferences and prescribe instruction accordingly. Modality-based teaching has strong intuitive appeal.

In this section we will define the modality concept and describe the test most often used for diagnosis in this area. Then we will examine the research. Later in the chapter we will present methods for diagnosing and teaching to specific modalities.

The most commonly recognized and diagnosed learning modalities are auditory, visual, kinesthetic, and a combination of all of these. When referred to in the literature, however, they are usually listed as VAKT, or visual, auditory, kinesthetic, and tactile. The term *kinesthetic* is an adjective derived from the noun *kinesthesia,* derived from *kinema,* or motion, and *aesthesis,* referring to perception. It means sensation of position or movement. The term tactile, of course, refers to the sense of touch. The term *VAKT* is also used for a teaching method very similar to the Fernald approach (Chapter 9). Since it would be almost impossible to use a kinesthetic without a tactile approach, the term *tactile* is often omitted.

The *Mills Learning Methods Test* was at one time one of the best known instruments for testing learning modalities. It is designed to determine whether a student learns words best by a phonic or auditory, visual, kinesthetic, or combination method. The *Learning Methods Test* contains a series of words supposedly representing the primer, first-, second-, and third-grade levels. Each of a set of cards has a word on one side and the same word and a picture representing it on the other side. The student is given the lists of words to pronounce until the lowest level is found in which he or she misses forty words. These forty words are divided into groups of ten. Each day ten words are taught in strict accordance with one of the four methods. Fifteen minutes is spent on each group of words. The *Learning Methods Test* can be used quite successfully by someone who is adept in it. However, it has a number of drawbacks that make it impractical in many situations. For example, after ten words are taught by one method, the student is given an immediate recall test. The next day the student takes a delayed recall test on the words learned the first day. After the delayed recall test the student is taught ten words by another method and is given another immediate recall test. The third day the student takes a delayed recall test on the words taught on the second day and learns ten more words by another method. It takes five days, since one day must elapse before the student can be given the delayed recall test on the last set of words. After the fifth day the clinician determines which method was most successful on the delayed recall test. The fact that it takes five days or more is a drawback for many clinicians, since they do not see the student on a daily basis or do not have a five-day period in which to complete their testing. It also presents a problem when the testing is not begun on a Monday, since it is then necessary to complete the testing during the following week, which does not allow equal periods to elapse before the delayed recall tests.

The methodology in several of the approaches has also been criticized. For example, as a part of the visual approach the student is presented the ten words picture side up and is told to look at the picture and then at the word. Maria A. Ceprano (1981), after doing a thorough review of the research, concluded that a number of sound studies using comparable methodology have produced conflicting results as to whether pictures do or do not help children learn sight words. Ceprano believed that the discrepant results may have been due to the differences in how the cues were presented. For this reason it seems that a particular method of presenting words and pictures may be more important for a specific student than the overall approach.

Perhaps a more serious problem is the fact that only a few concrete nouns and verbs can be illustrated. Many pictures thought of as being representative of a certain word by one student may represent another word to a second student. It stands to reason that if one used the *Learning Methods Test* and determined that a student learned best by the visual approach, it would still not guarantee success for that student, since so many words cannot be illustrated or would not be taught as in the test. In using the visual method Mills also suggests that a figure or outline of the shape or gestalt of each word be drawn on the board so that the student can match each word with this shape.

This practice has also been questioned by a number of modern writers. The major problem, of course, is that many words have exactly the same shape:

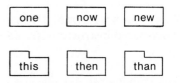

Therefore, the shape is of little value in helping a student distinguish between words. A third major criticism of the *Learning Methods Test* is that the directions are somewhat unclear. We have used it for some time in our remedial reading classes and have found that not all students interpret the directions the same way.

In spite of what may appear to be rather severe criticisms of the *Learning Methods Test,* it is a good training instrument for the concept of testing the various learning modalities, and we recommend that it be used for this purpose. However, when a reading clinician is able to see a student for only a short time, certain modifications in the Mills procedure need to be made. We also suggest certain modifications, even in a normal remedial situation. These techniques will be discussed later in the chapter.

Reviews of research on modality approaches have cast grave doubt about their efficacy. After reviewing fifteen studies, Sara Tarver and Margaret Dawson (1978) concluded that there was no evidence supporting an interaction between modality preference and method of teaching reading "when we are concerned with actual methods of teaching reading and measures of reading achievement rather than listening tasks and measures of recall or recognition." (p. 13) The authors concluded:

> It would seem efficacious at this time to devote more of our efforts to investigating the requirements of the reading task at the various stages of learning to read. . . . This information, in combination with assessment of each child's learning rate, may promote more effective individualization of reading instruction, individualization based on quantitative differences in rates of progression through an established sequence of reading skills rather than qualitative differences in perceptual functioning. (p. 16)

In Chapter 4 we quoted the opinion of Thomas Kampwirth and Marion Bates (1980), who reviewed twenty-two studies that compared auditory and visual preferences of children under ten to auditory and/or visual methods of teaching words to them. Kampwirth and Bates reported that twenty of the twenty-two studies indicated no significant correlation between modality preferences and teaching approaches. One study found that the auditory instructional approach was significantly more effective than the visual approach for both auditory and visual learners. One study found the visual approach to be most effective with both groups. Thus the reviewers concluded that there was little or no evidence to support the idea that remedial instruction should be based on modality preference.

In a response to Kampwirth and Bates, Walter Barbe, Raymond Swassing, and Michael Milone (1981) argued that modality-based instruction should not be rejected at present because:

1. The fact that "something has not been found does not mean it does not exist." (p. 263)
2. "The failure to discover significant aptitude-treatment interactions between modality strengths and reading instructional methods may reflect inadequacies of experimental design features rather than the lack of a relationship between the variables of interest." (p. 264)
3. "Unless the variable of teacher modality strength is controlled, the study of pupil modality strengths and reading may be flawed." (p. 265)
4. "The criteria for determining who is visual, auditory, and kinesthetic in preference are not well established." (p. 265)
5. "Modality is not a fixed characteristic." (p. 265)
6. Ninety-five percent of the teachers of learning-disabled children believe that the research supports this approach.

Barbe, Swassing, and Milone concluded, "Although no clear-cut evidence has been produced to support this practice, those who oppose it have not been able to muster proof that it is not useful." (p. 266)

Kampwirth (1981) responded to the response in part by writing:

If we concluded . . . that we should recommend a certain procedure in spite of there being no evidence to support it, then it removes educational practice from the realm of science and relegates it to a set of notions one tries because they have intuitive appeal or face (faith?) validity. (p. 267)

and:

The fact that 95 percent of these teachers believe in a concept does not make it true, it simply makes it popular. (p. 268)

There is also some indication that students' mode of learning may be cultural and experiential as well as constitutional. Frank Riessmann (1962) indicated that culturally disadvantaged students are often oriented toward physical and visual learning rather than aural learning. The fact that deprived students are often poor in listening abilities has been demonstrated in a number of other studies. Typical of these was one by Ronald Linder and Henry Fillmer (1970), who studied the comparative effectiveness of auditory, visual, and a combination of auditory-visual presentations in second-grade Southern black male students who were disabled readers. Linder and Fillmer found the total auditory performance to be significantly poorer than the total visual and the total auditory-visual for the tasks performed. However, there were no significant differences between students' performance on the total visual and the auditory-visual results. In concluding their study Linder and Fillmer stated,

> As in all studies, individual children in this study did demonstrate a preference for one modality over another. The results reported have been group performances rather than individual. But there are several cases in which the results of the group study were contradicted by individuals, making the listing of generalizations a hazardous undertaking. Once again research indicates that not all pupils may be expected to learn more effectively from one single type of presentation. (p. 22)

Etta Miller (1979) further expanded on this point and offered a possible solution to the confusion:

> Research on modality preference does not account for the findings that under any method used some children with a particular modality preference learn to read easily while others with the same strength, receiving the same instruction and using the same materials fail. With little research to indicate the best procedures, teachers need to continue *to present words in a variety of ways* [emphasis ours]. This repetition of presentation may help children to build associations, to remember word forms, to make use of linguistic and syntactic clues, and perhaps, to attract and to hold the attention of boys and girls who have poor attending behavior. It may turn out that cognitive skills are more important to initial reading success than perceptual ones. (pp. 103–104)

We conclude that the modality-preference approach can be justified only as a last resort or heroic approach, to be tried after other remedial techniques have failed. It is possible that in the future other evidence will suggest a broader application of this method. Diagnostic remedial procedures for discovering and teaching to dominant modalities should be viewed in this light. Albert Harris and Edward Sipay (1985) agree:

> . . . Perhaps the modality model is invalid, or it may be that the available assessment and instructional procedures are inadequate. . . . Or perhaps significant results were not obtained because the treatment worked for only a few children, and so any positive results were washed out in a comparison of mean scores. . . . (p. 430)

RESEARCH ON METHODS OF PRESENTATION OF MODALITIES

Some important generalizations on the kind of presentations that may be effective for learning were summarized by the landmark studies of Sam Duker (1965):

1. Combination presentations tend to be more efficient than auditory or visual presentation alone.
2. When the learner is familiar with the material, he or she is likely to retain more from an auditory presentation. If the material is unfamiliar, he or she is likely to retain more from a visual presentation.
3. Students with higher intelligence seem to benefit more from a visual presentation.
4. Students who read better seem to learn better through a visual presentation.
5. As students grow older they tend to learn better through a visual presentation. At the age of six they learn better as a group through an aural presentation; however, by the time they reach sixteen they learn better as a group through a visual presentation.
6. Difficult material seems to be learned better through a visual presentation, while easier material is learned better through an auditory presentation.
7. Students' immediate comprehension of information seems to favor a visual presentation, while long-term comprehension seems to favor an auditory presentation.
8. The efficiency of a visual presentation seems to decrease as the interval of delayed recall increases.
9. One of the advantages of a visual presentation is the opportunity for review of the material. When the material or the teaching situation is of such a nature that less referability is possible, the efficiency of a visual presentation is lessened.
10. Material that is well organized or follows a sequence is better understood with an auditory presentation. Material that is discrete and unrelated is better understood with a visual presentation.
11. A visual presentation tends to favor ease of learning, while retention seems to favor an oral presentation.

Robert Mills (1965) derived some interesting and pertinent generalizations from a study using his *Learning Methods Test* to evaluate various techniques of word recognition. Mills stressed that the findings pertained to the learning of words only, not necessarily to phonics or other reading skills. Mills studied a group of male and female subjects in grades two to four. His general conclusions:

1. The phonic method was least effective for the children with low intelligence (as a whole). The kinesthetic method was best for the same children in the greatest number of cases, but it was not statistically better than the visual or combinations methods.
2. For children with high intelligence the kinesthetic method was least effective.
3. The combination and visual methods were about equally good for children of average intelligence.
4. Children of high intelligence seemed to learn quite well by all methods; however, the visual method was superior to the kinesthetic method for this group.
5. For seven-year-olds the visual method appeared to be best, and the same group did poorest on the kinesthetic method. The phonic and combination methods did not appear to be especially effective or ineffective with this group.
6. The eight-year-olds did better with the kinesthetic method. Mills believed that the fact that this group was just becoming proficient with handwriting made some difference in this case.
7. For nine-year-olds no method was outstandingly effective or ineffective; however, the visual method did tend to be better than the kinesthetic method.
8. Mills found that children who had higher intelligence tended to learn words faster than those with lower intelligence; however, he found that there was no consistent relationship between age and a child's readiness to learn words.

In conclusion Mills stated:

Because different children learn to recognize words most efficiently by different teaching methods, the classroom teacher must be aware of these individual differences when he applies group-instruction techniques. Our research indicates the need for the teacher to familiarize himself with all the various techniques and to be versatile in the use of these if he is to teach all the children.

In individual cases of failure to make the expected growth in word-recognition skills, our research indicates the need for a diagnostic study of the child to determine the most appropriate method for the particular individual. (p. 225)

This suggests that at least some students may have a preferred mode of learning. It is possible that some students become disabled readers because they are exposed to teaching procedures that provide little opportunity for them to learn. To say that they do not learn because they are seldom or ever exposed to any portion of a certain method, however, would be an oversimplification, since it is virtually impossible for any student to go through school without being exposed to a combination of the various methods discussed by Mills.

DIAGNOSTIC TECHNIQUES FOR DISCOVERING DOMINANT MODALITIES, COGNITIVE STYLES, AND LEARNING RATES

After a student has had an initial diagnosis and remediation is begun, three questions may arise in the mind of the teacher: Is there a particular modality that seems most successful? Does the student seem to exhibit a particular cognitive style on which you can capitalize? How much instructional time is necessary; how much repetition? This section is designed to help develop the skills to answer these questions about each student.

DIAGNOSTIC TECHNIQUES FOR DISCOVERING DOMINANT MODALITIES

Before offering specific suggestions, we repeat that Mills's *Learning Methods Test* is designed to help you discover students' dominant modalities, and where time permits, it can be used successfully. On the other hand, certain features of Mills's test make it difficult to use. Furthermore, it is our opinion that several of its techniques have little or no value in the diagnostic-teaching process. What follows is a less formal technique for attempting to discover students' dominant modalities.

The Time Factor

Mills stresses, and we agree, that when testing various modalities on a particular student, it is important to control the amount of time spent on each one. Mills suggests fifteen minutes and exactly ten words for each modality. We have no argument with his time or the number of words that he suggests, except in many situations it is not practical to spend fifteen minutes per day on five successive days on each set of words. The essential point is that the same amount of time be spent in teaching using each modality. If your time is limited you may want to modify the time to five or ten minutes; however, the period chosen should remain consistent.

Material to Be Taught

Students' preferences for certain modalities are likely to affect the way they learn many things; however, in reading it usually shows up in the learning of words. This in itself presents problems, since some words cannot be illustrated with pictures. Edward Wolpert (1972) studied the relationships of word recognition to length, shape, and imagery. Wolpert was concerned with the ease with which forty-two first-grade children learned words varying in imagery value, length, and configuration. He found that his subjects learned a significantly greater number of three-letter words than five-letter words. His students also learned a significantly greater number of high-imagery words (such as *nose*) than low-imagery words (such as *same*). Word configuration did not seem to be so important as the other two factors. The point is that the results obtained in modality testing may to some extent depend on these extraneous factors, which may not always be apparent. For this reason results obtained from modality testing should be reconfirmed several times through careful diagnostic teaching as the student's remediation progresses.

Also, the words chosen for the Mills test should be of similar length and imagery value. Word length is quite easy to control, but imagery value presents a much more difficult problem. In our own reading centers we pick words that do not have high imagery value but that are generally in the speaking-listening vocabulary of the student.

In using the Mills learning test it is often difficult to find forty words at any level that older students do not know. However, in a less formal setting you can pick words from the basic sight word list in Chapter 4 or from any other good source such as Edward Fry's Instant Word List (1980).

Although words on lists may appear at preprimer, primer, first-, second-grade levels, etc., the preprimer or primer words are not necessarily easier to learn than the words on the second- or third-grade list. Preprimer words are so because they have traditionally been so. They usually appear more often in print than words at a higher grade level. However, if the student does not know them to begin with, there is very little difference in difficulty. On the other hand, after a student begins to read, he or she is likely to encounter high-utility words more often, and simply because of multiple exposure is likely to know them in a month or two. But, for recall a day or two later the imagery value of the word and its length are of more importance than its grade level. Therefore, if the words are in an older student's speaking-listening vocabulary, or in other words if the student can use them in a sentence, it does not make any difference if words from several levels are mixed for modality-testing purposes.

In some situations it is not practical to teach ten words by each of the modalities to be tested. If your time is limited, you may wish to cut the number to five or six and teach two sets per day. You must, however, present the same number of words using each learning modality.

The Teaching Procedure for Each Modality

Whatever learning modality is found to produce the best test results in delayed recall, the ultimate goal, it must be practical for everyday teaching. Many words cannot be illustrated by pictures, and, furthermore, many teachers are not artistic enough to illustrate them. For this reason it seems futile to concern yourself with whether a student can learn words through pictures.

This teaching procedure for four different modalities can be modified slightly for some students yet should in most cases be practical for daily use.

A. Phonic or Auditory Modality Approach
   1. Have the words to be learned on cards approximately 3½ in. × 8 in. Present the first card and pronounce it slowly while pointing to each phoneme. Do not try to pronounce it letter by letter if there are graphemes in the word that do not represent separate sounds. Do this a second time, asking the student to pronounce each part after you.
   2. Say the word rapidly and ask the student to say it rapidly after you.
   3. Ask the student to use the word in a sentence. If the student cannot, use it in a sentence for him or her. Then ask the student to make up a sentence.

(All students can do these first three steps and should be required to. Whether the following steps are done will depend on the phonics ability of the student. A sequence is suggested, but if the student cannot do some parts, do not waste time on them. Spend more time doing the parts with which the student is successful. In other words this approach may be modified from this point forward to fit the learning style of particular student.)

   4. Discuss the sounds in the word. If the student knows all of them, go on to the next word. If the student does not know them, point to the first one and ask the student to think of other words that begin with it. Do this same procedure with middle and ending sounds. Do not have the student look for little words in big words. If the student notes a little word in a larger word and its sound remains the same in the larger word, acknowledge that what he or she says is true, but do not encourage the practice. If the smaller word does not retain its sound in the larger word, explain that little words often change when they are a part of a longer word.
   5. If time allows, find and classify all words into piles that have the same beginning, middle, or ending sounds.
   6. The time spent on discussion of other words that rhyme with the beginning sounds of words will vary with the time allowed for teaching and the number of words to be taught. Gauge your time accordingly. Be sure to allow time to review all words to be taught by this method during the last minute or so before stopping.

B. Sight or Visual Modality Approach
   1. Have the words to be learned on cards approximately 3½ in. ×
      8 in. Point to the first word or sweep across it and pronounce it:
      "This word is *among.*"
   2. Ask the student to use the word in a sentence. If the student
      cannot, then use it in a sentence to demonstrate. Ask the student
      to make up a sentence of his or her own.
   3. Ask the student to look at the word and to look for anything
      about it that will help him or her to remember it, e.g., the double
      e's in *seen* or the length of the word. If the student does not
      respond well to this, repeat steps 1 through 3 with the next word
      and ask the student to tell you how the two words differ.
   4. After all words have been taught, ask the student to make a
      sentence out of the words, adding any other words necessary to
      complete the sentence.
   5. Have the student separate the words into categories that seem
      significant to him or her, e.g., all words with three letters and all
      words having no tall letters.
   6. Allow time to review all words before stopping.
C. Kinesthetic-Tactile Modality Approach
   1. Begin this approach with nothing on the cards and with the
      specific words to be taught on a small list beside you. Print the
      first word on a card, saying the part of the word as you write it.
      Then say the word and have the student repeat it.
   2. Have the student trace over the word several times using middle
      and index fingers. Be sure both fingers are in contact with the
      part being traced. Be sure the student says the word part while
      tracing it. Try to avoid emphasizing specific sounds.
   3. As with the other methods, have the student use the word in a
      sentence. If the student cannot, use it in a sentence yourself and
      then have the student use it in another sentence.
   4. After the student has traced it several times, give the student a
      new card and have him or her attempt to write it from memory.
      If the student begins to make a mistake, stop him or her, repeat
      steps 1 through 4, and have the student attempt it again. *Do not
      let the student write it wrong.*
   5. Allow time to review all words before stopping.
D. Combination Modality Approach
   1. Begin with the words printed on the cards. Tell the student the
      word and quickly trace over it, pronouncing it as you do so.
      Then pronounce it quickly.
   2. Have the student trace over it, again using middle and index
      fingers and saying the word parts as they are traced. Then have
      the student say the whole word quickly.
   3. Have the student use the word in a sentence. If the student

cannot, do so yourself and have the student make up a sentence
of his or her own.

4. Discuss any known sounds in the word and discuss the word
   length and any configuration that will help the student remember
   it.
5. Have the student classify words by stacking cards into piles with
   the same beginning, middle, or ending sounds, by word length or
   by specific configurations.
6. Allow time to review all words before stopping.

In using these procedures, keep the following important points in mind:

1. Do not attempt to teach too many words in too short a period. It is
   better to learn fewer words and review them than to be so hurried on
   the last few words that they are not covered well.
2. It is delayed recall (at least a day or more) that really matters in terms
   of the best approach for a particular student. Keep this in mind even
   though immediate recall using a particular approach seems quite effective.
3. If certain parts of some modality approaches seem successful while others do not, do not hesitate to combine the approaches that seem to be
   most successful.
4. Remember that as students learn, their modality strengths may change,
   so do not become permanently wedded to any one approach, but constantly diagnose as you teach to determine whether the original modality diagnosis was correct or whether slight changes from time to time
   may be in order.

Diagnosing and Teaching to Specific Cognitive Styles

For many years teachers have noted characteristics that relate to the learning
style of certain disabled readers. Cognitive styles are usually classified as impulsive or reflective and field-dependent or -independent as well as according
to modality preferences. Harryette B. Ehrhardt (1980) noted that cognitive
style is a matter of behavior as well as preference and that it cannot be measured quantitatively on a norm-referenced basis, as with general achievement.
Ehrhardt also said that teaching to cognitive style was usually based on the
premises that individuals have preferences in learning style and that individual
learning styles are identifiable.

Most teachers are familiar with the student who hurriedly guesses at words
even though he or she possesses adequate word-attack skills. Other students
continually make repetitions to correct omissions and/or insertions. Some students, even though they can repeat numerous rules for word-attack skills, seldom attempt to read an unfamiliar word. These are all types of impulsive-
reflective students.

Students who are classified as field-dependent are sensitive to social situations and prefer learning in the company of others. They also tend to be easily influenced and generally tend to conform (Harris & Sipay, 1985). Students who are field-independent tend to be impersonal, analytical, and not easily influenced.

Whether the practice of identifying and teaching to cognitive styles is valid is still questionable. Edward Scott and Frederick R. Annesley (1976) studied nine dimensions of cognitive style and suggested that two of the nine were significantly related to reading achievement. These two were dependence/independence and reflectivity/impulsivity. Scott and Annesley believed that field-dependent children make more global responses and have been shown to have a lower level of reading achievement than field-independent children, who, they say, perceive things analytically. They maintained that cognitive styles should be taken into consideration in determining which materials to use and in relation to the personality characteristics of the teacher.

Alan Neal (1974) studied reflectivity and impulsivity in fourth-grade students. He concluded that the impulsive student's behavior could be modified through verbal exhortation, a finding that should hold a great deal of hope for the teacher attempting to help the student who makes errors of what is often termed carelessness. Other researchers such as Ralph H. Huhn, Jr. (1981) have presented approaches to working with impulsive students classified as impulsive.

Torney-Miller (1981) and Christiansen (1980) have failed to support the hypotheses of diagnosing and teaching to cognitive styles.

It seems premature to attempt to launch large-scale programs to diagnose and remediate according to cognitive styles. On the other hand, it is prudent to be especially observant of the characteristics students display in the remedial reading classroom, especially in the area of field-independence/dependence and reflectivity/impulsivity.

From a practical standpoint, in dealing with cognitive styles, the remedial reading teacher can follow this diagnostic teaching procedure:

1. Note whether the student systematically applies word-attack skills. If not, teach the skills necessary for attacking similar words. Once the student has learned a few necessary rules, note whether he or she seems to be able to think through and apply these rules. If so, the more rule-oriented route may be correct. If the student can give the rules verbally but not apply them, give him or her some practice in the application of the rules. If after considerable practice the student still is not able to apply them, consider a more automatic or less rule-oriented approach to word attack. During the course of about three years (one hour per day), one popular phonics series teaches 120 to 130 phonic generalizations. Many students seem to do well with this program, but regardless of the time spent in the program, some students never apply these rules. For them the automatic approach may be called for. In

teaching it you may wish to teach automatic recall of most phonemes in the test in Appendix A when students see the written forms (graphemes). They can then learn phonograms or word families of high utility or compile lists of these on their own. Having learned the phonemes of high utility plus a number of word families or phonograms, a student will almost automatically be able to attack a great many words. Although this method may never be as systematic as rules and generalizations, it enables students to attack a great many words without a long reasoning process.

2. Through oral diagnosis note whether the student reads rapidly at the expense of comprehension. If so, discuss the need for more careful observation of word configuration and/or phonetic or structural analysis.[1]

3. Keep in mind that some students possess a sixth sense or innate psycholinguistic ability for learning the rules of the language. An occasional error that does not greatly change the meaning of a passage or that does not indicate lack of word-attack skills may not indicate the need for formal training in word attack. The student's time might better be spent in free reading or other worthy endeavors.

DIAGNOSING RATE OF LEARNING

Most classroom teachers get to know their students well enough to know which ones learn faster than the others. We often hear statements such as, "Denise just can't seem to learn no matter how hard I try to teach her," or "We must have gone over that word twenty times in class and Syril still doesn't know it." The first statement is quite unlikely to be true, but the second one may very well be true and be nothing extraordinary.

Most students require at least twenty exposures to a word before it becomes a sight word. It is not uncommon for slower students to require over 100 exposures before a word is instantly known; some may require as many as 200. Yet many remedial reading teachers feel that a student is almost incapable of learning if the student has not thoroughly learned a word exposed four or five times a day over three or four days. However, five times per day for three successive periods is only fifteen exposures, or fewer than the minimum required for a rapid learner in a developmental situation.

Marvin Wyne and Gary Stuck (1979) found that remedial students who received intervention to improve their time-on-task behavior achieved at a significantly higher rate in reading than their counterparts who did not receive the treatment. The improved performance of the experimental group was

---

[1]See Ekwall, E. E. *Locating and Correcting Reading Difficulties,* (3rd ed.), Columbus, OH: Charles E. Merrill, 1985, for a thorough analysis of the causes and remediation of specific types of errors.

maintained after their return to a regular classroom. Other recent research has confirmed the importance of pupils' on-task behavior as a critical factor in learning. Teachers should consider that one possible explanation for students' failure is that they do not always *attend* to material and information as it is being presented.

Most adults have forgotten how difficult it was to learn to read. Albert Einstein is reported to have said that learning to read was the most difficult task man has ever devised. You must be cognizant of just how difficult it is for some students to learn so that you can develop an adequate perspective on how much time you must expect to spend with each student on learning a new word, a vowel sound, a vowel rule, a syllable principle. When remedial reading teachers do this on an organized basis, they are often pleasantly surprised to find that many of their disabled readers are not slow learners at all.

From a practical standpoint learning rate can be judged by the following techniques:

1. Make note of one or two sight words that you wish to teach to a particular student. Then note on your daily record form (see Daily Lesson Plan Form in Chapter 15), as accurately as you can, how many times the word was taught and reviewed. You may also wish to ask the student to count the times he or she comes across the word in reading. After it is evident the student has mastered the word, check as nearly as possible the number of exposures or the amount of teaching it has taken.

2. Use the same recording procedure after teaching other concepts such as a vowel rule or syllabication principle. Then note whether the student can merely state the rule or whether he or she applies it regularly. If the student knows a principle but does not apply it, note the number of worksheets or application lessons it has generally taken before the student was actually able to apply the rule. Some never get to the point of actual application on a routine basis.

It would be unrealistic to do this sort of thing on a regular basis with every word or concept. On the other hand, we have found that university students who regularly do this exercise with disabled readers, often raise their perception of a student's ability to learn, and teacher expectation ultimately affects students' self-concepts.

Diagnosing and Using Information About Learning Styles

As we noted in Chapter 2, Public Law 94–142 mandates that an individual educational plan (IEP) be prepared for each handicapped student. The IEP must include "a specific statement describing the child's learning style."

Most researchers and writers agree that individuals have a preferred learning style; however, experts do not agree on how to define or explain learning styles. Lois R. Holtzclaw (1985) says, "The term 'learning style' refers to a student's constant way of responding and using stimuli in the context of learning." (p. 24) Waynne B. James and Michael W. Galbraith (1985) suggest that the learning styles of individuals be classified as perceptual, cognitive, emotional and social modes but not be limited to these. Perceptual style is the means by which a student extracts information from the environment using the senses. Cognitive modality is the mental processing of information; emotional style refers to the student's personal feelings, attitudes and personality states, all of which influence information gathering. Social modality deals with social sets that help or hinder learning.

James and Galbraith say that perceptual modality comprises seven parts:

Print: A student is print-oriented if he or she prefers to learn through reading.

Aural: A student who is aurally oriented is likely to learn best through listening. This person enjoys audio tapes and listening to what other learners have to say.

Interactive: An interactive student enjoys discussions with other students on a one-to-one basis or in small groups.

Visual: Visual learners do best through pictures, graphs, slides, demonstrations, films, etc.

Haptic: Haptic learners do best through the sense of touch. This type of person assimilates information through a hands-on approach.
James and Galbraith differentiate tactile from haptic learning: tactile refers to the fingers, while haptic implies the use of the entire hand.

Kinesthetic: The person who is kinesthetically oriented learns best while moving.

Olfactory: This refers to the use of the sense of smell in learning.

Although these authors are concerned with adult education, they offer the following two instruments to help in the identification of perceptual style. We believe the remedial reading teacher may find these useful, although in many cases the teacher may need to convert the instruments to interview style.

One of the most prolific advocates of the use of reading style and learning style inventories is Marie Carbo, also the author of the *Reading Style Inventory.* Carbo (1984*a*) states:

An impressive and growing body of research on the Dunn and Dunn (1978) model of learning style indicates that (a) reading achievement and attitudes improve significantly when youngsters are taught to read through their individual styles, (b) student learning style preferences for reading differ significantly across grade and achievement levels, and (c) the *Learning Style Inventory* and the *Reading Style Inventory* are valid and reliable instruments that can help educators improve reading instruction. (p. 72)

FIGURE 10–1   Questions Related to Perceptual Learning Style Identification

Questions Related to Identifying Strong Perceptual Elements		*Questions Related to Identifying Weak Perceptual Elements*
PRINT:		
Do you remember quickly and easily what you read?	OR	Do you have to read articles several times before grasping the important concepts?
Can you learn something better after seeing it or after writing it?		Do the words on the page all seem to run together?
AURAL:		
Do you tend to remember and repeat those ideas you heard verbally presented?	OR	Do you find it difficult to remember information presented in lectures?
Do you "hear" what others are telling you?		Do audio tapes leave you wanting to read the information?
INTERACTIVE:		
Do you like to use other people as sounding boards?	OR	Do you find that you do not get much information from small group/discussion activities?
Do you enjoy question/answer sessions or small group discussions?		Would you prefer not to discuss things with others, preferring instead to work alone?
VISUAL:		
Do you need to have a "picture" in your mind before comprehending something?	OR	Do visual representations such as graphs or tables leave you wanting an explanation?
Do you "see" what others are trying to tell you?		Do you find it difficult to picture things in your mind?
Do you create visual images as you think?		Do you fail to understand displays or charts?
HAPTIC:		
Do you feel that you have to touch the new things you are learning?	OR	Do you find it difficult to distinguish the feel of different items?
Are hands-on experiences important to you?		Does touching objects fail to create a visual image in your mind?
KINESTHETIC:		
Do you think you learn better when you are able to move during your learning?	OR	Do you find movement distracting?
Do you like to move your hands (knit, crochet, doodle) while learning, not from boredom, but because it helps you concentrate?		Is it hard to concentrate on learning something if you are also moving or doing something else?
OLFACTORY:		
Do smells have any special significance for you?	OR	Do you find smells basically offensive?
Can you associate a particular smell with specific past memories?		Do smells detract from your learning?
Are you frequently able to identify smells?		Do you find it hard to distinguish between different smells?

From *Lifelong Learning*. Vol. 8 #4, Waynne B. James and Michael W. Galbraith, Perceptual Learning Styles: Implications and techniques for the practitioner, p. 22.

FIGURE 10–2 Perceptual Learning Style Inventory

Check below the strategies/techniques through which you *think* you learn best.

1. ____ motion pictures
2. ____ lecture, information-giving
3. ____ group discussion
4. ____ reading assignments
5. ____ role playing with you as a participant
6. ____ project construction
7. ____ odor discrimination activities
8. ____ television programs
9. ____ autio tapes
10. ____ participant in panel discussions
11. ____ written reports
12. ____ nonverbal/body movements
13. ____ drawing, painting, or sculpturing
14. ____ tasting
15. ____ slides
16. ____ records
17. ____ question-answer sessions
18. ____ independent reading
19. ____ physical motion activities
20. ____ model building
21. ____ scented materials (such as scratch and sniff)
22. ____ graphs, tables, and charts
23. ____ recitations by others
24. ____ interviews
25. ____ writing
26. ____ participant in physical games
27. ____ touching objects
28. ____ photographs

CIRCLE THE NUMBERS YOU CHECKED IN PREVIOUS FIGURE.

If a majority of numbers for a particular style are circled, consider the possibility that you may have a learning style similiar to the one indicated. Identification of your learning style orientation should identify ways in which to expand your learning effectiveness.

STRATEGY NUMBERS	STYLE
1, 8, 15, 22, 28	VISUAL
2, 9, 16, 23	AURAL
3, 10, 17, 24	INTERACTIVE
4, 11, 18, 25	PRINT
5, 12, 19, 26	KINESTHETIC
6, 13, 20, 27	HAPTIC
7, 14, 21	OLFACTORY

From *Lifelong Learning,* Vol. 8 #4, Waynne B. James and Michael W. Galbraith, Perceptual Learning Styles: Implications and techniques for the practitioner, p. 23.

Carbo maintains that research in reading and learning style can be divided into five major categories: (1) environmental preferences, (2) perceptual strengths/preferences, (3) perceptual development, (4) comparisons across grade levels, and (5) comparisons across achievement levels.

Factors involved in environmental preferences include such things as the student's preferences for quiet versus noisy study areas, amount of light, and formal versus informal design such as sitting in a hard chair or at a desk versus sitting on rugs or pillows. Perceptual strengths are covered in detail in the preceding section. Perceptual development refers to age-grade factors regarding perceptual strengths and preferences. Carbo states that the youngest students are the most tactile and kinesthetic, with a gradual development of seeing and finally in grades five and six more dependence on hearing. Carbo also notes that students differ significantly in the way they learn depending upon their age-grade levels: primary students are more global than older students; older students are far less motivated to read; and second and fourth graders prefer more structure in the reading situation than sixth and eighth graders. She also states that older students like reading alone more than do second graders. Carbo says good readers preferred a formal environment, were responsible and persistent, and preferred to learn through hearing and seeing. Poor readers preferred learning tactually and kinesthetically and demonstrated a low preference for learning through visual and auditory modalities.

Carbo maintains that it is crucial to identify individual learning styles of certain students before they experience failure. In her summary Carbo states:

> Considering that most students enter school with an enthusiasm for learning to read and that many become increasingly less motivated to read, it is imperative that educators continue to research this area and to experiment with techniques for matching reading methods, materials, and teaching strategies to individual learning styles. (p. 75)

Shown below is an example of the *Reading Style Inventory* and what it attempts to measure and prescribe as explained by Carbo (1984*b*, 1984*c*).

Carbo's *Reading Style Inventory* may be administered with or without the aid of a computer, and when computer-scored, it provides a profile that advises on dealing with the particular reading style of each student.

Kenneth and Rita Dunn (1986) have listed other style inventories:

Grades K-12: *Learning Style Inventory:* Primary (Perrin). Obtainable from St. John's University Center for the Study of Learning and Teaching Styles, Utopia Parkway, Jamaica, NY 11439
Grades 3-12: *Learning Style Inventory* (Dunn, Dunn, & Price). Obtainable from Price Systems, Box 7818, Lawrence, KS 66046-0067
High School Students: *Productivity Environmental Preference Survey.* Obtainable from Price Systems, Box 7818, Lawrence, KS 66046-0067
Carbo's *Reading Style Inventory* is available from Learning Research Associates, Inc., P.O. Box 39, Roslyn Heights, NY 11577.

There is still much to be learned about the effectiveness of the application of learning styles to diagnosing and teaching. We are in agreement with Harris

FIGURE 10-3 Elements of Reading Style Identified by the *Reading Style Inventory*

I. Environmental Stimuli	***Does the student prefer to read:***
Sound	with music, with talking, in silence?
Light	in bright or dim light?
Temperature	in a warm or cool temperature?
Design	in a formal design (hard chair at a desk) or an informal design (soft chair, rug, floor)?
II. Emotion Stimuli	***When reading, is the student:***
Motivation	self-motivated, not self-motivated, motivated by peers, motivated by adults?
	Does the student:
Persistence	complete reading tasks?
Responsibility	do the reading work agreed upon or assigned?
Structure	prefer: little or much direction when reading? many or few choices of reading materials? reading work checked immediately or seldom? reading work checked by peers, adults, self?
III. Sociological Stimuli	***Does the student prefer to read:***
Peers	with five or six students?
Self	alone?
Pair	with one student?
Teacher	with a teacher?
Varied	with a teacher and students?
IV. Physical Stimuli	***Does the student read best:***
Perceptual	when taught through his/her visual modality, auditory modality, tactual modality, kinesthetic modality, and/or with a multisensory approach?
	Does the student prefer to read:
Intake	when permitted to eat and drink?
Time	in the morning, early afternoon, late afternoon, evening?
Mobility	when permitted to move?

From: The *Reading Style Inventory Manual* by Marie Carbo. 1981, p.2.

and Sipay (1985): "There is, however, no agreement as to what constitutes learning style, and research on its identification and use in reading instruction is still in its infancy." Again, we do not believe strongly in teaching to different modalities, although we have suggested methods of doing so. Carbo has presented considerable positive research information and a good argument for her *Reading Style Inventory*. We do, however, believe she has ignored some of the negative research in her zest for presenting it in a positive light.

SUMMARY

We are persuaded that most disabled readers will learn successfully if traditional diagnostic remedial procedures are employed over time. In rare cases it may be appropriate to try heroic approaches even if substantial research justification is lacking. In some cases it is desirable to diagnose for more than students' knowledge of reading skills. At present the notion that individual students possess different strengths and weaknesses in their sensory capabilities has not been proven. The accumulating evidence suggests that this approach does not lead to improved student performance and that a combination method is most effective. Nonetheless, we have presented techniques for diagnosing and teaching to dominant modalities in the hope that teachers will have a better understanding of this controversial approach and consider it when other approaches have failed.

There is a growing body of research to indicate that students possess different cognitive styles of learning. It appears feasible to note the cognitive style of a disabled reader so as to capitalize on it in teaching.

The remedial reading teacher should be aware of students' learning rates. Studies indicate that there is considerable variance in learning rates from individual to individual. Checking from time to time on the learning rates of individual students often reveals that a given disabled reader is not a slow learner. This can be beneficial to teacher expectation, which often influences student achievement.

During the past decade there has been considerable interest in and some research on the subject of particular learning/reading styles. Although learning style takes cognitive style into consideration, it also deals with a much broader spectrum. We have reviewed this concept as well as information pertaining to diagnosis and teaching to specific learning styles.

REFERENCES

Annesley, F. R. (1976). Cognitive style mapping and facilitation of reading competence—A position paper. (ED 200 913).

Barbe, W. B., Swassing, R. H., & Milone, M. N. (1981). Teaching to modality strengths: Don't give up yet! *Academic Therapy, 16,* 262–266.

Blackie, J. H. (1968). How children learn. *NEA Journal, 57,* 40–42.

Carbo, M. L. (1984). Research in learning style and reading implications. *Theory Into Practice, 23,* 72–76.

Carbo, M. L. (1984). Reading styles: How principals can make a difference. *Principal, 64,* 20–26.

Carbo, M. L. (1984). You can identify reading styles and then design a super reading program. *Early Years, 14,* 80–83.

Ceprano, M. A. (1981). A review of selected research on methods of teaching sight words. *Reading Teacher, 35,* 314–322.

Christiansen, J. C. (1980). Relationship between cognitive style and the acquisition of meaning in content reading. (ED 200 915).

Duker, S. (1965). Listening and reading. *Elementary School Journal, 65,* 321–329.

Dunn, R., Dunn, K., & Price, G. (1977). Diagnosing learning styles: A prescription for avoiding malpractice suits. *Phi Delta Kappan, 58,* 418–420.

Dunn, K., & Dunn, R. (1986). The look of learning styles. *Early Years, 16,* 49–53.

Ehrhardt, H. B. (1980). An overview of cognitive style. (ED 203 939).

Ekwall, E. E., & Oswald, L. D. (1971). *Rx reading program—teacher's manual.* Glenview, IL: Psychotechnics, Inc.

Fry, E. (1980). The new instant word list. *Reading Teacher, 34,* 284–289.

Harris, A. J., & Sipay, E. R. (1985). *How to increase reading ability* (8th ed.). NY: Longman.

Holtzclaw, L. R. (1985). Adult learner's preferred learning styles, choice of courses, and subject areas for prior experiential learning credit. *Lifelong Learning, 8,* 23–27.

Huhn, R. H., Jr. (1981). RSM2P: A meta-cognitive approach for teaching cognitive strategies to facilitate learning. (ED 211 946).

James, W. B., & Galbraith, M. W. (1985). Perceptual learning styles: Implications and techniques for the practitioner. *Lifelong Learning, 4,* 20–23.

Kampwirth, T. J., & Bates, M. (1980). Modality preference and teaching method: A review of the research. *Academic Therapy, 15,* 597–605.

Linder, R., & Fillmer, H. T. (1970). Auditory and visual performance of slow readers. *Reading Teacher, 24,* 17–22.

Miller, E. (1979). First-grade reading instruction and modality preference. *Elementary School Journal, 80,* 99–104.

Mills, R. E. (1965). An evaluation of techniques for teaching word recognition. *Elementary School Journal, 56,* 221–225.

Mills, R. E. (1970). *Learning methods test* (rev. ed.). Fort Lauderdale, FL: The Mills School.

Neal, A. J. (1974). *Reflectivity-impulsivity in grade four students and the apprehension of meanings of unfamiliar words. A study that relates cognitive study and reading behavior.* Paper presented at the International Reading Convention, New Orleans.

Riessmann, F. (1962). *The culturally deprived child.* NY: Harper & Brothers.

Tarver, S. G., & Dawson, M. M. (1978). Modality preference and the teaching of reading: A review. *Journal of Learning Disabilities, 11,* 5–17.

Torney-Miller, J. D. (1981). Relationships among cognitive style, learning style and reading skills. (ED 200 911).

Wolpert, E. M. (1972). Modality and reading: A perspective. *Reading Teacher, 26,* 180–186.

Wyne, M. V., & Stuck, G. B. (1979). Time-on-task and reading performance in under-achieving children. *Journal of Reading Behavior, 11,* 119–128.

11

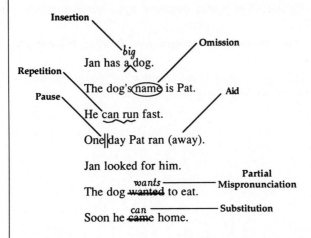

Using Informal Reading Inventories, the Cloze Procedure, and the Analysis of Oral Reading Errors

The first part of this chapter deals with a general description of informal reading inventories and why they are used. Detailed descriptions are given for their administration, scoring, and interpretation. Information on developing your own informal reading inventories is provided as well as information on using informal reading inventory criteria for matching students and instructional material. This is followed by a section on the analysis of error patterns from oral reading errors. The cloze procedure is explained along with information on developing, administering, and scoring cloze passages. Last is information on techniques for using the cloze procedure to place students in graded materials and on how to use the cloze procedure to select materials to meet the needs of students in a particular classroom.

THE INFORMAL READING INVENTORY

What Informal Reading Inventories Are and Why They Are Used

Informal reading inventories (IRIs) usually consist of a series of graded passages from preprimer to at least the seventh- or eighth-grade level. From the first-grade level on there are usually two passages, one to be read orally and one silently at each grade level. As the student reads orally, word-recognition errors are recorded, and from these a percentage of word recognition is computed. Following the reading of both passages (silent and oral) the student is asked a series of comprehension questions regarding the material. From these answers a percentage score for reading comprehension is derived. For older students oral reading is sometimes omitted.

Many people who work with children in reading on a day-to-day basis come to realize that standard measures of reading achievement often do not provide for the practical knowledge necessary for individualized instruction. In a thorough review of the issues involving IRIs Michael C. McKenna (1983) stated, "In the past half century, the informal reading inventory (IRI) has become a foremost weapon in the arsenal of reading and classroom teachers." (p. 670) McKenna also quoted these other authorities: Zintz (1981) called the IRI "the most accurate test measure that can be provided to evaluate the child's ability to use textbooks for instructional purposes." (p. 99) Dechant (1981) estimated that it is the most frequent means of determining reading levels and diagnosing reading behaviors. Johns (1977) said, "we cannot afford not to use informal reading inventories." (McKenna, p. 136)

Nancy B. Masztal and Lawrence L. Smith (1984) did a survey of a number of experienced teachers to determine the extent to which they actually used IRIs. They received responses from 125 teachers, of whom 81 percent said they were familiar with IRIs. Of that group 78 percent said they knew how to administer one. A total of 54 percent indicated that they actually administered IRIs in their classrooms. (This was not interpreted to mean that they administered IRIs to all students.) Of the group who administered IRIs within their classrooms, 27 percent used those that were commercially prepared and 24 percent used IRIs constructed by the teachers themselves, while 5 percent reported using an IRI constructed by other teachers. The 44 percent that remained reported using the IRI that accompanied their basal reading program.

There has been considerable controversy as to whether IRIs or other means of measurement are more accurate in placing students at their instructional level. Jo Ellen Oliver and Richard D. Arnold (1979) compared the results of a standardized test, teacher judgments, and an informal reading inventory using third-grade subjects:

> Based upon previous studies and the data gathered here, it would
> appear that scores from informal inventories place students in easier
> materials for instructional purposes than either standardized test scores
> or teacher judgment. Further, it would seem that as children proceed

through the elementary grades, they are placed in increasingly more difficult and perhaps even frustrating materials. The data suggest one-half to one grade level in primary grades . . . with up to two full years in the fifth and sixth grades. . . . If this interpretation is accurate, it is understandable why students are frustrated by reading materials in many schools and why they have problems in the secondary schools, where reading is prerequisite to most learning. (p. 58)

Jay S. Blanchard, Paul Borthwick, Jr., and Ann Hall (1983) also studied the use of standardized multiple choice tests, IRIs, and probed recall questions as measures of students' instructional reading levels. They concluded that one could not support the assumption that standardized test scores run too high or that reading instruction should begin at a lower level:

In summary, to interpret standardized reading test scores as not indicative of a pupil's instructional reading level, without caution in mind, is to ignore this research evidence. . . . (p. 688)

We believe that most teachers will benefit a great deal from the knowledge they gain in administering IRIs; however, the question as to which measure is best for determining students' instructional reading levels remains unanswered. It seems best for the teacher to use several measures of reading levels, if at all possible, and keep a running check on students' performance.

The Purpose of Informal Reading Inventories

One of the main purposes in using informal reading inventories is to place students in appropriate reading materials, to provide for a proper fit between student and study. Another is to determine students' independent, instructional, and frustration reading levels. This requires an assessment of students' reading comprehension, oral and silent, and of word recognition when reading orally. A third purpose of IRIs is to analyze the number and type of students' word-recognition errors and to assess reading comprehension for diagnostic-remedial purposes.

The IRI Criteria and Levels

Reading is essentially a process of recognizing and analyzing words and understanding words and ideas. In order to read efficiently one must reach a certain level of word recognition as well as a certain level of comprehension. In a thorough review of the history of IRIs Jerry L. Johns (1983) indicated that although they have been used considerably since the 1940s and even earlier, and although during the 1960s and especially the 1970s there was considerable research on the criteria for independent, instructional and frustration reading levels, no consensus was reached on the criteria. In looking to the future of IRIs Johns stated:

Perhaps the longest lasting and most perplexing issue concerns the appropriate criteria for the instructional level. Although a considerable amount of research has been done in this area, there is still no generally accepted and empirically validated criteria for the independent, instructional, or frustration levels. (p. 15)

Emmett Betts (1946) can probably be called the father of the IRI as we know it today. His original criteria have been widely used and accepted, although often questioned in the writing and research of various students of reading. William Powell (1970) and Powell (1971) questioned the original criteria and believed that for oral reading generally the percentage of errors a younger student could make without becoming frustrated was higher than for an older student. Earlier research by John Bormuth (1969) also indicated that the criteria should not remain static throughout the grade levels. One of the first and certainly most thorough explanations of the levels and the criteria for each was presented by Marjorie Johnson and Roy Kress (1965) and is summarized here:

Free or Independent Level (Criteria to be Met Without Examiner Aid)

Word recognition—99 percent or better
Comprehension—90 percent or better

This is the level at which children should read a library book or their textbooks *after* the teacher has introduced them to the new vocabulary and built up a proper background for comprehending the material. In general this is the level for when there is no one around to help. Although placement is normally based on these criteria, teachers associate certain behavioral characteristics with this level of reading. These characteristics were described by Johnson and Kress:

Rhythmical, expressive oral reading
Accurate observation of punctuation
Acceptable reading posture
Silent reading more rapid than oral
Response to questions in language equivalent to author's
No evidence of lip movement, finger pointing, head movement,
    vocalization, sub-vocalization, or anxiety about performance. (p. 6)

Instructional Level (Criteria to be Met Without Examiner Aid)

Word recognition—95 percent
Comprehension—75 percent

This is the level at which children normally read in their textbooks (social studies, science, basal reading) before the teacher has introduced them to the vocabulary and built up a background for comprehending the material. Placement is usually based on the same criteria, but the related behavioral characteristics while reading should be the same as for the independent reading level.

Everett E. Davis and Eldon E. Ekwall (1976) investigated some aspects of frustration as related to reading in elementary school children. They used a polygraph to assess certain physiological changes while the children were reading and concluded that for most children, reading passages for instructional purposes must be no more difficult than to allow for about 5 percent oral reading errors. Only a few children have special protective devices that enable them to withstand greater degrees of failure.

Frustration Level

Word recognition—90 percent or less
Comprehension—50 percent or less

This is the level at which the material is too difficult for sustained reading, and it is a level to avoid. Placement is again normally based on the criteria mentioned above but related behavioral characteristics are as follows:

Abnormally loud or soft voice
Arrhythmical or word-by-word oral reading
Lack of expression in oral reading
Inaccurate observation of punctuation
Finger pointing (at margin or every word)
Lip movement, head movement, sub-vocalization
Frequent requests for examiner help
Non-interest in the selection
Yawning or obvious fatigue
Refusal to continue. (p. 10)

Listening Comprehension Level (Criteria to be Met Without Examiner Aid)

Comprehension—75 percent (The responses to questions should generally be in language equivalent to the author's.)

The above criteria are from Kress and Johnson, cited earlier. Although other slightly different criteria for some reading levels are sometimes given by other authors, it should be emphasized that these are usually based on hunches. Research by Eldon E. Ekwall indicates that these criteria can probably be considered as correct providing *all* repetitions are counted as errors. (See Ekwall and English, 1971; Ekwall, Solis, and Solis, 1973.)

In order to determine the reading potential of disabled readers, examiners often begin to read passages at levels that are progressively higher than the students' frustration level. Students listen as these are read to them and the material is considered to be at their listening comprehension level as long as they can answer 75 percent of the comprehension questions. The highest grade level at which they can do this is their hearing comprehension level. For some disabled readers this may be one or more grade levels above their frustration level. However, hearing comprehension as a guide to reading potential is only a rough estimate, since some students possess less innate ability for listening than others. It has also been demonstrated that students from low socioeconomic levels often have listening skills inferior to those of students from middle- or upper-income levels. Therefore, misleading results can easily be obtained by putting too much reliance on the hearing comprehension level.

Administering Informal Reading Inventories

In administering an IRI the examiner sits preferably on one side of a table with the student facing from one side. A right-handed examiner places the student to the left; a left-handed examiner, to the right. In this way the student is less able to see and be distracted by the examiner's notetaking. The student is given a booklet containing a series of graded passages and usually starts at a level the examiner believes will be rather easy, equivalent to the student's independent reading level. In order to determine this level the examiner often administers a graded word list. Several of the commercially available inventories contain their own graded word lists for this purpose. (These are discussed later in this chapter.) We have found the San Diego Quick Assessment List (Chapter 4) to be quick and helpful for determining all three reading levels.

As the student takes the booklet, the examiner usually gives directions: "Here are some passages or stories I would like you to read. Please read them clearly and accurately and try to remember everything you read so you can answer some questions about them when you are done. If you come across a hard word, try to read it as best as you can, but I may help you if you cannot get it at all." In introducing each passage the examiner often makes some comment about the content of the passage. For example, in having a student read a passage about an airplane ride the examiner may say, "This is a story about a boy who went on an airplane ride. Have you ever ridden in an airplane?" When doing this, however, be sure to avoid answering any questions that will later be asked about the story. Handing the student the first passage, say, "Here is the first passage. Read it aloud. Again, try to remember everything you read so you can answer some questions about it when you are through. Go ahead and begin."

As the student reads, the examiner should have a copy of what the student is reading so that any word-recognition errors, hesitations, etc., can be recorded. It is better if the examiner's copy is double or triple spaced so that ample room is available for recording these errors. A code for marking oral reading errors is shown in the list that follows. Many people have learned another shorthand method of marking various kinds of word-recognition errors. We have found that students learn this code rather easily, but the important point is that you are able to look at the recorded errors and accurately interpret them immediately following the reading or even six months or a year later. For this reason you should become thoroughly familiar with either this or a modified version of this code. When giving an informal reading inventory, it is necessary to mark oral reading errors as the student proceeds, and it is usually a good idea to tape the reading. This enables the teacher to go back and check on the accuracy of the coding. This is especially important when major decisions are to be based on the student's performance on an informal reading inventory.

Code for Marking in Oral Diagnosis

To Be Scored as Errors in Marking Informal Reading Inventories
1. Encircle omissions.
2. Insert with a caret (ˆ) all insertions.
3. Draw a line through words for which substitutions or mispronunciations were made and write the substitution or mispronunciation above the word. Determine later whether the word missed was a substitution or mispronunciation.
4. If the student reads too fast to write in all mispronunciations, draw a line through the word and write a *P* for partial mispronunciation or a *G* for gross mispronunciation.
5. Mark inversions the same as substitutions and determine later whether the mistake was really an inversion or a substitution. Examples of inversions are *no* for *on, ont* for *not, saw* for *was,* etc.
6. Use parentheses ( ) to enclose words for which aid was given.
7. Underline repetitions with a wavy line.

Not to Be Scored as Errors in Marking Informal Reading Inventories
8. Make a check (✓) over words that were self-corrected.
9. Use an arced line to connect words where there was disregard for punctuation.
10. Make two vertical lines (‖) to indicate a pause before words.

Example of a coded passage:

Manuel ~~was~~ going to visit, his Uncle ~~Gilbert~~. He ~~packed~~ his (suitcase.) Then (his) mother took him to the ~~airport~~. Before he left he gave his mother a big ~~hug~~.

The errors:

Line 1: Substitution of *saw* for *was*. This is also a reversal.
Line 1: Insertion of the word *with* between the words *visit* and *Uncle*.
Line 1: Partial mispronunciation of the name *Gilbert*. A *P* is often written over words that were partially mispronounced. It is better if the

examiner can write the phonetic pronunciation. However, if the student reads too rapidly, the *P* is used.

Line 1: Gross mispronunciation of *packed*. It is better if the examiner can write the phonetic pronunciation. However, if the student reads too rapidly, the *G* is used.

Line 1: The examiner waited for five seconds and then pronounced the word *suitcase* for the student.

Line 2: The student repeated *Then*.

Line 2: The student omitted *his* but went back and reread *Then* and corrected the omission of *his*.

Line 2: The student partially mispronounced *airport* as *airpot*.

Line 2: The student repeated *he left*.

Line 3: The student substituted *bug* for *hug*. This might also be considered as a partial mispronunciation; however, when the student substitutes a real word for another real word, it is more often referred to as a substitution.

After the student has finished reading the passage, the examiner takes it back as casually as possible and then asks the prepared comprehension questions. These questions should appear on the same sheet as the word-recognition errors and can be marked with a plus sign for correct answers or a minus sign for wrong answers. If the student does not give a complete enough answer to score it accurately, the examiner asks a neutral question: "Can you tell me a little more about that?" or "Can you explain that a little more?" Questions that give the student a 50-50 chance of getting it right are avoided. After asking "What color was the car?" the examiner must not ask, "Was it blue or green?" There are also times to record verbatim what the student says in order to take more time in scoring it later. On some answers half credit is sometimes given where even after neutral questioning the answer is not clear-cut.

Some students occasionally do not give any answer to a question. The examiner gives ample time for the student to think about the question and try to answer it, usually five to ten seconds at least, then says, "Do you think you know that?" If not, the student will usually say, "No." This avoids wasting time waiting for an "I don't know."

After the student has read the first passage aloud and answered the questions, he or she reads silently the alternate passage at the same grade level, having received similar directions about remembering what is read. After the student has finished, the examiner asks the comprehension questions. If, however, it is obvious that the first passage was too difficult for the student, the examiner continues *downward* one or more grade levels with oral reading until the student's independent level is established. Then the process turns upward again, alternating from oral to silent at each level. The student continues upward until the frustration level is determined for both oral and silent reading.

After the student's frustration levels are reached, it is time to begin reading to the student to determine the listening comprehension level, using another set of graded reading passages so as not to spoil the original set for later.

Scoring and Interpreting Informal Reading Inventories

It often proves beneficial to code a passage exactly as a student reads it, although only the first seven types of errors (see the Code for Marking in Oral Diagnosis) are counted in computing the percentage of word-recognition errors. The coding symbols shown in 8 through 10 often provide information helpful in diagnosis of reading disability but are not used in computing the percentage of word-recognition errors. One of the main reasons that hesitations and lack of regard for punctuation are not counted as errors is that one cannot be objective in scoring them. For example, two scorers seldom reach perfect agreement on the exact number of times a student disregarded punctuation or hesitated too long, and low interscorer reliability would cost the informal reading inventory considerable validity. Items 1 through 7, however, are mistakes about which objective judgments can be made.

Most authorities agree (and we concur) that items 1 through 8 should be counted as errors. Some authors, however, feel that repetitions should not be counted as errors. Still others believe that only repetitions of more than one word should be counted as errors. These people sometimes argue, as Guszak does, "In his research on oral reading [Kenneth] Goodman has found that the repetition or regression is frequently the student's means of reprocessing a selective bit of data necessary to the emerging story line." (p. 667) They feel that since the repetition was made only to correct an error, it should not be counted as an error. Ekwall and English (1971), however, used the polygraph (lie detector) to measure students' frustration reading level as they read progressively more difficult passages. Their findings were also reported by Ekwall, Solis, and Solis (1973), and Ekwall (1974). These studies showed that when *all* repetitions are discounted as errors, students become physiologically frustrated before they reach the percentage of errors normally recognized as the frustration level. That is, students become so concerned about their reading performance that their hearts beat faster, they begin to perspire, etc., just as one does when frightened or extremely nervous. It seems beyond doubt that using the normally recognized criteria, *all* repetitions should be counted as errors.

Although it may not seem fair to a student to count repetitions, because the student ends up with more errors, it is less fair not to count these errors. If the student appears to be a better reader than is the case, subsequent reading material will be too difficult. On the other hand, seldom is students' reading material too easy for them as a result of this scoring.

One of the major problems teachers have encountered is that they did not understand how to interpret the scoring criteria as originally outlined by Betts and later explained by Johnson and Kress. Briefly summarized, their scoring criteria:

Reading level	Word Recognition	Comprehension
Free or independent	99% +	90% +
Instructional	95%	75%
Frustration	90% −	50% −

Figure 11–1 graphs scoring criteria for comprehension.

All of this seems easy enough until a teacher encounters several very confusing situations. The problem in interpretation often comes when the student scores between 50 percent and 75 percent. By adding the plus and minus to

FIGURE 11–1   Illustration of Various Levels of Comprehension

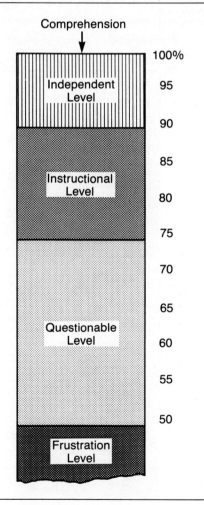

our criteria we have created four categories out of three levels. Although this is confusing for the first few times, it allows the teacher to make some subjective judgment based on the student's overall performance. The questionable area between 50 percent and 75 percent can be counted as instructional *or* frustration reading level based on how well the student performed on word recognition. With silent reading, the decision might be based on how interested the student appeared to be in the subject or how much difficulty the student *appeared* to have with word recognition while reading the passage.

The problem with percentages of comprehension is also encountered with percentages of word recognition. In order to clarify how to make decisions for placement based on both word recognition and comprehension, we will look at Figure 11–2, which shows the word recognition and comprehension

FIGURE 11–2 Illustration of Various Levels of Word Recognition and Comprehension

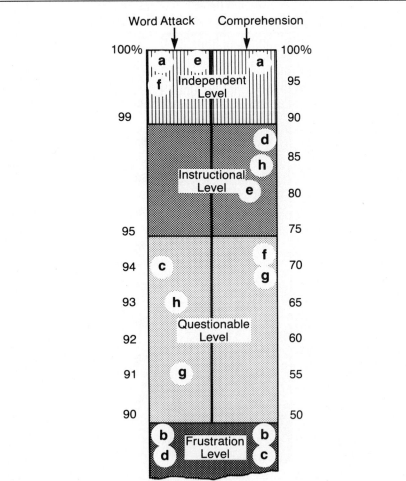

levels of student A through H). The exact percentages of word recognition and comprehension for each of these students on a particular reading passage are summarized below, then considered together for purposes of placement.

Student A: Above the minimum levels in both categories (comprehension and word recognition), he is reading at his free level.

Student B: Below the minimum levels in both categories, her overall reading is at her frustration level.

Student C: This student's word recognition score puts him in the high end of the questionable range; however, since his comprehension is at the frustration level, his overall reading level is also at the frustration level. When either score is in the frustration level, it is normally impossible for the student to be at any other level regardless of how high the score on the other factor.

Student D: Again, this student has a word-recognition score at frustration level, and although his comprehension score was rather high (85 percent), he is still at frustration level.

Student E: This student's score is in the independent level in word recognition and in the instructional level in comprehension. The overall score is not normally higher than the lower of the two scores. Therefore, her overall score is instructional level.

Student F: Also in the free level in word recognition, his score falls into the questionable range in comprehension. Since his word-recognition score is so high and his comprehension score is high in the range of instruction or frustration, we place him at the instructional level.

Student G: This student is in the low questionable range for word recognition and in the high questionable range for comprehension. We would not normally place a student in the instructional level without one score above the questionable level. Therefore, her overall level is frustration.

Student H: In about the middle of the questionable level for word recognition, he scored fairly high in the instructional range for comprehension but not high enough to make us definitely feel that there is any reason to place him above his frustration level. If the student was extremely interested in what he was reading or seemed to possess a great deal of perseverance, it would perhaps be proper for him to read at this level for a short time. As a general rule, however, students should not read material this difficult for them.

It is difficult to make decisions about the overall reading level of certain students even when given a certain amount of guidance (see Table 11-1). On the other hand, it is really only the teacher who knows the students, their

TABLE 11–1.   Placement of Students Based on Word Recognition and Comprehension.

Student	Word Recognition Percentage	Comprehension Percentage	Placement
a	99 or 100	100	Free or independent
b	Less than 90	Less than 50	Frustration
c	94	Less than 50	Frustration
d	Less than 90	85	Frustration
e	99 or 100	80	Instructional
f	99 or 100	70	Instructional
g	91	70	Frustration
h	93	85	Probably frustration but possibly instructional

interests, their ability to persevere, etc. And, the fact that IRI criteria are somewhat flexible is often beneficial.

Developing Your Own Informal Reading Inventories and Using the IRI Criteria

If determining students' free, instructional, and frustration reading levels is your purpose, as in an initial or final diagnosis by a reading specialist or clinician, it would probably be much easier to use one of the commercial IRIs discussed later in this chapter. It can take years to develop a good inventory of this nature, and there is little use in duplicating the efforts of experts. In addition to considerations of time, teachers will find difficulty in selecting proper passages. Lynn S. Fuchs, Douglas Fuchs, and Stanley L. Deno (1982) have made the point that the adequacy of the sampling procedure rests on the assumption that a passage found on any one page of a text is likely to be representative of the text as a whole. Fuchs, Fuchs, and Deno stated, "Investigations have established that extreme variation exists in the readability of basal readers . . . " (p. 8) and that this variation suggests that the practice of using arbitrarily drawn samples may lead to inadequate placements. These authors stated, "In sum, results indicate that IRI procedures for selecting passages from basal texts and for sampling pupils' reading performance may negatively affect current educational practice." (p. 23) In addition to this problem teachers will need to decide on their own scoring criteria and will find it much more difficult than most think to develop adequate questions for measuring comprehension. Applying the IRI criteria to materials used in your own school to determine proper balance between students and materials is one of their most valuable uses.

Whether you wish to make your own complete IRI or merely to select passages from existing materials, you will need certain guidelines. For lower-level passages (preprimer through first grade) often as few as twenty to forty words are used. As the material increases in difficulty, longer passages are usually selected (around 100 to 150 words at second- or third-grade level and up to 250 to 300 words at seventh- or eighth-grade level). Although it is difficult to measure comprehension skills, an attempt is usually made to devise comprehension questions over main ideas, important details, vocabulary, and inference. In order to insure a certain amount of validity, at least seven or eight questions are asked concerning each passage. One of the difficulties in constructing questions to accompany informal reading inventories is to be sure that the questions are passage-dependent. That is, you must try to eliminate questions that the student might answer correctly without reading the passage. It has been commonly assumed that factual questions are less likely to be passage-dependent than inferential questions. However, research by Frederick Duffelmeyer (1980) found that approximately two-thirds of the factual questions on a popular informal reading inventory were passage-dependent and only about one half of the inferential questions were passage-dependent. Duffelmeyer concluded that passage dependency is not a function of question type but rather a result of the item writer's ability to create good questions.

William Valmont (1972) provided some excellent guidelines for constructing questions for informal reading inventories:

1. Questions should be in the approximate order in which the information upon which they are based is presented in the passage.
2. It is generally preferable to place a main idea question first.
3. Ask the most important questions possible.
4. Check the sequence of questions to insure that a later question is not answered by an earlier one.
5. Check questions to insure that two or more questions do not call for the same response, fact, or inference.
6. A question that is so broad that any answer is acceptable is a poor question. If special questions to test divergent thinking are created, insure that reasonable, logical responses may be made.
7. A question that can be answered by someone who has not read the passage (except for vocabulary questions) is a poor question.
8. Avoid formulating questions whose answers call for knowledge based on something experienced by the pupil rather than from reading or application of information given in the story.
9. IRI questions are generally constructed to measure the student's comprehension of written matter. Therefore, insure that accompanying pictures do not aid the student in answering questions.
10. Keep your questions short and as simple as possible. Do not include irrelevant statements.
11. Generally, state questions so that they start with who, what, when, where, how, and why.

12. Do not let grammar or syntax unnecessarily complicate the questions.
13. Avoid stating questions in a negative manner.
14. Avoid overusing questions which require pupils to reconstruct lists, such as "list five ingredients" or "name four characters" or "tell six places." Anxiety or memory instead of comprehension may influence the pupil's performance.
15. Avoid writing questions with multiple answers which fail to establish specifications for the response.
Poor: What happened after Susan heard the telephone?
Better: What was the first thing that happened after Susan heard the telephone?
16. Do not mistake a question that calls for the reporting of several facts or details as an organization or sequence question.
17. To learn about a pupil's grasp of the vocabulary, ask the pupil to define the word, not to recall a word from the story.
Poor: What word told you about the age of the man?
Better: What does *old* mean?
18. Avoid stating a question as if to call for an opinion when asking the pupil to relate a fact.
Poor: How do you think Skip got to the store?
Better: How did Skip get to the store?
19. If a question is asking for a judgment, phrase it as "Why do you or don't you believe. . . ." Do not reveal the information called for.
20. Avoid asking questions on which the child has a fifty-fifty chance of being correct: "yes/no" questions, or "either/or." (pp. 511–512)[1]

In addition to Valmont's excellent suggestions, Michael C. McKenna (1983) wrote an outstanding article on the issues involved in the use of IRIs. McKenna's suggestions, we believe, should be followed in constructing and administering IRIs:

1. Do not assume that the stories in basal readers all represent the assigned readability level. Check readability with one or more of the better formulas. Once your IRI is complete, stay alert to readability problems as you begin to use it. If you use a commercial inventory, you can have more confidence in stated readability levels, but you should observe these same precautions.
2. Whether constructing your own instrument or selecting a commercial one, make sure the passages in each sequence are from the same general interest area, preferably one of moderate to high interest for both boys and girls of the ages at which the IRI will be given. It is a good idea to ask students individually about their

---

[1]Valmont, William J. "Creating Questions for Informal Reading Inventories," *Reading Teacher,* Vol. 25 (March 1972): 509–512. (Reprinted with permission of the author and the International Reading Association.)

interest in the subjects in the inventory. Make your inquiries prior to a student's exposure to the passages.

3. In writing questions, (1) state each clearly and simply; (2) limit the number of types, perhaps adopting the guidelines provided by Johnson and Kress; and (3) be alert to sets of questions which prove too easy or too hard. In using a commercial test, be wary of tally sheets which show students' responses delineated into a large number of comprehension subskills.

4. Ensure the passage dependency of questions by "field testing" them on some of your brighter students or by using an adult standard of prior knowledge in the subject area. Do not assume that questions in commercial instruments are passage dependent, and do not hesitate to replace some of them with your own.

5. Use the Betts criteria, but do not adhere to them too rigidly. Keep these points in mind: (1) In the lower grades, be lenient with the oral accuracy criteria when comprehension is good; (2) always look for signs of actual frustration in the student's behavior; and (3) when comprehension scores are between 65% and 75%, interpret the performance as instructional unless there is evidence of frustration.

6. Do count repetitions in your error tally. Do not consider the quality (semantic acceptability) of miscues, however. Consider quality in subjectively evaluating overall patterns once the levels have been determined, concentrating on miscues made at and below the instructional level.

7. If there is a difference between oral and silent comprehension scores, use the higher of the two.

8. For miscue analysis, do not allow students to read passages silently before oral reading. When oral accuracy is at frustration level and silent comprehension is at the instructional level, consider the level as instructional.

9. Avoid using word lists except as sight word tests. Look to other information in deciding where to begin in the passages.

10. At the secondary level, beware of commercial inventories that include passages at each of grades 7–12. If constructing your own IRI, combine the upper levels in pairs: 5–6, 7–8, 9–10, 11–12. When evaluating the performance of secondary students, give far more credence to silent comprehension than to oral accuracy scores.[2]

Thus far we have discussed using commercially published IRIs or developing your own. A third option may have particular merit for placing students in basal materials. Here we refer to the informal reading inventories that accompany the basal programs. Some are quite thorough and helpful, and others appear to be hastily constructed. We advise that teachers or reading specialists

[2]McKenna, M. C. Informal reading inventories: A review of the issues. *Reading Research Quarterly,* Vol. 36 (1983): 670–679. (Reprinted with permission of the author and the International Reading Association.)

examine these inventories carefully according to the guidelines we have presented. You may find that the materials are adequate for your needs or that they may be modified slightly. In some cases the inventories that accompany basal readers are inadequate and should be discarded.

A Reading Level Guide to Calculate Reading Levels and to Match Students and Materials

After working with beginning and practicing teachers for a number of years it is our feeling that few of them use reading inventories to advantage. For this reason Eldon E. Ekwall has created a Reading Level Guide. There are several reasons why teachers have not used informal reading inventories or the criteria of the IRI for placing students in materials:

1. Most teachers have not had enough training in the field of reading to understand how to use the IRI criteria either for scoring informal reading inventories or for placing students at the right reading level.
2. Teachers who have studied the IRI criteria can usually interpret the results they obtain providing both comprehension and word recognition clearly fall into the independent or the frustration reading level. However, when word recognition and comprehension differ considerably, the obtained results become much more difficult to interpret. The Reading Level Calculator eliminates the problems usually encountered in interpreting data.
3. Teachers are often hesitant to take the time to calculate the percentage of words recognized as well as the percentage of questions that were correct. The use of Tables 11–2 and 11–3 eliminates the need for calculating any percentages.

The purpose of the reading level guide. This is to help beginning and practicing teachers, or the reading specialist, place students at the proper reading level. This information will allow quick interpretation of information derived from informal reading inventories, and more important, help match the reading levels of children and books.

The use of the criteria for scoring informal reading inventories eliminates the need for teachers to work somewhat complicated and time-consuming readability formulas on classroom materials. It also eliminates the chore of attempting to assess the reading level of children. Furthermore, there is considerable chance that a book based on a reading level obtained by a readability formula will not be in accord with a teacher's assessed reading level. This is true for these two reasons:

1. Readability formulas at best produce only a rough approximation of the level of difficulty of reading material.
2. Most tests produce only a rough approximation of a child's reading

level. A reading level based on a subject about which the child is thoroughly familiar is likely to be artificially high because of the child's vocabulary and comprehension of the concepts, so the child may be placed in materials that are too difficult. On the other hand, material on subjects about which the child is unfamiliar may result in too low a placement. The important question is how well does a *certain* child read a *certain* set of materials.

The problem is that every book or set of reading materials presents somewhat different problems for different readers depending on their background of experiences. The only practical solution is to ask a child to read instructional materials and see how well *that* child reads *those* materials. This applies whether you are a parent attempting to determine whether a certain library book is easy enough for your child or a teacher trying to find the right level of basal reader for a student.

To determine whether reading material is at the proper level:

1. Have the student orally read a passage from the material. For students in grades one or two you will probably want to choose a passage of 25 to 100 words. For students at grade three or above you will probably want to use a passage of 100 to 200 words.
2. As the student reads, record oral errors using the Code for Marking in Oral Diagnosis. Either have a copy of the material on which to mark errors in word recognition or just count them on your fingers (without the student noticing).

Coding the exact type of error often lets you locate certain reading difficulties that might not otherwise become apparent. If you are interested only in placement, you may simply count each oral error. If you do not mark each error, be sure that you jot down the total number of word recognition errors.

3. Question the student concerning the material just read. You should ask at least four questions, preferably prepared in advance and designed to sample the following kinds of comprehension:
   a. Knowledge of the main ideas
   b. Knowledge of important details
   c. Knowledge of vocabulary
   d. Ability to infer from material read
   Note the number of questions asked and how many missed.
4. In the left-hand column of Table 11–2 you will find ranges for the length of passages. Count the words in your passage and find the range that corresponds. At the top of the table find the number of oral errors your student made. Read down this column and across the passage-

TABLE 11–2. Guide for Determining the Correct Percentage of Word Recognition

Number of words missed

Number of words in reading passage	1	2	3	4	5	6	7	8	9	10	11	12	13	14	15	16	17	18	19	20
20–25	96	91	F	F	F	F	F	F	F	F	F	F	F	F	F	F	F	F	F	F
26–30	96	93	F	F	F	F	F	F	F	F	F	F	F	F	F	F	F	F	F	F
31–35	97	94	91	F	F	F	F	F	F	F	F	F	F	F	F	F	F	F	F	F
36–40	97	95	92	F	F	F	F	F	F	F	F	F	F	F	F	F	F	F	F	F
41–45	98	95	93	91	F	F	F	F	F	F	F	F	F	F	F	F	F	F	F	F
46–50	98	96	94	92	F	F	F	F	F	F	F	F	F	F	F	F	F	F	F	F
51–55	98	96	94	92	91	F	F	F	F	F	F	F	F	F	F	F	F	F	F	F
56–60	98	97	95	93	91	F	F	F	F	F	F	F	F	F	F	F	F	F	F	F
61–65	98	97	95	94	92	F	F	F	F	F	F	F	F	F	F	F	F	F	F	F
66–70	99	97	96	94	93	F	F	F	F	F	F	F	F	F	F	F	F	F	F	F
71–75	99	97	96	95	93	92	F	F	F	F	F	F	F	F	F	F	F	F	F	F
76–80	99	97	96	95	94	92	92	F	F	F	F	F	F	F	F	F	F	F	F	F
81–85	99	98	96	95	94	93	92	F	F	F	F	F	F	F	F	F	F	F	F	F
86–90	99	98	97	95	94	93	92	91	F	F	F	F	F	F	F	F	F	F	F	F
91–95	99	98	97	96	95	94	93	91	F	F	F	F	F	F	F	F	F	F	F	F
96–100	99	98	97	96	95	94	93	92	F	F	F	F	F	F	F	F	F	F	F	F
101–105	99	98	97	96	95	94	93	92	91	F	F	F	F	F	F	F	F	F	F	F
106–110	99	98	97	96	95	94	94	93	92	F	F	F	F	F	F	F	F	F	F	F
111–115	99	98	97	96	96	95	94	93	92	91	F	F	F	F	F	F	F	F	F	F
116–120	99	98	97	96	96	95	94	93	92	91	F	F	F	F	F	F	F	F	F	F
121–125	99	98	98	97	96	95	94	93	93	92	91	F	F	F	F	F	F	F	F	F
126–130	99	98	98	97	96	95	95	94	93	92	92	91	F	F	F	F	F	F	F	F
131–135	99	98	98	97	96	95	95	94	93	92	92	91	F	F	F	F	F	F	F	F
136–140	99	99	98	97	96	96	95	94	93	93	92	92	91	F	F	F	F	F	F	F
141–145	99	99	98	97	97	96	95	94	94	93	92	92	91	F	F	F	F	F	F	F
146–150	99	99	98	97	97	96	95	95	94	93	93	92	92	91	F	F	F	F	F	F
151–155	99	99	98	97	97	96	95	95	94	93	93	92	92	91	F	F	F	F	F	F
156–160	99	99	98	97	97	96	96	95	94	94	93	92	92	91	91	F	F	F	F	F
161–165	99	99	98	98	97	96	96	95	94	94	93	93	92	91	91	F	F	F	F	F
166–170	99	99	98	98	97	96	96	95	95	94	93	93	92	92	91	F	F	F	F	F
171–175	99	99	98	98	97	97	96	95	95	94	94	93	92	92	91	91	F	F	F	F
176–180	99	99	98	98	97	97	96	95	95	94	94	93	93	92	92	91	F	F	F	F
181–185	99	99	98	98	97	97	96	96	95	95	94	93	93	92	92	91	91	F	F	F
186–190	99	99	98	98	97	97	96	96	95	95	94	94	93	93	92	91	91	F	F	F
191–195	99	99	98	98	97	97	96	96	95	95	94	94	93	93	92	92	91	91	F	F
196–200	99	99	98	98	97	97	96	96	95	95	94	94	93	93	92	92	91	91	F	F

length row. Your student's grade is where they intersect. This number represents the percentage correct.

5. Look in Table 11–3 and find the figure that corresponds to the number of questions asked. Then look across the top row of this table and find the figure that corresponds to the number of questions missed. Find the point at which the row intersects the column. This figure is the percent of correct comprehension responses.

6. Turn to the Reading Level Calculator (Table 11–4) and find the percentage of correct word recognition on the left-hand side and the percentage of correct comprehension at the top. If they intersect at an *F,* the student is reading at the frustration level; if in the area marked *Inst.,* at the instructional level. The area marked *Free* represents the independent level.

When in Table 11–2 or Table 11–3 your student's rows and columns intersect in an area marked *F,* the child is reading at the frustration level regardless of other scores. There is no need to use the Reading Level Calculator because the student's reading level is already determined.

In doing a quick check to determine whether certain materials are appropriate for a student, you may often omit the comprehension questions because of the time involved. Follow the same procedure, but instead of asking questions, consider the student's comprehension to be 100 percent when using the Reading Level Calculator as described in step 6 above.

To determine the grade level at which a student is reading, use the procedure that follows. You will need a series of reading passages of which the grade level of difficulty is already known:

Preprimer (PP)
Primer (P)

TABLE 11–3.   Guide for Determining the Correct Percentage of Comprehension

Number of questions missed

	0	1	2	3	4	5	6	7	8	9	10
10	100	90	80	70	60	F	F	F	F	F	F
9	100	90	80	65	55	F	F	F	F	F	F
8	100	90	75	65	F	F	F	F	F	F	F
7	100	85	70	60	F	F	F	F	F	F	F
6	100	85	65	F	F	F	F	F	F	F	F
5	100	80	60	F	F	F	F	F	F	F	F
4	100	75	F	F	F	F	F	F	F	F	F
3	100	65	F	F	F	F	F	F	F	F	F

Number of questions (row label at left)

TABLE 11–4. Reading Level Calculator

Percentage of comprehension

	55[a]	60	65	70	75	80	85	90	95	100
100	Inst.	Inst.	Inst.	Inst.	Inst.	Inst.	Inst.	Free	Free	Free
99	F	Inst.	Inst.	Inst.	Inst.	Inst.	Inst.	Free	Free	Free
98	F	F	Inst.	Inst.	Inst.	Inst.	Inst.	Inst.	Inst.	Inst.
97	F	F	F	Inst.	Inst.	Inst.	Inst.	Inst.	Inst.	Inst.
96	F	F	F	F	Inst.	Inst.	Inst.	Inst.	Inst.	Inst.
95	F	F	F	F	F	Inst.	Inst.	Inst.	Inst.	Inst.
94	F	F	F	F	F	F	Inst.	Inst.	Inst.	Inst.
93	F	F	F	F	F	F	F	Inst.	Inst.	Inst.
92	F	F	F	F	F	F	F	F	Inst.	Inst.
91	F	F	F	F	F	F	F	F	F	Inst.

Percent of word recognition

F = Frustration reading level
Inst. = Instructional reading level
Free = Free reading level

[a]The student is not considered to be at the frustration reading level below 75 percent if his or her word-recognition skills are still fairly high. Polygraph research indicated that if word recognition remains high, most students do not actually become frustrated until comprehension drops below 50 percent.

First Reader (F)
Second Reader, Book One (2–1)
Second Reader, Book Two (2–2)
Third Reader, Book One (3–1)
Third Reader, Book Two (3–2)
Fourth Reader (4)
Fifth Reader (5)
Sixth Reader (6)
Seventh Reader (7)
Eighth Reader (8)

Have the student begin reading at what you think will be the student's independent level and continue to read progressively harder passages. You may wish to determine this starting point by using the San Diego Quick Assessment List. Check the reading of each passage as described. Continue downward if necessary until the student's free level is reached, and then continue upward until the instructional and finally the frustration levels are reached.

Normally in giving informal reading inventories you wish to determine a student's three levels for both silent and oral reading. To do this you need two passages at each level of difficulty. Proceed the same as described before; however, this time at each grade level have the student read orally and then ask the comprehension questions. After doing this have the student read the other passage silently and again ask questions to determine the percentage of comprehension. To determine the proper level for passages that are read silently, find the comprehension percentage on Table 11–3 and look for it across the top of the Reading Level Calculator, considering the student's word recognition to be 100 percent. The point at which these two figures intersect represents the level at which the student is reading.

Briefly then, use the Reading Level Guide as follows:

1. Determine the number of word recognition errors.
2. Convert this to a percentage by using Table 11–2.
3. Determine the number of comprehension errors.
4. Convert this to a percentage by using Table 11–3.
5. Find the corresponding percentages derived on the Reading Level Calculator and determine the point at which they intersect. The coded intersection point represents the student's reading level.

Adapting Informal Reading Inventories for Use with Older Students

In most situations above grade six and even above the first and second grades a considerably larger amount of time is spent in having students read silently than orally. Some oral reading is done in such areas as poetry and choral reading. In addition, many teachers find that oral reading practice may benefit older students by helping them to apply new skills or improve reading fluency. However, except for these reasons it is difficult to justify oral reading for other than diagnostic purposes. For this reason, in designing informal reading inventories to determine the grade level at which students are capable of functioning or in applying the IRI criteria to match students and materials, there is often little need to have students read orally.

When a student obviously reads very poorly, further diagnosis including oral reading may be called for. However, a study by Robert Pehrsson (1974) indicated that students read better when they are not interrupted. When Pehrsson's students were told to read for meaning, their comprehension and rate of reading improved.

For these reasons we would suggest that in working with older students you first consider what you want to know about them. If it is, Can Cindy read this social studies book at her instructional level? Can Bill, who is in the ninth grade, read a particular trade book at his independent reading level? Then you may wish to omit the oral errors as a factor in making these decisions.

Commercially Developed Informal Reading Inventories

In recent years a number of new commercial IRIs have become available. These inventories generally include a series of graded passages that may be used to assess the reading levels of students for both oral and silent reading.

Assessment includes both word recognition and comprehension. The inventories also contain graded word lists for placement in the passages and/or additional diagnosis of word-recognition skills.

These commercial informal reading inventories were published in 1980 or later:

Bader, L. A. (1983). *Bader reading and language inventory.* New York: Macmillan.

Burns, P. C., & Roe, B. D. (1985). *Informal reading inventory* (2nd ed.). Chicago, IL: Rand McNally.

De Santi, R. J., Casbergue, R. M., & Sullivan, V. G. *The De Santi Cloze reading inventory.* Newton, MA: Allyn & Bacon.

Ekwall, E. E. (1986). *Ekwall reading inventory* (2nd ed.). Newton, MA: Allyn & Bacon.

Johns, J. L. (1985). *Basic reading inventory* (3rd ed.). Dubuque, IA: Kendall/Hunt.

Rinsky, L. A., & de Fossard, E. (1980). *The contemporary classroom inventory.* Dubuque, IA: Gorsuch Scarisbrick.

Silvaroli, N. J. (1986). *Classroom reading inventory* (5th ed.). Dubuque, IA: Wm. C. Brown.

Woods, M. L., & Moe, A. J. (1985). *Analytical reading inventory* (3rd ed.). Columbus, OH: Charles E. Merrill.

In Appendix B (Tests) you will find further information on each of these inventories: number of forms, range of reading levels, use of graded word lists, readability formulas used in developing the inventory, number of questions per passage, type of questions used, timing of reading rate, percentage of word recognition and comprehension for independent, instructional, and frustration reading levels, and other miscellaneous information that may be useful.

THE ANALYSIS OF ERROR PATTERNS FROM ORAL READING ERRORS

Although informal reading inventories can be useful for determining students' reading levels and for matching students and reading materials, one of their most important advantages is that they allow you to diagnose specific reading difficulties from patterns of oral reading errors. We believe that this analysis is the single most important and revealing area of reading diagnosis. It is true that oral reading may present a slightly distorted view of a student's reading ability. Unfortunately, however, there is no way of analyzing directly a student's decoding skills when the student is reading silently. Therefore, we feel that closely observing oral reading behavior is the most accurate barometer of a student's ability *in the act of reading.*

A shorthand method of marking each specific type of oral reading error was described earlier in this chapter. Once you have become familiar with this marking system, you will find that almost every student presents a pattern of errors that becomes a blueprint for instruction. This section is designed to help you analyze these patterns so as to provide more accurate and effective remediation.

You will recall that in the shorthand system it was suggested that you learn to mark several types of characteristics of students' reading that are not counted as errors in computing the percentage of word-recognition errors in informal reading inventories. Some of these characteristics, however, are important in the analysis of error patterns of disabled readers. This section contains a short description of each type of error, some possible reasons why students might make that particular type of error, and some remedial procedures for each error.

Omissions: Students sometimes leave out parts of words, such as -*s, -ed,* or -*ing;* however, this is considered to be a partial mispronunciation. Leaving out a whole word constitutes an omission. Omissions come in two general types, purposeful and nonpurposeful. If a student makes an omission and you wish to know which it is, ask the student to read the word when he or she has completed the passage. If the student immediately knows the omitted word, it was a nonpurposeful omission. If the student does not know the word, it was a purposeful omission.

If a great number of omissions are purposeful, the student will need work with word attack. If the student tends to make nonpurposeful omissions, you will need to help the student correct this habit. Karen D'Angelo and Marc Mahlios (1983) studied the insertion and omissions patterns of good and poor readers. In summarizing the seriousness of these two types of errors they stated:

> Stated positively, when these subjects made insertion and omission miscues, 99 percent of the time semantics were not distorted and 93 percent of the time syntax was not distorted. (p. 781)

As a result of this study the authors suggested that for the most part coding and interpreting these types of errors is of little value to the classroom teacher.

If certain students are making too many nonpurposeful omissions, try these suggestions for correcting them:

1. Call the student's attention to the omissions and discuss the necessity for accurate reading.
2. Tape record a student's oral reading and mark all omitted words. Then play this back to the student and discuss what is happening when the student reads aloud.
3. Have the student point to each word as it is read. We have found it much better to ask the student to pick the finger up and bring it down

on each word as it is read. Stress to the student that the word is only to be read as his or her finger comes down on the word. This will keep the student from reading ahead or behind.

4. One of the most effective procedures for correcting all types of errors is *repeated readings*. Give the student a passage to read. For third- or fourth-grade students the passage might be something rather difficult approximately 200 to 300 words in length. Code the student's oral reading errors. Then discuss each type of error. Ask the student to practice reading the passage until it can be read without a single error. Check the student's reading rate. You may also wish to make a graph that shows the number of errors and the number of words per minute each time the passage is practiced. The use of a graph will help the student to see progress in both reading rate and total number of errors. When doing this procedure it works well to let the student practice the passage alone and tell you when he or she is ready to make another attempt to read it perfectly.

Insertions: Insertions may arise from a lack of comprehension, from carelessness, or because the student's oral language ability surpasses reading ability. If the insertions are correct within the context of the sentence, it can usually be assumed that the student comprehends the passage. If these do not occur too often it may be best to ignore them. If they occur much too often, then you may wish to call the student's attention to them using the methods for corrections of omissions, i.e., tape the reading and discuss the errors; practice repeated readings; and use finger pointing.

If the student's insertions do not make sense in context, the student is probably having difficulty with comprehension. In such a case the comprehension exercises listed in Chapter 6 should prove helpful.

Substitutions or partial mispronunciations: Substitutions differ from mispronunciations in that one complete (correct) word is substituted for another, as *has* for *had*. This might also be termed a mispronunciation, but we classify the use of one basic sight word for another as a substitution. The use of one adjective for another is also a substitution. On the other hand, incorrect word endings or soft *c*'s and *g*'s for hard *c*'s and *g*'s or the wrong pronunciation of a letter or group of letters within a word is a partial mispronunciation.

A student who substitutes one word for another may be a careless reader or may lack word-recognition skills. The types of remediation for carelessness listed under omissions and insertions are also helpful for this problem. A student who mispronounces words may need help with word recognition as listed in Chapter 4; the student who makes partial mispronunciations will in most cases profit from work in word-analysis skills as listed in Chapter 5.

Substitutions or partial mispronunciations may result from the dialect of the reader. In such a case the examiner must distinguish between reading errors and miscues that are a function of dialect. A reading error is a substitution or mispronunciation that results in a loss of meaning for the student. The reader may translate the written material into his or her own dialect. When this happens, the reader is not losing meaning. In fact, this process may reflect good comprehension. For example, a black-dialect-speaking child may read the sentence, "Give me back my monkey," as, "Give me back my money." In this case the error resulted in a loss of meaning. However, this same student may read the sentence, "Have they gone there?" as, "Is they gone there?" Although a substitution was made for the first word, the sentence was read in accord with the child's dialect and there was no meaning loss.

Patricia Cunningham (1976–1977) found that graduate students enrolled in reading courses at four state universities in different regions corrected significantly more black-dialect-specific miscues than non-dialect-specific miscues. Her research indicated that the teachers would correct 78 percent of black-dialect-specific miscues and only 27 percent of nondialect-specific miscues. Cunningham determined that ignorance rather than racism accounted for the differential correction rate and recommended that teacher training emphasize the meaning equivalence between standard English and black dialect and the grammar of black dialect. Larry Ditto (1974) found that teachers who were informed of the nature of linguistic differences perceived fewer dialect-related responses as reading errors than those who were not.

Teachers may unfairly penalize students for dialect rendering and place them in instructional materials that are too low. Therefore, we recommend that teachers working with students who speak a nonstandard dialect become sufficiently familiar with the dialect to distinguish errors that result in meaning loss from those that do not.

Many partial mispronunciations are made because students put the wrong endings on words: *-ed* for *-ing,* etc. A helpful procedure for this type of student is to give sentences with various word endings. Where a word could have various endings, place several choices as shown in the sentence below. The student is to mark the correct ending:

> Jimmy was going to the airport with his father because he had always (wanting, wanted, wants) to see a large airplane.

Students who work with this kind of exercise soon become much more aware of word endings, and you are likely to find a rapid decrease in partial mispronunciations.

Gross mispronunciations.　These are distorted to the extent that the original can hardly be recognized. Students who constantly make gross mispronunciations usually require help in any or all of the word-analysis skills, but especially in phonics and structural analysis. They may also need help in the use of context clues. The student who grossly mispronounces words should be given a phonics test such as the one listed in Appendix A of this text and should be checked for knowledge of structural analysis and context clues.

Inversions or reversals.   Students make reversals—of entire words (*was* for *saw* or *on* for *no*), parts of words (*form* for *from*), or inversions of letters (*g* for *p, b* for *d, n* for *u*)—for a number of reasons. Many students below the age of seven or eight do so, but when they reach the seven and one half to eight years, they almost magically seem to gain the perceptual maturity needed to overcome the problem. Some children never realize that English words are written from left to right and that English sentences are read the same way. Other more severely disabled readers seem to possess some sort of neurological dysfunction that causes the images of words and letters to reach the brain in a scrambled order.

It is commonly assumed that students who make persistent reversal errors will be either poor readers or nonreaders. Helen Kaufman and Phyllis Biren (1976–1977) undertook a study to determine whether children who made persistent spatial errors after age seven were poor readers, spellers, and writers. In their preliminary study the researchers found no statistically significant correlation between the percentage of spatial errors and students' reading grades. They did, however, find that there may be a significant correlation between spatial errors and poor spelling and handwriting. More recent information such as came from Keith Stanovich (1982) has confirmed that students who make reversals or inversions are not more likely to be disabled than those who do not.

Since it is difficult to determine why a certain student makes reversals, the teacher will in most cases find it unprofitable to worry about the etiology of the problem but simply work on remediation.

Bill Hardin and Bonnie Bernstein (1976) suggest:

The best way to deal with reversals is to initiate specific corrective exercises, emphasizing the following principles: habit formation; directionality (left to right); writing of letters; multi-modal approaches that give the child the advantages that go with seeing, saying and writing simultaneously; peer reinforcement. (p. 104)

Among their specific recommendations:

1. Have the students trace letters or words while saying them to themselves.
2. Have the students copy words while pronouncing them.
3. Have the students write letters, then words, from dictation.
4. Work with a chalkboard.
5. Work with cursive writing as soon as interest develops.
6. Have the students count the number of *letters* in each word in a very

short selection or the number of *words* in a short selection to develop a left-right habit pattern.

7. Have the students "read" short selections by naming the first letter of each word.
8. Emphasize left-right movement yourself when working at the chalkboard.
9. Have children work in pairs, dictating words, letters, or phrases to each other on a chalkboard, slate, or paper and correcting each other's errors. (This will involve children in proofreading their own work.)

Other remedial procedures that have often proven helpful:

1. Let the student type words and see them take shape.
2. Use a blue letter at the beginning of words and an orange letter at the end. These colors should be removed as soon as the word has been mastered.
3. Use the nonvisual AKT approach in Chapter 9.
4. Use magnetic three-dimensional or felt or sandpaper letters and let the student trace these as he or she says them.
5. Use the Fernald approach in Chapter 9.
6. Uncover words from left to right and read them immediately after they are uncovered.
7. Explain to the student that English words and sentences are to be read from left to right.

Throughout this book we have emphasized the importance of providing instruction that closely parallels the act of reading. One study that contradicts this approach merits mention. Jack McKiernan and Margo Avakian (1980) reported on the effects of directional-awareness training on the remediation of receptive letter reversals. The researchers structured their study to maintain a distinction between directional awareness per se and letter recognition. The subjects received directional-awareness training *without* specific remediation on the letter-reversal problem. Using this approach, the researchers found significant improvement in the subjects' letter-reversal discrimination ability. The findings suggest that this may be one area where students' reading skills may be improved through training of a lower-level, nonreading skill.

Aid. Lacking the ability to attack a strange word, a student will usually ask for aid or simply wait until aid is given. Students who do this usually lack word-recognition and/or word-analysis skills and often lack confidence in their ability to attack strange words. When this happens, you should begin by testing the student's word-analysis skills. If the student is able to give various phonemes in isolation or knows certain rules but is unable to apply them, teach the student to *use* the word-attack skills presented in Chapter 5.

Repetitions. Students may make repetitions because of poor word-recognition or word-analysis skills or because they have a bad habit. Before attempting to remediate the problem you should first determine the cause, since remediation for repetitions of a bad habit is considerably different from that for repetitions of poor word-recognition or word-analysis skills.

If a student makes a number of repetitions in material written at the student's own grade level, you can usually determine the cause by having the student read material written several grade levels lower. If the student makes as many repetitions in the material at a lower grade level, the problem is probably a bad habit. If the student makes considerably fewer repetitions in the easier material, probably the problem is with word-recognition or word-analysis skills.

Repetitions of a bad habit can be treated much like habitual omissions, i.e., by having the student point to each word as it is read, cover the material with a small card as it is read, choral read with one or more good readers, read in conjunction with a tape recording, or do repeated readings. If it is determined that the problem is not a bad habit, determine whether the student is lacking in sight vocabulary (poor word-recognition skills) or has poor word-analysis skills, or both. Procedures for making these decisions are described in Chapters 4 and 5.

It should be emphasized that many students make repetitions to correct errors they discover as they continue to read. The errors are usually discovered from the context of the story line. Not all repetition errors are serious enough to interfere with comprehension or seriously retard a student's reading ability. However, whether serious or not, they are usually indicative of some type of difficulty.

Disregard of punctuation. Students may disregard punctuation because they are not familiar with the meanings of the marks, because they lack comprehension, or because the reading is so difficult that they fail to attend to punctuation. One of the first steps in determining the cause of the problem is to give the student easier material. If the student continues to disregard punctuation and appears to comprehend after being questioned, the student may need to work on the meaning of various punctuation marks. If the student does not disregard punctuation in the lower-level passage, it can be assumed that the problem is with comprehension or word recognition at higher levels. In this case it is necessary to do further diagnosis to pinpoint the problem. However, punctuation per se can be ignored as a problem.

Pauses before words. A student who pauses longer than is normal before words is usually either lacking in word-recognition or word-analysis skills or has formed a habit of word-by-word reading. If easier material can be given to a student who exhibits this problem, you can determine whether it is word-by-word reading or poor word recognition and/or word analysis. If the student continues to pause before words in material written at a lower grade level, try putting some of the words that appear after the pauses onto flash cards. If the student has almost instant recognition of the words on flash cards, you can feel fairly sure that the student merely has not learned to phrase properly. In this case, activities such as drill with sight phrases using flash cards or a tachistoscope would probably prove helpful. The student may also profit from choral readings with one or more good readers, from reading in conjunction with a tape recording, or from the use of repeated readings. Simply discussing the problem with the student and letting the student hear his or her reading via a tape recording compared with that of a good reader will often prove successful.

If a student improves when given easier material, the problem is usually with word recognition, word analysis, or both. The student who pauses before words and then says them correctly usually has good word-analysis but poor word-recognition skills, or in other words does not possess a sight vocabulary equal to his or her grade level. In this case, activities such as those suggested in Chapter 4 are appropriate. If the student pauses before words and is still unable to say them without aid, the student needs help with word-analysis skills. In this case the type of remediation suggested in Chapter 5 would be helpful.

Analyses of Specific Passages

The coded passages that follow describe typical oral reading errors of disabled readers. Following the passages are discussions of the types of errors and the kinds of remediation appropriate for these students. These are but brief samples. The analyses are presented to suggest some possibilities for remediation and to alert you to the value of diagnosing oral reading performance. You should not assume that a thorough diagnosis can be made from only one sample of oral reading.

Kathy had always wanted to go for a ride on an airplane. One day her father told her that she could ride on an airplane to visit her grandmother and grandfather. She was very happy and could hardly wait to get started.

When the time came to go, her father went to the ticket counter and paid for the airplane ticket. Her mother helped her get on the airplane. Then a lady told her to buckle her seat belt and she even helped her with it.

Soon the airplane was going very fast down the runway. Kathy was afraid at first but soon the airplane was in the air. Kathy peered out of the window at the ground below, where the houses and cars looked very small. The lady gave Kathy something to drink and a sandwich to eat.

(139 Words) (Number of word recognition errors _____)

(Continued on following page)

Questions:

F   1. __+__ What had Kathy always wanted to do? (Go for a ride on an airplane)

F   2. __+__ Who told Kathy that she could ride on an airplane? (Her father)

F   3. __+__ Whom was Kathy going to visit? (Her grandmother and grandfather)

F   4. __+__ How did Kathy feel about going? (She was very happy, happy, and/or she could hardly wait to get started)

F   5. __+__ Who helped Kathy get on the airplane? (Her mother)

F   6. __+__ What did the lady tell Kathy when she got on the airplane? (To buckle her seat belt)

F   7. __+__ How did Kathy feel when the airplane started going very fast? (She was afraid)

V   8. __+__ What did the word "peered" mean when it said, "Kathy peered out of the window?" (She looked, or she looked out of the window)

I   9. __+__ Why did the houses and cars look small below? (Because they were up in the air, far away, or high up in the air)

F 10. __+__ What did the lady give Kathy? (A drink and a sandwich) (Student must get both)[3]

After studying the errors on the student's passage we are able to make certain assumptions about his reading:

A number of words (*visit, runway, peered, window,* and *sandwich*) were not in this student's sight vocabulary, since he did not recognize them instantly, as indicated by pauses before them. However, it is evident that he does possess good word-analysis skills, since in most cases he was able to read the words after pausing briefly. He made repetitions a number of times before words at which he had paused. He may have been trying for a partial clue from the context but may have been stalling for time while he analyzed the word, knowing that the teacher would be likely to tell him if he hesitated too long. He seemed to have difficulty with *when* and *then*.

Knowing these things about this student's reading ability provides you with some valuable information for instruction:

1. He needs to develop a larger sight vocabulary, best done through wide reading. Since he can usually get unknown words right because of his good use of word-analysis skills, it is safe to assume that he would thus improve his word-recognition ability.
2. As just stated, he makes good use of word-analysis skills, including use of context; therefore, he probably needs very little more diagnosis or remediation in this area.
3. He should be given help with the words *when* and *then;* other than these two does not appear to be having difficulty with basic sight words.

[3]Reprinted by permission of Allyn and Bacon.

4. The student seems to be making repetitions before unknown words. It may be that the student is attempting to use context clues along with phonics and structural analysis; however, the repetitions will probably disappear when the student has developed a larger sight vocabulary, or when he is reading something easier.

5. The student seems to have excellent comprehension and not to need help in this area at all.

(Tuff) ~~was~~ *is* a big brown/bear. He ~~lived in~~ *lives on* a big ~~park~~. *P...* He ~~liked~~ *likes* to eat (honey) best of all. He also ~~liked~~ *likes* to eat/~~bread~~. *breakfast*

Some people were in the park having a ~~picnic~~. *party* They were ~~sitting by~~ *setting on* a big table. Tuff went to the ~~picnic~~ *party* too./(When) the (people) saw him they were (afraid.) *q...* They all jumped up and ran ~~away~~. *around the* ~~Then~~ *the* the bear ate all of ~~their~~ *the* food.

(71 Words) (Number of word recognition errors___18+___)

Questions:

F 1. __+__ Who was Tuff? (A big brown bear, (a bear,) or a brown bear)
F 2. __—__ Where did he live? (In a big park, or in a park)
F 3. __+__ What did he like to eat best of all? ((Honey)—If student says "bread" say, "But what did he like best of all?" Student must say "honey.")
F 4. __—__ What did he also like to eat? (Bread) (breakfast)
F 5. __—__ What were the people doing in the park? (Having a ~~picnic~~) *party*
F 6. __+__ Where were the people sitting? (By a table, or by a big table)
F 7. __½__ Where did Tuff go? (To the ~~picnic~~ too) *party*
F 8. __+__ What did the people think when they saw Tuff? (They were afraid))
F 9. __+__ What did they do when they saw Tuff? ((They jumped up and ran) away, or they ran away)
F 10. __+__ What did the bear do then? (He ate all of their food, or he ate the food)[4]

This passage is drawn from the Ekwall Reading Inventory and is written at the first-grade level. The student who read it was clearly at the frustration level. Interestingly, she did quite well on the preprimer selection. Teachers should remember that the jump from preprimer to first-grade level is much greater than the jump from say fifth-grade to sixth-grade level.

An examination of this passage reveals that a great deal of information can be gathered from an analysis of a student's oral reading, especially when the material is written at the student's frustration level. Obviously, the diagnostician must exercise caution and not ask the student to read numerous paragraphs at the frustration level. However, unless the student makes a significant

[4]Reprinted by permission of Allyn and Bacon.

number of errors or miscues, you will not have sufficient information on which to form an analysis.

Some of the assumptions you can make about this student's reading are as follows:

A number of basic sight words and other common words are not known, including *was, brown, lived, in, liked, by, when, away, then,* and *their.* These and others can be confirmed through a basic sight vocabulary test as described in Chapter 4. Fortunately, some basic sight words are known, and this may provide a foundation for future sight-word learning. Phonics skills also appear to be very weak, as this child was unable to unlock unknown words. On the other hand, there is evidence that this child has mastered the sound-symbol associations for most or all of the beginning single consonants. Even though this student was unable to read *park, bread,* and *picnic,* she did get the correct beginning sounds. A thorough assessment of phonics skills as described in Chapter 5 would be in order. This student appears to have a good ability to use context clues, revealed by the fact that all substitutions are words that make some sense, e.g., *is* for *was, lives on* for *lived in, likes* for *liked, breakfast* for *bread,* etc. This student most certainly lacks structural-analysis skills, which is to be expected of anyone who struggles to read at such a low level.

If the findings of this one oral reading passage are supported by additional testing of basic sight vocabulary and phonics skills, instruction will be required in the following areas:

1. She needs to develop a larger sight vocabulary. Unfortunately, her low reading level will preclude wide reading as a vehicle for this improvement, except for carefully chosen materials at preprimer level and perhaps language-experience stories. For some students who have a very meager sight vocabulary the use of the neurological impress method often proves beneficial. The specific procedures in Chapter 4 should prove effective for increasing this student's instant recognition of basic sight words. In our opinion the best thing for this student at this time is lots of language-experience stories to improve her overall sight vocabulary.

2. She needs to improve her phonics ability and learn how to analyze unknown words. Although she appears to know most initial consonants and perhaps vowels, she cannot systematically work her way through a word not in her sight vocabulary. For this reason more diagnosis should be done in phonic elements and in use of skills she already has. Procedures are in Chapter 5.

3. Her ability to use context clues is a relative strength. It is probable that this, combined with word-recognition and phonics skills, will enable her to improve her reading ability significantly.

4. It is difficult to make any concise judgment about her comprehension ability. Most of her errors in comprehension arose from miscalled words that altered the sense of the passage. Other than this it appears

that even though the student was reading at her frustration level, she seemed to maintain adequate comprehension.

> Kay was waiting by the door for the postman to come. Her father had promised to write her a letter. He told Kay the letter would have a blue stamp on it.
>
> Kay saw the postman walking toward the house. The man was carrying a big bag on his side. The man reached in his bag and gave Kay some letters. One of the letters had Kay's name on it. When Kay read the letter she was very happy. She was so happy when she read it that she began to jump up and down. In the letter Father told Kay he was going to buy her a pony.

(109 Words)

Time: __127__

(*in seconds*)

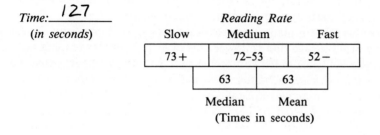

Reading Rate

	Slow	Medium	Fast
	73+	72–53	52–
		63	63
		Median	Mean

(Times in seconds)

Questions:

F   1. __t__ Whom was Kay waiting for by the door? (The postman)
F   2. __t__ Who had promised to write her a letter? (Her father, or Father)
F   3. __t__ What had her father told her the letter would have on it? (A blue stamp)
F   4. __t__ Whom did Kay see walking toward her house? (The postman)
F   5. __t__ What was the man carrying on his side? (A big bag)
F   6. __t__ What did the man do? (He reached in his bag and gave Kay some letters, or he gave Kay some letters)
I   7. __–__ How did Kay know that one of the letters was for her? (Because it had her name on it, or because it had a blue stamp on it.) *Don't Know*
F   8. __–__ How did Kay feel when she opened the letter? (Happy) *Don't know*
F   9. __t__ What did she do because she was so happy? (She began to jump up and down)
F 10. __t__ What did Father tell Kay in the letter? (That he was going to buy her a pony)[5]

This second-grade passage is also from the *Ekwall Reading Inventory*. The "B" indicates a silent passage. The student who read it was about halfway through the third grade (3.5) and had recently taken a group standardized reading achievement test. On that test she scored at the 2.3 grade level in total reading achievement and at 2.7 on vocabulary. She scored 80 percent, indicat-

[5]Reprinted by permission of Allyn and Bacon.

ing that she was reading at her instructional level. One of the two questions she missed was an inference type and the other was a factual question. The examiner timed the reading and found that it took 127 seconds. Both the median and mean times for this passage are 63 seconds when read by a second-grade student. A student who is in the third grade and reading up to grade level should read this passage *fast*—in 52 seconds or less. On the third-grade passage this student scored at frustration level on comprehension, although she made only two repetition errors. Some conclusions:

1. She is an extremely slow reader. Since group standardized achievement tests are timed, she probably did not finish the test. This would penalize her considerably and partially account for scoring below grade level.
2. Since she missed the inference question, she may need help in making inferences; however, use extreme caution in making such an interpretation based on only one question in one passage.
3. Since this student made only two word-recognition errors on the third-grade oral passage that followed this one, and yet was reading at frustration level because her comprehension was low, we believe that metacognition exercises (Chapter 6) would be very beneficial to her.
4. Her below-average group standardized test score on vocabulary could have been a product of her inability to read at a normal rate for a third-grade student. An oral vocabulary test would reveal whether the problem was slow reading or if her vocabulary was actually below grade normal. If an oral test indicated that her vocabulary was normal or above, she probably needed help in overall comprehension. If her score was also low, she should be helped with vocabulary development; this would probably help her overall comprehension.
5. One does not usually emphasize reading rate a great deal with students at the third-grade level. However, apparently a major problem for this student was her inability to read more rapidly. Perhaps she should do repeated readings, practicing both word recognition and reading rate.

The elephant is the largest animal in the world that lives on land. A full-grown elephant may have a weight of about four tons and may be nine feet tall. Because elephants are so large, they have no natural enemies other than man. Since elephants have so few enemies, they are usually easy to get along with and almost always act friendly.

Elephants usually live in herds with around thirty members of all ages. A female, or lady elephant, is called a cow. The herd usually has a cow as its leader, who is in charge of all the other elephants. During the hottest part of the day the herd will huddle together and attempt to find shade. Near sundown the entire herd usually goes to a nearby river or lake for a drink. Elephants normally continue to stay together in a herd for most of their lives.

(148 Words) (Number of word recognition errors___2___)

Questions:

F   1. __+__ What is the largest animal in the world that lives on land? (The elephant)

F   2. __+__ How heavy might a full-grown elephant be? (About four tons)

F   3. __+__ Why do elephants have no natural enemies other than man? (Because they are so ~~large~~) **big**

F   4. __+__ Why are elephants almost always easy to get along with or why do they act friendly? (Because they have no or few enemies or because they are so large)

V   5. __–__ What is a herd? (A group of something, a group of elephants, or a good synonym) **Don't Know**

F   6. __+__ How many elephants usually live in a herd? (About thirty)

F   7. __+__ Who is usually the leader of an elephant herd? (A cow, a female, or a lady elephant)

F   8. __+__ What do elephants do during the hottest part of the day? (They huddle together and/or attempt to find shade)

F   9. __+__ What do elephants usually do near sundown? (Go to get a drink or go to a nearby river or lake)

F 10. __+__ What did it say that would make you think elephants usually like each other? (They stay together for most of their lives, they stay together, or they stay in a herd)[6]

The student who read this passage was about a third of the way through the fifth grade (5.3). She paused before the words *natural, herd,* and *huddle* and then was able to pronounce each of the words correctly, with the exception of *huddle.* Since the student made only two word-recognition errors on the *Ekwall Reading Inventory* and missed only one comprehension question, she is considered to be reading at her independent level on this passage. Some tentative conclusions:

1. She is having some difficulty with vowel sounds. This is shown by the fact that she mispronounced the vowels in the words *tons, natural, herd, huddle,* and *hottest.* All of these words were self-corrected with the exception of *huddle.* After she mispronounced *tons, natural,* and *hottest,* she corrected them. She also self-corrected *herd* but seemed unsure of its meaning, as she missed question number five. This probably indicates that she had *tons, natural,* and *hottest* in her speaking-listening vocabulary and corrected them from context. On the other hand, she was unsure of the meaning of *huddle,* as she did not correct the original vowel sound.

2. She appears to need help with the two simplest vowel rules; i.e., in CVC words the vowel is usually short and in the VCE the vowel is more often long and the *e* is silent. Of these two rules, she appears to be having more difficulty with the CVC rule.

3. Although *tons, natural, herd, huddle,* and *hottest* are not in the stu-

[6]Reprinted by permission of Allyn and Bacon.

dent's sight vocabulary, this is not serious, as one expects as many as 5 percent of the words at a student's own grade level to be unknown.

Miscue Analysis

Kenneth Goodman (1969) and Yetta Goodman and Carolyn Burke (1972) have developed procedures for analyzing students' oral reading behavior based on Kenneth Goodman's psycholinguistic model of reading. These authors refer to students' errors as "miscues," based on the assumption that oral reading behavior arises from the student's underlying language competence.

Goodman and Burke's *Reading Miscue Inventory* is intended for use by teachers. The administration of this inventory is a time-consuming and complicated task. The examiner asks the student to read a complete passage that has not been previously seen by the student and that is one grade level above the material the student reads in class. The examiner may not aid the student in pronouncing unfamiliar words. After the passage is read, the student is required to retell the story. The examiner asks only general questions. After careful analysis, the examiner is presumably able to determine the reading strategies employed by the student.

In our experience teachers have not found the *Reading Miscue Inventory* to be practical or helpful in their work with remedial students. Some teachers do find, however, that this approach helps them understand the reading process. Eugene Jongsma (1978) found that teachers who were trained in miscue analysis became more aware of students' reading strengths as well as weaknesses.

George Spache (1981) summarized the criticisms of the *Reading Miscue Inventory:*

> Reviewers of the Reading Miscue Inventory point out that the analysis of oral reading errors as suggested by its authors has not been shown to be related to the reading level for instruction. Much of the scoring of miscues is completely subjective, and there are no data regarding the expected frequency of these miscues at any age or grade level. Even the evaluation of the child's recall of the story under guiding or leading questions is completely subjective. The Inventory lacks standardized directions and reading selections, criteria for interpreting diagnostic patterns, norms for interpreting scores, reliability or validity data, and evidence for its prescribed reading strategies. (p. 142)

After a critical review of the research, Karen Wixson (1979) summarized both the strengths and weaknesses of miscue analysis:

> Recent promotion of miscue analysis has served the field of reading well. The popularization of miscue analysis has succeeded in bringing about an awareness of reading as a language process, and in sensitizing people to the necessity for a method of evaluation which will accurately

reflect this process in operation. However, the exact nature of the relationship between oral reading errors, as analyzed by standard miscue analysis procedures, and the reading process remains unclear. Further, it is unknown whether miscue analysis succeeds in identifying the critical features of readers' oral reading performance which reveal their relative proficiency with the reading process. Accordingly, the current use of miscue analysis procedures as a basis for evaluation and planning in both research and instruction appears at best to be premature. (p. 172)

THE CLOZE PROCEDURE

Another useful technique for placing students, the procedure consists of deleting every *n*th word and replacing it with a blank line. Students are to read the material and fill in the blanks using the correct word according to the proper context of the sentence. The percentages of correct answers are calculated, and from these percentages free instructional and frustration reading levels are derived.

John Bormuth (1967, 1968) researched the use of the cloze procedure to derive the percentage of correct answers equivalent to the independent, instructional and frustration reading levels and to derive information on reliability. His studies were later duplicated and validated by Earl Rankin and Joseph Culhane (1969): "The results of this replication of two previous studies tend to corroborate the validity of the comparable cloze and multiple-choice percentage scores found by Bormuth. . . . " (p. 197) Rankin and Culhane also studied the cloze procedure and compared it to multiple-choice tests.

These substantial correlations indicate that the cloze procedure is a highly valid measure of reading comprehension. The average validity coefficient was .68. Since the multiple-choice tests took several weeks to construct, the cloze tests are preferable for measuring comprehension or readability, and they are measuring substantially the same thing. (p. 196)

Jones and Pikulski (1974) in a report on cloze procedures pointed out that their study concerned sixth graders only.

Given this limitation, the data suggested that the cloze test gave a considerably more accurate reading level placement than did the standardized test. If the cloze test can approximate reading levels on an informal reading inventory as much as 70 to 80 percent of the time, its relatively brief administration time recommends its use to the classroom teacher. Not only does cloze procedure appear to provide a reasonably valid determiner of instructional reading level, but its very ease of construction and administration makes it a practical tool for teachers who have had no special training in test administration. (p. 437)

However, there are some apparent problems in the use of the cloze procedure. Claire Ashby-Davis (1985) has said it may not always be a valid measure of reading comprehension. Ashby-Davis notes that students must be able to do more than comprehend well:

> . . . cloze probably favors students who are not only good readers but also good writers. While the scores of this kind of student are inflated in terms of reading comprehension, the scores of good, average, or poor readers are underestimated when they are deficient in writing skills, particularly in those skills needed to complete cloze. (p. 589)

Frederick A. Duffelmeyer (1983) pointed out that the original research on the recommended percentages for the independent, instructional, and frustration levels were done with only fourth- and fifth-grade students. Duffelmeyer feels that these same percentages do not necessarily apply when dealing with students at the secondary level. This will be discussed in more detail later in this chapter.

Developing, Administering, and Scoring Cloze Passages

In constructing cloze passages you could omit every third, fifth, tenth, etc., word. However, most of the research is based on the deletion of every fifth word. Uniform blank lines replace each word that has been deleted. It should also be stressed that the commonly used percentages for determining students' independent, instructional and frustration reading levels are based on the deletion of every fifth word. If every fourth or sixth word were deleted, these commonly used percentages would not apply.

Passages may vary in length depending on the grade level of the students; however, for students of third- or fourth-grade age or above, passages of about 250 words are often used. The entire first and last sentences are usually left intact. If passages of 250 words plus intact first and last sentences are used and if every fifth word is omitted, there are fifty blanks, and every blank or answer is equivalent to two percentage points.

Cloze passages may be administered like group standardized reading tests. However, in administering cloze passages there are usually no specific time limits.

For passages in which every fifth word has been deleted, Rankin and Culhane's percentage scores for the various reading levels:

> Independent level = 58 percent to 100 percent
> Instructional level = 44 percent through 57 percent
> Frustration level = 43 percent or below

Duffelmeyer studied tenth-grade students and found the mean scores for poor, average, and good readers to be considerably higher than those obtained for Rankin and Culhane's fifth graders. Duffelmeyer found the size of the difference was 12, 15, and 11 percent respectively for poor, average, and good readers. As a result of his study he recommended using more stringent criteria for secondary students, although he did not suggest specific percentages.

In scoring the passages only the exact word omitted is usually counted as correct; synonyms are not accepted. Bormuth's research has shown that the overall percentages change very little regardless of whether synonyms are accepted or not. If synonyms were counted, it would make the passages much more difficult to score. What one teacher considered adequate another would not. Thus is lost interscorer reliability. This point was further emphasized by William A. Henk and Mary L. Selders (1984), who studied synonymic scoring of cloze passages by various teachers:

> Generally this study shows that synonymic scoring of cloze tests is highly variable. An individual's synonym cloze score appears simply too dependent on who grades the test. When the total score may vary by 25 percentage points or more, judgments about the quality of performance are tenuous at best. Ranges may be so broad that the same test protocol may indicate independent level performance by one rater and frustration level by another. This instability renders the synonymic scoring method largely impractical. (p. 286)

Henk and Selders did, however, suggest that teachers examine certain students' passages for synonymic appropriateness. They believe that certain students might actually be penalized for having a very extensive vocabulary. We believe that if a student's score is just below a border line, the teacher should carefully examine the synonyms. If the student used many good or reasonable synonyms, the teacher might wish to consider the student as reading at the next higher level.

In scoring cloze passages students are not usually penalized for incorrect spelling as long as there is little or no doubt about which word was meant to be used.

A plastic overlay such as an overhead projector transparency of each cloze passage could have the correct answers on the overlay. When this is superimposed on the student's copy you can readily check the answers and convert them to percentages.

Using the Cloze Procedure to Place Students in Graded Materials[7]

Often a teacher receives a new student to be placed in one of several books that vary in difficulty or grade level. As an example, a fifth-grade teacher teaches in a school where there are several sections of fifth graders but all are grouped heterogeneously, so that each year she can expect to receive students

---

[7]The explanation given in this section is based on Bormuth, John R. "The Cloze Readability Procedure," *Readability—1968*. Prepared by a committee of the National Conference on Research in English, National Council of Teachers of English.

reading from perhaps the first- or second-grade level through the sixth- or seventh-grade level. She has a number of basal textbooks at various levels, but each time she receives a new student she is faced with the problem of which book to assign. To use the cloze procedure to place students, she would take these steps:

1. Select a number of passages from various parts of each book (six to twelve passages depending on the size of the book). Make sure each passage begins a new paragraph and is about 250 words in length.
2. Give the tests to twenty-five to thirty students from classes in which the texts will be used.
3. Determine the percentage of correct answers for each student on each passage. An example illustrating this is shown in Table 11–5. The mean score for each passage is calculated and the mean of the mean scores is determined. The mean of the means is determined by adding all the means and dividing by the number of passages, in this case eleven.

$$\frac{\begin{array}{c}65.4 + 48.1 + 74.0 + 39.8 + 60.4 + 42.4 \\ + \ 42.4 + 25.6 + 41.2 + 73.0 + 52.0\end{array}}{11} = 51.3$$

4. Select the passage score that is closest to the mean of the means, in this case number 11; its mean score is 52.0 and the mean of the means is 51.3. In other words this passage is most representative of the book as a whole.
5. The procedure described above is followed for each textbook the

TABLE 11–5. Percentage Scores Made on Eleven Passages from a Book by Each of Ten Students.

	1	2	3	4	5	6	7	8	9	10	11
Don	66	60	72	28	62	44	28	54	52	64	42
Dwight	72	52	76	32	38	62	48	26	38	72	52
Denise	56	38	64	42	42	38	52	14	30	64	74
Syril	42	20	86	46	74	28	38	22	28	88	44
Ed	74	42	84	42	56	22	42	18	50	78	50
Rick	76	48	72	48	72	74	54	14	52	86	62
Judy	72	62	64	38	58	64	46	26	36	56	58
Jack	58	73	58	52	64	28	38	28	34	72	34
Cindy	64	38	82	38	62	42	40	26	42	84	44
Dennis	74	48	82	32	76	22	38	28	50	66	60
Totals	654	481	740	398	604	424	424	256	412	730	520

Mean score for each passage
(Total ÷ 10)   65.4   48.1   74.0   39.8   60.4   42.4   42.4   25.6   41.2   73.0   52.0

teacher is likely to use. One cloze passage from each text is duplicated and compiled into booklets. When a new student or group of students enters the teacher's room, each is given a test booklet containing the cloze passages. A score between 44 and 57 percent indicates the instructional level. Above 57 percent is the independent level, and below 44 percent lies the frustration level.

The reliability of the procedure described above depends on the following three factors:

1. Test length—longer tests are more reliable but take longer to correct.
2. Number of passages used—the larger the number from each book, the likelier is the one chosen to be representative of the book.
3. Variance in difficulty from page to page—some materials vary widely. This is especially true of textbooks other than basal readers.

Using the Cloze Procedure to Select Materials to Meet the Needs of the Students

In many states a state textbook committee selects three to five basal textbooks from the many possible choices. These books may be purchased using state funds. Each school district often must select from the list one textbook that best meets the needs of the students. In other instances a teacher may be given a choice of books that best meet the needs of his or her students. Adequacy of teacher's manuals, supporting services and materials, and the format of the material itself are all important considerations in making such a choice. The most important factor, however, is whether the students can read the material. The following steps can be used to make this decision:

1. Select a number of random passages from each book or set of material. The same length of passages as described earlier can be used.
2. Select a random sample of the students with whom the book will be used.
3. Determine the mean of each passage from each set of materials or book.
4. Determine the mean of the means from each set of materials or book.
5. Any materials or books that fall within the range of 44 through 57 percent are appropriate for the students' instructional level. Materials at 58 percent or above are appropriate for the students' independent level, and materials below 44 percent are inappropriate, since they are at the students' frustration reading level.

In using the cloze procedure, exercise a certain amount of judgment when making decisions concerning the difficulty of materials. For example, if a student is highly interested in a subject, or if the student has the ability to persevere, it is permissible to consider material just below the 57 percent level as appropriate for independent reading. This is true especially if several of the student's errors were correct synonyms.

Analyzing errors on the cloze procedure can also provide useful information on the reading ability of the student. Although no specific procedures have been developed, an informal survey of a student's answers will give practical information concerning the student's ability to read and write. It shows whether the student can spell and about the student's overall comprehension and vocabulary by noting whether substitutions are synonyms or out of context. You can also tell whether the student has been able to remember details given earlier in the passage by noting whether the student uses these to answer questions later in the passage.

The cloze procedure has also been studied to determine its effectiveness as a teaching device. An excellent review of this research was done by Eugene Jongsma (1971). Jongsma indicates that most teachers who taught with the cloze procedure without any follow-up activities or discussion found it of little or no value in teaching comprehension. However, he did find several studies in which students' comprehension was improved when they discussed their answers on cloze passages.

SUMMARY

The reading level and reading disabilities of individual students cannot be accurately determined using most group tests. For this reason teachers should learn to administer, score, and interpret informal reading inventories, which can help determine students' independent, instructional, and frustration reading levels. The criteria used in scoring informal reading inventories are also useful in helping teachers find the proper fit between students and reading materials. By coding a student's oral reading errors teachers can often gain considerable insight into that particular student's reading disability.

The use of the cloze procedure is popular among specialists. The cloze procedure has been well researched and has an advantage over informal reading inventories in that it can be administered as a group test.

REFERENCES

Ashby-Davis, C. (1985). Cloze and comprehension: A qualitative analysis and critique. *Journal of Reading, 28,* 585–589.

Betts, E. A. (1946). *Foundations of reading instruction.* NY: American Book Co.

Blanchard, J. S., Borthwick, P., Jr., & Hall, A. (1983). Determining instructional reading level: Standardized multiple choice versus IRI probed recall questions. *Journal of Reading, 26,* 684–689.

Bormuth, J. R. (1967). Comparable cloze and multiple-choice comprehension test scores. *Journal of Reading, 10,* 291–299.

Bormuth, J. R. (1968). Cloze test reliability: Criterion reference scores. *Journal of Educational Measurement, 5,* 189–196.

Bormuth, J. R. (1969). Empirical determination of instructional level. In J. A. Figurel (Ed.), *Reading and realism* (pp. 716–721). Newark, DE: International Reading Association.

Cunningham, P. M. (1976–1977). Teachers' correction responses to black-dialect miscues which are non-meaning-changing. *Reading Research Quarterly, 12,* 637–653.

D'Angelo, K., & Mahlios, M. (1983). Insertion and omission miscues of good and poor readers. *Reading Teacher, 36,* 778–782.

Davis, E. E., & Ekwall, E. E. (1976). Modes of perception and frustration in reading. *Journal of Learning Disabilities, 9,* 448–454.

Dechant, E. (1981). *Diagnosis and remediation of reading disabilities.* Englewood Cliffs, NJ: Prentice-Hall.

Ditto, L. D. (1974). *The effects of language characteristics in oral reading.* Unpublished doctoral dissertation, Michigan State University, East Lansing.

Duffelmeyer, F. A. (1980). The passage independence of factual and inferential questions. *Journal of Reading, 23,* 131–134.

Duffelmeyer, F. A. (1983). The effect of grade on cloze test scores. *Journal of Reading, 26,* 436–441.

Ekwall, E. E. (1974). Should repetitions be counted as errors? *Reading Teacher, 27,* 365–367.

Ekwall, E. E., & Solis, J. E. (1971). *Use of the polygraph to determine elementary school students' frustration reading level* (Final Report Project No. OG078). Washington, DC: U.S. Department of Health, Education, and Welfare.

Ekwall, E. E., Solis, J. E., & Solis, E., Jr. (1973). Investigating informal reading inventory scoring criteria. *Elementary English, 50,* 271–274.

Fuchs, L. S., Fuchs, D., & Deno, S. L. (1982). Reliability and validity of curriculum-based informal reading inventories. *Reading Research Quarterly, 18,* 6–26.

Goodman, K. S. (1969). Analyses of reading miscues: Applied psycholinguistics. *Reading Research Quarterly, 5,* 9–30.

Goodman, Y. M., & Burke, C. L. (1972). *Reading miscue inventory.* NY: Macmillan.

Guszak, F. J. (1970). Dilemmas in informal reading assessments. *Elementary English, 47,* 666–670.

Hardin, B., & Bernstein, B. (1976). What about reversals? *Teacher, 94,* 104, 108.

Henk, W. A., & Selders, M. L. (1984). A test of synonymic scoring of cloze passages. *Reading Teacher, 38,* 282–287.

Johns, J. L. (1977). Matching students with books. *Contemporary Education, 48,* 133–136.

Johns, J. L. (1983). The informal reading inventory: 1910–1980. *Reading World, 23,* 8–19.

Johnson, M. S., & Kress, R. A. (1965). *Informal reading inventories.* Newark, DE: International Reading Association.

Jones, M. B., & Pikulski, E. C. (1974). Cloze for the classroom. *Reading Teacher, 17,* 432–438.

Jongsma, E. A. (1971). *The cloze procedure as a teaching technique.* Newark, DE: ERIC/CRIER and the International Reading Association.

Kaufman, H. S., & Biren, P. L. (1976–1977). Persistent reversers: Poor readers, writers, spellers? *Academic Therapy, 12,* 209–217.

Masztal, N. B., & Smith, L. L. (1984). Do teachers really administer IRIs? *Reading World, 24,* 80–83.

McKenna, M. C. (1983). Informal reading inventories: A review of the issues. *Reading Teacher, 36,* 670–679.

McKiernan, J., & Avakian, M. (1980). Directional awareness training: Remediation of receptive letter reversals. *Academic Therapy, 16,* 193–198.

Oliver, J. E., & Arnold, R. D. (1979). Comparing a standardized test, an informal reading inventory and teacher judgment on third grade reading. *Reading Teacher, 15,* 56–59.

Powell, W. R. (1970). Reappraising the criteria for interpreting informal reading inventories. In D. L. DeBoer (Ed.), *Reading diagnosis and evaluation* (pp. 100–109). Newark, DE: International Reading Association.

Powell, W. R. (1971). The validity of the instructional reading level. In R. L. Leibert (Ed.), *Diagnostic viewpoints in reading* (pp. 121–133). Newark, DE: International Reading Association.

Rankin, E. F., & Culhane, J. W. (1969). Comparable cloze and multiple choice comprehension scores. *Journal of Reading, 13,* 193–198.

Spache, G. D. (1981). *Diagnosing and correcting reading difficulties* (2nd ed.). Boston: Allyn and Bacon.

Stanovich, K. E. (1982). Individual differences on cognitive processes of reading: I. Word decoding. *Journal of Learning Disabilities, 15,* 485–493.

Valmont, W. J. (1972). Creating questions for informal reading inventories. *Reading Teacher, 25,* 509–512.

Wixson, K. L. (1979). Miscue analysis: A critical review. *Journal of Reading Behavior, 11,* 163–175.

Zintz, M. V. (1981). *Corrective reading* (4th ed.). Dubuque, IA: William C. Brown.

Diagnosis and Remediation
Through the Use of Interviews

The first part of this chapter contains a discussion of the interview as a source of information from parents and students. Specific techniques are discussed, including the pros and cons of using a checklist to guide or structure the interview. A good parent interview and a good student interview are illustrated and discussed. A poor student interview illustrates some common errors to be avoided.

THE INTERVIEW AS A SOURCE OF INFORMATION

Interviews can be an important part of the diagnostic remedial process, especially in a clinical setting or when it is evident that more information concerning the home environment is required. Some types of information obtained from an interview seldom become available elsewhere. However, interviews are often time consuming, and unless the remedial teacher or reading clinician believes that further useful information will be revealed, this step in the diagnostic process should be eliminated.

In some cases, however, a remark by the student or information on an initial application form (see Chapter 15) indicates that information from parents or a guardian would be of considerable value. Although the remedial teacher is not likely to interview the parents of every student or hold a lengthy interview with each disabled reader, there is still need to be able to conduct a skillful interview. Some types of information that can be derived from an initial parent interview:

Information Gained from Parent Interviews

Parental views of student's problems.   Having lived with a student for a number of years, parents generally have a great deal of information about a student's problems. This is especially true if the parents have other children who are not disabled readers so that they are able to make accurate comparisons. Parents are often able to describe a student's problems, although they may not necessarily use the terminology the remedial reading teacher might use.

It is important to determine whether parents understand the severity of the problem or whether they are concerned to the point of badgering the student. If they lack understanding, they may fail to provide a proper study environment, cooperation in library activities, motivation for improvement, etc.

One of the coauthors spent several hours one afternoon diagnosing the reading problems of a beginning second-grade student. This student was so hyperactive that it was nearly impossible to do the testing one to one. His teacher had told his mother that he "jumped around a lot and would not sit still." The mother had no other children with whom to compare the child and consequently believed that the teacher was overstating the problem. The child was referred to a pediatrician, who prescribed medication to calm him down, and the child's performance immediately improved. The important point was that the interview elicited the mother's views about the child and provided immediate feedback in suggestions for remediation.

Emotional climate of the home.   A skilled interviewer can learn a lot from parents about the emotional climate of the home. This might include information on parental discord or sibling discord or rivalry that may be harmful to the well-being of the student.

Health factors.   Although some information about a student's health shows up on forms and applications, it is often desirable to elaborate on certain aspects of it through the interview. For example, we often find in discussing eye examinations that a parent has been led to believe a student has had a thorough eye examination at school, when all the student may have had was a rough screening test for far-point vision using the Snellen chart. What may appear on a form to have been a minor ear infection during early childhood may in fact have been a chronic infection that has contributed to a student's inability to use phonics because of inadequate auditory discrimination.

It is difficult for a parent who is untrained in health education and reading education to realize the important relationships between the two. For this reason a parent interview should usually cover health factors that contribute to reading retardation.

Reading material available at home.   Most homes contain some books, magazines, and newspapers. Many family libraries, in fact, contain fairly large numbers of books that parents perceive as good reading material for their children. In a few cases this may be true, but in most cases very little of the home library is appropriate for a disabled reader. Through interviews the remedial reading teacher can thoroughly discuss reading level and interest and can advise parents about more appropriate materials.

Library habits and time spent in reading.   Through interviews the remedial reading teacher can also obtain a much deeper insight into the actual amount of time a student spends reading as well as the student's library habits. If a student is asked how much time is spent reading, the answer is quite likely to be meaningless, since the student has little basis for "a lot" or "a little" in comparison with other students. Furthermore, until students reach eleven or twelve, they tend to have little accurate perception of time. Parents can provide much more accurate information on such matters and on students' use of the school and city library. During the interview the teacher can also provide helpful information on how to select books for their children.

Study habits and study environment.   The interview can also provide excellent information concerning study habits and the study environment. Questions such as, "Is a specific *amount* of time set aside each evening for study?" "Is a specific *time* set aside each evening for study?" "Does the student have a room of his or her own?" often reveal a great deal. It is hard to get accurate information of this nature from students because of their inadequate perception of time and from a parent through forms or applications.

Parental expectation.   Parental expectation varies a great deal, depending on such factors as their educational and socioeconomic level and to some extent religious preference. Only through the interview can the remedial reading teacher begin to determine whether parent expectations are realistic. The interview also provides an opportunity to counsel parents in realistic expectations for the student. For this the teacher draws on tests for reading level and reading potential as indicated by IQ or better yet by ability to learn reading-related tasks.

Social adjustment.   It is easy to derive information on a student's social adjustment from parents by asking: "Tell me about Erica's friends." "Tell me how she gets along with her friends." "Does she have a lot of friends or does she prefer to play with one or two friends or play alone?" "Does she make friends easily?" or "Do other students seem to notice that she has a reading problem?" Information of this nature can be especially helpful if the parents have other children to compare.

Independence and self-concept.   The parents can also tell about the independent work habits and self-concept of a student. Questions that elicit such information: "Can Jim seem to do work on his own or does he need someone to urge him on?" "Tell me about Jim's work habits." "How does Jim feel about his reading?" "How does Jim feel about himself?" or more specifically, "What do you think about Jim's self-confidence?"

Duties at home.   Students who have duties at home are more likely to work independently on school assignments. These duties may include such things as emptying the garbage, mowing the lawn, and doing dishes. The parent can say how many of these duties a student is expected to perform as well as how well the student does them. The parent interview is also a good opportunity to suggest the need for such duties to build independent work habits in the student.

Sleep habits.   A partial reason for the poor performance of many students is that they do not get enough sleep. Reading clinicians often find applications and forms filled out by parents somewhat inaccurate. For example, a form may ask, "What time does the student normally go to bed?" Although a parent in all honesty may answer "9:00 PM," a careful interview will often reveal that this is the time when parents would *like* the student to go to bed. The student may often be allowed to stay up much later to watch television programs, or the family may socialize a great deal, keeping the student up much later than the official bedtime.

Successful practices with the student.   A student's parents often reveal methods they find successful in getting the best performance from the student. This might be, "Please do this for me," or a small reward for successful completion of a task. Ask, "What do you find is successful in getting Dan to do things you want him to do?"

Previous tutoring and results.   Many students who come to reading clinics or to a remedial reading classroom have previously been tutored. The parent interview presents an excellent opportunity to discover the length and to some extent the success of past tutoring. Many parents have some knowledge of the types and success of it. Others have records or examples that suggest what types of materials and activities to use or to avoid.

Information Gained from Student Interviews

An initial interview with a student may reveal information that is difficult to gain in other ways. Some examples:

Self-concept.   Studies quoted in Chapter 7 have shown the importance of self-confidence for success in reading. Statements or questions that often elicit how a student feels: "Tell me about yourself." "How do you feel about yourself when you read?"

The student's perception of the reading problem.   Since it is difficult to help someone who does not recognize that a problem exists, it is often beneficial to ask, "How do you feel about reading?" "Tell me about your reading." "Do you think you have a problem with reading?" Many disabled readers recognize their problems immediately; however, a rather large percentage either hesitate to admit to a reading problem or do not recognize that they are disabled readers. A student who does not admit to or recognize the problem will need to be diplomatically shown that compared to other students of his or her age-grade level, the student does not read well. This is an essential part of the eight-step counseling procedure described in Chapter 7.

Past experiences in reading.   Students who perceive themselves as having read a great deal may reveal that they have read almost nothing on their own. The disabled reader may perceive as reading looking at pictures in magazines or looking at comic books. Inventories dealing with such questions do not usually uncover this. An interviewer, however, can readily tell whether the student really reads: "Do you remember the name of the last book you read? . . . Tell me about it." . . . "Can you tell me the names of some books you have read this year?" One very common characteristic of severely disabled readers is never to have read a book on their own.

Attitudes about reading.   The initial student interview also lets the remedial teacher learn more about attitudes: Does the student like to read? Has he or she had extremely bad experiences with reading? Questions that may be helpful: "What do you think about reading?" "What are the good things you remember about reading?" "What are the bad or unpleasant things you remember about reading?" "Would you like to become a better reader?"

Reading interests.   Since the initial interview with a student normally comes the first time you have a chance to meet alone, it is a good time to derive information on the student's interests and hobbies. In this way you will be able to help the student find interesting materials. It should also be helpful in establishing initial rapport. The initial student interview can also tell about future ambitions, vocational plans, etc., all of which can work to your advantage in establishing motivation for reading.

Reading environment.   It is well known that students copy their peers' and parents' habits. The initial student interview usually provides an excellent opportunity to learn about the student's reading environment: Does the student have a quiet place to read at home? Does the student see various members of the family read a great deal? Does he or she come from an environment where reading is encouraged and rewarded?

Instructional techniques and materials the student has used.   For disabled readers who have failed with a particular program or technique it is generally a good practice to change the technique as well as the materials. For example, we do not usually teach disabled readers using a hardbound basal reader, since it might very well revive old failures. During the initial interview, the remedial teacher can often discover which materials the student has used. The student, while not particularly likely to remember the name of a book, probably will remember the names of characters in basal reader series he or she has used. In the El Paso Reading Center we use a list of characters in basal reading series. The interviewer asks: "Did you ever use a book about a little black dog named Tag?" "Did you use a book about Dot and Jim?" In many cases the instructional program will also have generally utilized a particular technique. To use this type of information the teacher must be somewhat familiar with the most commonly used basal reading series.

Information on technique alone can usually be obtained by using such questions as, "How did your teacher teach you words?" "What did your tutor do to teach you to sound out words?" "Although answers may be rather vague, further questioning will usually clarify which techniques have been successful and which unsuccessful.

The student interview can also provide useful information on such things as the amount of television the student watches each week, the student's duties at home, the time the student goes to bed, etc.

INTERVIEW TECHNIQUES

An interview can be either highly successful or of little value, depending on the interviewer. The skills for successful interviewing can quite easily be learned through a little experience and a few important techniques:

Make the Interviewee Comfortable

Whether it be student or parent, it is important to make the interviewee as comfortable as possible. Skilled counselors are usually masters at this.

One of the best ways to make parents comfortable is to get right down to business. They have usually come to the interview because they are concerned about their child. After greeting them and seating them in a comfortable chair, saying, "Tell me about Don's reading" is often sufficient to break the ice and get them started talking.

In interviewing students you may wish to say, "Tell me a little something about yourself." This leaves the student free to talk about anything he or she would like to. Sometimes, however, such a broad question is too open-ended. If the student replies, "Like what?" you may wish to probe further. "Well, tell me about some of your hobbies, your pets, or what you like to do."

Seat the student or parent to the side of your desk facing you rather than behind it so that the desk does not form a barrier.

Use Open-Ended Questions

Any experienced teacher knows that the tone of a class is set in the first few minutes. A professor who begins with a lecture and then tries to hold an open discussion is likely to get little or no response for the first few minutes after the lecture. The same principle holds true for interviewing. When the opening questions call for one- or two-word answers, a tone or mood that is difficult to change is often set. Open-ended questions usually set a tone for the interviewee to do much of the talking. All that may be needed is a nod of the head, an occasional "Yes" or "I see" or perhaps another open-ended question to redirect a response.

Some good examples of open-ended questions for parents: "Tell me about Susie's reading." "Why do you think she developed the problem?" "How does she feel about her ability to read?" Some good examples for students: "Tell me about your reading." "Why do you think you have this problem?" "Tell me what you like to read about."

Give the Interviewee Time to Think

It may at first seem foolish to emphasize that we often do not give the interviewee time to respond. The untrained interviewer, however, often feels the need for a constant chain of verbal exchanges. Remember that the interviewee is often asked to recall information and to gather thoughts and express opinions about matters to which he or she has not given much thought in the past.

In interviewing parents of disabled readers there is seldom any difficulty eliciting information, since they have in most cases pondered many of the questions that you are likely to ask. It is often more difficult to get students to open up and begin talking. During this time inexperienced interviewers often feel ill at ease and compelled to keep a constant conversation going. Instead, ask an open-ended question—"What do you think about your reading?" or "Tell me about a book you have read"—and then give the interviewee ample time to speak. In some cases this may be as long as fifteen to thirty minutes.

Ruth Strang, who was a world-renowned authority in counseling and reading, once interviewed a group of high school students in front of a graduate class that one of the coauthors was taking. In the beginning she asked a few questions, and there were several rather long silences. A little later every one of the high school students began to open up and became extremely talkative. After a while Dr. Strang left and invited students in her graduate course to continue interviewing the high school students. One of the first questions was why the interviewees suddenly became so talkative after being so quiet at first. They all agreed that Dr. Strang, who they did not realize was an expert in interview technique, seemed so helpless that they all felt a compassionate need to help her out by talking! We can all learn a lot from Dr. Strang's technique when we find a rather shy student.

Refrain from Expressing Negative Judgment or Attitudes

No interviewer is likely to agree with everything the interviewee says. In the beginning stages of counseling either students or parents, it is often wise to refrain from commenting on their opinions. This is not to say that an interviewer should not be honest, but that one may need to hold back some rather strong convictions. For example, many parents berate comic books and would prefer that their children not read them. On the other hand, most reading specialists probably feel that if a student has not developed the reading habit, even comic books are a step in improving his or her reading. During the initial interview, however, it is wise to refrain from strongly disagreeing with the interviewee, who will soon sense disapproval and probably terminate the interview. There is usually ample time at a slightly later date to counsel either the student or parent about changes in attitude.

Avoid the Use of Technical Terms

Most people have heard in conversation an unfamiliar term and been faced with the sometimes embarrassing situation of either having to ask or trying to bluff through until the subject is changed. This should be avoided in interviews, especially of parents. Those who have been working in education for a number of years often ask questions in teachers' jargon, for example, "How does Rose-Marie get along with her siblings?" "Has she had any traumatic experiences during the past year?" "Do you perceive her as an introvert?" Some people do not know what *siblings, traumatic, perceive,* and *introvert* mean. This causes a great deal of embarrassment for the person being interviewed.

Promise Only What You Know You Can Accomplish

If a doctor told you that you had cancer, you would immediately ask such questions as, "What are my chances for recovery?" "How long will it take to recover if I do recover at all?'' ''How much is it likely to cost?'' Parents are also naturally concerned about the remedial teacher's prognosis for success. However, there is a natural tendency to tell parents that everything will probably be all right in a short amount of time. A number of studies have demonstrated the effectiveness of remedial reading and that for most disabled readers, especially the severely disabled, regaining the ability to read at grade level is a long-term process.

Although parents should not be discouraged from seeking remediation for a disabled reader, they should be made to understand that most such children need to learn what normal-achieving students are learning in addition to making up for material they have already missed. In most cases this is rather a long process. A fairly good rule of thumb, although with many exceptions, is that with good tutoring a student takes nearly as long to recover from a reading disability as to develop it.

It is easy to explain to parents that their child made more rapid progress than you expected; it is much more difficult to say that after long tutoring their child has made little or no progress. For this reason parents should be reassured that progress from tutoring is usually forthcoming, but that the rate of achievement is likely to vary a great deal depending on such factors as potential for learning and the severity of the problem.

Do Not Undersell Your Own Knowledge and Abilities

Because people vary a great deal in their self-concept as well as in abilities, society demands a certain amount of modesty in dealings with others. Modesty in some areas is only natural; however, the remedial teacher should not be so modest that parents lose faith in the ability of the teacher. Most well-trained reading teachers realize that very little is known about certain types of severe reading disability. When students exhibit the symptoms of severe reading disability, it is usually wise to tell parents that progress is often very slow and that specialists know very little about remediation for their child's kinds of problems. However, well-trained teachers also convey to parents that they are as capable of dealing with the problem as any other expert in the field. It is also important to convey to parents that if symptoms the teacher is not qualified to deal with appear, the teacher will recommend someone who is qualified.

Do not sell yourself short. People do not want to think they are taking their car to a second-rate mechanic, let alone placing their child with a second-rate remedial reading teacher.

Avoid the Use of Words That May Offend Older Students

Family titles vary widely, so when dealing with students of any age, especially older students, it is usually a good practice to refer to parents as ''your mother'' and/or ''your father,'' since these terms are not cold and yet do not appear childish.

Avoid the Use of Overly Personal Questions

In interviewing parents you are likely to find a great variation in willingness to discuss certain factors that affect the well-being of a child. Avoid personal questions such as, "Do you have a happy marriage?" "Is there much conflict at home?" If a parent feels such matters are important, the same information can usually be elicited by open-ended, less personal questions such as, "Can you tell me something about the emotional climate of your home?"

Refer to Yourself in the First Person

Most experienced interviewers and teachers of older students refer to themselves in the first person. However, there is a tendency for inexperienced interviewers and teachers of young children to refer to themselves as "Mrs. Smith" or "your teacher." This is often quite offensive and should be avoided.

Ask Only One Question at a Time

A common mistake is asking several questions at one time. This reminds us of a presidential press conference; an overzealous reporter asks the president a whole series of questions, to which the president may reply, "Now which question do you want me to answer?" If he chooses to be less sarcastic, he may attempt to answer the first one or two questions. Parents or students usually answer the first question or the one they feel is most important and ignore the rest.

Remember That Children Usually Have an Inaccurate Perception of Time and Numbers

Teachers accustomed to working with students past the age of twelve, unless they have younger children of their own, often fail to realize that younger children have a very inaccurate perception of time and numbers. In interviewing eight- or nine-year-old students, there would be very little use in asking, "About how much television do you watch each week?" To get a good answer ask specific questions such as, "What programs did you watch last night?" or go through the listings with them.

The same procedure should be used with numbers. Do not ask, "About how many books have you read this year?" Instead list the titles the student remembers.

THE USE OF INTERVIEW GUIDES AND/OR CHECKLISTS

This may be advantageous or detrimental depending on skill. The interviewer who uses a very detailed checklist has the advantage of being reminded to cover all of the information. However, a detailed checklist can structure the interview to the point that it prevents the interviewer from carefully listening to responses. When this happens, the interviewer may fail to capitalize on significant remarks made by the interviewee.

Personal experience indicates that the use of a broad outline of points to be covered in an interview is often helpful but that when the outline or checklist becomes too detailed the spontaneity of the conversation is too often lost. For this reason we suggest a broad outline similar to the following for interviewing students.

1. Interests
    1.1. Clubs—church
    1.2. Hobbies
    1.3. Friends
    1.4. How is spare time spent?
2. Student's attitudes
    2.1. Toward family
    2.2. Toward school
        2.1.1. Favorite subjects and least-liked subjects
    2.3. Teachers
    2.4. Friends
    2.5. The reading problem
        2.5.1. Is the student aware of the problem?
        2.5.2. What does the student think the problem is?
        2.5.3. How much trouble has the student had?
        2.5.4. Why does the student have this difficulty?
        2.5.5. What are the student's suggestions for solutions?
        2.5.6. Does the student enjoy reading?
        2.5.7. What does the student read?
        2.5.8. Does the student go to the library or own books?
    2.6. The student
        2.6.1 How does the student feel about himself or herself in relation to other students?

A similar broad outline may be developed for interviewing parents; however, many parents will have filled out a form before meeting with the teacher. If so, it may serve as a guide for clarifying the student's health history, the onset of the reading problem, etc. The outline used with parents will also vary depending on whether it is used in the public schools, a university clinic, etc. For these reasons the interviewer should develop an outline for his or her own particular setting.

EXAMPLES OF INTERVIEWS

The first interview below was between a university student (I), who was meeting the mother (M) of a ten-year-old boy (Tim) for the first time. The boy was not present. After the first interview the university student asked the mother to wait in the reading center during a short interview with Tim (T).

As you read these two interviews, note techniques that seemed to work especially well, any information helpful in working with the boy, and any techniques that could be improved on.

Initial Interview with Tim's Mother

1.   I: Who recommended Tim for the reading center?
2.   M: Mrs. Jones had a friend who came here, so several of the teachers and I came up here last spring. She thought it would be good for Tim because they tried numerous things to pinpoint the problem.
3.   I: It is difficult to pinpoint the problem, especially if you don't have the right tools. What seems to be his main problem?
4.   M: I don't really know. I can't put my finger on it. He has difficulty, or maybe he doesn't even try to attack the words. I suppose he has the tools for them because he was tutored by the reading resource teacher.
5.   I: Oh yes.
6.   M: For a while she felt he was not happy because there were too many other children and she was afraid he felt he was being categorized as being not too bright. He has the tools for breaking the words down, so let's take him out of the tutoring and see how he does. He comprehends well, and if you read the material to him, he gets it.
7.   I: He understands what is read to him?
8.   M: He doesn't. Usually I read the whole chapter for him but I don't do his reading for him because they do this at school but say he doesn't really want to read. He doesn't take books. We belong to one of the Weekly Reader Book Clubs because he wanted to, and those books just sit on the shelf. They are only third-grade books, but he doesn't even try to read any of them. They are pretty long, and he really wants something quick so that he can read.
9.   I: He wants something that's real quick to read?
10.   M: He doesn't attempt words that he could sound out if he tried. He just guesses at them, and it's frustrating for me because I think he can do better. Sometimes I wonder if his memory needs training because he can look at those vowels and he can't tell you what they should say. I think by now he has had it every year.
11.   I: You say he has a hard time with the vowel sounds; what about the consonant sounds?
12.   M: Well when he first went to the second school, which was in the

second grade, the teacher that tested him said he had trouble with consonant blends and things like this, but she could not find anything like dyslexia.

13. I: This is something that I will not categorize Tim with. Teachers are getting away from this kind of thing.

14. M: Well he can't read fast enough, which makes all his achievement tests low because he doesn't get through with them. He does have a good attitude about school. I think the teachers say he does.

15. I: What kind of work does he do in his other subjects?

16. M: Well he doesn't . . . I don't know. He doesn't knock himself out studying, but he does try.

17. I: He tries?

18. M: Yes, he really puts forth lots of effort in everything he tries to do. My helping him at home is not good because I get frustrated, and he is in tears. When he was in the second grade I really tried hard to work with him, and it just made both of us nervous wrecks, and so in the third grade my husband said just let him go. Either he makes it or doesn't. You're not doing him any good by yelling.

19. I: I see. When did you notice that he had a specific reading problem?

20. M: Well, after first grade and he came out with a "C" in reading, but he couldn't read.

21. I: He couldn't read at all?

22. M: Really! Like nothing could he read, and he was not happy.

23. I: I imagine that this upset him.

24. M: I think that he felt kids would make fun of him and that stuff. They did this usually coming home because he couldn't keep up in reading with the rest of them, so we put him in another school and Mrs. Jones was his teacher. She would work with him on Saturdays. At the end of the year she realized how little he had to work with. She said that he had a poor foundation, or just had not retained what was given him. There was talk of holding him back, but they said he had the ability to do the work and that he would be bored with doing the same things. She said he was just like being in a cage and couldn't get through to the material. So he doesn't mind school. He gets upset if he gets too much homework and stuff, but he is eager to learn. He was just beside himself to come here. Tim said that he could not wait until he could read better.

25. I: Yes. That's a good sign. I'm glad he wants to come to the center. Now tell me, how does he get along with his peers?

26. M: He gets along with them all right, but since he goes to the new school, he doesn't know too many children in the immediate

neighborhood. He goes out and rides with them sometimes. I somehow think he is a little immature because . . . I don't know. I used to think that he was.

27. I: He just turned ten?

28. M: Yes, just in August. I think maybe he depended on everybody because he is the third child and close to the others. The daughter just older than him took care of him. She did things for him. He didn't have to talk as early as everybody because we were always handing him things. Of course, he had the hearing problem also.

29. I: Yes.

30. M: So I thought maybe he couldn't hear all of these sounds or distinguish them when writing and spelling. But supposedly his hearing is in normal limits now. The loss that he does have would be with the female voice range, which could have given him lots of trouble earlier in his schooling.

31. I: Yes, in the first grade when he was being taught to read. When did this problem get cleared up completely?

32. M: About two years ago. Whenever he gets a cold, his hearing level goes down. But he is not taking allergy shots now. We just give him an antihistamine when his nose starts running and this does all right. He hasn't had too many ear infections, but there is scarring in the ears. But anyway, the hearing tests indicate that his hearing is within the normal range.

33. I: I noticed this on the application. The previous hearing difficulties could have been a problem.

34. M: But in two years he should have been able to pick up all of the sounds.

35. I: He might have missed something important at the beginning that could be the cause of his reading problem. I hope to find out what it is. Do you read to Tim?

36. M: Well, we used to. My daughter used to read to him quite a bit. Nobody has read to him in the past year or so, and I'm sure he had less read to him than the older ones because I haven't had the time with the other children, you know. This isn't the right thing to do. Maybe there was too much television. So he didn't bother to read or listen.

37. I: Are his study habits good at home?

38. M: Oh no! I don't think they are particularly good. When I ask him what homework he has, he says none. They work individually at school, so most things he finishes there, unless he really goofs something up. Then he brings it home. Since he started this year, I haven't had to push him. I think he has kept up. Of course, he hasn't been in school very long. And he seems happy and content. Interested, at least. He comes home with tales of what has

gone on. So I think he is enjoying school. The other night he said that he surely will be glad to read better, so he can read the instructions on model airplanes.

39.   I: That is interesting. Does he like most models?

40. M: Yes, and he likes animals and stuff like that. He liked to read about them, but most of the books that have the information he wants are a little beyond him.

41.   I: Books that are more scientific?

42. M: He just can't break down the words. They are just too much. He is unfamiliar with the words so they don't mean anything to him. His vocabulary is not very big. I am sure that is why he can't read very well. I feel his vocabulary is not as good as most children his age. He seems to understand anything we say . . . all of us talking. He doesn't act like he can't understand.

43.   I: That's good. Besides his ear problem, has he had any other serious illness?

44. M: No. Just the normal things.

45.   I: Does Tim do much reading at home?

46. M: Not much. He joined the book club, but this lasted only a year. He would never finish a book. I tried to encourage him to go to the shelf and read these books, but he wasn't too interested.

47.   I: Is he interested in the comics?

48. M: Oh yes. Peanuts he always reads. Of course they don't have very much writing on them.

49.   I: But it is still reading!

50. M: But he doesn't have much interest in books. If there's nothing good on television, he might sit down and read. He reads comic books like Archie once in a while. I think they're really trash.

51.   I: What are his favorite television programs?

52. M: The cartoons of course. (*laugh*)

53.   I: Does he spend much time watching them?

54. M: Yes.

55.   I: Does Tim like sports?

56. M: He is not very well coordinated. He can't catch a ball well or anything like that. I'm sure that's partly our fault. We're not very athletic. His older brother gets very put out with him because he can't catch anything. So he doesn't want to bother. I think Tim would like to except he doesn't do as well as the others and this discourages him. The kids always make comments, you know.

57.   I: Kids are sometimes cruel to each other.

58. M: Yes, they are. But Tim still tries. He goes to the "Y" three times a week. . . . He took a physical fitness test, but did not do very well. He clobbered himself on the chin-ups and other things. He

doesn't do them at home. He did not ride a bicycle as soon as most children do. There are a lot of hills . . . but he rode a lot this summer with a friend.

59.   I: Does he make friends easily?
60. M: He doesn't go seeking new friends. Of course, not going to the same school as the other kids in the neighborhood is probably bad. On the weekends he stays at home or tries to get a friend from his school to play with that lives near us. Or he plays with his younger sister.
61.   I: I see. Well, would it be all right to get Tim's record from the school?
62. M: Yes. They said they would be glad to send the center anything that could be of help.
63.   I: That is good. You've been very helpful. I appreciate the time you have given me very much. Thank you.

Initial Interview with Tim

1.   I: Is there anything you want to start off telling me, Tim?
2.   T: Well, I'm in the fifth grade and ten years old.
3.   I: What do you like to do?
4.   T: I like to draw and I like to do drama at school, and paint and do papier-mâché, and all kinds of art.
5.   I: What kind of drawing do you like to do the best?
6.   T: Of people.
7.   I: Of people?
8.   T: No, I don't really draw them. I just make them up.
9.   I: So you just make them up. That's fine. What about your paintings?
10.   T: On my paintings, I paint like pictures of the sun, or the grass or something like that.
11.   I: I see. Getting back to people, what kind of people do you like to draw?
12.   T: Well some of the time I draw them with glasses and big ears, and big chins and things like that. . . .
13.   I: Funny things? They call them caricatures.
14.   T: Yes, that's right.
15.   I: What about the drama? Do you like to act?
16.   T: Yes.
17.   I: In plays?
18.   T: Well, in school the teacher would give us . . . well, like make up a pantomime for this week. So we would go home and practice and think of a pantomime and practice it, and the next time we had drama we'd do it. And we'd talk about it and make criticisms about it. So the next time we could do better.

19. I: What do you like to pantomime?
20. T: Well, really it depends . . . like in a . . . like something sad, well not sad, but something unusual . . . that doesn't happen very often or . . .
21. I: Something out of the ordinary. Something that doesn't happen every day. What are some of the things you have done?
22. T: Well, today, I don't know if this is very unusual, but I took a chair, put a table in front of me, act like the chair was a car and the table was a car and it was in the middle of the road, and I tried to get it out of the way. . . .
23. I: Did they guess what you were doing?
24. T: Yes.
25. I: What do you think about the way you read?
26. T: Well, I don't know. I guess I'm not too good.
27. I: What do you mean by that?
28. T: Like when I read, I don't know some of the words.
29. I: What do you do when you come to a word you don't know?
30. T: Sometimes I try to sound it out, but I can't do that most of the time.
31. I: Do you think we should try to help you with that?
32. T: Yeah, that would be all right.
33. I: Do you think you usually understand what you read?
34. T: Yeah, if I know all the words.
35. I: Well, tell me something, Tim. Do you like to read?
36. T: Yes.
37. I: What's your favority story? Or books?
38. T: Well, there's not many books about monkeys, but I'd like to read about monkeys.
39. I: What about the other animals?
40. T: Well, I like them, too. Dogs, cats, yes, I like them, too, and I like to read about them too—and Vikings.
41. I: And Vikings. You must like the seamen. What do you like about the Vikings?
42. T: Well, I'm not sure. They just seem brave and all this, and they only liked to live in the cold, and I also like things about the cold, like walruses, Eskimos, and things like this.
43. I: That's good. That's real good. That's interesting. I imagine you know a lot of things about these subjects.
44. T: Well, not a lot. But some.
45. I: You said you liked the Vikings. The Vikings were seamen. Do you like the sea?
46. T: Yes.
47. I: Have you ever seen the ocean?
48. T: Not in true life. In pictures and movies. But that's all.
49. I: That's good. Tim, how do you do your homework?

50. T: We don't have very much homework. We most of the time just do it at school.
51. I: What are you reading about in geography?
52. T: Well, we don't have geography. It's social science.
53. I: I see.
54. T: We talk about people and things. In the fifth chapter they talk about prehistoric things. They told us in the first of it that this railroad company was digging . . . well, making a path and came across this great, big, old rock; tried to move it aside, and when they did, there were five skeletons there. And skulls. And this guy . . . I forget what they called them . . . well, dug farther down and found their bodies . . . and this guy thinks they were prehistoric men.
55. I: That's kind of in line with your animals. You know they find a lot of prehistoric animals. Maybe we can find you some good books and stories about these.
56. T: Yes, that would be all right.
57. I: How much time, Tim, do you spend reading outside of school time?
58. T: Not much. Well, most of the time after school, I want to read but most of the books are too easy for me, or they're just . . . There's this one book that I was starting a long time ago. I stopped that one cause I was reading this other book, and another book, and finally I just read the same one to where I was before and quit.
59. I: And you quit at the same place?
60. T: Yes. That's all I read.
61. I: Well, maybe one of these days you can go back and finish it. Can you tell me the names of any of the books you have read this year?
62. T: Well, let's see. (*pause*) I guess I just can't remember any. There was this other book I told you about; but I guess I really don't read very much.
63. I: Do you think you would like to read if we could find something about monkeys or other animals?
64. T: Sure.
65. I: How much time do you spend watching television?
66. T: Well, let's see. On school days not much. Well, maybe a little, but most of the time I'm wrestling with my brother. Or I'm drawing pictures.
67. I: So you don't spend too much time watching television during the weekdays. How much do you watch during the weekends?
68. T: On Saturdays I watch quite a little bit. I like to watch Disney and things like that. I watch the cartoons.
69. I: Who do you watch them with?

70.   T: If Sarah's awake, I take her down with me on Saturday. I put her by the door where all of the toys are. She plays and I watch her and the T.V. She's my baby sister.
71.   I: Tim, how do you get along with your brothers and sisters?
72.   T: O.K. most of the time.
73.   I: Who do you play with most of the time?
74.   T: My brother.
75.   I: How old is he?
76.   T: He's fourteen.
77.   I: What are some of the things you do?
78.   T: Sometimes we make up things. Like I made a model of this mummy and we decided like it was the year 2000 or something and I'd look at the mummy and say some mumble jumble, and say, Mummy, come alive. And really, most of the time we pretend that a lot of things are real. And my brother likes to read also.
79.   I: Does your brother read to you?
80.   T: Well, he used to. But now he doesn't.
81.   I: Tim, I think that's about all for now. I want you to know that we're going to help you as much as possible during the coming weeks. You certainly have been helpful to me and I thank you.

In the preceding interviews each statement is numbered. These numbers are used for reference in the following discussion.

Techniques Used and Information Gained from Initial Interview with Tim's Mother

Note the following techniques:

3. Use of open-ended question to elicit what Tim's mother believed was his most important problem.
5. Use of simple "Oh yes" to get her to continue talking.
7. Question to clarify whether the mother believed Tim had a problem with comprehension.
9. Repetition of enough of the mother's statement to clarify what she meant *and* to let her know the interviewer was listening very carefully.
11. Further questioning to clarify the problem.
13. The interviewer diplomatically tells the mother that no one really knows what dyslexia is and the term should probably not be used.
17. Very short repetition (in question tones) to encourage the mother to continue.
21. Clarification of what the mother meant by "couldn't read."
23. Neutral statement that encouraged the mother to continue.
29. Again, the use of a simple "Yes" to get her to continue.
31. Clarifying the question.

41. Again, simple statement that encourages her to continue.
49. Interviewer does not disagree but lets her know that reading comic books is still reading, which indicates the interviewer's approval.
57. Encouraging, reassuring remark.
63. Expression of appreciation for mother's help.

Now note the following useful information:

4. Mother indicates that Tim probably has problems with word-attack skills.
4. He has been tutored before.
6. Indication of a possible problem with low self-concept.
6,8. There is some confusion about whether he comprehends well.
8. Tim does not read much, if any, on his own.
8. There is some indication that he might be encouraged to read if the interviewer could find something short that Tim could finish in a small amount of time.
10,12. Indication of difficulty with consonants, consonant blends, and vowels.
14. Mother perceives Tim's reading speed as too slow.
14. Tim has evidently maintained a good attitude towards school.
18. As with many parents, mother cannot work well with her son on his reading problem.
20,22. Indication of a problem from the very beginning of school.
24. More indication that Tim may have a low self-concept.
26. Mother believes he may be immature.
28. Some indication that he may lack initiative and/or self-confidence.
30,32,34. Possible explanation for Tim's poor start in school and a possible problem at the time he was interviewed. (Tests performed at the reading center indicated that he still had a severe hearing loss. When this was corrected he improved very rapidly.)
36,38. Some indication of poor study habits.
38. An indication of Tim's desire to learn to read better.
38,40. Information on what might motivate him to read.
42. His mother believes his vocabulary is low.
46. Indication that Tim does very little reading at home.
48. An indication that he does like comic books.
50. Mother has a negative attitude about comic books.
56. More indication of the possibility that Tim has a low self-concept.
60. Some indication that he does not have many friends his own age to play with at home.

Techniques Used and Information Gained from Initial Interview with Tim

Note the following techniques used by the interviewer:

1. Use of open-ended question to let Tim talk about anything he wished.
3. Another open-ended question to draw the student out.
5–23. Interviewer indicated deep interest in Tim's interests and thus helped establish rapport.
25. Open-ended question to uncover Tim's perception of his reading problem.
27. Further pursuit of Tim's perception of his reading problem.
29. Question to verify Tim's perception of his reading problem.
31. Solicitation of Tim's commitment that he needs help.
33. Diagnosis of Tim's perception of whether he has a comprehension problem.
35–47. Eliciting of information on reading interests.
55. Solicitation of Tim's commitment to read about things he is interested in.
57–61. Questioning to find out whether Tim really reads on his own. Note that in number 61 the interviewer pins him down, and discovers that Tim really doesn't read any books at all.
81. Assurance is offered that the interviewer will help him as much as possible, but no promises are made that cannot be kept.

Now note the following information derived from the interview:

4–24. What Tim likes to do in his spare time.
26. Tim's perception of his ability to read.
28–34. Tim's perception of his reading problem.
34–48. Guidelines for locating materials Tim should be interested in reading.
50. The amount of homework required by the teachers in the school he attends.
58–62. Student does not read anything that is not required.
66–70. How free time is spent.
62–80. Relationship with siblings.

Initial Interview with Danny

Although psychologists often say not to teach by showing bad examples, we have chosen one more example of an initial student interview to illustrate some problems. As with the two preceding interviews, it will be discussed more thoroughly at the end. However, as you read it, be sure to note the tremendous difference between this and the preceding student interview.

The interviewer was meeting nine-year-old Danny for the first time. An interview had already been conducted with his mother.

1. I: Hi, Danny. I'm Mrs. Stevens. How old are you?
2. D: Nine.
3. I: Nine years old, boy, that's getting up there, huh? What grade are you in?
4. D: Fourth.
5. I: Fourth grade. Did you have any trouble finding UTEP?
6. D: Ummm, yeah.
7. I: Did you help your mother?
8. D: Nope.
9. I: You didn't.
10. D: Nope.
11. I: She didn't know the way and I told her you probably could help her. Is this your first time here?
12. D: Uh huh.
13. I: It's kind of big, huh?
14. D: Uh huh.
15. I: Think you'd like to come here someday?
16. D: Uh huh.
17. I: Go to school when you're all grown up and out of high school.
18. D: Uh huh.
19. I: Think you might, huh?
20. D: Uh huh.
21. I: Well, where do you go to school?
22. D: Edwards.
23. I: Edwards, where is that—at Biggs Field?
24. D: Uh huh.
25. I: Do you live on post?
26. D: Nope.
27. I: You don't? Where do you live?
28. D: Biggs Field.
29. I: Biggs Field. I know where that is. We used to live at Fort Bliss. Do you know where Fort Bliss is?
30. D: Uh huh.
31. I: Do you go there often?
32. D: Uh huh.
33. I: Just to the PX, huh.
34. D: Uh huh.
35. I: That's a fun trip, huh? Do you participate in sports, play football, baseball?

36. D: Used to.
37. I: Which one—football or baseball?
38. D: Football and baseball.
39. I: You are not playing football this fall, huh?
40. D: Uh huh.
41. I: I understand your brother is playing and you wanted to go to the game tonight.
42. D: Uh huh.
43. I: That's just a practice one though, isn't it?
44. D: Uh huh.
45. I: So that's not too great, just to miss the practice one.
46. D: I don't know.
47. I: Do they play their games on Saturdays?
48. D: Uh huh.
49. I: Bet you won't miss many of them, huh? You won't miss any of them.
50. D: Maybe. I got to go to catechism.
51. I: Oh, you have to go to catechism on Saturdays. Well, what else do you do?
52. D: Nothing.
53. I: Nothing? Do you know why you came here?
54. D: Nope.
55. I: You don't know. Mother didn't tell you.
56. D: Nope.
57. I: Well, this is the reading center. Do you have any trouble with reading?
58. D: Uh huh.
59. I: Maybe you can tell me about it. What trouble do you have with it?
60. D: Hard words.
61. I: Hard words—when you say hard words, are they little words or big words?
62. D: Big words.
63. I: Big words, and why do they give you so much trouble?
64. D: (*cannot be understood*) They all have twenty letters.
65. I: They all have what?
66. D: Around twenty or fifteen letters in them.
67. I: They all have too many letters. Oh boy, you didn't learn how to break them down into syllables?
68. D: Yep.
69. I: Oh, you do know how.
70. D: Uh huh.
71. I: And they still give you trouble, huh?
72. D: Uh huh.

73.   I: Anything else about them that causes trouble?

74.   D: Nope.

75.   I: Nothing else. How about little words, do you have any trouble with them?

76.   D: Sometimes.

77.   I: Sometimes. Do you know when?

78.   D: Once in a while.

79.   I: Once in a while. Umm. Can you tell me one little word that gives you trouble? (*Long pause*) Can't think of any?

80.   D: Nope.

81.   I: Maybe there aren't too many that's giving you trouble, huh, just a few.

82.   D: Uh huh.

83.   I: How long have you had trouble with reading? Do you know?

84.   D: About a year.

85.   I: About a year. Do you have trouble talking about what you've read?

86.   D: Nope.

87.   I: When you read, you can tell the teacher what you have read, what it was all about.

88.   D: Uh huh.

89.   I: O.K. Does your teacher give you any special help with your reading?

90.   D: Nope.

91.   I: Do you have any trouble when you are in the reading group?

92.   D: Nope.

93.   I: You don't. Do you have any special friends?

94.   D: Yeah.

95.   I: How many?

96.   D: Five.

97.   I: Boys or girls?

98.   D: Boys.

99.   I: All boys.

100. D: Uh huh.

101. I: Does the teacher help you with your reading if you have trouble?

102. D: Sometimes.

103. I: Sometimes. Well, what does she do when she doesn't help you? What do you do? Well, what does the teacher do?

104. D: She just sits around.

105. I: She just sits around.

106. D: Uh huh.

107. I: Does she let you figure the word out on your own or does she help you?

108. D: She helps me.
109. I: She helps you with it. What do you like to read, Tom? I'm sorry, I called you Tom. That's my little boy's name. Dan, what do you like to read?
110. D: Books.
111. I: Any special kind of books?
112. D: Nope.
113. I: No special kind?
114. D: Nope.
115. I: Do you like comic books?
116. D: Yep.
117. I: How about books on sports, football players?
118. D: Yeah! (*Appears to be excited*)
119. I: Can you tell me one that you have about a football player maybe?
120. I: (*long pause*) You don't know, huh?
121. D: I know one but I can't . . . I don't know his name.
122. I: Who is it about—Oh, you don't know the football player's name.
123. D: Uh huh.
124. I: Ummm, it wouldn't be Roger Staubach, would it?
125. D: (*Negative headshake*)
126. I: No?
127. D: Nope.
128. I: Ah, is he an offensive player or a defensive player?
129. D: Defense.
130. I: Do you know which team?
131. D: Yep.
132. I: Dallas.
133. D: Nope.
134. I: Which one?
135. D: Minnesota.
136. I: Minnesota. Oh, boy I can't, I don't know many on the Minnesota team. O.K. Tom, I keep saying Tom. That's not great. O.K. Dan, can you tell me anything else about reading that bothers you?
137. D: Nope.
138. I: No! Can you tell me anything else that you like to do?
139. D: Nope.
140. I: Well, do you particularly like coming out here to the reading center?
141. D: Yeah.
142. I: Did you know I was a teacher?
143. D: Nope.

144.   I: I am. Your mother said she thought you knew. I teach first grade. What do you think about that? (*Pause*) They're all the little ones, huh?

145.   D: Uh huh.

146.   I: Is Mrs. James your friend?

147.   D: I don't know. (*very low*)

148.   I: Huh?

149.   D: I don't know.

150.   I: Did you like going to the special reading classes?

151.   D: Uh huh.

152.   I: You did. Did they help you?

153.   D: Yeah.

154.   I: How about Mrs. Edwards? Is that her name?

155.   D: Used to be.

156.   I: What's her name now?

157.   D: Her name is—(*unfinished*) She was it after school was out. Let's see, I'd go every Saturday.

158.   I: You would go every Saturday to her.

159.   D: Uh huh.

160.   I: And she would help you with reading.

161.   D: Yep.

162.   I: At her house.

163.   D: Yep!

164.   I: Did you like that?

165.   D: Yep!

166.   I: What did she help you with? Do you remember? What did she have you do?

167.   D: She'd write cards and write words on them and then I have to read it.

168.   I: Read the word—she would write words on the card and you would have to read it.

169.   D: Uh huh.

170.   I: Did you ever read any stories?

171.   D: Nope!

172.   I: Did you ever learn any sounds? Did she just write letters and have you say the sounds?

173.   D: Uh huh.

174.   I: Were you pretty good at that?

175.   D: Yeah.

176.   I: How about ending sounds?

177.   D: Nope.

178.   I: You weren't good at those?

179.   D: Nope.

180.   I: Oh, well, we'll have to work on the ending sounds then, huh?

181.   D: Uh huh.
182.   I: Right! Can you think of anything else that we'll have to work with? Can you think of anything that Mrs. Edwards did with you that you didn't get too good at that maybe I can help you with?
183.   D: Nope!
184.   I: You can't? O.K. Do you think that maybe the next time we talk you'll be able to think of something else I can help you with other than ending sounds? O.K.?
185.   D: O.K.
186.   I: Can you think of anything else I need to know?
187.   D: Nope.
188.   I: O.K.

Problems in Technique in Danny's Interview

This interviewer fell into the trap of dominating the conversation and mostly failed to use open-ended questions. This resulted in one-word responses. Other problems:

3. Failure to allow student time to think.
17. Interviewer talks down to student.
35. More than one question at once.
45. Argumentative statement that the student doesn't really believe.
55. Interviewer again talks down to student as she might to a preschool child.
59. This is a good open-ended question, but when the student said, "Hard words," the interviewer, instead of saying, "Tell me more," actually took away the incentive of the student to give more thought and his own explanation of his problem.
67. The interviewer expresses an assumption that may or may not be valid.
81. The interviewer puts words in the mouth of the student.
83. This statement should have been pursued in terms of the student's perception of why *he* thought he had had trouble with reading for just "one year."
103. Three questions at once!
109. The interviewer not only forgets the student's name but implies that he reminds her of her "little boy."
136. The interviewer again forgets the student's name.
144. Although there is nothing wrong with being a first-grade teacher, it is not necessary, or probably wise, to emphasize this fact when working with a fifth grader who may think a first-grade teacher should only teach "little boys and girls."

172. In this statement, as in a number of other instances, the interviewer practically tells the student how to respond.
188. The interview is ended very abruptly.

SUMMARY

Learning good techniques for interviewing students as well as parents is an important skill that should be practiced and developed. The interview can not only supplement the use of applications and questionnaires but also bring out information that may not readily be apparent. A number of techniques can help the interviewer by making the interviewee feel at ease and thus enhance responsiveness.

The Administration of the Remedial Reading Program

This chapter begins with a discussion of the roles and responsibilities of various reading specialists and the importance of two-way communication in defining these roles. This is followed by a discussion of ways in which the remedial reading teacher, administrator, and parents can help in the remedial reading program. Next come suggestions for selecting and scheduling students, and for developing and evaluating the remedial program. In conclusion we present the International Reading Association's code of ethics and qualifications for reading specialists.

THE ROLE OF THE READING SPECIALIST

A number of titles exist for reading specialists, depending on the role they are expected to serve. In 1979 the Evaluation Committee of the International Reading Association reported on a membership survey that identified the following official job titles: reading consultant, reading coordinator, reading diagnostician, reading specialist, reading supervisor, reading teacher, remedial reading teacher, and classroom teacher. More than 25 percent of the respondents had titles other than those mentioned above. *Reading specialist* is the generic term.

In 1986 the International Reading Association identified role responsibilities for all professionals involved in reading instruction. Ten professional roles were described under the three broad categories of classroom teachers, reading specialists, and allied professions:

ROLE RESPONSIBILITIES

Category I: Classroom Teachers
- Role 1—*Early Childhood and/or Elementary Teacher* (Preschool–8)
  Teaches in a regular classroom at the preschool, elementary, middle school or junior high school level; responsible for classroom reading or reading readiness instruction. Also responsible for the basic identification of and the prevention of reading problems.
- Role 2—*Secondary Teacher* (Grades 7–12)
  Teaches in a regular (self-contained or departmentalized content area) classroom at the middle school, junior high, or high school level; responsible for reading instruction in content areas (as opposed to instruction in specialized reading courses).

Category II: Reading Specialists
- Role 3—*Diagnostic-Remedial Specialist*
  Assesses, remediates, and plans instructional intervention at the elementary or secondary level, or in a laboratory, a clinic (public, private or commercial), or a resource center at all levels. Provides service to students designated as having reading disabilities, reading difficulties, or environmental/educational deprivation (e.g. Chapter 1). Coordinates reading services provided to each disabled learner in conjunction with the classroom teacher and those in allied professions.
- Role 4—*Developmental Reading-Study Skills Specialist*
  Teaches developmental and/or corrective reading, writing, and thinking skills at the secondary school, community college, college or university/professional school levels. May be responsible for teaching developmental reading in corporate, educational, vocational, penal, or social agencies.
  Responsible for teaching higher order developmental and study

skills as well as for providing diagnostic, corrective, and/or remedial services.

- Role 5 —*Reading Consultant/Reading Resource Teacher*
Organizes and administers a school site reading program.

  Responsible for providing leadership to classroom teachers, diagnostic-remedial specialists, and/or developmental reading-study skills specialists in planning, organizing, managing, and evaluating the school-wide reading program. The consultant's tasks may include a) applying current research/theory to practice in all programs; b) articulating a balanced reading-language-thinking program through the grades; c) providing staff development consistent with assessed needs of program and staff; d) coordinating the work of reading specialists and special services personnel; and e) advising administration and community about the school reading/language arts program.

- Role 6—*Reading Coordinator/Supervisor*
Supervises a district-wide reading and language arts program as central office staff person, or directs public, private, or corporate educational, vocational, penal, or social agency serving learners at any level.

  Responsible for student progress toward reading maturity through: a) improvement of curriculum, methodology, and management of district-wide reading/language arts programs and policies; b) application of current research/theory in the refinement of reading and language arts instruction; c) coordination and implementation of collaborative reading research; d) attainment of resources through budget processes and grant applications; e) development of community support for the reading/language arts program; f) supervision and evaluation of classroom teachers, diagnostic-remedial specialists, and reading consultants; and g) support of professional development through provision for attendance at workshops, conferences, and conventions.

- Role 7—*Reading Professor*
Teaches reading education courses at college or university level.

  Responsible for: a) providing preservice education, inservice education, and advanced study at college and university level to all reading professionals designated in this document; b) conducting research and evaluating the principles, practices, and needs of the fields; and c) disseminating state-of-the-art information goals and objectives to the educational community and community at large through collaborative efforts in publication and speaking.

Category III: Allied Professions
- Role 8—*Special Education Teacher*
Has direct instructional responsibilities in a self-contained learning disabilities or special education classroom or a resource room. Works with students who have specific disabilities in reading as well as those who are deficient in several academic areas.

- Role 9—*Administrator*
  Provides leadership to, and supervision of, elementary or secondary teachers at the building or district level. Is ultimately responsible for the school reading program.
- Role 10—*Support Service Provider*
  Provides service to students with reading problems in the role of a psychologist, a guidance counselor, a speech teacher/therapist, or a social worker in a public school or educational agency.[1]

Reading specialists (3 through 7 above) may serve a variety of roles and assume many different responsibilities. Remember that in most schools and school systems any one reading specialist may take on more than one of the roles listed above.

The Need for Clarification of the Role of Reading Personnel

Problems sometimes arise, especially in the case of newly assigned reading personnel, when roles are not clearly defined. The defining of roles should be a two-way process. That is, the reading specialist and the administrators and teachers should all perceive the specialist's job in the same way. Problems are often created when there are diverse concepts of the role of reading personnel.

The problem was illustrated by Richard Wylie (1969), who surveyed 100 classroom teachers and 100 reading consultants chosen randomly from four New England states. Wylie's questionnaire returns came from teachers in twenty-two communities and from consultants in sixty-three communities. Wylie asked several questions of consultants; two illustrate this problem:

> *Question 1:* "In what areas of reading instruction should the consultant give aid to the new teacher?" (p. 519)

The teachers' and consultants' answers are shown in Table 13–1.

It is important that the teachers expected the consultant to come into the classroom or at least invite teachers to demonstrations on how to teach certain concepts or how to use new materials. Unfortunately, the reading consultants did not consider this as a part of their job. The teachers also expected help with diagnostic and corrective procedures, but again, the consultants did not perceive this as a part of their job. The consultants were concerned with time allotments and the scope of the program, whereas the reading teachers did not consider these factors in evaluating the reading consultant's job.

---

[1]Reproduced by permission of the International Reading Association from a brochure entitled, *Guidelines for the specialized preparation of reading professionals.* Professional Standards and Ethics Committee of the International Reading Association, Newark, DE: April 1986.

TABLE 13–1. Comparison of Teacher and Consultant Views on Question 1

Teacher	Frequency	Percent	Consultant	Frequency	Percent
Materials	66	85	Materials	72	86
Demonstrations	63	81	Time allotments	68	81
Diagnostic and corrective procedures	63	81	Grouping	64	76
Grouping	58	74	Scope of total program	63	75
Interpretation of test results	57	73	Interpretation of test results	63	75

Reprinted with permission of Richard Wylie and the International Reading Association.

Question 2: "How should the consultant extend this aid?" (p. 519)

The results are shown in Table 13–2.

The teachers again believed that the consultant should do demonstration teaching and should free time for teachers to visit other classrooms or other schools. Yet the consultants evidently believed that these items were not a part

TABLE 13–2. Comparison of Teacher and Consultant Views on Question 2

Teacher	Frequency	Percent	Consultant	Frequency	Percent
In-service education; small groups, grade-level meetings	73	94	In-service education; grade-level meetings	79	94
Demonstration teaching	70	90	Orientation program early in year	74	88
			Bulletins or letters to teachers	70	83
Free time to visit other classrooms, schools	67	86	Suggestions of courses to take	61	73
Frequent meetings with reading specialists	62	79			
Workshops	44	56	Workshops	50	50

Reprinted with permission of Richard Wylie and the International Reading Association.

of their role. It is interesting that the kinds of activities the consultants believed they should perform would seldom take them out of their office and *never* take them into the classrooms to work with children.

Rita Bean (1979) studied teacher ratings of various reading specialist roles and analyzed the time spent by specialists in these roles in a Right to Read Special Emphasis Project in Pittsburgh, Pennsylvania. The most valued and least valued roles of the reading specialists as perceived by teachers:

Most valued
In-service role
Developing materials (with teachers)
Conferring with teachers
Individual instruction (out of classroom)

Least valued
Diagnosis—individual in the classroom
Diagnosis—group in the classroom
Group instruction in the classroom

The teachers rated the resource role the most highly. Yet an analysis of the time spent by the reading specialists revealed that this role is assumed only a small percentage of the time.

John Pikulski and Elliott Ross (1979) reported that reading specialists were seen as important and necessary personnel at all grade levels. The researchers also found that teachers wished reading specialists to spend some time in consulting; however, the teachers preferred that specialists spend the vast majority of their time providing direct instruction to students. Pikulski and Ross also reported that classroom teachers expected specialists to be knowledgeable about reading instruction, to possess positive attitudes about people, and to respond well in interpersonal relationships.

John Mangieri and Mary Heimberger (1980) reported on the contrast in role expectations between reading specialists and school administrators. Questionnaires completed by 160 reading consultants and 156 administrators from five states are summarized in Table 13–3.

According to the table the two roles most important to administrators were least important to reading consultants and vice versa. In this case the reading consultant's perceptions were consistent with those of the classroom teachers as reported by Bean, but somewhat in conflict with the teachers' perceptions reported by Pikulski and Ross.

This, as well as our own experience as consultants, leads us to conclude that before any new reading personnel begin their duties there should be a clear-cut understanding in writing of the roles of reading specialists. Karl Hesse, Richard Smith, and Aileen Nettleton (1973) studied content-area teachers' view of the role of the secondary reading consultant:

TABLE 13–3. Ranking of Reading Consultant's Roles (most important to least important)

By School Administrators	By Reading Consultants
Instructor	In-service Leader
Diagnostician	Resource Person
Evaluator	Investigator
Adviser	Adviser
Investigator	Evaluator
In-service Leader	Instructor
Resource Person	Diagnostician

Reprinted with the permission of John Mangieri and the International Reading Association.

There are differences in perceptions regarding the role of secondary school reading consultants among administrators, content area teachers, and reading consultants.

Perceptions differ within content area departments as well as among content area departments.

Because these differing perceptions do exist, for the sake of harmony and staff morale, it would probably be wise to assess the perceptions of all concerned personnel before the responsibilities of the consultant are decided. (p. 215)

Another problem has arisen from the implementation of P. L. 94–142 (discussed in Chapter 2) and the emergence of learning disabilities teachers. Many schools now employ both reading specialists and learning disabilities specialists. Since most students identified as learning disabled are primarily deficient in reading, the potential for conflict between the two types of specialists is great. Walter Sawyer and Bonnie Wilson (1979) suggest that learning disabilities teachers tend to use a medical model that focuses on the etiology (cause) of the problem, while reading specialists tend to evaluate the student's strengths and weaknesses along a "developmental skill hierarchy." These generalizations are broad and not accurate in all cases. However, there is a real possibility that students will suffer if one or the other specialist seeks to monopolize the remedial program, or worse, if both specialists work with students using drastically different approaches. Conflicting approaches may confuse students and negate the possibility for improvement. Sawyer and Wilson recommend that reading specialists focus on the acquisition and development of reading skills, while learning disabilities specialists assume primary responsibility for maintaining students in the least restrictive environment. Both specialists have roles to play in the development of the IEP. In order to be of greatest assistance to students, the school administrator and classroom teachers should participate with the specialists in defining and clarifying role expectations.

Problems are also likely to arise in the school administrative structure when dealing with various reading specialists. For example, the elementary school principal usually knows exactly how he or she fits into the administrative structure of school programs. This position might be illustrated as in Figure 13–1. Likewise the diagnostic remedial specialist, or even the part-time teacher and part-time consultant, usually falls into a common administrative structure (Figure 13–1) below the principal, as shown in Figure 13–2.

The problem sometimes becomes more complicated when dealing with full-time supervisors or consultants who work in several schools. In these cases the administrative structure may be more like that shown in Figure 13–3.

In this situation problems are often encountered when teachers realize they have more than one boss. Further difficulties are often encountered when there are no clear lines of authority between each school principal and consultants and supervisors. Where the consultant or supervisor and principal are congenial and diplomatic, this may matter very little. However, when their beliefs differ considerably, it is often difficult for them to work harmoniously together.

Before any reading position is filled, a needs assessment should be conducted. Participants should include all school administrators who are likely to work with the program, some classroom teachers, and if possible a competent

FIGURE 13–1 Administrative Structure Showing the Position of the Principal

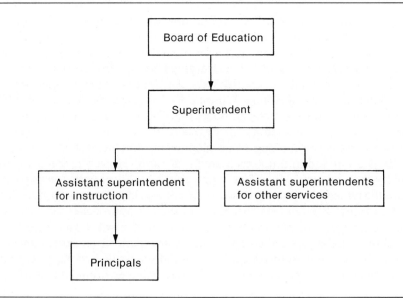

FIGURE 13-2 Administrative Structure Showing the Position of the Diagnostic Remedial Specialist or Reading Consultants Within Any One School

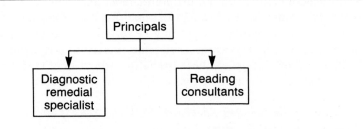

consultant from a college or university who is familiar with the training of reading specialists and their duties and titles.

The duties and title of the reading specialist will depend on such factors as the size of the district, the number of schools with which the specialist will be expected to work, the competencies of other teachers in the school system, and other reading specialists already employed.

FIGURE 13-3 A School Administrative Structure in Which There Are Supervisors and/or Consultants

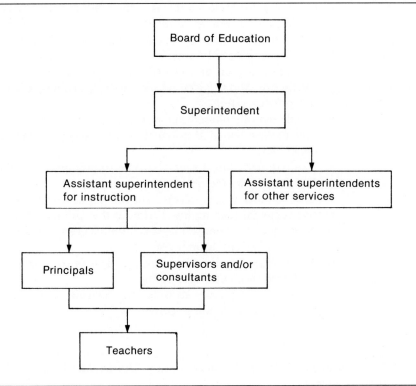

The Reading Specialist Position in Two School Districts

Many school districts do not differentiate among the roles of reading specialists as recommended by the International Reading Association. For example, in the Parkway School District in Chesterfield, Missouri, and the Hayward School District in Hayward, California, much time is spent in teaching remedial reading. However, these specialists do not limit their time to teaching. A description of the role of the reading specialist in both districts:

Role of the Reading Specialist, Parkway School District[2]

I. Remedial Reading

The primary role of the reading specialist in the Parkway School District is the instruction of pupils possessing deficient reading skills in relation to their reading potential.

A. Instruction

1. In the development of a caseload the following steps are taken:

a. A reading survey test is administered to these pupils to determine present reading ability.

b. The reading specialist, working with the staff, will obtain referrals of pupils considered to be disabled readers.

c. Guidance counselors will assist the reading specialists in administering individual intelligence tests to these pupils.

d. A "potential caseload" consisting of no less than 50 pupils is developed according to state guidelines. Normally, a total of 30 to 40 pupils will receive instruction at any given period of time, beginning with top priority pupils.

e. Pupils may be phased out of the program when it is felt that further remedial instruction is no longer considered beneficial.

f. The required state forms are to be submitted to the State Department by October 15.

2. A course of study is prescribed for the pupils selected to receive remedial reading instruction in the following manner:

a. A battery of diagnostic tests is administered to determine individual strengths and deficits.

b. The reading specialist attempts to identify the pupil's preferred modality of learning.

c. Awareness of pupil's attitudes and interests assists the specialist in motivating learners.

[2]Reproduced by permission of the Parkway School District. Marti Sellinriek, Language Arts Coordinator.

      d. Necessary data collected from the home, classroom, medical or other sources, as well as information used in the remedial process, will be placed in the folder required by the state for each child.

      e. A remedial reading program is planned for each student through the use of materials designed specifically to meet the needs of individual pupils.

      f. Cooperative planning by the reading specialist and the classroom teacher is necessary to provide methods and materials to be used in the classroom which correlate with the remedial reading program.

3. Schedules will be developed with the following consideration:

      a. A schedule is established for remedial classes on the basis of common needs for groups no larger than six students.

      b. Time will be allotted for staffing with teachers, clinic personnel, and other non-teaching responsibilities.

4. Instruction is conducted according to the following procedures:

      a. Parents are informed of pupil's inclusion in the remedial reading program.

      b. Instruction is given to remedial pupils, individually or in small groups.

      c. Evaluation is a continual process and the individual instructional program may be changed when necessary.

      d. During the process of remedial teaching, feedback and recommendations to the staff concerning the students should also be continuous.

      e. Pupils' progress will be reported to parents through conferences or other means of communication.

5. Referrals

      a. Referrals to the Parkway Right to Read Reading Clinic will be made when deemed advisable by the reading specialist.

      b. A reading specialist may initiate referrals to Special School District or other outside agencies according to Parkway guidelines.

B. Advisory and In-Service Education

The reading specialist serves as an advisor in the remedial area by working with administrators, teachers, guidance counselors, and the Parkway Right to Read Reading Clinic in the following ways:

1. To interpret the role of the reading specialist and the remedial program.

2. To help teachers administer diagnostic tests and interpret test results.

3. To assist the administration in planning the budget in the area of reading.
4. To help teachers understand materials used for remedial purposes.

C. Curriculum Development

In the area of Remedial Curriculum Development, the reading specialist has the following responsibilities:

1. To assist the district in development and/or location of materials for use by the disabled reader in the content areas.
2. To assist the district in development of programs for the early identification of student's potential learning style as it relates to the teaching of reading.
3. To provide orientation for new members of the reading specialist staff in the Parkway School system.
4. To participate in providing programs designed to improve the skills of the total reading staff. This may be done in cooperation with the staff of the Parkway Right to Read Reading Clinic.

    The reading specialist will have a secondary role of assisting in the areas of corrective and developmental reading instruction.

II. Corrective Reading

A. Instruction

1. The reading specialist will introduce corrective materials for classroom instruction, upon teacher request.
2. Emphasis will be placed on the use of alternative methods of instruction as a means of preventing reading disabilities.
3. Follow-up and evaluation of materials introduced shall be conducted.

B. Advisory and In-Service

The reading specialist will serve as a resource teacher in the following activities:

1. Assists classroom teachers in initiating diagnosis of pupils and interpreting results of data collected.
2. Assists the teacher with classroom organization for corrective instruction.
3. Observes disabled readers in a classroom situation, upon teacher request.
4. Evaluates pupil progress and performance in cooperation with the classroom teacher.
5. Assists in the evaluation and selection of appropriate materials utilized by the classroom teacher for corrective instruction.
6. Provides demonstration of new methods and materials.

C. Curriculum Development

1. The reading specialist will evaluate programs presently in use for corrective instruction.
2. New programs will be evaluated to assess their appropriateness for use in corrective instruction in Parkway.
3. The reading specialist, in conjunction with the Parkway Right to Read Reading Clinic, will give assistance to teachers in developing corrective reading techniques.

III. Developmental Reading

A. Instruction

The role of the reading specialist is to become familiar with the developmental programs of each assigned school. This will allow the specialist to make suggestions for pupils' past reading experiences and present abilities.

B. Advisory and In-Service

In helping teachers, at their request, to initiate and develop reading programs in their class groups, assistance will be given in an advisory capacity toward a diagnostic approach to developmental reading instruction. This method would include the following activities:

1. Reviews current information available from individual pupils.
2. Obtains new information about the pupils.
3. Selects a teaching approach (personalized, basal, etc.).
4. Groups pupils for instruction.
5. Selects appropriate materials.
6. Plans periodic evaluation to assess the need for changes in materials or grouping.
7. Assists teachers in developing goals and planning budgets in the area of developmental reading.

C. Curriculum Development

The reading specialist:

1. Serves as a liaison between the classroom teacher and the language arts coordinator.
2. Assists teachers to become familiar with new methods and materials.
3. Plans and develops special reading projects.
4. Interacts with the director of Research and Planning in those areas involving reading.

Role of the Reading Specialist
Priority Chart:
1. Primary responsibility
2. Secondary responsibility
3. Advisory responsibility

	Instruction	Advisory and In-service Education (within each school)	Curriculum Development
Remedial Reading	1	2	2
Corrective Reading	2	2	2
Developmental Reading	3	3	3

The position of reading specialist in the Parkway School District involves much more than simply being a teacher of reading. As outlined by the International Reading Association, in that district the reading specialist might be considered a special teacher of reading, a reading clinician (since all teachers are highly trained in the clinical aspects of reading), or a reading consultant. In some ways these same people take on the duties of a reading supervisor.

Evidence on the importance of task competencies that count among reading specialists was presented by V. V. Garry (1974). Garry developed an extensive list of various competencies using a research of the literature, interviews with reading authorities, and interviews with advisors from the State Department of Education and reading specialist training institutions. Garry's list of task competencies was presented to randomly chosen reading personnel, who were requested to assign a degree of importance to each. Task competencies were rated on a scale of five through one. From fifty items, twelve were rated in the highest quartile:

1. "Helping teachers plan and provide corrective and remedial reading instruction and suggesting remedial techniques for disabled readers both in the classroom and special reading program."
2. "Teaching small groups of disabled readers."
3. "Assisting in interpretation of standardized and informal reading test results."
4. "Assisting classroom teachers in diagnosing and analyzing students' strengths and weaknesses in various skills areas."
5. "Diagnosing and recommending treatment for more complex and severe reading disability cases."
6. "Referring pupils with special problems to proper agencies such as guidance and psychological services."
7. "Providing guidance in determining extent of reading retardation by utilizing various procedures."
8. "Providing guidance in selecting and identifying candidates for remedial reading classes or a reading clinic."
9. "Providing guidelines and practical assistance for evaluating student progress in remediation."
10. "Suggesting and demonstrating use of instructional materials and procedures to teachers."
11. "Selecting and developing materials to promote higher level reading competency."

12. "Encouraging, helping, and stimulating teachers to use different strategies of teaching reading such as programmed reading, language-experience, individualized reading." (pp. 609–612)

Note that in the Parkway School District, as well as in the study just quoted, the reading specialist is not expected to perform only one very specific role. This is healthy, since it allows the reading specialist, regardless of title, to communicate more with the classroom teacher. This communication provides for more effective in-service education and inevitably influences a school's reading program.

In the Unified School District of Hayward, California, thirty-four reading specialists serve twenty-four elementary schools. Each school has one reading specialist to serve either kindergarten to grade three or grades four to six, depending on the needs of the school. Ten of the schools have a second reading specialist, so that in these schools all elementary students and teachers are served.[3]

The program is supported by special state funds and district resources. James Shanker served as the district reading consultant. The primary emphasis is on an elementary reading specialist program to assist administrators and teachers in promoting effective reading instruction.

The following beliefs guide the Hayward program:

1. Leadership and support from the school board, the superintendent, and other district administrators are essential.
2. The principal, as key curriculum leader at the school site, should be involved in all efforts to improve reading instruction.
3. Only the most outstanding, fully qualified specialists should be hired.
4. The specialists must function as a coordinated group. It is the district's responsibility to provide leadership that will enable the reading specialists to clarify roles and responsibilities, define uniform procedures where needed, and develop essential materials and resources. Regular meetings of the group must occur.
5. The charge of the reading specialists must not be limited to remedial instruction. Their responsibilities should include assistance with all facets of the school reading program, especially the improvement of classroom teaching practices.
6. Reading specialists must receive ongoing supervision and assistance. They should be recognized for outstanding work and be provided with rewards and incentives to maintain their professional excellence.

[3]Some of the information in this section appeared in James L. Shanker, "The reading specialist position: The Hayward program," *Selected Proceedings from the Thirteenth Annual Conference of the California Reading Association,* San Diego, California, 1979.

Three steps in the district provided a framework for the effective implementation of the reading specialist program:

1. A Reading Planning Committee was formed to respond to the need for a well-thought-out, coherent, and district-sanctioned reading curriculum. This committee was composed of elementary and secondary teachers, district administrators, and the reading consultant. A subcommittee of this group prepared a K–6 Reading Guide for use by all elementary teachers and administrators. The development of this guide served to clarify district expectations and to coordinate the school reading programs.
2. The elementary schools adopted a new reading program, selected by teachers, to provide greater uniformity in the developmental reading curriculum.
3. All district principals and selected central office administrators participated in an eleven-week refresher course that emphasized content and methods of reading instruction.

All available positions were advertised. Candidates were sought from both inside and outside the district and selected after a thorough screening and interviewing procedure. This process is designed to determine the candidate's specific academic training, experience in both classroom and remedial reading instruction at the appropriate grade levels, ability to work effectively with classroom teachers and school administrators, and desire to serve children with special needs.

Each candidate is interviewed by a panel of district administrators, reading specialists, and the district reading consultant. At the outset many specialists accepted positions on temporary contracts because enrollment had declined and because there could be no guarantee of continued state funding.

Under the direction of the reading consultant, intensive initial training workshops were held at the district office. All reading specialists participated in the development of a position description, a performance review (evaluation) instrument, forms and procedures for the identification and selection of students to be served, diagnostic and record-keeping materials, and forms and procedures for monitoring the schoolwide reading program.

One goal of the training process is to establish uniformity in the materials and procedures for certain aspects of the job. The reading specialists recognize the advantages of a standardized position description, diagnostic battery, record-keeping forms, etc. Such an approach enables the district to prepare a wealth of supplementary materials, provide central office support for curriculum change at the school sites, and minimize confusion when students move from school to school.

In addition to developing standard materials and procedures, the training sessions provide an opportunity for reading specialists to share with each other their special skills and experiences. Camaraderie enhances the professionalism and job satisfaction of members of the group.

Finally, the training sessions provide for the development of task committees for future projects including professional growth plans, newsletters, materials sharing, test interpretation, kindergarten program planning, and position papers.

The in-service meetings are held on a regular basis on Friday afternoons. In order to encourage the sharing of ideas and techniques, many of the meetings are held in individual reading specialists' resource rooms.

A variety of resources are available to the reading specialists, including a meeting room in the district office convenient to duplication and laminating facilities. Another room houses materials and forms, which are printed in the nearby communications center. Numerous materials are also available at the district resource library, which is in the district office. These materials are delivered to the school on request.

Local district funds provide all reading specialists with essential materials and equipment, including furniture, textbooks, supplementary materials, audiovisual equipment, flash cards, stop watches, etc.

The reading specialists are primarily responsible to the building principals. They also receive regular supervision and assistance from the district reading consultant. The reading specialists complete an annual report that includes their own contributions to the school program and data on the performance of all students directly served.

A description of the role of the reading specialist in the Hayward School District follows:

Role of the Reading Specialist, Hayward Unified School District[4]

I. Qualifications

Credential: Any teaching credential authorizing service in the grade level or specialty indicated, and possession of the Reading Specialist Certificate or the Reading Specialist Credential issued by the California State Department of Education.

Provide evidence of adequate preparation, background, and experience for the position.

II. Conditions of Employment

A. Appointment and Term. The Reading Specialist shall be appointed by the Board of Education for a term of one year upon nomination and recommendation by the Superintendent.

B. Remuneration. Remuneration shall be determined by the official salary schedule for certificated personnel as adopted by the

[4]Reproduced by permission of the Hayward Unified School District, Hayward, California. Henry Nicolini, Assistant Superintendent, Instruction.

Board of Education. The salary paid shall include an additional sum above the official salary schedule of two hundred fifty dollars ($250) per teacher.

C. Work Year. The work year shall be the regular school year as established by the Board of Education for new and returning teachers.

D. Administrative Relationship. The Reading Specialist shall be responsible to the building principal. The central office staff shall assist the Reading Specialist in meeting the guidelines for the Reading Specialist program.

III. General Description of Position.

A. Primary Duties and Responsibilities

1. Devotes time to pupils in either the primary grades or the intermediate grades to meet their reading needs commensurate with their potential. The Reading Specialist shall spend a minimum of 50 percent of the work day in providing direct services to children. Other responsibilities shall be related directly to the program being served and shall not involve duties which are related to the general operation of the school.

2. Supplements the reading instruction otherwise provided in regular classes:

   a. The specialist teacher may work directly with pupils within the regular classroom during reading or outside of the classroom at designated times; train instructional aides or volunteers to work with pupils; or train peer tutors. The teacher should use the variety of human resources available to work with pupils.

   b. Guidelines suggest that group size should not exceed six; however, the teacher should use judgment in determining the most effective learning situation.

   c. The first priority for primary Reading Specialists in providing service is to supplement instruction in grade one. Primary Reading Specialists will provide service to supplement instruction in grades two and three to pupils who have been determined to have reading difficulties. Kindergarten pupils may receive instruction if other children have been served. Intermediate Reading Specialists will provide service to supplement instruction in grades four through six.

3. Provides demonstration teaching where appropriate.

4. Assists in administering and analyzing group tests given to pupils.

5. Assists in reading assessment of pupils identified for participation in specially funded programs.

6. Diagnoses identified pupils in reading using appropriate formal and informal tests, interprets results, and assesses and evaluates the pupil's growth with other persons responsible for the learner.
7. Assists the classroom teacher in developing prescriptions to meet the needs of pupils and assists in planning appropriate lessons and supplemental reading experiences to meet the diverse needs of pupils.
8. Assists the classroom teacher in developing within the child a positive attitude toward learning to read and in referring pupils who need specialized remedial help to professional personnel for specialized services.
9. Disseminates current research in reading to teachers and parents.
10. Assists the building principal and cooperates with other support staff in developing, planning, and implementing inservice programs for staff members in the area of reading and language, and in interpreting specially funded programs to school staff, parents, and community.
11. Assists the principal and cooperates with other support staff in maintaining systems of record keeping in reading.
12. Attends conferences in reading at the district, county, and state levels and shares information with other staff members.
13. Assists auxiliary staff members in developing programs to meet the learner's needs.
14. Participates in faculty meetings, curriculum planning, selection of additional personnel, and other program-related activities.
15. Performs adjunct duties when mutually agreed upon between teachers and immediate supervisor.

How Should Help Be Extended by the Reading Specialist?

A traditional method is to set up shop in a room and schedule students to come. Such an approach is often referred to as a *pull-out program,* since the students are pulled out of their regular classroom for special instruction. Although this often works quite well, it does not lend itself to opening two-way channels of communication. For example, the remedial reading teacher may omit to visit the homeroom of many of the students and thus miss the opportunity to coordinate the work of the students with their homeroom teachers. There is also little opportunity to provide the kind of information classroom teachers need. One solution is for reading specialists to provide a broader range of services.

In the Hayward School District, reading specialists provide both direct and indirect services. *Direct services* are instructional efforts aimed at low-achieving students. *Indirect services* refers to other roles such as resource person, staff development leader, and curriculum planner.

Hayward reading specialists devote at least 50 percent of their school day to providing direct services to students. The specialists are proscribed from supplanting the reading instruction of the classroom teacher. All direct services are provided over and above the regular classroom reading program. First priority is generally assigned to students in the lowest quartile, and second priority to students in the second lowest quartile on standardized reading tests.

For direct instruction the reading specialist may use the traditional *pull-out* format or work in the students' regular classrooms, either with small groups or using a team approach with the classroom teacher. Specialist services in the regular classroom are often referred to as a *push-in* or *in-class program*. The push-in program may be temporary and is designed not only to provide additional direct instruction to remedial pupils, but also to model effective teaching methods and otherwise assist the regular classroom teacher. This enables the reading specialist to observe students in their natural environment, facilitates the coordination of instruction and assignments, and promotes more effective communication with the classroom teacher. Carroll Green (1973) studied the attitude of teachers toward children. She found that both behavior and attitudes improved when the reading specialists actually went into the classroom to work with children: "When teachers received help in improving their skill in working with the children in the classroom, three out of five demonstrated behavioral changes and four out of five improved their score on the attitude test." (p. 2) This type of operation, however, requires that the reading specialist be flexible and particularly skilled at human relations, since many teachers feel threatened by the presence of the reading specialist in the classroom. One very effective way to ease the concerns of the classroom teacher is to offer to teach a lesson to a group or preferably to the whole class of students while the classroom teacher is present. If you indicate to the teacher that your purpose at this point is to get to know the children rather than to do a demonstration lesson, you will likely be welcome. Many reading specialists have found that a well-planned language-experience lesson with follow-up activities that can be displayed on a bulletin board serves not only to please the students but also to impress the teacher. Such an activity can be adapted for nearly any age level. It is also a good idea for the reading specialist to follow up the visit with a note to the teacher that emphasizes some of the positive aspects of the room or reflects appreciation of the teacher's work. Many reading specialists have won over reluctant or even hostile teachers in this way.

When a large-city school district modified its reading specialist program, Rita Bean and Tony Eichelberger (1985) studied the results and the perceptions of the affected reading specialists and teachers. This district eliminated pull-out instruction by reading specialists and substituted an in-class program. After one year Bean and Eichelberger reported three conclusions: (1) the reading specialists operated differently with the in-class program—more time was spent on instruction previously presented by the classroom teacher; (2) teachers and reading specialists supported the in-class approach; and (3) teachers and reading specialists had problems defining roles and working cooperatively in the classroom. The researchers suggested that special efforts be made to prepare staffs for an in-class program and that the best approach might well be a program that provides a balance between pull-out and push-in instruction.

There are other possible drawbacks to push-in instruction. It often requires the reading specialist to transport a considerable amount of materials from classroom to classroom. Also, the specialist may find it difficult to arrange for adequate and comfortable space. Perhaps the greatest potential problem is coping with the stress of working in a classroom where poor teaching practices occur. There is a tendency to assume that poor practices will cease if you are not there to observe them on a regular basis, or to conclude that such problems should be addressed only by the teacher's principal or other supervisor. However, our experience has shown that often the reading specialist is in a unique position to help teachers improve their skills. This is precisely because the reading specialist's role is one of assistance and not evaluation. If you are a reading specialist and you observe one or more teachers having significant difficulties in teaching effectively, we urge you not to ignore the problem but rather to discuss it with the principal and seek to work cooperatively, diplomatically, patiently, and persistently with the teacher. Indeed, we believe that no form of in-service training is more effective than direct one-to-one assistance. We are aware that the reading specialist who uses such an approach faces certain risks. However, if you have established credibility and can work effectively with people, these risks are minimized. Further, we believe that because good classroom instruction is crucial to the achievement of many students, some risk is worth taking.

Earlier we suggested that reading specialists may provide both direct and indirect services. The preceding paragraph illustrates a situation where direct services lead to indirect services. The two job descriptions include a number of indirect service responsibilities, which may account for up to 50 percent of Hayward reading specialists' time. What follows is a list of possible indirect services reading specialists may provide:

1. Working cooperatively with the school principal in developing, planning, and implementing the total school reading program.
2. Assisting classroom teachers in planning for and conducting classroom reading instruction. The reading specialist may assist the teacher in identifying individual student needs and planning appropriate lessons, or assist the teacher in the general organization and management of reading instruction.
3. Providing demonstration teaching lessons.
4. Providing a resource room for teachers, which includes instructional and supplementary materials, and information about current research and other professional matters.

5. Monitoring the progress of students in the basal program. The reading specialist may regularly gather data that show the groups of students and the progress they are making.
6. Organizing and conducting local school reading in-service meetings and other staff development efforts.[5]
7. Training aides, volunteers, and cross-age tutors.
8. Conducting parent conferences.
9. Making presentations before parent or community groups.
10. Assisting in administering and analyzing group test data.
11. Assisting in the assessment of students for special programs or services, such as participating in the development of IEPs.
12. Testing and placement of students new to the school.
13. Assisting in the development of the reading budget, the evaluation of new materials, and the ordering of basic and supplementary materials.
14. Providing leadership for schoolwide motivational reading activities.
15. Attending conferences, college courses, and meetings of professional groups and reporting to the school faculty.

In a school system where reading specialists have specific titles, it may be practical to have special remedial reading teachers who spend the greater proportion of their time in working with disabled readers. In such cases the reading consultant may take on many of the responsibilities for in-service education and may serve as a liaison between remedial and classroom teachers.

Some school systems have found it quite feasible to use mobile reading laboratories. These are usually trailer houses or campermobiles that have been converted to reading laboratories with bookshelves, study carrels, small tables and chairs, provisions for audiovisual equipment and viewing areas, etc. Where a reading specialist is expected to work in several schools on a rotating basis, a mobile laboratory often proves less costly on a long-term basis, since there is no necessity to duplicate rooms and equipment.

In such a case the mobile laboratory is moved to a new school two to three times weekly and all facilities become immediately available after a main power cord has been connected. This also allows the reading specialist to concentrate on providing only one attractive display of bulletin board materials and eliminates the upkeep and cleaning of two or more rooms. Most teachers report enthusiasm on the part of the students working in this type of facility.

Still another method that is proving worthwhile is to allow classroom teachers free time to work in the school's reading center or reading clinic either during a particular part of the day or for a semester or more. School districts providing such opportunities usually hire a permanent substitute teacher to take over the duties of the classroom teacher for the period.

Having the classroom teacher work in the reading clinic for one or more periods of the day allows for a great deal of coordination of the remedial

[5]For more information: James L. Shanker, *Guidelines for Successful Reading Staff Development.* Newark, DE: International Reading Association, 1982.

program of the classroom teacher and the reading clinician. Whether the classroom teacher is released for only one or two periods or for an entire semester or year, it provides an excellent opportunity to learn about materials and techniques of corrective teaching in the classroom.

The type of operation you choose will depend on the size of your school system and on the amount of materials, funds, and facilities available. Perhaps more important, it will depend on the reading specialists and their willingness to work within a given situation.

THE ROLE OF THE PRINCIPAL AND OTHER ADMINISTRATIVE PERSONNEL

Several researchers have summarized the characteristics of administrators who have successful reading programs (Mangieri and McWilliams, 1984; Manning and Manning, 1981; and Wilhite, 1984). One of the best descriptions is provided by Sidney Rauch (1974), who makes the point that the success of reading programs does not depend on any one special method, text, or type of organization. Rauch lists basic characteristics of a successful administrator:

1. The administrator should be knowledgeable about the reading process. His own experience as a classroom teacher, his observation of extremely competent teachers, enrollment in graduate courses in reading, attendance at conferences, or extensive reading in the field may contribute to his knowledge.
2. He takes advantage of the training and expertise of reading specialists. He recognizes his own limitations in the reading area and knows that he and his staff can benefit from the knowledge and experience of specialists. Above all, there is a close relationship between the specialist and himself.
3. He consults with supervisory and teaching personnel before new programs are instituted or changes are made. Before new programs are put into operation, he makes sure that the necessary in-service training is provided.
4. He realizes that teachers are severely handicapped if materials are lacking. Therefore, he makes certain that the budget includes the basic instructional materials, as well as the needed supplementary texts and other aids.
5. He encourages and supports experimentation and innovation. He is never satisfied with the status quo. At the same time, he doesn't abandon a successful program because of publicity given a "new" reading method, or because some school board member confuses exploratory research with a definitive study.
6. He has the support and respect of the community as a person and as an educational leader. (pp. 298–299)[6]

[6]Reprinted with permission. "Administrator's guidelines for more effective reading programs," from Sidney J. Rauch. *Journal of Reading,* January 1974, International Reading Association.

In addition to those qualities, other essential duties of the administrator:

1. Thorough familiarity with the state department of education's recommendations and/or requirements as well as those suggested by the International Reading Association for the training and background of various types of reading specialists.
2. Consistent striving to inform parents about the school's remedial reading program.
3. Scheduling adequate time for remedial teachers for conferences with students, parents, classroom teachers, and all other staff personnel directly related to the reading program.
4. Encouragement and provision for continual cooperative evaluation; necessary steps to improve the program.
5. Taking the initiative in developing a professional library accessible to all teachers.

Rauch also lists a number of excellent suggestions for administrators. We have paraphrased some of these and added others as follows:

1. Study and learn about reading. Observe reading specialists in action and observe the classroom reading instruction of master teachers.
2. Rauch says there is a specific need to clarify the role of various reading specialists, who should know exactly what is expected of them. Administrators and classroom teachers should view their roles in the same way. Rauch suggests a job description for each type of reading specialist similar to those for the Parkway School District and the Hayward School District.
3. Provide for continuous in-service training, not just lectures from experts or college professors but demonstrations and direct classroom assistance. The most successful in-service programs actively involve the teachers in day-to-day experiences over an extended period.
4. Provide for effective use of audiovisual materials and other facilities and/or materials needed by both classroom and remedial reading teachers.
5. Recognize that reading is a complex process and that what works with one student may or may not work with another. Provide an open environment where some structure is maintained, yet where experimentation based on research is encouraged.

In conclusion, we strongly agree with Rauch, who states, "An administrator who knows about the reading process, who takes advantage of the training and expertise of reading personnel, and who recognizes the many factors that determine reading progress can mean the difference between the success or failure of a school reading program." (p. 300)

PARENTS' ROLE IN THE REMEDIAL READING PROGRAM

An area often neglected by the remedial reading teacher is the active involvement of parents in the program. Some ways in which parents should help their children:

1. By creating a time and a place for home reading. This might be a time when every member of the household agrees that there will be no radio, no television, and if possible, no visiting friends. This includes the responsibility of making sure that adequate reading material is provided.
2. By helping the child develop habits of regularity in eating, sleeping, studying, and attending school.
3. By encouraging home responsibilities to develop feelings of satisfaction from successful accomplishments.
4. By exhibiting a genuine interest in the school and in the child.
5. By maintaining a relaxed, cooperative attitude toward the child's reading without undue pressure.
6. By taking and discussing excursions, such as trips to the zoo, planetariums, plays, parades, and sporting events, which will assist in developing language facility and a background of experiences for comprehension.
7. By supporting students' interest in hobbies such as stamp collecting, model building, collecting matchbook covers, pamphlets, animal raising and care, etc., all of which require reading.
8. By reading to the child frequently and using simple language-experience approaches at home.

There is controversy as to whether parents should attempt to teach their children at home. There is also considerable disagreement on whether disabled readers should be asked to read to their parents. There are no pat answers to such questions. Some parents are able to work with their children and maintain a completely relaxed manner. Yet other parents, including some teachers, cannot work with their own children without creating tension. One of the best ways to decide whether to recommend that parents work with their children is to ask the parents if they have a working relationship that is conducive to parent tutoring. It is also a good practice to ask students how they feel about it.

There is no pat answer to whether students should be asked to read to their parents. Again, if students wish to and if the parents are patient and calm, there is usually some benefit. Since many disabled readers have a low sight vocabulary caused by a lack of wide reading experience, oral reading is likely to be beneficial. Just be sure to provide materials that are at or below the students' independent reading levels. Students can learn from material that is too easy but will only become frustrated when trying to read material that is too difficult. Parents should generally be advised simply to tell children words the children do not know rather than to tell them to sound it out. Most students who know enough about word attack to analyze new words will do so without being told.

In Chapter 7, in the section on counseling parents of disabled readers, we reviewed the procedures of the Elementary Reading Clinic at California State University, Hayward, to acquaint parents with the clinic and to improve parents' effectiveness in assisting their own children. The activities have been adapted by reading specialists for use in their school programs. Helen Esworthy (1979) reports on a summer reading clinic that sponsors weekly workshops to involve parents in their children's reading instruction. Esworthy reports success in (1) orienting the parents to the purposes of the program, (2) furthering the parents' knowledge about reading by offering workable ideas for home, and (3) teaching parents about instructional devices by having them make some for the clinic program.

Alvin Granowsky, Frances Middleton, and Janice Mumford (1979) reported their experiences in developing a program that involved parents as equal partners in their children's education. Sadie Grimmett and Mae McCoy (1980) conducted a study in which written material sent by mail was used to train parents to assist their children in reading. They found that this communication stimulated parent involvement and resulted in accelerated reading achievement among third graders.

In the previous sections on the role of the reading specialist and the role of the principal and other administrative personnel, mention was made of the importance of effective communication and parent involvement. Enough evidence exists on the potential impact of parents on their children's reading achievement to warrant carefully planned cooperative efforts on the part of administrators and reading specialists to address this critical area.

SELECTING STUDENTS FOR REMEDIAL READING

Although the selection of students for participation in the remedial reading program may appear easy, a number of problems complicate the process. In the process you are likely to be confronted with the following questions: Who will make the initial recommendations and the final decision as to which students will join the program? What will measure reading disability? Will reading potential or expectancy be considered? What types of tests will be used to determine the degree of impairment?

Problems in the Selection Process

One of the first steps in the selection process is to define "disabled reader," or candidacy for remedial reading. One approach is to use a specified number of years of reading achievement below grade level (in many cases two) as the lone criterion.

A number of researchers, such as Charles Ullmann (1969) and Cecil Reynolds (1981), have pointed out that years below normal grade for age is a vague or inappropriate measure, likely to result in a misleading picture of the prevalence of reading disability:

> Whenever a fixed amount of grades or years below normal is set for defining reading disability, a progressively larger percentage of children, of each succeeding grade to which that standard amount is applied, will be defined as having a disability. This is due principally to deceleration in the average growth curve and the consequent reduction in the size of the steps from one grade to another. . . . It is no more appropriate to describe the gain between Grades 8 and 9 as equal to the gain between Grades 2 and 3, than it is to describe a 35-year-old man as 25 years taller than his 10-year-old son. (p. 557)

Another way of looking at this problem is on the basis of the percentage of knowledge lacking from normal, or 100 percent reading achievement. For example, a beginning third grader should have two years' reading knowledge, i.e., one year in the first grade and another year in the second grade. If this student is two years retarded in reading he or she has an achievement level of 1.0 (not really 0.0), or in other words, a 0 (zero) percent reading knowledge. But a student at the beginning of the sixth grade should have five years of knowledge. If he is retarded two years from his expected level, he is (5 − 2), or 3/5; at a 60 percent level. Obviously, the concept of a specified number of years of reading retardation is an inadequate measure.

Another method is by some measure of achievement level versus some measure of potential. James Reed (1970) illustrates the great variability in this method. He quotes a study indicating an eighth-grade student with a measured IQ of 120, reading at a seventh-grade level, to be two years, three years, or four and one-half years retarded as judged by the Bond-Tinker, Tiegs and Clark, or Harris formulas respectively. As Reed aptly states, "Obviously, the amount of retardation is not an absolute but depends on the procedure used to measure it." (p. 347) A concluding statement concerning Reed's study of the use of *WISC* IQs to measure reading potential:

> Teachers and reading specialists should view with considerable skepticism any statement pertaining to the so-called intellectual, cognitive, or perceptual deficiencies of retarded readers. Many of the statements are interesting speculations, but nothing more. The particular pattern of deficits may represent only an artifact of the investigator's decision to use one measure of potential instead of another. A child's potential for reading is probably much more closely related to the materials and methods used for teaching than some arbitrary index of expectancy. (p. 352)

The problem of errors in measurement in identifying disabled readers was also studied by Robert Bruininks, Gertrude Glaman, and Charlotte Clark (1973), who compared the percentages of disabled readers identified by use of five achievement expectancy formulas:

> Analysis revealed that the prevalence of third-grade children exhibiting reading difficulties varied widely because of survey techniques and type of IQ test (verbal or nonverbal) used in the five achievement expectancy formulas. Using a nonverbal intelligence test score, the percentage of poor readers among third-grade children ranged from 16 percent with the Bond and Tinker formula to 54.6 percent for the formula using mental age alone. (p. 180)

These authors believed that rather than an expectancy formula, it would be more realistic to use a criterion-referenced approach. In doing so one measures a student's attainment of specific reading skills with a certain program rather than achievement on a norm-referenced test. They also suggested that if reading retardation is measured according to the disparity between predicted and actual achievement, it should be done in relation to how long children have been exposed to systematic instruction (as in the Bond-Tinker formula) and that there should be a larger disparity between predicted and actual achievement at higher grade levels.

Perhaps the most useful approach is to consider any student as a candidate for remedial reading if he or she is reading at the frustration level in textbooks for his or her grade level.

The general philosophy of identifying as soon as possible students who are retarded in reading is strongly supported by research. A PREP (Putting Research into Educational Practice) summary entitled *Treating Reading Disabilities* and published by the Bureau of Research of the Office of Education stated:

> Early diagnosis is important, and the rule is "the earlier, the better." A four-year survey of some ten thousand children showed that when pupils with reading problems were identified by the second grade, they had a ten times greater chance for successful remediation than did those who were not identified until the ninth grade. (p. 5)

One of the major problems of the remedial reading teacher in working with older students is a low self-concept, apparently much more difficult to change than that of a younger student. This was illustrated by Erwin and Ralph Pearlman (1970), who studied the effect of the remedial reading training in a private clinic. They concluded that children in grades one through three made greater gains during remediation than children in grades four through six. The younger children also maintained their gains better. The authors believed this was because the younger children had faced fewer defeats and so maintained a greater degree of self-confidence.

A Suggested Procedure for Selecting Students for Remedial Reading

This six-step procedure for selecting the final case load is illustrated in Figure 13–4. Some of the procedures vary from those used in many schools today. The procedures used in many schools today are based on precedent. The following procedure may not be the easiest way of developing the final case load, but if followed carefully it will usually result in a successful program.

Step 1. This is initiation of a procedure for receiving recommendations from teachers. The success of this procedure depends to a large extent on

FIGURE 13–4 A Suggested Sequence for Selection of the Final Case Load

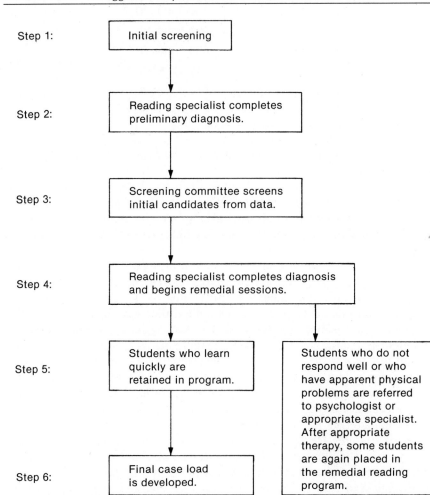

Step 1: Initial screening

Step 2: Reading specialist completes preliminary diagnosis.

Step 3: Screening committee screens initial candidates from data.

Step 4: Reading specialist completes diagnosis and begins remedial sessions.

Step 5: Students who learn quickly are retained in program.

Students who do not respond well or who have apparent physical problems are referred to psychologist or appropriate specialist. After appropriate therapy, some students are again placed in the remedial reading program.

Step 6: Final case load is developed.

classroom teachers' guidelines for the selection of students. The guidelines, developed by the administrative and reading staffs, should state the minimum degree of retardation for selection; age-grade preferences; and methods of assessing retardation. These guidelines should be communicated to all classroom teachers concerned with the program in an in-service meeting prior to the selection process.

The degree of retardation should vary according to the age-grade level of the student. Some general guidelines for selection of students:

Grade Level	Retardation for Recommendation
1	2 to 3 months
2	4 to 6 months
3	6 to 8 months
4	1 to 1½ years
5	1½ to 2 years
6+	2 years or more

The reading specialist should be sure to make classroom teachers feel they are participating in the selection of students. Two different forms for teacher referral are included in the next chapter. Each requires the teacher to spend some time in completing the referral. We believe this is preferable to having teachers simply list the names of the students they wish to refer. Completing a referral form makes teachers more likely to employ careful thought in selecting students.

At this stage the reading specialist should also examine the performance of referred students on group standardized achievement tests. In most schools such tests are given to all students on an annual basis. Although group tests provide no accurate measure of reading ability, they generally reveal whether the student is performing at grade level. The reading specialist can assume that most referrals are for students who are reading below grade level. By looking at group test scores the specialist can determine if one or more teachers are referring pupils who do not have an apparent need for remedial instruction. Furthermore, many specially funded programs require that students be drawn only from the bottom two quartiles as measured by standardized tests.

To complete the initial screening the reading specialist selects a suitable number of students for preliminary diagnosis. In some situations this is not difficult, since the number of students referred does not exceed the remedial teacher's potential case load. In many schools, however, preliminary selection is a difficult and delicate matter. The reading specialist may know, for instance, that the total case load cannot exceed thirty-five. However, classroom teachers may have referred seventy-five students, all but five of whom have scored below the fiftieth percentile on the standardized achievement test. In such a situation some students who are in need of special assistance will not receive it. The reading specialist, with the help and support of the principal, must communicate this problem to the teachers and seek an equitable approach. Often the specialist will choose first the students who have the lowest test scores. In some situations the specialist will select the students who are expected to make the greatest gains. Whichever approach is used, the faculty should understand the rationale and be willing to accept the decisions. Also, the specialist should try to balance the initial screening decisions so that if possible all teachers who referred students will have a similar number of students selected.

The reading specialist may screen approximately 20 percent more students than can be accommodated in the final program. Often the subsequent steps show that some listed students are not good candidates. A waiting list lets students quickly be brought in to the program as vacancies arise.

Step 2.   Once the preliminary screening is completed, the reading specialist begins diagnosis of individual students. The preliminary diagnosis should determine whether the student is a good candidate and identify some specific strengths and weaknesses. At this stage the specialist usually gives a pronunciation test such as the San Diego Quick Assessment Test and a basic sight vocabulary test (both described in Chapter 4) as well as an informal reading inventory (Chapter 11). These tests will demonstrate the degree and nature of disability. In some cases, depending on the number of students and the specialist's skill in administering tests, the students are tested in phonics, structural analysis, context clues, and comprehension.

Many reading specialists can complete the preliminary diagnoses (step 2) in about one week's time by testing, say, ten students per day. A thorough evaluation can be done in this period if the specialist is well organized and uses trained aides or parent volunteers. Under the supervision of the remedial teacher, paraprofessionals can administer and score the pronunciation and basic sight vocabulary tests while the reading teacher administers the informal reading inventory and specific skills tests. Many reading specialists find that with practice and expertise, the initial diagnosis can be completed in approximately thirty minutes per student. Since most classroom teachers are anxious for their remedial readers to begin receiving help immediately, it is important to complete the testing as efficiently as possible.

Step 3.   The reading specialist works with a screening committee to select the students who seem most likely to benefit from the program. In many schools screening is done by the remedial reading teacher without the aid of other school personnel. In some cases this works quite well, but the committee can be of great benefit to the remedial teacher. A committee composed of the remedial teacher, the principal, at least one classroom teacher, and perhaps the guidance counselor can eliminate a number of problems. For example, problems often arise when more pupils are taken from one teacher than from another. However, if a screening committee makes the decision, there is less likelihood that a teacher will feel that his or her students are not receiving equal consideration. Similarly, a committee can support the specialist in denying students who were referred because of discipline problems rather than reading problems per se. The principal and guidance counselor can add valuable input on such matters as scheduling and students' home conditions. Earlier in the book we discussed P.L. 94–142 and the importance of role clarification among professionals and proper educational assessment for the student with learning difficulties. The screening committee described in this section may address both issues.

Steps 4 and 5.   After the candidates have been selected, the reading specialist completes specific diagnostic tests and begins remedial sessions. At this point students may be tested for auditory discrimination and for vision. Students with problems in either area would be referred to a specialist for further testing (Chapter 8). During this period (perhaps two to four weeks) the remedial reading teacher might be working with a few more than a normal case load. Precise records should be kept indicating exactly how fast each student learns. A student weak in phonics would be given an individual phonics test during one of the first few sessions. After several weeks of work on missed phonemes or on unknown rules, the student would take another test to determine exactly how much the student had learned and retained. If the student had made considerable progress, the remedial teacher would probably wish to continue along the same lines as before. If nothing had been learned or retained, the teacher must decide whether altering instructional strategy or referral to a psychologist or other specialists was in order.

Step 6.   Students who seem to learn rather quickly should definitely be retained. Students who need auditory or visual correction should also join this final group. Students who seem not to benefit from instruction, as indicated in step 5, are referred to other specialists. For example, a child may need psychological help for an extended period, during which the psychologist or psychiatrist may or may not recommend that the student come to remedial reading. However, many students sooner or later become a part of the final case load.

SCHEDULING CLASSES FOR REMEDIAL READING

One major problem is from which courses to take students for remedial training. We suggest that where it is possible students be taken from either social studies or science to attend remedial reading. To begin with, much of these courses is based on textbooks. Candidates for remedial reading are in most cases not able to benefit from textbooks. Furthermore, there is no national science or social studies curriculum, as there is in reading and mathematics. For this reason overall school achievement test results are not adversely affected to any great extent by having students miss a portion of these classes. In fact, most achievement tests in social studies and science measure only vocabulary, and studies by Eldon E. Ekwall have shown that remedial reading students who were encouraged to read books about social studies and science gained as much and in many cases more vocabulary as the students in regular classes.

Students should not be taken from their regular reading classes or from physical education, art, or music classes. Much can be gained from their own reading classes if the teachers understand their problems. In the case of physical education, art, and music the student is likely to miss a great opportunity to have fun and compete on an equal basis.

THE NUMBER OF STUDENTS PER CLASS AND TOTAL CASE LOAD

The number of students in the remedial reading class varies to some extent on the age-grade levels of the students and on the similarity of the problems of students who can be scheduled together. A few students need such intensive training that it is imperative for them to receive individual help, especially in the beginning stages.

Many authorities have indicated that classes numbering up to six can be beneficial. In an evaluation of the El Paso Public Schools Title I Remedial Reading Program Edwa Steirnagle (1971) stated, "One surprising discovery was the fact that pupils who received one-to-one instruction from the teacher had not made the predicted progress. Classes consisting of five pupils who were instructed for a full hour, daily, produced the greatest gains." (p. 539) However, later research by Steirnagle indicated that gains began to drop off sharply when the number went beyond six to eight pupils.

Most reading authorities also agree that a teacher's total case load should not exceed forty pupils. In many cases, depending on severity of disabilities and the amount of consulting the teacher is expected to do, the maximum case load might well be thirty or fewer. The length of the instructional period and the number of remedial sessions per week for each pupil will be discussed in the following section.

FREQUENCY AND LENGTH OF CLASS SESSIONS

Several studies have been done on this. As pointed out earlier in the chapter, younger students have a much better chance of recovering from reading disabilities and of maintaining gains. Asher Cashdan and P. D. Pumfrey (1969) studied thirty-six junior high school students in three groups. One group was given remedial training in groups of four to six for thirty to sixty minutes twice weekly. Another group was taught in the same size group for thirty to sixty minutes once weekly. The third group served as a control and was given no remedial training at all. Twenty-two months later there were no significant differences in the achievement or attitudes of the three groups. The authors concluded that students of this age group needed a far more intensive and integrated program than this two-term project.

Robert Hicks et al. (1968) studied the gains made by third- and fourth-grade students. Their subjects were assigned to one of three experimental conditions. These conditions were half-hour remedial reading sessions, two, three, and four per week. No one received more than five hours of instruction per week. The experiment lasted approximately one school year. The third-grade group that was instructed three times per week made significantly greater gains than the group that was instructed only twice. They also found that the third graders who were instructed four times per week made significantly greater gains than the groups that were instructed only two or three times per week. On the other hand, at the fourth-grade level the number of sessions per week did not produce any significant differences. These authors stated:

> The results of this study tend to indicate that time allotments are an important consideration in the development of a third-grade remedial reading curriculum, i.e., there is a direct and reliable relationship between the number of sessions and the amount of improvement in reading shown over the school year. No such relationship was demonstrated for the fourth-grade pupils who served as S's in this study. Two sessions per week seem to be as beneficial as three or four. (pp. 439 and 744)

These findings were consistent with those of Oscar Jarvis (1965), who found that lengthening formalized reading instruction to more than fifty minutes per day had no significant effect on the gain of fourth, fifth, and sixth graders in a developmental situation. Jarvis stated, "These data strongly suggest that we teach reading in the other curricular areas of the elementary school curriculum as well as in the formalized reading class." (p. 204) However, the findings of Jarvis may not be applicable to children in grades one, two, and three.

Roger J. De Santi (1983) reported on the effects of varied duration and intensity of instruction for remedial readers in a clinic. He found that all students benefited from the instruction, but that gains were not necessarily enhanced by longer sessions or more total hours of tutoring. De Santi's conclusion: "The findings of this study imply that disabled readers profit from remedial services apparently regardless of the duration and intensity of scheduling." (p. 118)

It is difficult to summarize findings on frequency and length of class sessions because researchers report conflicting results. It appears that at third grade and probably below, students benefit from two or three sessions per week, but they will gain and retain more from four to five sessions per week. Students in the fourth grade and above are not likely to gain and retain progress in a short-term program (one year or less) regardless of the number of sessions. There are many exceptions to this rule. For example, at the El Paso Reading Center, students at the fourth-grade level and above have improved by one to two grade levels in remedial sessions held once per week for one semester. At the California State University, Hayward Reading Clinic, older elementary students have shown an average gain of two years after seven weeks of daily one-to-one instruction. In general, we conclude, students in any grade can be helped, and the more frequently the sessions are held the greater the chance for success. However, for students at fourth grade or above, the remedial process is likely to take much longer.

The length of class sessions in many cases depends on the administrative structure of the school. However, if possible a remedial period of twenty to thirty minutes for second and third graders and forty to fifty minutes for fourth graders and above is usually adequate to teach a good lesson and keep them from becoming overly restless. If possible, these periods should be broken up into several activities, particularly selection of books for outside reading. Although students often require some assistance in book selection, this also allows time for record keeping. Many reading specialists find it effective to overlap their schedules so that one group arrives five to ten minutes before the previous group is dismissed. When students in the arriving group enter the room, they know that they are to pick up a good book and enjoy some silent reading time. Thus, when the earlier group is dismissed, the teacher can expect that all of the members of the arriving group are present and in a good frame of mind for instruction.

TERMINATION OF STUDENTS FROM THE REMEDIAL READING PROGRAM

Ideally students should be terminated from the program when they are reading up to grade level. A number of studies have shown, however, that it is often necessary to continue remediation on a less intensive basis to maintain reading skills as well as to keep up with peers. Madeline Hardy (1968) studied the academic, vocational, and social adjustment of a group of young adults who had been disabled in reading and who had received clinical diagnosis and treatment during their elementary school years. She concluded that it was possible to reduce reading retardation by a remedial program, but the amount of retardation often increased at the end of the treatment. Gains were significant only during remedial work. Hardy also found that students who displayed deficiencies in visual, perceptual, and motor skills at referral tended to retain these deficiencies. She believed that because the disabled reader's problems tended to persist, remedial teachers should attempt to help the readers to understand, accept, and cope with their problems. Similarly, Paula Cornelius (1982) studied students identified as learning disabled and reported that these students:

> regress in their reading skills when they experience extended breaks in their educational programs and that a five-week summer reading program during either the first or last half of the summer can minimize this regression. (p. 412)

Bruce Balow (1965) studied three samples of boys and girls from the Psycho-Educational Clinic at the University of Minnesota. All were fifth and sixth graders who according to tests were bright enough to be reading at grade level or above, but who were reading three or more years below their expectancy level. Balow's subjects were mostly from a middle-class or lower-middle-class background. Prior to receiving remediation these students were achieving at approximately half the rate of normal students. During their period of remediation Samples I and II progressed at twelve and nine times their previous rates respectively. (There were no data available for Sample III.) Sample I did not receive any follow-up remedial assistance after being discharged from the clinic, while the students in Samples II and III were given less intensive but supportive help following their remedial period. The students in Sample I did not lose the reading skills acquired during their period of remediation, but they did not continue to develop on their own. Students in Samples II and III continued to gain in reading skills more rapidly than prior to entering the program, although they did not gain as rapidly as normally achieving readers.

Balow concluded:

> The unfortunate but highly instructive element of these findings is that severe reading disability is not corrected by short-term intensive courses of treatment, even though it is ameliorated by such help. Neither, it would appear, is the cure to be found in intensive treatment followed by maintenance sessions of an hour or so per week, although again such a program is far superior to no special help at all. The implication which follows naturally from these conclusions is that severe reading disability is probably best considered a relatively chronic illness needing long-term treatment rather than the short course typically organized in current programs. (p. 586)

Benjamin Willis (1971) studied the growth curves of third-year students in a remedial program. He found that the greatest growth in reading skills appeared to take place during the fourth month of instruction. Growth increased each month but seemed to level off by the fifth month. Although the results obtained by Willis were probably to some extent a function of the type of program provided and of the age of the students involved, there is definite evidence that if other factors are not hindering students' progress, they should show definite improvement after four months of instruction.

In summary:

1. The earlier disabled readers are identified (grades one to three) and placed in a remedial program, the more likely they are to learn to achieve on a level with their normal-reading peers. Even then, some follow-up program should be provided.
2. Students (grade four and above) who are severely disabled in reading should be considered as chronic cases who will need not only long-term treatment, but also follow-up help after discharge from the full program.
3. Most students, especially those at the third-grade level or below, should be referred to other specialists if they have not shown considerable gain after four to five months of instruction.

FACILITIES FOR REMEDIAL READING

There are several ways for the remedial reading teacher to operate: within the classroom, through a mobile reading center, or in a remedial reading class-room. The importance of a facility that is appealing to the eye cannot be over-emphasized. Although students may not appear to mind coming to a drab room, most will probably be adversely affected. Surroundings do make a major difference. This was pointed out to one of the coauthors when visiting a federal penitentiary to discuss their reading program. Some time before the visit to the institution, the reading classroom was in a basement. There was little or no sunlight, and a number of steam pipes running along the ceiling tended to drip water. The teacher of this class said that seldom had a day gone by that at least one physical fight did not break out in this classroom. However, after the reading class was moved into a sunny and brightly decorated classroom, there was not one incident even near the point of physical violence.

Most students are more inhibited than the inmates of this prison, but there is little doubt that students feel the influence of their surroundings as did the inmates of the federal penitentiary.

This is a list of some of the positive things we have observed in remedial classrooms:

1. Folders or carriers for each student.
2. Evidence of individual students' progress displayed in rooms.
3. Students' work prominently displayed in bright and attractive rooms.
4. Carpeted, comfortable area for free reading for early arrivals.
5. Lots of trade books properly displayed.
6. Numerous supplementary materials available, both commercial and homemade.
7. Use of materials to provide variety in directed instruction, such as chalkboard, chart rack, lap boards, pupil response devices.
8. Centers for variety in reinforcement, such as listening posts, record players, Language Masters, typewriters, recording studios.

9. The reading specialist's room serving as a central depository for basal materials and other reading materials, and thus as a resource center for classroom teachers.

In addition to a pleasant classroom atmosphere a number of other facilities are desirable:

1. Office space for record keeping and conferences with parents and students.
2. Storage for equipment, paper, books, and other materials.
3. A copier. This may be housed in or out of the classroom; however, the remedial reading teacher usually needs to copy a great many materials and for this reason should have easy access to duplicating facilities.
4. Chalkboard and bulletin board space.
5. Sufficient electrical outlets for overhead projectors, tape recorders, filmstrip projectors, etc.
6. Tables and chairs suitable for individual or small group work.
7. Study carrels with facilities for individual viewing of audiovisual materials.
8. Filing cabinets.

The general criteria for books, programs, and materials are discussed in Chapter 16.

EVALUATING PROGRESS IN REMEDIAL READING AND MEASURING THE EFFECTIVENESS OF THE PROGRAM

Most remedial reading teachers are concerned with evaluating two aspects of their program. One is the effect on individual students, and the other is the effectiveness of the program as a whole.

Individual Evaluation

Individual evaluation can be carried out in a number of ways. One is to keep very accurate records of pretest and posttest performance on individual diagnostic tests. For example, in giving a phonics test, the teacher notes exactly which phonemes were missed. After a period of teaching, the same test can again be given. Many teachers are used to thinking about progress in terms of grade-level scores. However, most standardized achievement tests do not measure individual achievement accurately enough to be of any real value for remedial work. Therefore, grade-level scores are often misleading. Criterion measures of gain in specific skills are much more meaningful for individual students.

Another method of measuring individual gains is a checklist of the characteristics and specific number of types of errors on informal reading inventories (Chapter 2). In the first administration of the IRI each characteristic and the number of each type of error is noted. After a period of remediation the same passages can be given and errors noted again. You can then figure the percentage of reduction in each type of error between the first and second test. If the overall grade level of the student has increased, however, it is important that the percentages be computed only on the same passages that were given (up to frustration level) in the first administration of the test.

The informal reading inventory is also useful for measuring individual gains. These may not always be apparent as the teacher works with students, and they often become very apparent on tape. The initial reading is recorded and after a period of remediation, the same passages are rerecorded after the first, on the same tape. Allowing students to hear their own progress in fluency and reduction in errors is highly motivating.

Group Evaluation

Group evaluation of remedial reading programs can also be difficult. One method of researching the effectiveness of special or compensatory programs is use of a control group. This method has some disadvantages. One is that there must be a control group. One does not wish to deprive the control group of the benefit of a promising new program for the sake of measuring significant differences in posttest results between the two groups. If students in another school are used as a control group, there is no assurance that students in the two schools are of equal ability; therefore, a comparison of the two would yield inaccurate results.

Another method for evaluating group gains is a comparison of pre- and posttest scores on standardized achievement tests. Students' growth can properly be reported in terms of grade equivalent units if you present a frequency distribution rather than attempt to average the students' gains. This type of report:

GE Gain Between Pre- and Posttesting	Number of Students Making This Gain	Percent	Cumulative Percent
1.5 and up	8	16%	100%
1.3–1.4	10	20%	84%
1.1–1.2	12	24%	64%
.9–1.0	10	20%	40%
.7– .8	5	10%	20%
.5– .6	3	6%	10%
less than .5	2	4%	04%
TOTAL	50		

From this, you could conclude that sixty percent of students seen by this reading specialist had gains greater than 1.0 grade equivalents between pre- and posttesting.

This is an explanation of a method of assessing gains that is relatively easy to interpret—children's ratio of learning. Although ratio of learning is not new, it is still unfamiliar to many people.[7]

It is a measurement of children's learning rate prior to entering a special program versus while they are in the program. Because of the unreliability of group test scores for individual students, you should determine the ratio of learning for all students in a special program rather than for individuals. The steps:

1. Determine the average number of years that all children in the special program were in school at the beginning of the program. The number of years in school equals grade level minus one, unless the child has failed. In that case the number of years in school equals the grade level they should have been in minus the number of failed years.

   Example:

Sara	— Grade 3 (never failed)	$3 - 1 = 2$
Blanca	— Grade 5 (never failed)	$5 - 1 = 4$
Elaine	— Grade 4 (failed one year)	$5 - 1 = 4$
Bill	— Grade 3 (failed two years)	$5 - 1 = 4$
Jennifer	— Grade 2 (never failed)	$2 - 1 = \underline{1}$

   $$\frac{\text{Total number of years in school}}{\text{Number of students}} \quad \frac{15}{5} = 3 \text{ years/student}$$

   This group has been in school for an average of 3 years per student.

2. Determine the average years of achievement of the group when they enter the program. Remember that achievement of 1.0 actually means no achievement at all; therefore, the number of years of achievement for each student is equal to each student's grade level score on an achievement test, minus one.

Example: *Name*	*Pretest Achievement Test Score*
Sarah	$1.5 - 1 = .5$
Blanca	$3.5 - 1 = 2.5$
Elaine	$2.5 - 1 = 1.5$
Bill	$2.5 - 1 = 1.5$
Jennifer	$\underline{1.0} - 1 = \underline{0.0}$
Total years on achievement test	11.0

   $$\frac{\text{Total years of achievement}}{\text{Number of students}} \quad \frac{6.0}{5.0} = 1.2$$

[7]The explanation for ratio of learning is largely adapted from an article by Eldon E. Ekwall, "Measuring gains in remedial reading." *Reading Teacher,* Vol. 26 (Novem-

The average number of years of achievement for this group when they entered the program was 1.2.

3. Divide the average years of achievement by the average years children have been in school. This will give you their average learning rate prior to entering the special program.

Example:

$$\frac{\text{Average number of years of achievement}}{\text{Average number of years in school}} \quad \frac{1.2}{3.0} = .40$$

The average learning rate for these children before entering the program was .40; they had learned only fourth tenths as much as they should have.

4. Determine how long children were in the special program.

Example:

September 15th to May 15th = 8 months

5. Determine the average gain per pupil during the special program.

Example: Name	*Posttest Achievement Test Score*
Sara	2.8
Blanca	4.8
Elaine	5.2
Bill	4.5
Jennifer	2.3
Total years (posttest)	19.6
Total years (pretest)	11.0
Years gained in program (difference between posttest and pretest)	$\frac{8.6}{5} = 1.72$ years/
Number of students	student

The average amount of gain during the special program was 1.72 years per student. Note that it is not necessary to subtract 1 from each student's score on the posttest and pretest since you are only finding the overall differences in the two scores. Subtracting 1 from each posttest score and each pretest score would give the same answer.

6. Determine the average learning rate during the special program by dividing the amount gained during the program by the number of years (or months) the students were in the program.

Example:

$$\frac{\text{Years gained during the program}}{\text{Years in program}} \quad \frac{1.72}{.8} = 2.15$$

The average learning rate was 2.15.

ber 1972): 138–141. Reproduced by permission of the International Reading Association.

7. Compare students' average learning rate before entering the special program with their rate while participating in it.

Students were learning 5.4 times as rapidly as they had been (2.15 ÷ .4 = 5.4); simply stated, they were now learning at a rate more than two times that of the average student. There is no doubt that this program was effective. Any learning rate greater than the students' rate prior to the special program indicates an improvement in the group rate of learning.

CODE OF ETHICS

All reading personnel, as well as administrators, should be familiar with the International Reading Association's Code of Ethics:

> The members of the International Reading Association who are concerned with the teaching of reading form a group of professional persons, obligated to society and devoted to the service and welfare of individuals through teaching, clinical services, research, and publication. The members of this group are committed to values which are the foundation of a democratic society—freedom to teach, write, and study in an atmosphere conducive to the best interests of the profession. The welfare of the public, the profession, and the individuals concerned should be of primary consideration in recommending candidates for degrees, positions, advancements, the recognition of professional activity, and for certification in those areas where certification exists.[8]

Ethical Standards in Professional Relationships
1. It is the obligation of all members of the International Reading Association to observe the Code of Ethics of the organization and to act accordingly so as to advance the status and prestige of the Association and of the profession as a whole. Members should assist in establishing the highest professional standards for reading programs and services, and should enlist support for these through dissemination of pertinent information to the public.
2. It is the obligation of all members to maintain relationships with other professional persons, striving for harmony, avoiding personal controversy, encouraging cooperative effort, and making known the obligations and services rendered by the reading specialist.
3. It is the obligation of members to report results of research and other developments in reading.
4. Members should not claim nor advertise affiliation with the International Reading Association as evidence of their competence in reading.

[8]Reprinted with permission of the International Reading Association.

Ethical Standards in Reading Services

1. Reading specialists must possess suitable qualifications . . . for engaging in consulting, clinical, or remedial work. Unqualified persons should not engage in such activities except under the direct supervision of one who is properly qualified. Professional intent and the welfare of the person seeking the services of the reading specialist should govern all consulting or clinical activities such as counseling, administering diagnostic tests, or providing remediation. It is the duty of the reading specialist to keep relationships with clients and interested persons on a professional level.

2. Information derived from consulting and/or clinical services should be regarded as confidential. Expressed consent of persons involved should be secured before releasing information to outside agencies.

3. Reading specialists should recognize the boundaries of their competence and should not offer services which fail to meet professional standards established by other disciplines. They should be free, however, to give assistance in other areas in which they are qualified.

4. Referral should be made to specialists in allied fields as needed. When such referral is made, pertinent information should be made available to consulting specialists.

5. Reading clinics and/or reading specialists offering professional services should refrain from guaranteeing easy solutions or favorable outcomes as a result of their work, and their advertising should be consistent with that of allied professions. They should not accept for remediation any persons who are unlikely to benefit from their instruction, and they should work to accomplish the greatest possible improvement in the shortest time. Fees, if charged, should be agreed on in advance and should be charged in accordance with an established set of rates commensurate with that of other professions.

Breaches of the Code of Ethics should be reported to IRA Headquarters for referral to the Committee on Professional Standards and Ethics for an impartial investigation.

SUMMARY

In initiating a remedial reading program it is especially important to develop a job description. There should be thorough communication among classroom teachers, administrative personnel, and reading personnel regarding the title and duties that various reading specialists are expected to perform.

Classroom teachers, administrators, reading specialists, and parents all have special talents to contribute to the remedial reading program. Each of these groups should become familiar with the program and learn about the unique contributions of the others.

An important aspect of the program is selection of students most likely to benefit from remedial instruction. It is important to obtain and/or develop materials appropriate for the specific difficulties of the students and to develop facilities conducive to learning.

Traditional methods of measurement in remedial reading are often inadequate. The methods suggested in this chapter may be found to be more appropriate.

Reading personnel must be highly qualified and perform their duties in a professional manner.

REFERENCES

Balow, B. (1965). The long-term effect of remedial reading instruction. *Reading Teacher, 18,* 581–586.

Bean, R. M. (1979). Role of the reading specialist: A multifaceted dilemma. *Reading Teacher, 32,* 409–413.

Bean, R. M., & Eichelberger, R. T. (1985). Changing the role of reading specialists: From pull-out to in-class programs. *Reading Teacher, 38,* 648–653.

Bruininks, R., Glaman, G., & Clark, C. R. (1973). Issues in determining prevalence of reading retardation. *Reading Teacher, 27,* 177–185.

Cashdan, A., & Pumfrey, P. D. (1969). Some effects of the teaching of remedial reading. *Educational Research, 11,* 138–142.

Cornelius, P. L. (1982). Effects of summer instruction on reading achievement regression of learning disabled students. *Journal of Learning Disabilities, 15,* 409–413.

De Santi, R. J. (1983). Varied duration and intensity of massed remedial reading instruction. *Reading Improvement, 20,* 114–119.

Esworthy, H. F. (1979). Parents attend reading clinic, too. *Reading Teacher, 32,* 831–834.

Evaluation Committee of the International Reading Association. (1979). What's in a name: Reading specialist? *Journal of Reading, 22,* 623–628.

Garry, V. V. (1974). Competencies that count among reading specialists. *Journal of Reading, 17,* 608–613.

Granowsky, A., Middleton, F. R., & Mumford, J. H. (1979). Parents as partners in education. *Reading Teacher, 32,* 826–830.

Green, C. R. (1973). Effects of reading supervisors on teacher attitudes toward children with reading problems. Abstract of unpublished doctoral dissertation, St. Louis University.

Grimmett, S. A., & McCoy, M. (1980). Effects of parental communication on reading performance of third grade children. *Reading Teacher, 34,* 303–308.

Hardy, M. I. (1968). Disabled readers: What happens to them after elementary school? *Canadian Education and Research Digest, 8,* 338–346.

Hesse, K. D., Smith, R. J., & Nettleton, A. (1973). Content teachers consider the role of the reading consultant. *Journal of Reading, 17,* 210–215.

Hicks, R. A., et al. (1968). Reading gains and instructional sessions. *Reading Teacher, 21,* 738–739.

Jarvis, O. T. (1965). Time allotment relationships to pupil achievement. *Elementary English, 42,* 201–204.

Mangieri, J. N., & Heimberger, M. J. (1980). Perceptions of the reading consultant's role. *Journal of Reading, 23,* 527–530.

Mangieri, J. M., & McWilliams, D. R. (1984). Providing effective leadership for reading programs. *National Association of Secondary School Principals (NASSP Bulletin), 68,* 64–68.

Manning, G. L., & Manning, M. (1981). What is the role of the principal in an excellent reading program? Principals give their views. *Reading World, 21,* 130–133.

Pearlman, E., & Pearlman, R. (1970). The effect of remedial reading training in a private clinic. *Academic Therapy, 5,* 298–304.

Pikulski, J. J., & Ross, E. (1979). Classroom teachers' perceptions of the role of the reading specialist. *Journal of Reading, 23,* 126–135.

Professional Standards and Ethics Committee of the International Reading Association. (1986). *Guidelines for the specialized preparation of reading professionals.* Newark, DE: International Reading Association.

Rauch, S. J. (1974). Administrator's guidelines for more effective reading programs. *Journal of Reading, 17,* 297–300.

Reed, J. C. (1970). The deficits of retarded readers—Fact or artifact? *Reading Teacher, 23,* 347–352.

Reynolds, C. R. (1981). The fallacy of "two years below grade level for age" as a diagnostic criterion for reading disorders. *Journal of School Psychology, 19,* 350–358.

Sawyer, W. S., & Wilson, B. A. (1979). Role clarification for remedial reading and learning disabilities teachers. *Reading Teacher, 33,* 162–166.

Steirnagle, E. (1971). A five-year summary of a remedial reading program. *Reading Teacher, 24,* 537–542.

Ullmann, C. A. (1969). Prevalence of reading disability as a function of the measure used. *Journal of Learning Disabilities, 2,* 556–558.

Wilhite, R. K. (1984). Principals' views of their role in the high school reading program. *Journal of Reading, 27,* 356–358.

Willis, B. C. (1971, December). Evaluation of the reading center's remedial program for the 1970–71 school year. Paper presented at the Broward County School Board, Fort Lauderdale, FA. Mimeographed.

Wylie, R. (1969). Diversified concepts of the role of the reading consultant. *Reading Teacher, 22,* 519–522.

14

Relaying Information, Record Keeping, and Writing Case Reports in Remedial Reading

This chapter contains a discussion of the necessity for accurately relaying information to and from individuals and agencies. A number of samples of forms for this are shown along with a short discussion of the use of each form. The latter part of the chapter contains a discussion of suggested techniques for writing case reports. This is followed by an example of a final case report.

THE PURPOSE OF REPORTING AND RECORD KEEPING

One of the most important and obvious reasons for reporting and record keeping is accurately transmitting information. Most people do not attempt to keep a record of a complex checking account in their head. Likewise, the information on disabled readers becomes too complex for one person to remember. Furthermore, often a number of people must deal with the same student, and it becomes necessary to relay information from person to person without taking the chance of misinterpretation or loss along the way.

A second, similar reason is to provide proper guidance to the student. Most people think they can remember more than they can. At a meeting of psychologists a questionnaire was circulated to listeners about one week after a speech. Only about 8 percent of the material the speaker presented was remembered at all, and half of the 8 percent (or 4 percent) was misinterpreted or inaccurately understood. As the remedial reading teacher works with each student, implications for further work and diagnosis constantly appear. If these implications are not written down, they are usually forgotten.

Accurate record keeping and reporting also serve as a measure of progress. In working with a disabled reader on a daily basis it is often difficult to observe progress, and it is necessary to keep accurate records to measure their growth in skills as well as to justify teaching them.

A third important purpose is in-service education. As the remedial teacher makes diagnoses and reports findings in written form and as he or she works with disabled readers and makes suggestions to classroom teachers for assignments, a great deal of reading education often takes place. When the classroom teacher sees positive results from the work of the remedial teacher and from work suggested by the remedial teacher, changes in the methods of the classroom teacher are likely to follow.

Legal requirements also make certain reporting necessary. Many programs are federally funded. This funding usually requires some sort of proof of success of the program. Depending on state and local district policies, it is also sometimes necessary to obtain written permission from parents in order to enroll children in remedial programs.

TYPES OF REPORTS AND RECORD KEEPING

The communication lines necessary for a successful remedial reading program are illustrated below. Either the remedial teacher does all of the diagnosis or at least part of the work is done by a diagnostician. Therefore, we have referred in some cases to the teacher and/or diagnostician, who may not be the same person.

1. Diagnostician or remedial teacher   Classroom teacher and administrators

2. Diagnostician or remedial teacher   Parents

3. Diagnostician or remedial teacher   Other educational agencies

Reporting Information from the Classroom Teacher to the Diagnostician or Remedial Reading Teacher

The forms that follow are used by the classroom teacher to relay information concerning candidates for remedial reading. Before these forms are used it is necessary for the remedial teacher to provide guidance in selecting students most in need of and most likely to benefit from remedial help. In most cases the forms that follow are distributed to the classroom teacher by the remedial reading teacher. If possible this should be done in an in-service meeting, at which time the use of the forms can be explained.

Form A is easy to use and helps teachers become aware of students' reading problems. Many teachers with little or no formal training in reading will need help in interpreting and using this form. However, this can be used to an advantage when at an in-service meeting the remedial teacher explains the categories of reading skills and how to identify problems in each category.

Form B is easy to understand; however, it is more time-consuming. Since the classroom teacher is in a position to observe students over a long period, this type of form can provide information of considerable value in working with disabled readers.

Reporting Information from the Diagnostician or Remedial Reading Teacher to Classroom Teachers

Form C reports the initial diagnosis. This is often helpful in placement of students at the proper reading levels and in pinpointing specific weaknesses, whether students appear to be proper candidates for remedial reading or not.

Forms D and E are to be used by the remedial teacher to report to the classroom teacher. It provides for continuous diagnostic information, work being carried on for correction of the student's problem, assignments for the student, and feedback from the classroom teacher. Form E is for assignments and goes either to the classroom teacher or to parents.

Reporting Information from the Diagnostician or Remedial Reading Teacher to Parents

In some districts permission from parents is required before enrolling students in programs such as remedial reading or special education. Form F is for this purpose.

Form G reports information from an initial diagnosis or from diagnostic teaching. This form also provides a checklist of activities for parents that are often beneficial to disabled readers.

(Form A)

Remedial Reading Referral

Teacher:_____   School:_____
Grade:_____   Date:_____

Nothing is so valuable in determining which students need remedial help as the opinion of the classroom teacher. If you have, or have had, students whom you feel need special help in reading, would you please list them in the space provided.

Following is a partial list of common weaknesses. If you feel any of these apply to students you are referring, please list the corresponding numbers after their names. If there are other difficulties that you have noted, please explain these also.

1. POOR SIGHT VOCABULARY
2. INABILITY TO USE CONTEXT CLUES
3. POOR USE OF PHONIC ANALYSIS
4. POOR USE OF STRUCTURAL ANALYSIS
5. MAKES REVERSALS (*saw* for *was*, etc.)
6. CANNOT ADJUST SPEED TO DIFFICULTY OF MATERIAL
7. WORD-BY-WORD READS
8. MAKES INSERTIONS, OMISSIONS, ETC.
9. POOR WORK AND STUDY HABITS
10. POOR CONCENTRATION
11. LACKS CONFIDENCE
12. EXHIBITS POOR ATTITUDE
13. POOR COMPREHENSION
14. PHRASES POORLY
15. OTHER (please explain)

If you have additional information, please enter it in the *remarks* blank. Please keep this form and it will be collected in the near future.

Student:_____
Remarks:_____
Student:_____
Remarks:_____
Student:_____
Remarks:_____
Student:_____
Remarks:_____
Student:_____
Remarks:_____

If you have additional students, please list their names on the back of this sheet.

Teacher's Report for Remedial Reading Referral

Student's Name:_____ Teacher's Name:_____

1. What do you think is the student's main problem(s) in reading?_____
_____
_____
_____

2. What is the student's reading level or what book is he or she presently using?_____
_____

3. How is this student grouped for reading?_____
_____

4. How is this student grouped for other subjects, and what is provided for any special reading problems that he or she may have?_____
_____
_____

5. What are some other weak points that you have observed in this student? (Other than in reading.)_____
_____
_____
_____

6. What are some of the student's strong points?_____
_____
_____

6. What are the student's reactions to reading? (Interests, attitude, etc.)__
_____
_____

7. What is the attitude of the student?
    Emotionally calm _____
    Apathetic _____
    Excitable _____
8. How does the student react to authority?
    Resistant _____
    Accepting _____
    Overly dependent _____
9. Describe the student's relationships to other students._____
_____

10. Have you noted any unusual emotional behavior by this student?_____
_____

11. How does this student react to a difficult task? Withdrawn:_____
Faces problem with little or no difficulty:_____
Acts impulsively:_____
12. How does the student act in the classroom? Calm and quiet: (If withdrawn please explain.)_____
Talkative:_____
Normal:_____
Other Information that you feel is important:_____
_____
_____

(Form C)

Individual Reading Diagnosis Report

Student:_____   Date tested:_____

School:_____   Teacher:_____

Student's age at time of testing:__   Student's grade at time of testing:__

In accordance with your referral the above-named student was tested and in my opinion does _____ does not _____ need to be in the remedial reading program.

COMPREHENSION (Combination of the *Gray Oral Reading Test* and an *Informal Reading Inventory*.)

```
                    100 │ +   +   +   +   +   +   +   +   +   +
  Percent of         75 │ +   +   +   +   +   +   +   +   +   +
  comprehension      50 │ +   +   +   +   +   +   +   +   +   +
                     25 │ +   +   +   +   +   +   +   +   +   +
                      x │
                        └──────────────────────────────────────
                          1   2   3   4   5   6   7   8   9   10
                              Reading grade level
                                (comprehension)
```

1. FREE READING LEVEL   Grade _____
2. INSTRUCTIONAL GRADE LEVEL   Grade _____
3. FRUSTRATION READING LEVEL   Grade _____

READING DIFFICULTIES:_____
_____

PHYSICAL OR OTHER DIFFICULTIES NOTED:_____
_____

TYPE OF HELP OR REMEDIATION RECOMMENDED:_____
_____
_____

1. FREE READING LEVEL: Reader level at which child can function adequately with no teacher help. Word recognition should be 99% accurate; comprehension of all types should average at least 90%.
2. INSTRUCTIONAL READING LEVEL: Reading level at which child can function adequately with teacher guidance and, at the same time, meet enough challenge to stimulate further growth. On a pretest at this level, word recognition should be 95% accurate and comprehension at least 75% accurate.
3. FRUSTRATION LEVEL: Reading level at which the child's abilities to function break down. Word recognition falls to 90% or below; comprehension, to 50% or below. May also be indicated by presence of symptoms of difficulty such as vocalization, tension movements, and so on. Serves as an indicator of rate of progress in that it shows how far above the instructional level learning can currently extend.

(Form D)

From:_____

To:_____

As you know, _____ is receiving help in reading. This time amounts to approximately thirty-five to forty-five minutes three times per week. That time is shared with from one to five other students. In order to make the most of that time, I hope we can work together with this student to his/her maximum benefit. I will try to give you a report from time to time on what I am working on with this particular student, and what I have asked the student to do between these sessions. If there is some question, please feel free to contact me or write a note at the bottom of this page and ask the student to return it to me.

Thank you.

Remedial reading teacher's diagnosis of the problem:_____
_____
_____

Work being carried on for correction of the above problem:_____
_____
_____
_____

Assignment for student:_____
_____

Comments from classroom teacher (to remedial reading teacher):_____
_____

(Form E)

ASSIGNMENT SHEET
Name:_____Date due:_____
Purpose of assignment:_____
_____

The following work has been assigned to be completed before the next meeting with the student's remedial reading instructor:

1._____
2._____
3._____
4._____
5._____
Remedial reading teacher_____

_____
(Signature of parent or teacher)

(Form F)

Parental Permission Form for Remedial Reading

To:_____

From:_____

Date:_____

     Your child, _____, has been given a series of reading and diagnostic tests, and it is my opinion that _____ should be given the help that we can provide in the remedial reading program. This is a class for children of normal intelligence who have some type of difficulty in reading.

     I would like to extend the opportunity for you to visit with me concerning your child's reading problem and to visit the class in which we would like to enroll him/her. If you would like to visit this class, it meets on _____ from _____ to _____ in Room _____. Please feel free to visit at any time.

     You have my permission to enroll _____ in the remedial reading program.

                               _____

                               (Signature of parent or guardian)

Note: Please ask your child to return this to me or send it to me at the following address:

_____

_____

_____

(Form G)

Progress Report to Parents

Date:_____

To:_____

From:_____(Remedial Reading Teacher)

     As you know, your child _____ has been receiving help in our remedial reading program. We feel that his/her primary need is:_____

_____

_____

     In addition to the help that your child has been getting at school, it would also be beneficial if he/she could receive help from you in the following areas:

1. ____ Show interest in homework assignments that have been given and check to see that these are completed on the date that they are due.

(Form G cont'd.)

2. ____ Take your child to the public library and help him/her to find books that he/she would like to read.

3. ____ Help your child by being a good listener when he/she reads to you. Do not be overly concerned with the teaching of specific skills. We will try to do this in the remedial reading program.

4. ____ Try to set aside a certain period of time each day for pleasure reading. This seems to work better if a *specific time* is set aside rather than a certain *amount* of time. In other words the amount of time is also important, for example, thirty to forty minutes, but it is important that it be done at the same time each day if possible.

5. ____ Please comment in the *remarks* space below whether you believe your child has taken an increased interest in reading on his/her own.

6. ____ Other:_____

_____

_____

Remarks:_____

_____

_____

_____
(Remedial Reading Teacher—Signature)

(Form H)

Date:_____

To:_____

_____

_____

_____

The following student _____, who lives at _____, is receiving remediation at the Reading Center at _____. In order to facilitate his/her remediation, we would appreciate any test results or records that you might have concerning this child.

Thank you.

_____, Director

Reading Center, _____

(Form H cont'd)

You have my permission to release any records
concerning my daughter ☐ son☐

_____
(student's name)

_____
                          Parent

Sent to:

Reporting Information from Parents to the Diagnostician and/or Remedial Reading Teacher

Teachers who work in university or public school reading clinics, as opposed to a regular remedial classroom, often come in contact with a greater percentage of seriously disabled readers. Although ample background information for any disabled reader is desirable, it is often especially helpful in order to diagnose the problems of seriously disabled readers. Some of this background information is usually available in the cumulative folders kept by the public schools or from the records of other educational agencies. Form H may be adapted to your specific situation as a request form for obtaining students' records from these various educational agencies. Note that it contains space for a parent's signature. Many educational agencies require parental permission before they will release student records.

Form I is used at the El Paso Reading Center. As the title indicates, it is an application for admission of students to the Reading Center. Most of the information requested on this form is directly applicable to a thorough diagnosis of each student. However, a few items, such as information on handedness and birth history, are used for research over a longer period. Personnel in reading clinics may wish to use an adaptation of this form, or remedial reading teachers may wish to use a shortened version to obtain information considered pertinent for an immediate, thorough diagnosis.

Form J is used for the initial case analysis of each student who enters the reading center. Note that space is provided for the number of reading errors and characteristics of the reader on an informal reading inventory on the first trial as the student enters the program. The same passages are again read at the end of the remedial period, and the percentage of change is computed. This type of information is often more valuable than a simple grade-level designation, which may or may not be accurate. The rest of the form is used to help the remedial teacher synthesize test results and other information collected in the initial diagnosis.

(Form I)

Application for Admission to Reading Center

(To be filled out by parents or guardians of student)

Name of Student: _____

            (Last)   (First)   (Middle)

Address: _____Telephone _____

_____

     (City)   (County)   (State)

Student's Birth Date: _____   Age: ____   Sex: ____   Race: ____

School: _____ Grade Level: _____

    (If not in school, indicate occupation of student)   (If not in school, last grade level reached)

Name of parent or guardian: _____

Address of parent or guardian: _____

Telephone number of parent or guardian: _____

Occupation of parent or guardian: (A) Father _____

                                       (be specific)

Employed by: _____ (B) Mother: _____

                                       (be specific)

_____   Employed by: _____

Father's place of birth: _____ Birth date: _____ Age: ____

Mother's place of birth: _____ Birth date: _____ Age: ____

Father's educational level _____ Mother's educational level: _____

Is this student adopted? _____ If so, student's age when acquired: _____

Does student know he is adopted? _____ Father dead? _____ Mother dead? _____

Cause of death? _____ Are parents separated? _____ Divorced? _____

Has either parent remarried? _____ Has either parent been married before? _____

           (which one?)   (which one?)

With whom does student live? _____

READING PROBLEM

1. Why is student being referred to the reading center? _____

(Form I cont'd.)

_____

_____

_____

_____

_____

_____

FAMILY HISTORY

1. List names, ages, and sex for other children, oldest to youngest: _____

_____

_____

_____

2. Which of the above children are living at home? _____

_____

3. Has anyone else ever lived in the home? If so, who? _____

_____

4. Has your family ever lived with anyone else? If so, who? _____

_____

5. What languages are spoken in the home? _____

_____

6. Do any other members of the family have a reading problem? _____

7. Has there been any physical deformity on either side of the family in any generation?

_____

8. How is the general health of other members of the family? _____

_____

DOMINANCE

1. Which hand does the student use to write? _____

Ever use other hand? _____ What for? _____

2. At what age did student show hand preference? _____

_____

3. Was student ever encouraged to use one hand more than the other? _____

(Explain — how, when and by whom?): _____

_____

_____

4. Are other members of the family left-handed? _____

(If yes, please list names) _____

BIRTH HISTORY

1. Was child born premature? _____If so, how much? _____

2. Was birth completely normal? If not, please explain _____

_____

_____

DEVELOPMENTAL HISTORY

1. At what age did child say first words? _____

2. At what age did child first walk? _____

3. Did this child walk and speak first words at an earlier or later date than other members of the family? (Please explain)

_____

_____

4. Has child ever had any serious illnesses? _____

_____

_____

5. Has child ever had any serious accidents? _____

_____

_____

6. Does student, or has student ever, worn glasses? _____

If yes, who prescribed them? _____

7. When did student have last examination by an eye doctor? What were the results? ___

_____

8. Has student ever had an ear infection? _____ If yes, please explain. _____

_____

9. Has student's hearing ever been checked by a doctor? _____

_____

10. Do you think student hears well? _____

SOCIO-EDUCATIONAL

1. Any special schools attended? _____ Name of school, type, where, when and how

long in attendance: _____

_____

Has student ever had an intelligence or other mental test? _____

If so: what test(s), by whom given, where and when, and results (findings)?

_____

_____

3. Has child ever failed in school? _____ What grades? _____ Why? _____

_____

4. Usual scholastic ratings? _____ 5. Best subjects? _____

6. Worst subjects? _____

7. How does student get along with siblings? _____

Other children? _____ Parents? _____

8. Disposition: Happy? _____ Affectionate? _____ Dependable? _____

Concentration? _____ Temper? _____ Fears? _____

_____(Other comments?) _____

9. Does student fatigue easily? _____ Symptoms observed: _____

10. How much does student sleep? _____ At night? _____ Daytime nap? _____

11. Interests and abilities: _____

12. What does student like to do in spare time? _____

(Form I cont'd.)

13. Does student like to compete with others? (Explain) _____

_____

REFERRAL INFORMATION

1. Who referred you to the University of Texas at El Paso Reading Center?

     Name: _____

     Address: _____

     _____

           (City)   (State)

2. Full name and address of family physician or student's physician:

     Name: _____

     Address: _____

     _____

           (City)   (State)

CASE RECORD INFORMATION

Name of person who has completed this form: _____

_____   _____

            (Signature)   (Date)

(Form J)

INITIAL CASE ANALYSIS

Student's Name: _____ Sex: _____

Grade: _____ Teacher: _____
                    (Person administering tests at UTEP
                    Reading Center)

School attended by student: _____

1. Results of tests administered at reading center

    1.1 Reading

        1.1.1 Graded word list

(Form J cont'd.)

San Diego Quick Assessment A measure of the student's ability to pronounce ten words at each grade level. It is not timed.

Other: _____ Description:

Test date: _____

Independent level   _____

Instructional level   _____

Frustration level   _____

1.1.2 Informal Reading Inventory

Ekwall Reading Inventory A series of graded passages designed to determine a student's independent, instructional, and frustration level both orally and silently.

Other: _____ Description:

Test date: _____

	Oral	Silent
Independent level	_____	_____
Instructional level	_____	_____
Frustration level	_____	_____
Listening comprehension level	_____	

Analysis of Graded Word List

Independent level:	Original word missed	Miscue used by student
	_____	_____
Instructional level	_____	_____
	_____	_____
Frustration level	_____	_____
	_____	_____
	_____	_____
	_____	_____
	_____	_____
	_____	_____

(Form J cont'd.)

Most common difficulties: _____

_____

_____

Analysis of Informal Reading Inventory

Types of Errors
(Indicate number of each type)

First Trial		Second Trial	Percent of increase (+) or decrease (−)
	Omissions		
	Insertions		
	Partial mispronunciations		

First Trial		Second Trial	Percent of increase (+) or decrease (−)
	Gross mispronunciations		
	Substitutions		
	Repetitions		
	Inversions		
	Aid		
	Self-corrected errors		

CHARACTERISTICS OF THE READER
Indicate with check mark (✔)

First Trial		Second Trial
	Poor word analysis skills	
	Head movement	
	Finger pointing	
	Disregard for punctuation	
	Loss of place	
	Overuse of phonics	
	Does not read in natural voice tones	

(Form J cont'd.)

First Trial

Second
Trial

	Poor enunciation	
	Word-by-word reading	
	Poor phrasing	
	Lack of expression	
	Pauses	

Some of the most common difficulties of the student as based on his/her informal reading inventory:

_____

_____

_____

_____

_____

_____

_____

_____

_____

1.1.3 Other tests administered at the reading center

1.1.4 Reading test results from outside sources

1.2 Other tests (administered at reading center)

1.2.1 Physical

Vision:
Wears glasses

          _____   _____
          yes   no

(Form J cont'd.)

Prescribed by whom _____

when _____

Results of visual screening test _____

Hearing:
Auditory discrimination test results

Audiometric test results

History of hearing problems   _____ _____
                                                yes   no
                                               (If yes, explain)

Present general health (level of energy, activity, sleep, diet)

Health history (severe illnesses, operations, accidents
                head and back injuries, allergies, etc.)

Other

1.2 Other tests (from outside sources)

2. Information from interviews and other sources

Environmental and personality factors

2.1 Home (parents, siblings, general environment)

(Form J cont'd.)

2.2 Home and family adjustment (security, dependence—
(independence, affection, warmth, etc.)

2.3 Attitude toward school (rebellious, submissive,
(indifferent, relations with teachers, etc.)

2.4 Emotional adjustment

3. Summary of results and possible and/or probable causes of reading difficulty

Maintaining Student Records

One of the reasons for record keeping is to help the remedial teacher keep up to date on each student. When a remedial teacher acquires a case load of twenty-five or more students, the task of analyzing the diagnostic test results and progress is likely to become overwhelming without a certain amount of record keeping. However, the type of records will vary with such factors as the number of students, their degree of disability, and the mode of operation of the teacher.

Most programs use one of two common types of operation. In one the remedial teacher works with each student or with only two to three students at a time. Information is often gained on planning the next session from diagnostic teaching. Form K may be used for this purpose. Teachers who work with a larger number of students during any one period usually find this somewhat burdensome. For this type of operation a daily worksheet such as Form L may be preferable. When using Form L the teacher often plans the activities of students a week or more in advance. This sheet may be posted or duplicated and put in individual student folders; the student, with some guidance, checks the plan and works on his or her own. This is somewhat more like a conventional lesson plan for a class of developmental readers. It also results in less individualization of instruction, which is highly important in remedial reading.

```
                                              (Form K)

                          Meeting Number_____

Student_____
Date_____
Time_____
Relevant conditions (if any) of meeting_____
_____
Length of session_____
Summary of activities_____
_____
_____
_____
_____
Plan for next session_____
_____
_____
_____
Diagnostic implications of today's activities_____
_____
_____
Teacher comments_____
_____
_____
_____
```

Reporting Information from Diagnostician or Remedial Reading Teacher to Other Educational Agencies

It is often necessary to send reports on students' progress to other educational agencies such as psychological evaluation centers, reading clinics, and schools. In many cases the diagnostician and/or remedial teacher may send copies of tests. Although test results are often valuable, they seldom contain the kind of information that the teacher can provide after working with a student. For example, an intelligence test may show that a certain student's IQ is 120, but if the student is unable to learn, the IQ of 120 has very little meaning. It is much more useful to know that the student learns best by a specific procedure or responds well with a certain type of reward, or or will read books on a certain subject.

In order to provide this type of information, the remedial reading teacher often must write a final case report on students' progress. This report can

```
                                                        (Form L)
                        Daily Worksheet

Date_____to_____Period_____Grade_____
RFU—Reading for Understanding    RX  —RX Reading Program
SRA—Reading lab                  RFM—Reading for Meaning
LS —Literature Sampler           S   —Story
PL —Pilot Library                O   —Oral Reading
L  —Listening                    BBR—Be a Better Reader
T  —Test                         Mc  —McCall Crabbs Tests
Ta —Tactics                      PP  —Programmed Phonics Books
SKS—Specific Skills Series       B   —Boardwork or Overhead
SE —Self Expression              WS  —Word Study
```

Name	Monday	Tuesday	Wednesday	Thursday	Friday

summarize test information, and more important, it can say how rapidly the student learns and what procedures and materials have been especially helpful.

SUGGESTED PROCEDURES FOR WRITING CASE REPORTS AND RECORD KEEPING

The writing of case reports, although worthwhile, can be very time consuming. For this reason the remedial teacher should develop the ability to include all pertinent information and exclude information of little value. This section contains a number of suggestions on procedures for writing case reports and keeping records. An example of a final case report is included.

1. *Use an outline form that will make sections and subsections clearly visible.* Each important section might be underlined and each subsection indented under the main heading. This will enable the reader to scan and spot specific information.

2. *Include important information but exclude information of no value in working with the student.* Suppose a student came to the teacher knowing only a few basic sight words. In the final case report it would be important to mention the number of basic sight words not known when the student entered the remedial program. If the student had learned nearly all of the basic sight words during remediation, there would be little or no value in listing which words were not known at the beginning of the remedial period. However, it would be important to say how the student seemed to learn best. It would also be helpful to list basic sight words still not known at the end of the remedial period. This eliminates the need for further testing by the person receiving the report.

3. *Where impressions are stated, they should be identified as such.* A statement such as, "Julie is highly intelligent because she learns phonics rules quickly" is inappropriate. It would be better to say, "Julie seems to learn phonics rules quickly." Some students possess a high potential for learning some tasks; however, this does not necessarily mean that the student has high intelligence.

4. *List specific test scores and the source of each score.* For example, "Irma's instructional reading level appears to be at the third-grade level, as shown by her scores on the *San Diego Quick Assessment,* the *Classroom Reading Inventory,* and the *Iowa Test of Basic Skills.*"

5. *List specific skills needing remediation.* Avoid vague statements such as "Martha seems to need help with word-attack skills." This is of little value, since there are five main types of word-attack skills and a number of subcategories. It would be much more helpful to be more specific: "Martha would benefit from instruction in context clues. She also needs to learn all of the short vowel sounds and the following blends. . . . "

6. *Give a brief interpretation of each test that may not be familiar to readers of the report.* For example, many people are not familiar with the norms of the *Wepman Auditory Discrimination Test.* To say, "Jerry missed six items on this test" would not mean much without the norms provided with this test. This statement would be more appropriate: "Jerry made six errors on this test. This indicates that he has difficulty discriminating among certain phonemes." It would also

be helpful to list the missed phonemes if that information is not given in the results.

7. *Keep sentence structure simple.* Make short, simple statements; long, complex sentences are often difficult to understand.

8. *Use third person when referring to yourself.* Rather than say "I think" or "It appears to me," it sounds more professional and perhaps less biased to say, "The clinician believes" or "The diagnostician interprets this to mean. . . ."

9. *Make specific recommendations for the remediation of difficulties.* The case report serves as a vehicle for in-service education. If it was noted that a student had a tendency to leave off or change endings such as *-s, -ed,* or *ing,* it would be beneficial to list specific workbooks and the pages of exercises for the remediation of problems such as these. It would also help to list exercises that would help, such as the following:

   a. Have the student fill in blanks in sentences from several choices as shown in this example:

      Pat _____ when she saw the snake.

         (jumps, jumping, jumped)

   b. Give the student a reading passage from a newspaper story and have him or her look for, pronounce, and circle all *-ing, -ed,* and *-s* endings.

10. *Give exact dates of the administration of each test.* Since students are constantly learning and changing, exact dates may be significant.

11. *Summarize significant strengths and weaknesses.* Some people who read reports are not directly involved with the student's problem; others are not likely to read an entire report with care. Furthermore, for the remedial teacher, clinician, or classroom teacher the summary will prove helpful in digesting the entire report.

12. *Include possible causal factors for weaknesses of the student.* In many cases it cannot be determined what caused a student to become a disabled reader. In other cases causes are so complex that it is extremely difficult to isolate any factor or small group of factors in a student's reading disability. On the other hand, a teacher who has worked with a student is likely to have insight into the causes of the reading disability. When there are definite signs that certain factors have contributed to a student's reading disability, these should be listed as "possible." Knowing about them may prevent reoccurrence.

THE FINAL CASE REPORT

This final case report is somewhat longer than practical in many cases. It was chosen because it illustrates most of the points in the previous section.

FINAL CASE REPORT

Name: Mark _____

School: _____   Age: 9   Birthday: 11/12/__

Grade: 4 (will be entering in September)

Examiner: _____

Period of diagnosis and remediation: September 5, 19__ to May 26, 19__

Date of report: June 3, 19__

General Background of Student

Home and Family Adjustment

Mark lives at home with his mother, stepfather, and five other children. Three of the children are his two sisters (10½ and 7) and a brother (9). The other two are half-brothers (6 and 4). After his mother's divorce from his father, Mark and his sisters and brother went to live with his grandmother. The four children lived with the grandmother approximately six years in Arizona. The parents feel that the adjustment of living with the grandmother to living with them was hard, but that he is fairly well adjusted now.

He reportedly gets along well with the other children in the family, though he has an occasional fight with the older brother. He is generous and does not mind sharing. He has several close friends and bowls weekly in a league.

Health History

His general health is reportedly fine and there is no record of his having any major illnesses. However, his mother stated that when he was quite small he used to run straight into things. His eyes were checked by a specialist in Arizona when he was about six years old, but no vision problem was apparent at that time. He was given a complete hearing examination at about the same time and was found to have no problem.

Education

Mark did not attend kindergarten. He attended school (first and second grade) in Arizona. The school was apparently an "Open Concept" type school. According to his parents, the school personnel were aware of his reading problem, but he has never attended any sort of special reading classes. During the past year, in the third grade, he has been in a self-contained classroom. This teacher has worked very closely with the examiner in carrying out various assignments and remedial activities.

Results of Diagnostic Tests

Wepman Auditory Discrimination Test
This test was administered on September 12, 19___. The student made only one error on this test. He was not able to discriminate between the letters "t" and "p" in the words "cap" and "cat."

Interpretation: At the time the test was administered Mark was eight years old. A child of eight years old is not considered to have an auditory discrimination problem if he makes only one error on this test.

Keystone Visual Survey Test
This test was administered on September 12, 19___. Mark failed all of the subtests for near-point vision and the subtest for fusion at near point. He scored in the expected range on the remainder of the subtests. Mark was tested again on September 14, 19___ using the same test. The results were the same.

Interpretation: Since the results of this test indicated referral for further visual examination, this was done. He was taken, by his mother, to an ophthalmologist on or about October 1, 19___. At that time he was given glasses to wear. He was told to wear them all of the time and has done so during the past school year.

San Diego Quick Assessment
This test was administered on September 13, 19___ and again on May 24, 19___. This is a word pronunciation test to estimate a student's Free or Independent, Instructional, and Frustration levels. The results were as follows:

Date: September 13, 19___
   Free or Independent Reading Level (Pre-Primer)
   Instructional Reading Level (Primer)
   Frustration Reading Level (First Grade)

Date: May 24, 19___
   Free or Independent Reading Level (First Grade)
   Instructional Reading Level (Second and Third Grade)
   Frustration Reading Level (Fourth Grade)

Interpretation: This is an indication that Mark's reading level (at least in terms of word knowledge) was no higher than First Grade Level at the time that he entered the remedial reading program. At the end of the program he had increased his word knowledge from two to three grade levels.

Diagnostic Reading Scales (Graded According to Informal Reading Inventory Criteria)

This test was administered on September 14, 19__ and again on May 25, 19__. Using the graded passages it enables one to obtain a student's Free or Independent, Instructional, and Frustration reading levels as the student reads both orally and silently. The results were as follows:

Date: September 14, 19__

	Oral Reading	Silent Reading
Independent reading level	None	None
Instructional reading level	None	None
Frustration reading level	First grade	First grade
Listening comprehension level	Fourth grade	

Date: May 25, 19__

Independent reading level	First grade	Second grade
Instructional reading level	Second grade	Third grade
Frustration reading level	Third grade	Fourth grade

Interpretation: This is an indication that Mark's reading level increased from one to three grade levels during the period of time that he spent in remedial reading. It should be noted that his silent reading tended to be about one level higher than his oral reading. This is because he still has some problems with certain word-attack skills; however, his ability to attack words has shown considerable improvement during the past year.

CRS Basic Sight Word Inventory

This test was administered on September 14, 19__ and again on May 24, 19__. It is a test of 299 basic sight words. These words are graded at the Pre-Primer, Primer, First Grade, Second Grade (first half), Second Grade (second half), and Third Grade (first half) levels. The results were as follows:

Date: September 14, 19__

At this time Mark knew only eighteen of the words at the Pre-Primer level and twelve of the words at the Primer level. Only seven words were known at the First Grade level. The test was stopped at the end of the First Grade level. Some examples of the errors made on this inventory are as follows:

Word	Error	Analysis of Error(s)
big	bat	Medial vowel and ending consonant
him	his	Ending consonant
come	came	Medial vowel
three	their	Initial blend and ending sound

Word	Error	Analysis of Error(s)
know	now	Vowel pair
your	yours	Insertion
play	pay	Substitution of initial consonant for blend

Date: May 24, 19___
At this time Mark knew all of the words on the *CRS Basic Sight Word Inventory.*

Interpretation: Mark seemed to learn basic sight words quite rapidly with very little difficulty.

Mills Learning Test
(Adapted form in which pictures were not used.) This test was given between September 19 and 22, 19___. It is a test to determine by which (if any) method a student can best learn words.

Interpretation: It was found that Mark learned best by using a combination approach. During the past school year nearly all sight words were taught by this method.

RX Phonics Survey
This is a phonics survey that tests students' knowledge of the eighty most useful phonemes. It was administered on September 19, 19 ___ and again on May 26, 19___.

Date: September 19, 19___
At this time Mark knew only about twelve initial consonant sounds and about three initial consonant blends. He knew only one vowel sound.

Date: May 26, 19___
At this time he knew all of the initial consonant sounds, and all of the initial consonant blends and digraphs with the exception of the following:
"sw" and "scr"
He also knew all of the vowels (both long and short), vowel combinations, and special letter combinations with the exception of the following:
"ow" (as in cow), "ew" (as in flew), "oi" (as in soil), and "aw" (as in paw)

Interpretation: At the beginning of the remedial period he knew very few phonic elements; however, he seemed to learn these quite rapidly. Much of the work in learning these was done using consonant substitution with known phonograms. The *Rx Reading Program* and *Webster Word Wheels* as well as the *Kenworthy Phonetic Drill Cards* were also very helpful in teaching phonics skills. Considerable teaching was also done using various commercial and homemade games.

No IQ tests were given, since Mark seemed to learn nearly everything that was taught to him very rapidly.

Gates-McKillop Reading Diagnostic Tests—Oral Vocabulary VIII–2

This test was administered on September 15, 19___. It is a test to determine the grade level of a student's oral vocabulary. The results:

Date: September 15, 19___
Grade Level 4.7

Interpretation: At the time this was given it indicated that this student's oral vocabulary was considerably above both his oral and silent reading levels. It would indicate that any problems that he might have encountered in comprehension did not stem from a lack of oral vocabulary.

Summary of Diagnosis

Significant Weaknesses
1. At the beginning of the remedial period Mark had an extremely low basic sight word vocabulary.
2. Mark had a tendency to ignore medial and terminal sounds.
3. He did not know but a few of the initial consonant sounds and almost no consonant blends, consonant digraphs, vowel pairs, and special letter combinations.
4. Mark had a tendency to repeat a number of words and phrases. However, this tendency seemed to disappear almost as soon as he began to develop a larger basic sight word vocabulary. For this reason the problem of repetitions was assumed to be caused from a lack of knowledge of words rather than from a bad habit.
5. A number of omissions were also noted at the beginning of the remedial period. This problem also seems to have been overcome with the learning of a number of sight words and an improvement in his word-attack skills.
6. At the beginning of the remedial period Mark showed definite signs of discomfort during testing. This problem also seems to have been overcome since he has come to know the examiner better and since he also seems to have gained some self-confidence.

Significant Strengths
1. Mark seems to learn almost any task rather quickly, especially when he receives tutoring in a rather small group or when he is tutored individually.
2. Although he seemed to have a rather low self-concept at the beginning of the remediation period, he now seems to have a

rather good opinion of himself and believes that he can learn as well as anyone else.

3. He is rather large for his age and seems to excel in most sports. This seems to have been an important factor in building his self-confidence.

4. His ability to comprehend what he read was rather low in the beginning, but this was evidently caused from his lack of word knowledge. Now that he has enlarged his sight vocabulary he is able to comprehend quite well.

5. Mark seems to have an intensive interest in sports and is an avid reader of books on this subject.

Causal Factors in the Student's Reading Disability

One of the causal factors in Mark's reading disability may have been the social adjustment of first going through the period in which his parents' divorce and then again having to go through social adjustment of moving in with his mother and stepfather after a period of about six years. Another cause of his reading disability may have been his eyesight. The tests conducted by the examiner, as well as those conducted by the ophthalmologist indicated that he had a serious visual problem. A third possible cause of his problem was the fact that he had attended a new "Open Concept" school that was in its initial stages of operation and he received no corrective help as his disability in reading began to develop.

Summary of Instructional Program

During the past year a lot of instruction was given on learning basic sight words and on increasing his sight vocabulary in general. This was accomplished through the following methods:

1. The use of drill with phrase cards.
2. The use of a programmed textbook in phonics and structural analysis.
3. The use of the language-experience approach.

    In the beginning stages the student dictated stories which the examiner wrote down. These were then compiled into booklets and later read back to the examiner by the student on a daily basis. Later the student wrote his own stories and illustrated them. These were also compiled into booklets, which he practiced reading over and over again. This material was sent home once he had mastered it to some extent. The stories were cut up into sentences or words and again assembled in order to recreate the original story or to make up a new one.

4. Whenever possible, the examiner gave a great deal of praise to the student for his accomplishments.
5. The student was taught the most useful vowel rules and syllabication principles.
6. A number of exercises were used in which sentences appeared with

one word left blank. This word was usually one which the student had previously missed. Wherever a blank appeared the student was given several choices of words to use in the blank. The word choices were normally those of similar configuration and would, in most cases, include the word that had been substituted by the student in place of the word missed.

7. Mark was encouraged to read a great deal on his own. At first he did very little of this, but after he had acquired a larger sight vocabulary he became an avid reader, especially of books concerning sports.

Prognosis for Success and Recommendations for Further Remediation

Prognosis

During the past year Mark has steadily improved in his reading ability. He appears to learn rapidly and there seems to be no physical or emotional problems that are now hindering his learning progress. At this point, however, he still needs to learn to use his newly acquired skills in vowel rules and syllabication principles. It would appear that he could profit from at least one more semester of remedial reading at which time another evaluation should be made. He has learned rapidly during the time that he spent in remedial reading this year and if the present rate of gain is maintained he should be reading up to grade level in a year or less.

Recommendations for Further Remediation

1. The student needs to do a great deal of free reading to increase his sight vocabulary through multiple exposure to many words.
2. Although he has become familiar with syllabication principles and vowel rules, he still needs more practice on using these skills.
3. Mark has been on a program of reading for approximately one hour per day during the past few months. His parents have set aside a certain time of day for him to read. This practice should be encouraged.
4. His parents should be encouraged to take him to the public library as often as possible.
5. It may be helpful to use some sort of reward system for a certain number of books read. He should, of course, be praised when he reads and encouraged to try to find books that he would like to read on his own.
6. Mark still needs to learn the vowel pairs "ow" (as in crow and cow), "ew," "oi," and "aw."
7. He seems to work best either by himself or in a small group. He seems to be highly distracted by large groups, especially when there is considerable noise in the room. Whenever possible, he should be taught either in a small group or individually.

SUMMARY

It is extremely important to develop a record-keeping system to communicate important information derived from testing and teaching. The system should be adequate but not burdensome, and should provide for communication among all who are likely to come into professional contact with each disabled reader. Record keeping also serves to measure the progress of disabled readers and as a training technique for classroom teachers and parents. Reading personnel must familiarize themselves with techniques for the writing of case reports.

15

Evaluation and Use of the Computer and Other Teaching Materials

This chapter contains some cautions that should be observed in using the computer. Although this information is lengthy, it should not be construed as meaning that we are anticomputer; the opposite is true. However, we believe that the cautions are so important that they should appear first. Next comes a list of common uses of the computer in the teaching of reading. A discussion of evaluation of software should help you choose this most important part of your computer system. There follow some factors to consider in the purchase of computer hardware and a section on evaluating other types of materials for the diagnosis and remediation of reading difficulties.

At the end of the chapter are listed some important sources of information for the computer user, including educational software directories, sources of software reviews, computer and software magazines, companies that publish or distribute software, and finally, a glossary of computer terminology.

SOME CAUTIONS TO BE OBSERVED

Perhaps the most important consideration is what you wish to do with the computer after it is purchased. All too many boards of education, administrators, and teachers have made the mistake of purchasing a particular computer because they "got a good deal." They then find that there is very little suitable software for their computer. In the case just cited, the purchasing process has been reversed. Teachers should first consult software directories (some of the best known are listed at the end of this chapter) and determine what programs are available for their purposes. Some in-house programming can be done; however, it is unlikely that the teacher will have the time or the inclination to develop software for everything. Therefore, before purchasing a computer, first study the software directories to determine specific needs.

Do the Materials Teach, Test, or Reinforce?

The cautions in purchasing software are much the same as for the purchase of nearly any educational materials. First determine what needs to be taught or what the computer is to do. There are three categories of materials for reading education. These are materials that *test,* that *teach,* and that *reinforce.* This is true whether it be software, books, or audiovisual materials.

Some materials actually teach, just as the teacher would in presenting a new concept. For example, if a student does not know the beginning *b* sound, the teacher might write some words beginning with *b* and ask the student to listen to them. The teacher might pronounce the words, pointing to the letter *b* as each word was pronounced, then ask the child to say the words. This is teaching plus testing.

For a beginning or seriously disabled reader, it would be difficult to duplicate this *teaching* procedure with the computer. It is possible to add a voice synthesizer to a computer and give the student practice in hearing the *b* sound, but voice synthesizers are in their infancy in terms of accuracy. They are, however, improving rapidly, and in the future will no doubt be able to do this task quite well. The second part of the teaching procedure, i.e., testing, is much more difficult for the computer. The computer could show pictures of various objects and ask the student to respond by pressing *Y* if a picture represented an object whose name began with a *b* sound or *N* if not. The problem is that a student may be able to identify objects that begin with *b;* however, that same student may be unable to reproduce the *b* sound when seeing it in print.

If the student is able to read with some understanding, a computer can teach quite well and interact with the student by giving an immediate response to an answer as well as providing reinforcement such as showing on the screen, GOOD, BILL, YOU'RE DOING FINE! when appropriate.

Computers in their present state of development can be used with a tape recorder or voice synthesizer for a narration and can provide a picture, although less clear than in a filmstrip or on an electronic card reader.

Computers can test many concepts as well as the teacher, although they are unable to interpret oral responses with accuracy, often necessary in teaching reading, especially at the lower levels. It would be unfair to say that students do not learn from testing. The computer has a distinct advantage over the usual paper-and-pencil test in that the student receives immediate feedback, enabling the student to learn from the test.

A large proportion of the software on the market most closely fits the description of materials that *reinforce.* The most common reinforcement device is probably traditional workbook exercises. Although teachers often feel that are teaching when using a workbook, it should be kept in mind that although reinforcement is a part of good teaching, the reinforcement device usually does not actually teach. Workbooks do only what they are designed to do, i.e., reinforce what has already been learned. Several colleagues of the author have recently said that what they have seen of reading software for word-attack skills are electronic workbooks.

Another caution is against purchasing software for teaching concepts that are not clearly defined or that have been shown by research to be less than worthwhile for the remediation of reading disabilities. For example, several programs supposedly diagnose student's abilities in reading comprehension. These programs are supposed to help the teacher decide whether a student is unable to determine the main idea of a passage or whether he or she can identify important details. At this time we know of no definitive research to prove that these skills exist as separate entities. If we cannot prove this with many years of the best research, then obviously a computer program cannot, in spite of the claims made by the vendors.

Other less than worthwhile programs are those that supposedly teach *visual discrimination.* Again, we know of no definitive research showing that working with students on visual discrimination ultimately helps alleviate their reading disabilities.

Still another kind of program to avoid purports to increase reading speed. In remedial reading one is usually not concerned with reading speed per se. Besides, most studies of the middle and late 1960s, when a great deal of federal money was available for tachistoscopes and controlled reading devices, showed that having students pace their reading with their hand usually improved their speed more than the most expensive mechanical devices.

Can the Computer Be Used in a Situation That Is Analogous to Reading?

There is a considerable difference between the ability to encode (write) and the ability to decode (read). Many of the skills that must be tested in reading require an oral response. One of the most important purposes of having a student read orally is to determine areas of weakness. The teacher may wish to know if the student reads word by word, an indication of a poor sight vocabulary. The teacher who listens to a student read aloud will also know if the student is making omissions, insertions, or partial or gross mispronunciations. Knowledge of the student-error pattern becomes a blueprint for instruction. The computer cannot perform this sort of task at this time. However, computer experts believe this will be possible in the near future.

One might assume that a student's knowledge of basic sight words could be tested by showing on a computer screen four or more words and pronouncing one of them using a tape recorder or voice synthesizer. The student chooses the word he or she hears. However, we have found that pronouncing a word when it is seen is much more difficult than identifying a word pronounced by the teacher. In fact, in a study done by the author it was found that students at the third, fourth, and fifth grade levels missed nearly six times as many words in pronouncing a word when it was shown to them as when they were asked to identify one of four words pronounced by the teacher. With our present state of technology the teacher using the computer could gain only a small amount of knowledge about a student's sight vocabulary.

In testing for most of the phonics skills an oral response is also the only way the teacher can have any degree of certainty that a student knows the concept. For example, the teacher could show a student four pictures and ask which of the four had a name that started with, for example, the *ch* sound. If the student could move the cursor under the proper picture or select a letter A, representing the picture, the student could probably identify the picture that stood for *ch;* however, the teacher could not be sure that the student could give the pronunciation of the sound in conjunction with a phonogram such as *ill,* to form *chill.* Admittedly, a student who could identify a picture beginning with *ch* would be more likely to be able to pronounce the sound; however, the teacher could not be assured of this.

One of the most common uses of the computer today is in the teaching of comprehension. In most of these exercises the student is asked to read a paragraph and then respond to a question pertaining to it. In this typical workbook exercise the computer has an advantage in that it can give the student an immediate response and perhaps even tell the student why a particular answer is not correct. However, giving a student material to read and then asking questions over the subject matter is not teaching but testing. Although if it is done enough, most students improve through this method, there are much more efficient ways of improving a student's comprehension—such as those described in Chapter 6.

In summary, then, the teacher who wishes to use the computer should constantly be asking such questions as: Am I using the computer to teach? If so, does the material being used really teach a new concept or only review what is already known? Am I using the computer to test? If I am, will the results be accurate enough for prescriptive teaching or will they only tell me that the student is weak in a certain broad area (that I may have already known)? Does the material test skills that are important for reading? At a minimum, the teacher should recognize whether materials being used are testing when they are supposed to teach as well as materials that only test or reinforce when they are represented as teaching.

PRESENT STATUS OF MICROCOMPUTERS IN THE DIAGNOSIS AND REMEDIATION OF DISABLED READERS

Following are some of the most common uses for microcomputers in the diagnosis and remediation of disabled readers. This is a rapidly changing field; information is constantly changing as programs are added and improved. At the end of this chapter you will find a listing of the various kinds of programs described below and the names of companies that publish or distribute programs.

Word Processing and Creative Writing

Perhaps the most important use to which computers have been put in the reading and language arts classroom is word processing. Several word processing packages are meant for use by students in grades one through eight. Others are intended for students above those grade levels but could be mastered by students in the upper elementary grades.

There are also several programs that are highly motivational for writing. One such program covers persuasion techniques and is designed to develop analytical skills. Another teaches sentence combining, an extremely useful technique in the improvement of students' writing skills. Still another permits the use of branching techniques to encourage creative writing. Some programs are designed to teach the mechanics of writing sentences and paragraphs, while others emphasize the proper use of various kinds of punctuation marks as well as proofreading skills.

Readability Formulas

The microcomputer has enabled the reading teacher to use readability formulas with considerably more ease than in the past. The most burdensome part of some readability formulas was going through each word in a passage to determine if it was on a list of "easy words." One program now available allows the teacher to type up to 100 words of the material on the computer screen. The teacher may then request complete information on the readability of the matter on the screen, or it may be printed for a permanent record. The program will search such long lists as the Dale List to determine a score on the Dale-Chall Readability Formula, meant to be used in grades 4–adult. It will then give complete information as to grade level. It will also enable the user to do an examination of readability formulas. Complete statistics on a passage may also be printed: number of sentences, of characters, of characters per word, of words with two syllables, of syllables, of words, of words per sentence, of syllables per word, of syllables per 100 words, and of sentences per 100 words. Having such information as syllables per 100 words and sentences per 100 words will enable the user to estimate the readability of the passage using the Fry Graph. The program will also quickly give an alphabetized list of the words in the passage. Using this type of program enables the user to see quickly the inadequacies of some of our most commonly used readability formulas, since it is not uncommon to see disagreement among the formulas of two to three years on a passage that is obviously written at the preprimer or primer level.

Use as a Record-Keeping System

Several programs enable the teacher quickly and easily to keep up-to-date records of students' grades on a weekly, monthly, quarterly, or semester basis. They write progress reports and keep track of missing grades as well as enable the teacher to curve total grades.

Some systems for teaching word attack and other reading skills also provide record-keeping systems, which enable the teacher to call up a student's name and information on lessons completed and performance on each lesson. For this the computer works extremely well; however, it is very difficult to provide meaningful lessons on word attack and the lower-level reading skills if the student is unable to read directions. Monitoring achievement is also somewhat difficult, since testing many of the lower-level skills requires an oral rather than a written response by the student.

Testing for Knowledge of Basic Sight Words

Most diagnosticians agree that students' knowledge of basic sight words can best be tested by means of a flash presentation, but attempting to manipulate flash cards and mark a score sheet at the same time can be difficult. The computer can help by flashing basic sight words. With a little experience the programmer can set the flash rate. In our reading center at the University of Texas at El Paso we use the Radio Shack Pocket Computer (PC-2) for this purpose. It is programmed to present a word every 1¾ seconds. This gives the person doing the testing an opportunity to record correct responses with a plus (+) mark and write incorrect responses in the blanks. It is important to use a computer that displays the words in lower case when testing for students' knowledge of basic sight words. Keep this point in mind when shopping for a computer for this purpose.

The Development of Comprehension

Numerous programs for the so-called teaching of comprehension are available. Most of these do what teachers have done for so long, i.e., present a reading passage and then ask a number of questions about that passage. Presenting information and then asking questions about it is not *teaching* comprehension but *testing* it. However, enough of this type of activity will improve students' comprehension through practice. Other programs, in spite of the traditional format, present material in a considerably more motivating way than traditional workbook form.

The Use of the Cloze Procedure

The use of the cloze procedure for the development of comprehension as well as vocabulary is becoming a popular computer activity. In the cloze procedure a word is omitted and the student is required to fill it in or choose from several words presented by the computer. The interaction provided by the computer makes this considerably more attractive to students than the traditional format.

No doubt the use of the cloze procedure for determining the proper match between students and materials will come into its own more in the future. For this purpose the teacher deletes every fifth word and replaces the words with blanks of uniform length. The student attempts to fill in the blanks using exactly the words omitted from the original selection. A percentage of correct responses is computed. A score of 43 percent or less is usually considered to indicate the frustration level; 44 through 56 percent, instructional level; and 57 percent or more, the independent level. A much more thorough explanation is presented in Chapter 6.

The Development of Word-Attack Skills

A number of programs for improving word-attack skills are available. Since the use of the computer requires some ability to read, it is much more difficult to provide meaningful activities than with the higher-level reading skills. Be extra careful in selecting these materials and consider the purpose for which they are to be used, i.e., for *testing, teaching,* or for *reinforcement* of previously taught skills.

The Neurological Impress Method

The neurological impress method has been thoroughly explained in Chapter 4. It can be extremely helpful in expanding students' sight vocabularies; however, it requires a great deal of the teacher's time. The teacher sits beside the student and points to words from material to be read. The student is to read the words and the teacher echoes the student. Or the student is to read immediately after the teacher. The teacher is to read slightly more loudly than usual and is to sit so that he or she reads directly into the student's ear. The reason for the success of the neurological impress method is apparently that it presents the student with numerous exposures to many words in a short time. Various researchers have attempted to duplicate the success of the one-on-one teaching situation using a tape recorder and asking the student to follow along in a reading passage as it is read via the tape recorder. This however, has not produced results comparable to those obtained when the teacher performs the activity personally with the student. It is our belief that the inability of the tape recorder to produce the same results as those obtained by a one-on-one teaching situation is because when the student reads in conjunction with a tape recorder, he or she may be looking ahead of or behind the word as it is being pronounced by the tape recorder and the student. As voice synthesizers continue to improve, the neurological impress method will no doubt become more widely used in this application, since it will be possible to ensure that the word being pronounced by the voice synthesizer is the same one at which the student is looking while pronouncing it. This can be done with the computer by underlining or highlighting the word on the computer screen as it is being pronounced by the voice synthesizer.

Spelling

The computer is having considerable success in the teaching of spelling. Some programs review and teach rules and generalizations and emphasize the spelling of the most common prefixes and suffixes. Others teach spelling of contractions, homonyms, synonyms, and antonyms. Some spelling programs adjust to the difficulty level of the student and allow the teacher to monitor progress. Still others allow the teachers to use their own word lists with the program format.

Life Skills

A number of programs teach life skills such as how to read labels, classified ads, and telephone directories; how to bank and get information needed for travel; and the like. Others teach how to budget and fill out commonly used forms for employment, financing, etc. A program is also available for teaching students to budget their time, even allowing them to print out their own schedule. Another teaches how to count money through a simulated shopping trip.

THE EVALUATION OF COMPUTER SOFTWARE[1]

You are likely to want the same features in computer software as in any good program for locating and correcting reading difficulties. However, in order to make an intelligent decision, it is necessary to know some of the capabilities of a computer in relation to traditional reading materials. The information that follows should help you to understand some of the capabilities and limitations of the computer in relation to the teaching of reading.

Remedial reading software can be divided into three categories—(*1*) management or record keeping, (*2*) supplements to the regular reading program, or (*3*) the main reading program. Remember that there are essentially three main kinds of teaching materials—those that teach, those that test, and those that reinforce. In evaluating software, you should first decide whether you want the materials for managing your reading program, for supplementing it, or for using it as a main curriculum (which will be doubtful, in the case of locating and correcting reading difficulties). In reading about the materials, or more likely in evaluating materials as you use them on a computer, you should decide how you might use them—to *teach,* to *test,* or to *reinforce.*

[1]From: Ekwall, Eldon E. *Locating and correcting reading difficulties,* 4th ed. Columbus, Ohio: Charles E. Merrill, 1985. (Reprinted by permission.)

Following are some characteristics to consider and questions to ask in evaluating reading software.

Purchasing of Software

1. The cost of the materials is an important factor. If the materials are quite expensive, it is a good idea to spend more time in evaluating them, just as if evaluating what kind of new automobile to buy rather than which dinner to have at a restaurant. However, an inexpensive program that is of little value should never be considered as an alternative to a more expensive program that meets all or most of the characteristics of an excellent teaching program.
2. In addition to the cost, consider whether or not the distributor will allow returns of unsatisfactory materials.
3. A number of writers suggest that most programs, especially the more expensive ones, should have been on the market for at least a year.
4. It is best to purchase from software companies that are well known and that have been in business for a considerable length of time.
5. When purchasing a major program, make sure the dealer will allow you to return older versions of the program for newer or updated ones as they become available.
6. Purchase only programs that have been tested and have proven worthwhile.
7. Purchase only materials for which you can make a back-up copy.
8. Was the material developed by someone well known in the field of reading or by a team of reading and computer consultants? Since most programmers do not have adequate knowledge in reading and many people in reading do not have adequate experience in programming, skills of a programmer, a reading expert, and an instructional expert make the ideal combination.

Teacher's Manual

1. Are the objectives for the program listed, so you will know exactly what is to be covered?
2. Does it tell the entry grade level of the student or necessary skills?
3. Are some sample frames shown, so that you will have some idea of the general format?
4. Are the directions for use of the materials clear and understandable?
5. Is information provided on minimum and maximum times that students will need to complete various lessons?
6. Are the directions for the student clear and at a reading level appropriate for the grade level of the skills taught? (This refers to any written materials that accompany the program. This same question should be asked of the material that appears on the screen; see Program Characteristics.)

Program Characteristics

1. If the program is linear, is the material in proper sequence? Most programs run in a linear sequence, so that a student must go through certain steps regardless of how well he performs on each step.
2. If the program is of the branching type, does it provide for a number of options? A branching program should allow the student to move ahead into more difficult material or back into easier material as needed.
3. If written material is necessary as a follow-up, is it provided with the program?
4. Does the lesson provide prompts or hints for answers with which the student is experiencing difficulty?
5. Are the contents free of racial and sexual bias?
6. Is this program a more effective way of presenting the information than other materials that may be less costly and more easily obtained?
7. Can the student load (boot) the program without having an extensive knowledge of computers?

User Control

1. Can the student determine the entry point, in terms of difficulty, of the materials being presented?
2. If the student cannot determine the entry point, can the teacher?
3. Can the student skip over material he already knows or increase the rate at which it is presented? (Keep in mind that this option exists with a book and that this and the ability to interact with the student should be two of the most important features of a computer.)
4. Can the student exit the program and reenter at another time?
5. Can the student review the directions?

Feedback Characteristics

1. Feedback should show whether the student has made the right or wrong response; and if it would be helpful, tell why a certain response is wrong.
2. Feedback should give praise for right answers but not scold for incorrect ones.
3. Praise or reinforcement should come only periodically for best results. Praise after each correct response loses force.
4. Feedback should be appropriate for the age-grade level of the student.

User Friendliness

1. Can the student easily understand the directions on the screen?
2. Can the student move from one part of a program to another without going through long elaborate directions? For example, a user friendly program might ask the student, ''Do you wish to go to an easier ques-

tion? *Y/N.''* If the student has been answering a number of questions wrong, he might press *Y* for *yes*.

Graphics
1. Do the graphics add to or detract from the material being taught?
2. Are the graphics in color?
3. Are the graphics appropriate for the grade level of the student?
4. Graphics *should not be* such that a wrong response will bring forth a more colorful or interesting display than a correct response.
5. Is the program free from violence or imitation of violent games used in arcades? (It should be.)

Evaluation System
1. Does the program have its own evaluation system?
2. Is there a record of student performance that will be useful to the teacher?
3. Does the program collect and store data and then prescribe appropriate lessons based on the student's performance?
4. What are the criteria for successfully completing the material?
5. Can the teacher transfer certain information to other programs to keep an overall record of a student's performance?
6. Can a student's record of performance be printed?

Compatibility
1. Will the software operate on your computer?
2. Does your computer have sufficient memory for the program? (A program designed for a 64K computer will not run on one with less memory.)
3. Does the program run on a computer using the same language as yours?

Peripheral Requirements
1. Does the program require a printer?
2. Does the program require a voice synthesizer?
3. Does it require one or two disk drives? (Some computers use a cassette to store information. This information is slower to retrieve than if stored on a disk; therefore, it is highly recommended that cassettes not be considered for serious instructional programs.)

THE EVALUATION OF COMPUTER HARDWARE[2]

Probably the worst mistake a user can make is to purchase a computer and then find that there is little software available for it. For this reason before

[2]Ekwall, Eldon E. *Locating and correcting reading difficulties,* 4th ed. Columbus, Ohio: Charles E. Merrill, 1985. (Reprinted by permission.)

considering the purchase of a computer, you should look at one of the more comprehensive software directories listed under *Educational Software Directories*. It will take only a minute or so to observe that most educational software available is for use on only a few brands of computers. After deciding what software you would like to use, you should consider some of the following factors in choosing a computer:

1. Is the dealer reputable? How long has the company been in business?
2. Does the dealer have a service plan?
3. What is the memory capacity of the computer? Will it handle all of the programs that you are likely to use?
4. Do you need one disk drive or two? Many programs require two disk drives and sometimes it is impossible to duplicate disks without two disk drives.
5. What languages does the computer use, or in what languages can it be programmed?
6. What peripherals are available for each computer, and which are you likely to need?
7. How large is the screen display? Most computers range in width from twenty to eighty characters, and the length of the display tends to run from sixteen to thirty-two lines. However, on word processors the screen display length may be fifty-four lines or more.
8. Do you need a color monitor? If any of the programs you will run are in color, you will. However, if the programs will be in black and white, you may actually get a better image with a black and white monitor.
9. What is the quality of the graphics on the monitor? The greater the number of dots on the monitor screen, the better your image will be.
10. Does the computer have built-in sound or music available? On some programs this is a necessity.
11. What is the cost of the computer in relation to comparable models?

After looking at numerous computers, you may wish to make an evaluation sheet for each computer to help you make your decision. Different factors will be worth different weights, depending upon which are most important to you. Your evaluation sheet for a particular computer might appear like the one on p. 556. In evaluating the final score you may find that two or three brands of computers have nearly the same score. On the other hand, you may find that others vary by twenty to thirty points. If the final scores are within a very close range (perhaps 2–6 or slightly more), reexamine various factors in relation to the numbers assigned to them as well as the computer rating and the numbers assigned to this category. Your ultimate decision will need to be based on the factors and ratings most important in your own situation.

Computer Evaluation Sheet

Brand of Computer ——————— *Dealer* ——————— *Date* ————

Factors	Factor Number[a]	×	Computer Rating[b]	=	Weighted Score
1. Dealer reputation	3		2		6
2. Dealer service plan	4		4		16
3. Memory capacity	5		5		25
4. Number of drives	5		5		25
5. Languages	3		2		6
6. Peripherals available	4		2		8
7. Screen display	3		1		3
8. Color monitor	3		3		9
9. Graphics	2		1		2
10. Sound/Music	3		3		9
11. Cost	5		3		15

Final Score ———— 124

[a] The factor number scale used in this case was arbitrarily set for one to five with five being extremely important. The factor number must be derived by the user depending upon specific needs.

[b] The computer rating is based on what you can determine about each of the eleven factors listed. Again, a rating scale of one to five was used with five being excellent and one being the lowest possible rating.

GUIDELINES OF THE INTERNATIONAL READING ASSOCIATION

The International Reading Association (1984) has also developed an excellent set of guidelines for educators using computers in the schools. These are as follows:[3]

> The Computer Technology and Reading Committee of the International Reading Association has compiled the following guidelines in an effort to encourage the effective use of technology in reading classrooms. The

[3] Reprinted by permission of the International Reading Association. (The authors would like to extend their thanks to the 1983–84 Computer and Technology Committee.) 1983–84 Computer Technology and Reading Committee: Alan E. Farstrup, Chair; Ossi Ahvenainen, Isabel Beck, Darlene Bolig, Jayne DeLawter, Shirley Feldmann, Peter Joyce, Michael Kamil, Gerald J. Kochinski, George E. Mason, Harry B. Miller, Jane D. Smith, Art Willer, Carmelita K. Williams; Linda Roberts, Consultant.

guidelines are designed to highlight important issues and provide guidance to educators as they work to make the best possible use of the many new technologies which are rapidly finding their way into schools and classrooms everywhere.

1. *ABOUT SOFTWARE*

   Curricular needs should be primary in the selection of instructional software. Above all, software designed for use in the reading classroom must be consistent with what research and practice have shown to be important in the process of learning to read or of reading to learn. The IRA believes that high quality instructional software should incorporate the following elements:

   - clearly stated and implemented instructional objectives.
   - learning to read and reading to learn activities which are consistent with established reading theory and practice.
   - lesson activities which are most effectively and efficiently done through the application of computer technology and are not merely replications of activities which could be better done with traditional means.
   - prompts and screen instructions to the student which are simple, direct and easier than the learning activity to be done.
   - prompts, screen instructions and reading texts which are at a readability level appropriate to the needs of the learner.
   - documentation and instructions which are clear and unambiguous, assuming a minimum of prior knowledge about computers for use.
   - screen displays which have clear and legible print with appropriate margins and between-line spacing.
   - documentation and screen displays which are grammatically correct, factually correct, and which have been thoroughly proofed for spelling errors.
   - a record keeping or information management element for the benefit of both the teacher and the learner, where appropriate.
   - provisions for effective involvement and participation by the learner, coupled with rapid and extensive feedback, where appropriate.
   - wherever appropriate, a learning pace which is modified by the actions of the learner or which can be adjusted by the teacher based on diagnosed needs.
   - a fair, reasonable and clearly stated publisher's policy governing the replacement of defective or damaged program media such as tapes, diskettes, ROM cartridges and the like.
   - a publisher's preview policy which provides pre-purchase samples or copies for review and which encourages a well-informed software acquisition process by reading educators.

2. *ABOUT HARDWARE*

   Hardware should be durable, capable of producing highly legible text displays, and safe for use in a classroom situation. Hardware should be chosen that conforms to established classroom needs. Some characteristics to be aware of include, but are not limited to, the following:

- compatibility with classroom software appropriate to the curriculum.
- proven durability in classroom situations.
- clear, unambiguous instruction manuals appropriate for use by persons having a minimum of technical experience with computers.
- sufficient memory (RAM) capability to satisfy anticipated instructional software applications.
- availability of disk, tape, ROM cartridge or other efficient and reliable data storage devices.
- screen displays which produce legible print, minimize glare, and which have the lowest possible screen radiation levels.
- a functional keyboard and the availability of other appropriate types of input devices.
- proven, accessible and reasonably priced technical support from the manufacturer or distributor.

3. *ABOUT STAFF DEVELOPMENT AND TRAINING*
Staff development programs should be available which encourage teachers to become intelligent users of technology in the reading classroom. Factors to consider include, but are not limited to, the following:

- study and practice with various applications of computer technology in the reading and language arts classroom.
- training which encourages thoughtful and informed evaluation, selection and integration of effective and appropriate teaching software into the reading and language arts classroom.

4. *ABOUT EQUITY*
All persons, regardless of sex, ethnic group, socioeconomic status, or ability, must have equality of access to the challenges and benefits of computer technology. Computer technology should be integrated into all classrooms and not be limited to scientific or mathematical applications.

5. *ABOUT RESEARCH*
Research which assesses the impact of computer technology on all aspects of learning to read and reading to learn is essential. Public and private funding should be made available in support of such research. Issues which need to be part of national and international research agendas include, but are not limited to:

- the educational efficacy of computer technology in the reading and language arts classroom.
- the affective dimensions of introducing computer technology into the schools.
- the cognitive dimensions of introducing computer technology into the reading classroom.

- the application of concepts of artificial intelligence to computer software which address issues of reading diagnosis, developmental reading, remedial reading, and instructional management.
- the impact of new technology on students, reading teachers, schools, curricula, parents, and the community.

6. *ABOUT NETWORKING AND SHARING INFORMATION*
Local area and national networks or information services should be established and supported which can be accessed through the use of computers. Such services should be designed to provide an information resource on reading related topics. Such services could also be used to provide linkage and information exchange among many institutions, including professional associations such as the IRA.

7. *ABOUT INAPPROPRIATE USES OF TECHNOLOGY*
Computers should be used in meaningful and productive ways which relate clearly to instructional needs of students in the reading classroom. Educators must capitalize on the potential of this technology by insisting on its appropriate and meaningful use.

8. *ABOUT LEGAL ISSUES*
Unauthorized duplication and use of copyrighted computer software must not be allowed. Developers and publishers of educational software have a right to be protected from financial losses due to the unauthorized use of their products. Consumers of educational software have a concomitant right to expect fair prices, quality products and reasonable publishers' policies regarding licensing for multiple copies, replacement of damaged program media, network applications and the like. Without mutual trust and cooperation on this important issue both parties will suffer and, ultimately, so will the learner.

OTHER MATERIALS FOR USE IN REMEDIAL READING

CRITERIA FOR EVALUATION

In purchasing materials for use in remedial reading there are certain criteria that may not be necessary for developmental reading. Remedial reading often deals with students who possess weaknesses or gaps in learning in specific areas, whereas in developmental reading the students usually start from the beginning and need to learn the entire scope of reading skills. Following is a list of some important criteria for materials for remedial reading.

Can Lessons Be Isolated for Teaching Specific Skills?

In most cases when teaching disabled readers it is not necessary to have them go through an entire phonics program, learn *every* commonly taught vowel rule, learn all basic sight words, etc. For this reason materials and programs for remedial reading should allow various lessons to be pulled out for use in teaching specific skills. For example, if you were using a phonics program and knew the student was weak in only the *fl, bl,* and *gr* blends, you should be able to isolate and use the parts of the program designed to teach these blends.

Some materials are such that a certain "level" of placement within the program is desirable. Where this is the case, the materials should contain a placement test.

Is the Cost Reasonable in Relation to the Lifetime of the Materials?

Some materials, such as workbooks, may appear to be relatively inexpensive. However, if they are quickly used up by students, their per-pupil cost may end up considerably higher than nonexpendable materials that cost somewhat more. Therefore, when purchasing materials consider the cost in relation to the total amount of usage for each pupil.

Another important factor is the amount of handling materials are likely to receive. Materials likely to be handled a great deal should be of a heavy card stock and if possible should be laminated to protect them from heavy use. Cost therefore should be considered in relation to construction quality.

How Many Students Can Be Serviced by the Material at One Time?

Some materials are such that only one student may use them at any one time, while others may be used by a number of students simultaneously. This is an extremely important factor. One new program requires the use of a rather expensive machine that will accommodate only one student at a time. Although each lesson is reasonably priced in relation to the total time it may last if handled carefully, the cost of the program is extremely high in relation to the number of students that can be serviced during a specified period. On the other hand, many programs in kit form contain duplicate lessons on which several students can work at one time. Furthermore, since students are not necessarily likely to be working on the same lesson at the same time, a small kit program may service a number of students at once.

Is the Cost Reasonable in Relation to the Spectrum of Skills Taught?

Some programs are extremely limited in relation to the number of reading skills taught, while others may cover a much greater spectrum of skills. If the lessons can be used without the aid of some expensive mechanical device, then a program that covers a greater spectrum of skills is likely to service more students. On the other hand, it is often desirable in remedial reading to cover certain concepts in depth. Where this is the case, a program with a number of lessons reviewing difficult skills may be desirable.

Can Lessons Be Replaced Without Purchasing a Completely New Program?

Any experienced teacher is likely to know that certain cards, tapes, sheets, etc., that are a part of a reading program are likely to be lost, especially where the material receives heavy usage. In purchasing a program you should consider the possibility that this may happen and give preference to materials whose various components can be replaced.

Another important factor to consider is the ease of access to replacement parts. For example, can a local dealer repair or replace broken or missing items? Is the program one that has established a good reputation, and is it manufactured by a large reputable company that is not likely to discontinue the item?

Is the Teacher's Manual Adequate or Burdensome?

No one is likely to read a manual that is extremely long or burdensome. We have also found that many of the sales representatives who sell these products have not read the manuals. Therefore, from a practical standpoint, before purchasing a new program you should examine the teacher's manual to see if it covers the program adequately and yet is not burdensome to read in its entirety.

Is the Format of the Material Different from That in Which Students Have Previously Experienced Failure?

It is common knowledge among reading personnel that certain types of materials, such as hardbound books, are often associated with failure by disabled readers. For this reason materials for remedial reading should not closely resemble mainstream materials. Softbound books, kits that contain easy, short lessons, programs with audio tapes, etc., are extremely popular with disabled readers. One way to select materials of this nature is to ask the sales people to allow you to use samples for a short period and ask students their reactions to these materials.

Are Materials Highly Motivating?

In visiting a reading center it soon becomes evident which programs and materials are popular with the students. For the teacher who is unfamiliar with various types of material it is advisable to visit other reading centers or remedial classrooms and ask more experienced teachers which are most popular with students of various ages. If possible, it is also advisable to obtain samples and try them out with students before buying them in larger quantities.

Are Books and Other Materials Graded According to a Well-Known Readability Formula or Are They Based on Publishers' Estimates?

Materials for remedial reading instruction should generally have a high interest level and yet contain a low vocabulary load. Numerous studies have shown that it is not uncommon for science and social studies textbooks used by students at the seventh-or eighth-grade level to vary in difficulty from page to page from approximately the third- or fourth-grade level up to the eleventh- or twelfth-grade level. Many publishers advertise their trade books as having a certain interest level and as "being at an appropriate reading level for students from third through sixth grade." Any kind of material in which the readability level varies so much is inappropriate for use in remedial reading.

When possible you should purchase reading materials that have been written at specific grade levels on the basis of one of the better-known readability formulas such as the Spache formula for grades one through three or the Dale-Chall formula for grades four upward.

SOFTWARE DIRECTORIES[4]

Software directories provide the teacher with a list of programs by subject matter. They also describe each program, including compatible computers. Included in the descriptions you will usually find the capacity needed to run the program as well as the necessary hardware accessories.

Addison-Wesley Book of Apple
  Computer Software
Addison-Wesley Publishing Co.,
  Inc.
Applications Software Division
Jacob Way
Reading, MA 01867

Best of Educational Software for
  Apple II Computers
SYBEX Computer Books
2344 6th Street
Berkeley, CA 94710

The Book of Apple Software &
  The Book of IBM Software
Arrays, Inc./Book Division
11223 South Hindry Ave.
Los Angeles, CA 90045

EISI Computer Courseware
2225 Grant Road, Suite 3
Los Altos, CA 94022

Guide to Free Computer Materials
Educators Progress Service, Inc.
214 Center Street
Randolph, WI 53956

[4]Ekwall, Eldon E. *Locating and correcting reading difficulties,* (4th ed.). Columbus, Ohio: Charles E. Merrill, 1985 (pp. 188–189). (Reprinted by permission of Charles E. Merrill.)

INSTRUCTOR
Fall Computer Directory for
  Schools
545 Fifth Avenue
New York, NY 10017

Parent/Teacher's Microcomputing
  Sourcebook for Children
R. R. Bowker Company
205 East Forty-second Street
New York, NY 10017

PC Telemart/Vanloves Apple
  Software Directory
R. R. Bowker Company
205 East Forty-second Street
New York, NY 10017

School Microwave Directory
Dresden Associates
Department CCN
P.O. Box 246
Dresden, ME 04343

Skarbek Software Director
Skarbek Corporation, Inc.
1531 Sugargrove Ct.
St. Louis, MO 63141

Swift's Directory of Educational
  Software for the IBM-PC
Sterling-Swift Publishing Co.
7901 South IH-35
Austin, TX 78744

TRS Educational Software
  Sourcebook
Radio Shack
Education Division
1400 One Tandy Center
Fort Worth, TX 76102

Wallace User's Guide to Apple
  Computers
Wallace Micro-Mart, Inc.
3010 North Sterling Ave.
Peoria, IL 61604

Where to Find Free Programs
  For Your TRS-80, Apple, or
  IBM Microcomputer
Mother Goose Distributing
512 Winston Ave.
Pasadena, CA 91107

Whole Earth Software Catalog
Quantum Press/Doubleday
Garden City, NY 11530

SOURCES OF SOFTWARE REVIEWS[5]

AEDS Bulletin
Association for Educational Data
  Systems
1201 Sixteenth Street, N.W.
Washington, DC

Apple Journal of Courseware
  Review
P.O. Box 28426
San Jose, CA 95159

Classroom Computer News
P.O. Box 266
Cambridge, MA 92138

Computers, Reading and Language
  Arts
P.O. Box 13247
Oakland, CA 94661

Courseware Report Card
150 West Carob St.
Compton, CA 90200

Electronic Education
1311 Executive Center Drive,
  Suite 220
Tallahassee, FL 32301

[5]Reprinted by permission of *Computers, Reading and Language Arts.* From: Ekwall, Eldon E. *Locating and correcting reading difficulties,* (4th ed.). Columbus, Ohio: Charles E. Merrill, 1985 (pp. 184–185). (Reprinted by permission of Charles E. Merrill.)

Electronic Learning
902 Sylvan Avenue
Englewood Cliffs, NJ 07632

EPIE Micro-Courseware PRO/
FILES
EPIE & Consumers' Union
Box 620
Stony Brook, NY 11790

InfoWORLD
375 Cochituate Road
P.O. Box 880
Framingham, MA 01701

MicroSIFT Reviews
Northwest Regional Educational
Laboratory
300 S.W. Sixth Avenue
Portland, OR 97204

Popular Computing
70 Main Street
Peterborough, NH 03458

School Microware Reviews
Dresden Associates
P.O. Box 246
Dresden, ME 04342

The Computing Teacher
Dept. of Computer Science
University of Oregon
Eugene, OR 97403

MAGAZINES WITH INFORMATION ABOUT COMPUTERS AND COMPUTER SOFTWARE[6]

ANALOG COMPUTING
P.O. Box 615
Holmes, PA 19043

BYTE
BYTE Subscriptions
P.O. Box 590
Martinsville, NJ 08836

Cider
Subscription Department
P.O. Box 911
Farmingdale, NY 11737

CLOSING THE GAP
P.O. Box 68
Henderson, MN 56004

COMPUTE
Compute Publications, Inc.
P.O. Box 5406
Greensboro, NC 27403

COMPUTERS, READING
AND LANGUAGE ARTS
P.O. Box 13247
Oakland, CA 94661

COMPUTER WORLD
375 Cochituate Road, Rte. 30
Framingham, MA 01701

CREATIVE COMPUTING
MICROSYSTEMS
PC
SYNC
COMPUTERS & ELECTRONICS
Ziff Davis Publications
Customer Service Group
39 East Hanover Ave.
Morris Plains, NJ 07950

[6]Ekwall, Eldon E. *Locating and correcting reading difficulties,* (4th ed.). Columbus Ohio: Charles E. Merrill, 1985 (pp. 187–188). (Reprinted by permission of Charles E. Merrill.)

EDUCOM
(Newsletter)
Computer Literacy Project
P.O. Box 364
Princeton, NJ 08540

ELECTRONIC EDUCATION
902 Sylvan Avenue
Englewood Cliffs, NJ 07632

ELECTRONIC LEARNING
902 Sylvan Avenue
Englewood Cliffs, NJ 07632

INSIDER
P.O. Box 911
Farmingdale, NY 11737

INSTRUCTOR
Computer Directory for Schools
  Instructor
757 Third Avenue
New York, NY 10017

MICROCOMPUTERS IN
  EDUCATION
Queue, Inc.
5 Chapel Hill Drive
Fairfield, CT 06432

PEACHWARE QUARTERLY
3445 Peachtree Road, N.E.
Atlanta, GA 30326

POPULAR COMPUTING
70 Main Street
Peterborough, NH 03458

SCHOOL MICROWARE
  REVIEWS
P.O. Box 246
Dresden, ME 04343

SOFTALK
Softalk Curriculum
P.O. Box 60
North Hollywood, CA 91603

THE COMPUTING TEACHER
Department of Computer
& Information Science
University of Oregon
Eugene, OR 97403

COMPANIES THAT PUBLISH OR DISTRIBUTE SOFTWARE MATERIALS FOR USE IN READING EDUCATION[7]

Adventure International
Box 3435
Longwood, FL 32750

Apple Computer, Inc.
Customer Relations, MS 18-F
20525 Mariani Ave.
Cupertino, CA 95014
(General Information)

Apple Educators' Newsletter
9525 Lucerne
Ventura, CA 93004

Atari, Inc.
2110 Powers Ferry Road, Suite
  303
Atlanta, GA 30339

A/V Concepts Corp.
30 Montauk Blvd.
Oakdale, NY 11769

Borg-Warner   Educational
  Systems
600 West University Drive
Arlington Heights, IL 60004

[7]Ekwall, Eldon E. *Locating and correcting reading difficulties,* (4th ed.). Columbus, Ohio: Charles E. Merrill, 1985 (pp. 185–187). (Reprinted by permission of Charles E. Merrill.)

BrainBank, Inc.
Suite 408
220 Fifth Ave.
New York, NY 10001

Compress
P.O. Box 102
Wentworth, NH 03282

Computer Curriculum Corporation
1701 W. Euless Boulevard, Suite
139
Euless, TX 76039

Creative Curriculum, Inc.
15632 Producer Lane
Huntington Beach, CA 92649

Creative Publications
3977 East Bashore Road
P.O. Box 10328
Palo Alto, CA 94303

Dale Seymour Publications
P.O. Box 10888
Palo Alto, CA 94303

Dormac, Inc.
P.O. Box 752
Beaverton, OR 97075

Dorsett Educational Systems,
Inc.
Golsby Airport
P.O. Box 1226
Norman, OK 73070

Educational Activities, Inc.
P.O. Box 392
Freeport, NY 11520

Educational Industrial Sales, Inc.
2225 Grant Rd., Suite 3
Los Altos, CA 94022

Educational Teaching Aids
159 West Kinzie Street
Chicago, IL 60610

Edutek Corporation
415 Cambridge #4
Palo Alto, CA 94306

EMC Publishing
300 York Avenue
St. Paul, MN 55101

George Earl
1302 So. General McMullen
San Antonio, TX 78237

Ginn & Company
1250 Fairwood Avenue
Columbus, OH 43216

Hartley Courseware, Inc.
123 Bride St.
Box 419
Dimondale, MI 48821

Holt, Rinehart & Winston
383 Madison Ave.
New York, NY 10017

I/CT Instructional/
Communications
Technology, Inc.
10 Stepar Place
Huntington Station, NY 11746

Ideal School Supply Co.
11000 S. Lavergne Ave.
Oak Lawn, IL 60453

Krell Software Corp.
1320 Stony Brook Road
Stony Brook, NY 11790

Kress Software Corporation
1320 Stony Brook Road
Stony Brook, NY 11790

Learning Well
Dept. 21
200 South Service Road
Roslyn Heights, NY 11577

Little Bee Educational Programs
P.O. Box 262
Massillon, OH 44648

The Micro Center
Department MK 28
P.O. Box 6
Pleasantville, NY 10570

Microcomputer Workshops
Courseware
225 Westchester Ave.
Port Chester, NY 10573

Mic-Ed Incorporated
8108 Eden Road
Eden Prairie, MN 55344

Micro Learningware
Highway 66 South Box 307
Mankato, MN 56002

Micromatics, Inc.
181 N. 200 W., Suite 5
Bountiful, UT 84010

Microphys
1737 West 2nd Street
Brooklyn, NY 11223

Micrograms, Inc.
P.O. Box 2146
Loves Park, IL 61130

Micro Power & Light Co.
12820 Hillcrest Road, Suite 219
Dallas, TX 75230

Milliken Publishing Company
1100 Research Blvd.
St. Louis, MO 63132

Milton Bradley Company
Springfield, MA 01101

Minnesota Educational Computing Consortium
3490 Lexington Ave. North
St. Paul, MN 55112

Nationwide Computer and Video
P.O. Box 61
1380 S. Pennsylvania Ave.
Morrisville, PA 19067

Orange Cherry Media
7 Delano Drive
Bedford Falls, NY 10507

Peachtree Software by Eduware
3445 Peachtree Road, N.E.
8th Floor
Atlanta, GA 30326

Powersoft, Inc.
P.O. Box 157
Pitman, NJ 08071

Program Design, Inc.
95 East Putnam Ave.
Greenwich, CT 06830

The Psychological Corporation
4640 Harry Hines Blvd.
Dallas, TX 75235

Queqe
5 Chapel Hill Drive
Fairfield, CT 06432

Radio Shack
Education Division
1400 One Tandy Center
Fort Worth, TX 76102

Random House, Inc.
2970 Brandywine Rd., Suite 201
Atlanta, GA 30341

Reader's Digest Services, Inc.
Educational Division
Pleasantville, NY 10570

Right On Programs
P.O. Box 977
Huntington, NY 11743

Scholastic Book Services
P.O. Box 1068
Jefferson City, MO 65102

Scholastic, Inc.
P.O. Box 7501
2931 E. McCarty Street
Jefferson City, MO 65102

Science Research Associates, Inc.
155 North Wacker Drive
Chicago, IL 60606

Skillcorp Software, Inc.
3741 Old Conejo Road
Newbury Park, CA 91320

Sliwa Enterprises, Inc.
2360-J George Washington
Highway
Yorktown, VA 23692

Society for Visual Education,
Inc.
Department LX
1345 Diversey Parkway
Chicago, IL 60614

Softside
10 Northern Boulevard
Amherst, NH 03031

Speco Educational Systems
3208 Daniels, Suite #6
Dallas, TX 75205

Sterling Swift Publishing Co.
7901 South IH 35
Austin, TX 78744

Sunburst Communications
Rm. Y 4747
39 Washington Avenue
Pleasantville, NY 01570

Tamarack Software
P.O. Box 247
Darby, MT 59829

TIEs
1925 West Country Road B2
St. Paul, MN 55113

Tycom Associates
68 Velma Ave.
Pittsfield, MA 01201

Unicom
297 Elmwood Ave.
Providence, RI 02907

Universal Systems for Education, Inc.
14901 East Hampden Ave., Suite 250
Aurora, CO 80014

COMPUTER TERMINOLOGY[8]

Access Time   The time required to retrieve a word from memory.

Add-On   A device for coupling a computer with a telephone for the transmission of data.

Applications Software   Computer programs written to perform actual tasks such as inventory, mail list, accounts payable/receivable.

Audio Device   Any computer device that accepts sound or produces sound. Examples include voice recognition and music or speech synthesis devices.

Auxiliary Storage   A storage device in addition to the "core" or main storage of the computer. Auxiliary storage is the permanent storage for information. It includes magnetic tapes, cassette tapes, cartridge tapes, hard disks, floppy disks. Auxiliary storage can't be accessed as fast as main storage.

BASIC   Beginner's All-Purpose Symbolic Instruction Code; a type of computer programming language.

Baud   Bits Per Second. Actually binary units of information per second. Teletypes transmit at 110 baud. Each character is 11 bits, and the teletype transmits at 10 characters per second.

Back Up   Duplicate data files, redundant equipment, or procedures used in the event of failure of a component or storage media.

Binary Number   Representation of a number in the binary system, using a series of zeros and ones.

Bit   The contraction of binary digit. A bit always has the value of zero or one. Bits are universally used in electronic systems to encode information, orders (instructions), and data. Bits are usually grouped in nybbles (four), bytes (eight), or larger units.

[8]This selected glossary of terminology is reprinted with permission of the R. R. Bowker Company from a compilation by Advanced Software Technology, Inc. Copyright © 1983.

Byte   A set of eight bits. A byte is universally used to represent a character. Microcomputer instructions require one, two, or three bytes. One byte includes two nybbles.

CAI   Computer Assisted Instruction.

Cassette   A small plastic cartridge that contains two spools of 1.8″ magnetic tape, and which has recently been applied to mass storage requirements of microcomputers and minicomputers.

Character   Any letter, number, symbol or punctuation mark that can be transmitted as output by the computer.

Character Printer   A printer that transfers a fully formed letter, number, or symbol with each impression stroke. The characters are generally more legible than those created by a dot matrix printer.

COBOL   Common Business Oriented Language. A high-level computer language using commands that resemble English. Cobol was designed specifically for business use.

Coding   The entering of a program or data into a computer, usually by means of a keyboard.

Command   An order to the computer in the form of words and numbers typed on a keyboard, words spoken into a microphone, positions of a game or joystick, etc.

Compile   To translate high-level language into a set of binary instructions.

Compiler   System software that produces a machine-code version of a program originally written in a high-level language such as Cobol, PL/1, etc.

Computer   A general purpose electrical system designed for the manipulation of information and incorporating a central processing unit (CPU), memory, input/output (I/O) facilities, power supply, and cabinet.

Computer Time Sharing   Permits one computer to serve several terminals in remote locating simultaneously and allows the cost of the computer to be divided among the users.

CP/M   Control Program/Monitor. One of the more common computer operating systems on which many computers are based and much software written.

CPU   Central Processing Unit. The computer module in charge of fetching, decoding, and executing instructions.

CRT   Cathode Ray Tube. The television tube used to display pictures or characters. Also the computer terminal made from a CRT.

Daisywheel   A style of printer or typewriter printing element in the shape of a disk. Each character is located at the end of a "petal" connected at the center of the disk, hence the name.

Data   Information stored or processed by the computer.

Database   Systematic organization of data files for easy access, retrieval, and update.

Dedicated   If a computer or a piece of hardware is assigned exclusively to one task, it is said to be a dedicated system.

Disk   A flat, circular object that resembles a phonograph record. A record "stores" music; a disk stores information. The disk is inserted into a disk drive that rotates at a high speed. The drive writes new information onto the disk and reads information that is already stored on the disk. There are two major types of disks found on small computers, flexible floppy disks and hard disks.

Diskette   Floppy disk. A circular mylar substrate coated with a magnetic oxide, rotating inside a special jacket that internally cleans the surface.

Display Screen   Same as CRT.

Dot Matrix   The type of printer in which characters are formed from multiple dots, much as a TV picture is created.

Dual Density   A reference to storage disks and disk drives that are capable of storing and reading twice the number of information tracks (80) per disk as the early standard (35–40).

Error Message   A one-sentence statement by the computer to the operator that something has been done incorrectly, e.g., "Does not compute."

External Memory   Used to store programs and information that would otherwise be lost if the computer was turned off. Cassette tapes, disks, bubble memory, and CCD (charge coupled devices) are also known as mass memory and removable memory.

File   A logical block of information, designated by name, and considered as a unit by a user. A file may be physically divided into smaller records.

Fixed Disk   A device in which the disk pack is sealed and cannot be removed. Being sealed it cannot be exposed to dust and dirt and, therefore, can be operated at higher speeds than removable units, with greater reliability.

Flexible Disk   Recent mass-storage device using a soft (floppy) disk to record information. The disk rotates in a cardboard jacket. Cutout holes provide access for the moving head (which must be applied against the disk in order to read and write) and for index information.

FORTRAN   FORmula TRANSlator. Early high-level language devised for numerical computations. Although complex, it is most frequently one of the programming languages used in scientific environments. Requires a compiler (by contrast, BASIC, derived from Fortran, can be interpreted).

Grid   A method of dividing the computer screen into evenly spaced horizontal and vertical lines. Used for locating points on the screen. These points are expressed as row and column coordinates.

Hard Copy   Computer output on paper.

Hard Disk   A data storage medium encompassing a permanently mounted disk and drive with a storage capacity 10 to 30 times that of the removable floppy disk.

Hardware   The bolts, nuts, boards, chips, wires, transformers, etc., in a computer. The physically existing components of a system.

Input   Any information coming into the computer.

Input Device   Any machine that allows you to enter commands or information into the computer's main (RAM) memory. An input device could be a typewriter keyboard, an organ keyboard, a tape drive, a disk drive, a microphone, a light pen, a digitizer, or electronic sensors.

Keyboard   A group of push buttons used for entering information into a computer system.

Kilo   A prefix meaning "1000."

Kilobyte   Term meaning "1000 bytes" (precisely, 1024 bytes).

Language   In relation to computers, any unified, related set of commands or instructions that the computer can accept. Low-level languages are difficult to use but closely resemble the fundamental operations of the computer. High-level languages resemble English.

LCD   Liquid Crystal Display.

LED   Light Emitting Diode.

Light Pen   An input device for a CRT. It records the emission of light at the point of contact with the screen. The timing relationship to the beginning of a scan determines the approximate position on the screen.

Letter Quality Printer   One that forms whole characters and provides output much like a standard office typewriter in quality.

Line Printer   A device that prints information from the computer at a high speed; produces a hard copy.

LOGO   A computer language, developed by scientists at MIT's Artificial Intelligence Laboratory, that has been used experimentally over the last several years in a children's learning laboratory as a tool to help youngsters master concepts in mathematics, art, and science.

Loop   A group of instructions that may be executed more than once.

Main Memory   The internal memory of the computer contained in its circuitry, as opposed to peripheral memory (tapes, disks).

Mainframe   The box that houses the computer's main memory and logic components—its CPU, RAM, ROM, interface input/output (I/O) circuitry, and so on. The word is also to distinguish the very large computer from the minicomputer or microcomputer.

Master File   A file that contains the main, permanent information used in a system. Other files are transaction files or files used as temporary work areas.

Matrix Printer   A matrix printer prints using a grid of dots usually 5 by 7. Characters are formed by striking certain dots in the grid.

Menu   A list of programs or applications that are available by making a selection. For example, a small home computer might display the following menu: "Do you want to 1. Balance checkbook? 2. See appointments for May? 3. See a recipe? Type number desired.

Microcomputer   A small but complete computer system, including CPU, memory, input/output (I/O) interfaces, and power supply.

Minicomputer   A small computer, intermediate in size between a microcomputer and a large computer.

Mini-Floppy   A 5¼″ diskette.

Modem   Modulator-demodulator. A device that transforms a computer's electrical pulses into audible tones for transmission over a phone line to another computer. A modem also receives incoming tones and transforms them into electrical signals that can be processed and stored by the computer.

Natural Language   A spoken, human language such as English, Spanish,

Arabic, or Chinese. In the future, small computers will probably be fast enough and have large enough vocabularies to enable you to talk to them using your natural language. Yet there will still be a need for special computer languages that are more efficient than natural languages for handling certain kinds of tasks

Network   A group of small computers communicating over telephone lines or by use of radio microwaves.

Nybble   Usually four bits, or half a byte.

Off Line   Equipment or information that is not currently part of an operating computer system.

On Line   Directly connected to the computer system and in performance-ready condition.

Operating System   Software required to manage the hardware and logical resources of a system, including scheduling and file (OS) management.

Output   Any processed information coming out of a computer, via any medium; print, CRT, etc.

Packaged Program   A program designed for a specific application of broad, general usage, unadapted to any particular installation.

Permanent Storage   Storage of computer data on a disk or magnetic tape.

Password   A code word or group of characters a computer system might require to allow that operator to perform certain functions. An operator's password might allow him to update payroll hours, but not run checks.

Pascal   A high-level programming language.

Peripheral   A human interface device connected to a computer.

Plotter   A mechanical device for drawing lines under computer control.

Program   A sequence of instructions that results in the execution of an algorithm. Programs are essentially written at three levels: (1) binary (can be directly executed by the MPU), (2) assembly language (symbolic representation of the binary), (3) high-level language (such as BASIC), requiring a compiler or interpreter.

Programming Language   A set of rules and conventions used to prepare the source program for translation by the computer. Each language has its own rules. Examples of programming languages are BASIC, COBOL, and RPG.

RAM   Random Access Memory. The portion of computer memory generally available to execute programs and store data. Memory locations can both be read from and written to at high speeds.

Random Access   An access method where each word can be retrieved directly by its address.

Retrieval   The reading of data from a permanent storage device and its transfer into memory.

ROM   Read Only Memory. A portion of computer memory where information is permanently stored. This information can be read at high speed but can never be altered. It is not available to execute programs or to store data.

Run   Execute a program.

Screen   Same as CRT.

Sign-Off The disconnect procedure that severs interactions between a user and a computer.

Sign-On The connect procedure that establishes contact between a user and a computer.

Software The programs (contrasted to hardware). Any set of coded instructions causing the computer to perform a task.

System A set of programs, a set of hardware, or a set of programs and hardware that work together for some specific purpose.

Synthesizer Any device that produces something that is based on digital signals stored in the computer. A voice synthesizer produces sounds that closely resemble a person talking. A music synthesizer makes music.

Terminal Usually a work station remote from the main computer allowing keyboard input and CRT and/or printer output.

Time Sharing Occurs when a single computer has multiple users who are each getting a ''slice'' of each second of the computer's processing time.

User Friendly Descriptive of both hardware and software that are designed to assist the user by being scaled to human dimensions, self-instructing, error proof, etc.

Video Monitor A computer picture screen.

Word A logical unit of information. It may have any number of bits, but it is usually four, eight, or sixteen for microcomputers.

SUMMARY

There is little doubt that the computer as a tool for the diagnosis and remediation of reading disabilities is here to stay. As programs and voice synthesizers as well as the ability of the computer to interpret oral responses improve, the computer will become an even more important tool for teaching students with reading and other learning disabilities.

REFERENCE

International Reading Association. *The Reading Teacher,* (October 1984) Vol. 18, 80–82.

16

Interpreting Test and Research Results in Reading

The first part of this chapter discusses the need for teachers to understand some common terms in order to interpret and evaluate test and research results. The next part contains an explanation of a number of terms for interpretation of test evaluations and results. The final part contains a discussion of the meaning of some common terms for the interpretation of research results in reading.

WHY TEACHERS NEED THE ABILITY TO INTERPRET TEST AND RESEARCH RESULTS

Under the present standards for certification in some states, teachers are not required to take a course in tests and measurements; and in most states teachers can begin teaching with little or no knowledge of basic statistical terms. However, teachers should know a number of terms commonly used in describing test results and accuracy. Without this basic knowledge it would be very difficult to evaluate test reviews such as those found in *Mental Measurements Yearbook* (1985) or in some cases even to evaluate the descriptive information provided by the publisher.

As the remedial reading teacher begins to work in the field, he or she is likely to find that knowledge gained in college course work eventually becomes outdated and requires supplementation with professional books and periodicals. Much of the information in these sources, especially in professional periodicals, presents the results of research in the field of reading. In order to understand much of this research at least some knowledge of statistical terms is needed.

The purpose of this chapter is only to define terms needed for interpreting test results and evaluations, and terms needed to interpret research results. No attempt is made to explain how to do the problems involved in evaluating tests and test results or how to apply the statistical procedures discussed.

THE MEANING OF SOME COMMON TERMS NEEDED FOR TEST INTERPRETATION

Mean

The *mean* is the arithmetic average, as illustrated below.

Julie	68
Syril	49
Enrique	38
Dennis	67
Judy	68
Denise	52
Total	342

The mean is the total divided by the number of scores: $342 \div 6 = 57$. The symbol for the mean is $\bar{x}$. A symbol for each raw score, i.e., is x, and n represents the total number of scores. The Greek capital letter *sigma* (Σ) represents the total sum, in this case 342. The formula:

$$\bar{x} = \frac{\Sigma x}{n}$$

Median

The *median* is the midpoint (not always a score); half of the ranked scores are above and half are below it. This is shown in the scores below.

Julie	68
Judy	68
Dennis	67
Denise	52
Syril	49
Enrique	38

Half the scores are above a point between 67 and 52 and half are below this point. When there are an even number of ranked scores, as in this case, the median is the midpoint of the two middle scores: $67 + 52 = 119 \div 2 = 59.5$.

If there is an uneven number of scores, then the median is an exact score, as in the example below.

Julie	68
Judy	43
Luis	41
Bob	40
Dolly	32

In this case 41 is the score at midpoint, or the median.

Mode

In a set of scores the *mode* is the one that appears most often. It is possible to have more than one mode if the two or more raw scores that appear most often occur an equal number of times. In the example shown below, 54 is the mode.

Raw scores = 22, 28, 34, 38, 42, 48, 54, 54, 57, 62

In the example that follows there are two modes, 32 and 53.

Raw scores = 28, 32, 32, 38, 43, 48, 53, 53, 58, 62

Range

The *range* is a measure of variability that indicates the distance between the smallest and largest score. It is calculated by subtracting the smallest score from the largest, as shown in the distribution below.

18, 23, 26, 32, 33

If x_n = the highest score (33) and x_1 = the lowest score (18), the range = x_n − x_1, or 33 − 18 = 15.

The Normal Curve

Figure 16-1 illustrates a *normal curve.* When measurements such as intelligence or height are taken, the largest number of scores falls at the mean, with slightly fewer above and slightly fewer below. When the distribution is "normal," i.e., with more scores at the median or mean and a gradually decreasing number at the extreme left (below the mean) and right (above the mean) in equal proportions, you get a smooth bell-shaped curve, as illustrated in Figure 16-1. It should also be noted that in a perfect bell curve the mean, median, and mode fall at the same point, the center, on the vertical line marked "0" in Figure 16-1. The highest point on a bell curve or normal curve represents the most scores, or measurements, and the lowest point represents the fewest scores or measurements. You are not likely to obtain a smooth normal-shaped curve when measuring any characteristic unless you are dealing with large numbers of scores.

Standard Deviation

Standard deviation, often designated by the lower case Greek letter sigma (σ), is used to describe the variability of scores in relation to the mean, a measure of central tendency. Think of standard deviation as a measure of the average distance from the mean of each score in a distribution. Robert Koenker (1961) points out that standard deviation, quartile deviation, and range are the most commonly used measures of dispersion:

> The purposes of measures of dispersion are as follows:
>
> 1. To find the spread or variability of a group of scores about the mean.
> 2. To compare the spread or variability of two or more groups.
> 3. To compare the spread or variability of one group on two different occasions. (p. 9)

The greater the range in scores, the larger the standard deviation. In a *normally* distributed set of scores 34.13 percent fall one standard deviation above the mean and 34.13 percent fall one standard deviation below the mean, as can be seen in Figure 16-1. Thus 68.26 (34.13 + 34.13) percent of scores fall within one standard deviation above or below the mean. It is fairly common to say that two thirds (or 66⅔ percent) of the scores in a normal distribution fall within one standard deviation (σ) of the mean. Likewise, as in Figure 16-1, 95.44 percent of the scores in a normal distribution fall within two sigmas of the mean.

FIGURE 16-1 The Normal Curve, Percentiles, and Standard Scores

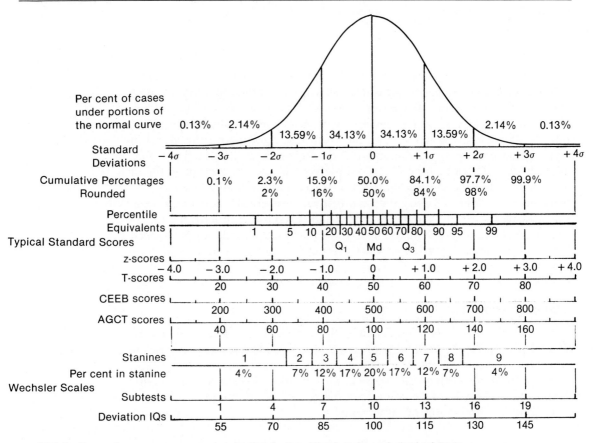

Distributions of scores on many standardized educational and psychological tests approximate the form of the normal curve shown at the top of this chart. Below it are shown some of the systems that have been developed to facilitate the interpretation of scores by converting them into numbers that indicate the examinee's relative status in a group.

The zero (0) at the center of the baseline shows the location of the mean (average) raw score on a test, and the symbol σ (sigma) marks off the scale of raw scores in standard deviation units.

Cumulative percentages are the basis of the percentile equivalent scale.

Several systems are based on the standard deviation unit. Among these standard score scales, the *z-score*, the *T-score* and the *stanine* are general systems that have been applied to a variety of tests. The others are special variants used in connection with tests of the College Entrance Examination Board, the World War II Army General Classification test, and the Wechsler Intelligence Scales.

Tables of norms, whether in percentile or standard score form, have meaning only with reference to a specified test applied to a specified population. The chart does not permit one to conclude, for instance, that a percentile rank of 84 on one test necessarily is equivalent to a *z-score* of +1.0 on another; this is true only when each test yields essentially a normal distribution of scores and when both scales are based on identical or very similar groups of people.

Courtesy of the Psychological Corporation. The scales on this chart are discussed in greater detail in *Test Service Bulletin No. 48*. The Psychological Corporation, New York, N.Y.

The standard deviation of a set of scores provides a standard of measurement of any score. This can be useful in comparing individual scores on various types of data.

Percentiles or Centiles

When a teacher wishes to describe the standing of a particular individual in relation to other members of a group, the teacher often uses *percentiles,* or less often quartiles or deciles. A percentile score is determined by the percentage of a group falling below that score. Thus an individual at the 65th percentile did better on a test than 65 percent of people taking the test. It should be kept in mind, however, that the percentile score is achieved in relation to the student's own group. For example, a student in a school district with poor achievement may score at the 86th percentile of local school norms. However, the same student may score at a different percentile based on national norms.

Percentile scores are not evenly spaced along a baseline, as can be seen in Figure 16–1. Since scores tend to cluster around the mean, the number of raw score points between, for example, the 40th and 45th percentiles may be considerably less than the number of points at the extreme ends.

One of the advantages of using percentiles is that they are usually readily understood, but they have one serious drawback. Suppose John ranked in the 56th percentile and Mary ranked in the 50th. Since it takes so few points to change percentile scores near the center of the distribution, John might easily have outranked Mary by chance.

There is no 100th percentile, only the percentage of cases that ranked below the number given. Therefore, a percentile rating of 99 for a student means that 99 percent of the group ranked below that student, who is in the top 1 percent.

Quartiles and Deciles

Quartiles and *deciles* also report an individual's relative standing in relation to other members of a group, just like percentiles. The 25th percentile is sometimes referred to as the 1st quartile and the 75th percentile as the 3rd. The 10th percentile is the 1st decile, the 20th percentile the 2nd decile, and so on. It should be remembered that the 1st or 3rd quartile or the 1st and 2nd decile are *points* in the distribution of scores and do not represent proportions of the distribution. No percentiles of any kind are equal units of measurement and cannot be averaged or treated arithmetically.

Standard Scores

Standard scores enable one to interpret an individual's score in terms of the number of standard deviations from the mean. Unlike percentiles, standard scores can be averaged and treated arithmetically. One of the most commonly used types is the *z*-score. In some statistics books the lower case *z* is used to indicate scores derived from the following formula:

$$z = \frac{x - \bar{x}}{s}$$

In this case *x* represents a student's raw score, $\bar{x}$ represents the mean for that set of scores, and *s* represents the standard deviation of that set of scores. For example, if a student scored 120 on a test on which the mean was 112 and the standard deviation was 10:

$$z = \frac{x - \bar{x}}{s}$$

$$z = \frac{120 - 112}{10}$$

$$= \frac{8}{10}$$

$$= .8$$

This tells us that the student's score was 8/10 or .8 standard deviation above the mean.

In other books (and in Figure 16–1) *z* is transformed to a standard score in which the mean is 50 and the standard deviation is 10; these are *T*-scores or *Z*-scores. The advantage of using *T*-scores is that they eliminate decimals and negative numbers, as in Figure 16–1.

Some tests, such as the *College Entrance Examination Board (CEEB)* and the old *Army General Classification Test (AGCT)* shown in Figure 16–1, are reported in transformed standard score form. The *CEEB* has a mean of 500 with a standard deviation of 100. This allows easy assessment of the value of a particular score. A score of 700 on the *CEEB* puts the student two standard deviation units above the mean. To interpret this score in terms of percentiles, follow the vertical line in Figure 16–1 up to the cumulative percentages. A score of 700 on the *CEEB* places the student at 97.7, or near the 98th percentile.

Stanines

The *stanine,* another form of standard score, carries a mean of 5 and a standard deviation of approximately 2. The term is derived from the words *standard* and *nine.* Figure 16–1 shows the approximate percentage of scores within each stanine. Only 4 percent of scores fall within the 1st stanine, but 20 percent fall within the 5th stanine.

The terms *percentile* and *stanine* are sometimes confusing. Percentiles and stanines are not equivalent. Note in Figure 16–1 that the beginning of the 2nd stanine is approximately even with the 5th percentile and the beginning of the

3rd stanine is approximately even with the 12th and 13th percentile. The 90th percentile falls near the beginning of the 8th stanine.

Standard Error

The *standard error* is an estimate of the reliability of a test score. It is calculated by using the test's standard deviation and reliability coefficient. The use of the standard error enables you to estimate a range of scores within which the individual "true" score will fall. Thus, a standard error of 5 indicates a 68 percent chance that the "true" score falls within five points of the obtained score. For example, if an individual scored 90 and the standard error was 5, you would estimate his "true" score to be 85 to 95, and you expect that your estimation will be confirmed 68 times out of 100–provided you could determine the so-called true score.

Wechsler Scales

The subtests of the *Wechsler Intelligence Scale for Children—Revised* and the Wechsler IQs both use standard scores. The Wechsler subtests have a mean of 10 with a standard deviation of 3. The IQ scale has a mean of 100 with a standard deviation of 15. This lets an experienced examiner easily interpret the values of the scores. For example, a scaled score of 7 on the "Picture Completion" subtest is one standard deviation below the mean. Likewise an overall Wechsler Full Scale IQ of 115 is one standard deviation above the mean. Assuming all scores to conform to a standard normal curve, the student's "Picture Completion" score places him or her at the 16th percentile and the overall Full Scale IQ score at the 84th percentile.

Reliability

Reliability refers to the consistency with which a test agrees with itself; it produces the same scores on several occasions when given to the same individual over a short period. High reliability in a test does not guarantee that it is worthwhile. However, for a test to be valid (which is discussed next) it must be reliable.

Some tests used in reading have high intrascorer reliability but poor interscorer reliability. That is, when the test is given by the same person to the same students (intra), the same results are obtained. However, when the same students take the test from different examiners (inter), the results often differ. This probably means that the examiners score answers differently; thus the test is subjective and can never be reliable.

Three methods of determining reliability are commonly used. One is to give the test and then repeat it at a later date (the *repeat* or *test-retest* method). If individual students get similar scores both times, or if the students are generally in the same rank order on both administrations, the correlation is high and it is considered reliable. Another method is to compare pupils' scores on the odd items with scores on the even-numbered items (the *split-half* technique) and again see if the scores are in the same rank order or if they have a high correlation. A third method is to compare one form of a test against another form (the *equivalent form* technique).

Validity

Validity describes whether a test measures what it should. It is quite possible for a test to be reliable without being valid. That is, it may give consistent scores but not measure what it purports to measure, as for example, the well-known basic sight word test that requires the student to circle one of four choices when the examiner says a word. Since word attack is a matter of seeing words and pronouncing them, this test is simply not valid. In phonics, also, if teachers do not test in a situation that is analogous to reading, the test does not measure the student's ability to use phonics, hence is not valid.

Several methods are used to determine the validity of a test. One is to correlate the results of a test with those of another well-known test to determine whether the students are generally in the same rank order on both tests. This method is fine if the well-known test is valid; however, being well-known, even widely used, does not make it valid. Another problem with this criterion is that the number of items missed by students may be in the same rank order, but there may be no correlation between missed items from test to test. For overall achievement tests this makes very little difference, but on a diagnostic test, which purports to diagnose specific blends, digraphs, etc., it would be very misleading.

Another method of establishing validity is to inspect the test or send it to a group of specialists in its field. If the inspection shows or group finds that the test measures what it purports to measure, it is considered valid. This is called *content* or *face* validity.

A third method is to give a test to individuals (for example, a reading readiness test) and then measure their performance in reading at a later date. If the scores correlate, we say the test has good *predictive* validity.

THE MEANING OF SOME COMMON NEEDED TERMS FOR INTERPRETING RESEARCH

Levels of Significance

In examining literature pertaining to research in reading as well as other fields, you will often encounter levels of significance, which are used in a number of statistical procedures to determine whether the results obtained are likely to have happened by chance. For example, in giving a reading test to two groups of fifth-grade students taught by different methods, you might find that one group had a mean grade-level achievement of 5.6 and the other, 5.9. This does not tell whether the higher-scoring group happened to do so by chance or the method of instruction used with them was superior. If it was superior teaching, these results could be expected nearly every year. To make comparisons between or among scores, use the level of significance, or *level of confidence.*

By applying the proper statistical procedure to the scores of the two groups of fifth-grade students, you can determine whether a mean grade-level achievement of 5.9 is significantly better than 5.6. If it is significantly better than 5.6 at the .05 level of confidence, you can conclude that these differences occur by chance only 5 times out of 100. If the 5.9 mean grade level of achievement is significantly better than the 5.6 at the .01 level of confidence, you can conclude that these differences happen by chance only once out of 100 times.

In significance or confidence levels you will often see the .05, .01, or .001 levels reported:

$p < .05$ The probability of that event's occurring is less than five in 100. A researcher usually selects the confidence level before the statistical procedure is completed. If level .05 is selected, $p < .05$ is considered significant. However, there is a greater chance that the scores occurred by chance than if $p < .01$ or $p < .001$.

$p > .05$ The probability of an event's occurring is greater than 5 in 100. Rather than show $p > .05$, researchers often write "NS," "not significant"; the odds of receiving random test scores are too great.

$p < .01$ The probability of that event's occurring is less than 1 in 100.

$p < .001$ The probability of that event's occurring is less than 1 in 1000.

There is a growing tendency for researchers to report levels of significance as computed, e.g., the .02 level, and the .10 level. Some statisticians believe that when this is done, researchers are likely to claim that a level of .10 or .15 is significant and therefore draw erroneous conclusions from their data.

Correlations

The term *correlation* is often used popularly to indicate some type of relationship or two things with something in common. However, when used in statistical research, the term usually refers to the coefficient of correlation (r) between two sets of variables. The most commonly used method of computing it is the Pearson Product Moment Correlation.

A correlation is a measure of the rank order in distance from the mean of two sets of data or scores. Correlations may be highly positive or highly negative. A perfect positive correlation is shown as 1.00 and a perfect negative correlation as − 1.00. In order to compute a correlation coefficient (*r*) there must be two values or scores for each individual in a group. The correlation coefficient is a measure of the rank order of scores on one test compared to the other. The more closely the rank orders match, or approach 1.00, the higher the chance that individuals in the group were in the same rank order on both tests. In negative correlation, high scores on the first test are associated with low scores on the second test and vice versa.

Richard C. Sprinthall (1987) points out that although exact values for correlations should usually be given, some broad categories are useful. Sprinthall uses one set given by J. P. Gilford, a noted statistician:[1]

r value	Interpretation
Less than .20	Slight; almost negligible relationship
.20–.40	Low correlation; definite but small relationship
.40–.70	Moderate correlation; substantial relationship
.70–.90	High correlation; marked relationship
.90–1.00	Very high correlation; very dependable relationship

The level of significance of a correlation should be reported in order to determine whether a high correlation has happened by chance. For example, three students, each taking two tests, could easily obtain the same rank order by chance. However, 300 students taking the two tests would not be likely to obtain the same rank order by chance. In order to evaluate a correlation, its level of significance is often reported.

There is often a danger in drawing conclusions based on certain correlation data. For example, you might find a high correlation between reading ability in the first grade and the scores on a certain test for eye-motor coordination. This would not necessarily mean that training in eye-motor coordination improves students' ability to read. In fact, numerous studies have shown that this does not occur. Evidently there is a common factor responsible for performance in both areas. However, that common factor may not be measured by either test.

t Tests and *F* tests

In researching problems in reading, it is often necessary to determine whether the test performance of one group is significantly different from that of another group. In other cases it is necessary to determine whether the test performance of a group is significantly different from the norm. When re-

[1]Reprinted by permission of the author and Prentice-Hall.

searchers wish to make decisions of this nature the t test or F test is often used. Since the purpose of this chapter is only to enable you to understand research reports when you read them, the differences in these statistical procedures will not be discussed. However, with either t or F tests you are concerned with whether differences between the means of two or more groups are significantly different. Assume a reading achievement test was given to two seventh-grade groups and the results showed a level of 7.2 for one group and 7.4 for the other group. Whether this difference occurred by chance depends on such factors as the number of students in each group and the standard deviation of the scores.

If the t or F test is used and the researcher reports significant differences between the means at high (.05, .01, or .001) confidence levels, you can conclude that the higher score indicates superior achievement.

Chi Square

The Chi Square Test (χ^2) is used to establish the distribution or ratio or frequency of a sample against another hypothetical or known distribution, ratio, or frequency; it tests the difference between *expected* and *observed* ratios, distributions, or frequencies.

One use of the Chi Square Test in reading: On a certain test previous research found that the expected distribution of mean scores was boys 75, girls 75. However, in a later testing the distribution of mean scores was boys 85, girls 65. Is this observed ratio different enough from the expected distribution to be considered significant? The Chi Square Test might reveal this distribution as either significant or not at .05, .01, or .001. If not significant, it could easily have happened by chance. If significant at the .05 level of confidence, it would not happen by chance more than five times out of 100.

THE BUROS MENTAL MEASUREMENTS YEARBOOKS AND OTHER SOURCES OF TEST INFORMATION

Those who find it necessary to use tests should become acquainted with the Mental Measurements Yearbooks (MMYs), a series of books published periodically (not yearly) since 1938. Now edited by James V. Mitchell, Jr. (1985), the books were originally edited by the late Oscar Buros. Buros (1968) stated the original objectives of the test section of the MMys.

    a. To provide comprehensive bibliographies of all standardized tests published in English-speaking countries.
    b. To provide frankly critical evaluations of tests, written by competent specialists representing a variety of viewpoints, to assist test users to choose the tests which will best meet their needs.
    c. To provide comprehensive bibliographies of articles, books, and theses dealing with the construction, validity, use, and limitations of specific tests.

    d. To impel test authors and publishers to place fewer but better tests on the market and to provide test users with detailed information on the validity and limitations of their tests at the time the tests are first published.

    e. To suggest to test users better methods of arriving at their own appraisals of both standardized and nonstandardized tests in light of their own particular values and needs.

    f. To stimulate contributing reviewers to reconsider and think through more carefully their own beliefs and values relevant to testing.

    g. To inculcate upon test users a keener awareness of both the values and dangers involved in the use and non-use of standardized tests.

    h. To impress test users with the desirability of suspecting all standardized tests—even though prepared by well-known authorities—accompanied by detailed data on their construction, validity, uses, and limitations. (pp. xv–xvi)

In 1985 the *Ninth Mental Measurements Yearbook* was published. Another source of information is *Tests in Print,* also edited by James V. Mitchell, Jr., and published by the Buros Institute. *Tests in Print III* was published in 1983.

Other sources of test information for the teacher of reading are books by Roger Farr and Robert F. Carey (1986), Robert Schreiner (Ed.) (1979), and Nicholas J. Silvaroli, Dennis J. Kear, and Michael C. McKenna (1982). See References.

SUMMARY

Remedial reading teachers must constantly review descriptive information on new tests and the professional literature in their field, much of which is concerned with the results of research. In order to evaluate test reviews and research results at least some understanding of various statistical terms or procedures is required. The most commonly used terms are *mean, median, mode, range, standard deviation, normal* or *bell curve, percentile, centile, quartile, decile, stanine,* and *standard score.* The teacher should understand the normal curve and understand when to use tests of significance such as *t* and *F* tests. Remedial reading teachers should also understand and be able to interpret studies dealing with reliability and validity. They must also be familiar with the values and limitations of correlations as well as some of the publications designed to help them evaluate tests.

REFERENCES

Buros, O. K. (Ed.). (1968). *Reading tests and reviews.* Highland Park, NJ: Gryphon Press.

Ekwall, E. E. (1973). *An analysis of children's test scores when tested with individually administered tests and when tested with group administered diagnostic tests.* Final research report, University Research Institute: University of Texas at El Paso.

Farr, R., & Carey, R. F. (1986). *Reading: What can be measured?* (2nd ed.). Newark, DE: International Reading Association.

Mitchell, J. Y., Jr. (Ed.). (1985). *The ninth mental mental measurements yearbook, Vol. 1 & II.* Lincoln, NE: Buros Institute of Mental Measurements of the University of Nebraska.

Mitchell, J. Y., Jr. (Ed.). (1983). *Tests in print III.* Lincoln, NE: Buros Institute of Mental Measurements of the University of Nebraska.

Schreiner, R. (Ed.). (1979). *Reading tests and teachers: A practical guide.* Newark, DE: International Reading Association.

Silvaroli, N., Kear, D. J., & McKenna, M. C. (1982). *A classroom guide to reading assessment and instruction.* Dubuque, IA: Kendall/Hunt.

Sprinthall, R. C. (1987). *Basic statistical analysis* (2nd ed.). Englewood Cliffs, NJ: Prentice-Hall.

APPENDIX A
The El Paso Phonics Survey

THE *QUICK SURVEY WORD LIST* AND THE *EL PASO PHONICS SURVEY*

The *Quick Survey Word List* and the *El Paso Phonics Survey* are designed to test the student's knowledge of phonics word-attack skills. The *Quick Survey Word List* is also designed to test the student's knowledge of such word-attack skills as syllabication; vowel rules; rules for *C, G,* and *Y;* and accent generalizations. Directions for using each of these instruments follow.

DIRECTIONS FOR ADMINISTERING THE *QUICK SURVEY WORD LIST*

The *Quick Survey Word List* is designed to enable the tester to determine quickly if a student has the necessary word-attack skills to read successfully material written at an adult level. It may be given to the student at approximately fourth-grade level and above to determine whether it is necessary to administer the *El Paso Phonics Survey.* The student is simply given the word list to look at and is asked to pronounce each word. If the student can pronounce each of them correctly, it will not be necessary to administer the *El Paso Phonics Survey,* since the ultimate purpose of learning sound-symbol correspondence is to enable the student to attack new words.

If it becomes apparent after one or two words that the student is not able to pronounce the words on the *Quick Survey Word List,* then it should be discontinued and the *El Paso Phonics Survey* should be administered.

The correct pronunciations of the words on the *Quick Survey Word List* are shown on p. 590. This key shows the correct pronunciation as well as the part of each word that should be stressed. It should be remembered, however, that accent rules or generalizations pertaining to the English language are not consistent; therefore, if the words are pronounced correctly except for the accent or stress shown on certain syllables, they should be considered as correct.

*Quick Survey Word List**

wratbeling	twayfrall
dawsnite	spreanplit
pramminciling	goanbate
whetsplitter	streegran

*Ekwall, Eldon E. *Elkwall Reading Inventory.* Boston, MA: Allyn and Bacon, 1979. Reproduced by permission of Allyn and Bacon, Inc.

gincule   glammertickly

cringale   grantellean

slatrungle   aipcid

Pronunciation of Quick Survey Words

răt´-bĕl-ĭng   twā´-fräl

däs´-nit   sprēn´-plĭt

prăm´-mĭn-cĭl-ĭng   gōn´-bāt

hwĕt´-splĭt-tər   strē´-grăn

jĭn´-kyo͞ol   glăm´-mər-tĭck-ly

crĭn´-gāl   grăn´-tĕl-lēn

slăt´-rŭn-gəl   āp´-sĭd

Pronunciation Key

l—litt<u>le</u>   ə—tamp<u>er</u>

ə—<u>a</u>bout   hw—<u>wh</u>at

ä—f<u>a</u>ther   kyo͞o—c<u>u</u>te

EL PASO PHONICS SURVEY: GENERAL DIRECTIONS†

1. Before beginning the test, make sure the student has instant recognition of the test words that appear in the box at the top of the first page of the survey. These words should be known instantly by the student. If they are not, re-schedule the test at a later date, after the words have been taught and the student has learned them.
2. Give the student the El Paso Phonics Survey stimulus sheet pages.
3. Point to the letter in the first column and have the student say the name of that letter (not the sound it represents). Then point to the word in the middle column and have the student pronounce it. Then point to the nonsense word in the third column and have the student pronounce it.
4. If the student can give the name of the letter, the word in the middle column, and the nonsense word in the third column, mark the answer sheet with a plus (+). If the student cannot pronounce the nonsense word after giving the name of the letter and the word in the middle column, mark the answer sheet with a minus (−), or you may wish to write the word phonetically as the student pronounced it.
5. If the student can tell you the name of the letter and the small word in the middle column but cannot pronounce the nonsense word, you may wish to have him or her give the letter sound in isolation. If he or she can give the sound in isolation, either the student is unable to "blend" or does not know the letter well enough to give its sound and blend it at the same time.
6. Whenever a superior letter appears on the answer sheet, you may wish to refer to the Special Directions sheet.

†Reproduced by permission of Allyn and Bacon, Inc.

7. To the right of each answer blank on the answer sheet, you will note a grade-level designation under the heading "PEK." This number represents the point at which most basal reading series would have already taught that sound. Therefore, at that point, you should expect it to be known. The designation 1.9 means the ninth month of the first year, and so forth.

8. When the student comes to two- or three-letter consonant digraphs or blends, as with *qu* in number 22, he or she is to say "*q-u*" as with the single letters. *Remember:* the student never gives letter sounds in isolation when engaged in actual reading.

9. When the student comes to the vowels (number 59), he or she is to say "short *a*," and so forth, and then the nonsense word in column two. If the student does not know that the breve (˘) over the vowels means short *a, e,* and so forth, then explain this. Do the same with the long vowels where the macron (—) appears.

10. All vowels and vowel combinations are put with only one or two of the first eight consonants. If any of these first eight consonants are not known, they should be taught before you attempt to test for vowel knowledge.

11. You will note that words appear to the right of some of the blanks on the answer sheet. These words illustrate the correct consonant or vowel sound that should be heard when the student responds.

12. Only phonic elements have been included that have a high enough utility to make them worthwhile learning. For example, the vowel pair *ui* appears very seldom, and when it does it may stand for the short *i* sound as in "build," the long *oo* sound as in "fruit," or the short *u* sound as in "luck." Therefore, there is really no reason to teach it as a sound. However, some letters, such as *oe*, may stand for several sounds but most often stand for one particular sound. In the case of *oe*, the long *o* sound should be used. In cases such as this, the most common sound is illustrated by a word to the right of the blank on the answer sheet. If the student gives another correct sound for the letter(s) then say, "Yes, but what is another way that we could say this nonsense word?" The student must then say it as illustrated in the small word to the right of the blank on the answer sheet. Otherwise, count the answer as wrong.

13. Stop the test after five consecutive misses or if the student appears frustrated from missing a number of items even though he or she has not missed five consecutive items.

EL PASO PHONICS SURVEY: SPECIAL DIRECTIONS*

[a]3. If the student uses another *s* sound as in "sugar" *(sh)* in saying the nonsense word "sup," ask, "What is another *s* sound?" The student must use the *s* as in "sack."

[b]15. If the student uses the soft *c* sound as in "cigar" in saying the nonsense word "cam," ask, "What is another *c* sound?" The student must use the hard *c* sound as in "coat."

[c]16. If the student uses the soft *g* sound as in "gentle" in saying the nonsense word "gup," ask, "What is another *g* sound?" The student must use the hard *g* sound as in "gate."

[d]17. Ask, "What is the *y* sound when it comes at the beginning of a word?"

[e]23. The student must use the *ks* sound of *x,* and the nonsense word "mox" must rhyme with "box."

*Reproduced by permission of Allyn and Bacon, Inc.

^f33. If the student use the *th* sound heard in "that," ask, "What is another *th* sound?" The student must use the *th* sound heard in "thing."

^g34. If the student uses the *hoo* sound of *wh* in saying the nonsense word "whup," ask, "What is another *wh* sound?" The student must use the *wh* sound as in "when."

^h69. The student may give either the *oo* sound heard in "moon" or the *oo* sound heard in "book." Be sure to note which one is used.

ⁱ70. If the same *oo* sound is given this time as was given for item 69, say, "Yes, that's right, but what is another way we could pronounce this nonsense word?" Whichever sound was *not* used in item 69 must be used here; otherwise, it is incorrect.

^j71. The student may give either the *ea* sound heard in "head" or the *ea* sound heard in "meat." Be sure to note which one is used.

^k72. If the same *ea* sound is given this time as was given for item 71, say "Yes, that's right, but what is another way we could pronounce this nonsense word?" Whichever sound was *not* used in item 71 must be used here; otherwise, it is incorrect.

^l78. The student may give either the *ow* sound heard in "cow" or the *ow* sound heard in "crow." Be sure to note which one is used.

^m79. If the same *ow* sound is given this time as was given for item 78, say, "Yes, that's right, but what is another way we could pronounce this nonsense word?" Whichever sound was *not* used in item 78 must be used here; otherwise, it is incorrect.

EL PASO PHONICS SURVEY: ANSWER SHEET*

Name _____ Sex _____ Date _____

School _____ Examiner _____

Mark answers as follows
Pass   +
Fail   − (or write word as pronounced)

PEK
Point at which phonic element is expected to be known

		Answers	PEK			Answers	PEK
INITIAL CONSONANT SOUNDS				12. j	jin	_____	1.9
1. p	pam	_____	1.9	13. k	kam	_____	1.9
2. n	nup	_____	1.9	14. l	lin	_____	1.9
^a3. s	sup	_____	1.9	^b15. c	cam	_____	1.9
4. t	tup	_____	1.9	^c16. g	gup	_____	1.9
5. r	rin	_____	1.9	^d17. y	yin	_____	1.9
6. m	min	_____	1.9	18. v	vam	_____	1.9
7. b	bup	_____	1.9	19. z	zin	_____	1.9
8. d	dup	_____	1.9	20. c	cin	_____	2.5 (sin)
9. w	wam	_____	1.9	21. g	gin	_____	1.9 (jin)
10. h	hup	_____	1.9	22. qu	quam	_____	1.9
11. f	fin	_____	1.9				

*Superior letters indicate notes listed in El Paso Phonics Survey: Special Directions. Material reproduced by permission of Allyn and Bacon, Inc.

	Answers	*PEK*

		Answers	*PEK*

ENDING CONSONANT X

ᵉ23. x   mox   _____ 1.9

INITIAL CONSONANT CLUSTERS

24. pl   plup   _____ 1.9
25. fr   frin   _____ 1.9
26. fl   flam   _____ 1.9
27. st   stup   _____ 1.9
28. bl   blin   _____ 1.9
29. tr   trin   _____ 1.9
30. gr   grup   _____ 1.9
31. br   brin   _____ 1.9
32. sh   shup   _____ 1.9
ᶠ33. th   thup   _____ 1.9   (thing)
ᵍ34. wh   whup   _____ 1.9   (when)
35. ch   cham   _____ 2.   (church)
36. dr   drup   _____ 2.5
37. pr   pram   _____ 2.5
38. sl   slup   _____ 2.5
39. cl   clin   _____ 2.5
40. gl   glam   _____ 2.5
41. sm   smin   _____ 2.5
42. sk   skam   _____ 2.5
43. cr   crin   _____ 2.5
44. tw   twam   _____ 2.5
45. sn   snup   _____ 2.5
46. sch   scham   _____ 2.5
47. sp   spam   _____ 2.9
48. sc   scup   _____ 2.9
49. str   stram   _____ 2.9
50. thr   thrup   _____ 2.9
51. shr   shrup   _____ 2.9
52. squ   squam   _____ 2.9
53. sw   swup   _____ 3.5
54. spr   spram   _____ 3.5
55. spl   splin   _____ 3.5
56. wr   wrin   _____ 4.5
57. dw   dwin   _____ 4.5
58. scr   scrup   _____ 4.5

VOWELS, VOWEL TEAMS, AND SPECIAL LETTER COMBINATIONS

59. ă   pam   _____ 1.9
60. ĭ   rit   _____ 1.9
61. ĕ   nep   _____ 1.9
62. ŏ   sot   _____ 1.9
63. ŭ   tum   _____ 1.9
64. ī   tipe   _____ 2.5
65. ē   rete   _____ 2.5
66. ā   sape   _____ 2.5
67. ū   pune   _____ 2.5
68. ō   sote   _____ 2.5
ʰ69. oo   oot   _____ 2.5   (moon or book)
ⁱ70. oo   oot   _____ 2.5   (moon or book)
ʲ71. ea   eap   _____ 2.5   (head or meat)
ᵏ72. ea   eam   _____ 2.5   (head or meat)
73. ai   ait   _____ 2.5   (ape)
74. ay   tay   _____ 2.5   (hay)
75. oe   poe   _____ 2.5   (hoe)
76. oa   oan   _____ 2.5   (soap)
77. ee   eem   _____ 2.5   (heed)
ˡ78. ow   owd   _____ 2.5   (cow or crow)
ᵐ79. ow   fow   _____ 2.5   (cow or crow)
80. or   orm   _____ 2.5   (corn)
81. ir   irt   _____ 2.5   (hurt)
82. ur   urd   _____ 2.5   (hurt)
83. aw   awp   _____ 2.9   (paw)
84. oi   doi   _____ 2.9   (boy)
85. ou   tou   _____ 2.9   (cow)
86. ar   arb   _____ 2.9   (harp)
87. oy   moy   _____ 2.9   (boy)
88. er   ert   _____ 2.9   (her)
89. ew   bew   _____ 2.9   (few)
90. au   dau   _____ 2.9   (paw)

EL PASO PHONICS SURVEY*

Test Words

in	up	am

#					#			
1.	p	am	pam		46.	sch	am	scham
2.	n	up	nup		47.	sp	am	spam
3.	s	up	sup		48.	sc	up	scup
4.	t	up	tup		49.	str	am	stram
5.	r	in	rin		50.	thr	up	thrup
6.	m	in	min		51.	shr	up	shrup
7.	b	up	bup		52.	squ	am	squam
8.	d	up	dup		53.	sw	up	swup
9.	w	am	wam		54.	spr	am	spram
10.	h	up	hup		55.	spl	in	splin
11.	f	in	fin		56.	wr	in	wrin
12.	j	in	jin		57.	dw	in	dwin
13.	k	am	kam		58.	scr	up	scrup
14.	l	in	lin		59.	ă	pam	
15.	c	am	cam		60.	ĭ	ri	
16.	g	up	gup		61.	ĕ	nep	
17.	y	in	yin		62.	ŏ	sot	
18.	v	am	vam		63.	ŭ	tum	
19.	z	in	zin		64.	ī	tipe	
20.	c	in	cin		65.	ē	rete	
21.	g	in	gin		66.	ā	sape	
22.	qu	am	quam		67.	ū	pune	
23.	m	ox	mox		68.	ō	sote	
24.	pl	up	plup		69.	oo	oot	
25.	fr	in	frin		70.	oo	oot	
26.	fl	am	flam		71.	ea	eap	
27.	st	up	stup		72.	ea	eam	
28.	bl	in	blin		73.	ai	ait	
29.	tr	in	trin		74.	ay	tay	
30.	gr	up	grup		75.	oe	poe	
31.	br	in	brin		76.	oa	oan	
32.	sh	up	shup		77.	ee	eem	
33.	th	up	thup		78.	ow	owd	
34.	wh	up	whup		79.	ow	fow	
35.	ch	am	cham		80.	or	orm	
36.	dr	up	drup		81.	ir	irt	
37.	pr	am	pram		82.	ur	urd	
38.	sl	up	slup		83.	aw	awp	
39.	cl	in	clin		84.	oi	doi	
40.	gl	am	glam		85.	ou	tou	
41.	sm	in	smin		86.	ar	arb	
42.	sk	am	skam		87.	oy	moy	
43.	cr	in	crin		88.	er	ert	
44.	tw	am	twam		89.	ew	bew	
45.	sn	up	snup		90.	au	dau	

*Reproduced by permission of Allyn and Bacon, Inc.

APPENDIX B
Reading and Reading-Related Tests and Inventories

We believe, as stated a number of times in this text, that a test, in order to be valid, should test in a situation where the student is doing the same thing in taking the test that he or she will be doing in using that skill in reading. All too often, it has been taken for granted that a test is valid simply because it has been published. This is, of course, often a false assumption. We believe that many of the most commonly used tests in the field of reading do not actually diagnose what they were actually designed to diagnose. In order to help the prospective user of some of the most commonly used tests evaluate their characteristics before purchasing them, we have designed Part I of this appendix somewhat differently from the traditional test appendix. In Part I, a number of the most commonly published reading diagnostic tests are presented so that the prospective user may see, not only what subtest each test contains but how each subtest is administered. Knowing this information should help the prospective user decide whether various subtests are likely to be valid measures of the skills they are designed to test.

We have also presented the same information for most of the commonly used informal reading inventories published since 1980. Following are a list of the tests and/or inventories listed in Part I:

Reading Diagnostic Tests

Botel Reading Inventory
Diagnostic Reading Scales
Durrell Analysis of Reading Difficulty
Gates-McKillop-Horowitz Reading Diagnostic Tests
Learning Styles Inventory
Prescriptive Reading Performance Test
Roswell-Chall Diagnostic Reading Test
Sipay Word Analysis Tests
Test of Early Language Development
Test of Language Development
Wide Range Achievement Tests
Woodcock Reading Mastery Tests

Informal Reading Inventories

Analytical Reading Inventory
Bader Reading and Language Inventory
Basic Reading Inventory
Burns/Roe-Informal Reading Inventory
Classroom Reading Inventory
Contemporary Classroom Reading Inventory
DeSanti Cloze Reading Inventory
Ekwall Reading Inventory

Part II of this appendix lists various information about other tests commonly used in reading diagnosis.

Part I: READING DIAGNOSTIC TESTS

BOTEL READING INVENTORY—FOLLETT PUBLISHING CO. ©1978

PURPOSE: To measure general comprehension and oral reading fluency for placement.

Age/Grade: First grade–high school

| Four tests |
| Time: Varies |

ITEMS TESTED	RATIONALE	METHOD: GROUP/INDIVIDUAL
I. Decoding Test	Assesses decoding competency.	Tests 1–3 group Tests 4–12 individual
1. Letter naming	Assesses letter knowledge.	Examiner produces letters. Student designates letter named, choosing from six listed.
2. Beginning consonant sound/letter awareness	Estimates knowledge of initial sounds.	Examiner pronounces two words. Student selects word with same beginning sound from group of four.
3. Rhyme sound/letter pattern awareness	Measures awareness of sound/spelling correspondence.	Examiner pronounces pair of rhyming words. Student underlines word from list of four which rhymes with those examiner reads.
4. 12 decoding syllable/spelling patterns	Measures student's ability to decode one-syllable words (#12 contains multiple syllable nonsense words).	Student reads ten words on each of nine graduated word lists. These tests are administered individually.
II. Spelling placement test	Estimates student's ability to spell words of high utility.	Examiner dictates words on five graded word lists and student writes them. There are twenty words on each list.
III. Word recognition test	Evaluates student's oral reading fluency.	Student reads words on graduated word lists aloud. The lists begin with pre-primer level and go through fourth grade.
IV. Word opposites test	Estimates student's comprehension.	Student selects word from list of three which is opposite in meaning from stimulus word. There are ten lists of ten words each ranging from first grade level through senior high school.

DIAGNOSTIC READING SCALES—MCGRAW-HILL ©1981

PURPOSE: To assess oral and silent reading abilities and phonics
knowledge.

Age/Grade: Grades One through Seven

Seventeen tests: three word recognition, two reading, and twelve word analysis and phonics tests. Time: Approximately one hour

ITEMS TESTED	RATIONALE	METHOD: INDIVIDUAL
1. Word recognition lists	Estimates student's instructional level.	Student reads aloud words from three graduated word lists. The word levels are preprimer to 5th grade.
2. Reading selections a. Oral reading	Identifies student's oral reading errors, silent reading level, classroom instructional level, and need for remediation.	Student reads graded selections aloud, and examiner asks 6–8 questions concerning each. Time required is recorded.
b. Silent reading	Identifies student's independent reading level.	Student reads silently passage one level beyond last oral reading. Examiner asks comprehension questions. Time recorded.
3. Word analysis and phonics tests	Supplements reading selections. Recommended for levels below Grade A.	Student pronounces one-syllable nonsense words, or examiner reads words to student (auditory tests).
a. Initial consonants	Assesses student's ability to pronounce initial consonants.	Student pronounces nine one-syllable real words and thirteen one-syllable nonsense words that begin with a consonant.
b. Final consonants	Assesses student's ability to pronounce final consonants.	Student reads fifteen one-syllable nonsense words aloud. Examiner checks only for final consonant sound.
c. Consonant digraphs	Assesses student's ability to pronounce digraphs.	Student reads aloud fifteen one-syllable nonsense words. Only digraphs are examined.
d. Consonant blends	Assesses student's ability to pronounce consonant blends.	Student pronounces twenty-four one-syllable nonsense words.
e. Initial consonant substitution	Examines student's ability to substitute one consonant for another.	Student reads word, then substitutes letter for the first letter in the word.

(continued)

ITEM TESTED	RATIONALE	METHOD: INDIVIDUAL
f. Initial consonants (auditory)	Assesses student's ability to hear and identify initial consonants.	Examiner reads words. Student responds by naming initial consonant of each.
g. Auditory discrimination	Determines student's ability to hear differences in pairs of words.	Examiner reads similar or same pairs of words aloud. Student responds "same" or "different."
h. Short and long vowel sounds	Examines student's knowledge of short and long vowel sounds.	Student reads 15 pairs of words containing short and long vowels.
i. Vowels with "R"	Assesses knowledge of "R"-controlled vowels.	Student pronounces ten nonsense words containing vowels and "R's."
j. Vowel dipthongs and digraphs	Assesses student's knowledge of vowel combinations.	Student pronounces thirty words and nonsense words (one-syllable).
k. Common syllables or phonograms	Examines knowledge of word elements.	Student pronounces thirty-four phonograms.
l. Blending	Assesses student's ability to blend word parts into words.	Student reads two or three word parts, then pronounces as one word. Ten items.

DURRELL ANALYSIS OF READING DIFFICULTY—THE PSYCHOLOGICAL CORPORATION
© 1980

PURPOSE: Observation and evaluation of reading abilities.

> Fifteen tests
> Time: Varies

Age/Grade: Pre-primer through 6th grade

ITEMS TESTED	RATIONALE	METHOD: INDIVIDUAL
1. Oral reading	Estimates reading level and analysis of problems	Student reads 3 paragraphs aloud. Length of time taken and errors recorded.
2. Silent reading	Compares silent reading with oral reading.	Student silently reads paragraphs progressively more difficult until time norms are not met or there are too many recall errors on subsequent questions.
3. Listening comprehension	Estimates student's reading ability through listening.	Teacher reads paragraphs aloud, then questions students on material.

ITEM TESTED	RATIONALE	METHOD: INDIVIDUAL
4. Word recognition/word analysis	Assesses child's knowledge of recognition of sight words and solving of unknowns.	Student reads aloud words on graduated word lists (3).
5. Listening vocabulary	Assesses listening vocabulary	Each child is tested on five word lists concerning accompanying pictures.
6. Sounds in isolation	Assesses mastery of sound/symbol relationships.	Student sounds out 16 letters, 12–16 blends and digraphs, 16–18 phonograms, 7–8 initial affixes, and 6–8 final affixes.
7. Spelling	Assesses phonetic spelling and visual recall.	Teacher reads words followed by sentences using the words on graded word lists. List 1 for grades 2 and 3, list 2 for grades 4, 5, and 6.
8. Phonic spelling of words	Assesses ability to spell words phonetically.	Teacher reads nonsense words aloud to student, who records them. Several answers may be correct. The test has 15 words for students in grades 4–6.
9. Visual memory of words-primary	Checks student's ability to remember visual word patterns.	Teacher says letter as child looks at word, student is to circle letter dictated. Exercises 4–15: Student selects word teacher reads from a list of 4 to 7 words, using tachistoscope. Grade 3 and below.
10. Visual memory of words-intermediate	Assesses ability of student to retain word pattern and record it.	Teacher shows word on tachistoscope for three seconds. Student records it. Fifteen words.
11. Identifying sounds in words	Assesses ability to discriminate among phonemes and identify graphemes.	Teacher says a word as child looks at a group of three words. Child is to circle the word containing the same initial and/or final sound as the work spoken by the teacher. Grades 3–6.
12. Prereading phonics abilities inventories (non-readers)	Estimates readiness or problems of children having difficulties.	
a. Syntax matching	Checks awareness of separate words in spoken sentences.	Teacher reads short sentences and asks child to point to specific word.

(continued)

ITEM TESTED	RATIONALE	METHOD: INDIVIDUAL
b. Identifying letter names in spoken words	Assesses knowledge of 22 direct phonics elements.	Child identifies the first letter of twenty-two words pronounced by teacher.
c. Identifying phonemes in spoken words	Checks awareness of nineteen phonemes.	Teacher reads sentence. Child is asked to give initial phoneme of last word.
d. Naming letters (lower case)	Assesses mastery at letter recognition.	Child looks at picture and word naming it. Teacher reads word and child names letters in it.
e. Writing letters	Assesses relevation of letter form.	Child looks at picture. Teacher identifies object and student writes the initial letter of the object's name adjacent to it.
f. Writing from copy	Checks attention to latter form.	Child looks at picture and writes word naming it. Words are from Naming Lower Case Letters list.
g. Naming letters (upper case)	Given to child who had difficulty in lower case recognition.	Teacher moves finger along non-ordered alphabet. Student names letters.
h. Identifying letters named	This test given only to children who cannot name letters.	Teacher names letter in a row of four and child points to the letter named.

GATES-MCKILLOP-HOROWITZ READING-DIAGNOSTIC TESTS—TEACHERS COLLEGE PRESS
© 1981

PURPOSE: Individual diagnosis of reading strengths and weaknesses.

Eight tests
Time: One hour

Age/Grade: First through sixth grade and older children with reading problems.

ITEMS TESTED	RATIONALE	METHOD: INDIVIDUAL
1. Oral reading	Assesses student's oral reading level.	Student reads orally seven paragraphs of increasing difficulty.
2. Reading sentences	Assesses student's oral reading ability.	Student reads orally four sentences.
3. Words: flash	Assesses sight word knowledge.	Student pronounces forty words on a tachistoscope, with thirty second time limit.

ITEM TESTED	RATIONALE	METHOD: INDIVIDUAL
4. Words: untimed	Assesses word analysis skills.	Student pronounces words on graduated list of eighty until ten are missed.
5. Knowledge of word parts: word attack		
a. Syllabication	Assesses student's ability to divide words into syllables.	Student pronounces seventeen nonsense words.
b. Reading words	Assesses student's word attack skills.	Student pronounces fifteen nonsense words.
c. Giving letter sounds	Measures knowledge of letter sounds.	Student looks at stimulus sheet and gives one or two sounds for twenty-six letters in isolation, and five phonemes.
d. Naming capital letters	Measures letter recognition.	Student looks at letter and names it.
f. Naming lower case letters	Measures lower case letter recognition.	Student looks at letter and names it.
6. Recognizing the visual forms of sounds	Assesses ability to hear sounds and transfer to letters.	Examiner pronounces one of three nonsense words as student looks at the words. Student points out the one the examiner reads.
7. Auditory Tests		
a. Blending	Measures student's ability to blend.	Teacher pronounces word parts. Student puts sounds together to form words.
b. Auditory discrimination	Measures student's ability to distinguish sounds.	Examiner pronounces pairs of words. Student responds "same" or "different."
8. Written expression		
a. Spelling	Assesses spelling competency.	Examiner dictates forty words from graduated word list until six consecutive errors are made. Student writes words.
b. Informal writing sample	Assesses composition skills.	Examiner gives student topic of interest. Student writes brief composition.

LEARNING STYLES INVENTORY—CREATIVE LEARNING PRESS © 1978

PURPOSE: To measure student attitude toward nine general modes of instruction.

| Sixty-five questions |
| Time: 30 minutes |

Age/Grade: Grades four through twelve

ITEMS TESTED	RATIONALE	METHOD: GROUP
1. Projects 2. Drill and recitation 3. Peer teaching 4. Discussion 5. Teaching games 6. Independent study 7. Programmed instruction 8. Lecture 9. Simulation	Assesses student's learning style preferences in order to obtain a more complete characterization of the learner, resulting in better response by the individual student to his/her learning environment.	Students are given a questionnaire containing sixty-five items concerning types of academic instruction. The test items concern their feelings about certain classroom activities. Answer choices range from "very pleasant" to "very unpleasant." The scoring is computerized.

PRESCRIPTIVE READING PERFORMANCE TEST—WESTERN PSYCHOLOGICAL SERVICE © 1978

PURPOSE: To evaluate reading and spelling patterns and identify performance errors.

| Sixteen tests |
| Time: Varies |

Age/Grade: Prereading/Adult

ITEMS TESTED	RATIONALE	METHOD: GROUP
I. List R (Readiness)	Assesses reading readiness.	
1. See and Say	Assesses alphabet knowledge.	Examiner points to lower case letter, child names letter.
2. Hear and Write	Assesses child's ability to hear and record letters.	Examiner dictates five letters and child writes them down.
3. Hear and Say	Assesses ability to blend.	Examiner pronounces word. Child gives rhyming nonsense word.
4. See and Say	Assesses ability to blend initial letter sounds.	Child looks at letter and phoneme and blends orally.
II. PP Through A (Preprimer through Adult)	Identifies reading difficulties.	Student pronounces words from graduate word lists, beginning two levels below his/her grade level. There are fifteen lists of twenty words each.

ROSWELL-CHALL DIAGNOSTIC READING TEST—ESSAY PRESS © 1978

PURPOSE: To evaluate word analysis and word recognition.

| Five tests |
| Time: Ten minutes |

Age/Grade: First to fourth grade and higher levels where decoding difficulties are suspected

ITEMS TESTED	RATIONALE	METHOD: INDIVIDUAL
Words	Assesses knowledge of words of high frequency.	Student pronounces thirty-five words of increasing difficulty until six consecutive errors are made.
1A. Single Consonant Sounds	Assesses student's knowledge of single consonant sounds.	Student gives one or two sounds for nineteen letters.
1B. Consonant Digraphs	Assesses knowledge of three digraph sounds.	Student pronounces three digraphs.
1C. Consonant Blends	Assesses child's ability to attach initial blends to phonograms.	Student pronounces five phonograms with sixteen initial consonant blends.
2A. Short Vowel Sounds	Assesses student's knowledge of short vowel sounds.	Student pronounces ten one-syllable words.
2B. Short and Long Vowel Sounds	Assesses student's ability to pronounce short and long vowel sounds in isolation.	Student pronounces five vowels giving both long and short sounds.
2C. Rule of Silent E	Assesses student's ability to pronounce one syllable words ending in E.	Student reads four pairs of one syllable words, the first word having short vowel sound and second ending in E with the long vowel sound.
3A. Vowel Digraphs	Assesses student's ability to pronounce eight vowel digraphs.	Student pronounces eight words containing vowel digraphs.
3B. Common Dipthongs and R-Controlled Vowels	Assesses student's ability to pronounce words containing digraphs and R-controlled vowels.	Student pronounces three one-syllable words containing R-controlled vowels and three words containing dipthongs.
4. Syllabication and Compound Words	Assesses student's ability to pronounce compound words.	Student pronounces eight multi-syllable words.
Extended Evaluation w. Naming Capital Letters	Assesses student's ability to name capital letters.	Student names fourteen capital letters.

(continued)

ITEM TESTED	RATIONALE	METHOD: INDIVIDUAL
x. Naming Lower Case Letters	Assesses student's ability to pronounce lower case letters.	Student pronounces nineteen lower case letters.
y. Encoding Single Consonants	Assesses student's ability to hear initial consonant sounds.	Examiner reads list of fourteen one-syllable words. Student writes the initial letter of each word.
z. Encoding Phonically Regular Words	Assesses student's ability to spell consonant-vowel-consonant words.	Examiner reads five one-syllable words and used each in a sentence. Student writes the word.

SWAT (SIPAY WORD ANALYSIS TESTS)—EDUCATORS PUBLISHING SERVICE © 1980

PURPOSE: Diagnosis of reading difficulties Age/Grade: Every age and level	Sixteen tests plus survey. Time: Varies, ten to twenty minutes per test.

ITEM TESTED	RATIONALE	METHOD: INDIVIDUAL
SURVEY TEST	To sample various skills measured by the SWAT.	Student reads words and nonsense words from stimulus cards. There are fifty-seven items tested.
1. Letter names A. Lower case B. Upper case	Assesses knowledge of alphabet.	Student pronounces letters one at a time from twenty-six stimulus cards.
2. Symbol-sound association: single letters	Measures ability to associate sound with letter.	Student looks at letter on stimulus card and gives sound or sounds.
3. Substitution: single letters	Measures ability to blend visually and assess phonic analysis.	Student reads nonsense words from stimulus cards.
4. Consonant-Vowel-Consonant Trigrams	Assesses ability to decode trigrams.	Student reads nonsense words from stimulus cards.
5. Initial consonant blends and digraphs	Measures ability to make symbol-sound associations for initial blends and digraphs.	Student pronounces nonsense words from stimulus cards. Examiner may select from sixty-two blends and digraphs.
6. Final consonant blends and digraphs	Assesses ability to make symbol-sound associations for final blends and digraphs.	Student pronounces nonsense words from fifty-seven stimulus cards.

ITEM TESTED	RATIONALE	METHOD: INDIVIDUAL
7. Vowel combinations	Measures ability to make symbol-sound associations for vowel combinations.	Student pronounces real and nonsense words from stimulus cards.
8. Open-syllable generalization	Measures student's ability to recognize long vowel sound at the end of an accented syllable.	Student pronounces first syllable of a multi-syllable nonsense word from stimulus card.
9. Final silent E generalization	Assesses student's knowledge of long vowel-consonant-silent E rule.	Student pronounces words and nonsense words from stimulus cards.
10. Vowel versatility	Measures student's ability to sound single vowel in various spelling patterns.	Student pronounces words or nonsense words from twenty stimulus cards.
11. Vowels + R	Assesses knowledge of vowel sounds followed by R.	Student pronounces fifteen nonsense words from stimulus cards.
12. Silent consonants	Assesses knowledge of symbol-sound associations for consonant clusters containing a silent consonant.	Student pronounces twenty-one words with consonant cluster endings from stimulus cards.
13. Vowel sounds of y	Assesses ability to make symbol-sound associations of vowel sounds of y.	Student pronounces words from stimulus cards with y in initial, medial, and final position.
14. Visual analysis	Measures ability to divide words into parts to decode unknown words.	Student pronounces multi-syllable words and words with affixes, and gives reasons for syllabication
15. Visual blending	Measures skill in blending elements into syllables or words.	Student pronounces twelve words which have been divided into parts.
16. Contractions	Measure skill in recognizing/decoding contractions.	Student pronounces eighteen contractions and tells from what words it is made.

TELD (THE TEST OF EARLY LANGUAGE DEVELOPMENT)—PRO-ED © 1981

PURPOSE: To evaluate a student's progress in the instructional program and identify children with social needs.	Thirty-eight items Time: 15 to 20 minutes

Age/Grade: Ages three to seven

ITEMS TESTED	RATIONALE	METHOD: INDIVIDUAL
1. Language abilities (form and content)	1. To identify children of poor language development. 2. To document progress. 3. To suggest instructional practice.	Child is shown thirty-eight picture cards and is asked appropriate questions concerning them. There may be different starting points according to age.

TOLD (THE TEST OF LANGUAGE DEVELOPMENT) PRO ED © 1977

PURPOSE: To diagnose specific strengths and weaknesses in language development.	Five tests, two supplemental tests Time: Varies

Age/Grade: Above 6.0 years of age

ITEMS TESTED	RATIONALE	METHOD: INDIVIDUAL
A. Semantics	To test aptitude of language with words.	
1. Picture vocabulary	Measures meanings associated with words.	Student points to correct picture of four items named by examiner.
2. Oral vocabulary	Measures ability to give oral definition.	Examiner pronounces a word. Student identifies with descriptors. Twenty words are given and responses are very specific.
B. Syntax	Measures knowledge of word order.	
1. Grammatic understanding	Assesses comprehension of syntactic forms.	Examiner shows three pictures and gives stimulus sentence. Child points to appropriate picture.
2. Sentence imitation	Measures ability to produce correct sentences.	Student repeats sentence verbatim after examiner reads it.

ITEM TESTED	RATIONALE	METHOD: INDIVIDUAL

SUPPLEMENTAL TESTS

ITEM TESTED	RATIONALE	METHOD: INDIVIDUAL
A. Phonology 1. Word discrimination	Assesses ability to recognize differences in sounds.	Examiner reads word pairs. Student responds "same" or "different."
2. Word articulation	Measures ability to produce important sounds of speech.	Examiner shows stimulus pictures and gives sentences. Student responds with correct word. Perfect articulation required.

WIDE RANGE ACHIEVEMENT TESTS (WRAT)—JASTAK ASSOCIATES © 1978

PURPOSE: To assess reading, spelling, and math difficulties.

> Four tests
> Time: Twenty to thirty minutes per test

Age/Grade: Level I Age 5.5 to 11.11
          Level II Age 12.0 to Adult

ITEMS TESTED	RATIONALE	METHOD: SMALL GROUP/INDIVIDUAL
Level I 1. Pre-Reading	Measures letter knowledge.	Student pronounces twenty-three letters from stimulus sheet, and names letters of his/her name.
2. Reading	Assesses word recognition.	Student pronounces words on graduated list of seventy-five words until twelve consecutive errors occur.
3. Spelling a. Copying Marks	Measures ability to differentiate angles, curves, and spatial orientation.	Student copies marks from stimulus.
b. Name	Measures child's ability to write his/her name.	Child writes his/her name within one minute.
c. Dictation	Assesses student's spelling knowledge.	Examiner pronounces forty-five words from graduated word list. Student writes words until ten consecutive ones are misspelled.

(continued)

ITEM TESTED	RATIONALE	METHOD: INDIVIDUAL
4. Arithmetic a. Written	Assesses knowledge of basic skills.	Student computes answers to forty-three problems within ten minutes. Can be done in group.
b. Oral	Assesses ability to count.	Student counts and reads numbers from stimulus and does these simple computations.
Level II	The same format as Level I but designed for ages twelve to adult.	

WOODCOCK READING MASTERY TESTS—AMERICAN GUIDANCE ASSOCIATION © 1975

PURPOSE: To measure precise reading achievement and predict success at different levels of difficulty.

Five tests
Time: Varies

Age/Grade: Kindergarten through Grade Twelve

ITEMS TESTED	RATIONALE	METHOD: INDIVIDUAL
1. Letter identification	Measures ability to name letters of the alphabet.	Student is shown 45 letters in various kinds of type. There are ten letters on each card. Child names them.
2. Word identification	Measures word knowledge but not comprehension.	Student reads 150 words in range of difficulty from pre-primer to twelfth grade.
3. Word attack	Measures ability to pronounce nonsense words through phonics and structural analysis.	Student sounds out 50 nonsense words of increasing difficulty.
4. Word comprehension	Measures knowledge of word meanings.	By analogy, student selects second word of a pair and gives it orally to the teacher.
5. Passage comprehension	Measures comprehension, word attack, and word-meaning skills.	Student reads silently a passage with a word missing (Modified Cloze Procedure). S/he gives examiner the appropriate word.

INFORMAL READING INVENTORIES

ANALYTICAL READING INVENTORY—CHARLES E. MERRILL © 1985

PURPOSE: To help analyze the reading performance of students in grades 2 through 9

TEST INCLUDES - Thirty graded reading selections
Seven graded word lists per form A, B, and C
Ten passages per grade level primer through 9 in forms A, B, and C

AGE/GRADE - 2 through 9
levels primer through grade 9

ITEMS TESTED	RATIONALE	METHOD/INDIVIDUAL
1. Graded Word List	Helps to facilitate the selection of the appropriate reading passage. Can also be used for limited diagnoses of reading difficulties.	Student is given one Graded Word List and pronounces each word on the list. Teacher records miscues. Continue until student misses 5 out of 20 words on the list. Teacher selects words at random and asks student to use the word in a sentence. Teacher records the sentences.
2. Graded Oral Passages	Helps identify word recognition skills. Find independent, instructional and frustration and listening capacity levels. Assess oral and/or silent reading performance and level of comprehension.	Teacher reads motivational statement. (May add more prereading, if needed). Student reads progressively difficult passages. At the end of each passage the student is asked to retell the story in his own words. Guidelines are given to check retelling of content. Depending on the thoroughness of the retelling, the student may be asked comprehension questions. There are 6–8 questions which cover main idea, facts, terminology, cause/effect inference, and drawing conclusions. Student continues reading until frustration level is reached.

****Alternate forms may be used if silent reading passages are also desired.

3. Listening Capacity	Determine the level of comprehension that a student has when a passage is read to him.	After the frustration level is reached in the oral reading passages, teacher reads the next passage aloud to the student. Student retells the story and/or answers comprehension questions. Stop when student's comprehension falls below 75%.

THE BADER READING AND LANGUAGE INVENTORY—MACMILLAN, INC. © 1983

PURPOSE: To determine appropriate placement of students in instructional materials, diagnose student's special needs and levels in reading.

TEST INCLUDES - Thirty-six Graded Reading Passages-preprimer through grade 12, three forms
Graded Word Lists
Phonics
Spelling
Cloze
Visual Discrimination
Auditory Discrimination
Unfinished Sentences
Arithmetic
Oral Language
Writing
TIME - Varies
AGE/GRADE - Preprimer through grade 12

ITEMS TESTED	RATIONALE	METHOD/INDIVIDUAL
1. Word Recognition Lists	A guide for a starting point to administer reading passages and measure word attack skills in isolation.	Student pronounces words on progressively more difficult list. Teacher may use diacritical marks on miscues for later analysis. Stop when student misses 3 words on the list to determine instructional level. Proceeding to frustration level is optional.
2. Supplementary Word Lists	Use to assess whether student recognizes frequently seen words. Titles are: instructions/directions, experience I, experience II, functional literacy.	See method for word lists above.
3. Graded Reading Passages a. Oral Reading	Used to obtain instructional *reading level;* accuracy and comprehension are used for this determination.	Student reads aloud progressively difficult passages. Teacher tapes reading and also marks miscues on another copy of the passage. For prepared reading, student may read the passage first silently before reading it aloud. For unprepared reading, student may not read the passage silently beforehand.
b. Silent Reading	Used to obtain instructional reading level during silent reading.	Begin with student's highest instructional level during oral reading. Student reads progressively harder passages. At the end of each passage, student retells what happened in the passage or answers comprehension questions.

ITEMS TESTED	RATIONALE	METHOD/INDIVIDUAL
c. Listening Comprehension	Used to obtain the level at which student can listen to a passage which the teacher reads aloud and have adequate comprehension	Begin with highest instructional level passage. Teacher reads passages aloud until student no longer attains the minimum level of comprehension when passage is retold or when comprehension questions are asked.
4. Phonics and Word Attack	Get data on student's knowledge of sound-symbol association, ability to blend sounds and use of structural analysis.	Select tests which are felt to be needed. Read directions aloud and mark responses as student responds.
5. Spelling	Diagnose information related to student's ability to spell	Start with list that is closest to student's reading level. Use separate sheet of paper for each test. Give instructions orally. Say word, use it in a sentence then say it again. Lists include: phonetic, nonphonetic, rules, commonly misspelled words
6. Cloze	Used to obtain information about student's ability to use previous experiences and knowledge about language structure	Cloze Passage for beginners-Student tries to read the story by supplying the missing words in the blanks. Semantic Cloze-Student tries to complete the sentences based on his or her background of experiences. Syntactic Cloze-Student must supply missing words that are semantically and syntactically correct. Grammatical Cloze-Student must supply word that is grammatically correct.
7. Visual Discrimination	Used to determine if student can tell the difference between different letters, words and phrases	Two tests-Directions are the same. Student is to circle the items in the box which are the same. PP-1 use test 1, grade 2 and up use test 2.
8. Auditory Discrimination	Used to determine if student can hear whether certain word pairs are alike or different	Teacher reads word pairs aloud and student tells whether the words are the same or different. Those students who know the names of letters can be tested for the ability to hear letter names in words in order to assess a basic area of phonemic discrimination.

(continued)

ITEMS TESTED	RATIONALE	METHOD/ INDIVIDUAL
9. Unfinished Sentences	Reveals student interests and concerns	Should be administered and responded to orally but it may be given in writing. Teacher reads aloud the beginning of a sentence and the student responds as quickly as possible to finish it.
10. Arithmetic	To obtain evidence of student's potential or of other underlying problems	Give the test sheet and some scrap paper to use and tell student to do as many problems as he can as quickly as possible. Allow 5 minutes.
11. Oral Language a. Describing b. Retelling c. Dictating d. Sentence Completion e. Repeating Sentences	Assess student's Oral Language Development	Show student a picture appropriate to his age and ask student to tell as much as possible about it. Teacher tapes for later analysis. Teacher reads a 60–100 word passage of suitable maturity level, then asks student to retell the story. Have student make up a story and dictate it to examiner. Analyze and record. See directions for Cloze Test. Read sentence; student repeats it, then teacher points out individual words to repeat.
12. Writing a. Handwriting b. Near and Far Point Copying c. Writing from Dictation d. Expressing Ideas in Writing	Obtain data about student's abilities in writing	Obtain a sample of student's best effort at handwriting or have student write what teacher reads aloud in his best handwriting. Students copy different passages of the same length and difficulty from 10–12 feet away and on the desk in front of the student. Comparisons of both passages may reveal problems. Examiner dictates a passage and student writes it down. Sample of student's best may be found to use or give the student a picture and ask him to write a story about it. Give all the time needed but note how long it takes to produce the story.

BASIC READING INVENTORY-THIRD EDITION—KENDALL/HUNT © 1985

PURPOSE: To assess student's independent, instructional, frustration, and listening levels and to evaluate student's strengths and weaknesses in word attack skills and comprehension.

TEST INCLUDES: Thirty graded word lists pp-grade 8, forms A, B and C

Thirty reading passages pp-grade 8, forms, A, B and C

TIME: Varies

ITEMS TESTED	RATIONALE	METHOD/INDIVIDUAL
1. Graded Word Lists	Estimate starting level at which student begins graded passages	Student pronounces words on lists from successive grade levels; Stop when student misses 7–6 words on a list; Begin at highest level where student pronounces 19–20 words.
2. Graded Passages a. Oral Reading Word analysis skills Comprehension	Estimate student's independent, instructional, frustration and listening capacity levels; diagnose student's strengths and weaknesses in word attack skills and comprehension.	Student reads passage aloud of increased difficulty. After each passage is read, the teacher asks comprehension questions. There are 10 questions which cover main idea, fact, inference, vocabulary and evaluation. Teacher marks all miscues for later analysis and diagnoses. Student continues reading passages until frustration level is reached.
b. Silent Reading (optional) Suggested strongly for students above primary level	Assess student's silent reading ability, gain information about student's reading level, diagnose strengths/weaknesses in comprehension	Use graded passages from a form not used for oral reading. Begin with passage at student's highest independent level. After each passage teacher asks comprehension questions. Continue until student is unable to answer half of the comprehension questions.
c. Listening Capacity	Assess student's listening comprehension ability.	Use graded passage that is one level beyond student's frustration level. Teacher reads passage aloud then asks comprehension questions. Stop when student answers less than 75% of the comprehension questions.

BURNS/ROE INFORMAL READING INVENTORY—HOUGHTON MIFFLIN CO. © 1985

PURPOSE: To measure comprehension, oral reading fluency for placement; diagnose individual strengths and weaknesses.

TEST INCLUDES: Two forms of Graded Word List-pp through 12

Four forms of Graded Passages-pp through 12

TIME: Varies

AGE/GRADE: First through Grade Twelve

ITEMS TESTED	RATIONALE	METHOD/INDIVIDUAL
1. Graded word lists-word analysis	Estimates, independent, instructional and frustration reading levels. Measures knowledge of sight vocabulary. Miscues can be analyzed in lieu of administering the complete IRI.	Words may be put on 3 × 5 cards or the complete list can be given to the student. Student pronounces each word aloud. Miscues are marked on scoring sheet as they occur. Student reads progressively more difficult lists until frustration is reached.
2. Graded Reading Passages a. Oral Reading	Identifies oral reading errors and student's different reading levels.	Each passage begins with a motivating sentence read aloud by the teacher. Student reads aloud progressively more difficult passages until the frustration reading level is reached. Oral reading errors are coded by the teacher, using Miscue Analysis form. After each passage is read, the student is asked comprehension questions based upon traditional comprehension skills (main idea, detail, sequence, cause/effect, inference).
b. Silent Reading	Identifies student independent, instructional and frustration levels during silent reading.	Student reads a passage silently and at the same level as the oral reading passage. Student answers comprehension questions after each passage. Stop when student reaches frustration level.
c. Capacity or Listening Level	Estimates level at which student can hear a passage and comprehend at least 75% of the material.	Teacher chooses the first successive passage after the reader has achieved the frustration level and continues until the student cannot answer at least 75% of the questions asked.

CLASSROOM READING INVENTORY—WILLIAM C. BROWN © 1986

PURPOSE: Attempts to identify student's specific word recognition and comprehension skills. Used to determine student's independent, instructional, frustration, and listening capacity levels.

TEST INCLUDES:
Four forms of Graded Oral Passages
A and B for Primary
C for Junior High/Middle School
D for High School to adult
Graded word lists for each form and grade level
Spelling Survey

TIME:
Administration-Twelve minutes or less

AGE/GRADE
Preprimer through high school/adult

ITEMS TESTED	RATIONALE	METHOD/INDIVIDUAL
1. Graded Word Lists, Form A and B	Identifies word recognition errors and estimates approximate starting level to begin reading graded oral paragraphs	Present graded word lists to students. Reader pronounces each word. Teacher records all responses so that they can be analyzed later.
2. Part II Graded Paragraphs Form A and B	Estimate student's independent and instructional reading levels. Identify word recognition errors and estimate extent of comprehension. Note: Each paragraph has an illustration and a motivational statement which the teacher reads to the student.	Student reads paragraphs orally at progressively higher levels. When the student has finished reading a passage, five comprehension questions are asked (2-factual, 2-vocabulary and 1-inference) Passages cover fiction as well as different content areas.

Stop when student reaches frustration in word recognition or comprehension.

***Although silent reading passages are not given, form A and B may be used interchangeably so that form A can be read orally and form B could be read silently. There is no provision for this with form C and D since form C is geared toward junior high and middle school and form D is used for high school to adult

3. Part 3 Spelling Survey Form A and B	Obtain additional information on student's ability to integrate and express letter-form, letter-sound relationships	After completing parts 1 and 2, begin at level 1. Teacher pronounces word, uses it in a sentence, then says the word again. The student is then asked to spell the word. Stop when 5 out of 10 words are missed on the list. *Doesn't state whether student spells the words out loud or on paper.

(continued)

ITEMS TESTED	RATIONALE	METHOD/ INDIVIDUAL
4. Part 1 Graded Word Lists Form C and D	Identify specific word recognition errors and estimate starting point at which mature student should begin reading Graded Oral Paragraphs	Student is given list and told to pronounce each word. Stop when student misses 5 out of 20 words. Record all responses for later analysis.
5. Part 2 Graded Oral Paragraphs Form C and D Independent level Instructional level Frustration level Listening capacity	Estimate student's independent and instructional level. Identify reading and comprehension levels. *These passages do not include an illustration; all passages are nonfiction.	See Graded Oral Paragraph Method Form A and B.

***This inventory is designed to be administered only to students who may need additional help in reading.

THE CONTEMPORARY CLASSROOM READING INVENTORY—GORSUCH SCARISBRICK © 1980

PURPOSE: Determine students' reading levels in fiction, social studies and science; evaluate word attack strategies and comprehension and student strengths and weaknesses.

TEST INCLUDES: Graded Word Lists–fiction, social studies and science–grades primer through seven;

Selections for Oral Reading–fiction, social studies and science–grades primer through seven;

Cloze Selections–fiction, social studies and science–grades 4 through 9.

TIME: Varies for administration @ 15 minutes per area

AGE/GRADE: primer through grade nine
           grades 2–9

ITEMS TESTED	RATIONALE	METHOD/INDIVIDUAL
1. Graded Word Lists- fiction, social studies and science Word Recognition Abilities	Estimate approximate grade level where students should begin reading the selection and helps identify specific word recognition problems	Teacher presents list (fiction, social studies or science). Student pronounces each word. Stop when student misses 5–6 words on the list. Start reading at highest instructional level. *Instructions do not state whether all of the word lists for each content area are given at once or just prior to reading that particular content area selection.
2. Selections for Oral Reading fiction, social studies and science	Each passage begins with a motivational statement read aloud by the teacher; used to determine student's individual reading levels, determine word attack and comprehension abilities. Passage at	Grades 1–3, administer only one section of test at a sitting (fiction, social studies or science). Students read progressively more difficult passages until frustration is reached. After the student reads each passage the teacher

ITEMS TESTED	RATIONALE	METHOD/ INDIVIDUAL
	primer-grade 2 levels include an illustration.	asks 5 comprehension questions (main idea, supporting details, inference sequence, vocabulary, reasoning/conclusion and evaluation)
c. Supplementary Cloze Procedure Placement in Reading Materials	Assess the match between a grade level selection and a student's reading ability	Students read a passage and insert words in the cloze blanks which make sense within the passage. Cloze Passages may be given in fiction, social studies or science. In grades 4–5 administer only one passage per day; In grades 6–9 administer two selections per day.

DE SANTI CLOZE READING INVENTORY—ALLYN AND BACON, INC. © 1986

PURPOSE: To identify individual's reading abilities, attendant strengths and weaknesses, and the difficulty levels most appropriate for instructional purposes.

TEST INCLUDES: Thirty Cloze Passages
                Coding Form and Answer Keys
                28 Word Lists
                Summary Sheets

TIME: Administration: 30–45 minutes
     Scoring   8–12 minutes per individual

AGE/GRADE: Grades 3 through 12*

ITEMS TESTED	RATIONALE	METHOD: GROUP/IND.* *ADMINISTRATOR'S CHOICE
1. Graded word list-word recognition and analysis	Assesses the reader's vocabulary, and word analysis skills; estimates independent, instructional and frustration reading levels.	Words are flashed at one-second intervals to reader; responses are recorded on scoring sheet; student answers orally. Stop when student reaches frustration level.
2. Cloze passages for silent reading	Measures reader's comprehension, logical language production and ability to deal with grammatical structure of printed language	Student reads through entire selected Cloze passage first, then fills in each blank which is most appropriate. Responses are entered on the coding form provided. Only one Cloze Passage should be given per session. Passages are provided for pretest, posttest and alternate forms. No test is provided to test oral reading.

*Graded word lists are included from PP-Grade 12

EKWALL READING INVENTORY—ALLYN & BACON © 1986

PURPOSE: Used to measure student's oral, silent, and listening comprehension levels and to diagnose student's strengths and weaknesses in reading. It also assesses student knowledge of phonics, letters, basic sight words, vowel rules, syllable principles, and contractions.

TEST INCLUDES:
Graded Word List—PP-9
Student Reading Passages—Forms, A, B, C, and D—PP-9
Quick Survey Word List
El Paso Phonics Survey
Letter Knowledge Test
Ekwall Basic Sight Word Test
Materials for Testing Knowledge of Vowel Rules and Syllable Principles
Knowledge of Contractions Test
Diagnostic Flow Chart

TIME—Administration time for the informal reading section varies by grade level, however, overall time usually varies from 13–34 minutes. The time for the El Paso Phonics Survey varies from 7–25 minutes.

AGE/GRADE—Preprimer through grade nine

ITEMS TESTED	RATIONALE	METHOD/INDIVIDUAL
1. Graded word list	Used to determine the level to begin the student reading passages and to determine the student's ability to pronounce words in isolation. This, of course, gives some measure of the student's word attack skills.	Begin at approximately 2 years below present grade placement. Student pronounces words on lists at progressively higher levels. Teacher marks wrong miscues with ($-$) and correct responses with ($+$). Continue until student misses three or more words on any one list.
2. Student reading passages	Used to determine student's oral and silent reading levels-independent, instructional, frustration, and listen-comprehension.	Start at level which corresponds to independent level on the graded word list. Student first reads oral passages (A for oral and B for silent). (If using alternate forms use C for oral and D for silent.) As student reads orally, examiner codes miscues on teacher answer sheet. Stop when student reaches frustration level on both oral and silent reading based on either word recognition errors or comprehension for the oral passages and on comprehension for the silent passages.
Listening Comprehension	Enables the tester to quickly determine whether there is a discrepancy between the level at which a student can read and comprehend and between what he or she can listen and comprehend.	Start at passage which is at the student's highest instructional level. Read passage aloud to student and ask comprehension questions. Stop when student is no longer able to answer at least 70–75 percent of the questions correctly.

ITEMS TESTED	RATIONALE	METHOD: INDIVIDUAL
3. El Paso Phonics Survey	Assesses student's knowledge of sound symbol correspondence	Each initial consonant and consonant cluster is tested using the consonant or consonant cluster with ence. Any of the following endings: "in," "am," "up." Student is not tested unless he or she knows these words before beginning the test. All vowels, vowel pairs, and special letter combinations are tested using a nonsense word made from one of the first eight consonants tested. Unless a student gets these correct he or she is not tested on any of the vowels, vowel pairs, or special letter combinations.
4. Letter Knowledge	Assesses student's recognition of the upper and lower case letters of the alphabet	Student is asked to name letters presented in random order. If student cannot do this he or she is asked to proceed to progressively easier tasks in assessing letter knowledge.
5. Basic Sight Word Knowledge	To assess student's instant recognition of words on the *Ekwall Basic Sight Word List*	Student is presented with a stimulus sheet with sight words in random order and asked to pronounce each of them. If the student does not respond within a very short time the answer is counted as incorrect even if he or she eventually is able to pronounce it.
6. Knowledge of Syllable Principles and Vowel rules	To assess student's knowledge of vowel rules, syllable principles, and accent generalizations	For syllable principles student is shown cards with nonsense words on them. Student is to tell the examiner where to divide words if they were real words. For Vowel Rules student is shown nonsense words to pronounce.
7. Knowledge of contractions	To assess student's knowledge of contractions	Student is given stimulus sheet and asked to pronounce each contraction and tell what two words it stands for.
8. Diagnostic Flow Chart	To aid examiner in the most effective and efficient diagnosis of reading disability.	The Flow Chart takes the examiner through a step-by-step procedure in an attempt to avoid giving diagnostic instruments that are needed.

Part II: OTHER TESTS COMMONLY USED IN READING DIAGNOSIS

Auditory Discrimination Tests

Name and date of test	Vocabulary	Comprehension	Word attack	Speed	Listening	Other	Time for administration	Number of forms	Grade level	Group (G) or Individual (I)	Publisher
Goldman-Fristoe-Woodcock Test of Auditory Discrimination (no date given)					X	Measures speech-sound discrimination	10–15 min.	1	Ages 4 and over	I	American Guidance Service
Wepman Auditory Discrimination Test (1973)					X	Recognize the sound differences between minimal pairs	15–20 min.	2	K–3	I	Language Research Associates

Skills or Areas Measured

Basic Sight Word Inventories

Name and date of test	Skills or Areas Measured						Time for administration	Number of forms	Grade level	Group (G) or individual (I)	Publisher
	Vocabulary	Comprehension	Word attack	Speed	Listening	Other					
Dolch Basic Sight Word Test (1942)						Tests recognition of 220 high-utility words	Varies	1	All levels	G	Garrard Press
The Group Instant Words Recognition Test (no date given)						Sight recognition of 600 most common words	Varies	2	All levels	G&I	Jamestown Publishers
Harris-Jacobson List (1985)						Tests recognition of 335 high-utility words	Varies	1	All levels	I	Harris, A. J., Sipay, E. R. (1985). *How to increase reading ability.* NY: Longman. pp. 376–377.
The Instant Words Criterion Test (1981)						Sight recognition of 300 most common words	Varies	1	All levels	I	Jamestown Publishers
Johnson Basic Sight Vocabulary Test (1973)						Tests recognition of 300 high-utility words	Varies	2	1–3	I	Personal (University of Wisconsin, Madison, Wisconsin)

Content-Area Inventories

| Name and date of test | Skills or Areas Measured | | | | | | Time for administration | Number of forms | Grade level | Group (G) or individual (I) | Publisher |
	Vocabulary	Comprehension	Word attack	Speed	Listening	Other					
Content Inventories: English, Social Studies, Science (1979)	X	X				Cloze tests, study skills	Varies	1	4–12; English, 7–12	G	Kendall/Hunt

Decoding Inventories

| Name and date of test | Skills or Areas Measured | | | | | | Time for administration | Number of forms | Grade level | Group (G) or individual (I) | Publisher |
	Vocabulary	Comprehension	Word attack	Speed	Listening	Other					
Decoding Inventory, 3 levels (1979)			X			Auditory and visual discrimination, context clues	Varies	1	Pre-primer-4 and above	I	Kendall/Hunt

Intelligence Tests

Skills or Areas Measured

Name and date of test	Vocabulary	Comprehension	Word attack	Speed	Listening	Other	Time for administration	Number of forms	Grade level	Group (G) or individual (I)	Publisher
McCarthy Scales of Children's Abilities (1972)						Assess motor and intellectual development	45 min. for age 5 and under; 1 hour for older children	1	Ages 2½–8½	I	Psychological Corporation
Peabody Picture Vocabulary Test-Revised (PPVT-R) (1981)						For testing verbal intelligence through pictures	15 min. or less	1	Ages 2½–40	I	American Guidance Service
Slosson Intelligence Test (1981)						A measure of intelligence	10-30 min.	1	Age 1-adult	I	Slosson Educational Publications

Intelligence Tests (continued)

Name and date of test		Skills or Areas Measured											
	Vocabulary	Comprehension	Word attack	Speed	Listening	Other	Time for administration	Number of forms	Grade level	Group (G) or individual (I)	Publisher
Stanford-Binet Intelligence Scale, Form LM (1972 Norms)	X	X				A measure of overall intelligence	45–90 min.	1	2–12 and sometimes older	I	Houghton Mifflin
Wechsler Adult Intelligence Scale—Revised (WAIS-R) (1980)	X	X				A measure of intelligence using subtests	1 hr.	1	Ages 16–74	I	Psychological Corporation
Wechsler Intelligence Scale for Children—Revised (WISC-R) (1974)	X	X				A measure of intelligence using subtests	1 hr.	1	Ages 6.0–16.11	I	Psychological Corporation
Wechsler Preschool and Primary Scale of Intelligence (WPPSI) (1967)	X	X				A measure of intelligence using subtests	50–70 min.	1	Ages 4–6½	I	Psychological Corporation

Language Dominance and/or Assessment Tests

Name and date of test	Skills or Areas Measured					Other	Time for administration	Number of forms	Grade level	Group (G) or individual (I)	Publisher
	Vocabulary	Comprehension	Word attack	Speed	Listening						
Ambiguous Word Language Dominance Test (1978)						Spanish/English language dominance	30 min.	1	Age 10 and above	I	Publishers Test Service, Mc-Graw-Hill
Flexibility Language Dominance Test (1978)						Spanish/English language dominance	30 min.	1	Age 10 and above	G	Publishers Test Service, Mc-Graw-Hill
Houston Test for Language Development (1978)	X	X	X		X	Also nonverbal communication	20–40 min. depending on age	2	Infancy–6 yrs.	I	Stoelting
Language Assessment Battery (LAB) (1977) English Edition Spanish Edition					X	Subtests in reading, writing, speaking	41 min. 41 min.	1 1	K-12 K-12	K-2, I; 3-12, G&I	Riverside Publishing

625

Readiness Tests (including Bilingual)

Name and date of test	Skills or Areas Measured						Time for administration	Number of forms	Grade level	Group (G) or individual (I)	Publisher
	Vocabulary	Comprehension	Word attack	Speed	Listening	Other					
Comprehensive Tests of Basic Skills, Readiness Test (1977)					X	Letter names, letter forms, phonics	2 hrs. 39 min.	1	K-1.3	G	CTB/McGraw-Hill
Cooperative Preschool Inventory						Knowledge of self, ability to follow directions, verbal expression, number concepts					Addison-Wesley
English Edition (1970)							Approx. 15 min.	1	Preschool	I	
Spanish Edition (1974)							Approx. 30 min.	1	Preschool	I	
Metropolitan Readiness Tests, 2 levels (1976)		X			X	Auditory and visual discrimination, phonics, math	Level 1, 90 min.; Level 2, 3 hrs.	2	K-1	G	Psychological Corporation

Reading Tests

Skills or Areas Measured

Name and date of test	Vocabulary	Comprehension	Word attack	Speed	Listening	Other	Time for administration	Number of forms	Grade level	Group (G) or individual (I)	Publisher
Assessment of Reading Growth (1981) Level 9 Level 13 Level 17		X X X					50 min. 50 min. 42 min.	1 1 1	2-4 6-8 10-12	G G G	Jamestown Publishers
California Achievement Tests, C & D (Reading) (1977)	X	X					45–60 min.	2	K-12	G	CTB/McGraw-Hill
Comprehensive Tests of Basic Skills, Español (Reading) (1978)	X	X				Based on CTBS S & T	45–60 min.	1	K-8	G	CTB/McGraw-Hill
Comprehensive Tests of Basic Skills, S & T (Reading) (1973)	X	X					45–60 min.	2	K-12	G	CTB/McGraw-Hill

627

Reading Tests (continued)

Name and date of test	Skills or Areas Measured						Time for administration	Number of forms	Grade level	Group (G) or individual (I)	Publisher
	Vocabulary	Comprehension	Word attack	Speed	Listening	Other					
Comprehensive Tests of Basic Skills, U & V (Reading) (1981)	X	X	X				45–70 min.	2	K-12	G	CTB/McGraw-Hill
Doren Diagnostic Reading Test of Word Recognition Skills (1973)			X			Spelling and sight words	1–3 hrs.	1	1-6	G	American Guidance Service
Gates-MacGinitie Reading Tests (1978) Basic R	X	X					65 min.	2	1.0-1.9	G	Riverside Publishing
A	X	X							1.5-1.9	G	
B	X	X							2	G	
C	X	X							3	G	
D	X	X							4-6	G	
E	X	X							7-9	G	
F	X	X							10-12	G	
Iowa Silent Reading Tests, 3 levels (1973)	X	X		X		Study skills	56 min.-1½ hrs. depending on level	2	6-12, college	G	Psychological Corporation

					Time	Forms	Grades		Publisher
Iowa Tests of Basic Skills (1982)									Riverside Publishing
Early Primary Battery	X		X	Also subtests in language, mathematics	2 hrs.-2 hrs. 40 min.	1	K-1.9	G	
Primary Battery	X		X	Same as above plus work-study skills	3 hrs. 55 min.	1	1.7-3.5	G	
Multilevel Battery	X	X		Language, math, work-study skills	4 hrs. 4 min.	2	3-8	G	
Iowa Tests of Educational Development (1978)	X	X		Language arts and mathematics	2¼ hrs.	2	9-12	G	SRA
McCarthy Individualized Diagnostic Reading Inventory (1976)	X	X		Study skills	Part 1, 35 min.-1 hr.; Part 2, 34 min.	1	2-12	I	Stoelting
Metropolitan Achievement Tests (Reading) (1978)		X			30-50 min. depending on level	2	K-12	G	Psychological Corporation

(continued)

Name and date of test	Vocabulary	Comprehension	Word attack	Speed	Listening	Other	Time for administration	Number of forms	Grade level	Group (G) or individual (I)	Publisher
Nelson-Denny Reading Test (1981)	X	X		X			35 min.	2	9-12, college, adult	G	Riverside Publishing
Nelson Reading Skills Test (1977)	X	X				Word meaning	33 min.	2	3-9	G	Houghton Mifflin
Oral Reading Criterion Test (no date given)		X				To determine independent and instructional levels	Varies	1	1-7	I	Jamestown Publishers
Peabody Individual Achievement Test (no date given)	X	X				Spelling, math, general information	30-40 min.	1	K-adult	I	American Guidance Service
Performance Assessment in Reading (PAIR) (1978)	X	X				Study skills	Varies	1	Jr. high	G	CTB/McGraw-Hill
Pressey Diagnostic Reading Tests (no date given)	X	X		X			25 min. per section (3)	2	3-9	G	Bobbs-Merrill
School and College Ability Tests (SCAT), Series III (1979)	X	X					20 min.	2	3.5-12.9	G	Addison-Wesley

						Administration time	Forms/Levels	Grade/age range	Type	Publisher
Sequential Tests of Educational Progress (STEP III) Primary Levels A-D (1974)		X		X		Untimed: 30–40 min. (approx.)	2	Pre-pri-mary–3.5	G	Addison-Wesley
Intermediate and Advanced E-J (1979)	X	X				40 min.	2	3.5–12.9	G	
Skills Monitoring System—Reading (1977)		X				Untimed	1	3–5	I	Psychological Corporation
Slosson Oral Reading Test (1977)			X			3 min.	1	Preschool–high school	I	Slosson Educational Publications
SRA Achievement Series (1978) Primary Levels (Levels A-D)	X	X		X	Reading, math, language arts	2½–3 hrs. depending on level	2	K–3	G	SRA
Upper Levels (3rd edition) (Levels E-H)	X	X			Auditory Discrimination	3 hrs.	2	4–12	G	

(continued)

Name and date of test	Vocabulary	Comprehension	Word attack	Speed	Listening	Other	Time for administration	Number of forms	Grade level	Group (G) or individual (I)	Publisher
						Skills or Areas Measured					
Stanford Achievement Test (1973)	X	X	X		X	Spelling	75–150 min. depending on level	2	1.5–9.9	G	Psychological Corporation
Stanford Diagnostic Reading Test (1978)	X	X	X	X		Auditory discrimination	96–145 min. depending on level	2	1.6–13	G	Harcourt Brace Jovanovich
Stanford Test of Academic Skills (TASK) (1973)		X					40 min.	2	8–13	G	Psychological Corporation
Tests of Achievement and Proficiency (1982)		X				Subtests in study skills and other subject areas	4 hrs.	1	9–12	G	Riverside Publishing
Tests of Adult Basic Education, 3 levels of difficulty (1978)	X	X				Also language, math for vocational-bound persons	1½–2½ hrs. depending on level	1	Adult	G	CTB/McGraw-Hill
Test of Reading Comprehension (1978)	X	X					Varies	1	2–12	G	Pro-Ed
The 3-R's Test (1982)						Subtests in reading, math, language	130 min.	2	K–12	G	Riverside Publishing

Some Recommended Books for Use in Teaching Remedial Reading

Publisher/Title	Description	Reading Grade Level	Interest Grade Level
Bantam Books School and College Dept. 666 Fifth Ave. New York, NY 10103			
Be an Interplanetary Spy	Twelve full-length fiction stories challenge the reader like a video game. In each book the reader is the interplanetary spy sent to different galaxies on important missions.	3	4 and up
Choose Your Own Adventure Series	Reluctant readers identify with exciting plot options, with hundreds of possible outcomes. Fifty-three books are both fantasy adventures and entertaining games.	4	4–6
Time Machine	Eight new books of historically accurate time-travel adventure. The reader travels to another time and place to search for a famous person or event, plots choices in this combination game and novel.	4	5 and up
Bowmar/Nobel Publishers P.O. Box 25308 1901 N. Walnut Oklahoma City, OK 73125			
Starting Line	Multimedia reading series provides beginning readers with opportunities for recreational reading. The program contains four reading programs: Cats, Racing, Wheels, and Kickoff. Filmstrip, cassettes, and duplicating masters are available.	pp–2	4–6
The Monster Series	A lovable monster and his friends and adventures in series 1 and 2. Carefully controlled vocabulary in the language of the child comprise set (Ten books each of twelve titles). Filmstrips, records, and cassettes.		Series 1: K–1 Series 2: 2–4

(continued)

Publisher/Title	Description	Reading Grade Level	Interest Grade Level
Gold Dust Books	Success-oriented program for the less-able intermediate student consists of mystery, adventure, humor, science fiction, and sports selections. Two libraries contain three copies of six different titles.	2.0–2.9	4–6
Reading Incentive Program	Classroom reading kits combine high interest, low readability with informal language to hold the older reader's attention. Examples of the twenty titles include Motorcycles, Horses, Dune Buggies, Slot Car Racing.	3–5	4–12
Children's Press 1224 W. Van Buren St. Chicago, IL 60607			
The Mania Books	Thirteen books with a controlled first-grade vocabulary. High-interest format covering diverse topics: cowboys, dogs, hot rods, volcanos.	1	K–5
Ready, Get Set, Go	Eighteen books at three levels; stories contain color photographs with an easy-to-read format.		
Ready Books		1.1–1.5	1–6
Get Set Books		1.9–2.5	1–6
Go Books		2.5–3.0	1–6
New True Books	Ten groups (147 titles) of easy-to-understand content-area readers. Full color photographs and printed in large type. Science, social studies, math, and language arts.	2.0–3.4	K–4
Junior Detective Books	Two young sleuths ply their trade through the pages of these colorful cartoonlike books.	2–6	4–6
Doomsday Journals	Six exciting novels about out-of-control events. *Children's Press publishes an Early Childhood Catalog containing numerous books in diverse subject areas individually listed by grade level and interest level. Most are appropriate for the less-able reader.	2.8–4.4	6–12
The Continental Press 520 E. Bainbridge St. Elizabethtown, PA 17022			
Spiral Kits	These kits improve older students' reading ability. Three copies of twelve titles in	2.0–4.5	7–12

Publisher/Title	Description	Reading Grade Level	Interest Grade Level
	each kit. Themes such as teenage problems, mystery-supernatural, sports, biography, true adventure, and the future.		
Crestwood House P.O. Box 3427 Mankato, MN 56002-3427			
The Adventures of Beast	Entertaining books that teach a lesson.	2	K-3
Boulder Gang	Problems common to all children.	2-3	K and up
Teammates	Action and a little romance for the older students.	3-4	3 and up
Sports Legends	Biographies of famous athletes.	3-4	3 and up
Survival	Documented stories of people facing actual survival situations.	3-4	3 and up
Roundup	A little of everything: mysteries, adventure, and intrigue.	3-4	3 and up
Funseekers	Color photos and action-packed sports for young readers.	3-4	3 and up
Galaxy I	Many titles in science fiction.	3-5	3 and up
Monsters	Classic monster stories rewritten for the young reader.	3-5	3 and up
Movie Monsters	A new series based on classic monster movies.	3-5	3 and up
Crisis	Serious books that will attract reluctant readers through real-life crisis.	4-5	3 and up
Behind the Scenes	Exciting and informative reading that can indirectly be used as a career series.	4-5	4-5
Horses	Nonfiction horse books that take a close look at some of the well-known members of the horse family.	4-5	4 and up
Wildlife	Many well-known but little-understood animals are depicted.	5	5-6
Technology	This series takes a close look at how things are made.	5	4 and up
Working Dogs	This popular topic focuses on special dogs that go beyond being just pets.	5-6	5 and up
Movin' On	A new series on airplanes, trucks, trains, vans, etc.	5-6	4 and up
Back to Nature Sports	These books deal with outdoor sports.	5-6	4 and up
SCU-2	These books feature today's sports stars.	5-6	4 and up

(continued)

Publisher/Title	Description	Reading Grade Level	Interest Grade Level
Curriculum Associates, Inc. 5 Esquire Rd. North Billerica, MA 01862–2589			
Fable Plays for Oral Reading	Aesop's Fables come to life in these twelve selections. Speaking parts use controlled vocabulary and vary in length and difficulty so that the teacher may assign parts selectively.	1–3	1–5
Fairy Tale Plays for Oral Reading	Ample opportunity for oral reading practice is available when children play the characters of their favorite fairy tales.	1–3	2–5
Primary Plays for Oral Reading More Primary Plays for Oral Reading	Contemporary topics about people and their problems appeal to the young reader. Both sets come in a spirit master book and average ten to fifteen minutes in length.	2	2–4
Walker Plays for Oral Reading	Four collections of plays give an abundance of interesting topics for students to dramatize. These high-interest plays are short and easy to understand, which motivates students of varying levels. All are selections of classic stories or myths. A brief introduction to each play presents necessary background information.		3–8
	Walker Holiday Plays for Reading	3.1–5.2	
	Walker American Plays for Reading	3.1–5.5	
	Walker Mythology Plays for Reading	3.3–4.3	
	Walker Plays for Reading	3.4–5.4	
Dale Seymour Publications P.O. Box 10888 Palo Alto, CA 94303			
Giant First Start Readers	Eight easy-to-read stories with lots of repetition make excellent practice for the beginning reader.	1	K–2
Troll First-Start Easy Readers	These ten little stories, colorfully illustrated, are ideal for the remedial reader. Simple sentences and controlled vocabulary with a word list for each book are a few of the highlights.	1	K–3
I Can Read and Write Books	Six books in this supplementary reading series consist of one-page stories on subjects such as turtles, birds, fossils, etc. Each story is reproducible and intended to be traced over and copied on	1–2	2–5

Publisher/Title	Description	Reading Grade Level	Interest Grade Level
	the child's own paper. Each student makes his own book.		
Stamp-A-Story Minibooks	Thirty humorous story poems, each on a reproducible page that folds into a four-page minibook. Children love these short, interesting readings that earn a "story stamp" on the cover when mastered. Reinforce the Dolch Sight Vocabulary.	1–3	1–5
Thunder the Dinosaur Books	Ten books star Thunder the friendly brontosaurus and his escapades. The stories were actually written by a classroom of children; they contain the children's language and natural phrasing, which adds a new dimension for the reader.	2	K–4
City Kids	Funny pictures and school topics that all children can relate to keep the hesitant reader interested in these twelve books.	2–3	2–6
Fish Alley Five	Five friends—a horse, a crab, a pelican, a cat, and a tiny spider—live and play along the wharf. Set up their story scenes with 3-D models.	2.6	2–4
Easy-to-Read Mysteries	Simple plots and lots of adventure turn even the most reluctant reader into an eager one. Ten books in the set.	3	2–4
The Mr. Books and Little Miss Books	Each book features one character whose special trait causes a common problem. The simple, humorous format of these little books has given them instant popularity.	4	3–6
Freddy Higginbottom Books	Freddy Higginbottom is a young inventor whose fast action and zany antics quickly captivate the reader. A teacher's guide includes vocabulary, comprehension, and writing activities.	4	4–8
Dell Publishing Co., Inc. Educational Department 245 E. 47th St. New York, NY 10017			
Hi-Lo, Historical Fiction and Adventure	Eight diverse books packed with suspense and adventure. Slightly enlarged format, well-spaced type, and inviting photographs.	2–3	4 and up

(continued)

Publisher/Title	Description	Reading Grade Level	Interest Grade Level
The Economy Company 1200 Northwest 63rd St. P.O. Box 25308 Oklahoma City, OK 73125			
Keytext	The Keytext program offers the student having difficulty in reading a complete basal program. High-interest selections are presented in short segments. Readabilities are carefully controlled using the Spache and Dale-Chall formulas.	1–8	Content is carefully written to interest disabled reader
EMC Publishing Changing Times Education Service 300 York Ave. St. Paul, MN 55101			
Science Content	Three high-interest colorful science content kits will fascinate the most reluctant reader.	2–3	2–9
	Animals Around Us	2	2–6
	Four Awful Creatures	3	4–9
	Creatures Wild and Free	3	4–9
Fiction Content	Four diverse paperback sets of exciting themes for the intermediate student. Ghosts, danger, courage, science fiction, dinosaurs, problems of growing up are a few subjects.	3	4–9
Encounters	Adolescent readers will relate to these sixteen exciting, easy-reading books. Encounters is a complete reading program that includes a follow-up skills program.	3–4.5	7–12
Biography Content	These photo-illustrated, easy-to-read biographies intrigue the reluctant reader while reinforcing basic skills. Henry Winkler, Jane Pauley, Sylvester Stallone, The Osmonds, Natalie Cole, and Stevie Wonder are examples. Each kit contains four books with cassettes and activities.	3–5	4–12
	Superstars	3	3–9
	Headliners 1	4	4–12
	Headliners 2	4	4–12
	Center Stage	4	4–12
	Black American Athletes	5	4–12
	Man Behind the Bright Lights	5	4–12
Easy-to-Read Classics	Students with special needs can be intro-	3–6	7–12

Publisher/Title	Description	Reading Grade Level	Interest Grade Level
	duced to outstanding literature. Selections have been shortened and simplified but still keep the original flavor. Each book contains comprehension and discussion questions.		
Monsters and Mysteries	Eight exciting titles to read about the unexplainable, the unsolved . . . stories about the undersea, the solar system, the world of spies, and more.	5–6	4–12
Fearon Education David S. Lake Publishers 19 Davis Dr. Belmont, CA 94002			
Jim Hunter Books	The slower reader can find enjoyment in these high-action spy adventures. Sixteen illustrated books follow the escapades of daring Jim Hunter.	1.0–3.0	6–12
Galaxy 5	Six easy-to-read space fantasy adventures with evil kings, robots, and space pirates. DramaTape cassettes are available for the first two chapters of each book.	1.8–3.0	6–12
Space Police	Six action-packed space-age cops and robbers books include good topics for classroom discussion. Themes such as crime, jealousy, the generation gap, and prejudice are included.	1.8–3.0	6–12
BesTellers	Three distinct programs are thrilling pleasure books, a skill-development program, and action-filled magazines. This high-interest, easy-reading program offers something for every student in need.	1.8–4.0	6–12
	BesTellers	1.8–4.0	6–12
	BesTellers Reading Program	2.0–4.0	6–12
	BesTeller Magazines	3.0–4.0	6–12
Specter	The student who enjoys reading about mystery, weird events, and psychic phenomena will love these easy-to-read books. Short sentences and easy vocabulary will enthuse the most reluctant reader.	1.9–2.8	7–12
Laura Brewster	The six Laura Brewster mysteries will entertain the disabled reading student with fast-paced excitement. Skill-builder workbooks are available for each title.	2.0–2.9	6–12

(continued)

Publisher/Title	Description	Reading Grade Level	Interest Grade Level
Pacemaker Classics	Twelve timeless stories are abridged to an easy reading level. This series will introduce the remedial reader to well-known adaptations of classic novels.	2.0–2.9	5–12
Pacemaker True Adventures	Eleven books describe some of history's most terrifying and exciting adventures. These motivating themes and well-illustrated stories help students turn on to books	2.0–2.9	5–12
SporTellers	Sports are the topic of these eight novels designed for the young adults with reading difficulties.	2.0–3.6	6–12
Crisis Series	Teenage problems are confronted in these six realistic stories. Positive attitudes are promoted in up-to-date settings.	2.3–4.5	6–12
TaleSpinners	Eight diverse novels with cliff-hanging situations that appeal to the more mature student needing high interest/easy reading.	2.6–4.5	7–12
Doomsday Journals	Six doomsday titles entice even the most reluctant reader. Skill-builder workbooks are available for each story.	2.8–4.4	7–12
Quicksilver Books	High-interest themes about horses, dogs, cars, fads, aviation, and crime fighters are highlighted in this reading/writing program. Stories are short and easy to read. At the end of each book are questions to guide the student through book reports.	3.0–4.5	4–8
South City Cops	These exciting paperbacks follow the adventures of Eddy Hall and Kate Brightwater, two police patrol officers. Six titles are filled with interesting dialog and full-color covers.	3.5–4.0	6–12
Super Specter Series	Six diverse stories are filled with ghosts, witches, and other scary characters. Skill-builder workbooks are also available.	3.5–4.5	6–12
Sum-Way Books	Teach math-word problems and involve the reader in making decisions. The student actually directs the plot in this content-area adventure series.	4.0–4.5	4–8
Fastback Books	Fastbacks include six different sets—spy, mystery, romance, crime, horror, and sports—of exciting, color-filled stories	4.5–5.0	7–12

Publisher/Title	Description	Reading Grade Level	Interest Grade Level
	that come pocket-sized to help develop the habit of reading.		
Double Fastbacks	Four action books designed for the older student who is ready for a lengthier book than the Fastback Series. These books have none of the usual comprehension checks and drill pages. They are intended to create a regular habit of pleasure reading.	4.5–5.0	7–12
Garrard Publishing Co. 1607 N. Market St. P.O. Box A Champaign, IL 61820			
Begin-to-Read with Duck and Pig	Four books with full-color illustrations and a comical story line about the antics of Duck and Pig.	1	K–4
The Old Witch Books	Written by Ida DeLage, these fifteen beginning readers have a common factor: children like to read them.	1–2	K–4
Small Bear Adventures	Small Bear starts a series of his own. Seven delightful adventure stories with captivating illustrations.	2	K–4
Kleep: Space Detective	Three illustrated books with exciting space adventures including giants, evil magicians, and invasions from other planets.	2–3	2–6
Garrard's Dolch Series			
First Reading Books	Seventeen titles reinforced in sturdy cloth bindings. These Dolch readers are written with the easier half of the Dolch 220 Basic Sight Words. Beginners can read them on their own.	1	1–4
Basic Vocabulary Books	These stories about animals are written almost entirely with the Dolch 220 Basic Sight Words. The wide interest range provides easy to read format. Seventeen books with full page illustrations.	2	1–6
Folklore of the World Books	Wonderfully appealing Dolch stories that unlock new worlds of adventure. Stories consist of the folklore of fourteen other countries.	3	2–8
Pleasure Reading Books	Old classics have been rewritten with the First Thousand Words for Children's Reading, a list scientifically derived by Dr. Dolch. Thirteen titles.	4	3 and up

(continued)

Publisher/Title	Description	Reading Grade Level	Interest Grade Level
Globe Book Company, Inc. 50 W. 23rd St. New York, NY 10010			
Journeys to Fame	These twenty-two biographies tell of men and women who achieved success despite an obstacle encountered early in life.	2–3	7–12
Weird and Mysterious	Twenty-seven nonfiction stories and exercises with emphasis on word analysis, vocabulary, and reading comprehension.	2–3	7–12
The World of Vocabulary Series	Seven softcover text-workbooks, each containing short nonfiction selections for building vocabulary and other skills.	2–7	7–12
Stories of Surprise and Wonder	These eighteen thrillers are adaptations of famous tales.	3	7–12
Legends for Everyone	Twenty-four unforgettable stories of such characters as Rip Van Winkle, Paul Bunyan, Calamity Jane. Original drawings in many different styles. Vocabulary aids and comprehension questions are also provided.	3	6–8
Stranger than Fiction	Thirty-six short, factual selections adapted from newspaper and magazine stories. The emphasis is on off-beat subjects and situations.	3	7–12
Beyond Time and Space	Twenty-two science-fiction stories by well-known writers. These stories are designed to get students thinking, talking, and writing.	3–5	7–12
Something True, Something Else	An anthology of fictional adventure, true adventure and science fiction. Each story is four to seven pages on interesting subjects such as bears, Bigfoot, astronauts, UFOs, and ESP.	4–5	7–12
A Better Reading Workshop	A series of four softcover text-workbooks for less-able students. Each self-contained book covers a new skill area.	4–6	7–12
Holt, Rinehart and Winston 383 Madison Ave. New York, NY 10017			
Accent on Reading Skills	For students who need a second chance at reading. Skills lessons use high-interest stories and articles.	2–8	4–8

Publisher/Title	Description	Reading Grade Level	Interest Grade Level
Impact on Reading	This series provides high-interest, high-quality literature by well-known authors. Each book contains literary selections in different genres: sports, poems, plays, and more.	3–7	7–12
Houghton Mifflin Company One Beacon Street Boston, MA 02108			
Vistas	Stories for reluctant readers chosen for their high interest and appeal. A complete reading program includes anthology selections—fiction, nonfiction, poems, cartoons.	4–6	7–12
Jamestown Publishers P.O. Box 6743 Providence, RI 02840			
Attention Span Stories	These five low-readability stories consist of one-page episodes with three cliff-hangers at the bottom of the page. Each time the story is read the student can create a different adventure by determining the direction he would like the story to take. The characters come from diverse racial and ethnic backgrounds and are in their teens.	2–3	6–9
Adult Learner Series	The books in this fast-paced novel-length set have been adapted for older beginning readers. Nine books contain adventure and mystery plots to motivate the reluctant reader.	2–3	9–12
Jamestown Classics	Each one of the twenty-four classic short stories carries a mature theme designed for low-level readers. All stories are illustrated and chosen for their strong characterization, provocative ideas, and intriguing plots.	4.5–5.5	6–12
Modern Curriculum Press 13900 Prospect Rd. Cleveland, OH 44136			
Double Scoop Readers	Trolls and cows keep beginning readers glued to print. These twelve books have carefully controlled vocabulary from the most widely used basals.	Preprimer–Primer 1.3–1.5	1–3
Primary Sight-Word Readers	Twenty sight-word books offer students the opportunity to read about friendships, animals, and adventures. The	Preprimer–first	1–2

(*continued*)

Publisher/Title	Description	Reading Grade Level	Interest Grade Level
	bright, colorful artwork found in each book is a plus.		
Beginning to Read Books	Over 100 titles in paperback or hardbound editions. Book sets begin at pre-primer levels and continue through second grade. This series is designed to make beginning students independent readers.	Preprimer–second	1–3
Phonics Practice Readers Series A and B	Eighty primary phonetic readers now supplement the basal program. Students needing practice in words containing short vowels, long vowels, consonant blends and digraphs will love these exciting little books.	1–2	1–2
V2/Vowels and Values Readers	These easy-to-read books follow the progression of the Phonic Practice Readers with one new dimension—values. Each of the twenty books focuses on a specific value such as sharing, following directions, and protecting the environment.	1–2	1–2
First Ideas Books	Eight topics in colorful, easy-to-read format teach students basic skills in the content areas.	1–2	1–3
Bright Ideas Books	Sixteen books blend fantasy and reality with stories and poems as well as art projects. Each book focuses on a topic such as wheels, the zoo, in the air, flying to the moon.	1–2	1–3
Star Series Readers	Classic literature at beginning levels will establish reading for pleasure at an early age. Eight levels of difficulty offer every child the opportunity to enjoy literature.	1–2	1–3
See How I Read Books	Controlled vocabulary and sentence structure are features of this six-book sight word program. Duplicating masters follow each story to reinforce skills.	1.3–1.7	2–3
The High Action Treasure Chest	Forty-four action-packed titles for middle-grade students. Motivation is the key element in this series. Each book comes with a self-correcting skill card that ties pleasure reading in with skill development.	2.1–3.5	4–adult
Fourways Readers	More than independent reading, these eight titles are called Fourway Readers	2.5–5.0	4–6

Publisher/Title	Description	Reading Grade Level	Interest Grade Level
	for a reason. The student first reads a suspenseful episode; he then listens, discusses, and writes about what he would do in a similar situation.		
Traditional Tales Books	The theme is world cultures in this collection of six classic folk tales for the intermediate student.	3.0–4.9	4–6
Intermediate Readers	Older reluctant readers can explore current topics on friendship, science fiction, horses, and mysteries. A teacher's guide includes story summaries and discussion questions.	4–5	4–6
	*MCP has numerous other low-level, high-interest books from which to choose. These books have simple sentence structure, controlled vocabularies, and are colorfully illustrated for the primary student as well as for the older student with difficulties in learning to read.		
Scholastic Inc. 2931 E. McCarty Street P.O. Box 7502 Jefferson City, MO 65102			
Sprint Libraries	Exciting grown-up novels for students needing a remedial reading program. These sets come in several ranges of difficulty. Students love reading these fully illustrated novels.	1.0–5.0	4–6
	Sprint Starter Level	1.0–2.0	
	First Level	2.0–3.0	
	Second Level	3.0–4.0	
	Third Level	4.0–5.0	
	Starter Libraries A-D	1.5–1.9	
	Sprint Libraries (15)	2.0–4.0	
Action Libraries	These series offer the older student original novelettes with high-appeal themes at easy-to-read levels. Realistic and contemporary settings and characters with whom teenagers can identify. Twelve unique libraries.	2.0–4.0	7–12
Action Theme Collections	Even the most reluctant readers are motivated by these action-adventure, mystery, and science fiction themes. Three collections.	2.0–4.0	7–12

(continued)

Publisher/Title	Description	Reading Grade Level	Interest Grade Level
Double Action Libraries	Novels for the older student who is ready for more mature paperbacks but not yet ready for on-level materials. Six libraries.	3.0–5.0	7–12
Double Action Theme Collections	Two special collections of adventure-mystery and personal-growth themes.	3.0–5.0	7–12
Scope Activity Kits	Twenty activity kits contain thirty copies each of student booklets. Students explore timeless themes at their own level. They cover critical skills, reading comprehension, language skills, listening skills, and more.	4–6	7–12
Scope Plays	Eight exciting, illustrated plays for secondary students reading below grade level. Many opportunities for role-play and dramatic readings with each paperback anthology.	4–6	7–12
Science Research Associates, Inc. **155 N. Wacker Dr.** **Chicago, IL 60606**			
Development Reading Laboratory, Kit 1	Six levels of low-difficulty, high-interest reading selections.	1.2–2.2	2–6
Super A, Super AA, and Super BB Kits	Comic book readers; high-interest stories with controlled vocabulary. Up-to-date content includes science and space fiction, spy stories, comedy, fantasy, mystery, and more.	2–5	4–8
Pilot Library Series	Unaltered excerpts from selected juvenile books. Each library contains seventy-two selections sixteen to thirty-two pages in length, of graded levels of difficulty.	3–8	2–12
Scott, Foresman and Company **1900 E. Lake Ave.** **Glenview, IL 60025**			
Focus	This complete basal program is designed for students who have not succeeded in the regular basal. Beautifully illustrated content, organized to the readability and interest levels of the disabled reader. One main comprehension and study skill in each section.	K–8	Each book is especially written to interest designated level.

Publisher/Title	Description	Reading Grade Level	Interest Grade Level
Sunburst Communciations Room W J 6 39 Washington Ave. Pleasantville, NY 10570–9971			
The Best of Hi/Lo	Fifteen easy-to-read literature books offer exciting reading for the intermediate and junior high school student.	3–5	4–9
Hi/Lo Sports	Nine paperback books represent a variety of sports topics.	3–6	5–9
Hi/Lo High School I	Nineteen paperbacks with high-interest formats for lower-level readers.	4–6	8–12
Hi/Lo High School II	A set of eleven individualized paperbacks with captivating stories for today's teenagers.	4–6	8–12
Hi/Lo Fantasy	Eighteen fantasy-filled paperbacks for the intermediate to high school student needing an easier-to-read format.	5–7	5–12
Turman Publishing Co., Ed. Div. 200 W. Mercer St. Seattle, Washington 98119			
Bestsellers Paperback Books	High-interest, easy-reading paperbacks. Action-packed stories feature vampires, bomber pilots, ghosts, space warriors and more. Full-color covers and dramatic illustrations give these books an adult look that appeals to children and young adults. Ten books in set.	2	4–12
Stars	High-interest, low-level materials for older students. Each lesson has a 500-word article, photo of subject, and quiz at end. Published monthly. Students love to read about their favorite stars.	3	4–12

APPENDIX D
Commercial Materials for Teaching Reading Skills in a Remedial Reading Center

Publisher/Program	Reading Skills	Grade Level
American Guidance Services, Inc. Publishers Building Circle Pines, MN 55014–1796		
Goldman-Lynch Sounds and Symbols Development Kit	Phonetic analysis skills	Primary-Intermediate-ESL

Sixty-four lesson plans stimulate production of English speech sounds and recognition of associated symbols. Puppet, tape cassettes, posters, picture cards, magnetic symbols and adventure story books.

Barnell Loft, Ltd. 958 Church St. Baldwin, NY 11510		
Auditory Readiness Series	Auditory skills	Primary

Instruction in the basic auditory skills with an enjoyable gamelike technique that captures students' interest. Related classroom activities for reinforcement.

Visual Readiness	Visual matching skills	Primary

Instruction in visual readiness skills: match letters, words, initial and final consonants.

Capitalization and Punctuation	Capitalization and punctuation	1–9

Ninety-four key concepts. For individual or group instruction. Duplicating masters included.

Cloze Connections	Comprehension skills	1–9

To improve the student's comprehension skills by highlighting semantic, grammatical, and phonic cues to unlock meaning.

Instructional Aid Kits	Decoding skills Vocabulary development	Primary–Junior High

Each kit contains fifty cards and answer keys. Examples:

Time for Sounds		1–2
Riddle Riddle Rhyme Time		1–2
One Too Many		1–2
Fun With Words		1–6
Pronoun Parade		1–5

Multiple Skills Series	All	1–9

Comprehensive program is designed to teach all basic reading skills from basic sight words to comprehension. Teachers purchase according to skills or grade level desired. Four booklets on each level,

Publisher/Program	Reading Skills	Grade Level

a teacher's manual, duplicating masters for worksheets, and a class record sheet are included. Also in Spanish.

Picto-Cabulary Series	Vocabulary development (sight and meaning)	Primary-Intermediate-Junior High

Illustrated booklets stimulate interest in words and enlarge vocabularies. Worksheets and teacher's manual with each set. Three levels available.

Specific Skill Series	Comprehension skills, study skills, word analysis skills	Primary–Senior High

Specific and concentrated experiences in reading for different purposes. Practice material for pupils from kindergarten through high school. Additional drill in areas of need. Each booklet is concerned with one reading skill on one reading level. Titles: Following Directions, Working with Sounds, Locating the Answer, Getting the Facts, Detecting the Sequence, Getting the Main Idea, Drawing Conclusions, Identifying Inferences, Using the Context.

Supportive Reading Skills	All	1–9

This is a diagnostic and prescriptive reading program that supplements the Specific Skills Series.

Bell and Howell Company
7100 McCormick Rd.
Chicago, IL 60645

Language Master	Reading readiness (visual, auditory, alphabetical skills) Word attack Vocabulary	Primary–Adult

This is a card reader. The student inserts a card, watches and listens, records, and immediately compares responses to the instructor track. Program employs sight, speech, touch, and hearing in coordinated, effective instruction. Includes a compact, portable unit with self-contained dual track recording and playback capability. Used with sets of cards containing visual material and a strip of magnetic recording tape.

Bowmar/Noble Publishers
1901 N. Walnut
P.O. Box 25308
Oklahoma City, OK 73125

Letter Sounds All Around	Alphabet Beginning Sounds Vocabulary	1–3

Multimedia program contains filmstrip/cassette lessons to motivate students. Artwork, music, and exciting dialogue hold interest of pupils.

Primary Reading Series	Comprehension	Reading: 1.3–2.5 Interest: 4–8

Six kits consist of high-interest story cards at the interest level of younger readers. On the back of each card are questions to teach and evaluate basic comprehension skills. Teacher's guide included.

Best	Word analysis	1–Adult

(continued)

Publisher/Program	Reading Skills	Grade Level

Basic phonic skills are taught and reinforced through this tutorial kit. Decoding skills developed with pictures and letter cards, orientation tape, and a record pad.

| Sports Reading Series | Comprehension | Reading: 2.0–4.3 |
| | | Interest: 4–8 |

Three reading kits consist of high-interest, low-readability story cards about professional sports—Olympics, Big League Baseball, Pro Basketball. On the back of each card are questions to check comprehension.

| Major Sports | Comprehension | Reading: 2.0–4.3 |
| | | Interest: 4–8 |

Ten books capitalize on students' interest in sports. Each has a slightly higher reading level. Comprehension checks and teacher's guide.

Double Play Reading Series	Oral reading	Reading: 2.5–5.9
	Inferential comprehension	Interest: 4–9
Triple Play Reading Series	Vocabulary	Reading: 2.0–7.0
		Interest: 4–9

Each series contains five kits with plays and accompanying cassette tapes by professional actors. Each play includes duplicating masters and worksheets on vocabulary and comprehension, including inference skills. Students listen and participate in drama, comedy, and adventure.

| Reading Comprehension Series | Comprehension | Reading: 3.0–4.4 |
| | | Interest: 4–8 |

Eight kits of high-interest story cards at an easier level. On the back of each card are questions designed to teach and evaluate basic comprehension skills. Teacher's guide included.

| Quicksilver Books | Comprehension | Reading: 3.0–4.5 |
| | Writing skills | Interest: 4–8 |

Six sets of books in display boxes. Five copies of each book and a teaching guide contain the same high-interest categories as Reading Comprehension Series.

Charles E. Merrill Publishing Co.
1300 Alum Creek Dr.
P.O. Box 508
Columbus, OH 43216

| New Diagnostic Reading Skill-text Series | Comprehension | K–6 |

Workbook series combines an easy-to-use format with short stories and skill development. Concentration on main idea, following directions, vocabulary, and independent thinking.

| Merrill Phonics Skilltext Series | Phonics | Reading: 1.0–4.0 |
| | | Interest: 1–8 |

Seven colorful workbooks put phonics instruction in immediate context. Uses a step-by-step sequential skills presentation; each book concentrates on new skills while reviewing the old. Teacher's guide reviews all basic phonic generalizations.

Reading Reinforcement Skill-text Series	Vocabulary	Reading: 1.0–5.2
	Word structure	Interest: 1–8
	Comprehension	
	Dictionary skills	

Publisher/Program	Reading Skills	Grade Level

This supplemental program is aimed at the less-able reader who needs high-interest stories with low readability and carefully developed skills. Ten workbooks introduce and review reading skills while giving confidence.

Reading for the Real World	Vocabulary	Reading: 4.0–7.5 Interest: 7–10

For students reading below grade level, program offers short, high-interest lessons using real-life happenings. Two skill books; each level contains thirty-eight narratives about people and their work. Stories are followed by skills page and presented in magazine format.

College Skills Center
Department 855502
320 W. 29th St.
Baltimore, MD 21211–2891

66 Passages to Learn to Read Better	Comprehension Vocabulary	Reading: 3–6 Interest: ages 10 and up

Student workbook is aimed at the reluctant reader. Clear explanations. Reading selections, mainly nonfiction, for older students include Sports, Humor, Nature, and Social Science. Instruction moves from sentence and paragraph to reading short passages. Vocabulary workbook, software, cassette tapes.

88 Passages to Develop Reading Comprehension	Comprehension Vocabulary	Reading: 6–10 Interest: ages 12 and up

Workbook teaches five comprehension skills; context clues present the vocabulary program. Selections stimulate the remedial student. Vocabulary workbook, software, and cassette tapes available.

100 Passages to Develop Reading Comprehension	Comprehension Vocabulary	Reading: 9–adult Interest: ages 15 and up

Workbook presents nine distinct types of comprehension skills. Reading selections never over two pages. Vocabulary workbook and software available.

Curriculum Associates, Inc.
5 Esquire Rd.
N. Billerica, MA 01862–2589

Sound Start	Phonics Sight vocabulary	K–1

Flip-chart easel, spirit masters, and a binder with teacher's manual are components of forty-lesson step-by-step program to help beginning readers make the transition from speech to print.

My Short Book My Long Book I Can Write a Book	Phonics	1–3

Three skill books reinforce short and long vowels. Brightly illustrated workbooks practice vowels through context clues, identification of missing letter, rhyming patterns.

Clues for Better Reading	Comprehension	1–9

Detailed illustrations, a varied format offer high interest for all readers. Three kits and primary workbook contain stories, activity and answer cards, spirit masters, and entry tests for each skill area.

(continued)

Publisher/Program	Reading Skills	Grade Level
Clues	Grades	Average Readability
Workbook A	1–2	1.5
Kit I	2–3	2.5
Kit II	4–6	4.3
Kit III	7–9	6.2
Listening Comprehension Skills Program	Listening skills	1–10

Each kit contains activity cards for practice in oral reading, listening, and comprehension. All activities are self-directing. Skills reinforced include main idea, sequence, prediction, details, inference, finding logical consequences.

Kit	Listening Grade	Reading Grade
A	1–4	2–5
B	3–6	4–7
C	5–8	6–9
D	7–10	8–10
Reading Skills Practice Kit Level I	Comprehension Vocabulary Structural analysis	2–4

Appropriate for older students needing skill practice. Two hundred activity cards emphasize words, vocabulary, and study skills.

Context Phonetic Clues	Word analysis	3–6 and remedial

Intensive phonics program for remedial readers. Its fast-action and interesting approach can increase students' vocabulary by 900 words. Clue cards have words on one side and context clues on the other. The teacher reads the clues and the student indicates the answer.

Lessons in Vowel and Consonant Sounds	Phonics	3–8

Comprehensive phonics program provides upper elementary and junior high students with high-interest drill lessons of increasing difficulty to reinforce all vowel and consonant sounds.

Vocabulary Fluency	Vocabulary	4–6
Book A		7–9
Book B		

Two oral vocabulary programs use a speaking-into-reading approach. Emphasis on reading, writing, and speaking skills for intermediate and ESL students with minimal reading skills. Books come with ten reusable student books and cassette tapes.

Reading Skills Practice Kit	Level II	Reading comprehension Vocabulary Structural analysis Story analysis Research skills	4–8

Supplemental practice lessons add interest along with skill mastery to students reading below grade level. New ESL teacher's guide included.

Publisher/Program	Reading Skills	Grade Level

DLM Teaching Resources
P.O. Box 4000
One DLM Park
Allen, TX 75002

Cove School Reading Program	Sight words Phonetic analysis	K–2

Simple format with large lettering provides carefully sequenced instruction for students with difficulty learning to read. Six workbooks stress consonants, short vowels, blends and digraphs, vowel digraphs, and long vowels.

Sight Word Readers (1 and 2) Sight Word Lab (1 and 2)	Sight words Study skills	1–2 (Interest level 2–6)

Carefully developed program uses Sight Word Labs to teach high-frequency words and gives practice using them in context with the Sight Word Readers. Sixteen illustrated books in each set.

Swain Beginning Reading Program	Phonetic analysis Comprehension	1–3

For the student who is not ready for a basal program or who is having difficulty learning to read. Children first learn how to read in sentences, then move on to plays and stories. Two lesson books, blackline masters, five student readers.

Essential Sight Words Program	Sight words	1–4 (Interest level 4 up)

Slow-paced, structured sight word program for low-achieving readers offers recurring exposure to difficult words through over 200 different activities.

Survival Words Program	Sight words	1–4 (Interest level Junior High)

Sequel to Essential Sight Words Program. Words and phrases are taught through worksheets and storybooks.

Sound Foundations Programs	Word attack	1–6

Four programs teach and reteach basic phonetic elements in this carefully structured approach. Each program includes 150 student activity cards.

The Reading Comprehension Series	Comprehension	Grades 2–7

Program teaches comprehension skills to remedial students reading one to three grades below level. Eight workbooks teach context, main idea, details, sequence, spatial relationships, comparison, cause and effect, and study skills.

*DLM also carries extensive games that teach and practice all reading skill areas.

Educators Publishing Service, Inc.
75 Moulton St.
Cambridge, MA 02238–9101

Starting Comprehension: Stories to Advance Reading and Thinking	Comprehension Vocabulary	pre-primer–2

Essential comprehension skills (literal, inferential, and organizational) from picture to paragraph level. Unique program is written in two different strands: phonetic or sight method. Twelve workbooks.

(continued)

Publisher/Program	Reading Skills	Grade Level
Primary Phonics; More Primary Phonics	Word analysis	K–4

Two series supplement a phonetic reading series. Individual readers and accompanying workbooks increase in difficulty in a sequential, structured phonetic approach.

Wordly Wise Reading Series	Vocabulary	1–4

Six readers with an accompanying workbook offer the beginning reader practice in systematically learning vocabulary.

Sound-Off	Word analysis Vocabulary Comprehension	1–5

Five workbooks cover five phonic skill areas (consonants, short vowels, initial and consonant blends and digraphs, long vowels, and *r*-controlled vowels). Exercises for the beginning or disabled reader provide practice to strengthen proficiency in these areas.

Explode the Code	Word analysis Structural analysis	1–6

Twelve illustrated workbooks supplement a linguistic or phonetic basal reading program. Basic phonic presentations and vocabulary.

EMC Publishing
Changing Times Education Service
300 York Ave.
St. Paul, MN 55101

Passport to Reading	Comprehension Vocabulary Study skills	Junior High–Senior High (Reading levels: 2.0–5.0)

The more mature student learns basic study skills using this set of six text-workbooks. Each workbook contains interesting stories with follow-up skill activities.

Schmerler Reading Program	Word attack Sight words	All

Two systems include S.T.A.R.T. for reading readiness and beginning reading skills, Instructional Sequence for a comprehensive language arts program. For the student needing special help in reading skills. Activity books, tests, paperback readers, flashcards, and wall charts.

Globe Book Company, Inc.
50 W. 23rd St.
New York, NY 10010

The Reading for Survival Series	Word analysis, comprehension, and writing Skills	1–8 (decoding level)

Seven soft-cover texts for the older poor reader as well as the non-reader. Students move from the alphabet to third-grade reading level. Lessons are organized around up-to-date life skills.

The World of Vocabulary	Alphabetizing, prefixes, context clues, analogies	2–7

Build vocabulary skills for the less-able reading student. Each lesson contains eight to ten new words and accompanying comprehension questions.

Publisher/Program	Reading Skills	Grade Level
A Need to Read	Comprehension and vocabulary development	3–6

Written for three levels of difficulty, these comprehension and vocabulary books help less-able students make reading progress.

The Real Stories Series	Comprehension and vocabulary development	3–6

Four softcover texts build comprehension and vocabulary skills. Nonfiction short stories feature writing lessons and open-ended discussion questions.

A Better Reading Workshop	Comprehension development, study skills	4–6

Four workbooks teach basic reading skills in smaller, more manageable steps. Materials also improve test-taking abilities.

Reading Power Through Cloze	Comprehension development, vocabulary development, writing skills	4–7

Four workbooks hold the interest of the older student while teaching (and testing) with the cloze procedure. Word meanings are discovered using context, prefixes, and suffixes. Comprehension skills include main idea, details, and predicting outcomes.

Hayes School Publishing Co., Inc.
321 Pennwood Ave.
Wilkinsburg, PA 15221–3398

Hayes Company Materials	Word-analysis skills Dictionary skills Vocabulary Study skills	Primary–senior high

Workbooks and liquid duplicating material to teach and emphasize fundamental and individualized instruction in all reading skills.

Houghton Mifflin
One Beacon St.
Boston, MA 02108

The Listening Corner	Phonetic analysis Structural analysis Comprehension Vocabulary	K–3

Reading skills are taught through listening with this audio-cassette program. Formats include narrators, story tellers, music, and sound effects.

Vistas	Comprehension Reference/study skills Survival skills	Reading: 4–6 Interest: Junior High–High School

Program offers short, appealing text (including biographies, poems, cartoons) that interest the older less able student. Three levels of texts and accompanying materials.

(continued)

Publisher/Program	*Reading Skills*	*Grade Level*
Individualized Reading Skills Program	Phonics Comprehension Reference/study skills	Intermediate–Junior High

Three instructional levels in an individualized setting. Booklets, answer cards, and tests.

Jamestown Publishers
P.O. Box 9168
Providence, RI 02940

Comprehension Crossroads	Vocabulary Comprehension	Reading: 3–12 Interest: 6–12

Crossword puzzles stimulate interest at the student's level. Puzzles carefully restricted to noted reading levels. Duplicating masters included.

Comprehension Skills Series	Comprehension	Reading: 4–12 Interest: 6–adult

Each booklet develops a specific comprehension skill. Description of the skill, a lesson, and exercises to evaluate students' progress. Read-along cassettes available.

Skills Drills	Comprehension	Reading: 4.5, 5.5, and 6.5 Interest: 6–12

Below-level students progress through three levels with these reproducible worksheets. Five comprehension skills: context, details, sequence, inference, and main idea. The lively illustrations and subject matter (biographies, entertainment, science, and sports) are components of this high-interest, low-level program.

Reading Drills	Vocabulary Comprehension	Reading: 4–10 Interest: 4–adult

These text-workbooks contain thirty timed passages, each followed by comprehension questions, cloze tests, and a vocabulary exercise. Middle level is for elementary and junior high school. The advanced level is for high school and above.

Mafex Associates, Inc.
90 Cherry St.
P.O. Box 519
Johnstown, PA 15907

Phonetic Reading Chain	Phonetic analysis skills Sight words	Ages 8 to adult

Poor readers learn multisyllabic words in structured program with controlled content. Components include oral reading books, tests, cassettes, flashcards, and reading chain sets.

Modern Curriculum Press
13900 Prospect Rd.
Cleveland, OH 44136

Starting Off with Phonics Workbooks	Phonics	K–1

Publisher/Program	Reading Skills	Grade Level

Complete readiness program uses six workbooks focusing on a specific concept. Lessons with games, songs, and tactile exercises. Auditory, visual, motor skills, the alphabet, consonant sounds, short vowels and long vowels.

MCP Phonics Workbook Program	Phonics	1–6

Phonics workbook program remains popular. Each page focuses on one skill. Extensive review is an integral part of each book. The logical scope and sequence help make workbooks effective.

Thinking About Reading	Comprehension	2–6

Unusual comprehension program uses latest techniques to develop critical-thinking skills. Students read a story, stopping periodically to predict and review (Directed Reading Thinking Activity), then map key elements of what they have read (developing story synthesis). Next, students choose two vocabulary words (motivational device for vocabulary building), then enter into convergent and divergent thinking through discussion or written work. Student workbook with teacher's guide for each level.

Skill-by-Skill Workbooks	Comprehension	2–6

Colorful formats, high-interest material and easy-to-follow directions help students concentrate on comprehension skills. A workbook for each grade on getting the main idea, increasing comprehension, organizing information, using references, working with facts and details, following directions.

High Action Reading Workbooks	Comprehension	2–6

Five workbook levels in comprehension, vocabulary, study skills. Students read and practice skills on topics such as mysteries, myths, and magic.

Reach for Reading	Phonics	4–6

Sequential decoding workbook for the older student offers motivation through high-action stories, puzzles, and comic book formats. Skill practice is kept short and to the point.

Reader's Digest
Random House
School Division
400 Hahn Rd.
Westminister, MD 21157

Reading Skill Builders	Vocabulary Comprehension	1–9

Program builds comprehension and vocabulary skills while providing interest for the reader. Exercises focus on comprehension skills such as main idea, cause and effect, sequence, etc. Less-able students read from lower level selections. Duplicating masters for each level are available.

Triple Takes	Critical thinking Comprehension	3–8 (reading level 1–8)

Real-life topics make content enjoyable. Every unit contains three types of exercises: functional (using maps, schedules, advertisements), content area (science, math, social studies), and recreational (news articles, selections from many genres).

RD 2000	Vocabulary Comprehension	5–12 (reading level 0–6.9)

(*continued*)

Publisher/Program	Reading Skills	Grade Level

Comprehensive reading program has colorfully illustrated, high-interest magazine format. Problem readers enjoy sports, mysteries, science fiction, and famous people. Audio lessons, activity books, and follow-up testing materials. Available in kit form.

The Riverside Publishing Co.
8420 Bryn Mawr Ave.
Chicago, IL 60631

Discovering Phonics We Use	Word analysis	1–6

Supplemental phonics series includes seven workbooks to teach and practice skill application through a variety of appealing strategies. Puzzles, riddles, word games, and letter substitution.

Comprehension We Use	Comprehension	1–6

Six workbooks teach the elementary child survival and content-area comprehension skills. Program shows the student how to understand what he or she reads.

Scholastic Inc.
P.O. Box 7501
2931 E. McCarty St.
Jefferson City, MO 65102

Language Arts Phonics	Phonetic analysis Vocabulary Writing skills	1–3

Three books combine reading and language skills. Lessons begin with poems, stories, games, broken down to teach individual skills.

Phonics	Phonetic analysis	1–3

Each of six workbooks concentrates on a phonic element (initial consonants, final consonants, short vowels, long vowels, digraphs, consonant blends, word patterns).

Listening Skills	Listening skills Comprehension	1–6

Students practice listening as they follow with a cassette and skills worksheet. Pupils are motivated by the radio-style storytime.

Word Mastery with Puzzles and Games	Vocabulary Spelling Phonetic analysis	1–6

Three game-style workbooks drill important reading skills. Each workbook spans two reading levels.

Vocabulary Skills	Vocabulary skills Context clues Structural analysis skills	1–6

Six workbooks can be used remedially as well as on grade level to teach and practice vocabulary skills. Format helps prepare students for standardized tests.

Publisher/Program	Reading Skills	Grade Level
Reading Comprehension	Comprehension	3–6

While reading exemplary literature, students practice literal, interpretive, and critical reading skills.

Reluctant Reader Libraries	Comprehension Vocabulary	5–6

Captivating titles entice the most reluctant reader in these three library sets. Fifty books in each library (thirty in the mini-collection) plus reading skills worksheets.

Science Research Associates, Inc.
155 N. Wacker Dr.
Chicago, IL 60606

BRS Satellites Kit	Fluency building	1–2

Extra practice selections for beginning readers who learn slowly. Five levels of difficulty make pleasure reading possible for all students.

Reading for Understanding 1, 2, 3	Comprehension	Kit 1: 1–3 Kit 2: 3–7 Kit 3: 7–12

Kits teach inferential comprehension. Students are encouraged to work at their own pace while learning to analyze ideas and make judgments.

Schoolhouse Series	Phonetic analysis Vocabulary Structural analysis Comprehension	1–3 2–4 3–4 3–8

Each kit concentrates on one reading skill. Kits consist of exercise cards, plastic overlays, markers, and progress sheets.

SRA Skills Series	Phonetic analysis Structural analysis Comprehension	1–3 3–7 4–8

Student focuses on one reading skill at a time. Each kit has forty-eight teaching units and contains skill cards, cassette lessons, activity sheets, tests, and student progress folders.

Mark 11 Reading Laboratory Kits	Word study/comprehension Study skills/vocabulary Listening/study skills	Kit 2A: level 4 Kit 2B: level 5 Kit 2C: level 6

Each kit has ten levels. Students start at their present reading level and progress at their own rate. Students check their own work and chart their own progress. Built-in mechanisms tell them when given skills need extra practice. Each kit contains 150 power-builder cards, rate-builder cards, skill development cards-each with a key card.

Cracking the Code	Word attack skills	4–9

Reader and workbook give the older less-able student basic word attack skills. Selections have themes that appeal to the more mature student.

(continued)

Publisher/Program	*Reading Skills*	*Grade Level*

Scribner Educational Publishers
Front and Brown St.
Riverside, NJ 08075

SUPER Books	Comprehension	1–3
	Vocabulary	
	Fluency practice	

Three kits at three levels have easy-to-read stories to take home for practice. Job cards and duplicating masters reinforce skills for the beginning-to-read students. Kits contain 550 books.

| Reading with Phonics | Phonics | 1–4 |

The older student with a weak phonic background will find this a logical program for presenting the forty-four basic speech sounds. Three workbooks.

| ReadAbility | Comprehension | 4–9 |

Each of six workbooks contains two-page lessons taken from content area reading as well as fictional reading selections.

| Reading for Meaning | Comprehension | 4–12 |
| | Vocabulary | |

For poor readers to improve reading rate, comprehension, and vocabulary. Nine workbooks begin at the fourth-grade reading level but can be used with older students.

Sunburst Communications
Room WJ6
39 Washington Ave.
Pleasantville, NY 10570–9971

Strange Strange World	Comprehension	Reading: 2.0–2.8
Hi/Lo Series	Vocabulary	Interest: 5–12
	Writing skills	

Three programs (Real or Unreal?, Amazing Animal Stories, Weird Adventures) combine filmstrips and magazines. Worksheets improve reading skills.

| Stories of the Unusual | Comprehension | Reading: 2–6 |
| | Study Skills | Interest: 4–10 |

High-interest multisensory reading program provides the less-able reader with reading at a workable level. Each playlet ends in a cliff-hanger. The student finishes the story by reading a short selection. Content-area materials and study skills lessons accompany each unit.

| Reading for Every Day | Survival reading skills | Reading: 4 |
| | | Interest: 4–7 |

Students apply reading skills to everyday experiences. Examples include road maps, menus, and want ads. Fifty activity cards, worksheets, and student record sheets.

| You Can Be a Better Reader | Comprehension | 5–10 |
| | Vocabulary | |

Filmstrip and cassette interview format involves student in looking for main ideas and inferences. Amusing stories provide new vocabulary and figures of speech. Worksheets and a guide included.

Publisher/Program	Reading Skills	Grade Level
Steck-Vaughn Company P.O. Box 2028 Austin, TX 78768		
Building Sight Vocabulary	Sight words	Interest level: K–3

Game formats and stories in three-book series introduce and reinforce basic sight words. Placement tests and take-home materials included.

Reading Comprehension Series	Comprehension	Interest level: 1–6

Short selections with controlled vocabulary enhance this supplementary comprehension program. Seven workbooks contain illustrations to build enthusiasm.

Power Words Program	Sight words	Interest level: 2–6

Four-book series is for the upper elementary student who cannot identify necessary sight words. Testing materials included.

Mastering Basic Reading Skills	Comprehension Vocabulary Structural analysis Study skills	Interest level: 2–9 (4 and up)

Middle-grade students progress through eight soft-cover books on fundamental reading skills. Lesson format: teaser paragraphs, vocabulary words and definitions, a short story, and carefully designed exercises for practice.

Superstars	Comprehension Vocabulary	Interest level 5–12 (4–6)

Brief biographical sketches of popular singers, athletes, and entertainers give supplemental reading practice while reinforcing comprehension and vocabulary skills. Each of six books contains fourteen or fifteen minibiographies.

Some Publishers of Games	Reading Skills	Grade Level
Barnell-Loft, Ltd. 958 Church St. Baldwin, NY 11510	Basic sight words Vocabulary development (sight and meaning)	Primary Intermediate
Creative Publications 5005 W. 110th St. Oak Lawn, IL 60453	Word-analysis skills Dictionary skills	Junior High Senior High
DLM Teaching Resources P.O. Box 4000 One DLM Park Allen, TX 75002	Comprehension skills Study skills Oral reading skills	Adult
Garrard Publishing Company P.O. Box A 1607 N. Market St. Champaign, IL 60453		

(*continued*)

Some Publishers of Games	Reading Skills	Grade Level
Kenworthy Educational Service, Inc. 138 Allen St. Ellicott Station, P.O. Box 60 Buffalo, NY 14205–0060		
Mafex Associates, Inc. 90 Cherry St. P.O. Box 519 Johnstown, PA 15902		
Milton Bradley Co. Springfield, Massachusetts		
Science Research Associates, Inc. 155 N. Wacker Dr. Chicago, IL 60606		
Trend Enterprises, Inc. St. Paul, MN 55164		

Names and Addresses of Companies That Publish Materials in Reading

Abingdon Press
201 8th Avenue South
Nashville, TN 37202

Abrahams Magazine Service
56 East 13th Street
New York, NY 10003

Academic Press
111 Fifth Avenue
New York, NY 10003

Academic Therapy Publications
20 Commercial Blvd.
Novato, CA 94947

Acropolis Books Ltd.
2400 17th Street N.W.
Washington, DC 20009

Addison-Wesley Publishing Co., Inc.
Jacob Way
Reading, MA 01867

Addison-Wesley Testing Services
2725 San Hill Road
Menlo Park, CA 94025

Allied Educational Press
P.O. Box 337
Niles, MI 49120

Allied School & Office Products
P.O. Box 25147
4900 Menaul N.E.
Albuquerque, NM 87125

Allyn and Bacon, Inc.
470 Atlantic Ave.
Boston, MA 02210

American Council on Educ.
One Dupont Circle
Washington, DC 20036

American Guidance Service
Publisher's Building
Circle Pines, MN 55014

American Library Association
50 East Huron Street
Chicago, IL 60611

American Printing House for the Blind
P.O. Box 6085
Louisville, KY 40206

Amsco School Publications, Inc.
315 Hudson Street
New York, NY 10013

Apple Computer
20525 Miriana Ave.
Cupertino, CA 94015

Ann Arbor Publishers, Inc.
P.O. Box 7249
Naples, FL 33940

Arista Corporation
2 Park Ave.
New York, NY 10016

ARO Publishing Inc.
P.O. Box 193
Provo, UT 84601

Association for Childhood Education
  International
3615 Wisconsin Avenue N.W.
Washington, DC 20016

A-V Concepts Corporation
30 Montauk Boulevard
Oakdale, NY 11769

Avon Books
1790 Broadway
New York, NY 10019

Baker and Taylor Co.
1515 Broadway
New York, NY 10036

Baker Street Publications Ltd.
502 Range St.
Box 3610
Mankato, MN 56084

Ballantine/Del Rey Fawcett Books
201 E. 50th St.
New York, NY 10022

Bantam Books, Inc.
School and College
Marketing Division
666 Fifth Avenue
New York, NY 10019

Barnell Loft, Ltd.
958 Church Street
Baldwin, NY 11510

Barnes/Sale & Noble Annex
126 Fifth Ave.
New York, NY 10011

Clarence L. Barnhart, Inc.
Box 250—1 Stone Place
Bronxville, NY 10708

Basic Skills Program
Office of Basic Skills Improvement
400 Maryland Avenue, S.W.
Room 1167—Donohoe Building
Washington, DC 20202

Bell and Howell
Audio-Visual Products Div.
7100 N. McCormick Road
Chicago, IL 60645

Benefit Press
1250 Sixth Avenue
San Diego, CA 92101

Berrent Educational Press
444 Community Dr.
Manhasset, NY 11030

Bobbs-Merrill Educational Publishing
4300 West 62nd Street
P.O. Box 7080
Indianapolis, IN 46206

Borg-Warner Educational Systems
600 West University Drive
Arlington Heights, IL 60004

R.R. Bowker Co.
1180 Avenue of the Americas
New York, NY 10036

Bowmar Noble Publishers Inc.
4563 Colorado Blvd.
Los Angeles, CA 90039

Boynton/Cook Publishers, Inc.
Forge Lane
Box 598
Lakeville, CT 06039

Burgless Publishing Co.
7108 Ohms Lane
Minneapolis, MN 55435

Carlson-Dellosa Publishing
1946 S. Arlington Road
Akron, OH 44306

C B H Publishing Inc.
Box 236
Glencol, IL 60022

C.C. Publications, Inc.
P.O. Box 23699
Tigaro, OR 97223

Center for Applied Research in
  Education, Inc.
P.O. Box 130
West Nyack, NY 10995

Centurion Industries, Inc.
167 Constitution Drive
Menlo Park, CA 94025

Chapman Brook & Kent
1215 Del la Vina Street, Suite F
P.O. Box 21008
Santa Barbara, CA 93121

Chicago Tribune
435 North Michigan Avenue
Chicago, IL 60611

The Children's Book Council
67 Irving Place
New York, NY 10003

Children's Press
1224 West Van Buren Street
Chicago, IL 60607

Clarion Books
52 Vanderbilt Ave.
New York, NY 10017

Cliff's Notes
1701 P Street
Lincoln, NE 68508

Cobblestone Publishing, Inc.
20 Grove St.
Peterborough, NH 03458

College Board
45 Columbus Ave.
New York, NY 10023

College Skills Center
Department 865052
320 West 29th Street
Baltimore, MD 21211

Conference Book Service, Inc.
80 South Early St.
Alexandria, VA 22304

Communacad
Box 541
Wilton, CT 06897

Compress
A Division of Wadsworth, Inc.
P.O. Box 102
Wentworth, NH 03282

Consulting Psychologists Press, Inc.
577 College Ave.
Palo Alto, CA 94306

Contemporary Books Inc.
180 North Michigan Avenue
Chicago, IL 60601

Continental Press Inc.
520 East Bainbridge St.
Elizabeth Town, PA 17022

Coronado Publishers, Inc.
1250 Sixth Avenue
San Diego, CA 92101

Coronet
65 East South Water Street
Chicago, IL 60601

Council for Exceptional Children
1920 Association Drive
Reston, VA 22091

Crane Publishing Co.
PO Box 3713
Trenton, NJ 08629

Creative Classroom
Macmillan Book Clubs
866 Third Street
New York, NY 10022

Creative Curriculum, Inc.
15681 Commerce Lane
Huntington Beach, CA 92649

Creative Publications
P.O. Box 10328
Palo Alto, CA 94303

Crestwood House
Box 3427
Mankato, MN 58001

Crown Publishers, Inc.
One Park Avenue
New York, NY 10016

CTB/McGraw-Hill
Del Monte Research Park
Monterey, CA 93940

Curriculum Associates, Inc.
6620 Robin Willow Ct.
Dallas, TX 75248

Curriculum Associates, Inc.
Sound Start
5 Esquire Road
North Billerica, MA 01862

Curriculum Innovations, Inc.
3500 Western Avenue
Highland Park, IL 60035

Curriculum Review
517 S. Jefferson St.
Chicago, IL 60607

Cushman-Fowler Learning Associates
P.O. Box 6196
Olympia, WA 98502

C. Lucas Dalton
5720 Caruth Haven
Suite 130
Dallas, TX 75206

Delacorte Press
c/o Montville Warehousing Co., Inc.
Changebridge Road
Pine Brook, NJ 07058

Dell Publishing Co.
Education Dept.
245 East 47th St.
New York, NY 10017

Department of Defense
Office of Dependent Schools
2461 Eisenhower Avenue
Alexandria, VA 22331

DES Educational Publications
25 South Fifth Ave
P.O. Box 1291
Highland Park, NJ 08904

Developmental Learning Materials
P.O. Box 4000
One DLM Park
Allen, TX 75002

A B Dick Co.
5700 Touhy Avenue
Chicago, IL 60648

Dome Press, Inc.
1169 Logan Ave.
Elgin, IL 60120

Dormac, Inc.
P.O. Box 752 (1983 PO 1699)
Beaverton, OR 97075

Doubleday & Co., Inc.
501 Franklin Ave
Garden City, NY 11530

Dreier Educational Systems
25 South Fifth Avenue
P.O. Box 1291
Highland Park, NJ 08904

DRP Services
The College Board
45 Columbus Avenue
New York, NY 10023

Dura-Clad Books
PO Box 82
LaBelle, MO 63447

E.P. Dutton
2 Park Ave.
New York, NY 10016

Duvall Publishing
422 W. Appleway
Coer d'Alene, ID 83814

E & R Development Co.
Vandalia Road
Jacksonville, FL 62650

Early Years/K-8
PO Box 3330
Westport, CT 06880

Earier-to-Learn
Box 329
Garden City, NY 11530

EBSCO Curriculum Materials
Box 11521
Birmingham, AL 35202

Econoclad Books
2101 N. Topeka Blvd.
P.O. Box 1777
Topeka, KS 66601

The Economy Company
Box 25308
1901 North Walnut Street
Oklahoma City, OK 73125

EDITS
P.O. Box 7234
San Diego, CA 92107

EDL Division
Artista Corporation
2440 Estandway
P.O. Box 6146
Concord, CA 94524

EDL/McGraw-Hill
1221 Avenue of the Americas
New York, NY 10020

EDUCAT Publishers, Inc.
P.O. Box 2158
Berkeley, CA 94702

The Education Center
1411 Mill Street
P.O. Box 9753
Greensboro, NC 27408

Educational Activities
P.O. Box 392
Freeport, NY 11520

Educational Activities, Inc.
1937 Grand Ave.
Baldwin, NY 11510

Educational Book Division
Prentice-Hall
Englewood Cliffs, NJ 07632

Educational Development Corp
8141 East 44th
P.O. Box 45663
Tulsa, OK 74145

Educational Programs and Promotions
2227-A Michigan Ave.
Arlington, TX 76013

Educational Development Corp
P.O. Box 45663
Tulsa, OK 74145

Educational Services, Inc.
P.O. Box 219
Stevensville, MI 49127

Educational Teaching Aids Division
555 West Adams Street
Chicago, IL 60606

Educational Testing Service
Mail Stop 50-D
Rosedale Rd.
Princeton, NJ 08541

Educational Testing Service
Box 999
Princeton, NJ 08540

Educators Publishing Service
75 Moulton Street
Cambridge, MA 02238

Educulture
1 Dubuque Plaza
Suite 150
Dubuque, IA 52001

Elsevier-Dutton Publishing Co., Inc.
2 Park Avenue
New York, NY 10016

EMC Publishing
300 York Avenue
St. Paul, MN 55101

Encyclopedia Britannica Educational
  Corp.
425 North Michigan Ave.
Chicago, IL 60601

ERIC Clearinghouse on Reading
  and Communication Skills
1111 Kenyon Rd.
Urbana, IL 61801

ESP, Inc.
1201 E. Johnson Ave.
P.O. Drawer 5037
Jonesboro, AR 72401

Essay Press, Inc.
P.O. Box 2323
La Jolla, CA 92037

ETA (Educational Teaching Aids)
159 West Kinzie St.
Chicago, IL 60610

Gallaudet College Press
800 Florida Avenue N.E.
Washington, DC 20002

Gamco Industries, Inc.
Box 1911
Big Springs, TX 79720

Garrard Publishing Co.
1607 North Market Street
Champaign, IL 61820

Ginn & Company Publishers
9888 Monroe Drive
Dallas, TX 75220

Globe Book Co.
50 West 23rd Street
New York, NY 10010

Global Computer Supplies
9135 Hemlock Drive
Hempstead, NY 11550

Goldencraft
1224 West Van Buren St.
Chicago, IL 60607

Good Apple, Inc.
Box 299
Carthage, IL 62321

Gralan Distributors, Inc.
PO Box 45134
Baton Rouge, LA 70895

Greenhaven Press, Inc.
577 Shoreview Park Road
St. Paul, MN 55112

Grosset & Dunlap, Inc.
Education Division
51 Madison Avenue
New York, NY 10010

Grove Press, Inc.
196 West Houston Street
New York, NY 10014

E. M. Hale and Company
Harvey House Publishers
128 West River Street
Chippewa Falls, WI 54729

Hammond, Inc.
515 Valley Street
Maplewood, NJ 07040

Hampden Publications, Inc.
P.O. Box 4873
Baltimore, Maryland 21211

Harper & Row, Inc.
10 East 53rd Street
New York, NY 10022

Hartley Courseware, Inc.
133 Bridge Street
Dimondale, MI 48821

Hawthorn Books Inc.
260 Madison Avenue
New York, NY 10016

Hayden Book Company, Inc.
50 Essex Street
Rochelle Park, NJ 07662

Hayes School Publishing Co., Inc.
321 Pennwood Avenue
Wilkinsburg, PA 15221

D. C. Heath and Company
125 Spring St.
Lexington, MA 02173

Heinemann
70 Court Street
Portsmouth, NH 03801

Hertzberg-New Method Inc.
Vandalia Road
Jacksonville, IL 62650

High Noon Books
20 Commercial Blvd.
Novata, CA 94947

Highlights for Children
2300 West Fifth Avenue
P.O. Box 269
Columbus, OH 43216

The Highsmith Co., Inc.
P.O. Box 800 B
Highway 106 East
Fort Atkinson, WI 53538

Holiday House, Inc.
18 East 53rd St.
New York, NY 10022

Holt, Rinehart and Winston
CBS Inc.
383 Madison Avenue
New York, NY 10017

Humanics Limited
P.O. Box 7447
Atlanta, GA 30309

Hutchinson Books, Inc.
Chestnut Street
Lewiston, ME 04240

Ideal School Supply Company
11000 S. Lavergne Ave.
Oak Lawn, IL 60453

I/CT-Instructional/Communications
   Technology, Inc.
10 Stepar Place
Huntington Station, NY 11746

Ideal School Supply Co.
11000 South Lavergne Avenue
Oak Lawn, IL 60453

Imperial International Learning
   Corporation
P.O. Box 548
Kankakee, IL 60901

Incentive Publications
2400 Crestmoor Road
Nashville, TN 37215

Incentives for Learning Inc.
600 West Van Buren Street
Chicago, IL 60607

Innovative Sciences, Inc.
300 Broad Street
Stanford, CT 06901

Instructional Fair
Box 1650
Grand Rapids, MI 49501

Instructor Publications, Inc.
545 Fifth Ave.
New York, NY 10017

Instructor Publications
7 Bank Street
Dansville, NY 14437

International Reading Association
800 Barksdale Road
Newark, DE 19711

ITA
A Non-Profit Educational Foundation
Hofstra University
Hempstead, NY 11550

Jamestown Publishers
P.O. Box 6743
Providence, RI 02940

Janus Book Publishers
2501 Industrial Pkwy. West
Hayward, CA 94545

Jostens Learning Systems
800 East Business Center Drive
Mount Prospect, IL 60056

Harcourt Brace Jovanovich, Inc.
School Division
6277 Sea Harbor Dr.
Orlando, FL 32887

Harcourt Brace Jovanovich, Publishers
Trade Children's Books
1250 Sixth Ave.
San Diego, CA 92101

Kenworthy Educational Services, Inc.
Box 60
138 Allen Street
Buffalo, NY 14205

Keystone View
Division of Mast Development Co.
2212 East 12th Street
Davenport, IA 52803

Kimbo Educational
P.O. Box 477
Long Branch, NJ 07740

King Features
235 East 45th Street
New York, NY 10017

The Kingsbury Center
2138 Bancroft Place, N.W.
Washington, DC 20008

The Klamath Printery
628 Oak Street
Klamath Falls, OR 97601

Knowledge Industry Publications, Inc.
701 Westchester Avenue
White Plains, NY 10604

H. P. Kopplemann
140 Van Block Ave.
Hartford, CT 06141

Kraus-Thomson Organization Ltd.
Millwood, NY 10546

Ladybird Books, Inc.
Chestnut St.
Lewiston, ME 04240

Laidlaw Educational Publishers
Thatcher & Madison
River Forest, IL 60305

Landmark Editions, Inc.
1420 Kansas Ave.
Kansas City, MO 64127

Language Research Associates, Inc.
P.O. Drawer 2085
Palm Springs, CA 92262

Lansford Publishing Co.
1088 Lincoln Avenue
P.O. Box 8711
San Jose, CA 95155

LDM Teaching Resources
One DLM Park
Allen, TX 75002

Learning Arts
P.O. Box 179
Wichita, KS 67201

Learning Associates, Inc.
P.O. Box 561167
Miami, FL 33156

The Learning Line
Box 1200
Palo Alto, CA 94302

Learning Links Inc.
11 Wagon Rd.
Roslyn Heights, NY 11577

Learning Multi-Systems
340 Coyier Lane
Madison, WI 53713

Learning Periodicals Group
19 Darvis Drive
Belmont, CA 94002

Learning Resources Corporation
8517 Production Avenue
San Diego, CA 92121

Learning Systems Corp.
60 Conolly Parkway
Hamden, CT 06514

Learning Tree Publishing Inc.
7108 South Alton Way
Englewood, CO 80112

Learning Well
200 South Service Road
Roslyn Heights, NY 11577

Lerner
241 First Avenue North
Minneapolis, MN 55401

Leswing Press
P.O. Box 3577
San Rafael, CA 94901

Library of Congress
National Library Service for the
    Blind and Physically Handicapped
1291 Taylor Street N.W.
Washington, DC 20542

Listening Library, Inc.
P.O. Box L
1 Park Avenue
Old Greenwich, CT 06870

Little, Brown and Company
College Division
34 Beacon Street
Boston, MA 02106

Litton Educational Publishing, Inc.
7625 Empire Drive
Florence, KY 41042

Longman Inc.
College and Professional Book Division
1560 Broad
New York, NY 10036

Longman Inc.
95 Church St.
White Plains, NY 10601

Longwood Division
Allyn & Bacon Inc.
Link Drive
Rockleigh, NJ 07647

Lumen Publications
1500 Palisade Ave.
Fort Lee, NJ 07024

Macmillan Children's Book Group
115 Fifth Ave.
New York, NY 10003

Macmillan Instant Activities Program
6 Commercial Street
Hicksville, NY 11801

Macmillan Publishing Co., Inc.
866 3rd Avenue
New York, NY 10022

Mafex Associates, Inc.
90 Cherry St.
Box 519
Johnstown, PA 15907

Mast Development Co.
2212 East 12th Street
Davenport, IA 52803

Mastery Education Corp.
85 Main Street
Watertown, MA 02172

McCormick-Mathers Publishing
   Company
A Division of Litton Ed. Publishing Inc.
7625 Empire Drive
Florence, KY 41042

McDonald Publishing Co.
925 Demun Avenue
St. Louis, MO 63105

McDougal, Littell & Company
P.O. Box 1667-C
Evanston, IL 60204

McGraw-Hill Book Co.
8171 Redwood Highway
Novato, CA 94947

McGraw-Hill Ryerson Ltd.
330 Progress Avenue
Scarbrough, Ontario
Canada, M1P 2Z5

McGraw-Hill School Division
(Webster Division, The Economy
   Company)
Bomar/Noble Publishers
PO Box 25308
Oklahoma City, OK 25308

Rand McNally and Co.
Box 7600
Chicago, IL 60680

Media Basics
Larchmont Plaza
Larchmont, NY 10538

Media Materials, Inc.
Department MDR
2936 Remington Avenue
Baltimore, MD 21211

Media-Pak/82
Box 541
Wilton, CT 06897

Melody House Publishing Co.
819 N.W. 92nd Street
Oklahoma City, OK 73114

Charles E. Merrill Publishing Co.
A Bell & Howell Company
1300 Alum Creek Dr.
Columbus, OH 43216

G & C Merriam Company
Publishers of Merriam-Webster
   Reference Books
47 Federal Street
Springfield, MA 01101

Julian Messner
1230 Avenue of the Americas
New York, NY 10020

Microcomputer Workshops Courseware
225 Westchester Ave.
Port Chester, NY 10573

Midwest Publications
P.O. Box 448
Pacific Grove, CA 93950

Milliken Publishing Company
1100 Research Blvd
P.O. Box 21579
St Louis, MO 63132

Milton Bradley Co.
Springfield, MA 01101

Houghton Mifflin
One Beacon Street
Boston, MA 02107

Modern Curriculum Press, Inc.
13900 Prospect Rd.
Cleveland, OH 44136

The Morgan Company
4510 N. Ravenswood Ave.
Chicago, IL 60640

William Morrow & Company, Inc.
105 Madison Ave.
New York, NY 10016

National Association for the Deaf
814 Thayer Avenue
Silver Springs, MD 20910

National Council of Teachers of English
1111 Kenyon Road
Urbana, IL 61801

National Public Radio
2025 M Street, N.W.
Washington, DC 20036

National Textbook Company
4255 W. Touhy
Lincolnwood, IL 60646

NCS/Educational Systems Division
4402 West 76th Street
Minneapolis, MN 55435

The New American Library, Inc.
1633 Broadway
New York, NY 10019

Newsweek
444 Madison Ave.
New York, NY 10022

Nystrom
3333 Elston Ave.
Chicago, IL 60618

Oceana Educational Communications
75 Main Street
Dobbs Ferry, NY 10522

Open Court Publishing Company &
  Cricket Magazine
315 Fifth St.
Peru, IL 61354

Optimal Corporation
Open Court Publishing Company
LaSalle, IL 61301

Oryx Press
2214 N. Central
Phoenix, AZ 85004

Richard C. Owen, Publishers
P.O. Box 14007
Chicago, IL 60614

Richard C. Owen Publishers, Inc.
Rockefeller Center
Box 819
New York, NY 10185

Oxford University Press
200 Madison Avenue
New York, NY 10016

THE A. N. Palmer Company
1720 West Irving Park Road
Schaumburg, IL 60193

Paperback Sales, Inc.
425 Michigan Ave.
Chicago, IL 60611

Parachute Press
P.O. Box 26186
Tempe, AZ 85282

Pendulum Press, Inc.
The Academic Building
237 Saw Mill Rd.
West Haven, CT 06516

Penguin Books
299 Murry Hill Parkway
East Rutherford, NJ 07073

Viking Penguin, Inc.
625 Madison Avenue
New York, NY 10022

Perfection Form Company
1000 North Second Avenue
Logan, IA 51546

Phonovisual Products, Inc.
12216 Parklawn Drive
P.O. Box 2007
Rockville, MD 20852

PIRT
c/o Tact
P.O. Box 1052
Daylestown, PA 18901

Pitman Learning, Inc.
(formerly Fearon Pitman Publishers,
  Inc.)
19 Davis Drive
Belmont, CA 94002

Plays, Inc.
8 Arlington Street
Boston, MA 02116

PLAYS Inc.
120 Boylston Street
Boston, MA 02116

Pleasantville Media
Suite E-61
P.O. Box 415
Pleasantville, NY 10570

Pocket Books
1230 Avenue of the Americas
New York, NY 10020

Polaroid Corporation
575 Technology Square
Cambridge, MA 02139

Prentice-Hall
Englewood Cliffs, NJ 07632

Pro-Ed
5341 Industrial Oaks Blvd.
Austin, TX 78735

Programs for Achievement in Reading,
   Inc.
Abbott Park Place
Providence, RI 02903

Pruett Publishing Company
3235 Prairie Avenue
Boulder, CO 80301

The Psychological Corporation
555 Academic Court
San Antonio, TX 78204

Psychological Test Specialists
Box 9229
Missoula, MT 59807

Publishers Test Service
2500 Garden Road
Monterey, CA 93940

The Putnam Publishing Group
51 Madison Ave.
New York, NY 10010

Radio Shack
Publicity Department
300 One Tandy Center
Fort Worth, TX 76102

Raintree Publishers, Inc.
310 W. Wisconsin Ave.
Milwaukee, WI 53203

Random House/Knopf/Patheon/
   Villard/Times Books
201 East 50th St.
New York, NY 10022

Reader's Digest Services, Inc.
Educational Division
Pleasantville, NY 10570

Readers Theatre Script Service
P.O. Box 178333
San Diego, CA 92117

The Reading Laboratory
P.O. Box 681
South Norwalk, CT 06854

Reflections & Images
6607 Northridge Drive
San Jose, CA 95120

Regents Publishing Co., Inc.
Two Park Avenue
New York, NY 10016

Remedia Publications
PO Box 1174
Scottsdale, AZ 85252

Resources
Instructional Communication
   Technology, Inc.
Huntington Station, NY 11746

Resources for the Gifted
P.O. Box 15050
Phoenix, AZ 85060

Frank E. Richards Publishing Co., Inc.
P.O. Box 66
Phoenix, NY 13135

Riverside Publishing Co.
8420 Bryn Mawr Ave.
Chicago, IL 60631

Rourke Publishing Group
P.O. Box 711
Windermere, FL 32786

Santillana Publishing Co.
575 Lexington Avenue
New York, NY 10022

Scarecrow Press, Inc.
52 Liberty Street
Box 656
Metuchen, NJ 08840

Frank Schaffer Publications
1028 Via Mirabel, Dept. 34
Palos Verdes Estates, CA 90274

Scholastic, Inc.
730 Broadway
New York, NY 10003

Scholastic Inc.
2931 E. McCarty St.
Jefferson City, MO 65102

Scholastic Book Service
904 Sylvan Avenue
Englewood Cliffs, NJ 07632

School Days Magazine
19711 Magellan Dr.
Torrance, CA 90502

Schoolhouse Press
191 Spring St.
Lexington, MA 02173

SRA
Science Research Assoc., Inc.
155 North Wacker Dr.
Chicago, IL 60606

Science Research Associates, Inc.
College Division
1540 Page Mill Road
P.O. Box 10021
Palo Alto, CA 94303

Scott, Foresman and Company
1900 East Lake Ave.
Glenview, IL 60025

Scott, Foresman and Company
11310 Gemini Lane
Dallas, TX 75229

Scribner Educational Publishers
866 Third Ave.
New York, NY 10022

Dale Seymour Publications
P.O. Box 10888
Palo Alto, CA 94303

Silver Burdett & Ginn
191 Spring Street
Lexington, MA 02173

Simon & Schuster Building
1230 Avenue of the Americas
New York, NY 10020

Simon & Schuster/Pocket Books
1230 Avenue of the Americas
New York, NY 10020

Sirs
P.O. Box 2507
Boca Raton, FL 33432

Skillcorp Publishers, Inc.
P.O. Box 712
Columbus, OH 43216

Slosson Educational Publications
P.O. Box 280
East Aurora, NY 14052

Smithsonian Institution
475 L'Enfant Plaza
Suite 4800
Washington, DC 20560

Southwestern Publishing Co.
5101 Madison Road
Cincinnati, OH 45227

Special Learning Corporation
42 Boston Post Rd.
P.O. Box 306
Guilford, CT 06437

Spectrum Educational Media, Inc.
P.O. Box 611
Mattoon, IL 61938

Sports Illustrated
Educational Program
10 North Main St.
Yardley, PA 19067

Steck-Vaughn Co.
Box 2028
807 Brazos St.
Austin, TX 78767

Stemmer House
2627 Caves Road
Owings Mills, NY 21117

Step Inc.
P.O. Box 887
Mukilteo, WA 98275

Sterling Swift Publishing Co.
7901 South IH-35
Austin, TX 78744

Stoelting Co.
1350 So. Kostner Avenue
Chicago, IL 60623

Story House Corp.
Bindery Lane
Charlettsville, NY 12036

Strine Publishing Co.
P.O. Box 149
York, PA 17405

Sundance Publishers & Distributors
Newtown Road
Littleton, MA 01460

Sunburst Communications
Room D 57
39 Washington Avenue
Pleasantville, NY 10570

SVE
Society for Visual Education
A Business Corporation
Dept. LX
1345 Diversey Parkway
Chicago, IL 60614

SVE Teacher's Choice
2750 North Wayne Avenue
Chicago, IL 60614

Swan Books
PO Box 332
Fair Oaks, CA 95628

Taylor & Francis Inc.
114 East 32nd Street
New York, NY 10016

Taylor & Francis Inc.
242 Cherry Street
Philadelphia, PA 19106

Teachers & Writers Collaborative
5 Union Square West
New York, NY 10003

Teachers College Press
1234 Amsterdam Ave.
New York, NY 10027

Teaching and Computers
Scholastic, Inc.
P.O. Box 645
Lyndhurst, NJ 07071

Teaching Resources Corporation
50 Pond Park Road
Hingham, MA 02043

Thinking Skills
P.O. Box 448
Pacific Grove, CA 93950

Time Education Program
10 North Main Street
Yardley, PA 19067

TPAssociates/TP Press
22181 Wood Island Land
Huntington Beach, CA 92646

Treetop Publishing
220 Virginia Street
Racine, WI 53405

Trend Enterprises
P.O. Box 64073
St. Paul, MN 55164

Trillium Press, Inc.
PO Box 209
Monroe, NY 10950

Troll Associates
100 Corporate Drive
Mahwah, NJ 07430

TSC
A Houghton Mifflin Co.
Dept. 70
Box 683
Hanover, NH 03755

Turman Publishing
200 West Mercer
Seattle, WA 98119

Turman Publishing Co.
809 East Pike Street
Seattle, WA 98122

Tutor/Tape
107 France Street
Toms River, NJ 08753

United Learning
6633 West Howard Street
Niles, IL 60648

University of Chicago Press
5801 South Ellis Avenue
Chicago, IL 60637
or
Journals Dept.
11030 South Langley Avenue
Chicago, IL 60672

University of Illinois Press
Urbana, IL 61601

University of Michigan Press
P.O. Box 1104
Ann Arbor, MI 48106

University of Nebraska Press
318 Nebraska Hall
901 North 17th Street
Lincoln, NE 68588

University Press of America
4720 Boston Way
Lanham, MD 20706

U.S. Government Printing Office
Washington, DC 20402

The Viking Press
Viking Penguin Inc.
625 Madison Avenue
New York, NY 10022

J. Weston Walch, Publisher
321 Valley St.
Portland, Maine 04104

Jane Ward Co.
Dept. 4
1642 South Beech St.
Lakewood, CO 80228

Franklin Watts, Inc.
730 Fifth
New York, NY 10019

E.H. White & Company
Suite 710
1025 Vermont Avenue, N.W.
Washington, DC 20005

The White Rabbit Children's Books,
  Inc.
7777 Girard Ave.
La Jolla, CA 92037

Albert Whitman and Company
5747 West Howard Street
Niles, IL 60648

H.W. Wilson Company
950 University Avenue
Bronx, NY 10452

The World Almanac
Education Division
1278 West Ninth Street
Cleveland, OH 44113

World Book-Childcraft
International, Inc.
Merchandise Mart Plaza
Chicago, IL 60654

World Book, Inc.
Merchandise Mart Plaza
Chicago, IL 60654

The Wright Group/Story Box
7620 Miramar Road
Suite 4200
San Diego, CA 92126

Xerox Education Publications
1250 Fairwood Avenue
Columbus, OH 43216

Youngheart Records
P.O. Box 27784
Los Angeles, CA 90027

Zaner-Bloser
2500 West Fifth Avenue
P. O. Box 16764
Columbus, OH 43216

Richard L. Zweig Associates
20800 Beach Boulevard
Huntington Beach, CA 92648

Index